USING ECONOMETRICS
A PRACTICAL GUIDE

The Addison-Wesley Series in Economics

USING ECONOMETRICS

FOURTH EDITION

A PRACTICAL GUIDE

A. H. Studenmund

Occidental College

Boston   San Francisco   New York
London   Toronto   Syndey   Tokyo   Singapore   Madrid
Mexico City   Munich   Paris   Cape Town   Hong Kong   Montreal

Executive Editor: Denise J. Clinton

Sponsoring Editor: Victoria Warneck

Senior Project Manager: Mary Clare McEwing

Managing Editor: James Rigney

Production Supervisor: Katherine Watson

Senior Designer: Regina Hagen

Cover Design: Dick Hannus

Senior Project Manager, Technology: Melissa Honig

Marketing Manager: Dara Lanier

Market Research Coordinator: Dorothea Dennis

Project Coordination and Text Design: Nesbitt Graphics, Inc.

Electronic Page Makeup: Nesbitt Graphics, Inc.

Senior Manufacturing Buyer: Hugh Crawford

For permission to use copyrighted material, grateful acknowledgment is made to the copyright holders:
Table B-1: Reprinted with permission of Hafner Press, a division of Macmillan Publishing Company from *Statistical Methods for Research Workers*, 14th Edition, by Ronald A. Fisher. Copyright © 1970 by University of Adelaide. Tables B-2 and B-3: Abridged from M. Merrington and C. M. Thompson, "Tables of percentage points of the inverted beta (*F*) distribution," *Biometrika*, Vol. 38, 1951, pp. 159–77. By permission of the Biometrika Trustees. Table B-4: From N. E. Savin and Kenneth White, "The Durbin-Watson Test for Serial Correlation with Extreme Sample Sizes or Many Regressors," *Econometrica*, Nov. 1977, p. 1994. Reprinted with permission. Tables B-5 and B-6: From J. Durbin and G. S. Watson, "Testing for serial correlation in least squares regressions," *Biometrika*, Vol. 38, 1951, pp. 159–77. By permission of the Biometrika Trustees. Tables B-7 and B-8: Based on *Biometrika Tables for Statisticians*, Vol. 1, 3rd ed. (1966). By permission of the Biometrika Trustees.

Library of Congress Cataloging-in-Publication Data

Studenmund, A. H.
    Using econometrics: a practical guide / A.H. Studenmund.--4th ed.
        p. cm. -- (The Addison Wesley series in economics)
    Includes index.
    ISBN 0-321-06481-X
        1. Econometrics. 2. Regression analysis. I. Title. II. Series.

    HB139 .S795 2000
    330'.01'5195--dc21

Please visit our website at www.awl.com/studenmund

ISBN 0-321-06481-X
    345678910—MA—030201

Dedicated to
Brent Ripley Studenmund Morse

CONTENTS

PREFACE

Econometric education is a lot like learning to fly a plane; you learn more from actually doing it than you learn from reading about it.

Using Econometrics represents a new approach to the understanding of elementary econometrics. It covers the topic of single-equation linear regression analysis in an easily understandable format that emphasizes real-world examples and exercises. As the subtitle, *A Practical Guide*, implies, the book is aimed not only at beginning econometrics students but also at regression users looking for a refresher and at experienced practitioners who want a convenient reference.

The material covered by this book is traditional, but there are five specific features that we feel distinguish *Using Econometrics*:

1. Our approach to the learning of econometrics is simple, intuitive, and easy to understand. We do not use matrix algebra, and we relegate proofs and calculus to the footnotes.

2. We include numerous examples and example-based exercises. We feel that the best way to get a solid grasp of applied econometrics is through an example-oriented approach.

3. Although most of this book is at a simpler level than other econometrics texts, Chapters 6 and 7 on specification choice are among the most complete in the field. We think that an understanding of specification issues is vital for regression users.

4. We use a unique kind of learning tool, called an interactive regression learning exercise, to help students simulate econometric analysis by giving them feedback on various kinds of decisions without relying on computer time or much instructor supervision.

5. We offer the student version of EViews, the premier econometric software package for Windows computers, as an option with each copy of the text at an extremely low additional cost. We're excited about adding EViews to our package, because students appreciate the program's accuracy and easy-to-use Windows interface. Although we use EViews to produce the regression results in the book, *Using Econometrics* is not tied to EViews in any way, so the text fits well with all standard regression programs.

The formal prerequisites for using this book are few. Readers are assumed to have been exposed to some microeconomic and macroeconomic theory, basic mathematical functions, and elementary statistics (even if they have forgotten most of it). Students with little or no statistical background are encouraged to begin their study of econometrics by reading Chapter 16, Statistical Principles.

Because the prerequisites are few and the statistics material is self-contained, *Using Econometrics* can be used not only in undergraduate courses but also in MBA-level courses in quantitative methods. We also have been told that the book is a helpful supplement for graduate-level econometrics courses.

New in the Fourth Edition

A recent survey of econometricians ranked *Using Econometrics* as the most adopted text in the field. As a result, we've tried hard to retain the clarity and practicality that have made the book a success while adding a new statistics chapter, the EViews option, and more coverage of modern regression topics.

Specific new items include:

1. A completely new elementary statistics chapter that was written by Gary Smith, the author of one of the most highly regarded statistics textbooks in the field.

2. The optional inclusion of the student version of EViews with each copy of the text at an additional cost that is far lower than even the wholesale price of the program. This EViews option is discussed in more depth in the section that follows.

3. An increased emphasis on modern regression topics, including the White test, heteroskedasticity-corrected standard errors, the AR(1) adjustment for serial correlation, Akaike's Information Criterion, the Schwarz criterion, and nonstationarity.

4. A website <www.awl.com/studenmund> which includes additional interactive regression learning exercises, the text's datasets already formatted so that they can be downloaded for use in some of the most popular econometric software packages (EViews, SAS, SHAZAM, and EXCEL) as well as in ASCII form, and a detailed guide, written by Robert Johnson, on using EViews to complete the text's exercises.

5. Improved, expanded, and updated exercises, examples, and data sets.

6. An expanded Instructor's Manual, which includes answers to odd-numbered exercises, lecture notes, sample examinations, and an additional interactive exercise.

The EViews Option

We're excited to be able to offer our readers the chance to purchase the student version of EViews at an extremely low price. EViews is the number one Windows-based econometric software package in the world; it's accurate, easy to use, and provides support for a wide range of advanced options.

We urge professors and students alike to take advantage of this low-cost EViews option even if a different regression package is used for class exercises. The advantages to students of owning their own regression software are many: they can run regressions when they are off campus, and, most importantly, they'll have a regression package to use for research after the class is over, and even after they've graduated.

Acknowledgments

If this book has a spiritual father, it's Henry Cassidy of the Federal Home Loan Mortgage Corporation. It was Henry who saw the need for a follow-on to Rao and Miller's legendary *Applied Econometrics,* and who coauthored the first edition of *Using Econometrics* as an expansion of his own work of the same name.

For four straight editions, Carolyn Summers of the National Education Association has been the text's editorial consultant, proofreader, and indexer. It's hard to overstate the value of Carolyn's contribution to this long-term project because of her precise editing, her practical econometric experience, her infectious wit, and her undaunted enthusiasm.

The excellent new chapter on statistics was written by Gary Smith of Pomona College. His book, *Introduction to Statistical Reasoning* (McGraw Hill, 1998; ISBN: 0-07-059276-4) would be a perfect text for a course that acts as a prerequisite for an elementary econometrics class.

Doug Steigerwald of the University of California at Santa Barbara reviewed the entire text, provided in-depth feedback on new material, and offered analyses of the recommendations of the outside reviewers (particularly when they disagreed). In all these roles, he was superb. The other reviewers in this excellent group included Anne Alexander (University of Wyoming), Kurt Beron (Univeristy of Texas at Dallas), Manfred Keil (Claremont McKenna), Chris Lacke (Rowan University), Larry Ringer (Texas A&M University), Helen Roberts (University of Illinois at Chicago), Marc Tomljanovich (Union College), and Tore Wentzel-Larsen (Bodo/Norway).

Invaluable in the editorial and production process were Gina Hagen, Lois Lombardo, Jim Rigney, Frank Ruggirello, Victoria Warneck, Katy Watson, and, especially, Mary Clare McEwing. Others who provided timely and useful assistance to this edition were Bernard Grofman, Tami Hooker, Robert Johnson, George Jougantos, David Lilien, Amber McClain, Silver Oak, Barbara Passarelle, Cynthia Szady, George Thomas, and, of course, my family (Jaynie, Scott, and Connell Studenmund). In addition, we appreciate the permission of William F. Lott and Subhash C. Ray and their publisher, Harcourt Brace and Company, for permission to reproduce a number of data-intensive exercises that originally were published in their excellent text, *Applied Econometrics: Problems with Data Sets* (1992). Finally, but perhaps most importantly, I'd like to thank my superb Occidental College colleagues and students for their feedback and encouragement. These especially include Steve Babbington, Mary Hirschfeld, Katie Holford, Joaquin Lujan, Bich Ly, Matt Mihm, Robby Moore, Mike Tamada, and Caroline van Oosterom.

A. H. Studenmund
June, 2000

USING ECONOMETRICS
A PRACTICAL GUIDE

THE BASIC

REGRESSION MODEL

An Overview of Regression Analysis

1.1   What Is Econometrics?

"Econometrics is too mathematical; it's the reason my best friend isn't majoring in economics."

"There are two things you don't want to see in the making—sausage and econometric research."[1]

"Econometrics may be defined as the quantitative analysis of actual economic phenomena."[2]

"It's my experience that 'economy-tricks' is usually nothing more than a justification of what the author believed before the research was begun."

Obviously, econometrics means different things to different people. To beginning students, it may seem as if econometrics is an overly complex obstacle to an otherwise useful education. To skeptical observers, econometric results should be trusted only when the steps that produced those results are completely known. To professionals in the field, econometrics is a fascinating set

---

1. Attributed to Edward E. Leamer.

2. Paul A. Samuelson, T. C. Koopmans, and J. R. Stone, "Report of the Evaluative Committee for *Econometrica*," *Econometrica*, 1954, p. 141.

of techniques that allows the measurement and analysis of economic phenomena and the prediction of future economic trends.

You're probably thinking that such diverse points of view sound like the
statements of blind people trying to describe an elephant based on what they
happen to be touching, and you're partially right. Econometrics has both a
formal definition and a larger context. Although you can easily memorize the
formal definition, you'll get the complete picture only by understanding the
many uses of and alternative approaches to econometrics.

That said, we need a formal definition. **Econometrics,** literally "economic
measurement," is the quantitative measurement and analysis of actual economic and business phenomena. It attempts to quantify economic reality
and bridge the gap between the abstract world of economic theory and the
real world of human activity. To many students, these worlds may seem far
apart. On the one hand, economists theorize equilibrium prices based on
carefully conceived marginal costs and marginal revenues; on the other,
many firms seem to operate as though they have never heard of such concepts. Econometrics allows us to examine data and to quantify the actions of
firms, consumers, and governments. Such measurements have a number of
different uses, and an examination of these uses is the first step to understanding econometrics.

1.1.1   Uses of Econometrics

Econometrics has three major uses:

1. describing economic reality

2. testing hypotheses about economic theory

3. forecasting future economic activity

The simplest use of econometrics is **description.** We can use econometrics
to quantify economic activity because econometrics allows us to put numbers in equations that previously contained only abstract symbols. For example, consumer demand for a particular commodity often can be thought of as
a relationship between the quantity demanded (Q) and the commodity's
price (P), the price of a substitute good (P_s), and disposable income (Yd). For
most goods, the relationship between consumption and disposable income
is expected to be positive, because an increase in disposable income will be
associated with an increase in the consumption of the good. Econometrics
actually allows us to estimate that relationship based upon past consumption, income, and prices. In other words, a general and purely theoretical
functional relationship like:

$$Q = f(P, P_s, Yd) \qquad\qquad (1.1)$$

can become explicit:

$$Q = 31.50 - 0.73P + 0.11P_s + 0.23Yd \qquad (1.2)$$

This technique gives a much more specific and descriptive picture of the function.[3] Let's compare Equations 1.1 and 1.2. Instead of expecting consumption merely to "increase" if there is an increase in disposable income, Equation 1.2 allows us to expect an increase of a specific amount (0.23 units for each unit of increased disposable income). The number 0.23 is called an estimated regression coefficient, and it is the ability to estimate these coefficients that makes econometrics valuable.

The second and perhaps the most common use of econometrics is **hypothesis testing,** the evaluation of alternative theories with quantitative evidence. Much of economics involves building theoretical models and testing them against evidence, and hypothesis testing is vital to that scientific approach. For example, you could test the hypothesis that the product in Equation 1.1 is what economists call a normal good (one for which the quantity demanded increases when disposable income increases). You could do this by applying various statistical tests to the estimated coefficient (0.23) of disposable income (Yd) in Equation 1.2. At first glance, the evidence would seem to support this hypothesis because the coefficient's sign is positive, but the "statistical significance" of that estimate would have to be investigated before such a conclusion could be justified. Even though the estimated coefficient is positive, as expected, it may not be sufficiently different from zero to imply that the true coefficient is indeed positive instead of zero. Unfortunately, statistical tests of such hypotheses are not always easy, and there are times when two researchers can look at the same set of data and come to slightly different conclusions. Even given this possibility, the use of econometrics in testing hypotheses is probably its most important function.

The third and most difficult use of econometrics is to **forecast** or predict what is likely to happen next quarter, next year, or further into the future, based on what has happened in the past. For example, economists use econometric models to make forecasts of variables like sales, profits, Gross Domestic Product (GDP), and the inflation rate. The accuracy of such forecasts depends in large measure on the degree to which the past is a good guide to the future. Business leaders and politicians tend to be especially in-

---

3. The results in Equation 1.2 are from a model of the demand for chicken that we will examine in more detail in Section 6.1.

terested in this use of econometrics because they need to make decisions about the future, and the penalty for being wrong (bankruptcy for the entrepreneur and political defeat for the candidate) is high. To the extent that econometrics can shed light on the impact of their policies, business and government leaders will be better equipped to make decisions. For example, if the president of a company that sold the product modeled in Equation 1.1 wanted to decide whether to increase prices, forecasts of sales with and without the price increase could be calculated and compared to help make such a decision. In this way, econometrics can be used not only for forecasting but also for policy analysis.

1.1.2   Alternative Econometric Approaches

There are many different approaches to quantitative work. For example, the fields of biology, psychology, and physics all face quantitative questions similar to those faced in economics and business. However, these fields tend to use somewhat different techniques for analysis because the problems they face aren't the same. "We need a special field called econometrics, and textbooks about it, because it is generally accepted that economic data possess certain properties that are not considered in standard statistics texts or are not sufficiently emphasized there for use by economists."[4]

Different approaches also make sense within the field of economics. The kind of econometric tools used to quantify a particular function depends in part on the uses to which that equation will be put. A model built solely for descriptive purposes might be different from a forecasting model, for example.

To get a better picture of these approaches, let's look at the steps necessary for any kind of quantitative research:

1. specifying the models or relationships to be studied
2. collecting the data needed to quantify the models
3. quantifying the models with the data

Steps 1 and 2 are similar in all quantitative work, but the techniques used in step 3, quantifying the models, differ widely between and within disciplines. Choosing the best technique for a given model is a theory-based skill that is often referred to as the "art" of econometrics. There are many alternative approaches to quantifying the same equation, and each approach may

---

4. Clive Granger, "A Review of Some Recent Textbooks of Econometrics," *Journal of Economic Literature*, March 1994, p. 117.

give somewhat different results. The choice of approach is left to the individual econometrician (the researcher using econometrics), but each researcher should be able to justify that choice.

This book will focus primarily on one particular econometric approach: *single-equation linear regression analysis.* The majority of this book will thus concentrate on regression analysis, but it is important for every econometrician to remember that regression is only one of many approaches to econometric quantification.

The importance of critical evaluation cannot be stressed enough; a good econometrician can diagnose faults in a particular approach and figure out how to repair them. The limitations of the regression analysis approach must be fully perceived and appreciated by anyone attempting to use regression analysis or its findings. The possibility of missing or inaccurate data, incorrectly formulated relationships, poorly chosen estimating techniques, or improper statistical testing procedures implies that the results from regression analyses should always be viewed with some caution.

1.2   What Is Regression Analysis?

Econometricians use regression analysis to make quantitative estimates of economic relationships that previously have been completely theoretical in nature. After all, anybody can claim that the quantity of compact discs demanded will increase if the price of those discs decreases (holding everything else constant), but not many people can put specific numbers into an equation and estimate *by how many* compact discs the quantity demanded will increase for each dollar that price decreases. To predict the *direction* of the change, you need a knowledge of economic theory and the general characteristics of the product in question. To predict the *amount* of the change, though, you need a sample of data, and you need a way to estimate the relationship. The most frequently used method to estimate such a relationship in econometrics is regression analysis.

1.2.1   Dependent Variables, Independent Variables, and Causality

Regression analysis is a statistical technique that attempts to "explain" movements in one variable, the **dependent variable**, as a function of movements in a set of other variables, called the **independent** (or **explanatory**) **variables**, through the quantification of a single equation. For example in Equation 1.1:

$$Q = f(P, P_s, Yd) \tag{1.1}$$

Q is the dependent variable and P, P_s, and Yd are the independent variables. Regression analysis is a natural tool for economists because most (though not all) economic propositions can be stated in such single-equation functional forms. For example, the quantity demanded (dependent variable) is a function of price, the prices of substitutes, and income (independent variables).

Much of economics and business is concerned with cause-and-effect propositions. If the price of a good increases by one unit, then the quantity demanded decreases on average by a certain amount, depending on the price elasticity of demand (defined as the percentage change in the quantity demanded that is caused by a one percent change in price). Similarly, if the quantity of capital employed increases by one unit, then output increases by a certain amount, called the marginal productivity of capital. Propositions such as these pose an if-then, or causal, relationship that logically postulates that a dependent variable's movements are causally determined by movements in a number of specific independent variables.

Don't be deceived by the words dependent and independent, however. Although many economic relationships are causal by their very nature, a regression result, no matter how statistically significant, cannot prove causality. All regression analysis can do is test whether a significant quantitative relationship exists. Judgments as to causality must also include a healthy dose of economic theory and common sense. For example, the fact that the bell on the door of a flower shop rings just before a customer enters and purchases some flowers by no means implies that the bell causes purchases! If events A and B are related statistically, it may be that A causes B, that B causes A, that some omitted factor causes both, or that a chance correlation exists between the two.

The cause-and-effect relationship is often so subtle that it fools even the most prominent economists. For example, in the late nineteenth century, English economist Stanley Jevons hypothesized that sunspots caused an increase in economic activity. To test this theory, he collected data on national output (the dependent variable) and sunspot activity (the independent variable) and showed that a significant positive relationship existed. This result led him, and some others, to jump to the conclusion that sunspots did indeed cause output to rise. Such a conclusion was unjustified because regression analysis cannot confirm causality; it can only test the strength and direction of the quantitative relationships involved.

1.2.2 Single-Equation Linear Models

The simplest single-equation linear regression model is:

$$Y = \beta_0 + \beta_1 X \tag{1.3}$$

Equation 1.3 states that Y, the dependent variable, is a single-equation linear function of X, the independent variable. The model is a single-equation model because no equation for X as a function of Y (or any other variable) has been specified. The model is linear because if you were to plot Equation 1.3 on graph paper, it would be a straight line rather than a curve.

The βs are the **coefficients** that determine the coordinates of the straight line at any point. β_0 is the **constant** or **intercept** term; it indicates the value of Y when X equals zero. β_1 is the **slope coefficient,** and it indicates the amount that Y will change when X increases by one unit. The solid line in Figure 1.1 illustrates the relationship between the coefficients and the graphical meaning of the regression equation. As can be seen from the diagram, Equation 1.3 is indeed linear.

The slope coefficient, β_1, shows the response of Y to a change in X. Since being able to explain and predict changes in the dependent variable is the essential reason for quantifying behavioral relationships, much of the emphasis in regression analysis is on slope coefficients such as β_1. In Figure 1.1 for example, if X were to increase from X_1 to X_2 (ΔX), the value of Y in Equation 1.3 would increase from Y_1 to Y_2 (ΔY). For linear (i.e., straight-line) regression models, the response in the predicted value of Y due to a change in X is constant and equal to the slope coefficient β_1:

$$\frac{(Y_2 - Y_1)}{(X_2 - X_1)} = \frac{\Delta Y}{\Delta X} = \beta_1$$

where Δ is used to denote a change in the variables. Some readers may recognize this as the "rise" (ΔY) divided by the "run" (ΔX). For a linear model, the slope is constant over the entire function.

We must distinguish between an equation that is linear in the variables and one that is linear in the coefficients. This distinction is important because if linear regression techniques are going to be applied to an equation, that equation *must be* linear in the coefficients.

An equation is **linear in the variables** if plotting the function in terms of X and Y generates a straight line. For example, Equation 1.3:

$$Y = \beta_0 + \beta_1 X \tag{1.3}$$

is linear in the variables, but Equation 1.4:

$$Y = \beta_0 + \beta_1 X^2 \tag{1.4}$$

is not linear in the variables because if you were to plot Equation 1.4 it

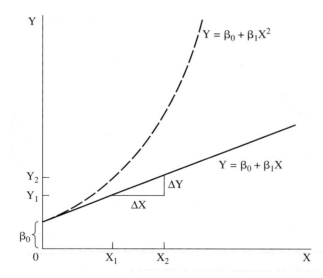

Figure 1.1 Graphical Representation of the Coefficients of the Regression Line

The graph of the equation $Y = \beta_0 + \beta_1 X$ is linear with a constant slope equal to $\beta_1 = \Delta Y / \Delta X$. The graph of the equation $Y = \beta_0 + \beta_1 X^2$, on the other hand, is nonlinear with an increasing slope (if $\beta_1 > 0$).

would be a quadratic, not a straight line. This difference[5] can be seen in Figure 1.1.

An equation is **linear in the coefficients** only if the coefficients (the βs) appear in their simplest form—they are not raised to any powers (other than one), are not multiplied or divided by other coefficients, and do not themselves include some sort of function (like logs or exponents). For example, Equation 1.3 is linear in the coefficients, but Equation 1.5:

$$Y = \beta_0 + X^{\beta_1} \tag{1.5}$$

is not linear in the coefficients β_0 and β_1. Equation 1.5 is not linear because there is no rearrangement of the equation that will make it linear in the βs of original interest, β_0 and β_1. In fact, of all possible equations for a single explanatory variable, *only* functions of the general form:

$$f(Y) = \beta_0 + \beta_1 f(X) \tag{1.6}$$

5. Equations 1.3 and 1.4 have the same β_0 in Figure 1.1 for comparison purposes only. If the equations were applied to the same data, the estimated β_0s would be different.

are linear in the coefficients β_0 and β_1. In essence, any sort of configuration of the Xs and Ys can be used and the equation will continue to be linear in the coefficients. However, even a slight change in the configuration of the βs will cause the equation to become nonlinear in the coefficients.

Although linear regressions need to be linear in the coefficients, they do not necessarily need to be linear in the variables. Linear regression analysis can be applied to an equation that is nonlinear in the variables if the equation can be formulated in a way that is linear in the coefficients. Indeed, when econometricians use the phrase "linear regression," they usually mean "regression that is linear in the coefficients."[6]

1.2.3   The Stochastic Error Term

Besides the variation in the dependent variable (Y) that is caused by the independent variable (X), there is almost always variation that comes from other sources as well. This additional variation comes in part from omitted explanatory variables (e.g., X_2 and X_3). However, even if these extra variables are added to the equation, there still is going to be some variation in Y that simply cannot be explained by the model.[7] This variation probably comes from sources such as omitted influences, measurement error, incorrect functional form, or purely random and totally unpredictable occurrences. By *random* we mean something that has its value determined entirely by chance.

Econometricians admit the existence of such inherent unexplained variation ("error") by explicitly including a stochastic (or random) error term in their regression models. A **stochastic error term** is a term that is added to a regression equation to introduce all of the variation in Y that cannot be explained by the included Xs. It is, in effect, a symbol of the econometrician's ignorance or inability to model all the movements of the dependent variable.

---

6. The application of regression analysis to equations that are nonlinear in the variables is covered in Chapter 7. The application of regression techniques to equations that are nonlinear in the *coefficients*, however, is much more difficult.

7. The exception would be the extremely rare case where the data can be explained by some sort of physical law and are measured perfectly. Here, continued variation would point to an omitted independent variable. A similar kind of problem is often encountered in astronomy, where planets can be discovered by noting that the orbits of known planets exhibit variations that can be caused only by the gravitational pull of another heavenly body. Absent these kinds of physical laws, researchers in economics and business would be foolhardy to believe that *all* variation in Y can be explained by a regression model because there are always elements of error in any attempt to measure a behavioral relationship.

The error term (sometimes called a disturbance term) is usually referred to with the symbol epsilon (ϵ), although other symbols (like u or v) are sometimes used.

The addition of a stochastic error term (ϵ) to Equation 1.3 results in a typical regression equation:

$$Y = \overbrace{\beta_0 + \beta_1 X}^{\text{deterministic}} + \overbrace{\epsilon}^{\text{stochastic}} \tag{1.7}$$

Equation 1.7 can be thought of as having two components, the *deterministic* component and the *stochastic*, or random, component. The expression $\beta_0 + \beta_1 X$ is called the *deterministic* component of the regression equation because it indicates the value of Y that is determined by a given value of X, which is assumed to be nonstochastic. This deterministic component can also be thought of as the **expected value** of Y given X, the mean value of the Ys associated with a particular value of X. For example, if the average height of all 14-year-old girls is 5 feet, then 5 feet is the expected value of a girl's height given that she is 14. The deterministic part of the equation may be written:

$$E(Y|X) = \beta_0 + \beta_1 X \tag{1.8}$$

which states that the expected value of Y given X, denoted as $E(Y|X)$, is a linear function of the independent variable (or variables if there are more than one).[8]

Unfortunately, the value of Y observed in the real world is unlikely to be exactly equal to the deterministic expected value $E(Y|X)$. After all, not all 14-year-old girls are 5 feet tall. As a result, the stochastic element (ϵ) must be added to the equation:

$$Y = E(Y|X) + \epsilon = \beta_0 + \beta_1 X + \epsilon \tag{1.9}$$

---

8. This property holds as long as $E(\epsilon|X) = 0$ [read as "the expected value of X, given epsilon" equals zero], which is true as long as the Classical Assumptions (to be outlined in Chapter 4) are met. It's easiest to think of $E(\epsilon)$ as the mean of ϵ, but the expected value operator E technically is a summation of all the values that a function can take, weighted by the probability of each value. The expected value of a constant is that constant, and the expected value of a sum of variables equals the sum of the expected values of those variables.

The stochastic error term must be present in a regression equation because there are at least four sources of variation in Y other than the variation in the included Xs:

1. Many minor influences on Y are _omitted_ from the equation (for example, because data are unavailable).

2. It is virtually impossible to avoid some sort of _measurement error_ in at least one of the equation's variables.

3. The underlying theoretical equation might have a _different functional form_ (or shape) than the one chosen for the regression. For example, the underlying equation might be nonlinear in the variables for a linear regression.

4. All attempts to generalize human behavior must contain at least some amount of unpredictable or _purely random_ variation.

To get a better feeling for these components of the stochastic error term, let's think about a consumption function (aggregate consumption as a function of aggregate disposable income). First, consumption in a particular year may have been less than it would have been because of uncertainty over the future course of the economy. Since this uncertainty is hard to measure, there might be no variable measuring consumer uncertainty in the equation. In such a case, the impact of the omitted variable (consumer uncertainty) would likely end up in the stochastic error term. Second, the observed amount of consumption may have been different from the actual level of consumption in a particular year due to an error (such as a sampling error) in the measurement of consumption in the National Income Accounts. Third, the underlying consumption function may be nonlinear, but a linear consumption function might be estimated. (To see how this incorrect functional form would cause errors, see Figure 1.2.) Fourth, the consumption function attempts to portray the behavior of people, and there is always an element of unpredictability in human behavior. At any given time, some random event might increase or decrease aggregate consumption in a way that might never be repeated and couldn't be anticipated.

These possibilities explain the existence of a difference between the observed values of Y and the values expected from the deterministic component of the equation, $E(Y|X)$. These sources of error will be covered in more detail in the following chapters, but for now it is enough to recognize that in econometric research there will always be some stochastic or random element, and, for this reason, an error term must be added to all regression equations.

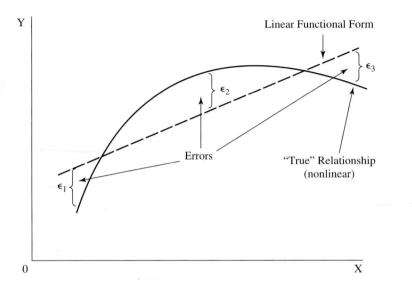

Figure 1.2 Errors Caused by Using a Linear Functional Form to Model a Nonlinear Relationship

One source of stochastic error is the use of an incorrect functional form. For example, if a linear functional form is used when the underlying relationship is nonlinear, systematic errors (the ϵs) will occur. These nonlinearities are just one component of the stochastic error term. The others are omitted variables, measurement error, and purely random variation.

1.2.4   Extending the Notation

Our regression notation needs to be extended to include reference to the number of observations and to allow the possibility of more than one independent variable. If we include a specific reference to the observations, the single-equation linear regression model may be written as:

$$Y_i = \beta_0 + \beta_1 X_i + \epsilon_i \qquad (i = 1, 2, \ldots, n) \qquad (1.10)$$

where: Y_i = the ith observation[9] of the dependent variable
X_i = the ith observation of the independent variable
ϵ_i = the ith observation of the stochastic error term
β_0, β_1 = the regression coefficients
n = the number of observations

---

9. A typical observation (or unit of analysis) is an individual person, year, or country. For example, a series of annual observations starting in 1950 would have Y_1 = Y for 1950, Y_2 for 1951, etc.

This equation is actually n equations, one for each of the n observations:

$$Y_1 = \beta_0 + \beta_1 X_1 + \epsilon_1$$
$$Y_2 = \beta_0 + \beta_1 X_2 + \epsilon_2$$
$$Y_3 = \beta_0 + \beta_1 X_3 + \epsilon_3$$
$$\vdots$$
$$Y_n = \beta_0 + \beta_1 X_n + \epsilon_n$$

That is, the regression model is assumed to hold for each observation. The coefficients do not change from observation to observation, but the values of Y, X, and ϵ do.

A second notational addition allows for more than one independent variable. Since more than one independent variable is likely to have an effect on the dependent variable, our notation should allow these additional explanatory Xs to be added. If we define:

X_{1i} = the ith observation of the first independent variable
X_{2i} = the ith observation of the second independent variable
X_{3i} = the ith observation of the third independent variable

then all three variables can be expressed as determinants of Y in a **multivari-ate** (more than one independent variable) linear regression model:

$$Y_i = \beta_0 + \beta_1 X_{1i} + \beta_2 X_{2i} + \beta_3 X_{3i} + \epsilon_i \qquad (1.11)$$

The **meaning of the regression coefficient β_1** in this equation is the impact of a one unit increase in X_1 on the dependent variable Y, *holding constant* the other included independent variables (X_2 and X_3). Similarly, β_2 gives the impact of a one-unit increase in X_2 on Y, holding X_1 and X_3 constant. These **multivariate regression coefficients** (which are parallel in nature to partial derivatives in calculus) serve to isolate the impact on Y of a change in one variable from the impact on Y of changes in the other variables. This is possible because multivariate regression takes the movements of X_2 and X_3 into account when it estimates the coefficient of X_1. The result is quite similar to what we would obtain if we were capable of conducting controlled laboratory experiments in which only one variable at a time was changed.

In the real world, though, it is almost impossible to run controlled experiments, because many economic factors change simultaneously, often in opposite directions. Thus the ability of regression analysis to measure the impact of one variable on the dependent variable, *holding constant the influence of the other variables in the equation,* is a tremendous advantage. Note that if a variable is not included in an equation, then its impact is *not* held constant in the estimation of the regression coefficients. This will be discussed further in Chapter 6.

The general multivariate regression model with K independent variables thus is written as:

$$Y_i = \beta_0 + \beta_1 X_{1i} + \beta_2 X_{2i} + \cdots + \beta_K X_{Ki} + \epsilon_i \qquad (1.12)$$
$$(i = 1, 2, \ldots, n)$$

If the sample consists of a series of years or months (called a **time series**), then the subscript i is usually replaced with a t to denote time.[10]

1.3   The Estimated Regression Equation

Once a specific equation has been decided upon, it must be quantified. This quantified version of the theoretical regression equation is called the **estimated regression equation** and is obtained from a sample of actual Xs and Ys. Although the theoretical equation is purely abstract in nature:

$$Y_i = \beta_0 + \beta_1 X_i + \epsilon_i \qquad (1.13)$$

the estimated regression equation has actual numbers in it:

$$\hat{Y}_i = 103.40 + 6.38 X_i \qquad (1.14)$$

Estimated regression coefficients

The observed, real-world values of X and Y are used to calculate the coefficient estimates 103.40 and 6.38. These estimates are used to determine $\hat{Y}$ (read as "Y-hat"), the *estimated* or *fitted* value of Y.

Let's look at the differences between a theoretical regression equation and an estimated regression equation. First, the theoretical regression coefficients β_0 and β_1 in Equation 1.13 have been replaced with *estimates* of those coefficients like 103.40 and 6.38 in Equation 1.14. We can't actually observe the values of the true[11] regression coefficients, so instead we calculate estimates of those coefficients from the data. The **estimated regression coefficients,**

---

10. It also does not matter if X_{1i}, for example, is written as X_{i1} as long as the appropriate definitions are presented. Often the observational subscript (i or t) is deleted, and the reader is expected to understand that the equation holds for each observation in the sample.

11. Our use of the word *true* throughout the text should be taken with a grain of salt. Many philosophers argue that the concept of truth is useful only relative to the scientific research program in question. Many economists agree, pointing out that what is true for one generation may well be false for another. To us, the true coefficient is the one that you'd obtain if you could run a regression on the entire relevant population. Thus, readers who so desire can substitute the phrase "population coefficient" for "true coefficient" with no loss in meaning.

more generally denoted by $\hat{\beta}_0$ and $\hat{\beta}_1$ (read as "beta-hats"), are empirical best guesses of the true regression coefficients and are obtained from data from a sample of the Ys and Xs. The expression

$$\hat{Y}_i = \hat{\beta}_0 + \hat{\beta}_1 X_i \qquad (1.15)$$

is the empirical counterpart of the theoretical regression Equation 1.13. The calculated estimates in Equation 1.14 are examples of estimated regression coefficients $\hat{\beta}_0$ and $\hat{\beta}_1$. For each sample we calculate a different set of estimated regression coefficients.

$\hat{Y}_i$ is the *estimated value* of Y_i, and it represents the value of Y calculated from the estimated regression equation for the *i*th observation. As such, $\hat{Y}_i$ is our predication of $E(Y_i|X_i)$ from the regression equation. The closer $\hat{Y}_i$ is to Y_i, the better the fit of the equation. (The word *fit* is used here much as it would be used to describe how well clothes fit.)

The difference between the estimated value of the dependent variable ($\hat{Y}_i$) and the actual value of the dependent variable (Y_i) is defined as the **residual** (e_i):

$$e_i = Y_i - \hat{Y}_i \qquad (1.16)$$

Note the distinction between the residual in Equation 1.16 and the error term:

$$\epsilon_i = Y_i - E(Y_i|X_i) \qquad (1.17)$$

The *residual* is the difference between the observed Y and the estimated regression line ($\hat{Y}$), while the *error term* is the difference between the observed Y and the true regression equation (the expected value of Y). Note that the error term is a theoretical concept that can never be observed, but the residual is a real-world value that is calculated for each observation every time a regression is run. Most regression techniques not only calculate the residuals but also attempt to select values of $\hat{\beta}_0$ and $\hat{\beta}$ that keep the residuals as low as possible. The smaller the residuals, the better the fit, and the closer the $\hat{Y}$s will be to the Ys.

All these concepts are shown in Figure 1.3. The (X, Y) pairs are shown as points on the diagram, and both the true regression equation (which cannot be seen in real applications) and an estimated regression equation are included. Notice that the estimated equation is close to but not equivalent to the true line. This is a typical result. For example, $\hat{Y}_6$, the computed value of Y

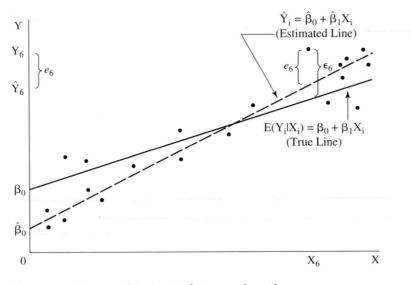

Figure 1.3 True and Estimated Regression Lines

The true relationship between X and Y (the solid line) cannot typically be observed, but the estimated regression line (the dotted line) can. The difference between an observed data point (for example, i = 6) and the true line is the value of the stochastic error term (ϵ_6). The difference between the observed Y_6 and the estimated value from the regression line ($\hat{Y}_6$) is the value of the residual for this observation, e_6.

for the sixth observation, lies on the estimated (dashed) line, and it differs from Y_6, the actual observed value of Y for the sixth observation. The difference between the observed and estimated values is the residual, denoted by e_6. In addition, although we usually would not be able to see an observation of the error term, we have drawn the assumed true regression line here (the solid line) to see the sixth observation of the error term, ϵ_6, which is the difference between the true line and the observed value of Y, Y_6.

Another way to state the estimated regression equation is to combine Equations 1.15 and 1.16, obtaining:

$$Y_i = \hat{\beta}_0 + \hat{\beta}_1 X_i + e_i \qquad (1.18)$$

Compare this equation to Equation 1.13. When we replace the theoretical regression coefficients with estimated coefficients, the error term must be replaced by the residual, because the error term, like the regression coefficients β_0 and β_1, can never be observed. Instead, the residual is observed and measured whenever a regression line is estimated with a sample of Xs and Ys. In this sense, the residual can be thought of as an estimate of the error term, and e could have been denoted as $\hat{\epsilon}$.

The following chart summarizes the notation used in the true and estimated regression equations:

True Regression Equation	Estimated Regression Equation
β_0	$\hat{\beta}_0$
β_1	$\hat{\beta}_1$
ϵ_i	e_i

The estimated regression model can be extended to more than one independent variable by adding the additional Xs to the right side of the equation. The multivariate estimated regression counterpart of Equation 1.12 is:

$$\hat{Y}_i = \hat{\beta}_0 + \hat{\beta}_1 X_{1i} + \hat{\beta}_2 X_{2i} + \cdots + \hat{\beta}_K X_{Ki} \qquad (1.19)$$

1.4   A Simple Example of Regression Analysis

Let's look at a fairly simple example of regression analysis. Suppose you've accepted a summer job as a weight guesser at the local amusement park, Magic Hill. Customers pay 50 cents each, which you get to keep if you guess their weight within 10 pounds. If you miss by more than 10 pounds, then you have to give the customer a small prize that you buy from Magic Hill for 60 cents each. Luckily, the friendly managers of Magic Hill have arranged a number of marks on the wall behind the customer so that you are capable of measuring the customer's height accurately. Unfortunately, there is a five-foot wall between you and the customer, so you can tell little about the person except for height and (usually) gender.

On your first day on the job, you do so poorly that you work all day and somehow manage to lose two dollars, so on the second day you decide to collect data to run a regression to estimate the relationship between weight and height. Since most of the participants are male, you decide to limit your sample to males. You hypothesize the following theoretical relationship:

$$Y_i = f(\overset{+}{X}_i) + \epsilon_i = \beta_0 + \beta_1 X_i + \epsilon_i \qquad (1.20)$$

where: Y_i = the weight (in pounds) of the ith customer
   X_i = the height (in inches above 5 feet) of the ith customer
   ϵ_i = the value of the stochastic error term for the ith customer

TABLE 1.1   DATA FOR AND RESULTS OF THE WEIGHT-GUESSING EQUATION

Obser-vation i (1)	Height Above 5' X_i (2)	Weight Y_i (3)	Predicted Weight $\hat{Y}_i$ (4)	Residual e_i (5)	$ Gain or Loss (6)
1	5.0	140.0	135.3	4.7	+.50
2	9.0	157.0	160.8	−3.8	+.50
3	13.0	205.0	186.3	18.7	−.60
4	12.0	198.0	179.9	18.1	−.60
5	10.0	162.0	167.2	−5.2	+.50
6	11.0	174.0	173.6	0.4	+.50
7	8.0	150.0	154.4	−4.4	+.50
8	9.0	165.0	160.8	4.2	+.50
9	10.0	170.0	167.2	2.8	+.50
10	12.0	180.0	179.9	0.1	+.50
11	11.0	170.0	173.6	−3.6	+.50
12	9.0	162.0	160.8	1.2	+.50
13	10.0	165.0	167.2	−2.2	+.50
14	12.0	180.0	179.9	0.1	+.50
15	8.0	160.0	154.4	5.6	+.50
16	9.0	155.0	160.8	−5.8	+.50
17	10.0	165.0	167.2	−2.2	+.50
18	15.0	190.0	199.1	−9.1	+.50
19	13.0	185.0	186.3	−1.3	+.50
20	11.0	155.0	173.6	−18.6	−.60
					TOTAL = $6.70

Note: This data set, and every other data set in the text, is available on the text's website in four formats and on the EViews CD-ROM. This data set's filename is HTWT1

In this case, the sign of the theoretical relationship between height and weight is believed to be positive (signified by the positive sign above X_i in the general theoretical equation), but you must quantify that relationship in order to estimate weights given heights. To do this, you need to collect a data set, and you need to apply regression analysis to the data.

The next day you collect the data summarized in Table 1.1 and run your regression on the Magic Hill computer, obtaining the following estimates:

$$\hat{\beta}_0 = 103.40 \qquad \hat{\beta}_1 = 6.38$$

This means that the equation

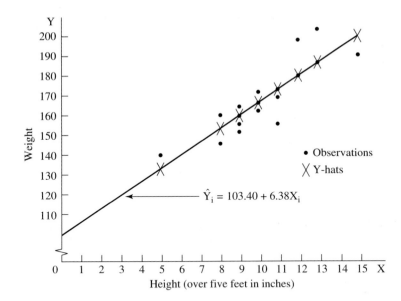

Figure 1.4 A Weight-Guessing Equation

If we plot the data from the weight-guessing example and include the estimated regression line, we can see that the estimated $\hat{Y}$s come fairly close to the observed Ys for all but three observations. Find a male friend's height and weight on the graph; how well does the regression equation work?

$$\text{Estimated weight} = 103.40 + 6.38 \cdot \text{Height (inches above five feet)}$$

$$(1.21)$$

is worth trying as an alternative to just guessing the weights of your customers. Such an equation estimates weight with a constant base of 103.40 pounds and adds 6.38 pounds for every inch of height over 5 feet. Note that the sign of $\hat{\beta}_1$ is positive, as you expected.

How well does the equation work? To answer this question, you need to calculate the residuals (Y_i minus $\hat{Y}_i$) from Equation 1.21 to see how many were greater than ten. As can be seen in the last column in Table 1.1, if you had applied the equation to these 20 people you wouldn't exactly have gotten rich, but at least you would have earned $6.70 instead of losing $2.00. Figure 1.4 shows not only Equation 1.21 but also the weight and height data for all 20 customers used as the sample.

Equation 1.21 would probably help a beginning weight guesser, but it could be improved by adding other variables or by collecting a larger sample. Such an equation is realistic, though, because it's likely that every successful weight guesser uses an equation like this without consciously thinking about that concept.

Our goal with this equation was to quantify the theoretical weight/height equation, Equation 1.20, by collecting data (Table 1.1) and calculating an estimated regression, Equation 1.21. Although the true equation, like observations of the stochastic error term, can never be known, we were able to come up with an estimated equation that had the sign we expected for $\hat{\beta}_1$ and that helped us in our job. Before you decide to quit school or your job and try to make your living guessing weights at Magic Hill, there is quite a bit more to learn about regression analysis, so we'd better move on.

1.5   Using Regression to Explain Housing Prices

As much fun as guessing weights at an amusement park might be, it's hardly a typical example of the use of regression analysis. For every regression run on such an off-the-wall topic, there are literally hundreds run to *describe* the reaction of GDP to an increase in the money supply, to *test* an economic theory with new data, or to *forecast* the effect of a price change on a firm's sales.

As a more realistic example, let's look at a model of housing prices. The purchase of a house is probably the most important financial decision in an individual's life, and one of the key elements in that decision is an appraisal of the house's value. If you overvalue the house, you can lose thousands of dollars by paying too much; if you undervalue the house, someone might outbid you.

All this wouldn't be much of a problem if houses were homogeneous products, like corn or gold, that have generally known market prices with which to compare a particular asking price. Such is hardly the case in the real estate market. Consequently, an important element of every housing purchase is an appraisal of the market value of the house, and many real estate appraisers use regression analysis to help them in their work.

Suppose your family is about to buy a house in Southern California, but you're convinced that the owner is asking too much money. The owner says that the asking price of $230,000 is fair because a larger house next door sold for $230,000 about a year ago. You're not sure it's reasonable to compare the prices of different-sized houses that were purchased at different times. What can you do to help decide whether to pay the $230,000?

Since you're taking an econometrics class, you decide to collect data on all local houses that were sold within the last few weeks and to build a regression model of the sales prices of the houses as a function of their sizes.[12] Such a data set is called **cross-sectional** because all of the observations are from the same point in time and represent different individual economic entities (like countries, or in this case, houses) from that same point in time.

To measure the impact of size on price, you include the size of the house as an independent variable in a regression equation that has the price of that house as the dependent variable. You expect a positive sign for the coefficient of size, since big houses cost more to build and tend to be more desirable than small ones. Thus the theoretical model is:

$$P_i = f(\overset{+}{S_i}) + \epsilon_i = \beta_0 + \beta_1 S_i + \epsilon_i \qquad (1.22)$$

where: P_i = the price (in thousands of $) of the ith house
S_i = the size (in square feet) of that house
ϵ_i = the value of the stochastic error term for that house

You collect the records of all recent real estate transactions, find that 43 local houses were sold within the last 4 weeks, and estimate the following regression of those 43 observations:

$$\hat{P}_i = 40.0 + 0.138 S_i \qquad (1.23)$$

What do these estimated coefficients mean? The most important coefficient is $\hat{\beta}_1 = 0.138$, since the reason for the regression is to find out the impact of size on price. This coefficient means that if size increases by 1 square foot, price will increase by 0.138 thousand dollars ($138). $\hat{\beta}_1$ thus measures the change in P_i associated with a one-unit increase in S_i. It's the slope of the regression line in a graph like Figure 1.5.

What does $\hat{\beta}_0 = 40.0$ mean? $\hat{\beta}_0$ is the estimate of the constant or intercept term. In our equation, it means that price equals 40.0 when size equals zero. As can be seen in Figure 1.5, the estimated regression line intersects the price axis at 40.0. While it might be tempting to say that the average price of a vacant lot is $40,000, such a conclusion would be unjustified for a number of

---

12. It's unusual for an economist to build a model of price without including some measure of quantity on the right-hand side. Such models of the price of a good as a function of the attributes of that good are called *hedonic* models and will be discussed in greater depth in Section 11.7. The interested reader is encouraged to skim the first few paragraphs of that section before continuing on with this example.

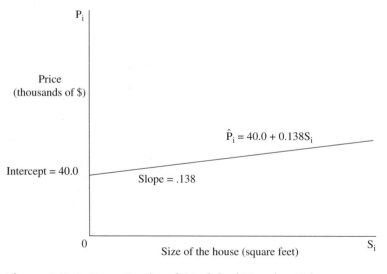

Figure 1.5 A Cross Sectional Model of Housing Prices

A regression equation that has the price of a house in Southern California as a function of the size of that house has an intercept of 40.0 and a slope of 0.138, using Equation 1.23.

reasons, which will be discussed in later chapters. It's much safer either to interpret $\hat{\beta}_0 = 40.0$ as nothing more than the value of the estimated regression when $S_i = 0$, or to not interpret $\hat{\beta}_0$ at all.

How can you use this estimated regression to help decide whether to pay $230,000 for the house? If you calculate a $\hat{Y}$ (predicted price) for a house that is the same size (1,600 square feet) as the one you're thinking of buying, you can then compare this $\hat{Y}$ with the asking price of $230,000. To do this, substitute 1600 for S_i in Equation 1.23, obtaining:

$$\hat{P}_i = 40.0 + 0.138(1600) = 40.0 + 220.8 = 260.8$$

The house seems to be a good deal. The owner is asking "only" $230,000 for a house when the size implies a price of $260,800! Perhaps your original feeling that the price was too high was a reaction to the steep housing prices in Southern California in general and not a reflection of this specific price.

On the other hand, perhaps the price of a house is influenced by more than just the size of the house. (After all, what good's a house in Southern California unless it has a pool or air-conditioning?) Such multivariate models are the heart of econometrics, but we'll hold off adding more independent variables to Equation 1.23 until we return to this housing price example later in the text.

1.6   Summary

1. Econometrics, literally "economic measurement," is a branch of economics that attempts to quantify theoretical relationships. Regression analysis is only one of the techniques used in econometrics, but it is by far the most frequently used.

2. The major uses of econometrics are description, hypothesis testing, and forecasting. The specific econometric techniques employed may vary depending on the use of the research.

3. While regression analysis specifies that a dependent variable is a function of one or more independent variables, regression analysis alone cannot prove or even imply causality.

4. Linear regression can only be applied to equations that are *linear in the coefficients*, which means that the regression coefficients are in their simplest possible form. For an equation with two explanatory variables, this form would be:

$$f(Y_i) = \beta_0 + \beta_1 f(X_{1i}) + \beta_2 f(X_{2i}) + \epsilon_i$$

5. A stochastic error term must be added to all regression equations to account for variations in the dependent variable that are not explained completely by the independent variables. The components of this error term include:
    a. omitted or left-out variables
    b. measurement errors in the data
    c. an underlying theoretical equation that has a different functional form (shape) than the regression equation
    d. purely random and unpredictable events

6. An estimated regression equation is an approximation of the true equation that is obtained by using data from a sample of actual Ys and Xs. Since we can never know the true equation, econometric analysis focuses on this estimated regression equation and the estimates of the regression coefficients. The difference between a particular observation of the dependent variable and the value estimated from the regression equation is called the residual.

Exercises

(Answers to even-numbered exercises are in Appendix A.)

1. Write the meaning of each of the following terms without referring to the book (or your notes), and compare your definition with the version in the text for each:
   a. stochastic error term
   b. regression analysis
   c. linear in the variables
   d. slope coefficient
   e. multivariate regression model
   f. expected value
   g. residual
   h. linear in the coefficients

2. Use your own computer's regression software and the weight (Y) and height (X) data from Table 1.1 to see if you can reproduce the estimates in Equation 1.21. There are three different ways to load the data: You can type in the data yourself, you can open datafile HTWT1 on the EViews CD, or you can download datafile HTWT1 (in any of four formats: SAS, EXCEL, SHAZAM, and ASCII) from the text's website: www.awlonline.com/studenmund/ Once the datafile is loaded, then run $Y = f(X)$, and your results should match Equation 1.21. Different programs require different commands to run a regression. For help in how to do this with EViews, for example, see the answer to this question in Appendix A.

3. Decide whether you would expect relationships between the following pairs of dependent and independent variables (respectively) to be positive, negative, or ambiguous. Explain your reasoning.
   a. Aggregate net investment in the U.S. in a given year and GDP in that year.
   b. The amount of hair on the head of a male professor and the age of that professor.
   c. The number of acres of wheat planted in a season and the price of wheat at the beginning of that season.
   d. Aggregate net investment and the real rate of interest in the same year and country.
   e. The growth rate of GDP in a year and the average hair length in that year.
   f. The quantity of canned heat demanded and the price of a can of heat.

4. Let's return to the height/weight example in Section 1.4:
   a. Go back to the data set and identify the three customers who seem to be quite a distance from the estimated regression line. Would we have a better regression equation if we dropped these customers from the sample?
   b. Measure the height of a male friend and plug it into Equation 1.21. Does the equation come within ten pounds? If not, do you think you see why? Why does the estimated equation predict the same weight for all males of the same height when it is obvious that all males of the same height don't weigh the same?
   c. Look over the sample with the thought that it might not be randomly drawn. Does the sample look abnormal in any way? (*Hint:* Are the customers who choose to play such a game a random sample?) If the sample isn't random, would this have an effect on the regression results and the estimated weights?
   d. Think of at least one other factor besides height that might be a good choice as a variable in the weight/height equation. How would you go about obtaining the data for this variable? What would the expected sign of your variable's coefficient be if the variable were added to the equation?

5. Continuing with the height/weight example, suppose you collected data on the heights and weights of 29 more customers and estimated the following equation:

$$\hat{Y}_i = 125.1 + 4.03X_i \qquad\qquad (1.24)$$

where: Y_i = the weight (in pounds) of the *i*th person
         X_i = the height (in inches over five feet) of the *i*th person

   a. Why aren't the coefficients in Equation 1.24 the same as those we estimated previously (Equation 1.21)?
   b. Compare the estimated coefficients of Equation 1.24 with those in Equation 1.21. Which equation has the steeper estimated relationship between height and weight? Which equation has the higher intercept? At what point do the two intersect?
   c. Use Equation 1.24 to "predict" the 20 original weights given the heights in Table 1.1. How many weights does Equation 1.24 miss by more than ten pounds? Does Equation 1.24 do better or worse than Equation 1.21? Could you have predicted this result beforehand?
   d. Suppose you had one last day on the weight-guessing job. What equation would you use to guess weights? (*Hint:* There is more than one possible answer.)

6. Not all regression coefficients have positive expected signs. For example, a *Sports Illustrated* article by Jaime Diaz reported on a study of golfing putts of various lengths on the Professional Golfers Association (PGA) Tour.[13] The article included data on the percentage of putts made (P_i) as a function of the length of the putt in feet (L_i). Since the longer the putt, the less likely even a professional is to make it, we'd expect L_i to have a negative coefficient in an equation explaining P_i. Sure enough, if you estimate an equation on the data in the article, you obtain:

$$\hat{P}_i = f(\overline{L}_i) = 83.6 - 4.1L_i \qquad (1.25)$$

a. Carefully write out the exact meaning of the coefficient of L_i.
b. Use Equation 1.25 to determine the percent of the time you'd expect a PGA golfer to make a 10-foot putt. Does this seem realistic? How about a 1-foot putt or a 25-foot putt? Do these seem as realistic?
c. Your answer to part b should suggest that there's a problem in applying a linear regression to these data. What is that problem? (*Hint:* If you're stuck, first draw the theoretical diagram you'd expect for P_i as a function of L_i, then plot Equation 1.25 onto the same diagram.)
d. Suppose someone else took the data from the article and estimated:

$$P_i = 83.6 - 4.1L_i + e_i$$

Is this the same result as that in Equation 1.25? If so, what definition do you need to use to convert this equation back to Equation 1.25?

7. Return to the housing price model of Section 1.5 and consider the following equation:

$$\hat{S}_i = 72.2 + 5.77P_i \qquad (1.26)$$

where: S_i = the size (in square feet) of the *i*th house
P_i = the price (in thousands of $) of that house

a. Carefully explain the meaning of each of the estimated regression coefficients.
b. Suppose you're told that this equation explains a significant portion (more than 80 percent) of the variation in the size of a house. Have we shown that high housing prices cause houses to be large? If not, what have we shown?
c. What do you think would happen to the estimated coefficients of

---

13. Jaime Diaz, "Perils of Putting," *Sports Illustrated*, April 3, 1989, pp. 76–79.

this equation if we had measured the price variable in dollars instead of in thousands of dollars? Be specific.

8. If an equation has more than one independent variable, we have to be careful when we interpret the regression coefficients of that equation. Think, for example, about how you might build an equation to explain the amount of money that different states spend per pupil on public education. The more income a state has, the more they probably spend on public schools, but the faster enrollment is growing, the less there would be to spend on each pupil. Thus, a reasonable equation for per pupil spending would include at least two variables: income and enrollment growth:

$$S_i = \beta_0 + \beta_1 Y_i + \beta_2 G_i + \epsilon_i \qquad (1.27)$$

where: S_i = educational dollars spent per public school student in the ith state
Y_i = per capita income in the ith state
G_i = the percent growth of public school enrollment in the ith state

a. State the economic meaning of the coefficients of Y and G. (*Hint:* Remember to hold the impact of the other variable constant.)

b. If we were to estimate Equation 1.27, what signs would you expect the coefficients of Y and G to have? Why?

c. In 1995 Fabio Silva and Jon Sonstelie estimated a cross-sectional model of per student spending by state that is very similar to Equation 1.27.[14]

$$\hat{S}_i = -183 + 0.1422 Y_i - 5926 G_i \qquad (1.28)$$
$$n = 49$$

Do these estimated coefficients correspond to your expectations? Explain Equation 1.28 in common sense terms.

d. The authors measured G as a decimal, so if a state had a 10 percent growth in enrollment, then G equaled .10. What would Equation 1.28 have looked like if the authors had measured G in percentage points, so that if a state had 10 percent growth, then G would have equaled 10? (*Hint:* Write out the actual numbers for the estimated coefficients.)

---

14. Fabio Silva and Jon Sonstelie, "Did Serrano Cause a Decline in School Spending?" *National Tax Review*, June 1995, pp. 199–215. The authors also included the tax price for spending per pupil in the ith state as a variable.

9. Your friend estimates a simple equation of bond prices in different years as a function of the interest rate that year (for equal levels of risk) and obtains:

$$\hat{Y}_i = 101.40 - 4.78X_i$$

where: Y_i = U.S. government bond prices (per \$100 bond) in the ith year
X_i = the federal funds rate (percent) in the ith year

a. Carefully explain the meanings of the two estimated coefficients. Are the estimated signs what you would have expected?
b. Why is the left-hand variable in your friend's equation $\hat{Y}$ and not Y?
c. Didn't your friend forget the stochastic error term in the estimated equation?
d. What is the economic meaning of this equation? What criticisms would you have of this model? (*Hint:* The federal funds rate is a rate that applies to overnight holdings in banks.)

10. Housing price models can be estimated with time-series as well as cross-sectional data. If you study aggregate time-series housing prices (see Table 1.2 for data and sources), you have:

$$\hat{P}_t = f(\overset{+}{GDP}) = 7404.6 + 19.8Y_t$$
$$n = 31 \text{ (annual 1964–1994)}$$

where : P_t = the nominal median price of new single-family houses in the U.S. in year t
Y_t = the U.S. GDP in year t (billions of current \$)

a. Carefully interpret the economic meaning of the estimated coefficients.
b. What is Y_t doing on the right side of the equation? Shouldn't it be on the left side?
c. Both the price and GDP variables are measured in nominal (or current, as opposed to real, or inflation-adjusted) dollars. Thus a major portion of the excellent explanatory power of this equation (more than 99 percent of the variation in P_t can be explained by Y_t alone) comes from capturing the huge amount of inflation that took place between 1964 and 1994. What could you do to eliminate the impact of inflation in this equation?
d. GDP is included in the equation to measure more than just inflation. What factors in housing prices other than inflation does the

TABLE 1.2   DATA FOR THE TIME-SERIES MODEL OF HOUSING PRICES

t	Year	Price(P_t)	GDP(Y_t)
1	1964	18,900	648.0
2	1965	20,000	702.7
3	1966	21,400	769.8
4	1967	22,700	814.3
5	1968	24,700	889.3
6	1969	25,600	959.5
7	1970	23,400	1010.7
8	1971	25,200	1097.2
9	1972	27,600	1207.0
10	1973	32,500	1349.6
11	1974	35,900	1458.6
12	1975	39,300	1585.9
13	1976	44,200	1768.4
14	1977	48,800	1974.1
15	1978	55,700	2232.7
16	1979	62,900	2488.6
17	1980	64,600	2708.0
18	1981	68,900	3030.6
19	1982	69,300	3149.6
20	1983	75,300	3405.0
21	1984	79,900	3777.2
22	1985	84,300	4038.7
23	1986	92,000	4268.6
24	1987	104,500	4539.9
25	1988	112,500	4900.4
26	1989	120,000	5250.8
27	1990	122,900	5546.1
28	1991	120,000	5724.8
29	1992	121,500	6020.2
30	1993	126,500	6343.3
31	1994	130,000	6736.9

P_t = the nominal median price of new single family houses in the U.S. in year t.
   (Source: *The Statistical Abstract of the U.S.*)

Y_t = the U.S. GDP in year t (billions of current dollars).
   (Source: *The Economic Report of the President*)

Note: EViews filename = HOUSE1

GDP variable help capture? Can you think of a variable that might do a better job?

11. The distinction between the stochastic error term and the residual is one of the most difficult concepts to master in this chapter.
   a. List at least three differences between the error term and the residual.

b. Usually, we can never observe the error term, but we can get around this difficulty if we assume values for the true coefficients. Calculate values of the error term and residual for each of the following six observations given that the true β_0 equals 0.0, the true β_1 equals 1.5, and the estimated regression equation is $\hat{Y}_i = 0.48 + 1.32X_i$:

Y_i	2	6	3	8	5	4
X_i	1	4	2	5	3	4

(*Hint:* To answer this question, you'll have to solve Equation 1.13 for ϵ and substitute Equation 1.15 into Equation 1.16.)
Note: filename = EX1

12. Look over the following equations and decide whether they are linear in the variables, linear in the coefficients, both, or neither.

a. $Y_i = \beta_0 + \beta_1 X_i^3 + \epsilon_i$

b. $Y_i = \beta_0 + \beta_1 \log X_i + \epsilon_i$

c. $\log Y_i = \beta_0 + \beta_1 \log X_i + \epsilon_i$

d. $Y_i = \beta_0 + \beta_1 X_i^{\beta_2} + \epsilon_i$

e. $Y_i^{\beta_0} = \beta_1 + \beta_2 X_i^2 + \epsilon_i$

13. What's the relationship between the unemployment rate and the amount of help-wanted advertising in an economy? In theory, the higher the unemployment rate, the lower the number of help-wanted ads, but is that what happens in the real world? Damodar Gujarati[15] tested this theory using time-series data for six years. You'd think that six years' worth of data would produce just six observations, far too few with which to run a reliable regression. However, Gujarati used one observation per quarter, referred to as "quarterly data," giving him a total of 24 observations. If we take his data set and run a linear-in-the-variables regression, we obtain:

$$\widehat{HWI}_t = 364 - 46.4UR_t \qquad (1.29)$$
$$n = 24 \text{ (quarterly 1962–1967)}$$

where: HWI_t = the U.S. help-wanted advertising index in quarter t
UR_t = the U.S. unemployment rate in quarter t

a. What sign did you expect for the coefficient of UR? (*Hint:* HWI rises as the amount of help-wanted advertising rises.) Explain your reasoning. Do the regression results support that expectation?

15. Damodar Gujarati, "The Relation Between the Help-Wanted Index and the Unemployment Index," *Quarterly Review of Economics and Business*, Winter 1968, pp. 67–73.

b. This regression is linear both in the coefficients and in the variables. Think through the underlying theory involved here. Does the theory support such a linear-in-the-variables model? Why or why not?

c. The model includes only one independent variable. Does it make sense to model the help-wanted index as a function of just one variable? Can you think of any other variables that might be important?

d. (optional) We have included Gujarati's data set, in Table 1.3 on our website, and on the EViews CD (as file HELP1). Use the EViews program (or any other regression software) to estimate Equation 1.29 on your own computer. Compare your results with Equation 1.29; are they the same?

TABLE 1.3

Observation	Quarter	HWI	UR
1	1962:1	104.66	5.63
2	1962:2	103.53	5.46
3	1962:3	97.30	5.63
4	1962:4	95.96	5.60
5	1963:1	98.83	5.83
6	1963:2	97.23	5.76
7	1963:3	99.06	5.56
8	1963:4	113.66	5.63
9	1964:1	117.00	5.46
10	1964:2	119.66	5.26
11	1964:3	124.33	5.06
12	1964:4	133.00	5.06
13	1965:1	143.33	4.83
14	1965:2	144.66	4.73
15	1965:3	152.33	4.46
16	1965:4	178.33	4.20
17	1966:1	192.00	3.83
18	1966:2	186.00	3.90
19	1966:3	188.00	3.86
20	1966:4	193.33	3.70
21	1967:1	187.66	3.63
22	1967:2	175.33	3.83
23	1967:3	178.00	3.93
24	1967:4	187.66	3.96

Note: filename = HELP1

CHAPTER 2

Ordinary Least Squares

The bread and butter of regression analysis is the estimation of the coefficients of econometric models with a technique called Ordinary Least Squares (OLS). The first two sections of this chapter summarize the reasoning behind and the mechanics of OLS. Regression users usually rely on computers to do the actual OLS calculations, so the emphasis here is on understanding what OLS attempts to do and how it goes about doing it.

How can you tell a good equation from a bad one once it has been estimated? One factor is the extent to which the estimated equation fits the actual data. The rest of the chapter is devoted to developing an understanding of the most commonly used measures of this fit: R^2 and the adjusted R^2, $\overline{R}^2$, pronounced R-bar-squared. The use of R^2 is not without perils, however, so the chapter concludes with an example of the misuse of this statistic.

2.1   Estimating Single-Independent-Variable Models with OLS

The purpose of regression analysis is to take a purely theoretical equation like:

$$Y_i = \beta_0 + \beta_1 X_i + \epsilon_i \qquad (2.1)$$

and use a set of data to create an estimated equation like:

$$\hat{Y}_i = \hat{\beta}_0 + \hat{\beta}_1 X_i \qquad (2.2)$$

where each "hat" indicates a sample estimate of the true population value. (In the case of Y, the "true population value" is $E[Y|X]$.) The purpose of the estimation technique is to obtain numerical values for the coefficients of an otherwise completely theoretical regression equation.

The most widely used method of obtaining these estimates is Ordinary Least Squares (OLS). OLS has become so standard that its estimates are presented as a point of reference even when results from other estimation techniques are used. **Ordinary Least Squares** is a regression estimation technique that calculates the $\hat{\beta}$s so as to minimize the sum of the squared residuals, thus:[1]

$$\text{OLS minimizes } \sum_{i=1}^{n} e_i^2 \quad (i = 1, 2, \ldots, n) \quad (2.3)$$

Since these residuals (e_is) are the differences between the actual Ys and the estimated Ys produced by the regression (the $\hat{Y}$s in Equation 2.2), Equation 2.3 is equivalent to saying that OLS minimizes $\sum (Y_i - \hat{Y}_i)^2$.

2.1.1 Why Use Ordinary Least Squares?

Although OLS is the most-used regression estimation technique, it's not the only one. Indeed, econometricians have invented what seems like zillions of different estimation techniques, a number of which we'll discuss later in this text.

There are at least three important reasons for using OLS to estimate regression models:

1. OLS is relatively easy to use.
2. The goal of minimizing $\sum e_i^2$ is quite appropriate from a theoretical point of view.
3. OLS estimates have a number of useful characteristics.

The first reason for using OLS is that it's the simplest of all econometric estimation techniques. Most other techniques involve complicated nonlinear

---

1. The summation symbol, $\sum$, means that all terms to its right should be added (or summed) over the range of the i values attached to the bottom and top of the symbol. In Equation 2.3, for example, this would mean adding up e_i^2 for all integer values between 1 and n:

$$\sum_{i=1}^{n} e_i^2 = e_1^2 + e_2^2 + \cdots + e_n^2$$

Often the $\sum$ notation is simply written as $\sum_i$ as in Equation 2.5, and it is assumed that the summation is over all observations from i = 1 to i = n. Sometimes, the i is omitted entirely, as in Equation 2.16, and the same assumption is made implicitly. For more practice in the basics of summation algebra, see Exercise 2.

formulas or iterative procedures, many of which are extensions of OLS itself. In contrast, OLS estimates are simple enough that, if you had to, you could compute them without using a computer or a calculator (for a single-independent-variable model).

The second reason for using OLS is that minimizing the summed, squared residuals is an appropriate theoretical goal for an estimation technique. To see this, recall that the residual measures how close the estimated regression equation comes to the actual observed data:

$$e_i = Y_i - \hat{Y}_i \qquad (i = 1, 2, \ldots, n) \qquad (1.16)$$

Since it's reasonable to want our estimated regression equation to be as close as possible to the observed data, you might think that you'd want to minimize these residuals. The main problem with simply totaling the residuals and choosing that set of βs that minimizes them is that e_i can be negative as well as positive. Thus, negative and positive residuals might cancel each other out, allowing a wildly inaccurate equation to have a very low ɡ e_i. For example, if Y = 100,000 for two consecutive observations and if your equation predicts 1.1 million and −900,000, respectively, your residuals will be +1 million and −1 million, which add up to zero!

We could get around this problem by minimizing the sum of the absolute values of the residuals, but this approach has problems as well. Absolute values are difficult to work with mathematically, and summing the absolute values of the residuals gives no extra weight to extraordinarily large residuals. That is, it often doesn't matter if a number of estimates are off by a small amount, but it's important if one estimate is off by a huge amount. For example, recall the weight-guessing equation of Chapter 1; you lost only if you missed the customer's weight by 10 or more pounds. In such a circumstance, you'd want to avoid large residuals.

Minimizing the summed squared residuals gets around these problems. Squared functions pose no unusual mathematical difficulties in terms of manipulations, and the technique avoids canceling positive and negative residuals because squared terms are always positive. In addition, squaring gives greater weight to big residuals than it does to smaller ones because e_i^2 gets relatively larger as e_i increases. For example, one residual equal to 4.0 has a greater weight than two residuals of 2.0 when the residuals are squared ($4^2 = 16$ vs. $2^2 + 2^2 = 8$).

The final reason for using OLS is that its estimates have at least three desirable characteristics:

1. The estimated regression line (Equation 2.2) goes through the means of Y and X. That is, if you substitute $\overline{Y}$ and $\overline{X}$ into Equation 2.2, the equation holds *exactly*: $\overline{Y}_i = \beta_0 + \beta_1 \overline{X}_i$.

2. The sum of the residuals is exactly zero.

3. OLS can be shown to be the "best" estimator possible under a set of fairly restrictive assumptions.

An **estimator** is a mathematical technique that is applied to a sample of data to produce real-world numerical **estimates** of the true population regression coefficients (or other parameters). Thus, Ordinary Least Squares is an estimator, and a $\hat{\beta}$ produced by OLS is an estimate.

2.1.2   How Does OLS Work?

How would OLS estimate a single-independent-variable regression model like Equation 2.1?

$$Y_i = \beta_0 + \beta_1 X_i + \epsilon_i \tag{2.1}$$

OLS selects those estimates of β_0 and β_1 that minimize the squared residuals, summed over all the sample data points:

$$\sum_{i=1}^{n} e_i^2 = \sum_{i=1}^{n} (Y_i - \hat{Y}_i)^2 \qquad (i = 1, 2, \ldots, n) \tag{2.4}$$

However, $\hat{Y}_i = \hat{\beta}_0 + \hat{\beta} X_{1i}$, so OLS actually minimizes

$$\sum_i e_i^2 = \sum_i (Y_i - \hat{\beta}_0 - \hat{\beta}_1 X_i)^2 \tag{2.5}$$

by choosing the $\hat{\beta}$s that do so. In other words, OLS yields the $\hat{\beta}$s that minimize Equation 2.5. For an equation with just one independent variable, these coefficients are[2]:

$$\hat{\beta}_1 = \frac{\sum_{i=1}^{n} [(X_i - \overline{X}) \cdot (Y_i - \overline{Y})]}{\sum_{i=1}^{n} (X_i - \overline{X})^2} \tag{2.6}$$

and, given this estimate of β_1,

---

2. For those with a moderate grasp of calculus and algebra, the derivation of these equations is informative. See Exercise 12.

$$\hat{\beta}_0 = \overline{Y} - \hat{\beta}_1\overline{X} \qquad (2.7)$$

where $\overline{X}$ = the mean of X, or $\sum X/n$, and $\overline{Y}$ = the mean of Y, or $\sum Y/n$.

What do these equations mean? Equation 2.6 sets $\hat{\beta}_1$ equal to the joint variation of X and Y (around their means) divided by the variation of X around its mean. It measures the portion of the variation in Y that is associated with variations in X. Equation 2.7 defines $\hat{\beta}_0$ to ensure that the regression equation does indeed pass through the means of X and Y. In addition, it can be shown that Equations 2.6 and 2.7 provide $\hat{\beta}$s that minimize the summed square residuals. Note that for each different data set, we'll get different estimates of β_1 and β_0, depending on the sample.

2.1.3 Total, Explained, and Residual Sums of Squares

Before going on, let's pause to develop some measures of how much of the variation of the dependent variable is explained by the estimated regression equation. A comparison of the estimated values with the actual values can help the researcher get a feeling for the adequacy of the hypothesized regression model.

Various statistical measures can be used to assess the degree to which the $\hat{Y}$s approximate the corresponding sample Ys, but all of them are based on the degree to which the regression equation estimated by OLS explains the values of Y better than a naive estimator, the sample mean, denoted by $\overline{Y}$. That is, econometricians use the squared variations of Y around its mean as a measure of the amount of variation to be explained by the regression. This computed quantity is usually called the **total sum of squares**, or TSS, and is written as:

$$TSS = \sum_{i=1}^{n} (Y_i - \overline{Y})^2 \qquad (2.8)$$

For Ordinary Least Squares, the total sum of squares has two components, that variation which can be explained by the regression and that which cannot:

$$\sum_i (Y_i - \overline{Y})^2 = \sum_i (\hat{Y}_i - \overline{Y})^2 + \sum_i e_i^2 \qquad (2.9)$$

Total Sum of Squares (TSS)	= Explained Sum of Squares (ESS)	+ Residual Sum of Squares (RSS)

This is usually called the "decomposition of variance."

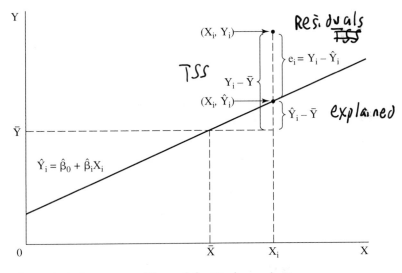

Figure 2.1 Decomposition of the Variance in Y

The variation of Y around its mean $(Y - \overline{Y})$ can be decomposed into two parts: (1) $(\hat{Y}_i - \overline{Y})$, the difference between the estimated value of Y $(\hat{Y})$ and the mean value of Y $(\overline{Y})$; and (2) $(Y_i - \hat{Y}_i)$, the difference between the actual value of Y and the estimated value of Y.

Figure 2.1 illustrates the decomposition of variance for the simple regression model. All estimated values of Y_i lie on the estimated regression line $\hat{Y}_i = \hat{\beta}_0 + \hat{\beta}_1 X_i$. The total deviation of the actual value of Y_i from its sample mean value is decomposed into two components, the deviation of $\hat{Y}_i$ from the mean and the deviation of the actual value of Y_i from the fitted value $\hat{Y}_i$. Thus, the first component of Equation 2.9 measures the amount of the squared deviation of Y_i from its mean that is explained by the regression line. This component of the total sum of the squared deviations, called the **explained sum of squares,** or ESS, is attributable to the fitted regression line.

The ESS is the explained portion of the TSS. The unexplained portion (that is, unexplained in an empirical sense by the estimated regression equation), is called the **residual sum of squares,** or RSS.[3]

We can see from Equation 2.9 that the smaller the RSS is relative to the TSS, the better the estimated regression line appears to fit the data. Thus, given the TSS, which no estimating technique can alter, researchers desire an estimating technique that minimizes the RSS and therefore maximizes the ESS. That technique is OLS.

---

3. Note that some authors reverse the definitions of TSS, RSS, and ESS (defining ESS as $\sum e^2$), and other authors reverse the order of the letters, as in SSR.

2.1.4 An Illustration of OLS Estimation

The equations for calculating regression coefficients might seem a little forbidding, but it's not hard to apply them yourself to data sets that have only a few observations and independent variables. Although you'll usually want to use regression software packages to do your estimation, you'll understand OLS better if you work through the following illustration.

To keep things simple, let's attempt to estimate the regression coefficients of the height and weight data given in Section 1.4. For your convenience in following this illustration, the original data are reproduced in Table 2.1. As was noted in Section 2.1.2, the formulas for OLS estimation for a regression equation with one independent variable are Equations 2.6 and 2.7:

$$\hat{\beta}_1 = \frac{\sum_{i=1}^{n} [(X_i - \overline{X}) \cdot (Y_i - \overline{Y})]}{\sum_{i=1}^{n} (X_i - \overline{X})^2} \tag{2.6}$$

$$\hat{\beta}_0 = \overline{Y} - \hat{\beta}_1 \overline{X} \tag{2.7}$$

If we undertake the calculations outlined in Table 2.1 and substitute them into Equations 2.6 and 2.7, we obtain these values:

$$\hat{\beta}_1 = \frac{590.20}{92.50} = 6.38$$

$$\hat{\beta}_0 = 169.4 - (6.38 \cdot 10.35) = 103.4$$

If you compare these estimates, you'll find that the manually calculated coefficient estimates are the same as the computer regression results summarized in Section 1.4.

Table 2.1 can also be used to exemplify some of the characteristics of OLS estimates. For instance, the sum of the $\hat{Y}$s (column 8) equals the sum of the Ys (column 2), so the sum of the residuals (column 9) does indeed equal zero (except for rounding errors). Another property of OLS estimates, that the estimated regression line goes through the means of Y and X, can be shown by substituting $\overline{Y}$ and $\overline{X}$ from Table 2.1 into the estimated regression equation. (Of course, this is hardly a surprise, since OLS calculates $\hat{\beta}_0$ so as to ensure that this property holds.)

The figures in Table 2.1 can also be used to derive the total sum of squares (TSS), the explained sum of squares (ESS), and the residual sum of squares (RSS). The TSS equals $\sum (Y_i - \overline{Y})^2$, or the sum of the squares of the values in column four, which equals 5,065. The ESS equals $\sum (\hat{Y}_i - \overline{Y})^2$, or the sum of the squared differences between the values in column eight and $\overline{Y}$, which

TABLE 2.1 THE CALCULATION OF ESTIMATED REGRESSION COEFFICIENTS FOR THE WEIGHT/HEIGHT EXAMPLE

Raw Data			Required Intermediate Calculations					
i (1)	Y_i (2)	X_i (3)	$(Y_i - \overline{Y})$ (4)	$(X_i - \overline{X})$ (5)	$(X_i - \overline{X})^2$ (6)	$(X_i - \overline{X})(Y_i - \overline{Y})$ (7)	$\hat{Y}_i$ (8)	$e_i = Y_i - \hat{Y}_i$ (9)
1	140	5	−29.40	−5.35	28.62	157.29	135.3	4.7
2	157	9	−12.40	−1.35	1.82	16.74	160.8	−3.8
3	205	13	35.60	2.65	7.02	94.34	186.3	18.7
4	198	12	28.60	1.65	2.72	47.19	179.9	18.1
5	162	10	−7.40	−0.35	0.12	2.59	167.2	−5.2
6	174	11	4.60	0.65	0.42	2.99	173.6	0.4
7	150	8	−19.40	−2.35	5.52	45.59	154.4	−4.4
8	165	9	−4.40	−1.35	1.82	5.94	160.8	4.2
9	170	10	0.60	−0.35	0.12	−0.21	167.2	2.8
10	180	12	10.60	1.65	2.72	17.49	179.9	0.1
11	170	11	0.60	0.65	0.42	0.39	173.6	−3.6
12	162	9	−7.40	−1.35	1.82	9.99	160.8	1.2
13	165	10	−4.40	−0.35	0.12	1.54	167.2	2.8
14	180	12	10.60	1.65	2.72	17.49	179.9	0.1
15	160	8	−9.40	−2.35	5.52	22.09	154.4	5.6
16	155	9	−14.40	−1.35	1.82	19.44	160.8	−5.8
17	165	10	−4.40	−0.35	0.12	1.54	167.2	−2.2
18	190	15	20.60	4.65	21.62	95.79	199.1	−9.1
19	185	13	15.60	2.65	7.02	41.34	186.3	−1.3
20	155	11	−14.40	0.65	0.42	−9.36	173.6	−18.6
Sum	3388	207	0.0	0.0	92.50	590.20	3388.3	−0.3
Mean	169.4	10.35	0.0	0.0			169.4	0.0

equals 3,765. The RSS, $\sum e_i^2$, is the sum of the squares of the values in column nine, which equals 1,305. Note that TSS = ESS + RSS except for rounding errors.[4] For practice in the use of these concepts, see Exercise 4.

2.2 Estimating Multivariate Regression Models with OLS

Let's face it, only a few dependent variables can be explained fully by a single independent variable. A person's weight, for example, is influenced by more than just that person's height. What about bone structure, percent body fat, exercise habits, or diet?

As important as additional explanatory variables might seem to the

---

4. If there is no constant term in the equation, TSS will not necessarily equal ESS + RSS, nor will $\sum e$ necessarily equal zero.

height/weight example, there's even more reason to include a variety of independent variables in economic and business applications. Although the quantity demanded of a product is certainly affected by price, that's not the whole story. Advertising, aggregate income, the prices of substitutes, the influence of foreign markets, the quality of customer service, possible fads, and changing tastes all are important in real-world models. As a result, we feel that it's vital to move from single-independent-variable regressions to *multivariate regression models*, equations with more than one independent variable.

2.2.1   The Meaning of Multivariate Regression Coefficients

The general multivariate regression model with K independent variables can be represented by Equation 1.12:

$$Y_i = \beta_0 + \beta_1 X_{1i} + \beta_2 X_{2i} + \cdots + \beta_K X_{Ki} + \epsilon_i \qquad (1.12)$$

where *i*, as before, goes from 1 to n and indicates the observation number. Thus, X_{1i} indicates the *i*th observation of independent variable X_1, while X_{2i} indicates the *i*th observation of another independent variable, X_2.

The biggest difference between a single-independent-variable regression model and a multivariate regression model is in the interpretation of the latter's slope coefficients. These coefficients, often called *partial*[5] regression coefficients, are defined to allow a researcher to distinguish the impact of one variable on the dependent variable from that of other independent variables.

> Specifically, a **multivariate regression coefficient** indicates the change in the dependent variable associated with a one-unit increase in the independent variable in question *holding constant the other independent variables in the equation.*

This last italicized phrase is a key to understanding multiple regression (as multivariate regression is often called). The coefficient β_1 measures the impact on Y of a one-unit increase in X_1, holding constant X_2, X_3, . . . and X_K but *not* holding constant any relevant variables that might have been omitted

---

5. The term "partial regression coefficient" will seem especially appropriate to those readers who have taken calculus, since multivariate regression coefficients correspond to partial derivatives. Indeed, in Equation 1.12 the partial derivative of Y_i with respect to X_{1i} is β_1, etc.

from the equation (e.g., X_{K+1}). The coefficient β_0 is the value of Y when all the Xs and the error term equal zero. As we'll learn in Section 7.1, you should always include a constant term in a regression equation, but you should not rely on estimates of β_0 for inference.

As an example of multivariate regression, let's consider the following annual model of the per capita demand for beef in the United States:

$$\hat{B}_t = 37.54 - 0.88P_t + 11.9Yd_t \qquad (2.10)$$

where: B_t = the per capita consumption of beef in year t (in pounds per person)

P_t = the price of beef in year t (in cents per pound)

Yd_t = the per capita disposable income in year t (in thousands of dollars)

The estimated coefficient of income, 11.9, tells us that beef consumption will increase by 11.9 pounds per person if per capita disposable income goes up by \$1,000, holding constant the price of beef. The ability to hold price constant is crucial because we'd expect such a large increase in per capita income to stimulate demand, therefore pushing up prices and making it hard to distinguish the effect of the income increase from the effect of the price increase. The multivariate regression estimate allows us to focus on the impact of the income variable by holding the price variable constant.

Note, however, that the equation does not hold constant other possible variables (like the price of a substitute) because these variables are not included in Equation 2.10. Before you move on to the next section, take the time to think through the meaning of the estimated coefficient of P in Equation 2.10; do you agree that the sign and relative size fit with economic theory?

2.2.2   OLS Estimation of Multivariate Regression Models

The application of OLS to an equation with more than one independent variable is quite similar to its application to a single-independent-variable model. To see this, let's follow the estimation of the simplest possible multivariate model, one with just two independent variables:

$$Y_i = \beta_0 + \beta_1 X_{1i} + \beta_2 X_{2i} + \epsilon_i \qquad (2.11)$$

The goal of OLS is to choose those $\hat{\beta}$s that minimize the summed square residuals, but now these residuals are from a multivariate model. For Equation 2.11, OLS would minimize:

$$\sum e_i^2 = \sum (Y_i - \hat{Y}_i)^2 = \sum (Y_i - \hat{\beta}_0 - \hat{\beta}_1 X_{1i} - \hat{\beta}_2 X_{2i})^2 \quad (2.12)$$

While OLS estimation of multivariate models is identical in general approach to that of single-independent-variable models, the equations themselves are more cumbersome. For Equation 2.11, the estimated coefficients are:

$$\hat{\beta}_1 = \frac{(\sum yx_1)(\sum x_2^2) - (\sum yx_2)(\sum x_1 x_2)}{(\sum x_1^2)(\sum x_2^2) - (\sum x_1 x_2)^2} \quad (2.13)$$

$$\hat{\beta}_2 = \frac{(\sum yx_2)(\sum x_1^2) - (\sum yx_1)(\sum x_1 x_2)}{(\sum x_1^2)(\sum x_2^2) - (\sum x_1 x_2)^2} \quad (2.14)$$

$$\hat{\beta}_0 = \bar{Y} - \hat{\beta}_1 \bar{X}_1 - \hat{\beta}_2 \bar{X}_2 \quad (2.15)$$

where lower case variables indicate deviations from the mean, as in $y = Y_i - \bar{Y}$; $x_1 = X_{1i} - \bar{X}_1$; and $x_2 = X_{2i} - \bar{X}_2$.

For the reader who is just about to throw this book away because of the complexity of the previous equations, there's both bad and good news. The bad news is that Equations 2.13 through 2.15 are for a regression model with only two independent variables; with three or more, the situation really gets out of hand! The good news is that numerous user-friendly computer packages can calculate all of the above in less than a second of computer time. Indeed, only someone lost in time or stuck on a desert island would bother estimating a multivariate regression model without a computer. The rest of us will use EViews, SHAZAM, SAS, TSP, RATS, BIOMED, MINITAB, or any of the other commercially available regression packages. The purpose of presenting these equations is to help you understand what multivariate estimation involves, not to teach you how to do it without a computer.

2.2.3   An Example of a Multivariate Regression Model

As an example of the estimation of a multivariate regression model, let's return to the beef demand equation of the previous section, Equation 2.10:

$$\hat{B}_t = 37.54 - 0.88 P_t + 11.9 Yd_t \quad (2.10)$$

where: B_t = the per capita consumption of beef in year t (in pounds per person)

P_t = the price of beef in year t (in cents per pound)

Yd_t = the per capita disposable income in year t (in thousands of dollars)

TABLE 2.2 DATA FOR THE DEMAND FOR BEEF EXAMPLE			
Year	**B**	**Yd**	**P**
1960	85.1	6.036	20.40
1961	87.8	6.113	20.20
1962	88.9	6.271	21.30
1963	94.5	6.378	19.90
1964	99.9	6.727	18.00
1965	99.5	7.027	19.90
1966	104.2	7.280	22.20
1967	106.5	7.513	22.30
1968	109.7	7.728	23.40
1969	110.8	7.891	26.20
1970	113.7	8.134	27.10
1971	113.0	8.322	29.00
1972	116.0	8.562	33.50
1973	108.7	9.042	42.80
1974	115.4	8.867	35.60
1975	118.9	8.944	32.20
1976	127.4	9.175	33.70
1977	123.5	9.381	34.40
1978	117.9	9.735	48.50
1979	105.4	9.829	66.10
1980	103.2	9.722	62.40
1981	104.2	9.769	58.60
1982	103.7	9.725	56.70
1983	105.7	9.930	55.50
1984	105.5	10.419	57.30
1985	106.5	10.625	53.70
1986	107.3	10.905	52.60
1987	103.3	10.970	61.10

Note: filename = BEEF2

These coefficients were calculated by a computer program using Equations 2.13–2.15 with the data in Table 2.2.

How would we go about graphing a multivariate regression result? We could use a three-dimensional diagram to graph Equation 2.10, as can be seen in Figure 2.2, but any additional variables would push us into four or more dimensions. What can we do? The answer is to draw a diagram of the dependent variable as a function of one of the independent variables *holding the other independent variable(s) constant.* In geometric terms, this means restricting the diagram to just one slice (or plane) of its actual multidimensional space.

To illustrate, look at Figures 2.3 and 2.4. These figures contain two different views of Equation 2.10. Figure 2.3 is a diagram of the effect of P on B,

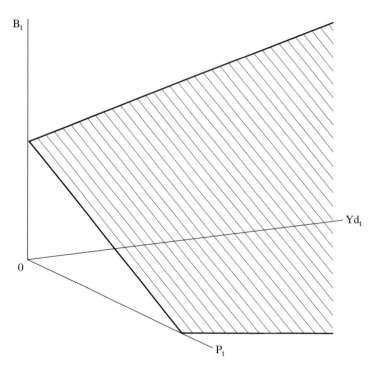

Figure 2.2 Beef Consumption as a Function of Price and Income

A three-dimensional rendering of Equation 2.10 is a plane that rises as per capita disposable income rises but falls as the price of beef rises.

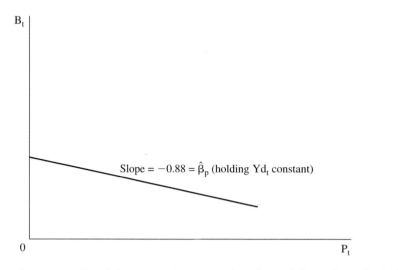

Slope $= -0.88 = \hat{\beta}_p$ (holding Yd_t constant)

Figure 2.3 Beef Consumption as a Function of the Price of Beef

In Equation 2.10, an increase in the price of beef by a penny decreases per capita beef consumption by 0.88 pounds, holding disposable income (per capita) constant.

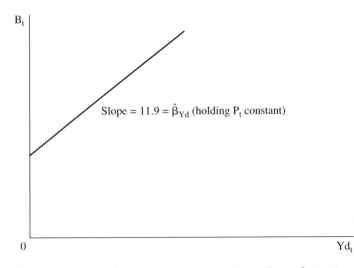

Figure 2.4   Beef Consumption as a Function of Per Capita Disposable Income

In Equation 2.10, an increase in per capita disposable income of a thousand dollars increases per capita beef consumption by 11.9 pounds, holding the price of beef constant.

holding Yd constant, and Figure 2.4 shows the effect of Yd on B, holding P constant. These two figures are graphical representations of multivariate regression coefficients, since they measure the impact on the dependent variable of a given independent variable, holding constant the other variables in the equation.

2.3   Evaluating the Quality of a Regression Equation

If the bread and butter of regression analysis is OLS estimation, then the heart and soul of econometrics is figuring out how good these OLS estimates are.

Many beginning econometricians have a tendency to accept regression estimates as they come out of a computer, or as they are published in an article, without thinking about the meaning or validity of those estimates. Such blind faith makes as much sense as buying an entire wardrobe of clothes without trying them on. Some of the clothes will fit just fine, but many others will turn out to be big (or small) mistakes.

Instead, the job of an econometrician is to carefully think about and evaluate every aspect of the equation, from the underlying theory to the quality of the data, before accepting a regression result as valid. In fact, most good econometricians spend quite a bit of time thinking about what to expect from an equation *before* they estimate that equation.

Once the computer estimates have been produced, however, it's time to evaluate the regression results. The list of questions that should be asked during such an evaluation is long. For example:

1. Is the equation supported by sound theory?
2. How well does the estimated regression as a whole fit the data?
3. Is the data set reasonably large and accurate?
4. Is OLS the best estimator to be used for this equation?
5. How well do the estimated coefficients correspond to the expectations developed by the researcher before the data were collected?
6. Are all the obviously important variables included in the equation?
7. Has the most theoretically logical functional form been used?
8. Does the regression appear to be free of major econometric problems?

The goal of this text is to help you develop the ability to ask and appropriately answer these kinds of questions. In fact, the number in front of each question above roughly corresponds to the chapter in which we'll address the issues raised by that question. Since this is Chapter 2, it'll come as no surprise to you to hear that the rest of the chapter will be devoted to the second of these topics, the overall fit of the estimated model.

2.4   Describing the Overall Fit of the Estimated Model

Let's face it, we expect that a good estimated regression equation will explain the variation of the dependent variable in the sample fairly accurately. If it does, we say that the estimated model fits the data well.

Looking at the overall fit of an estimated model is useful not only for evaluating the quality of the regression, but also for comparing models that have different data sets, functional forms, or combinations of independent variables. We can never be sure that one estimated model represents the truth any more than another, but evaluating the quality of the fit of the equation is one ingredient in a choice between different formulations of a regression model. The simplest commonly used measure of that fit is the coefficient of determination, R^2.

2.4.1 R^2, The Coefficient of Determination

The **coefficient of determination** is the ratio of the explained sum of squares to the total sum of squares:

$$R^2 = \frac{ESS}{TSS} = 1 - \frac{RSS}{TSS} = 1 - \frac{\sum e_i^2}{\sum (Y_i - \bar{Y})^2} \qquad (2.16)$$

The higher R^2, the closer the estimated regression equation fits the sample data. Measures of this type are called "goodness of fit" measures. Since TSS, RSS, and ESS are all nonnegative (being squared deviations), and since ESS ≤ TSS, R^2 must lie in the interval

$$0 \le R^2 \le 1 \qquad (2.17)$$

A value of R^2 close to one shows an excellent overall fit, whereas a value near zero shows a failure of the estimated regression equation to explain the values of Y_i better than could be explained by the sample mean $\bar{Y}$. In other words, R^2 can be defined by the percentage of the variation of Y around $\bar{Y}$ that is explained by the regression equation. Since OLS selects the parameter estimates that minimize RSS, OLS provides the largest possible R^2, given the linear specification of the model.

Figures 2.5 through 2.7 demonstrate some extremes. Figure 2.5 shows an X and Y that are unrelated. The fitted regression line might as well be $\hat{Y} = \bar{Y}$, the same value it would have if X were omitted. As a result, the estimated linear regression is no better than the sample mean as an estimate of Y_i. The explained portion, ESS, = 0, and the unexplained portion, RSS, equals the total squared deviations TSS; thus, $R^2 = 0$. In this case, the residuals are large relative to the deviations in Y from its mean, implying that a regression line is not useful in describing the relationship between X and Y.

Figure 2.6 shows a relationship between X and Y that can be "explained" quite well by a linear regression equation: the value of R^2 is .95. This kind of result is typical of a time-series regression with a good fit. Most of the variation has been explained, but there still remains a portion of the variation that is essentially random or unexplained by the model. Goodness of fit is relative to the topic being studied. If the sample is cross-sectional, an R^2 of .50 might be considered a good fit. In other words, there is no simple method of determining how high R^2 must be for the fit to be considered satisfactory. Instead, knowing when R^2 is relatively large or small is a matter of experience. It should be noted that a high R^2 does not imply that changes in X lead to changes in Y, as there may be an underlying variable whose changes lead to changes in both X and Y simultaneously.

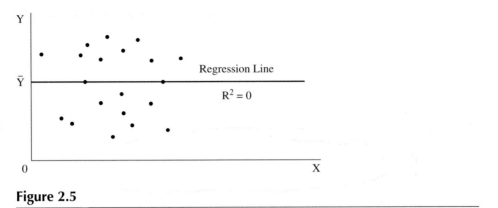

Figure 2.5

X and Y are not related; in such a case, R^2 would be 0.

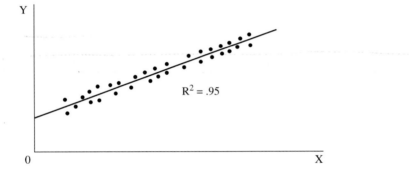

Figure 2.6

A set of data for X and Y that can be "explained" quite well with a regression line ($R^2 = .95$).

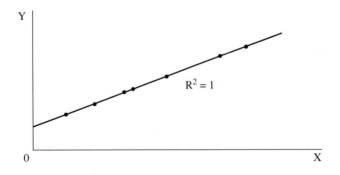

Figure 2.7

A perfect fit: all the data points are on the regression line, and the resulting R^2 is 1.

Figure 2.7 shows a perfect fit of $R^2 = 1$. Such a fit implies that no estimation is required. The relationship is completely deterministic, and the slope and intercept can be calculated from the coordinates of any two points. In fact, reported equations with R^2s equal to (or very near) one should be viewed with suspicion; they very likely do not explain the movements of the dependent variable Y in terms of the causal proposition advanced, even though they explain them empirically.

2.4.2 $\overline{R}^2$, The Adjusted R^2

A major problem with R^2 is that adding another independent variable to a particular equation can never decrease R^2. That is, if you compare two identical regressions (same dependent variable and independent variables), except that one has an additional independent variable, the equation with the greater number of independent variables will always have a better (or equal) fit as measured by R^2. To see this, recall the equation for R^2, Equation 2.16:

$$R^2 = 1 - \frac{RSS}{TSS} = 1 - \frac{\sum e_i^2}{\sum (Y_i - \overline{Y})^2} \qquad (2.16)$$

Since the dependent variable has not changed, TSS is still the same. Also, since OLS ensures that adding a variable will not increase the summed squared residuals, RSS will only decrease or stay the same.[6] If RSS decreases, RSS/TSS will also decrease and $1 - RSS/TSS$ will increase. Thus, adding a variable to an equation virtually guarantees that R^2 will increase.

Perhaps an example will make this clear. Let's return to our weight guessing regression, Equation 1.21:

Estimated weight $= 103.40 + 6.38 \cdot$ Height (over five feet)

The R^2 for this equation is .74. If we now add a completely nonsensical variable to the equation (say, the campus post office box number of each individual in question), then it turns out that the results become:

Estimated weight $= 102.35 + 6.36$ (height $>$ five feet) $+ 0.02$ (box#)

but the R^2 for this equation is .75! Thus, an individual using R^2 alone as the measure of the quality of the fit of the regression would choose the second version as better fitting.

---

6. You know that RSS will never increase because the OLS program could always set the coefficient of the added variable equal to zero, thus giving the same fit as the previous equation. The coefficient of the newly added variable being zero is the only circumstance in which R^2 will stay the same when a variable is added. Otherwise, R^2 will always increase when a variable is added to an equation.

The inclusion of the campus post office box variable not only adds a nonsensical variable to the equation, but it also requires the estimation of another coefficient. This lessens the **degrees of freedom,** or the excess of the number of observations (n) over the number of coefficients (including the intercept) estimated (K + 1). For instance, when the campus box number variable is added to the weight/height example, the number of observations stays constant at 20, but the number of estimated coefficients increases from 2 to 3, so the number of degrees of freedom falls from 18 to 17. This decrease has a cost, since the lower the degrees of freedom, the less reliable the estimates are likely to be.[7] Thus, the increase in the quality of the fit caused by the addition of a variable needs to be compared to the decrease in the degrees of freedom before a decision can be made with respect to the statistical impact of the added variable.

In essence, R^2 is of little help if we're trying to decide whether adding a variable to an equation improves our ability to meaningfully explain the dependent variable. Because of this problem, econometricians have developed another measure of the quality of the fit of an equation. That measure is $\overline{R}^2$ (pronounced R-bar-squared), which is R^2 adjusted for degrees of freedom:

$$\overline{R}^2 = 1 - \frac{RSS/(n - K - 1)}{TSS/(n - 1)} = 1 - \frac{\sum e_i^2/(n - K - 1)}{\sum (Y_i - \overline{Y})^2/(n - 1)} \qquad (2.18)$$

Notice that the only difference between R^2 and $\overline{R}^2$ is that the latter has been adjusted to take account of the K degrees of freedom that were lost in the calculations of the estimated slope coefficients. As a result, it's no surprise to learn that one can be expressed in terms of the other. If we substitute Equation 2.16 into Equation 2.18, it turns out that $\overline{R}^2$ can be expressed as a function of R^2:

$$\overline{R}^2 = 1 - (1 - R^2) \cdot \frac{(n - 1)}{(n - K - 1)} \qquad (2.19)$$

$\overline{R}^2$ will increase, decrease, or stay the same when a variable is added to an equation, depending on whether the improvement in fit caused by the addition of the new variable outweighs the loss of the degree of freedom. Indeed, the $\overline{R}^2$ for the weight-guessing equation *decreases* to .72 when the mail box variable is added. The mail box variable, since it has no theoretical relation to

---

7. For more on degrees of freedom, see Section 3.1.4.

weight, should never have been included in the equation, and the $\overline{R}^2$ measure supports this conclusion.

The highest possible $\overline{R}^2$ is 1.00, the same as for R^2. The lowest possible $\overline{R}^2$, however, is not .00; if R^2 is extremely low, $\overline{R}^2$ can be slightly negative. To see this, substitute 0 for R^2 into Equation 2.19.

$\overline{R}^2$ can be used to compare the fits of equations with the same dependent variable and different numbers of independent variables. Because of this property, most researchers automatically use $\overline{R}^2$ instead of R^2 when evaluating the fit of their estimated regression equations. In fact, $\overline{R}^2$ has become so popular that it replaces R^2 in most reported regression results.

Finally, a warning is in order. Always remember that the quality of fit of an estimated equation is only one measure of the overall quality of that regression. As mentioned above, the degree to which the estimated coefficients conform to economic theory and the researcher's previous expectations about those coefficients are just as important as the fit itself. For instance, an estimated equation with a good fit but with an implausible sign for an estimated coefficient might give implausible predictions and thus not be a very useful equation. Other factors, such as theoretical relevance and usefulness, also come into play. Let's look at an example of these factors.

2.5   An Example of the Misuse of $\overline{R}^2$

Section 2.4 implies that the higher the overall fit of a given equation, the better. Unfortunately, many beginning researchers assume that if a high $\overline{R}^2$ (or R^2) is good, then maximizing $\overline{R}^2$ is the best way to maximize the quality of an equation. Such an assumption is dangerous because a good overall fit is only one measure of the quality of an equation.

Perhaps the best way to visualize the dangers inherent in maximizing $\overline{R}^2$ without regard to the economic meaning or statistical significance of an equation is to look at an example of such misuse. This is important because it is one thing for a researcher to agree in theory that "$\overline{R}^2$ maximizing" is bad, and it is another thing entirely for that researcher to avoid subconsciously maximizing $\overline{R}^2$ on projects. It is easy to agree that the goal of regression is not to maximize $\overline{R}^2$, but many researchers find it hard to resist that temptation.

As an example, assume that you've been hired by the State of California to help the legislature evaluate a bill to provide more water to Southern California.[8] This issue is important because a decision must be made whether or not

---

8. The principle involved in this section is the same one that was discussed during the actual research, but these coefficients are hypothetical because the complexities of the real equation are irrelevant to our points.

to ruin, through a system of dams, one of the state's best trout fishing areas. On one side of the issue are Southern Californians who claim that their desert-like environment requires more water; on the other side are outdoors lovers and environmentalists who want to retain the natural beauty for which California is famous. Your job is to forecast the amount of water demanded in Los Angeles County, the biggest user of water in the state.

Because the bill is about to come before the state legislature, you are forced to choose between two regressions that have already been run for you, one by the state econometrician and the other by an independent consultant. You will base your forecast on one of these two equations. The state econometrician's equation:

$$\hat{W} = 24{,}000 + 48{,}000\text{PR} + 0.40\text{P} - 370\text{RF} \qquad (2.20)$$
$$\overline{R}^2 = .859 \quad \text{DF} = 25$$

The independent consultant's equation:

$$\hat{W} = 30{,}000 + 0.62\text{P} - 400\text{RF} \qquad (2.21)$$
$$\overline{R}^2 = .847 \quad \text{DF} = 26$$

where: $\hat{W}$ = the total amount of water consumed in Los Angeles County in a given year (measured in millions of gallons)

PR = the price of a gallon of water that year (measured in real dollars)

P = the population in Los Angeles County that year

RF = the amount of rainfall that year (measured in inches)

DF = degrees of freedom, which equal the number of observations (n = 29, since the years in the sample are 1970 through 1998) minus the number of coefficients estimated

Review these two equations carefully before going on with the rest of the section. What do you think the arguments of the state econometrician were for using his equation? What case did the independent econometrician make for her work?

The question is whether or not the increased $\overline{R}^2$ is worth the unexpected sign in the price of water coefficient in Equation 2.20. The state econometrician argued that given the better fit of his equation, it would do a better job of forecasting water demand. The independent consultant argued that it did not make sense to expect that an increase in price in the future would, holding the other variables in the equation constant, increase the quantity of water demanded in Los Angeles. Furthermore, given the unexpected sign of the coefficient, it seemed much more likely that the demand for water was unrelated to price during the sample period or that some important variable (such as real per capita income) had been left out of both equations. Since the amount of money spent on water was fairly low compared with other expenditures during the sample years, the consultant pointed out, it was possible that the demand for water was fairly price inelastic. The economic argument for the positive sign observed by the state econometrician is difficult to justify; it implies that as the price of water goes up, so does the quantity of water demanded.

Was this argument simply academic? The answer, unfortunately, is no. If a forecast is made with Equation 2.20, it will tend to overforecast water demand in scenarios that foresee rising prices and underforecast water demand with lower price scenarios. In essence, the equation with the better fit would do a worse job of forecasting.[9]

Thus, a researcher who uses $\overline{R}^2$ as the sole measure of the quality of an equation (at the expense of economic theory or statistical significance) increases the chances of having unrepresentative or misleading results. This practice should be avoided at all costs. No simple rule of econometric estimation is likely to work in all cases. Instead, a combination of technical competence, theoretical judgment, and common sense makes for a good econometrician.

To help avoid the natural urge to maximize $\overline{R}^2$ without regard to the rest of the equation, you might find it useful to imagine the following conversation:

You: Sometimes, it seems like the best way to choose between two models is to pick the one that gives the highest $\overline{R}^2$.

Your Conscience: But that would be wrong.

You: I know that the goal of regression analysis is to obtain dependable estimates of the true population coefficients and not to get a high $\overline{R}^2$, but my results "look better" if my fit is good.

Your Conscience: Look better to whom? It's not at all unusual to get a high $\overline{R}^2$ but find that some of the regression coefficients have signs that are contrary to theoretical expectations.

You: Well, I guess I should be more concerned with the logical relevance of the explanatory variables than with the fit, huh?

Your Conscience: Right! If in this process we obtain a high $\overline{R}^2$, well and good, but if $\overline{R}^2$ is high, it doesn't mean that the model is good.

You: Amen.

---

9. A couple of caveats to this example are in order. First, the purpose of the rainfall variable in both equations was to explain past behavior. For forecasting purposes, average rainfall figures would likely be used because future rainfall would not be known. Second, the income variable suggested by the independent consultant turned out to have a relatively small coefficient. This is because water expenditure is so minor in relation to the overall budget that the demand for water turned out to be fairly income inelastic as well as fairly price inelastic.

2.6   Summary

1. Ordinary Least Squares (OLS) is the most frequently used method of obtaining estimates of the regression coefficients from a set of data. OLS chooses those $\hat{\beta}$s that minimize the summed squared residuals ($\sum e_i^2$) for a particular sample.

2. The coefficient of determination, R^2, is the simplest measure of the degree of statistical fit of an estimated equation. It can be thought of as the percentage of the variation of Y around its mean that has been explained by a particular regression equation and is defined as the explained sum of squares (ESS) divided by the total sum of squares (TSS). A major fault of R^2 is that it always increases (technically, never decreases) when a variable is added to an equation.

3. R-bar-squared ($\overline{R}^2$) is the coefficient of determination (R^2) adjusted for degrees of freedom. $\overline{R}^2$ increases when a variable is added to an equation only if the improvement in fit caused by the addition of the new variable more than offsets the loss of the degree of freedom that is used up in estimating the coefficient of the new variable. As a result, most researchers will automatically use $\overline{R}^2$ instead of R^2 when evaluating the fit of their estimated regression equations.

4. Always remember that the quality of fit of an estimated equation is only one of the measures of the overall quality of that regression. The degree to which the estimated coefficients conform to economic theory and expectations developed by the researcher before the data were collected is at least as important as the size of $\overline{R}^2$ itself.

Exercises

(Answers to even-numbered exercises are in Appendix A.)

1. Write the meaning of each of the following terms without referring to the book (or your notes), and compare your definition with the version in the text for each:
   a. ordinary least squares
   b. the meaning of a multivariate regression coefficient
   c. total, explained, and residual sums of squares
   d. coefficient of determination
   e. degrees of freedom
   f. $\overline{R}^2$

2. To get more practice in the use of summation notation, use the data in question 4 below on Income (Y) and Percent of the labor force on farms (X) to answer the following questions. (*Hint*: Before starting this exercise, reread footnote 1 in this chapter which defines $\sum X = X_1 + X_2 + \cdots + X_n$.)
    a. Calculate $\sum X$. (*Hint*: Note that n = 10.)
    b. Calculate $\sum Y$.
    c. Calculate $\sum 3X$. Does it equal $3\sum X$?
    d. Calculate $\sum(X + Y)$. Does it equal $\sum X + \sum Y$?

3. a. In a single-independent variable model, what is the relationship between $\hat{\beta}_0$ and $\hat{\beta}_1$? More specifically, if $\hat{\beta}_1$ is known to be "too high" in a given equation, would you expect $\hat{\beta}_0$ to be too high, too low, or unaffected? Why?
    b. Suppose you estimate equations A and B on the same data and find that $\hat{\beta}_1 = \hat{\alpha}_1$. What values for $\hat{\beta}_0$, $\hat{\alpha}_0$, and/or $\hat{\alpha}_2$ does this result imply?

$$A: Y_i = \beta_0 + \beta_1 X_{1i} + \epsilon_{ai}$$

$$B: Y_i = \alpha_0 + \alpha_1 X_{1i} + \alpha_2 X_{2i} + \epsilon_{bi}$$

4. Just as you are about to estimate a regression (due tomorrow), massive sunspots cause magnetic interference that ruins all electrically powered machines (e.g., computers). Instead of giving up and flunking, you decide to calculate estimates from your data (on per capita income in thousands of U.S. dollars as a function of the percent of the labor force in agriculture in 10 developed countries) using methods like those used in Section 2.1.4 *without* a computer. Your data are:

Country	A	B	C	D	E	F	G	H	I	J
Income	6	8	8	7	7	12	9	8	9	10
Percent on farms	9	10	8	7	10	4	5	5	6	7

    a. Calculate $\hat{\beta}_0$ and $\hat{\beta}_1$.
    b. Calculate R^2 and $\bar{R}^2$.
    c. If the percentage of the labor force in agriculture in another developed country was 8 percent, what level of per capita income (in thousands of U.S. dollars) would you guess that country had?

5. Consider the following two least-squares estimates[10] of the relationship between interest rates and the federal budget deficit in the United States:

$$\text{Model A: } \hat{Y}_1 = 0.103 - 0.079X_1 \qquad R^2 = .00$$

where: Y_1 = the interest rate on Aaa corporate bonds
X_1 = the federal budget deficit as a percentage of GNP
(quarterly model: n = 56)

$$\text{Model T: } \hat{Y}_2 = 0.089 + 0.369X_2 + 0.887X_3 \qquad R^2 = .40$$

where : Y_2 = the interest rate on 3-month Treasury bills
X_2 = the federal budget deficit in billions of dollars
X_3 = the rate of inflation (in percent)
(quarterly model: n = 38)

a. What does "least-squares estimates" mean? What is being estimated? What is being squared? In what sense are the squares "least"?
b. What does it mean to have an R^2 of .00? Is it possible for an R^2 to be negative?
c. Calculate $\bar{R}^2$ for both equations. Is it possible for $\bar{R}^2$ to be negative?
d. Compare the two equations. Which model has estimated signs that correspond to your prior expectations? Is Model T automatically better because it has a higher $\bar{R}^2$? If not, which model do you prefer and why?

6. In an effort to determine whether going to class improved student academic performance, David Romer[11] developed the following equation:

$$G_i = f(ATT_i, PS_i) + \epsilon_i$$

where: G_i = the grade of the ith student in Romer's class
(A = 4, B = 3, etc.)
ATT_i = the fraction of class lectures that the ith student attended
PS_i = the fraction of the problem sets that the ith student completed

---

10. These estimates are simplified versions of results presented in the June/July 1984 issue of the *Review* of the Federal Reserve Bank of St. Louis (Model A) and the Summer 1983 issue of the *Review* of the Federal Bank of San Francisco (Model T).

11. David Romer, "Do Students Go to Class? Should They?" *Journal of Economic Perspectives,* Summer 1993, pp. 167–174.

a. What signs do you expect for the coefficients of the independent variables in this equation? Explain your reasoning.
b. Romer then estimated the equation:

$$\hat{G}_i = 1.07 + 1.74ATT_i + 0.60PS_i$$
$$n = 195 \quad R^2 = .33$$

Do the estimated results agree with your expectations?
c. It's usually easier to develop expectations about the signs of coefficients than about the *size* of those coefficients. To get an insight into the size of the coefficients, let's assume that there are 25 hours of lectures in a semester and that it takes the average student approximately 50 hours to complete all the problem sets in a semester. If a student in one of Romer's classes had only one more hour to devote to class and wanted to maximize the impact on his or her grade, should the student go to class for an extra hour or work on problem sets for an extra hour? (*Hint:* Convert the extra hour to percentage terms and then multiply those percentages by the estimated coefficients.)
d. From the above, it'd be easy to draw the conclusion that the bigger a variable's coefficient, the greater its impact on the dependent variable. To test this conclusion, what would your answer to part c have been if there had been 50 hours of lecture in a semester and if it had taken 10 hours for the average student to complete the problem sets? Were we right to conclude that the larger the estimated coefficient, the more important the variable?
e. What's the real-world meaning of having $R^2 = .33$? For this specific equation, does .33 seem high, low, or just about right?
f. Is it reasonable to think that only class attendance and problem-set completion affect your grade in a class? If you could add just one more variable to the equation, what would it be? Explain your reasoning. What should adding your variable to the equation do to R^2? to $\bar{R}^2$?

7. Suppose that you have been asked to estimate an econometric model to explain the number of people jogging a mile or more on the school track to help decide whether to build a second track to handle all the joggers. You collect data by living in a press box for the spring semester, and you run two possible explanatory equations.

$$A: \hat{Y} = 125.0 - 15.0X_1 - 1.0X_2 + 1.5X_3 \qquad \bar{R}^2 = .75$$
$$B: \hat{Y} = 123.0 - 14.0X_1 + 5.5X_2 - 3.7X_4 \qquad \bar{R}^2 = .73$$

where:
Y = the number of joggers on a given day
X_1 = inches of rain that day
X_2 = hours of sunshine that day
X_3 = the high temperature for that day (in degrees F)
X_4 = the number of classes with term papers due the next day

a. Which of the two (admittedly hypothetical) equations do you prefer? Why?
b. How is it possible to get different estimated signs for the coefficient of the same variable using the same data?

8. David Katz[12] studied faculty salaries as a function of their "productivity" and estimated a regression equation with the following coefficients:

$$\hat{S}_i = 11{,}155 + 230B_i + 18A_i + 102E_i + 489D_i + 189Y_i + \cdots$$

where:
S_i = the salary of the ith professor in dollars per year
B_i = the number of books published, lifetime
A_i = the number of articles published, lifetime
E_i = the number of "excellent" articles published, lifetime
D_i = the number of dissertations supervised
Y_i = the number of years teaching experience

a. Do the signs of the coefficients match your prior expectations?
b. Do the relative sizes of the coefficients seem reasonable?
c. Suppose a professor had just enough time (after teaching, etc.) to write a book, write two excellent articles, or supervise three dissertations. Which would you recommend? Why?
d. Would you like to reconsider your answer to part b above? Which coefficient seems out of line? What explanation can you give for that result? Is the equation in some sense invalid? Why or why not?

9. What's wrong with the following kind of thinking: "I understand that R^2 is not a perfect measure of the quality of a regression equation because it always increases when a variable is added to the equation. Once we adjust for degrees of freedom by using $\overline{R}^2$, though, it seems to me that the higher the $\overline{R}^2$, the better the equation."

---

12. David A. Katz, "Faculty Salaries, Promotions, and Productivity at a Large University," *American Economic Review*, June 1973, pp. 469–477. Katz's equation included other variables, as well, as indicated by the "+ $\cdots$" at the end of the equation.

10. In 1985 Charles Lave[13] published a study of driver fatality rates. His overall conclusion was that the variance of driving speed (the extent to which vehicles sharing the same highway drive at dramatically different speeds) is important in determining fatality rates. As part of his analysis, he estimated an equation with cross-state data from two different years:

$$1981: \quad \hat{F}_i = \hat{\beta}_0 + 0.176V_i + 0.0136C_i - 7.75H_i$$
$$\overline{R}^2 = .624 \qquad n = 41$$

$$1982: \quad \hat{F}_i = \hat{\beta}_0 + 0.190V_i + 0.0071C_i - 5.29H_i$$
$$\overline{R}^2 = .532 \qquad n = 44$$

where: F_i = the fatalities on rural interstate highways (per 100 million vehicle miles traveled) in the ith state
$\hat{\beta}_0$ = an unspecified estimated intercept
V_i = the driving speed variance in the ith state
C_i = driving citations per driver in the ith state
H_i = hospitals per square mile (adjusted) in the ith state

a. Think through the theory behind each variable, and develop expected signs for each coefficient. (*Hint:* Be careful with C.) Do Lave's estimates support your expectations?
b. Should we attach much meaning to the differences between the estimated coefficients from the two years? Why or why not? Under what circumstances might you be concerned about such differences?
c. The 1981 equation has the higher $\overline{R}^2$, but which equation has the higher R^2? (*Hint:* You can calculate the R^2s given the information above, or you can attempt to figure the answer theoretically.)

11. In Exercise 5 in Chapter 1, we estimated a height/weight equation on a new data set of 29 male customers, Equation 1.24:

$$\hat{Y}_i = 125.1 + 4.03X_i \qquad\qquad (1.24)$$

where: Y_i = the weight (in pounds) of the ith person
X_i = the height (in inches above five feet) of the ith person

13. Charles A. Lave, "Speeding, Coordination, and the 55 MPH Limit," *American Economic Review*, December 1985, pp. 1159–1164.

Suppose that a friend now suggests adding F_i, the percent body fat of the ith person, to the equation.

a. What is the theory behind adding F_i to the equation? How does the meaning of the coefficient of X change when you add F?

b. Assume you now collect data on the percent body fat of the 29 males and estimate:

$$\hat{Y}_i = 120.8 + 4.11X_i + 0.28F_i \qquad (2.22)$$

Do you prefer Equation 2.22 or Equation 1.24? Why?

c. Suppose you learn that the $\overline{R}^2$ of Equation 1.24 is .75 and the $\overline{R}^2$ of Equation 2.22 is .72. Which equation do you prefer now? Explain your answer.

d. Suppose that you learn that the mean of F for your sample is 12.0. Which equation do you prefer now? Explain your answer.

12. For students with a background in calculus, the derivation of Equations 2.6 and 2.7 is useful. Derive these two equations by carrying out the following steps. (*Hint:* Be sure to write out each step of the proof; if you get stuck, compare your answer to that in the back of the book.)

a. Differentiate Equation 2.5 with respect to $\hat{\beta}_0$ and then with respect to $\hat{\beta}_1$.

b. Set these two derivatives equal to zero, thus creating what are called the "normal equations."

c. Solve the normal equations for $\hat{\beta}_1$, obtaining Equation 2.6.

d. Solve the normal equations for $\hat{\beta}_0$, obtaining Equation 2.7.

13. To get more practice in using EViews or your computer's regression program, estimate Equation 2.10 using the data from Table 2.2 (or the BEEF2 datafile on the website or the EViews disk). Can you replicate the results in the text? What are R^2 and $\overline{R}^2$?

Learning to Use Regression Analysis

From a quick reading of Chapter 2, it'd be easy to conclude that regression analysis is little more than the mechanical application of a set of equations to a sample of data. Such a notion would be similar to deciding that all there is to golf is hitting the ball well. Golfers will tell you that it does little good to hit the ball well if you've used the wrong club or have hit the ball toward a trap, tree, or pond. Similarly, experienced econometricians spend much less time thinking about the OLS estimation of an equation than they do about a number of other factors. Our goal in this chapter is to introduce some of these "real world" concerns.

The first section, an overview of the six steps typically taken in applied regression analysis, is the most important in the chapter. We believe that the ability to learn and understand a specific topic, like OLS estimation, is enhanced if the reader has a clear vision of the role that specific topic plays in the overall framework of regression analysis. In addition, the six steps make it hard to miss the crucial function of theory in the development of sound econometric research.

This is followed by a complete example of how to use the six steps in applied regression, a location analysis for the "Woody's" restaurant chain that is based on actual company data and to which we will return in future chapters to apply new ideas and tests.

3.1   Steps in Applied Regression Analysis

Although there are no hard and fast rules for conducting econometric research, most investigators commonly follow a standard method for applied regression analysis. The relative emphasis and effort expended on each step

---

63

may vary, but normally all the steps are considered necessary for successful research. Note that we don't discuss the selection of the dependent variable; this choice is determined by the purpose of the research. After that, it is logical to follow this sequence:

1. Review the literature and develop the theoretical model.
2. Specify the model: Select the independent variables and the functional form.
3. Hypothesize the expected signs of the coefficients.
4. Collect the data.
5. Estimate and evaluate the equation.
6. Document the results.

The purpose of suggesting these steps is not to discourage the use of innovative or unusual approaches but rather to develop in the reader a sense of how regression ordinarily is done by professional economists and business analysts.

3.1.1   Step 1: Review the Literature and Develop the Theoretical Model

The first step in any applied research is to get a good theoretical grasp of the topic to be studied. That's right, the best data analysts don't start with data; they start with theory. This is because many econometric decisions, ranging from which variables to use to which functional form to employ, are determined by the underlying theoretical model. It's virtually impossible to build a good econometric model without a solid understanding of the topic you're studying.

For most topics, this means that it's smart to review the scholarly literature before doing anything else. If a professor has investigated the theory behind your topic, you want to know about it. If other researchers have estimated equations for your dependent variable, you might want to apply one of their models to your data set. On the other hand, if you disagree with the approach of previous authors, you might want to head off in a new direction. In either case, you shouldn't have to "reinvent the wheel"; you should start your investigation where earlier researchers left off. Any academic paper on an empirical topic should begin with a summary of the extent and quality of previous research.

The most convenient approaches to reviewing the literature are to obtain several recent issues of the *Journal of Economic Literature* or a business-oriented publication of abstracts, or to run an Internet search on your topic. Using these resources, find and read several recent articles on your topic. Pay attention to the bibliographies of these articles. If an older article is cited by a number of current authors, or if its title hits your topic on the head, trace back through the literature and find this article as well. We'll have more advice on reviewing the literature in Chapter 11.

In some cases, a topic will be so new or so obscure that you won't be able to find any articles on it. What then? We recommend two possible strategies. First, try to transfer theory from a similar topic to yours. For example, if you're trying to build a model of the demand for a new product, read articles that analyze the demand for similar, existing products. Second, if all else fails, pick up the telephone and call someone who works in the field you're investigating. For example, if you're building a model of housing in an unfamiliar city, call a real estate agent who works there.

3.1.2 Step 2: Specify the Model: Select the Independent Variables and the Functional Form

The most important step in applied regression analysis is the **specification** of the theoretical regression model. After selecting the dependent variable, the following components should be specified:

1. the independent variables and how they should be measured,
2. the functional (mathematical) form of the variables, and
3. the type of stochastic error term.

A regression equation is specified when each of these elements has been treated appropriately. We'll discuss the details of these specification decisions in Chapters 6, 7, and 4, respectively.

Each of the elements of specification is determined primarily on the basis of economic theory, rather than on the results of an estimated regression equation. A mistake in any of the three elements results in a **specification error.** Of all the kinds of mistakes that can be made in applied regression analysis, specification error is usually the most disastrous to the validity of the estimated equation. Thus, the more attention paid to economic theory at the beginning of a project, the more satisfying the regression results are likely to be.

The emphasis in this text is on estimating behavioral equations, those that describe the behavior of economic entities. We focus on selecting independent variables based on the economic theory concerning that behavior. An explanatory variable is chosen because it is a theoretical determinant of the dependent variable; it is expected to explain at least part of the variation in the dependent variable. Recall that regression gives evidence but does not prove economic causality. Just as an example does not prove the rule, a regression result does not prove the theory.

There are dangers in specifying the wrong independent variables. Our goal should be to specify only relevant explanatory variables, those expected theoretically to assert a "significant" influence on the dependent variable. Variables suspected of having little effect should be excluded unless their possible impact on the dependent variable is of some particular (e.g., policy) interest.

For example, an equation that explains the quantity demanded of a consumption good might use the price of the product and consumer income or wealth as likely variables. Theory also indicates that complementary and substitute goods are important. Therefore, you might decide to include the prices of complements and substitutes, but which complements and substitutes? Of course, selection of the closest complements and/or substitutes is appropriate, but how far should you go? The choice must be based on theoretical judgment.

When researchers decide that, for example, the prices of only two other goods need to be included, they are said to impose their *priors* (i.e., previous theoretical belief) or their working hypotheses on the regression equation. Imposition of such priors is a common practice that determines the number and kind of hypotheses that the regression equation has to test. The danger is that a prior may be wrong and could diminish the usefulness of the estimated regression equation. Each of the priors therefore should be explained and justified in detail.

Some concepts (for example, gender) might seem impossible to include in an equation because they're inherently qualitative in nature and can't be quantified. These variables can be quantified by using dummy (or binary) variables. A **dummy variable** takes on the values of one or zero depending on whether a specified condition holds. We'll discuss dummy variables in detail in Chapters 7 and 13.

As an illustration, suppose that Y_i represents the salary of the ith high school teacher, and that the salary level depends primarily on the type of degree earned and the experience of the teacher. All teachers have a B.A., but some also have an M.A. An equation representing the relationship between earnings and the type of degree might be:

$$Y_i = \beta_0 + \beta_1 X_{1i} + \beta_2 X_{2i} + \epsilon_i \qquad (3.1)$$

where: $X_{1i} = \begin{cases} 1 \text{ if the } i\text{th teacher has an M.A.} \\ 0 \text{ otherwise} \end{cases}$

$X_{2i} =$ the number of years of teaching experience of the ith teacher

The variable X_1 only takes on values of zero or one, so X_1 is called a dummy variable, or just a "dummy." Needless to say, the term has generated many a pun. In this case, the dummy variable represents the condition of having a master's degree. The coefficient β_1 indicates the additional salary that can be attributed to having an M.A., holding teaching experience constant.

3.1.3   Step 3: Hypothesize the Expected Signs of the Coefficients

Once the variables are selected, it is important to carefully hypothesize the signs you expect their regression coefficients to have based on the underlying theory. For example, in the demand equation for a final consumption good, the quantity demanded (Q_d) is expected to be inversely related to its price (P) and the price of a complementary good (P_c), and positively related to consumer income (Y) and the price of a substitute good (P_s). The first step in the written development of a regression model usually is to express the equation as a general function:

$$Q_d = f(\overset{-}{P}, \overset{+}{Y}, \overset{-}{P_c}, \overset{+}{P_s}) + \epsilon \qquad (3.2)$$

The signs above the variables indicate the hypothesized sign of the respective regression coefficient in a linear model.

In many cases, the basic theory is general knowledge, so that the reasons for each sign need not be discussed. However, if any doubt surrounds the selection of an expected sign, you should document the opposing forces at work and the reasons for hypothesizing a positive or negative coefficient.

3.1.4   Step 4: Collect the Data

Data collection may begin after the specification of the regression model. This step entails more than a mechanical recording of data, though, because the type and size of the sample must also be chosen. Often, analysis begins as researchers examine the data and look for typographical, conceptual, or definitional errors. For more on the details of data collection, see Section 11.4.

A general rule regarding sample size is the more observations the better as long as the observations are from the same general population. Ordinarily, researchers take all the roughly comparable observations that are readily available. In regression analysis, all the variables must have the same number of observations. They also should have the same frequency (monthly, quarterly, annual, etc.) and time period. Often, the frequency selected is determined by the availability of data.

The reason there should be as many observations as possible concerns the statistical concept of *degrees of freedom* first mentioned in Section 2.4.2. Consider fitting a straight line to two points on an X, Y coordinate system, as in Figure 3.1. Such an exercise can be done mathematically without error. Both points lie on the line, so there is no estimation of the coefficients involved. The two points determine the two parameters, the intercept and the slope, precisely. Estimation takes place only when a straight line is fitted to three or more points that were generated by some process that is not exact. The excess of the number of observations (three) over the number of coefficients to be estimated (in this case two, the intercept and slope) is called the **degrees of freedom.**[1] All that is necessary for estimation is a single degree of freedom, as in Figure 3.2, but the more degrees of freedom there are, the less likely it is that the stochastic or purely random component of the equation (the error term) will affect inferences about the deterministic portion, the portion of primary interest. This is because when the number of degrees of freedom is large, every positive error is likely to be balanced by a large negative error. With only a few points, the random element is likely to fail to provide such offsetting observations. For example, the more a coin is flipped, the more likely it is that the observed proportion of heads will reflect the true underlying probability (namely, 0.5).

Another area of concern has to do with the *units of measurement of the variables.* Does it matter if an independent variable is measured in dollars or thousands of dollars? Does it matter if the measured variable differs consistently from the true variable by ten units? Interestingly, such changes don't matter in terms of regression analysis except in interpreting the scale of the

---

1. Throughout the text, we will calculate the number of degrees of freedom (d.f.) in a regression equation as d.f. = $(n - K - 1)$, where K is the number of independent variables in the equation. Equivalently, some authors will set $K' = K + 1$ and define d.f. = $(n - K')$. Since K' equals the number of independent variables plus one (for the constant), it equals the number of coefficients to be estimated in the regression.

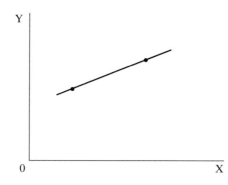

Figure 3.1 Mathematical Fit of a Line to Two Points

If there are only two points in a data set, as in Figure 3.1, a straight line can be fitted to those points mathematically without error, because two points completely determine a straight line.

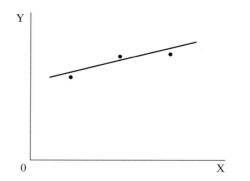

Figure 3.2 Statistical Fit of a Line to Three Points

If there are three (or more) points in a data set, as in Figure 3.2, then the line must almost always be fitted to the points statistically, using the estimation procedures of Section 2.1.

coefficients. All conclusions about signs, significance, and economic theory are independent of units of measurement.[2]

That is, it makes little difference whether an independent variable is measured in dollars or thousands of dollars. The constant term and measures of overall fit remain unchanged. Such a multiplicative factor does change the

---

2. The units of measurement of the dependent variable also do not alter the interpretation of the regression equation (except, as above, in interpreting the magnitude of the regression coefficients), hypothesis testing, or measures of fit such as R^2.

slope coefficient, but only by the exact amount necessary to compensate for the change in the units of measurement of the independent variable. Similarly, a constant factor added to a variable alters only the intercept term without changing the slope coefficient itself.

As an example, recall the weight/height regression of Section 1.4. The explanatory variable was measured as inches above 5 feet, so that 5 feet, or 60 inches, was a constant factor that was subtracted from each observation. If we reestimate the equation with the absolute height in inches (Z) as the independent variable, we get:

$$\hat{Y}_i = -279.2 + 6.38Z_i \tag{3.3}$$

Since the original equation was

$$\hat{Y}_i = 103.4 + 6.38X_i \tag{3.4}$$

only the constant term has changed, and for each height we would obtain the same estimated weight. To see this, substitute 60 for Z and 0 for X; Y = 103.4 in both cases! The essential relationship between Y and Z is the same as between Y and X. That is, adding a constant to a variable will not change the slope coefficients of a linear equation (but it will in most equations that are nonlinear in the coefficients).

3.1.5   Step 5: Estimate and Evaluate the Equation

The Ordinary Least Squares (OLS) technique, discussed in Section 2.1, is the method typically used to estimate econometric equations. Where alternative techniques might be appropriate, estimates from the alternatives should be compared to OLS estimates. The alternatively estimated equations must be evaluated carefully and judgment applied before a choice is made.

Once the model has been estimated, the results should be checked for errors. Data transformations and coefficient estimation are usually done in the same computer program, so it is wise to obtain a printout of the data set exactly as it was used in the regression estimation. Check one or two values of any variables that were transformed. If these values are correct, it may be assumed that the computer did not make any mistakes transforming the rest of the observations. Also obtain a printout or a plot of the data and look for outliers. An **outlier** is an observation that lies outside the range of the rest of the observations. Looking for outliers is a very economical way to look for data entry or transcription errors. It's also a good habit to make sure that the mean, maximum, and minimum of each variable seem reasonable.

After checking for data errors, examine the signs, magnitudes, and significance of the coefficients and the overall measures of fit. Regression results are rarely what one expects. Usually, additional model development is required or alternative estimating techniques are called for. Be sure to reevaluate the model and make any necessary changes before jumping into fancy regression "fix-up" routines. Sometimes these routines improve the overall measures of goodness of fit or some other statistic while playing havoc with the reliability of estimates of the model's parameters. A famous econometrician, Zvi Griliches, warned that errors in the data coming from their measurement, usually computed from samples or estimates, imply that the fancier estimating techniques should be avoided because they are more sensitive to data errors than is OLS.[3] Such *errors in the variables* are dealt with in Section 14.6. Also, when faced with unexpected regression results (which happen all too often), a reexamination of the theoretical basis of the model is in order. However, one should avoid adjusting the theory merely to fit the data, thus introducing researcher bias. The researcher has to walk the fine line between making appropriate and inappropriate adjustments to the model. Choosing proper modifications is one of the artistic elements in applied regression analysis.

3.1.6 Step 6: Document the Results

A standard format usually is used to present estimated regression results:

$$\hat{Y}_i = 103.40 + 6.38X_i$$
$$(0.88)$$
$$t = 7.22$$
$$n = 20 \quad \overline{R}^2 = .73$$

(3.5)

The number in parentheses is the estimated standard error of the estimated coefficient, and the t-value is the one used to test the hypothesis that the true value of the coefficient is different from zero. These and other measures of the quality of the regression will be discussed in later chapters. What is important to note is that the documentation of regression results using an easily understood format is considered part of the analysis itself. For time-series data sets, the documentation also includes the frequency (e.g., quarterly or annual) and the time period of the data.

Most computer programs present statistics to eight or more digits, but it is important to recognize the difference between the number of digits computed and the number of *significant figures*, which may be as low as two or three.

---

3. Zvi Griliches, "Data and Econometricians—The Uneasy Alliance," *American Economic Review*, May 1985, p. 199. See also, B. D. McCullough and H. D. Vinod, "The Numerical Reliability of Econometric Software," *Journal of Economic Literature*, June 1999, pp. 633–665.

One of the important parts of the documentation is the explanation of the model, the assumptions, and the procedures and data used. The written documentation must contain enough information so that the entire study could be replicated[4] exactly (except for rounding errors) by others. Unless the variables have been defined in a glossary or table, short definitions should be presented along with the equations. If there is a series of estimated regression equations, then tables should provide the relevant information for each equation. All data manipulations as well as data sources should be documented fully. When there is much to explain, this documentation usually is relegated to a data appendix. If the data are not available generally or are available only after computation, the data set itself might be included in this appendix.

3.2   Using Regression Analysis to Pick Restaurant Locations

To solidify our understanding of the six basic steps of applied regression analysis, let's work through a complete regression example. Suppose that you've been hired to determine the best location for the next Woody's restaurant, where Woody's is a moderately priced, 24-hour, family restaurant chain.[5] You decide to build a regression model to explain the gross sales volume at each of the restaurants in the chain as a function of various descriptors of the location of that branch. If you can come up with a sound equation to explain gross sales as a function of location, then you can use this equation to help Woody's decide where to build their newest eatery. Given data on land costs, building costs, and local building and restaurant municipal codes, the owners of Woody's will be able to make an informed decision.

1. *Review the literature.* You do some reading about the restaurant industry, but your review of the literature consists mainly of talking to various experts within the firm to get their hypotheses, based on experience, as to the particular attributes of a location that contribute to success at selling food at Woody's. The experts tell you that all of the chain's restaurants are identical (indeed, this is sometimes a criticism of the chain) and that all the locations are in what might be called "subur-

---

4. For example, the *Journal of Money, Credit, and Banking* has requested authors to submit their actual data sets so that regression results can be verified. See W. G. Dewald et al., "Replication in Empirical Economics," *American Economic Review*, September 1986, pp. 587–603.

5. The data in this example are real (they're from a sample of 33 Denny's restaurants in southern California), but the number of independent variables considered is much smaller than was used in the actual research.

ban, retail, or residential" environments (as distinguished from central cities or rural areas, for example). Because of this, you realize that many of the reasons that might help explain differences in sales volume in other chains do not apply in this case because all the Woody's locations are similar. (If you were comparing Woody's to another chain, such variables might be appropriate.)

In addition, discussions with the people in the Woody's strategic planning department convince you that price differentials and consumption differences between locations are not as important as is the number of customers a particular location attracts. This causes you to be concerned for a while because the variable you had planned to study originally, gross sales volume, would vary as prices changed between locations. Since your company controls these prices, you feel that you would rather have an estimate of the "potential" for such sales. As a result, you decide to specify your dependent variable as the number of customers served (measured by the number of checks or bills that the waiters and waitresses handed out) in a given location in the most recent year for which complete data are available.

2. *Specify the model: Select the independent variables and the functional form.* Your discussions and personal investigations lead to a number of suggested variables that should help explain the attractiveness of a particular site to potential customers. After a while, you realize that there are three major determinants of sales (customers) on which virtually everyone agrees. These are the number of people who live near the location, the general income level of the location, and the number of direct competitors close to the location. In addition, there are two other good suggestions for potential explanatory variables. These are the number of cars passing the location per day and the number of months that the particular restaurant has been open. After some serious consideration of your alternatives, you decide not to include the last possibilities. All the locations have been open long enough to have achieved a stable clientele, so the number of months open would not be likely to be important. In addition, data are not available for the number of passing cars for all the locations. Should population prove to be a poor measure of the available customers in a location, you'll have to decide whether to ask your boss for the money to collect complete traffic data.

The exact definitions of the independent variables you decide to include are:

N = Competition: the number of direct market competitors within a two-mile radius of the Woody's location

P = Population: the number of people living within a three-mile radius of the Woody's location

I = Income: the average household income of the population measured in variable P

Since you have no reason to suspect anything other than a linear functional form and a typical stochastic error term, that's what you decide to use.

3. *Hypothesize the expected signs of the coefficients.* After thinking about which variables to include, you expect hypothesizing signs will be easy. For two of the variables, you're right. Everyone expects that the more competition, the fewer customers (holding constant the population and income of an area), and also that the more people that live near a particular restaurant, the more customers (holding constant the competition and income). You expect that the greater the income in a particular area, the more people will choose to eat away from home and the more people will choose to eat in a family restaurant instead of in the lower-priced fast-food chains. However, people in especially high-income areas might want to eat in a restaurant that has more "atmosphere" than a family restaurant. Some investigation reveals that it is virtually impossible to get zoning clearance to build a 24-hour facility in a "ritzy" residential neighborhood. You remain slightly worried that the income variable might not be as unambiguous a measure of the appeal of a location as you had thought. To sum, you expect:

$$Y_i = f(\overset{-}{N_i}, \overset{+}{P_i}, \overset{+}{I_i}) + \epsilon_i = \beta_0 + \beta_n N_i + \beta_p P_i + \beta_I I_i + \epsilon_i \quad (3.6)$$

where the signs above the variables indicate the expected impact of that particular independent variable on the dependent variable, holding constant the other two explanatory variables, and ϵ_i is a typical stochastic error term.

4. *Collect the data.* You want to include every local restaurant in the Woody's chain in your study, and, after some effort, you come up with data for your dependent variable and all your independent variables for all 33 locations. You're confident that the quality of your data is excellent for three reasons: each manager measured each variable identically, you've included each restaurant in the sample, and all the information is from the same year. [The data set is included in this section (Table 3.1), along with a sample computer output for the regression estimated (Table 3.2).]

5. *Estimate and evaluate the equation.* You take the data set and enter it into the computer. You then run an OLS regression on the data, but you do so only after thinking through your model once again to see if there are hints that you've made theoretical mistakes. You end up admitting that although you cannot be sure you are right, you've done the best you can, and so you estimate the equation, obtaining:

$$\hat{Y}_i = 102{,}192 - 9075N_i + 0.355P_i + 1.288I_i \qquad (3.7)$$
$$\phantom{\hat{Y}_i = 102{,}192} (2053) \quad (0.073) \quad (0.543)$$
$$t = -4.42 \quad\;\; 4.88 \quad\;\;\;\; 2.37$$
$$n = 33 \quad \overline{R}^2 = .579$$

This equation satisfies your needs in the short run. In particular, the estimated coefficients in the equation have the signs you expected. The overall fit, although not outstanding, seems reasonable for such a diverse group of locations. To predict sales at potential locations, you obtain the values of N, P, and I for each location and then plug them into Equation 3.7. Other things being equal, the higher the predicted Y, the better the location from Woody's point of view.

6. *Document the results.* The results summarized in Equation 3.7 meet our documentation requirements. (Note that we include the standard errors of the estimated coefficients and t-values[6] for completeness even though we won't make use of them until Chapter 5.) However, it's not easy for a beginning researcher to wade through a computer's regression output to find all the numbers required for documentation. You'll probably have an easier time reading your own computer system's printout if you take the time to "walk through" the sample computer output for the Woody's model on the previous two pages. This sample output was produced by the EViews computer program, but it's similar to those produced by SAS, SHAZAM, TSP, and others.

Page one of the computer output summarizes the input data. The first items listed are the actual data. These are followed by a table of the simple correlation coefficients between all pairs of variables in the data set.

The second page summarizes the OLS estimates generated from the data. It starts with a listing of the estimated coefficients, their estimated

---

6. Throughout the text, the number in parentheses below a coefficient estimate will be the standard error of that estimated coefficient. Some authors put the t-value in parentheses, though, so be alert when reading journal articles or other books.

TABLE 3.1   DATA FOR THE WOODY'S RESTAURANTS EXAMPLE

obs	Y	N	P	I
1	107919.0	3.000000	65044.00	13240.00
2	118866.0	5.000000	101376.0	22554.00
3	98579.00	7.000000	124989.0	16916.00
4	122015.0	2.000000	55249.00	20967.00
5	152827.0	3.000000	73775.00	19576.00
6	91259.00	5.000000	48484.00	15039.00
7	123550.0	8.000000	138809.0	21857.00
8	160931.0	2.000000	50244.00	26435.00
9	98496.00	6.000000	104300.0	24024.00
10	108052.0	2.000000	37852.00	14987.00
11	144788.0	3.000000	66921.00	30902.00
12	164571.0	4.000000	166332.0	31573.00
13	105564.0	3.000000	61951.00	19001.00
14	102568.0	5.000000	100441.0	20058.00
15	103342.0	2.000000	39462.00	16194.00
16	127030.0	5.000000	139900.0	21384.00
17	166755.0	6.000000	171740.0	18800.00
18	125343.0	6.000000	149894.0	15289.00
19	121886.0	3.000000	57386.00	16702.00
20	134594.0	6.000000	185105.0	19093.00
21	152937.0	3.000000	114520.0	26502.00
22	109622.0	3.000000	52933.00	18760.00
23	149884.0	5.000000	203500.0	33242.00
24	98388.00	4.000000	39334.00	14988.00
25	140791.0	3.000000	95120.00	18505.00
26	101260.0	3.000000	49200.00	16839.00
27	139517.0	4.000000	113566.0	28915.00
28	115236.0	9.000000	194125.0	19033.00
29	136749.0	7.000000	233844.0	19200.00
30	105067.0	7.000000	83416.00	22833.00
31	136872.0	6.000000	183953.0	14409.00
32	117146.0	3.000000	60457.00	20307.00
33	163538.0	2.000000	65065.00	20111.00

Correlation Matrix

	Y	N	P	I
Y	1.000000	-0.144225	0.392568	0.537022
N	-0.144225	1.000000	0.726251	-0.031534
P	0.392568	0.726251	1.000000	0.245198
I	0.537022	-0.031534	0.245198	1.000000

Dependent Variable: Y
Method: Least Squares
Date: 02/29/00   Time: 14:55
Sample: 1 33
Included observations: 33

Variable	Coefficient	Std. Error	t-Statistic	Prob.
C	102192.4	12799.83	7.983891	0.0000
N	-9074.674	2052.674	-4.420904	0.0001
P	0.354668	0.072681	4.879810	0.0000
I	1.287923	0.543294	2.370584	0.0246

R-squared	0.618154	Mean dependent var	125634.6
Adjusted R-squared	0.578653	S.D. dependent var	22404.09
S.E. of regression	14542.78	Akaike info criterion	22.12079
Sum squared resid	6.13E+09	Schwarz criterion	22.30218
Log likelihood	-360.9930	F-statistic	15.64894
Durbin-Watson stat	1.758193	Prob(F-statistic)	0.000003

obs	Actual	Fitted	Residual	Residual Plot
1	107919.	115090.	-7170.56	
2	118866.	121822.	-2955.74	
3	98579.0	104786.	-6206.86	
4	122015.	130642.	-8627.04	
5	152827.	126346.	26480.5	
6	91259.0	93383.9	-2124.88	
7	123550.	106976.	16573.7	
8	160931.	135909.	25021.7	
9	98496.0	115677.	-17181.4	
10	108052.	116770.	-8718.09	
11	144788.	138503.	6285.43	
12	164571.	165550.	-979.034	
13	105564.	121412.	-15848.3	
14	102568.	118275.	-15707.5	
15	103342.	118896.	-15553.6	
16	127030.	133978.	-6948.11	
17	166755.	132868.	33886.9	
18	125343.	120598.	4744.90	
19	121886.	116832.	5053.70	
20	134594.	137986.	-3391.59	
21	152937.	149718.	3219.43	
22	109622.	117904.	-8281.51	
23	149884.	171807.	-21923.2	
24	98388.0	99147.7	-759.651	
25	140791.	132537.	8253.52	
26	101260.	114105.	-12845.4	
27	139517.	143412.	-3895.30	
28	115236.	113883.	1352.60	
29	136749.	146335.	-9585.91	
30	105067.	97661.9	7405.12	
31	136872.	131544.	5327.62	
32	117146.	122564.	-5418.45	
33	163538.	133021.	30517.0	

standard errors, and the associated t-values, and follows with R^2, $\overline{R}^2$, the standard error of the regression, RSS, and the F-ratio. This is followed by a listing of the observed Ys, the predicted Ys, and the residuals for each observation. Numbers followed by "E+06" or "E−01" are expressed in a scientific notation indicating that the printed decimal point should be moved six places to the right or one place to the left, respectively.

In future chapters, we'll return to this example in order to apply various tests and ideas as we learn them.

3.3   Summary

1. Six steps typically taken in applied regression analysis are:
    a. Review the literature and develop the theoretical model.
    b. Specify the model: Select the independent variables and the functional form.
    c. Hypothesize the expected signs of the coefficients.
    d. Collect the data.
    e. Estimate and evaluate the equation.
    f. Document the results.

2. A dummy variable takes on only the values of one or zero, depending on whether or not some condition is met. An example of a dummy variable would be X equals 1 if a particular individual is female and 0 if the person is male.

Exercises

(Answers to even-numbered exercises are in Appendix A.)

1. Write the meaning of each of the following terms without referring to the book (or your notes), and compare your definition with the version in the text for each:
    a. the six steps in applied regression analysis
    b. dummy variable
    c. cross-sectional data set
    d. specification error
    e. degrees of freedom

2. Contrary to their name, dummy variables are not easy to understand without a little bit of practice:
    a. Specify a dummy variable that would allow you to distinguish be-

tween undergraduate students and graduate students in your econometrics class.

b. Specify a regression equation to explain the grade (measured on a scale of 4.0 for an A) each student in your class received on his or her first econometrics test (Y) as a function of the student's grade in a previous course in statistics (G), the number of hours the student studied for the test (H), and the dummy variable you created above (D). Are there other variables you would want to add? Explain your answer.

c. What is the hypothesized sign of the coefficient of D? Does the sign depend on the exact way in which you defined D? (*Hint:* In particular, suppose that you had reversed the definitions of one and zero in your answer to part a.) How?

d. Suppose that you collected the data and ran the regression and found an estimated coefficient for D that had the expected sign and an absolute value of 0.5. What would this mean in real-world terms? By the way, what would have happened if you had only undergraduates or only graduate students in your class?

3. Do liberal arts colleges pay economists more than they pay other professors? To find out, we looked at a sample of 2,929 small-college faculty members and built a model of their salaries that included a number of variables, four of which were (standard errors in parentheses):

$$\hat{S}_i = 36{,}721 + 817M_i + 426A_i + 406R_i + 3539T_i + \cdots \quad (3.8)$$
$$(259) \quad (456) \quad (24) \quad (458)$$
$$\overline{R}^2 = .77 \quad n = 2929$$

where: S_i = the salary of the *i*th college professor
   M_i = a dummy variable equal to 1 if the *i*th professor is a male and 0 otherwise
   A_i = a dummy variable equal to 1 if the *i*th professor is African American and 0 otherwise
   R_i = the years in rank of the *i*th professor
   T_i = a dummy variable equal to 1 if the *i*th professor teaches economics and 0 otherwise

a. Carefully explain the meaning of the estimated coefficient of M.

b. The equation indicates that African Americans earn $426 more than members of other ethnic groups, holding constant the other variables in the equation. Does this coefficient have the sign you expected? Why or why not?

c. Is R a dummy variable? If not, what is it? Carefully explain the meaning of the coefficient of R.

d. What's your conclusion? Do economists earn more than other professors at liberal arts colleges? Explain.

e. Assume that your professor is a white, male economist who has been an assistant professor at your college for three years. How much money does the equation predict that he is earning? (*Hint:* As tempting as it might be, please don't ask your professor how much he or she earns.)

4. Return to the Woody's regression example of Section 3.2.

a. In any applied regression project there is the distinct possibility that an important explanatory variable has been omitted. Reread the discussion of the selection of independent variables and come up with a suggestion for an independent variable that has not been included in the model (other than the variables already mentioned). Why do you think this variable was not included?

b. What other kinds of criticisms would you have of the sample or independent variables chosen in this model?

5. Suppose you were told that, while data on traffic for Equation 3.7 are still too expensive to obtain, a variable on traffic, called T_i, *is* available that is defined as 1 if more than 15,000 cars per day pass the restaurant and 0 otherwise. Further suppose that when the new variable (T_i) is added to the equation the results are:

$$\hat{Y}_i = 95{,}236 - 7307N_i + 0.320P_i + 1.28I_i + 10{,}994T_i \qquad (3.9)$$
$$\phantom{\hat{Y}_i = 95{,}236} (2153) \quad (0.073) \quad (0.51) \quad (5577)$$
$$\phantom{\hat{Y}_i = 95{,}236} t = -3.39 \quad 4.24 \quad 2.47 \quad 1.97$$
$$\phantom{\hat{Y}_i = 95{,}236} n = 33 \qquad \overline{R}^2 = .617$$

a. What is the expected sign of the coefficient of the new variable?

b. Would you prefer this equation to the original one? Why?

c. Does the fact that $\overline{R}^2$ is higher in Equation 3.9 mean that it is *necessarily* better than Equation 3.7?

6. Suppose that the population variable in Section 3.2 had been defined in different units as in:

P = Population: thousands of people living within a three-mile radius of the Woody's location

a. Given this definition of P, what would the estimated slope coefficients in Equation 3.7 have been?

b. Given this definition of P, what would the estimated slope coefficients in the equation in question 5 above have been?

c. Are any other coefficients affected by this change?

7. Use EViews or your own computer regression software to estimate Equation 3.7 using the data in Table 3.1.

8. The Graduate Record Examination (GRE) subject test in economics is a multiple-choice measure of knowledge and analytical ability in economics that's used mainly as an entrance criterion for students applying to Ph.D. programs in the "dismal science." For years, critics have claimed that the GRE, like the Scholastic Aptitude Test (SAT), is biased against women and some ethnic groups. To test the possibility that the GRE subject test in economics is biased against women, Mary Hirschfeld, Robert Moore, and Eleanor Brown[7] estimated the following equation (standard errors in parentheses):

$$\widehat{GRE_i} = 172.4 + 39.7G_i + 78.9GPA_i + 0.203SATM_i + 0.110SATV_i$$
$$(10.9) \quad (10.4) \qquad (0.071) \qquad (0.058)$$
$$n = 149 \quad \overline{R}^2 = .46 \qquad\qquad (3.10)$$

where: GRE_i = the score of the ith student in the Graduate Record Examination subject test in economics

G_i = a dummy variable equal to 1 if the ith student was a male, 0 otherwise

GPA_i = the GPA in economics classes of the ith student (4 = A, 3 = B, etc.)

$SATM_i$ = the score of the ith student on the mathematics portion of the Scholastic Aptitude Test

$SATV_i$ = the score of the ith student on the verbal portion of the Scholastic Aptitude Test

a. Carefully explain the meaning of the coefficient of G in this equation. (*Hint:* Be sure to specify what 39.7 stands for.)

b. Does this result prove that the GRE is biased against women? Why or why not?

c. If you were going to add one variable to Equation 3.10, what would it be? Explain your reasoning.

d. Suppose that the authors had defined their gender variables as G_i = a dummy variable equal to 1 if the ith student was a female, 0

---

7. Mary Hirschfeld, Robert L. Moore, and Eleanor Brown, "Exploring the Gender Gap on the GRE Subject Test in Economics," *Journal of Economic Education*, Winter 1995, p. 13.

otherwise. What would the estimated Equation 3.10 have been in that case? (*Hint:* Only the intercept and the coefficient of the dummy variable change.)

9. Michael Lovell[8] estimated the following model of the gasoline mileage of various models of cars (standard errors in parentheses):

$$\hat{G}_i = 22.008 - 0.002W_i - 2.76A_i + 3.28D_i + 0.415E_i$$
$$\quad\quad\quad (0.001) \quad (0.71) \quad (1.41) \quad (0.097)$$
$$\overline{R}^2 = .82$$

where: G_i = miles per gallon of the *i*th model as reported by Consumers' Union based on actual road tests
W_i = the gross weight (in pounds) of the *i*th model
A_i = a dummy variable equal to 1 if the *i*th model has an automatic transmission and 0 otherwise
D_i = a dummy variable equal to 1 if the *i*th model has a diesel engine and 0 otherwise
E_i = the U.S. Environmental Protection Agency's estimate of the miles per gallon of the *i*th model

a. Hypothesize signs for the slope coefficients of W and E. Which if any, of the signs of the estimated coefficients are different from your expectations?
b. Carefully interpret the meanings of the estimated coefficients of A_i and D_i.
c. Lovell included one of the variables in the model to test a specific hypothesis, but that variable wouldn't necessarily be in another researcher's gas mileage model. What variable do you think Lovell added? What hypothesis do you think Lovell wanted to test?

10. Your boss is about to start production of her newest box office smash-to-be, *Invasion of the Economists, Part II,* when she calls you in and tells you to build a model of the gross receipts of all the movies produced in the last five years. Your regression is[9] (standard errors in parentheses):

$$\hat{G}_i = 781 + 15.4T_i - 992F_i + 1770J_i + 3027S_i - 3160B_i + \cdots$$
$$\quad\quad (5.9) \quad (674) \quad (800) \quad (1006) \quad (2381)$$
$$\overline{R}^2 = .485 \quad n = 254$$

8. Michael C. Lovell, "Tests of the Rational Expectations Hypothesis," *American Economic Review*, March 1986, pp. 110–124.

where: G_i = the final gross receipts of the ith motion picture (in thousands of dollars)

T_i = the number of screens (theaters) on which the ith film was shown in its first week

F_i = a dummy variable equal to 1 if the star of the ith film is a female and 0 otherwise

J_i = a dummy variable equal to 1 if the ith movie was released in June or July and 0 otherwise

S_i = a dummy variable equal to 1 if the star of the ith film is a superstar (like Tom Cruise or Milton) and 0 otherwise

B_i = a dummy variable equal to 1 if at least one member of the supporting cast of the ith film is a superstar and 0 otherwise

a. Hypothesize signs for each of the slope coefficients in the equation. Which, if any, of the signs of the estimated coefficients are different from your expectations?

b. Milton, the star of the original *Invasion of the Economists*, is demanding $4 million from your boss to appear in the sequel. If your estimates are trustworthy, should she say "yes" or hire Arnold (a nobody) for $500,000?

c. Your boss wants to keep costs low, and it would cost $1.2 million to release the movie on an additional 200 screens. Assuming your estimates are trustworthy, should she spring for the extra screens?

d. The movie is scheduled for release in September, and it would cost $1 million to speed up production enough to allow a July release without hurting quality. Assuming your estimates are trustworthy, is it worth the rush?

e. You've been assuming that your estimates are trustworthy. Do you have any evidence that this is not the case? Explain your answer. (*Hint:* Assume that the equation contains no specification errors.)

---

9. This estimated equation (but not the question) comes from a final exam in managerial economics given at the Harvard Business School in February 1982, pp. 18–30.

CHAPTER 4

The Classical Model

The classical model of econometrics has nothing to do with ancient Greece or even the classical economic thinking of Adam Smith. Instead, the term *classical* refers to a set of fairly basic assumptions required to hold in order for OLS to be considered the "best" estimator available for regression models. When one or more of these assumptions do not hold, other estimation techniques sometimes may be better than OLS.

As a result, one of the most important jobs in regression analysis is to decide whether the classical assumptions hold for a particular equation. If so, the OLS estimation technique is the best available. Otherwise, the pros and cons of alternative estimation techniques must be weighed. These alternatives are usually adjustments to OLS that take account of the particular assumption that has been violated. In a sense, most of the rest of this book deals in one way or another with the question of what to do when one of the classical assumptions is not met. Since econometricians spend so much time analyzing violations of them, it is crucial that they know and understand these assumptions.

4.1   The Classical Assumptions

The **Classical Assumptions** must be met in order for OLS estimators to be the best available. Because of their importance in regression analysis, the assumptions are presented here in tabular form as well as in words. Subsequent chapters will investigate major violations of the assumptions and introduce estimation techniques that may provide better estimates in such cases.

The Classical Assumptions

I. The regression model is linear in the coefficients, is correctly specified, and has an additive error term.

II. The error term has a zero population mean.

III. All explanatory variables are uncorrelated with the error term.

IV. Observations of the error term are uncorrelated with each other (no serial correlation).

V. The error term has a constant variance (no heteroskedasticity).

VI. No explanatory variable is a perfect linear function of any other explanatory variable(s) (no perfect multicollinearity).

VII. The error term is normally distributed (this assumption is optional but usually is invoked).

An error term satisfying Assumptions I through V is called a **classical error term,** and if Assumption VII is added, the error term is called a **classical normal error term.**

I. *The regression model is linear in the coefficients, is correctly specified, and has an additive error term.* The regression model is assumed to be linear in the coefficients:

$$Y_i = \beta_0 + \beta_1 X_{1i} + \beta_2 X_{2i} + \cdots + \beta_K X_{Ki} + \epsilon_i \qquad (4.1)$$

On the other hand, the regression model does not have to be linear in the variables because OLS can be applied to equations that are nonlinear in the variables. The good properties of OLS estimators hold regardless of the functional form of the *variables* as long as the form of the equation to be estimated is linear in the *coefficients.* For example, an exponential function:

$$Y_i = e^{\beta_0} X_i^{\beta_1} e^{\epsilon_i} \qquad (4.2)$$

where e is the base of the natural log, can be transformed by taking the natural log of both sides of the equation:

$$\ln(Y_i) = \beta_0 + \beta_1 \ln(X_i) + \epsilon_i \qquad (4.3)$$

The variables can be relabeled as $Y_i^* = \ln(Y_i)$ and $X_i^* = \ln(X_i)$, and the form of the equation is linear in the coefficients:

$$Y_i^* = \beta_0 + \beta_1 X_i^* + \epsilon_i \qquad (4.4)$$

In Equation 4.4, the properties of the OLS estimator of the βs still hold because the equation is linear in the coefficients. Equations that are nonlinear in the variables will be discussed in Chapter 7.

Two additional properties also must hold.[1] First, we assume that the equation is correctly specified. If an equation has an omitted variable or an incorrect functional form, the odds are against that equation working well. Second, we assume that a stochastic error term has been added to the equation. This error term must be an additive one and cannot be multiplied by or divided into any of the variables in the equation.

II. *The error term has a zero population mean.* As was pointed out in Section 1.2.3, econometricians add a stochastic (random) error term to regression equations to account for variation in the dependent variable that is not explained by the model. The specific value of the error term for each observation is determined purely by chance. Probably the best way to picture this concept is to think of each observation of the error term as being drawn from a random variable distribution such as the one illustrated in Figure 4.1.

Classical Assumption II says that the mean of this distribution is zero. That is, when the entire population of possible values for the stochastic error term is considered, the average value of that population is zero. For a small sample, it is not likely that the mean is exactly zero, but as the size of the sample approaches infinity, the mean of the sample approaches zero.

To compensate for the chance that the mean of the population ϵ might not equal zero, the mean of ϵ_i for any regression is forced to be zero by the existence of the constant term in the equation. If the mean of the error term is not equal to zero, then this nonzero amount is implicitly (because error terms are unobservable) subtracted from each error term and added instead to the constant term. This leaves the equation unchanged except that the new error term has a zero mean (and thus conforms to Assumption II). In addition, the constant term has been changed by the difference between the sample mean of the error term and zero. Partially because of this difference, it is risky to place much importance on the estimated magnitude of the constant term. In essence, the constant term equals the fixed portion of Y that cannot

---

1. Many authors make these two assumptions implicitly rather than explicitly, but the two properties must hold nonetheless.

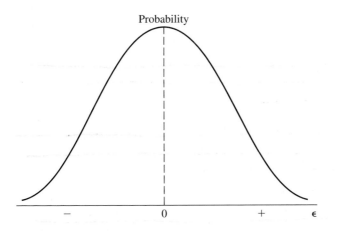

Figure 4.1 An Error Term Distribution with a Mean of Zero

Observations of stochastic error terms are assumed to be drawn from a random variable distribution with a mean of zero. If Classical Assumption II is met, the expected value (the mean) of the error term is zero.

be explained by the independent variables, whereas the error term represents the stochastic portion of the unexplained value of Y.

Although it's true that the error term can never be observed, it's instructive to pretend that we can do so to see how the existence of a constant term forces the mean of the error term to be zero in a sample. Consider a typical regression equation:

$$Y_i = \beta_0 + \beta_1 X_i + \epsilon_i \tag{4.5}$$

For example, if the mean of ϵ_i is 3 instead of 0, then[2] $E(\epsilon_i - 3) = 0$. If we add 3 to the constant term and subtract it from the error term, we obtain:

$$Y_i = (\beta_0 + 3) + \beta_1 X_i + (\epsilon_i - 3) \tag{4.6}$$

Since equations 4.5 and 4.6 are equivalent (do you see why?), and since $E(\epsilon_i - 3) = 0$, then Equation 4.6 can be written in a form that has a zero mean for the error term:

$$Y_i = \beta_0^* + \beta_1 X_i + \epsilon_i^* \tag{4.7}$$

2. Here, as in Chapter 1, the "E" refers to the expected value (mean) of the item in parentheses after it. Thus $E(\epsilon_i - 3)$ equals the expected value of the stochastic error term epsilon minus 3. In this specific example, since we've defined $E(\epsilon_i) = 3$, we know that $E(\epsilon_i - 3) = 0$. One way to think about expected value is as our best guess of the long-run average value a specific item will have.

where $\beta_0^* = \beta_0 + 3$ and $\epsilon_i^* = \epsilon_i - 3$. As can be seen, Equation 4.7 conforms to Assumption II. This form is always assumed to apply for the true model. Therefore, the second classical assumption is assured as long as there is a constant term included in the equation. This statement is correct as long as all other classical assumptions are met.

III. *All explanatory variables are uncorrelated with the error term.* It is assumed that the observed values of the explanatory variables are determined independently of the values of the error term. Explanatory variables (Xs) are considered to be determined outside the context of the regression equation in question.

If an explanatory variable and the error term were instead correlated with each other, the OLS estimates would be likely to attribute to the X some of the variation in Y that actually came from the error term. If the error term and X were positively correlated, for example, then the estimated coefficient would probably be higher than it would otherwise have been (biased upward), because the OLS program would mistakenly attribute the variation in Y caused by ϵ to have been caused by X instead. As a result, it's important to ensure that the explanatory variables are uncorrelated with the error term.

An important economic application that violates this assumption is any model that is simultaneous in nature. In most economic applications, there are several related propositions that, when taken as a group, suggest a *system* of regression equations. In most situations, interrelated equations should be considered simultaneously instead of separately. Unfortunately, such simultaneous systems violate Classical Assumption III.

To see why, let's look at an example. In a simple Keynesian macroeconomic model, an increase in consumption (caused perhaps by an unexpected change in tastes) will increase aggregate demand and therefore aggregate income. An increase in income, however, will also increase consumption; so, income and consumption are interdependent. Note, however, that the error term in the consumption function (which is where an unexpected change in tastes would appear) and an explanatory variable in the consumption function (income) have now moved together. As a result, Classical Assumption III has been violated; the error term is no longer uncorrelated with all the explanatory variables. This will be considered in more detail in Chapter 14.

IV. *Observations of the error term are uncorrelated with each other.* The observations of the error term are drawn independently from each other. If a systematic correlation exists between one observation of the error term and another, then it will be more difficult for OLS to get precise estimates of the coefficients of the explanatory variables. For example, if the fact that the ϵ from one observation is positive increases the probability that the ϵ from another observation also is positive, then the two observations of the error term are positively correlated. Such a correlation would violate Classical Assumption IV.

In economic applications, this assumption is most important in time-series models. In such a context, Assumption IV says that an increase in the error term in one time period (a random shock, for example) does not show up in or affect in any way the error term in another time period. In some cases, though, this assumption is unrealistic, since the effects of a random shock sometimes last for a number of time periods. If, over all the observations of the sample, ϵ_{t+1} is correlated with ϵ_t, then the error term is said to be **serially correlated** (or *autocorrelated*), and this assumption is violated. Violations of this assumption are considered in more detail in Chapter 9.

(V.) *The error term has a constant variance.* The variance (or dispersion) of the distribution from which the observations of the error term are drawn is constant. That is, the observations of the error term are assumed to be drawn continually from identical distributions (for example, the one pictured in Figure 4.1). The alternative would be for the variance of the distribution of the error term to change for each observation or range of observations. In Figure 4.2, for example, the variance of the error term is shown to increase as the variable Z increases; such a pattern violates Classical Assumption V. This type of violation makes precise estimation difficult, because a particular deviation from a mean (in this case an error term) can be called a statistically large or small deviation only when it is compared with the standard deviation (which is the square root of the variance) of the distribution in question. If you assume that all error term observations are drawn from a distribution with a constant variance when in reality they are drawn from distributions with different variances, then the relative importance of changes in Y is very hard to judge. Even though the actual values of the error term are not directly observable, the lack of a constant variance for the distribution of the error term causes OLS to generate imprecise estimates of the coefficients of the independent variables.

In economic applications, Assumption V is most important in cross-sectional data sets. For example, in a cross-sectional analysis of household consumption patterns, the variance (or dispersion) of the consumption of certain goods might be greater for higher-income households because they have more discretionary income than do lower-income households. Thus the ab-

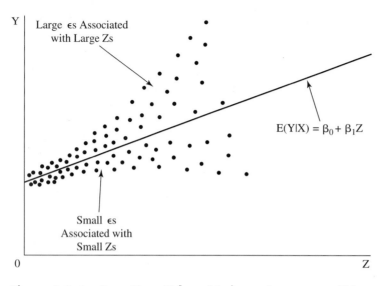

Figure 4.2 An Error Term Whose Variance Increase as Z Increases (Heteroskedasticity)

One example of Classical Assumption V not being met is when the variance of the error term increases as Z increases. In such a situation (called heteroskedasticity), the observations are on average farther from the true regression line for large values of Z than they are for small values of Z.

solute amount of the dispersion is greater even though the percentage dispersion is the same. The violation of Assumption V is referred to as heteroskedasticity and will be discussed in more detail in Chapter 10.

VI. *No explanatory variable is a perfect linear function of any other explanatory variable(s).* Perfect **collinearity** between two independent variables implies that they are really the same variable, or that one is a multiple of the other, and/or that a constant has been added to one of the variables. That is, the relative movements of one explanatory variable will be matched exactly by the relative movements of the other even though the absolute size of the movements might differ. Because every movement of one of the variables is matched exactly by a relative movement in the other, the OLS estimation procedure will be incapable of distinguishing one variable from the other.

Many instances of perfect collinearity (or **multicollinearity** if more than two independent variables are involved) are the result of the researcher not accounting for identities (definitional equivalences) among the independent variables. This problem can be corrected easily by dropping one of the perfectly collinear variables from the equation.

Suppose you were attempting to explain home purchases and had included both real and nominal interest rates as explanatory variables in your equation for a time period in which inflation (and expected inflation) was constant. In such an instance, real and nominal interest rates would differ by a constant amount, and the OLS procedure would not be able to distinguish between them. Note that perfect multicollinearity can be caused by an accident in the sample at hand. While real and nominal interest rates would be perfectly multicollinear if inflation were constant in a given sample, they would not be perfectly multicollinear in samples where there was some change in inflation.

Perfect multicollinearity also can occur when two independent variables always sum to a third. For example, the explanatory variables "games won" and "games lost" for a sports team that has a constant number of games played and no ties will always sum to that constant, and perfect multicollinearity will exist. In such cases, the OLS computer program (or any other estimation technique) will be unable to estimate the coefficients unless there is a rounding error. The remedy is easy in the case of perfect multicollinearity: just delete one of the two perfectly correlated variables.

Finally, it's also possible to violate Assumption VI if one of the explanatory variables has a variance of zero. In this case, the variable will be perfectly collinear with the constant term, and OLS estimation will be impossible. Luckily, it's quite unusual to encounter perfect multicollinearity, but, as we shall see in Chapter 8, even imperfect multicollinearity can cause problems for estimation.

(VII.) *The error term is normally distributed.* Although we have already assumed that observations of the error term are drawn independently (Assumption IV) from a distribution that has a zero mean (Assumption II) and that has a constant variance (Assumption V), we have said little about the shape of that distribution. Assumption VII states that the observations of the error term are drawn from a distribution that is normal (that is, bell shaped, and generally following the symmetrical pattern portrayed in Figure 4.1).

This assumption of normality is not required for OLS estimation. Its major use is in **hypothesis testing,** which uses the estimated regression statistics to accept or reject hypotheses about economic behavior. One example of such a test is deciding whether a particular demand curve is elastic or inelastic in a particular range. Hypothesis testing is the subject of Chapter 5, and, without the normality assumption, most of the tests in that chapter would be invalid.

4.2   The Normal Distribution of the Error Term

In this section we briefly introduce the concept of the normal distribution and explain why the Central Limit Theorem tends to justify the assumption of normality for a stochastic error term.

The only assumption that is optional to the definition of the classical model is that the error term is normally distributed. It is usually advisable to add the assumption of normality to the other six assumptions for two reasons:

1. The error term ϵ_i can be thought of as the composite of a number of minor influences or errors. As the number of these minor influences gets larger, the distribution of the error term tends to approach the normal distribution. This tendency is called the Central Limit Theorem.

2. The *t*-statistic and the *F*-statistic, which will be developed in Chapter 5, are not truly applicable unless the error term is normally distributed.

4.2.1   The Normal Distribution

The normal distribution is a symmetrical, continuous, bell-shaped curve. The parameters that describe normal distributions and allow us to differentiate between various normal distributions are the *mean* (μ, the measure of central tendency), and the *variance* (σ^2, the measure of dispersion). Two such normal distributions are shown in Figure 4.3. In normal distribution I, the mean is 0 and the variance is 1; in normal distribution II, the mean is 2, and the variance is 0.5.

A quick look at Figure 4.3 shows how normal distributions differ when the means and variances are different. When the mean is different, the entire distribution shifts. For example, distribution II is to the right of distribution I because its mean, 2, is greater than the mean of distribution I. When the variance is different, the distribution becomes fatter or skinnier. For example, distribution II is distributed more compactly around its mean than is distribution I because distribution II has a smaller variance. Observations drawn at random from distribution II will tend to be closer to the mean than those drawn from distribution I, while distribution I will tend to have a higher likelihood of observations quite far from its mean.

In Figure 4.3, distribution I represents what is called the **standard normal distribution** because it is a normal distribution with a mean equal to zero and a variance equal to one. This is the usual distribution given in statistical tables, such as Table B-7 in the back of this book. Often the parameters of a normal distribution will be listed in a compact summary form: $N(\mu, \sigma^2)$. For distribution I, this notation would be $N(0,1)$ and would stand for a normal distribution with mean zero and variance one.

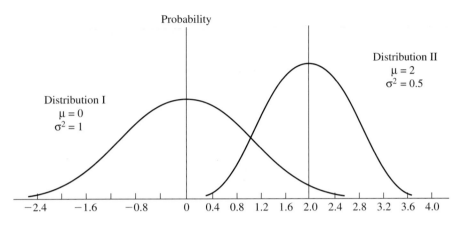

Figure 4.3 Normal Distributions

Although all normal distributions are symmetrical and bell shaped, they do not necessarily have the same mean and variance. Distribution I has a mean of 0 and a variance of 1, whereas distribution II has a mean of 2 and a variance of 0.5. As can be seen, the whole distribution shifts when the mean changes, and the distribution gets fatter as the variance increases.

4.2.2 The Central Limit Theorem and the Normality of the Error Term

As mentioned in Chapter 1, the error term in a regression equation is assumed to be caused in part by the omission of a number of variables from the equation. These variables are expected to have relatively small individual effects on the hypothesized regression equation, and it is not advisable to include them as independent variables. The error term represents the combined effects of these omitted variables. This component of the error term is usually cited as the justification for the assumption of normality of the error term. In general, a random variable generated by the combined effects of a number of omitted, individually unimportant variables will be normally distributed according to the **Central Limit Theorem,** which states:

> *The mean (or sum) of a number of independent, identically distributed random variables will tend to be normally distributed, regardless of their distribution, if the number of different random variables is large enough.*

The Central Limit Theorem becomes more valid as the number of omitted variables approaches infinity, but even a few are sufficient to show the tendency toward the normal bell-shaped distribution. The more variables omitted, the more quickly the distribution of the error term approaches the normal distri-

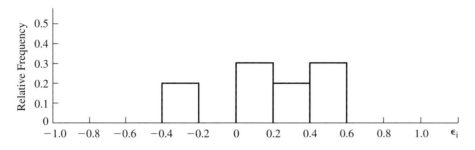

Figure 4.4 Relative Frequency of the Error Term as an Average of 2 Omitted Variables: 10 Observations

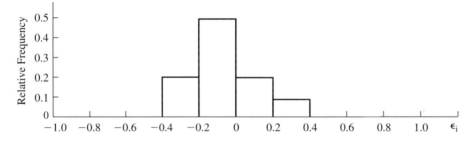

Figure 4.5 Relative Frequency of the Error Term as an Average of 10 Omitted Variables: 10 Observations

As the number of different omitted variables increases, the distribution of the sum of those variables approaches the normal distribution. This tendency (called the Central Limit Theorem) can be seen in Figures 4.4 and 4.5. As the number of omitted variables increases from 2 to 10, the distribution of their average does indeed become more symmetrical and bell shaped.

bution because the various omitted variables are more likely to cancel out extreme observations. As a result, it is good econometric practice to assume a normally distributed stochastic error term in a regression that must omit a number of minor unrelated influences. Purposely omitting a few variables to help achieve normality for the error term, however, should *never* be considered.

Let's look at an example of the Central Limit Theorem and how the error term tends to be normally distributed if the number of omitted variables is large enough. First, suppose that only two potentially relevant variables are so minor that they are not included in an equation. Figure 4.4 shows 10 computer-generated observations of a stochastic error term that is the sum of two identically distributed variables.[3] Note that although the observations of the error term are near zero, their distribution is hardly normal looking.

Suppose that we now increase the number of omitted variables from 2 to 10. Figure 4.5 shows 10 computer-generated observations of a stochastic error term that is the sum of 10 identically distributed variables. As we'd expect from the Central Limit Theorem, the resulting distribution is much more bell shaped (normal) than is Figure 4.4. If we were to continue to add variables, the distribution would tend to look more and more like the normal distribution.

These figures show the tendency of errors to cancel each other out as the number of omitted variables increases. Why does this occur? Averaging the Xs, each of which is distributed according to the uniform distribution, bunches the observations toward the middle (because extreme values of any X tend to be offset by the others) resulting in a fairly normal distribution. The more Xs to be averaged, the more normal this distribution becomes.

By the way, the omitted variables do not have to conform to the uniform distribution to produce this result; they can follow *any* probability distribution. Indeed, if the omitted variables were normally distributed, the error term would be normally distributed by definition, since the sum (or average) of normally distributed variables is also a normally distributed variable.

4.3   The Sampling Distribution of $\hat{\beta}$

Just as the error term follows a probability distribution, so too do the estimates of the true slope βs (the $\hat{\beta}$s, or "β-hats") follow such a probability distribution. In fact, each different sample of data typically produces a different set of $\hat{\beta}$s. These $\hat{\beta}$s usually are assumed to be normally distributed because the normality of the error term implies that the OLS estimator of the $\hat{\beta}$s in the simple linear regression model is normally distributed as well. The probability distribution of the $\hat{\beta}$s is called a **sampling distribution** because it is based on a number of sample drawings of the error term. To show this, we will discuss the general idea of the sampling distribution of the $\hat{\beta}$s and then use a computer-generated example to demonstrate that such distributions do indeed tend to be normally distributed.

---

3. In generating these figures, we assumed that all variables were uniformly distributed (every value equally and uniformly likely), that the other components of the error term were small in size compared with the omitted variables, and that the coefficients of the omitted variables were 1.0. These assumptions made the computations easier; the property shown holds even without them.

4.3.1 Sampling Distributions of Estimators

Recall that an *estimator* is a formula, such as the OLS formula in Equation 2.13, that tells you how to compute $\hat{\beta}_k$, and an *estimate* is the value of $\hat{\beta}_k$ computed by that formula. We have noted that the purpose of regression analysis is to obtain good estimates of the true (or population) coefficients of an equation from a sample of that population. In other words, given an equation like:

$$Y_i = \beta_0 + \beta_1 X_{1i} + \beta_2 X_{2i} + \epsilon_i \tag{4.8}$$

we want to estimate βs by taking a sample of the population and calculating those estimates (typically by OLS if the classical assumptions are met). Since researchers usually have only one sample, beginning econometricians often assume that regression analysis can produce only one estimate of the βs. In reality, each different sample from a given population will produce a different set of estimates of the βs. For example, one sample might produce an estimate considerably higher than the true β whereas another might come up with a $\hat{\beta}$ that is lower. We need to discuss the properties of the distribution of these $\hat{\beta}$s, even though in most real applications we will encounter only a single draw from it.

A simplified example will help clarify this point. Suppose you were attempting to estimate the average age of your class from a sample of the class; let's say that you were trying to use a sample of 5 to estimate the average age of a class of 30. Your estimate would obviously depend on the exact sample you picked. If your random sample accidentally included the five youngest or the five oldest people in the class, then your estimated age would be dramatically different from the one you would get if your random sample were more centered. In essence, then, there is a distribution of all the possible estimates that will have a mean and a variance just as the distribution of error terms does. To illustrate this concept, assume that the population is distributed uniformly between 19 and 23. Here are three samples from this population:

    sample 1:   19, 19, 20, 22, 23;   mean = 20.6
    sample 2:   20, 21, 21, 22, 22;   mean = 21.2
    sample 3:   19, 20, 22, 23, 23;   mean = 21.4

Each sample yields an estimate of the true population mean (which is 21), and the distribution of the means of all the possible samples has its own mean and variance. For a "good" estimation technique, we would want the mean of the distribution of sample estimates to be equal to the true population mean. This is called *unbiasedness*. Although the mean of our three samples is a little over 21, it seems likely that if we took enough samples, the mean of our group of samples would eventually equal 21.0.

In a similar way, the $\hat{\beta}$s estimated by OLS for Equation 4.8 form a distribution of their own. Each sample of observations of Y and the Xs will produce different $\hat{\beta}$s, but the distribution of these estimates for all possible samples has a mean and a variance like any distribution. When we discuss the properties of estimators in the next section, it will be important to remember that we are discussing the properties of the distribution of estimates generated from a number of samples (a sampling distribution).

Properties of the Mean

A desirable property of a distribution of estimates is that its mean equals the true mean of the variable being estimated. An estimator that yields such estimates is called an unbiased estimator.

> An **unbiased estimator** is an estimator whose sampling distribution has as its expected value the true value of β.
>
> $$E(\hat{\beta}_k) = \beta_k \qquad (4.9)$$

Only one value of $\hat{\beta}$ is obtained in practice, but the property of unbiasedness is useful because a single estimate drawn from an unbiased distribution is more likely to be near the true value (assuming identical variances of the $\hat{\beta}$s) than one taken from a distribution not centered around the true value. If an estimator produces $\hat{\beta}$s that are not centered around the true β, the estimator is referred to as a **biased estimator.**

We cannot ensure that every estimate from an unbiased estimator is better than every estimate from a biased one because a particular unbiased estimate[4] could, by chance, be farther from the true value than a biased estimate might be. This could happen by chance, for example, or because the biased estimator had a smaller variance. Without any other information about the distribution of the estimates, however, we would always rather have an unbiased estimate than a biased one.

Properties of the Variance

Just as we would like the distribution of the $\hat{\beta}$s to be centered around the true population β, so too would we like that distribution to be as narrow (or pre-

---

4. Technically, since an estimate has just one value, an estimate cannot be unbiased (or biased). On the other hand, the phrase "estimate produced by an unbiased estimator" is cumbersome, especially if repeated 10 times on a page. As a result, many econometricians use "unbiased estimate" as shorthand for "a single estimate produced by an unbiased estimator."

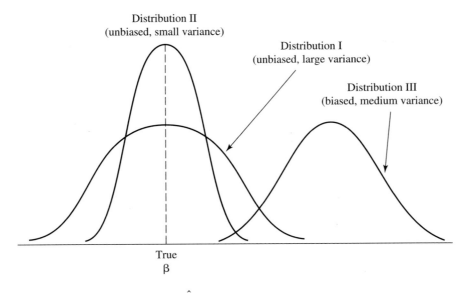

Distribution II
(unbiased, small variance)

Distribution I
(unbiased, large variance)

Distribution III
(biased, medium variance)

True
β

Figure 4.6 Distributions of β̂

Different distributions of β̂ can have different means and variances. Distributions I and II, for example, are both unbiased, but distribution I has a larger variance than does distribution II. Distribution III has a smaller variance than distribution I, but it is biased.

cise) as possible. A distribution centered around the truth but with an extremely large variance might be of very little use because any given estimate would quite likely be far from the true β value. For a β̂ distribution with a small variance, the estimates are likely to be close to the mean of the sampling distribution. To see this more clearly, compare distributions I and II (both of which are unbiased) in Figure 4.6. Distribution I, which has a larger variance than distribution II, is less precise than distribution II. For comparison purposes, a biased distribution (distribution III) is also pictured; note that bias implies that the expected value of the distribution is to the right or left of the true β.

The variance of the distribution of the β̂s can be decreased by increasing the size of the sample. This also increases the degrees of freedom, since the number of degrees of freedom equals the sample size minus the number of coefficients or parameters estimated. As the number of observations increases, other things held constant, the distribution of β̂s becomes more centered around its sample mean, and the variance of the sampling distribution tends to decrease. Although it is not true that a sample of 15 will always produce estimates closer to the true β than a sample of 5, it is quite likely to do

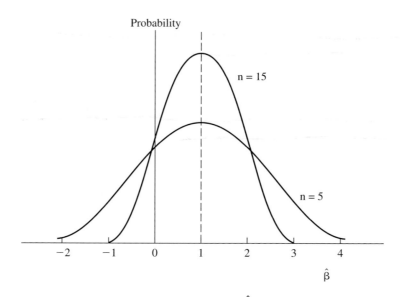

Figure 4.7 Sampling Distribution of $\hat{\beta}$ for Various Observations (n)

As the size of the sample increases, the variance of the distribution of βs calculated from that sample tends to decrease. In the extreme case (not shown) a sample equal to the population would yield only an estimate equal to the mean of that distribution, which (for unbiased estimators) would equal the true β, and the variance of the estimates would be zero.

so; such larger samples should be sought. Figure 4.7 presents illustrative sampling distributions of $\hat{\beta}$s for 15 and 5 observations for OLS estimators of β when the true β equals 1. The larger sample indeed produces a sampling distribution that is more closely centered around β.

In econometrics, general tendencies must be relied on. The element of chance, a random occurrence, is always present in estimating regression coefficients, and some estimates may be far from the true value no matter how good the estimating technique. However, if the distribution is centered around the true value and has as small a variance as possible, the element of chance is less likely to induce a poor estimate. If the sampling distribution is centered around a value other than the true β (that is, if $\hat{\beta}$ is *biased*) then a lower variance implies that most of the sampling distribution of $\hat{\beta}$ is concentrated on the wrong value. However, if this value is not very different from the true value, which is usually not known in practice, then the greater precision will still be valuable.

A final item of importance is that as the variance of the error term increases, so too does the variance of the distribution of $\hat{\beta}$. The reason for the increased variance of $\hat{\beta}$ is that with the larger variance of ϵ_i, the more extreme values of ϵ_i are observed with more frequency, and the error term becomes more important in determining the values of Y_i. Thus, the relative portion of the movements of Y_i explained by the deterministic component βX_i is less, and there are more unexplained changes in Y_i caused by the stochastic element ϵ_i. This implies that empirical inferences about the value of β are more tenuous. The R^2 of the equation will tend to decrease as the variance of the error term increases, symptomatic of this tendency.

Properties of the Standard Error

Since the standard error of the estimated coefficient, $SE(\hat{\beta})$, is the square root of the estimated variance of the $\hat{\beta}$s, it too is affected by the size of the sample and other factors. To see this, let's look at an equation for $SE(\hat{\beta}_1)$, the standard error of the estimated slope coefficient from a model with two independent variables:

$$SE(\hat{\beta}_1) = \sqrt{\frac{\sum e_i^2 /(n-3)}{\sum (X_{1i} - \bar{X}_1)^2 (1 - r_{12}^2)}} \qquad (4.10)$$

Take a look[5] at Equation 4.10. What happens if the sample size, n, increases? As n increases, so too will $\sum e_i^2$ and $\sum (X_{1i} - \bar{X}_1)^2$. The denominator of Equation 4.10 will rise unambiguously, but the numerator will not, because the increase in $\sum e_i^2$ will tend to be offset by the increase in n. As a result, an increase in sample size will cause $SE(\hat{\beta})$ to fall; the larger the sample, the more precise our coefficient estimates will be.

How about when $\sum e_i^2$ increases, holding the sample size constant? In this case, $SE(\hat{\beta}_1)$ will increase. Because estimates of $VAR[\epsilon_i]$ (the variance of the error term) increase as $\sum e_i^2$ increases, such a relationship makes sense because a more widely varying error term will make it harder for us to obtain precise coefficient estimates. The more ϵ varies, the less precise the coefficient estimate will be.

Finally, what about that $\sum (X_i - \bar{X})^2$ term? When $\sum (X_i - \bar{X})^2$ increases, holding the sample size constant, $SE(\hat{\beta}_1)$ decreases. Thus, the more X varies around its mean, the more precise the coefficient estimate will be. This makes sense, since a wider range of X will provide more information on which to base the β. As a result, the $\hat{\beta}$s will be more accurate, and $SE(\hat{\beta}_1)$ will fall. Although we've used an equation from a three-variable model to show these properties, they also hold for $SE(\hat{\beta})$s from equations with any number of variables.

---

5. r_{12}^2 in Equation 4.10 is the simple correlation coefficient between X_1 and X_2. For more on r, see Section 5.3.3.

4.3.2 A Demonstration that the β̂s Are Normally Distributed

One of the properties of the normal distribution is that any linear function of normally distributed variables is itself normally distributed. Given this property, it is not difficult to prove mathematically that the assumption of the normality of the error terms implies that the β̂s are themselves normally distributed. This proof is not as important as an understanding of the meaning of such a conclusion, so this section presents a simplified demonstration of that property.

To demonstrate that normal error terms imply normally distributed β̂s, we'll use a number of computer-generated samples and then calculate β̂s from these samples in much the same manner as mean ages were calculated in the previous section. All the samples generated will conform to the same arbitrarily chosen true model, and the error term distribution used to generate the samples will be assumed to be normally distributed as is implied by the Central Limit Theorem. An examination of the distribution of β̂s generated by this experiment not only shows its normality, but is also a good review of the discussion of the sampling distribution of β̂s.

For this demonstration, assume that the following model is true:

$$Y_i = \beta_0 + \beta_1 X_i + \epsilon_i = 0 + 1X_i + \epsilon_i \qquad (4.11)$$

This is the same as stating that, on average, $Y = X$. If we now assume that the error term is (independently) normally distributed with mean 0 and variance of 0.25, and if we further choose a sample size of 5 and a given set of fixed Xs, we can use the computer to generate a large number of random samples (data sets) conforming to the various assumptions listed above. We then can apply OLS and calculate a β̂ for each sample, resulting in a distribution of β̂s as discussed in this section. The sampling distribution for 5,000 such computer-generated data sets and OLS-calculated β̂s is shown in Figure 4.8.

Two conclusions can be drawn from an examination of Figure 4.8:

1. The distribution of β̂s appears to be a symmetrical, bell-shaped distribution that is approaching a continuous normal distribution as the number of samples of β̂s increases.

2. The distribution of the β̂s is unbiased but shows surprising variations. β̂s from –2.5 to +4.5 can be observed even though the true value of β is 1.0. Such a result implies that any researcher who bases an important conclusion on a single regression result runs the risk of overstating the case. This danger depends on the variance of the estimated coefficients, which decreases with the size of the sample. Note from Figure 4.7 that as the sample size increases from 5 to 15, the chance of

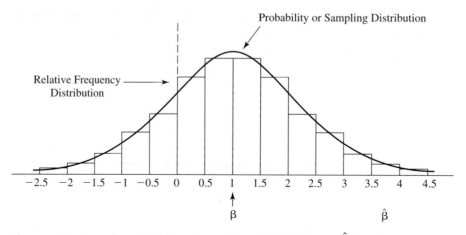

Figure 4.8 Sampling Distribution of the OLS Estimate $\hat{\beta}$ for $\beta = 1$ and $\sigma^2 = 0.25$

To demonstrate that the distribution of $\hat{\beta}$s is indeed normal, we calculated 5,000 estimates of $\hat{\beta}$ from 5,000 samples where the true β was known to be 1.0. As can be seen, the resulting distribution of the $\hat{\beta}$s is not only centered around 1.0, the true β, but it is also symmetrical and bell shaped, as is the normal distribution.

observing a single $\hat{\beta}$ far from its true value falls; this demonstrates the desirability of larger samples.

Computer-generated simulations of this kind are usually referred to as **Monte Carlo experiments.** Monte Carlo experiments typically have seven steps:

1. Assume a "true" model with specific coefficient values (for example, $Y = 3.0 + 1.2X_1 - 5.3X_2$) and an error term distribution (for example, N[0,1.0]).

2. Select values for the independent variables.

3. Select an estimating technique (usually OLS).

4. Create various samples of values of the dependent variable, using the assumed model, by randomly generating error terms from the assumed distribution.

5. Compute the estimates of the βs from the various samples using the estimating technique.

6. Evaluate the results.

7. Return to step 1 and choose other values for the coefficients, independent variables, or error term variance; compare these results with the first set. (This step, which is optional, is called *sensitivity analysis* and is discussed in more detail in Section 6.4.5).

4.4 The Gauss–Markov Theorem and the Properties of OLS Estimators

The Gauss–Markov Theorem proves two important properties of OLS estimators. This theorem is proven in all advanced econometrics textbooks and readers interested in the proof should see Exercise 8 and its answer in Appendix A. For a regression user, however, it's more important to know what the theorem implies than to be able to prove it. The **Gauss–Markov Theorem** states that:

> Given Classical Assumptions I through VI (Assumption VII, normality, is not needed for this theorem), the Ordinary Least Squares estimator of β_k is the minimum variance estimator from among the set of all linear unbiased estimators of β_k, for k = 0, 1, 2, . . . , K.

The Gauss–Markov Theorem is perhaps most easily remembered by stating that "OLS is BLUE" where **BLUE** stands for "*Best* (meaning minimum variance) *Linear Unbiased Estimator*." Students who might forget that "best" stands for minimum variance might be better served by remembering "OLS is MvLUE," but such a phrase is hardly catchy or easy to remember.

If an equation's coefficient estimation is unbiased (that is, if each of the estimated coefficients is produced by an unbiased estimator of the true population coefficient), then:

$$E(\hat{\beta}_k) = \beta_k \qquad (k = 0, 1, 2, . . . , K)$$

Best, as mentioned above, means that each $\hat{\beta}_k$ has the smallest variance possible (in this case, out of all the linear unbiased estimators of β_k). An unbiased estimator with the smallest variance is called **efficient**, and that estimator is said to have the property of efficiency.

The Gauss–Markov Theorem requires that just the first six of the seven classical assumptions be met. What happens if we add in the seventh assumption, the assumption that the error term is normally distributed? In this case, the result of the Gauss–Markov Theorem is strengthened because the OLS estimator can be shown to be the best (minimum variance) unbiased estimator out of *all* the possible estimators, not just out of the linear estimators. In other words, if all seven assumptions are met, OLS is "BUE." It also turns out that the OLS estimator is equivalent to another estimation technique, the maximum likelihood estimator (which we will discuss in Chapter 13).

Given all seven classical assumptions, the OLS coefficient estimators can be shown to have the following properties:

1. *They are unbiased.* That is, $E(\hat{\beta})$ is β. This means that the OLS estimates of the coefficients are centered around the true population values of the parameters being estimated.

2. *They are minimum variance.* The distribution of the coefficient estimates around the true parameter values is as tightly or narrowly distributed as is possible for an unbiased distribution. No other unbiased estimator has a lower variance for each estimated coefficient than OLS.

3. *They are consistent.* As the sample size approaches infinity, the estimates converge on the true population parameters. Put differently, as the sample size gets larger, the variance gets smaller, and each estimate approaches the true value of the coefficient being estimated.

4. *They are normally distributed.* The $\hat{\beta}$s are $N(\beta, VAR[\hat{\beta}])$. Thus various statistical tests based on the normal distribution may indeed be applied to these estimates, as will be done in Chapter 5.

If the seven classical assumptions are met and if OLS is used to calculate the $\hat{\beta}$s, then it can be stated that an estimated regression coefficient is an unbiased, minimum variance estimate of the impact on the dependent variable of a one-unit increase in a given independent variable, holding constant all other independent variables in the equation. Such an estimate is drawn from a distribution of estimates that is centered around the true population coefficient and has the smallest possible variance for such unbiased distributions.

4.5   Standard Econometric Notation

Whereas Section 4.3 portrayed graphically the notions of central tendency and dispersion, this section presents the standard notation used throughout the econometrics literature for these concepts.

The measure of the central tendency of the sampling distribution of $\hat{\beta}$, which can be thought of as the mean of the $\hat{\beta}$s, is denoted as $E(\hat{\beta})$, read as "the expected value of beta-hat." The expected value of a random variable is the population mean of that variable (with observations weighted by the probability of observation).

The variance of $\hat{\beta}$ is the typical measure of dispersion of the sampling distribution of $\hat{\beta}$. The variance has several alternative notational representations, including $VAR(\hat{\beta})$ and $\sigma^2(\hat{\beta})$. Each of these is read as the "variance of beta-hat" and represents the degree of dispersion of the sampling distribution of $\hat{\beta}$.

TABLE 4.1 NOTATION CONVENTIONS			
Population Parameter (True Values, but Unobserved)		**Estimate (Observed from Sample)**	
Name	**Symbol(s)**	**Name**	**Symbol(s)**
Regression coefficient	β_k	Estimated regression coefficient	$\hat{\beta}_k$
Expected value of the estimated coefficient	$E(\hat{\beta}_k)$		
Variance of the error term	σ^2 or $VAR(\epsilon_i)$	Estimated variance of the error term	s^2 or $\hat{\sigma}^2$
Standard deviation of the error term	σ	Standard error of the equation (estimate)	s or SEE
Variance of the estimated coefficient	$\sigma^2(\hat{\beta}_k)$ or $VAR(\hat{\beta}_k)$	Estimated variance of the estimated coefficient	$s^2(\hat{\beta}_k)$ or $\widehat{VAR}(\hat{\beta}_k)$
Standard deviation of the estimated coefficient	$\sigma_{\hat{\beta}k}$ or $\sigma(\hat{\beta}_k)$	Standard error of the estimated coefficient	$\hat{\sigma}(\hat{\beta}_k)$ or $SE(\hat{\beta}_k)$
Error or disturbance term	ϵ_i	Residual (estimate of error in a loose sense)	e_i

Table 4.1 presents various alternative notational devices used to represent the different population (true) parameters and their corresponding estimates (based on samples).

To review Table 4.1, the true coefficient β_k is estimated by $\hat{\beta}_k$. The estimator is stochastic, or random, because its value depends on the values of the stochastic error term in the true function. Thus, $\hat{\beta}$ has a sampling distribution based on the distribution of the ϵ_is. If the ϵ_is are normally distributed, as usually is assumed by invoking the Central Limit Theorem, then the $\hat{\beta}$s are normally distributed.

Two population parameters, the mean and the variance, fully describe the $\hat{\beta}$ distribution. The mean, the measure of central tendency of the sample distribution, is $E(\hat{\beta}_k)$, which equals β_k if the estimator is unbiased. The variance (or, alternatively, the square root of the variance, called the **standard deviation**) is a measure of dispersion in the sampling distribution of $\hat{\beta}_k$. The variance of the estimates is a population parameter that is never actually observed in practice; instead, it is estimated with $\hat{\sigma}^2(\hat{\beta}_k)$, also written as $s^2(\hat{\beta}_k)$. Note, by the way, that the variance of the true β, $\sigma^2(\beta)$, is zero, since there is only one true β_k with no distribution around it. Thus, the estimated variance of the estimated coefficient is defined and observed, the true variance of the estimated coefficient is unobservable, and the true variance of the true coefficient is zero. The square root of the estimated variance, or the coefficient estimate, is the standard error of $\hat{\beta}$, $SE(\hat{\beta}_k)$, which we will use extensively in hypothesis testing.

4.6 Summary

1. The seven Classical Assumptions state that the regression model is linear with an error term that has a mean of zero, is uncorrelated with the explanatory variables and other observations of the error term, has a constant variance, and is normally distributed (optional). In addition, explanatory variables must not be perfect linear functions of each other.

2. The two most important properties of an estimator are unbiasedness and minimum variance. An estimator is unbiased when the expected value of the estimated coefficient is equal to the true value. Minimum variance holds when the estimating distribution has the smallest variance of all the estimators.

3. Given the Classical Assumptions, OLS can be shown to be the minimum variance, linear, unbiased estimator (or BLUE, for best linear unbiased estimator) of the regression coefficients. This is the Gauss–Markov Theorem. When one or more of the classical properties do not hold (excluding normality), OLS is no longer BLUE, although it still may provide better estimates in some cases than the alternative estimation techniques discussed in subsequent chapters.

4. Because the sampling distribution of the OLS estimator of $\hat{\beta}_k$ is BLUE, it has desirable properties. Moreover, the variance, or the degree of dispersion of the sampling distribution of $\hat{\beta}_k$, decreases as the number of observations increases.

5. An OLS-estimated regression coefficient from a model that meets the classical assumptions is an unbiased, minimum variance estimate of the impact on the dependent variable of a one-unit increase in the independent variable in question, holding constant the other independent variables in the equation.

6. There is a standard notation used in the econometric literature. Table 4.1 presents this fairly complex set of notational conventions for use

_handwritten: 3/5,7,8 4/3,6,9

in regression analysis. This table should be reviewed periodically as a refresher.

Exercises

(Answers to even-numbered exercises are in Appendix A.)

1. Write the meaning of each of the following terms without referring to the book (or to your notes), and compare your definition with the version in the text for each:
    a. the Classical Assumptions
    b. classical error term
    c. standard normal distribution
    d. the Central Limit Theorem
    e. unbiased estimator
    f. BLUE
    g. sampling distribution

2. Which of the following pairs of independent variables would violate Assumption VI? (That is, which pairs of variables are perfect linear functions of each other?)
    a. right shoe size and left shoe size (of students in your class)
    b. consumption and disposable income (in the United States over the last 30 years)
    c. X_i and $2X_i$
    d. X_i and $(X_i)^2$

3. Consider the following estimated regression equation (standard errors in parentheses):

$$\hat{Y}_t = -120 + 0.10F_t + 5.33R_t \qquad \bar{R}^2 = .50$$
$$(0.05) \quad (1.00)$$

    where: Y_t = the corn yield (bushels/acre) in year t
    F_t = fertilizer intensity (pounds/acre) in year t
    R_t = rainfall (inches) in year t

    a. Carefully state the meaning of the coefficients 0.10 and 5.33 in this equation in terms of the impact of F and R on Y.
    b. Does the constant term of −120 really mean that *negative* amounts of corn are possible? If not, what is the meaning of that estimate?
    c. Suppose you were told that the true value of β_F is *known* to be 0.20. Does this show that the estimate is biased? Why or why not?

    d. Suppose you were told that the equation does not meet all the classical assumptions and, therefore, is not BLUE. Does this mean that the true β_R is definitely *not* equal to 5.33? Why or why not?

4. The Gauss–Markov Theorem shows that OLS is BLUE, so we, of course, hope and expect that our coefficient estimates will be unbiased *and* minimum variance. Suppose, however, that you had to choose one or the other.

    a. If you had to pick one, would you rather have an unbiased non-minimum variance estimate or a biased minimum variance one? Explain your reasoning.

    b. Are there circumstances in which you might change your answer to part a? (*Hint:* Does it matter *how* biased or less-than-minimum variance the estimates are?)

    c. Can you think of a way to systematically choose between estimates that have varying amounts of bias and less-than-minimum variance?

5. In 1993 Edward Saunders published an article that tested the possibility that the stock market is affected by the weather on Wall Street. Using daily data from 1962 through 1989, he estimated an equation with the following significant variables (standard errors in parentheses):[6]

$$\widehat{DJ}_t = \hat{\beta}_0 + 0.10R_{t-1} + 0.0010J_t - 0.017M_t + 0.0005C_t$$
$$(0.01)(0.0006)(0.004)(0.0002)$$
$$n = 6{,}911 \text{ (daily)}\quad \overline{R}^2 = .02$$

where: DJ_t = the percentage change in the Dow Jones industrial average on day t

              R_t = the daily index capital gain or loss for day t

              J_t = a dummy variable equal to 1 if the *i*th day was in January and equal to 0 otherwise

              M_t = a dummy variable equal to 1 if the *i*th day was a Monday and equal to 0 otherwise

              C_t = a variable equal to 1 if the cloud cover was 20 percent or less, equal to –1 if the cloud cover was 100 percent and equal to 0 otherwise

---

6. Edward M. Saunders, Jr., "Stock Prices and Wall Street Weather," *American Economic Review,* December 1993, pp. 1337–1346. Saunders also estimated equations for the New York and American Stock Exchange indices, both of which had much higher R^2s than did this equation. R_{t-1} was included in the equation "to account for nonsynchronous trading effects" (p. 1341).

    a. Saunders did not include an estimate of the constant term in his published regression results. Which of the Classical Assumptions supports the conclusion that you shouldn't spend much time analyzing estimates of the constant term? Explain.

    b. Which of the Classical Assumptions would be violated if you decided to add a dummy variable to the equation that was equal to 1 if the ith day was a Tuesday, Wednesday, Thursday, or Friday, and equal to 0 otherwise? (*Hint:* The stock market is not open on weekends.)

    c. Carefully state the meaning of the coefficients of R and M, being sure to take into account the fact the R is lagged in this equation (for valid theoretical reasons).

    d. The variable C is a measure of the percentage of cloud cover from sunrise to sunset on the ith day and reflects the fact that approximately 85 percent of all New York's rain falls on days with 100 percent cloud cover. Is C a dummy variable? What assumptions (or conclusions) did the author have to make to use this variable? What constraints does it place on the equation?

    e. Saunders concludes that these findings cast doubt on the hypothesis that security markets are entirely rational. Based just on the small portion of the author's work that we include in this question, would you agree or disagree? Why?

6.   Consider a random variable that is distributed $N(0, 0.5)$, that is, normally distributed with a mean of zero and a variance of 0.5. What is the probability that a single observation drawn from this distribution would be greater than one or less than minus one? [*Hint:* To answer this question, you will need to convert this distribution to a standard normal one (with mean equal to zero and standard deviation equal to one) and then refer to Table B-7 in the back of the book. The table includes a description of how to make such a transformation.]

7.   W. Bowen and T. Finegan[7] estimated the following regression equation for 78 cities (standard errors in parentheses):

$$\hat{L}_i = 94.2 - 0.24U_i + 0.20E_i - 0.69I_i - 0.06S_i + 0.002C_i - 0.80D_i$$
$$\quad\quad\quad (0.08)\quad (0.06)\quad (0.16)\quad (0.18)\quad (0.03)\quad (0.53)$$
$$n = 78 \quad R^2 = .51$$

---

7. W. G. Bowen and T. A. Finegan, "Labor Force Participation and Unemployment," in Arthur M. Ross (ed.), *Employment Policy and Labor Markets* (Berkeley: University of California Press, 1965), Table 4-2.

where: L_i = percent labor force participation (males ages 25 to 54) in the ith city

U_i = percent unemployment rate in the ith city

E_i = average earnings (hundreds of dollars/year) in the ith city

I_i = average other income (hundreds of dollars/year) in the ith city

S_i = average schooling completed (years) in the ith city

C_i = percent of the labor force that is nonwhite in the ith city

D_i = a dummy equal to 1 if the city is in the South and 0 otherwise

a. Interpret the estimated coefficients of C and D. What do they mean?
b. How likely is perfect collinearity in this equation? Explain your answer.
c. Suppose that you were told that the data for this regression were from one decade and that estimates on data from another decade yielded a much different coefficient of the dummy variable. Would this imply that one of the estimates was biased? If not, why not? If so, how would you determine which year's estimate was biased?
d. Comment on the following statement. "I know that these results are not BLUE because the average participation rate of 94.2 percent is way too high." Do you agree or disagree? Why?

8. A typical exam question in a more advanced econometrics class is to prove the Gauss–Markov Theorem. How might you go about starting such a proof? What is the importance of such a proof? (*Hint:* If you're having trouble getting started answering this question, see Appendix A.)

9. For your first econometrics project you decide to model sales at the frozen yogurt store nearest your school. The owner of the store is glad to help you with data collection because she believes that students from your school make up the bulk of her business. After countless hours of data collection and an endless supply of tutti-frutti frozen yogurt, you estimate the following regression equation (standard errors in parentheses):

$$\hat{Y}_t = 262.5 + 3.9T_t - 46.94P_t + 134.3A_t - 152.1C_t$$
$$\quad\quad\quad (0.7)\quad (20.0)\quad\quad (108.0)\quad\quad (138.3)$$
$$n = 29 \quad \overline{R}^2 = .78$$

where: Y_t = the total number of frozen yogurts sold during the tth
two-week time period

T_t = average high temperature (in degrees F) during period t

P_t = the price of frozen yogurt (in dollars) at the store in
period t

A_t = a dummy variable equal to 1 if the owner places an ad
in the school newspaper during period t, 0 otherwise

C_t = a dummy variable equal to 1 if your school is in regular session in period t (early September through early
December and early January through late May), 0
otherwise

a. This is a demand equation without any supply equation specified.
Does this violate any of the Classical Assumptions? What kind of
judgments do you have to make to answer this question?

b. What is the real-world economic meaning of the fact that the estimated coefficient of A_t is 134.3? Be specific.

c. You and the owner are surprised at the sign of the coefficient of C_t.
Can you think of any reason for this sign? (*Hint:* Assume that your
school has no summer session.)

d. If you could add one variable to this equation, what would it be?
Be specific.

10. The middle third of this text (Chapters 6 through 11) concentrates on
analyzing violations of the six Classical Assumptions required to
prove the Gauss–Markov Theorem. If you're going to understand
these chapters, it's good advice to know the Classical Assumptions
cold before you start them. (It turns out to be fairly difficult to make
sense of a whole chapter about the violation of a particular assumption if you're not really sure what that assumption is all about!) To
help accomplish this task, complete the following exercises:

a. Write out the Classical Assumptions without looking at your book
or notes. (*Hint:* Don't just say them to yourself in your head—put
pen or pencil to paper!)

b. After you've completed writing out all six assumptions, compare your
version with the text's. What differences are there? Are they important?

c. Get together with a classmate and take turns explaining the assumptions to each other. In this exercise, try to go beyond the definition of the assumption to give your classmate a feeling for the
real-world meaning of each assumption.

Hypothesis Testing

The most important use of econometrics for many researchers is in testing their theories with data from the real world, so hypothesis testing is more meaningful to them than are the other major uses of econometrics (description and forecasting). This chapter starts with a brief introduction to the topic of hypothesis testing. We then examine the *t*-test, the statistical tool typically used for hypothesis tests of individual regression coefficients, and the *F*-test of overall significance.

We are merely returning to the essence of econometrics—an effort to quantify economic relationships by analyzing sample data—and asking what conclusions we can draw from this quantification. Hypothesis testing goes beyond calculating estimates of the true population parameters to a much more complex set of questions. Hypothesis testing determines what we can learn about the real world from a sample. Is it likely that our result could have been obtained by chance? Can our theories be rejected using the results generated by our sample? If our theory is correct, what are the odds that this particular sample would have been observed?

Hypothesis testing and the *t*-test should be familiar topics to readers with strong backgrounds in statistics, who are encouraged to skim this chapter and focus only on those applications that seem somewhat new. The development of hypothesis testing procedures is explained here in terms of the regression model, however, so parts of the chapter may be instructive even to those already skilled in statistics. Students with a weak background in statistics are encouraged to read Chapter 16 before beginning Chapter 5.

Our approach will be classical in nature, since we assume that the sample data are our best and only information about the population. An alternative, **Bayesian statistics,** adds prior information to the sample to draw statistical inferences.[1]

5.1 What Is Hypothesis Testing?

Hypothesis testing is used in a variety of settings. The Food and Drug Administration (FDA), for example, tests new products before allowing their sale. If the sample of people exposed to the new product shows some side effect significantly more frequently than would be expected to occur by chance, the FDA is likely to withhold approval of marketing that product. Similarly, economists have been statistically testing various relationships between consumption and income for half a century; theories developed by John Maynard Keynes and Milton Friedman, among others, have been tested on macroeconomic and microeconomic data sets.

Although researchers are always interested in learning whether the theory in question is supported by estimates generated from a sample of real-world observations, it's almost impossible to *prove* that a given hypothesis is correct. All that can be done is to state that a particular sample conforms to a particular hypothesis. Even though we cannot prove that a given theory is "correct" using hypothesis testing, we *can* often *reject* a given hypothesis with a certain degree of confidence. In such a case, the researcher concludes that it is very unlikely the sample result would have been observed if the hypothesized theory were correct. If there is conflicting evidence on the validity of a theory, the question is often put aside until additional data or a new approach shed more light on the issue.

Let's begin by investigating three topics that are central to the application of hypothesis testing to regression analysis:

1. the specification of the hypothesis to be tested,

---

1. Bayesian econometrics combines estimates generated from samples with estimates based on prior theory or research. For example, suppose you attempt to estimate the marginal propensity to consume (MPC) with the coefficient of income in an appropriately specified consumption regression equation. If your prior belief is that the MPC is 0.9 and if the estimated coefficient from your sample is 0.8, then a Bayesian estimate of the MPC would be somewhere between the two, depending on the strength of your belief. Bayesians, by being forced to state explicitly their prior expectations, tend to do most of their thinking before estimation, which is a good habit for a number of important reasons. For more on this approach, see Dale Poirier, *Intermediate Statisics and Econometrics: A Comparative Approach* (Cambridge, MA: MIT Press, 1995).

2. the decision rule to use in deciding whether to reject the hypothesis in question, and

3. the kinds of errors that might be encountered if the application of the decision rule to the appropriate statistics yields an incorrect inference.

5.1.1 Classical Null and Alternative Hypotheses

The first step in hypothesis testing is to state explicitly the hypothesis to be tested. To ensure fairness, the researcher should specify the hypothesis *before* the equation is estimated. The purpose of prior theoretical work is to match the hypothesis to the underlying theory as completely as possible. Hypotheses formulated after generation of the estimates are at times justifications of particular results rather than tests of their validity. As a result, most econometricians take pains to specify hypotheses before estimation.

In making a hypothesis, you must state carefully what you think is not true and what you think is true. These reflections of the researcher's expectations about a particular regression coefficient (or coefficients) are summarized in the null and alternative hypotheses. The **null hypothesis** is typically a statement of the range of values of the regression coefficient that would be expected to occur if the researcher's theory were *not* correct. The **alternative hypothesis** is used to specify the range of values of the coefficient that would be expected to occur if the researcher's theory were correct. The word *null* also means "zero," and the null hypothesis can be thought of as the hypothesis that the researcher does *not* believe.[2] The reason it's called a null or zero hypothesis is that a variable would not be included in an equation if its expected coefficient were zero.

We set up the null and alternative hypotheses in this way so we can make rather strong statements when we reject the null hypothesis. It is only when we define the null hypothesis as the result we do *not* expect that we can control the probability of rejecting the null hypothesis accidentally when it is in fact true. The converse does not hold. That is, we can never actually know the probability of agreeing accidentally that the null hypothesis is correct when it

---

2. Researchers occasionally will have to switch the null and alternative hypotheses. For instance, some tests of rational expectations theory have put the preferred hypothesis as the null hypothesis in order to make the null hypothesis a specific value. In such cases of tests of specific nonzero values, the reversal of the null and alternative hypotheses is regrettable but unavoidable. An example of this kind of reversal is a two-sided null hypothesis involving a nonzero value, as in the second example in Section 5.3.2. Except for these rare cases, all null hypotheses in this text will be the result we expect not to occur.

is in fact false. As a result, we can never say that we *accept* the null hypothesis; we always must say that we *cannot reject* the null hypothesis, or we put the word "accept" in quotes.

Hypotheses in econometrics usually do not specify particular values, but instead they state the particular signs that the researcher expects the estimated coefficients to take. We typically hypothesize that a particular coefficient will be positive (or negative). In such cases, the null hypothesis represents what is expected not to occur, but that expectation is now a range; the same is true for the alternative hypothesis.

The notation used to refer to a null hypothesis is "H_0:," and this notation is followed by a statement of the value or range of values you do *not* expect the particular parameter to take. If, for example, you expect a negative coefficient, then the correct null hypothesis is:

$$H_0: \beta \geq 0 \qquad \text{(the values you do not expect)}$$

The alternative hypothesis is expressed by "H_A:" followed by the parameter value or values you expect to observe:

$$H_A: \beta < 0 \qquad \text{(the values you expect to be true)}$$

Another way to state the null and alternative hypotheses is to test the null hypothesis that β is not significantly different from zero in either direction. In this second approach, the null and alternative hypotheses would be:

$$H_0: \beta = 0$$
$$H_A: \beta \neq 0$$

Since the alternative hypothesis has values on both sides of the null hypothesis, this approach is called a **two-sided test** (or *two-tailed test*) to distinguish it from the **one-sided test** of the previous example (in which the alternative hypothesis was only on one side of the null hypothesis).[3]

---

3. Some researchers prefer to use a two-tailed test around zero for this hypothesis because they feel that the classical approach requires the null hypothesis to contain a single value. We feel that the use of a two-tailed test in such a circumstance is a mistake. However, we have no quarrel with using $\beta = 0$ as the null hypothesis as long as the alternative hypothesis remains the same. These two versions of the null hypothesis give identical answers because to test a null hypothesis that is a range like $\beta \leq 0$, you must focus on the value in that range that is closest to the range implied by the alternative hypothesis. If you can reject that value, you can reject values that are farther away as well. Truncating the range of the null hypothesis in this way has no practical importance.

5.1.2 Type I and Type II Errors

The typical testing technique in econometrics is to hypothesize an expected sign (or value) for each regression coefficient (except the constant term) and then to determine whether to reject the null hypothesis. Since the regression coefficients are only estimates of the true population parameters, it would be unrealistic to think that conclusions drawn from regression analysis will always be right.

There are two kinds of errors we can make in such hypothesis testing:

Type I. We reject a true null hypothesis.
Type II. We do not reject a false null hypothesis.

We will refer to these errors as **Type I** and **Type II Errors**, respectively.[4] Suppose we have the following null and alternative hypotheses:

$$H_0: \beta \leq 0$$
$$H_A: \beta > 0$$

There are two distinct possibilities. The first is that the true β in the population is equal to or less than zero, as specified by the null hypothesis. When the true β is not positive, unbiased estimates of β will be distributed around zero or some negative number, but any given estimate is very unlikely to be exactly equal to that number. Any single sample (and therefore any estimate of β calculated from that sample) might be quite different from the mean of the distribution. As a result, even if the true parameter β is not positive, the particular estimate obtained by a researcher may be sufficiently positive to lead to the rejection of the null hypothesis that $\beta \leq 0$. This is a Type I Error; we have rejected the truth! A Type I Error is graphed in Figure 5.1.

The second possibility is that the true β is greater than 0, as stated in the alternative hypothesis. Depending on the specific value of the population β (and other factors), it's possible to obtain an estimate of β that is close enough to zero (or negative) to be considered "not significantly positive." This occurs because the sampling distribution of $\hat{\beta}$, even if unbiased, has a portion of its area in the region of $\beta \leq 0$. Such a result may lead the researcher to "accept" the hypothesis that $\beta \leq 0$ when in truth $\beta > 0$. This is a Type II Error; we have failed to reject a false null hypothesis! A Type II Error is graphed in Figure 5.2 on page 118. (The specific value of $\beta = 1$ was selected as the true value in that figure purely for illustrative purposes.)

---

4. Some authors refer to these as α and β errors, respectively.

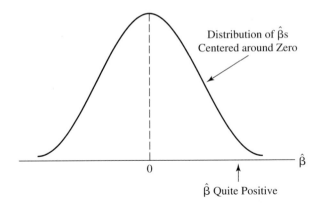

Figure 5.1 Rejecting a True Null Hypothesis Is a Type I Error

If $\beta = 0$, but you observe a $\hat{\beta}$ that is very positive, you might reject a true null hypothesis, $H_0: \beta \le 0$, and conclude incorrectly that the alternative hypothesis $H_A: \beta > 0$ is true.

As an example of Type I and Type II Errors, let's suppose that you're on a jury in a murder case.[5] In such a situation, the presumption of "innocent until proven guilty" implies that:

 H_0: *The defendant is innocent.*

 H_A: *The defendant is guilty.*

What would a Type I Error be? Rejecting the null hypothesis would mean sending the defendant to jail, so a Type I Error, rejecting a true null hypothesis, would mean:

   Type I Error = Sending an innocent defendant to jail.

Similarly,

   Type II Error = Freeing a guilty defendant.

Most reasonable jury members would want both levels of error to be quite small, but such certainty is almost impossible. After all, couldn't there be a mistaken identification or a lying witness? In the real world, decreasing the probability of a Type I Error (sending an innocent defendant to jail) means increas-

---

5. This example comes from and is discussed in much more detail in Edward E. Leamer, *Specification Searches* (New York: John Wiley and Sons, 1978), pp. 93–98.

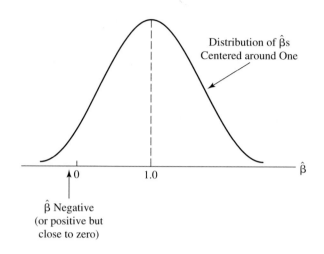

Distribution of $\hat{\beta}$s
Centered around One

0   1.0 $\hat{\beta}$

$\hat{\beta}$ Negative
(or positive but
close to zero)

Figure 5.2 Failure to Reject a False Null Hypothesis Is a Type II Error

If $\beta = 1$, but you observe a $\hat{\beta}$ that is negative or close to zero, you might fail to reject a false null hypothesis, $H_0: \beta \leq 0$, and incorrectly ignore that the alternative hypothesis, $H_A: \beta > 0$, is true.

ing the probability of a Type II Error (freeing a guilty defendant). If we never sent an innocent defendant to jail, we'd be freeing quite a few murderers!

5.1.3   Decision Rules of Hypothesis Testing

In testing a hypothesis, a sample statistic must be calculated that allows the null hypothesis to be "accepted" or rejected depending on the magnitude of that sample statistic compared with a preselected *critical* value found in tables such as those at the end of this text; this procedure is referred to as a **decision rule.**

A decision rule is formulated before regression estimates are obtained. The range of possible values of $\hat{\beta}$ is divided into two regions, an *"acceptance"* region and a *rejection region*, where the terms are expressed relative to the null hypothesis. To define these regions, we must determine a *critical value* (or, for a two-tailed test, two critical values) of β. Thus, a **critical value** is a value that divides the "acceptance" region from the rejection region when testing a null hypothesis. Graphs of these "acceptance" and rejection regions are presented in Figures 5.3 and 5.4.

To use a decision rule, we need to select a critical value. Let's suppose that the critical value is 1.8. If the observed $\hat{\beta}$ is greater than 1.8, we can reject the null hypothesis that β is zero or negative. To see this, take a look at the one-sided test in Figure 5.3. Any $\hat{\beta}$ above 1.8 can be seen to fall into the rejection region,

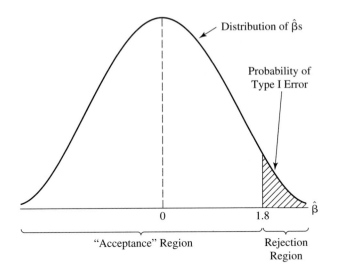

Figure 5.3 "Acceptance" and Rejection Regions for a One-Sided Test of β

For a one-sided test of H_0: $\beta \le 0$ vs. H_A: $\beta > 0$, the critical value divides the distribution of $\hat{\beta}$ (centered around zero on the assumption that H_0 is true) into "acceptance" and rejection regions.

whereas any $\hat{\beta}$ below 1.8 can be seen to fall into the "acceptance" region.

The rejection region measures the probability of a Type I Error if the null hypothesis is true. Take another look at Figure 5.3. Note that we've labeled the rejection region as the probability of a Type I Error. Why? If the null hypothesis is true and we reject it, we've made a Type I Error, but the only time we can reject the truth is when $\hat{\beta}$ falls in the rejection region.

Some students react to the news that the rejection region measures the probability of a Type I Error by suggesting that we make the rejection region as small as possible. Unfortunately, decreasing the chance of a Type I Error means increasing the chance of a Type II Error (not rejecting a false null hypothesis). This is because if you make the rejection region so small that you almost never reject a true null hypothesis, then you're going to "accept" almost every null hypothesis, whether they're true or not! As a result, the probability of a Type II Error will rise.

As an example of the trade-off between the probability of a Type I Error and the probability of a Type II Error, think back to the murder case example of the previous section:

Type I Error = Sending an innocent defendant to jail.
Type II Error = Freeing a guilty defendant.

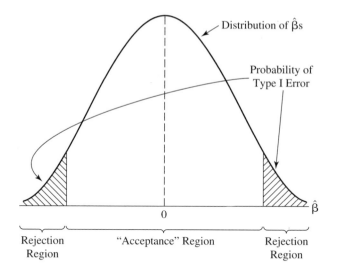

Figure 5.4 "Acceptance" and Rejection Regions for a Two-Sided Test of β

For a two-sided test of H_0: $\beta = 0$ vs. H_A: $\beta \neq 0$, we divided the distribution of $\hat{\beta}$ into an "acceptance" region and *two* rejection regions.

The only way to ensure a low probability of Type I Error is to free almost every defendant, but that would mean freeing quite a few guilty ones. Thus decreasing the probability of a Type I Error does, indeed, increase the probability of a Type II Error.

Given that, how do you choose between Type I and Type II Errors? Is it worse to send an innocent defendant to jail or to free a murderer? The answer is easiest if you know that the cost (to society or the decision maker) of making one kind of error is dramatically larger than the cost of making the other. If you worked for the FDA, for example, you'd want to be very sure that you hadn't released a product that had horrible side effects. Without such information about costs, however, most econometricians focus on Type I Error while choosing a critical value that keeps the probability of either kind of error from getting unreasonably large. In Section 5.2.3, we'll discuss our specific solution to this dilemma for the *t*-test.

5.2   The *t*-Test

The *t*-test is the test that econometricians usually use to test hypotheses about individual regression slope coefficients. Tests of more than one coefficient at a time (joint hypotheses) are typically done with the *F*-test, presented in Sections 5.5 and 7.7.

The *t*-test is easy to use because it accounts for differences in the units of measurement of the variables and in the standard deviations of the estimated coefficients (both of which would affect the shape of the distribution of β and the location of the critical value). More important, the *t*-statistic is the appropriate test to use when the stochastic error term is normally distributed and when the variance of that distribution must be estimated. Since these usually are the case, the use of the *t*-test for hypothesis testing has become standard practice in econometrics.

5.2.1 The t-Statistic

For a typical multiple regression equation:

$$Y_i = \beta_0 + \beta_1 X_{1i} + \beta_2 X_{2i} + \epsilon_i \tag{5.1}$$

we can calculate t-values for each of the estimated coefficients in the equation. For reasons that will be explained in Section 7.1.2, *t*-tests are usually done only on the slope coefficients; for these, the relevant general form of the **t-statistic** for the *k*th coefficient is

$$t_k = \frac{(\hat{\beta}_k - \beta_{H_0})}{SE(\hat{\beta}_k)} \qquad (k = 1, 2, \ldots, K) \tag{5.2}$$

where: $\hat{\beta}_k$ = the estimated regression coefficient of the *k*th variable
β_{H_0} = the border value (usually zero) implied by the null hypothesis for β_k
$SE(\hat{\beta}_k)$ = the estimated standard error of $\hat{\beta}_k$ (that is, the square root of the estimated variance of the distribution of the $\hat{\beta}_k$; note that there is no "hat" attached to SE because SE is already defined as an estimate)

How do you decide what *border* is implied by the null hypothesis? Some null hypotheses specify a particular value. For these, β_{H_0} is simply that value; if $H_0: \beta = S$, then $\beta_{H_0} = S$. Other null hypotheses involve ranges, but we are concerned only with the value in the null hypothesis that is closest to the border between the "acceptance" region and the rejection region. This border value then becomes the β_{H_0}. For example, if $H_0: \beta \geq 0$ and $H_A: \beta < 0$, then the value in the null hypothesis closest to the border is zero, and $\beta_{H_0} = 0$.

Since most regression hypotheses test whether a particular regression coefficient is significantly different from zero, β_{H_0} is typically zero, and the most-used form of the t-statistic becomes

$$t_k = \frac{(\hat{\beta}_k - 0)}{SE(\hat{\beta}_k)} \qquad (k = 1, 2, \ldots, K)$$

which simplifies to

$$t_k = \frac{\hat{\beta}_k}{SE(\hat{\beta}_k)} \qquad (k = 1, 2, \ldots, K) \qquad (5.3)$$

or the estimated coefficient divided by the estimate of its standard error. This is the *t*-statistic formula used by most computer programs.

For an example of this calculation, let's consider the equation for the check volume at Woody's restaurants from Section 3.2:

$$\hat{Y}_i = 102{,}192 - 9075N_i + 0.3547P_i + 1.288I_i \qquad (5.4)$$
$$(2053) \qquad (0.0727) \qquad (0.543)$$
$$t = -4.42 \qquad 4.88 \qquad 2.37$$
$$n = 33 \qquad \overline{R}^2 = .579$$

In Equation 5.4, the numbers in parentheses underneath the estimated regression coefficients are the estimated standard errors of the estimated $\hat{\beta}$s, and the numbers below them are t-values calculated according to Equation 5.3. The format used to document Equation 5.4 above is the one we'll use whenever possible throughout this text. Note that the sign of the t-value is always the same as that of the estimated regression coefficient, while the standard error is always positive.

Using the regression results in Equation 5.4, let's calculate the t-value for the estimated coefficient of P, the population variable. Given the values in Equation 5.4 of 0.3547 for $\hat{\beta}_P$ and 0.0727 for $SE(\hat{\beta}_P)$, and given $H_0: \beta_P \leq 0$, the relevant t-value is indeed 4.88, as specified in Equation 5.4:

$$t_P = \frac{\hat{\beta}_P}{SE(\hat{\beta}_P)} = \frac{0.3547}{0.0727} = 4.88$$

The larger in absolute value this t-value is, the greater the likelihood that the estimated regression coefficient is significantly different from zero.

5.2.2 The Critical t-Value and the *t*-Test Decision Rule

To decide whether to reject or not to reject a null hypothesis based on a calculated t-value, we use a critical t-value. A *critical t-value* is the value that distinguishes the "acceptance" region from the rejection region. The critical t-value, t_c, is selected from a t-table (see Statistical Table B-1 in the back of the book) depending on whether the test is one sided or two sided, on the level of Type I Error you specify and on the degrees of freedom, which we have defined as the number of observations minus the number of coefficients estimated (including the constant) or $n - K - 1$. The level of Type I Error in a hypothesis test is also called the *level of significance* of that test and will be discussed in more detail later in this section. The t-table was created to save time during research; it consists of critical t-values given specific areas underneath curves such as those in Figure 5.3 for Type I Errors. A critical t-value is thus a function of the probability of Type I Error that the researcher wants to specify.

Once you have obtained a calculated t-value and a critical t-value, you reject the null hypothesis if the calculated t-value is greater in absolute value than the critical t-value and if the calculated t-value has the sign implied by H_A.

Thus, the rule to apply when testing a single regression coefficient is that you should:

Reject H_0 if $|t_k| > t_c$ and if t_k also has the sign implied by H_A.
Do Not Reject H_0 otherwise.

This decision rule works for calculated t-values and critical t-values for one-sided hypotheses around zero:

$$H_0: \beta_k \leq 0$$
$$H_A: \beta_k > 0$$

$$H_0: \beta_k \geq 0$$
$$H_A: \beta_k < 0$$

for two-sided hypotheses around zero:

$$H_0: \beta_k = 0$$
$$H_A: \beta_k \neq 0$$

for one-sided hypotheses based on hypothesized values other than zero:

$$H_0: \beta_k \leq S$$
$$H_A: \beta_k > S$$

$$H_0: \beta_k \geq S$$
$$H_A: \beta_k < S$$

and for two-sided hypotheses based on hypothesized values other than zero:

$$H_0: \beta_k = S$$
$$H_A: \beta_k \neq S$$

The decision rule is the same: Reject the null hypothesis if the appropriately calculated t-value, t_k, is greater in absolute value than the critical t-value, t_c, as long as the sign of t_k is the same as the sign of the coefficient implied in H_A. Otherwise, "accept" H_0. Always use Equation 5.2 whenever the hypothesized value is not zero.

Statistical Table B-1 contains the critical values t_c for varying degrees of freedom and levels of significance. The columns indicate the levels of significance according to whether the test is one sided or two sided, and the rows indicate the degrees of freedom. For an example of the use of this table and the decision rule, let's return once again to the estimated model of gross check volume at Woody's restaurants and, in particular, to the t-value for $\hat{\beta}_P$ calculated in Section 5.2.1. Recall that we hypothesized that population's coefficient would be positive, so this is a one-sided test:

$$H_0: \beta_P \leq 0$$
$$H_A: \beta_P > 0$$

There are 29 degrees of freedom (equal to $n - K - 1$, or $33 - 3 - 1$) in this regression, so the appropriate t-value with which to test the calculated t-value is a one-tailed critical t-value with 29 degrees of freedom. To find this value, pick a level of significance, say 5 percent, and turn to Statistical Table B-1. The number there is 1.699; should you reject the null hypothesis?

The decision rule is to reject H_0 if $|t_k| > t_c$ and if t_k has the sign implied by H_A. Since the 5 percent, one-sided, 29 degrees of freedom critical t-value is 1.699, and since the sign implied by H_A is positive, the decision rule (for this specific case) becomes:

$$\text{Reject } H_0 \text{ if } |t_P| > 1.699 \text{ and if } t_P \text{ is positive}$$

or, combining the two conditions:

$$\text{Reject } H_0 \text{ if } t_P > 1.699$$

What is t_P? In the previous section, we found that t_P was $+4.88$, so we would reject the null hypothesis and conclude that population does indeed tend to have a positive relationship with Woody's check volume (holding the other variables in the equation constant).

This decision rule is based on the fact that since both $\hat{\beta}$ and $SE(\hat{\beta})$ have known sampling distributions, so does their ratio, the t-statistic. The sampling distribution of $\hat{\beta}$ was shown in Chapter 4 and is based on the assumption of the normality of the error term ϵ_i and on the other Classical Assumptions. Consequently, the sampling distribution of the t-statistic is also based on the same assumption of the normality of the error term and the Classical Assumptions. If any of these assumptions are violated, t_c will not necessarily follow the t-distribution detailed in Statistical Table B-1. In many cases, however, the t-table is used as a reasonable approximation of the true distribution of the t-statistic even when some of these assumptions do not hold.

In addition, as was mentioned above, the critical t-value depends on the number of degrees of freedom, on the level of Type I Error (referred to as the level of statistical significance), and on whether the hypothesis is a one-tailed or two-tailed one. Figure 5.5 illustrates the dependence of the critical t_c on two of these factors. For the simple regression model with 30 observations and two coefficients to estimate (the slope and the intercept), there are 28 degrees of freedom. The "acceptance" and rejection regions are stated in terms of the decision rule for several levels of statistical significance and for one-sided ($H_A: \beta > 0$) and two-sided ($H_A: \beta \neq 0$) alternatives.

Note from Statistical Table B-1 that the critical t-value for a one-tailed test at a given level of significance is exactly equal to the critical t-value for a two-tailed test at twice the level of significance as the one-tailed test. This property arises because the t-statistic is symmetrical. For example, if 5 percent of the area under the curve is to the right of t_c, then 5 percent will also be to the left of $-t_c$, and the two tails will sum to 10 percent. This relationship between one-sided and two-sided tests is illustrated in Figure 5.5. The critical value $t_c = 1.701$ is for a one-sided, 10 percent level of significance, but it also represents a two-sided, 10 percent level of significance because if one tail represents 5 percent, then both tails added together represent 10 percent.

5.2.3 Choosing a Level of Significance

To complete the previous example, it was necessary to pick a level of significance before a critical t-value could be found in Statistical Table B-1. The words "significantly positive" usually carry the statistical interpretation that H_0 ($\beta \leq 0$) was rejected in favor of H_A ($\beta > 0$) according to the preestablished decision rule, which was set up with a given level of significance. The

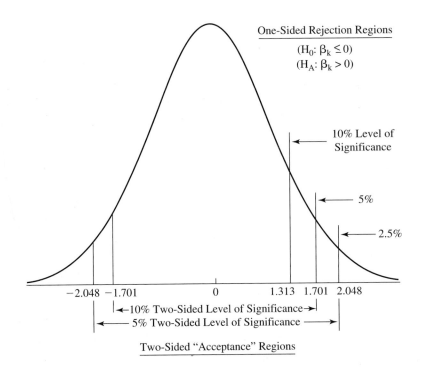

One-Sided Rejection Regions
$$(H_0: \beta_k \leq 0)$$
$$(H_A: \beta_k > 0)$$

10% Level of
Significance

5%

2.5%

−2.048 −1.701   0   1.313 1.701 2.048

|←—10% Two-Sided Level of Significance—→|
|←———— 5% Two-Sided Level of Significance ————→|

Two-Sided "Acceptance" Regions

Figure 5.5 One-Sided and Two-Sided *t*-Tests for Various Levels of Significance and 28 Degrees of Freedom

The critical t-value depends on whether the *t*-test is two sided or one sided and on the chosen level of significance. In particular, the t_c for a one-sided test at a given level of significance is equal exactly to the t_c for a two-sided test with twice the level of significance of the one-sided test. For example, $t_c = 1.701$ for a 10 percent two-sided *and* as a 5 percent one-sided test.

level of significance indicates the probability of observing an estimated t-value greater than the critical t-value if the null hypothesis were correct. It measures the amount of Type I Error implied by a particular critical t-value. If the level of significance is 10 percent and we reject the null hypothesis at that level, then this result would have occurred only 10 percent of the time that the null hypothesis was indeed correct.

How should you choose a level of significance? Most beginning econometricians (and many published ones too) assume that the lower the level of significance, the better. After all, they say, doesn't a low level of significance guarantee a low probability of making a Type I Error? Unfortunately, an extremely low level of significance also dramatically increases the probability of making a Type II Error. Therefore, unless you're in the unusual situation of not caring about mistakenly "accepting" a false null hypothesis, minimizing the level of significance is *not* good standard practice.

Instead, we recommend using a 5 percent level of significance except in those circumstances when you know something unusual about the relative costs of making Type I and Type II Errors. If we can reject a null hypothesis at the 5 percent level of significance, we can summarize our results by saying that the coefficient is "statistically significant" at the 5 percent level. Since the 5 percent level is arbitrary, we shouldn't jump to conclusions about the value of a variable simply because its coefficient misses being significant by a small amount; if a different level of significance had been chosen, the result might have been different.

Some researchers avoid choosing a level of significance by simply stating the lowest level of significance possible for each estimated regression coefficient. Such a use of the t-value should be regarded as a descriptive rather than a hypothesis-testing use of statistics.

Now and then researchers will use the phrase "degree of confidence" or "level of confidence" when they test hypotheses. What do they mean? The *level of confidence* is nothing more than 100 percent minus the level of significance. Thus a *t*-test for which we use a 5 percent level of significance can also be said to have a 95 percent level of confidence. Since the two terms have identical meanings, for all intents and purposes, we will tend to use level of significance throughout this text. Another reason we prefer the term level of significance to level of confidence is to avoid any possible confusion with the related concept of confidence intervals.

5.2.4 Confidence Intervals

A **confidence interval** is a range within which the true value of an item is likely to fall a specified percentage of the time.[6] This percentage is the level of confidence associated with the level of significance used to choose the critical t-value in the interval. For an estimated regression coefficient, the confidence interval can be calculated using the two-sided critical t-value and the standard error of the estimated coefficient:

$$\text{Confidence interval} = \hat{\beta} \pm t_c \cdot SE(\hat{\beta}) \tag{5.5}$$

As an example, let's return to Equation 5.4 and our *t*-test of the significance of the estimate of the coefficient of population in that equation:

---

6. Although it is common usage to call this interval a "confidence interval," it technically is a "prediction interval."

$$\hat{Y}_i = 102{,}192 - 9075N_i + 0.3547P_i + 1.288I_i \qquad (5.4)$$
$$(2053) \qquad (0.0727) \quad (0.543)$$
$$t = -4.42 \qquad 4.88 \qquad 2.37$$
$$n = 33 \qquad \overline{R}^2 = .579$$

What would a 90 percent confidence interval for $\hat{\beta}_p$ look like? Well, $\hat{\beta}_p = 0.3547$ and $SE(\hat{\beta}_p) = 0.0727$, so all we need is a 90 percent two-sided critical t-value for 29 degrees of freedom. As can be seen in Statistical Table B-1, this $t_c = 1.699$. Substituting these values into Equation 5.5, we get:

$$CI = \hat{\beta} \pm t_c \cdot SE(\hat{\beta})$$

90 percent confidence interval around $\hat{\beta}_p = 0.3547 \pm 1.699 \cdot 0.0727$
$$= 0.3547 \pm 0.1235$$

In other words, we expect that 90 percent of the time the true coefficient will fall between 0.2312 and 0.4782.

There's an interesting relationship between confidence intervals and two-sided hypothesis testing. It turns out that if a hypothesized border value, β_{H_0}, falls within the 90 percent confidence interval for an estimated coefficient, then we will not be able to reject the null hypothesis at the 10 percent level of significance in a two-sided test. If, on the other hand, β_{H_0} falls outside the 90 percent confidence interval, then we can reject the null hypothesis.

Perhaps the most important econometric use of confidence intervals is in forecasting. Many decision makers find it practical to be given a forecast of a range of values into which the forecasted item is likely to fall some percentage of the time. In contrast, decision makers find that a specific point forecast provides them with little information about the reliability or variability of the forecast. For more on this application of confidence intervals, see Section 15.2.3.

5.3 Examples of *t*-Tests

5.3.1 Examples of One-Sided *t*-Tests

The most common use of the one-sided *t*-test is to determine whether a regression coefficient has the sign predicted by theory. Let's face it, if you expect a positive sign for a coefficient and you get a negative $\hat{\beta}$, it's hard to reject the possibility that the true β might be negative (or zero). On the other hand, if you expect a positive sign and get a positive $\hat{\beta}$, things get a bit tricky. If $\hat{\beta}$ is positive, but fairly close to zero, then a one-sided *t*-test should be used to determine whether the $\hat{\beta}$ is different enough from zero to allow the rejection of the null hypothesis. Recall that in order to be able to control the amount of Type I Error we make, such a theory implies an alternative hypothesis of

H_A: $\beta > 0$ (the expected sign) and a null hypothesis of H_0: $\beta \leq 0$. Let's look at some complete examples of these kinds of one-sided t-tests.

Consider a simple model of the aggregate retail sales of new cars that hypothesizes that sales of new cars (Y) are a function of real disposable income (X_1) and the average retail price of a new car adjusted by the consumer price index (X_2). Suppose you spend some time reviewing the literature on the automobile industry and are inspired to test a new theory. You decide to add a third independent variable, the number of sports utility vehicles sold (X_3), to take account of the fact that some potential new car buyers now buy car-like trucks instead. You therefore hypothesize the following model:

$$Y = f(\overset{+}{X}_1, \overset{-}{X}_2, \overset{-}{X}_3) + \epsilon \tag{5.6}$$

β_1 is expected to be positive and β_2 and β_3, negative. This makes sense, since you'd expect higher incomes, lower prices, or lower numbers of sports utility vehicles sold to increase new cars sales, holding the other variables in the equation constant. Although in theory a single test for all three slope coefficients could be applied here, nearly every researcher examines each coefficient separately with the t-test. The four steps to use when working with the t-test are:

1. Set up the null and alternative hypotheses.
2. Choose a level of significance and therefore a critical t-value.
3. Run the regression and obtain an estimated t-value (or t-score).
4. Apply the decision rule by comparing the calculated t-value with the critical t-value in order to reject or "accept" the null hypothesis.

1. *Set up the null and alternative hypotheses.*[7] From Equation 5.6, the one-sided hypotheses are set up as:

1. H_0: $\beta_1 \leq 0$
   H_A: $\beta_1 > 0$

2. H_0: $\beta_2 \geq 0$
   H_A: $\beta_2 < 0$

3. H_0: $\beta_3 \geq 0$
   H_A: $\beta_3 < 0$

---

7. Recall from footnote 3 that a one-sided hypothesis can be stated either as H_0: $\beta \leq 0$ or H_0: $\beta = 0$ because the value used to test H_0: $\beta \leq 0$ is the value in the null hypothesis closest to the border between the acceptance and the rejection regions. When the amount of Type I Error is calculated, this border value of β is the one that is used because, over the whole range of $\beta \leq 0$, the value $\beta = 0$ gives the maximum amount of Type I Error. The classical approach limits this maximum amount to a preassigned level, the chosen level of significance.

Remember that a *t*-test typically is not run on the estimate of the constant term β_0.

2. *Choose a level of significance and therefore a critical t-value.* Assume that you have considered the various costs involved in making Type I and Type II Errors and have chosen 5 percent as the level of significance with which you want to test. There are 10 observations in the data set that is going to be used to test these hypotheses, and so there are $10 - 3 - 1 = 6$ degrees of freedom. At a 5 percent level of significance (or a 95 percent level of confidence), the critical t-value, t_c, can be found in Statistical Table B-1 to be 1.943. Note that the level of significance does not have to be the same for all the coefficients in the same regression equation. It could well be that the costs involved in an incorrectly rejected null hypothesis for one coefficient are much higher than for another, and so lower levels of significance would be used. In this equation, though, for all three variables:

$$t_c = 1.943$$

3. *Run the regression and obtain an estimated t-value.* You now use the data (annual from 1990 to 1999) to run the regression on your computer's OLS package, getting:

$$\hat{Y}_t = 1.30 + 4.91X_{1t} + 0.00123X_{2t} - 7.14X_{3t} \qquad (5.7)$$
$$\phantom{\hat{Y}_t = 1.30 +} (2.38) \quad\;\; (0.00022) \quad (71.38)$$
$$\phantom{\hat{Y}_t = 1.30 +} t = 2.1 \qquad\quad 5.6 \qquad\quad -0.1$$

where: Y = new car sales (in hundreds of thousands of units) in year t

X_1 = real U.S. disposable income (in hundreds of billions of dollars)

X_2 = the average retail price of a new car in year t (in dollars)

X_3 = the number of sports utility vehicles sold in year t (in millions)

Once again, we use our standard documentation notation, so the figures in parentheses are the estimated standard errors of the $\hat{\beta}$s. The t-values to be used in these hypothesis tests are printed out by most standard OLS programs, because the programs are written to test the null hypothesis that $\beta = 0$ (or, equivalently, $\beta \leq$ or ≥ 0). If the program does not calculate the t-scores automatically, one may plug the

$\hat{\beta}$s and their estimated standard errors into Equation 5.3, repeated here:

$$t_k = \frac{\hat{\beta}_k}{SE(\hat{\beta}_k)} \qquad (k = 1, 2, \ldots, K) \qquad (5.3)$$

For example, the estimated coefficient of X_3 divided by its estimated standard error is $-7.14/71.38 = -0.1$. Note that since standard errors are always positive, a negative estimated coefficient implies a negative t-value.

4. *Apply the decision rule by comparing the calculated t-value with the critical t-value in order to reject or "accept" the null hypothesis.* As stated in Section 5.2, the decision rule for the *t*-test is to

Reject H_0 if $|t_k| > t_c$ and if t_k also has the sign implied by H_A. Do not reject H_0 otherwise.

What would these decision rules be for the three hypotheses, given the relevant critical t-value (1.943), and the calculated t-values?

For β_1: Reject H_0 if $|2.1| > 1.943$ and if 2.1 is positive.

In the case of disposable income, you reject the null hypothesis that $\beta_1 \le 0$ with 95 percent confidence since 2.1 is indeed greater than 1.943. The result (that is, $H_A: \beta_1 > 0$) is as you expected on the basis of theory since the more income in the country, the more new car sales you'd expect.

For β_2: Reject H_0: if $|5.6| > 1.943$ and if 5.6 is negative.

For prices, the t-statistic is large in absolute value (being greater than 1.943) but has a sign that is contrary to our expectations, since the alternative hypothesis implies a negative sign. Since both conditions in the decision rule must be met before we can reject H_0, you cannot reject the null hypothesis that $\beta_2 \ge 0$. That is, you cannot reject the hypothesis that prices have a zero or positive effect on new car sales! This is an extremely small data set that covers a time period of dramatic economic swings, but even so, you're surprised by this result. Despite your surprise, you stick with your contention that prices belong in the equation and that their expected impact should be negative.

Notice that the coefficient of X_2 is quite small, 0.00123, but that this size has no effect on the t-calculation other than its relationship to the standard error of the estimated coefficient. In other words, the absolute magnitude of any $\hat{\beta}$ is of no particular importance in determining statistical significance because a change in the units of measurement of X_2 will change both $\hat{\beta}_2$ and $SE(\hat{\beta}_2)$ in exactly the same way, so the calculated t-value (the ratio of the two) is unchanged.

For β_3: Reject H_0 if $|-0.1| > 1.943$ and if -0.1 is negative.

For sales of sports utility vehicles, the coefficient $\hat{\beta}_3$ is not statistically different from zero since $|-0.1| < 1.943$, and you cannot reject the null hypothesis that $\beta \geq 0$ even though the estimated coefficient has the sign implied by the alternative hypothesis. After thinking this model over again, you come to the conclusion that you were hasty in adding the variable to the equation.

Figure 5.6 illustrates all three of these outcomes by plotting the critical t-value and the calculated t-values for all three null hypotheses on a t-distribution that is centered around zero (the value in the null hypothesis closest to the border between the acceptance and rejection regions). Students are urged to analyze the results of tests on the estimated coefficients of Equation 5.7 assuming different numbers of observations and different levels of significance. Exercise 4 has a number of such specific combinations, with answers in the back of the book.

Researchers sometimes note in their results the maximum level of confidence achieved by an estimated coefficient. For example, in Figure 5.6, the area under the t-statistic curve to the right of 2.1 for β_1 is the level of significance (about 4 percent in this case). Since the level of significance chosen is subjective, such an approach allows readers to form their own conclusions about the acceptance or rejection of hypotheses. It also conveys the information that the null hypothesis can be rejected with more confidence for some estimated coefficients than for others. Computer programs often give such probabilities of significance, P-values, for t-values, and if the probability given is less than or equal to the preselected level of significance, then the null hypothesis can be rejected. The availability of such probabilities should not deceive beginning researchers into waiting to state the levels of significance to be used until after the regressions are run, however, because the researchers run the risk of adapting their desired significance levels to the results.

The purpose of this example is to provide practice in testing hypotheses, and the results of such a poorly thought-through equation for such a small number of observations should not be taken too seriously. Given all that, however, it's still instructive to note that you did not react the same way to your inability to reject the null hypotheses for the price and sports utility vehicle variables. That is, the failure of the sports utility vehicle variable's coefficient to be significantly negative caused you to realize that perhaps the addition of this

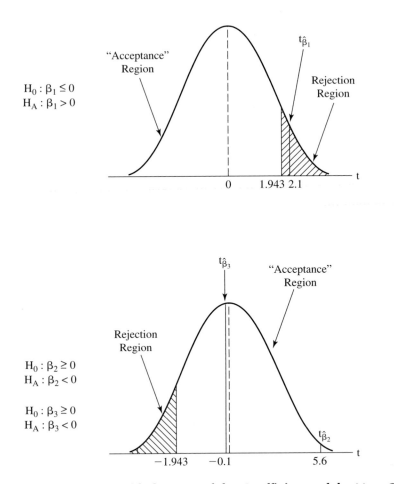

$H_0 : \beta_1 \leq 0$
$H_A : \beta_1 > 0$

$H_0 : \beta_2 \geq 0$
$H_A : \beta_2 < 0$

$H_0 : \beta_3 \geq 0$
$H_A : \beta_3 < 0$

Figure 5.6 One-Sided *t*-Tests of the Coefficients of the New Car Sales Model

Given the estimates in Equation 5.7 and the critical t-value of 1.943 for a 5 percent level of significance, one-sided, 6 degrees of freedom *t*-test, we can reject the null hypothesis for $\hat{\beta}_1$, but not for $\hat{\beta}_2$ or $\hat{\beta}_3$.

variable was ill advised. The failure of the price variable's coefficient to be significantly negative did not cause you to consider the possibility that price has no effect on new car sales. Put differently, estimation results should never be allowed to cause you to want to adjust theoretically sound variables or hypotheses, but if they make you realize you have made a serious mistake, then it would be foolhardy to ignore that mistake. What to do about the positive coefficient of price, on the other hand, is what the "art" of econometrics is all about. Surely a positive coefficient is unsatisfactory, but throwing the price variable out of the equation seems even more so. Possible answers to such issues are addressed more than once in the chapters that follow.

5.3.2 Examples of Two-Sided *t*-Tests

Although most hypotheses in regression analysis can be tested with one-sided *t*-tests, two-sided *t*-tests are appropriate in particular situations. Researchers sometimes encounter hypotheses that should be rejected if estimated coefficients are significantly different from zero, or a specific nonzero value, in either direction. This situation requires a two-sided *t*-test. The kinds of circumstances that call for a two-sided test fall into two categories:

1. Two-sided tests of whether an estimated coefficient is significantly different from zero, and

2. Two-sided tests of whether an estimated coefficient is significantly different from a specific nonzero value.

1. **Testing whether a $\hat{\beta}$ is statistically different from zero.** The first case for a two-sided test of $\hat{\beta}$ arises when there are two or more conflicting hypotheses about the expected sign of a coefficient. For example, in the Woody's restaurant equation of Section 3.2, the impact of the average income of an area on the expected number of Woody's customers in that area is ambiguous. A high-income neighborhood might have more total customers going out to dinner, but those customers might decide to eat at a more formal restaurant than Woody's. As a result, you could run a two-sided *t*-test around zero to determine whether or not the estimated coefficient of income is significantly different from zero in *either* direction. In other words, since there are reasonable cases to be made for either a positive or a negative coefficient, it is appropriate to test the $\hat{\beta}$ for income with a two-sided *t*-test:

$$H_0: \beta = 0$$
$$H_A: \beta \neq 0$$

As Figure 5.7 illustrates, a two-sided test implies two different rejection regions (one positive and one negative) surrounding the "acceptance" region. A critical t-value, t_c, must be increased in order to achieve the same level of significance with a two-sided test as can be achieved with a one-sided test.[8] As a result, there is an advantage to testing hypotheses with a one-sided test if the underlying theory allows because, for the same t-values, the possibility of Type I Error is half as much for a one-sided test as for a two-sided test. In cases where there are powerful

---

8. See Figure 5.5 in Section 5.2. In that figure, the same critical t-value has double the level of significance for a two-sided test as for a one-sided test.

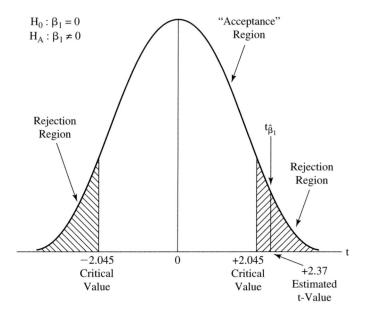

$H_0 : \beta_1 = 0$
$H_A : \beta_1 \neq 0$

"Acceptance" Region

Rejection Region

$t_{\hat{\beta}_1}$

Rejection Region

t

−2.045
Critical
Value

0

+2.045
Critical
Value

+2.37
Estimated
t-Value

Figure 5.7 Two-Sided *t*-Test of the Coefficient of Income in the Woody's Model

Given the estimates of Equation 5.4 and the critical t-values of ±2.045 for a 5 percent level of significance, two-sided, 29 degrees of freedom *t*-test, we can reject the null hypothesis that $\beta_1 = 0$.

theoretical arguments on both sides, however, the researcher has no alternative to using a two-sided *t*-test around zero. To see how this works, let's follow through the Woody's income variable example in more detail.

1. *Set up the null and alternative hypotheses.*

$$H_0: \beta_I = 0$$
$$H_A: \beta_I \neq 0$$

2. *Choose a level of significance and therefore a critical t-value.* You decide to keep the level of significance at 5 percent, but now this amount must be distributed between two rejection regions for 29 degrees of freedom. Hence, the correct critical t-value is 2.045 (found in Statistical Table B-1 for 29 degrees of freedom and a 5 percent, two-sided test). Note that, technically, there now are two critical t-values, +2.045 and −2.045.

3. *Run the regression and obtain an estimated t-value.* Since the value implied by the null hypothesis is still zero, the estimated t-value of $+2.37$ given in Equation 5.4 is applicable.

4. *Apply the decision rule by comparing the calculated t-value with the critical t-value in order to reject or "accept" the null hypothesis.* We once again use the decision rule stated in Section 5.2, but since the alternative hypothesis specifies either sign, the decision rule simplifies to:

$$\text{For } \beta_I \quad \text{Reject } H_0 \text{ if } |2.37| > 2.045$$

In this case, you reject the null hypothesis that β_I equals zero because 2.37 is greater than 2.045 (see Figure 5.7). Note that the positive sign implies that, at least for Woody's restaurants, income increases customer volume (holding constant population and competition). Given this result, we might well choose to run a one-sided t-test on the next year's Woody's data set. For more practice with two-sided t-tests, see Exercise 6.

2. **Two-sided t-tests of a specific nonzero coefficient value.** The second case for a two-sided t-test arises when there is reason to expect a specific nonzero value for an estimated coefficient. For example, if a previous researcher has stated that the true value of some coefficient almost surely equals a particular number, β_{H_0}, then that number would be the one to test by creating a two-sided t-test around the hypothesized value, β_{H_0}. To the extent that you feel that the hypothesized value is theoretically correct, you also violate the normal practice of using the null hypothesis to state the hypothesis you expect to reject.[9]

In such a case, the null and alternative hypotheses become:

$$H_0: \beta_k = \beta_{H_0}$$
$$H_A: \beta_k \neq \beta_{H_0}$$

where β_{H_0} is the specific nonzero value hypothesized.

---

9. Instead of being able to reject an incorrect theory based on the evidence, the researcher who violates the normal practice is reduced to "not rejecting" the β value expected to be true. This makes a big difference because to "accept" H_0 is merely to say that H_0 is not rejected by the data. However, there are many theories that are not rejected by the data, and the researcher is left with a regrettably weak conclusion. One way to accommodate such violations is to increase the level of significance, thereby increasing the likelihood of a Type I Error.

Since the hypothesized β value is no longer zero, the formula with which to calculate the estimated t-value is Equation 5.2, repeated here:

$$t_k = \frac{(\hat{\beta}_k - \beta_{H_0})}{SE(\hat{\beta}_k)} \qquad (k = 1, 2, \ldots, K) \qquad (5.2)$$

This t-statistic is still distributed around zero if the null hypothesis is correct, because we have subtracted β_{H_0} from the estimated regression coefficient whose expected value is supposed to be β_{H_0} when H_0 is true. Since the t-statistic is still centered around zero, the decision rules developed earlier are still applicable. In other words, the techniques used above are precisely the same as for a two-sided *t*-test of a specific nonzero coefficient. For practice with this kind of *t*-test, see Exercise 6.

5.3.3 The *t*-Test of the Simple Correlation Coefficient, r

From the previous sections, it'd be easy to get the impression that the *t*-test is used only for tests of regression coefficients, but that's hardly the case. It turns out that there is a variety of applications for the *t*-test that don't involve $\hat{\beta}$s.

The most immediately useful of these applications is a *t*-test of the simple correlation coefficient. The **simple correlation coefficient, r,** is a measure of the strength and direction of the linear relationship between two variables. The simple correlation coefficient between X_1 and X_2 is:

$$r_{12} = \frac{\sum[(X_{1i} - \bar{X}_1)(X_{2i} - \bar{X}_2)]}{\sqrt{\sum(X_{1i} - \bar{X}_1)^2 \sum(X_{2i} - \bar{X}_2)^2}} \qquad (5.8)$$

If two variables are perfectly positively correlated, then $r = +1$. To see this, assume that $X_{1i} = X_{2i}$ and substitute into Equation 5.8:

$$r_{12} = \frac{\sum[(X_{1i} - \bar{X}_1)(X_{1i} - \bar{X}_1)]}{\sqrt{\sum(X_{1i} - \bar{X}_1)^2 \sum(X_{1i} - \bar{X}_1)^2}} \qquad (5.9)$$

$$= \frac{\sum[(X_{1i} - \bar{X}_1)^2]}{\sum[(X_{1i} - \bar{X}_1)^2]} = +1$$

If two variables are perfectly negatively correlated, then r = −1. To see this, substitute $X_{2i} = -X_{1i}$ into Equation 5.8:

$$r_{12} = \frac{\sum[(X_{1i} - \overline{X}_1)(-X_{1i} + \overline{X}_1)]}{\sqrt{\sum(X_{1i} - \overline{X}_1)^2 \sum(-X_{1i} + \overline{X}_1)^2}} \tag{5.10}$$

$$= \frac{-\sum[(X_{1i} - \overline{X}_1)^2]}{\sum[(X_{1i} - \overline{X}_1)^2]} = -1$$

If two variables are totally uncorrelated, then r = 0.

One of the major uses of the simple correlation coefficient r is to test the hypothesis that two explanatory variables are correlated in a less than perfect but still significant (multicollinear) way. For imperfect multicollinearity to occur in this two-variable case, the simple correlation coefficient must be fairly large in the direction indicated by theory. In order to test this hypothesis, r can be converted into a t-statistic using:

$$t = \frac{r\sqrt{n - 2}}{\sqrt{(1 - r^2)}} \tag{5.11}$$

where n is the size of the sample. The statistic defined in Equation 5.11 follows the t-distribution with n − 2 degrees of freedom. Since t is directly related to r, a large positive r will convert into a large positive t, and so on.

Tests of hypotheses about t (and therefore about r) can be undertaken using the critical t-values and decision rules outlined in Section 5.2 and Statistical Table B-1. For example, suppose you encounter a simple correlation coefficient of 0.946 between two variables you expect to be positively correlated in a data set with 28 observations. In this case,

$$H_0: r \le 0$$
$$H_A: r > 0$$

and we can reject the null hypothesis of no positive correlation if the calculated t-score is larger in absolute value than the critical t-value of 1.706 (for 26 degrees of freedom at the 5 percent, one-sided level of significance) and if t has the positive sign implied by the alternative hypothesis. If we substitute r = 0.946 and n = 28 into Equation 5.11, we obtain 14.880, and the null hypothesis of no positive collinearity can be rejected. (If theory provides no expected direction, a two-sided test should be used.) For practice in hypothesis tests of simple correlation coefficients, see Exercise 10.

5.4   Limitations of the *t*-Test

A problem with the *t*-test is that it is easy to misuse; t-scores are so frequently printed out by computer regression packages and the *t*-test seems so easy to work with that beginning researchers sometimes attempt to use the *t*-test to "prove" things that it was never intended to even test. For that reason, it's probably just as important to know the limitations of the *t*-test as it is to know the applications of that test. Perhaps the most important of these limitations, that the usefulness of the *t*-test diminishes rapidly as more and more specifications are estimated and tested, is the subject of Section 6.4. The purpose of the present section is to give additional examples of how the *t*-test should *not* be used.

5.4.1   The *t*-Test Does Not Test Theoretical Validity

Recall that the purpose of the *t*-test is to help the researcher make inferences about a particular population coefficient based on an estimate obtained from a sample of that population. Some beginning researchers conclude that any *statistically* significant result is also a *theoretically* correct one. This is dangerous because such a conclusion confuses statistical significance with theoretical validity.

Consider for instance, the following estimated regression that explains the consumer price index in the United Kingdom:[10]

$$\hat{P} = 10.9 - 3.2C + 0.39C^2 \tag{5.12}$$
$$(0.23) \quad (0.02)$$
$$t = -13.9 \quad 19.5$$
$$\overline{R}^2 = .982 \quad n = 21$$

Apply the *t*-test to these estimates. Do you agree that the two slope coefficients are statistically significant? As a quick check of Statistical Table B-1 shows, the critical t-value for 18 degrees of freedom and a 5 percent two-

---

10. These results, and others similar to them, can be found in David F. Hendry, "Econometrics—Alchemy or Science?" *Economica*, November 1980, pp. 383–406.

tailed level of significance is 2.101, so we can reject the null hypothesis of no effect in these cases and conclude that C and C^2 are indeed statistically significant variables in explaining P.

The catch is that P is the consumer price index and C is the cumulative amount of rainfall in the United Kingdom! We have just shown that rain is statistically significant in explaining consumer prices; does that also show that the underlying theory is valid? Of course not. Why is the statistical result so significant? The answer is that at 5 percent level of significance, there is a 1-in-20 chance of rejecting a true null hypothesis. If we try 20 or more different tests, the odds are good that eventually we will be able to reject a correct null hypothesis. This almost always inappropriate technique (called data mining) was used to obtain the unrealistic results above. The moral should be clear: Never conclude that statistical significance, as shown by the t-test, is the same as theoretical validity.

Occasionally, estimated coefficients will be significant in the direction opposite from that hypothesized, and some beginning researchers may be tempted to change their hypotheses. For example, a student might run a regression in which the hypothesized sign is positive, get a "statistically significant" negative sign, and be tempted to change the theoretical expectations to "expect" a negative sign after "rethinking" the issue. Although it is admirable to be willing to reexamine incorrect theories on the basis of new evidence, that evidence should be, for the most part, theoretical in nature. In the case cited above, the student should have been concerned that the evidence did not support the theory, but that lack of support should not have caused the theory itself to change completely. If the evidence causes a researcher to go back to the theoretical underpinnings of a model and find a mistake, then the null hypothesis should be changed, but then this new hypothesis should be tested using a completely different data set. After all, we already know what the result will be if the hypothesis is tested on the old one.

5.4.2 The t-Test Does Not Test "Importance"

One possible use of a regression equation is to help determine which independent variable has the largest relative effect (importance) on the dependent variable. Some beginning researchers draw the unwarranted conclusion that the most statistically significant variable in their estimated regression is also the most important in terms of explaining the largest portion of the movement of the dependent variable. Statistical significance indicates the likelihood that a particular sample result could have been obtained by chance, but it says little if anything about which variables determine the major portion of the variation in the dependent variable. To determine importance, a measure such as the size of the coefficient multiplied by the average size of the independent variable would make much more sense.[11] Consider the following hypothetical equation:

$$\hat{Y} = 300.0 + 10.0X_1 + 200.0X_2 \tag{5.13}$$
$$(1.0) \qquad (25.0)$$
$$t = 10.0 \qquad 8.0$$
$$\overline{R}^2 = .90 \qquad n = 30$$

where: Y = mail-order sales of "O'Henry's Oyster Recipes"
X_1 = hundreds of dollars of advertising expenditures in "Gourmets' Magazine"
X_2 = hundreds of dollars of advertising expenditures on the "Julia Adult TV Cooking Show"

(Assume that all other factors, including prices, quality, and competition, remain constant during the estimation period.)

Where should O'Henry be spending his advertising money? That is, which independent variable has the biggest impact per dollar on Y? Given that X_2's coefficient is 20 times X_1's coefficient, you'd have to agree that X_2 is more important as defined above, and yet which coefficient is more statistically significantly different from zero? With a t-score of 10.0, X_1 is more statistically significant than X_2 and its 8.0, but all that means is that we have more confidence that the coefficient is positive, not that the variable itself is necessarily more important in determining Y. The theoretical underpinnings of a result and the actual result itself are at least as important as the statistical significance of that result.

5.4.3 The *t*-Test Is Not Intended for Tests of the Entire Population

The *t*-test helps make inferences about the true value of a parameter from an estimate calculated from a sample of the *population* (the group from which the sample is being drawn). As the size of the sample approaches the size of the population, an unbiased estimated coefficient approaches the true population value. If a coefficient is calculated from the entire population, then an unbiased estimate already measures the population value and a significant *t*-test adds nothing to this knowledge. One might forget this property and at-

---

11. Some useful statistical measures of "importance" have been developed, but none is fully satisfactory because of the presence of multicollinearity (to be discussed in Chapter 8). See J. M. Shanks, "The Importance of Importance" (Berkeley: Survey Research Center, University of California, 1982).

tach too much importance to t-scores that have been obtained from samples that approximate the population in size. All the *t*-test does is help decide how likely it is that a particular small sample will cause a researcher to make a mistake in rejecting hypotheses about the true population parameters.

This point can perhaps best be seen by remembering that the t-score is the estimated regression coefficient divided by the standard error of the estimated regression coefficient. If the sample size is large enough to approach the population, then the standard error will fall close to zero because the distribution of estimates becomes more and more narrowly distributed around the true parameter (if this is an unbiased estimate). The standard error will approach zero as the sample size approaches infinity. Thus, the t-score will eventually become:

$$t = \frac{\hat{\beta}}{0} = \infty$$

The mere existence of a large t-score for a huge sample has no real substantive significance because if the sample size is large enough, you can reject almost any null hypothesis! It is true that sample sizes in econometrics can never approach infinity, but many are quite large; and others, even though fairly small, are not really samples of a population but contain the entire population in one data set.[12]

5.5   The *F*-Test of Overall Significance

Although the *t*-test is invaluable for hypotheses about individual regression coefficients, it can't be used to test hypotheses about more than one coefficient at a time. Such a limitation is unfortunate, since it's possible to imagine quite a few interesting hypotheses that involve more than one coefficient. For example, suppose you wanted to test the hypothesis that two regression coefficients were equal to each other? In such a situation, most researchers would use a different statistical test, the *F*-test.

The *F*-test is a method of testing a null hypothesis that includes more than one coefficient; it works by determining whether the overall fit of an equation is significantly reduced by constraining the equation to conform to the null hypothesis. If the fit is significantly reduced, then we can reject the null hypothesis. If the fit is not reduced significantly, then we can't reject the null hypothesis. The *F*-test is used most frequently in econometrics to test the overall significance of a regression equation, the topic of this section. We'll investigate other uses of the *F*-test in Section 7.7.

---

12. D. N. McCloskey, "The Loss Function Has Been Mislaid: The Rhetoric of Significance Tests," *American Economic Review*, May 1985, p. 204.

Although R^2 and $\overline{R}^2$ measure the overall degree of fit of an equation, they don't provide a formal hypothesis test of that overall fit. Such a test is provided by the F-test. The null hypothesis in an F-test of overall significance is that all the slope coefficients in the equation equal zero simultaneously. For an equation with K independent variables, this means that the null and alternative hypotheses would be[13]:

$$H_0: \beta_1 = \beta_2 = \cdots = \beta_K = 0$$
$$H_A: H_0 \text{ is not true}$$

To show that the overall fit of the estimated equation is statistically significant, we must be able to reject this null hypothesis using the F-test. The equation for the F-test of overall significance is:

$$F = \frac{\text{ESS}/K}{\text{RSS}/(n - K - 1)} = \frac{\sum (\hat{Y}_i - \overline{Y})^2/K}{\sum e_i^2/(n - K - 1)} \qquad (5.14)$$

This is the ratio of the explained sum of squares (ESS) to the residual sum of squares (RSS), adjusted for the number of independent variables (K) and the number of observations in the sample (n). In this case, the "constrained equation" to which we're comparing the overall fit is:

$$Y_i = \beta_0 + \epsilon_i \qquad (5.15)$$

which is nothing more than saying $\hat{Y}_i = \overline{Y}$. Thus the F-test of overall significance is really testing the null hypothesis that the fit of the equation isn't significantly better than that provided by using the mean alone. The decision rule to use in the F-test is to reject the null hypothesis if the calculated F-value (F) from Equation 5.14 is greater than the appropriate critical F-value (F_c):

$$\text{Reject} \qquad H_0 \text{ if } F \geq F_c$$
$$\text{Do Not Reject } H_0 \text{ if } F < F_c$$

The critical F-value, F_c, is determined from Statistical Tables B-2 or B-3 depending on a level of significance chosen by the researcher and on the de-

---

13. Note that we don't hypothesize that $\beta_0 = 0$. This would imply that $E(\overline{Y}) = 0$.

grees of freedom. The F-statistic has two types of degrees of freedom: the degrees of freedom for the numerator of Equation 5.14 (K, the number of constraints implied by the null hypothesis) and the degrees of freedom for the denominator of Equation 5.14 (n − K − 1, the degrees of freedom in the regression equation). The underlying principle here is that if the calculated F-value (or F-ratio) is greater than the critical value, then the estimated equation's fit is significantly better than the constrained equation's fit (in this case, just using $\overline{Y}$), and we can reject the null hypothesis of no effect.

As an example of the use of the *F*-test, let's test the overall significance of the Woody's restaurant model of Equation 3.4. Since there are three independent variables, the null and alternative hypotheses are:

$$H_0: \beta_N = \beta_P = \beta_I = 0$$
$$H_A: H_0 \text{ is not true}$$

To decide whether to reject or not reject this null hypothesis, we need to calculate Equation 5.14 for the Woody's example. There are three constraints in the null hypothesis, so K = 3. If we check the EViews computer output for the Woody's equation on page 77, we can see that n = 33 and RSS = 6,130,000,000. In addition, it can be calculated[14] that ESS equals 9,929,450,000. Thus the appropriate F-ratio is:

$$F = \frac{ESS/K}{RSS/(n - K - 1)} = \frac{9,929,450,000/3}{6,130,000,000/29} = 15.65 \qquad (5.16)$$

In practice, this calculation is never necessary, since virtually every computer regression package routinely provides the computed F-ratio for a test of overall significance as a matter of course. On the Woody's computer output, the value of the F-statistic (15.64894) can be found near the bottom of the right-hand column.

Our decision rule tells us to reject the null hypothesis if the calculated F-value is greater than the critical F-value. To determine that critical F-value, we need to know the level of significance and the degrees of freedom. If we assume a 5 percent level of significance, the appropriate table to use is Statistical Table B-2. The numerator degrees of freedom equal 3 (K), and the denominator degrees of freedom equal 29 (n − K − 1), so we need to look in Statistical Table B-2 for the critical F-value for 3 and 29 degrees of freedom.

---

14. To do this calculation, note that $R^2 = ESS/TSS$ and that $TSS = ESS + RSS$. If you substitute the second equation into the first and solve for ESS, you obtain $ESS = RSS \cdot (R^2)/(1 - R^2)$. Since both RSS and R^2 are included in the EViews computer output on page 77, you can then calculate ESS.

As the reader can verify,[15] $F_c = 2.93$ is well below the calculated F-value of 15.65, so we can reject the null hypothesis and conclude that the Woody's equation does indeed have a significant overall fit.

Two final comments about the *F*-test of overall significance are in order. First, if there is only one independent variable, then an *F*-test and a *t*-test of whether the slope coefficient equals zero will always produce the same answer. (Indeed, it can be shown mathematically that the two tests are identical.) This property does not hold if there are two or more independent variables. In such a situation, an *F*-test could determine that the coefficients *jointly* are not significantly different from zero even though a *t*-test on one of the coefficients might show that *individually* it is significantly different from zero (or vice versa).

Finally, the F-statistic can be shown to be a direct function of R^2. The larger R^2 is, the larger the F-ratio. Thus the *F*-test of overall significance is a test of the significance of R^2 itself. For more on this property, see Exercise 8.

5.6 Summary

1. Hypothesis testing makes inferences about the validity of specific economic (or other) theories from a sample of the population for which the theories are supposed to be true. The four basic steps of hypothesis testing (using a *t*-test as an example) are:
    a. Set up the null and alternative hypotheses.
    b. Choose a level of significance and, therefore, a critical t-value.
    c. Run the regression and obtain an estimated t-value.
    d. Apply the decision rule by comparing the calculated t-value with the critical t-value in order to reject or "accept" the null hypothesis.

2. The null hypothesis states the range of values that the regression coefficient is expected to take on if the researcher's theory is not correct. The alternative hypothesis is a statement of the range of values that the regression coefficient is expected to take if the researcher's theory is correct.

3. The two kinds of errors we can make in such hypothesis testing are:

    Type I: We reject a null hypothesis that is true.

---

15. Note that this critical F-value must be interpolated. The critical value for 30 denominator degrees of freedom is 2.92, and the critical value for 25 denominator degrees of freedom is 2.99. Since both numbers are well below the calculated F-value of 15.65, however, the interpolation isn't necessary to reject the null hypothesis. As a result, many researchers don't bother with such interpolations unless the calculated F-value is inside the range of the interpolation.

Type II: We do not reject a null hypothesis that is false.

4.   A decision rule states critical t-values above or below which observed sample t-values will lead to the rejection or "acceptance" of hypotheses concerning population parameters. Critical values are selected from a t-distribution table, depending on the chosen level of significance, the degrees of freedom involved, and the specifics of the particular hypothesis.

5.   The *t*-test tests hypotheses about individual coefficients from regression equations. The general form for the t-statistic is

$$t_k = \frac{(\hat{\beta}_k - \beta_{H_0})}{SE(\hat{\beta}_k)} \qquad (k = 1, 2, \ldots, K)$$

In many regression applications, β_{H_0} is zero. Once you have calculated a t-value and chosen a critical t-value, you reject the null hypothesis if the t-value is greater in absolute value than the critical t-value and if the t-value has the sign implied by the alternative hypothesis.

6.   The *t*-test is easy to use for a number of reasons, but care should be taken when using the *t*-test to avoid confusing statistical significance with theoretical validity or empirical importance.

7.   The *F*-test is a method of testing a null hypothesis that includes more than one coefficient. The *F*-test is used most frequently in econometrics to test the overall significance of a regression equation with the following equation:

$$F = \frac{ESS/K}{RSS/(n - K - 1)} = \frac{\sum (\hat{Y}_i - \bar{Y})^2/K}{\sum e_i^2/(n - K - 1)}$$

Once you've calculated an F and chosen a critical F-value, F_c, then you can reject the null hypothesis that implies that the overall fit of an equation is not significant if $F \geq F_c$.

Exercises

(Answers to even-numbered exercises are in Appendix A.)

1.   Write the meaning of each of the following terms without referring to the book (or your notes), and compare your definition with the version in the text for each.
     a. null hypothesis

    b. alternative hypothesis
    c. Type I Error
    d. level of significance
    e. two-sided test
    f. decision rule
    g. critical value
    h. t-statistic
    i. *t*-test of the simple correlation coefficient
    j. *F*-test
    k. confidence interval

2. Create null and alternative hypotheses for the following coefficients:
   a. the impact of height on weight (Section 1.4)
   b. all the coefficients in Equation A in Exercise 7, Chapter 2
   c. all the coefficients in $Y = f(X_1, X_2, \text{ and } X_3)$ where Y is total gasoline used on a particular trip, X_1 is miles traveled, X_2 is the weight of the car, and X_3 is the average speed traveled
   d. the impact of the decibel level of the grunt of a shot-putter on the length of the throw involved (shot-putters are known to make loud noises when they throw, but there is little theory about the impact of this yelling on the length of the put). Assume all relevant "non-grunt" variables are included in the equation.

3. Think of examples other than the ones in this chapter in which:
   a. It would be more important to keep Type I Error low than to keep Type II Error low.
   b. It would be more important to keep Type II Error low than to keep Type I Error low.

4. Return to Section 5.3 and test the hypotheses implied by Equation 5.6 with the results in Equation 5.7 for all three coefficients under the following circumstances:
   a. 10 percent significance and 15 observations
   b. 90 percent confidence and 28 observations
   c. 99 percent confidence and 10 observations

5. Return to Section 5.2 and test the appropriate hypotheses with the results in Equation 5.4 for all three coefficients under the following circumstances:
   a. 5 percent significance and 6 degrees of freedom
   b. 90 percent confidence and 29 degrees of freedom
   c. 99 percent confidence and 2 degrees of freedom

6. Using the techniques of Section 5.3, test the following two-sided hypotheses:

a. For Equation 5.13, test the hypothesis that:

$$H_0: \beta_2 = 160.0$$
$$H_A: \beta_2 \neq 160.0$$

at the 5 percent level of significance.

b. For Equation 5.4, test the hypothesis that:

$$H_0: \beta_3 = 0$$
$$H_A: \beta_3 \neq 0$$

at the 99 percent level of confidence.

c. For Equation 5.7, test the hypotheses that:

$$H_0: \beta_2 = 0$$
$$H_A: \beta_2 \neq 0$$

at the 5 percent level of significance.

7. For all three tests in Exercise 6, under what circumstances would you worry about possible violations of the principle that the null hypothesis contains that which you do not expect to be true? In particular, what would your theoretical expectations have to be in order to avoid violating this principle in Exercise 6a?

8. It turns out that the F-ratio can be expressed as a function of R^2.
   a. As an exercise, substitute Equation 2.16 into Equations 5.14 to derive the exact relationship between F and R^2.
   b. If one can be expressed as a function of the other, why do we need both? What reason is there for computer regression packages to typically print out both R^2 and the F-ratio?

9. Test the overall significance of equations that have the following F-values (Using Statistical Table B-2):
   a. F = 5.63 with   4 degrees of freedom in the numerator and 30 degrees of freedom in the denominator
   b. F = 1.53 with   3 degrees of freedom in the numerator and 24 degrees of freedom in the denominator
   c. F = 57.84 with   5 degrees of freedom in the numerator and 60 degrees of freedom in the denominator

10. Given the following simple correlation coefficients between two explanatory variables, use the *t*-test (and Equation 5.11) to test the possibility of significant collinearity in the specified circumstances:
    a. r = .905, n = 18, 5 percent level, positive expected relationship
    b. r = .958, n = 27, 2.5 percent level, positive expected relationship

c. $r = .821$, $n = 7$, 1 percent level, positive expected relationship

d. $r = -.753$, $n = 42$, 10 percent level, negative expected relationship

e. $r = .519$, $n = 30$, 5 percent level, ambiguous expected relationship

11. Consider the following hypothetical equation for a sample of divorced men who failed to make at least one child support payment in the last four years (standard errors in parentheses):

$$\hat{P}_i = 2.0 + 0.50M_i + 25.0Y_i + 0.80A_i + 3.0B_i - 0.15C_i$$
$$\qquad\quad (0.10) \quad (20.0) \quad (1.00) \quad (3.0) \quad (0.05)$$

where: P_i = the number of monthly child support payments that the ith man missed in the last four years

M_i = the number of months the ith man was unemployed in the last four years

Y_i = the ratio of the dollar value of the average child support payment to average monthly disposable income for the ith man

A_i = the age in years of the ith man

B_i = the religious beliefs of the ith man (a scale of 1 to 4, with 4 being the most religious)

C_i = the number of children the ith man has fathered

a. Your friend expects the coefficients of M and Y to be positive. Test these hypotheses. (Use the 95 percent level and $n = 20$.)

b. Test the hypothesis that the coefficient of A is different from zero. (Use the 1 percent level and $n = 25$.)

c. Develop and test hypotheses for the coefficients of B and C. (Use the 90 percent level and $n = 17$.)

12. Test the overall significance of the Magic Hill weight/height estimated question in Section 1.4 by using the F ratio and Statistical Table B-2 in the back of the book. (*Hint:* The first step is to calculate the F-ratio from the information given in Table 2.1.)

13. Thomas Bruggink and David Rose[16] estimated a regression for the annual team revenue for Major League Baseball franchises:

$$\hat{R}_i = -1522.5 + 53.1P_i + 1469.4M_i + 1322.7S_i - 7376.3T_i$$
$$\qquad\qquad (9.1) \qquad (233.6) \qquad (1363.6) \qquad (2255.7)$$
$$\qquad t = 5.8 \qquad\quad 6.3 \qquad\qquad 1.0 \qquad\qquad -3.3$$
$$\overline{R}^2 = .682 \quad n = 78 \ (1984-1986) \quad F = 42.2$$

16. Thomas H. Bruggink and David R. Rose, Jr., "Financial Restraint in the Free Agent Labor Market for Major League Baseball: Players Look at Strike Three," *Southern Economic Journal*, April 1990, pp. 1029–1043.

where: R_i = team revenue from attendance, broadcasting, and
                concessions (in thousands of dollars)
           P_i = the *i*th team's winning rate (their winning percentage
                multiplied by a thousand, 1000 = high)
           M_i = the population of the *i*th team's metropolitan area
                (in millions)
           S_i = a dummy equal to 1 if the *i*th team's stadium was
                built before 1940, 0 otherwise
           T_i = a dummy equal to 1 if the *i*th team's city has two
                Major League Baseball teams, 0 otherwise

a. Develop and test appropriate hypotheses about the individual coefficients and the overall fit at the 5 percent level. (*Hint:* You do not have to be a sports fan to do this question correctly.)

b. The authors originally expected a negative coefficient for S. Their explanation for the unexpected positive sign was that teams in older stadiums have greater revenue because they're better known and have more faithful fans. Since this $\hat{\beta}$ is just one observation from the sampling distribution of $\hat{\beta}$s, do you think they should have changed their expected sign?

c. On the other hand, Keynes reportedly said, "When I'm wrong, I change my mind; what do you do?" If one $\hat{\beta}$ lets you realize an error, shouldn't you be allowed to change your expectation? How would you go about resolving this difficulty?

d. Assume that your team is in last place with $P = 350$. According to this regression equation, would it be profitable to pay $4 million a year to a free agent who would raise the team's winning rate (P) to 500? Be specific.

14. Develop appropriate hypotheses for each slope coefficient in each of the following equations, and then calculate t-scores and test each null hypothesis at the 5 percent level:
    a. Exercise 9 in Chapter 4
    b. Exercise 9 in Chapter 3 (*Hint:* Assume 28 degrees of freedom. Would your answer change if there were only 5 degrees of freedom? How?)
    c. Exercise 10 in Chapter 3

15. Consider the following equation estimated by Fred McChesney[17] to determine whether the *Washington Post's* Pulitzer Prize winning cover-

---

17. Fred S. McChesney, "Sensationalism, Newspaper Profits, and the Marginal Value of Watergate," *Economic Inquiry,* January 1987, pp. 135–144. (n is hypothetical.)

age of the Watergate political crisis of the 1970s had an effect on the newspaper's circulation (t-scores in parentheses):

$$\hat{C}_t = 290.10 + 0.761J_t + 0.325S_t + 0.058W_t$$
$$\qquad\qquad\quad (14.27)\quad (6.07)\quad\quad (1.31)$$
$$\overline{R}^2 = .97\quad n = 26\ (\text{annual})\quad F = 168.05$$

where: C_t = circulation of the *Post* in year t
   J_t = circulation of the *Wall Street Journal* in year t
   S_t = the number of months during year t that the *Washington Star*, the *Post*'s main local competitor at the time, did not publish
   W_t = a dummy variable equal to 1 during years of Watergate coverage and 0 otherwise

a. Develop appropriate hypotheses about the slope coefficients of this equation. (*Hint:* The *Wall Street Journal* had little coverage of Watergate and serves a much different market than does the *Post*. As a result, McChesney considered the *Journal*'s circulation to be a measure of the non-Watergate demand for newspapers.)
b. Test these hypotheses at the 5 percent level. (*Hint:* Note that t-scores, not standard errors, are given in parentheses. As mentioned in the chapter, not all published regression results follow our documentation format.)
c. Test the overall significance of the equation using the *F*-test (at the 1 percent level).
d. What economic conclusion can you draw about the effect of Watergate on the *Post*'s circulation?

16. In 1986 Frederick Schut and Peter VanBergeijk[18] published an article in which they attempted to see if the pharmaceutical industry practiced international price discrimination by estimating a model of the prices of pharmaceuticals in a cross section of 32 countries. The authors felt that if price discrimination existed, then the coefficient of per capita income in a properly specified price equation would be strongly positive. The reason they felt that the coefficient of per capita income would measure price discrimination went as follows: the higher the ability to pay, the lower (in absolute value) the price elas-

---

18. Frederick T. Schut and Peter A. G. VanBergeijk, "International Price Discrimination: The Pharmaceutical Industry," *World Development*, 1986, pp. 1141–1150. The estimated coefficients we list are those produced by EViews using the original data and differ slightly from those in the original article.

ticity of demand for pharmaceuticals and the higher the price a price discriminator could charge. In addition, the authors expected that prices would be higher if pharmaceutical patents were allowed and that prices would be lower if price controls existed, if competition was encouraged, or if the pharmaceutical market in a country was relatively large. Their estimates were (standard errors in parentheses):

$$\hat{P}_i = 38.22 + 1.43GDPN_i - 0.6CVN_i + 7.31PP_i \qquad (5.17)$$
$$(0.21) \qquad (0.22) \qquad (6.12)$$
$$t = \qquad 6.69 \qquad -2.66 \qquad 1.19$$

$$-15.63DPC_i - 11.38IPC_i$$
$$(6.93) \qquad (7.16)$$
$$t = \qquad -2.25 \qquad -1.59$$

$$n = 32 \text{ (national 1975 data)} \quad \overline{R}^2 = .775 \quad F = 22.35$$

where: P_i = the pharmaceutical price level in the ith country divided by that of the United States

   $GDPN_i$ = per capita domestic product in the ith country divided by that of the United States

   CVN_i = per capita volume of consumption of pharmaceuticals in the ith country divided by that of the United States

   PP_i = a dummy variable equal to 1 if patents for pharmaceutical products are recognized in the ith country and equal to 0 otherwise

   DPC_i = a dummy variable equal to 1 if the ith country applied strict price controls and 0 otherwise

   IPC_i = a dummy variable equal to 1 if the ith country encouraged price competition and 0 otherwise

a. Develop and test appropriate hypotheses concerning the regression coefficients using the t-test at the 5 percent level.

b. Test the overall significance of the estimated equation using the F-test at the 5 percent level.

c. Set up 90 percent confidence intervals for each of the estimated slope coefficients.

d. Do you think Schut and VanBergeijk concluded that international price discrimination exists? Why or why not?

e. How would the estimated results have differed if the authors had not divided each country's prices, per capita income, and per capita pharmaceutical consumption by that of the United States? Explain your answer.

f. Reproduce their regression results by using the EViews computer program (datafile DRUGS5) or your own computer program and the data from Table 5.1.

TABLE 5.1   DATA FOR THE PHARMACEUTICAL PRICE DISCRIMINATION EXERCISE

Country	P	GDPN	CV	N	CVN	PP	IPC	DPC
Malawi	60.83	4.9	0.014	2.36	0.6	1	0	0
Kenya	50.63	6.56	0.07	6.27	1.1	1	0	0
India	31.71	6.56	18.66	282.76	6.6	0	0	1
Pakistan	38.76	8.23	3.42	32.9	10.4	0	1	1
Sri Lanka	15.22	9.3	0.42	6.32	6.7	1	1	1
Zambia	96.58	10.3	0.05	2.33	2.2	1	0	0
Thailand	48.01	13.0	2.21	19.60	11.3	0	0	0
Philippines	51.14	13.2	0.77	19.70	3.9	1	0	0
South Korea	35.10	20.7	2.20	16.52	13.3	0	0	0
Malaysia	70.74	21.5	0.50	5.58	8.9	1	0	0
Colombia	48.07	22.4	1.56	11.09	14.1	0	1	0
Jamaica	46.13	24.0	0.21	0.96	22.0	1	0	0
Brazil	63.83	25.2	10.48	50.17	21.6	0	1	0
Mexico	69.68	34.7	7.77	28.16	27.6	0	0	0
Yugoslavia	48.24	36.1	3.83	9.42	40.6	0	1	1
Iran	70.42	37.7	3.27	15.33	21.3	0	0	0
Uruguay	65.95	39.6	0.44	1.30	33.8	0	0	0
Ireland	73.58	42.5	0.57	1.49	38.0	1	0	0
Hungary	57.25	49.6	2.36	4.94	47.8	0	1	1
Poland	53.98	50.1	8.08	15.93	50.7	0	1	1
Italy	69.01	53.8	12.02	26.14	45.9	0	0	1
Spain	69.68	55.9	9.01	16.63	54.2	0	0	0
United Kingdom	71.19	63.9	9.96	26.21	38.0	1	1	1
Japan	81.88	68.4	28.58	52.24	54.7	0	0	1
Austria	139.53	69.6	1.24	3.52	35.2	0	0	0
Netherlands	137.29	75.2	1.54	6.40	24.1	1	0	0
Belgium	101.73	77.7	3.49	4.59	76.0	1	0	1
France	91.56	81.9	25.14	24.70	101.8	1	0	1
Luxembourg	100.27	82.0	0.10	0.17	60.5	1	0	1
Denmark	157.56	82.4	0.70	2.35	29.5	1	0	0
Germany, West	152.52	83.0	24.29	28.95	83.9	1	0	0
United States	100.00	100.0	100.00	100.00	100.0	1	1	0

Source: Frederick T. Schut and Peter A.G. VanBergeijk, "International Price Discrimination: The Pharmaceutical Industry," *World Development,* 1986, p. 1144.

Note: filename = DRUGS5

VIOLATIONS OF THE
CLASSICAL ASSUMPTIONS

CHAPTER 6

Specification: Choosing the Independent Variables

Before any equation can be estimated, it must be completely *specified*. Specifying an econometric equation consists of three parts: choosing the correct independent variables, the correct functional form, and the correct form of the stochastic error term.

A **specification error** results when any one of these choices is made incorrectly. This chapter is concerned with only the first of these, choosing the variables; the second and third will be taken up in later chapters.

That researchers can decide which independent variables to include in regression equations is a source of both strength and weakness in econometrics. The strength is that the equations can be formulated to fit individual needs, but the weakness is that researchers can estimate many different specifications until they find the one that "proves" their point, even if many other results disprove it. A major goal of this chapter is to help you understand how to choose variables for your regressions without falling prey to the various errors that result from misusing the ability to choose.

The primary consideration in deciding if an independent variable belongs in an equation is whether the variable is essential to the regression on the basis of theory. If the answer is an unambiguous yes, then the variable definitely should be included in the equation, even if it seems to be lacking in statistical significance. If theory is ambivalent or less emphatic, a dilemma arises. Leaving a relevant variable out of an equation is likely to bias the remaining estimates, but including an irrelevant variable leads to higher variances of the estimated coefficients. Although we'll develop statistical tools to help us deal with this decision, it's difficult in practice to be sure that a variable is relevant, and so the problem often remains unresolved.

We devote the fourth section of the chapter to specification searches and the pros and cons of various approaches to such searches. For example, techniques like stepwise regression procedures and sequential specification searches often cause bias or make the usual tests of significance inapplicable, and we do not recommend them. Instead, we suggest trying to minimize the number of regressions estimated and relying as much as possible on theory rather than statistical fit when choosing variables. There are no pat answers, however, and so the final decisions must be left to each individual researcher.

6.1 Omitted Variables

Suppose that you forget to include all the relevant independent variables when you first specify an equation (after all, no one's perfect!). Or suppose that you can't get data for one of the variables that you *do* think of. The result in both these situations is an **omitted variable,** defined as an important explanatory variable that has been left out of a regression equation.

Whenever you have an omitted (or *left-out*) variable, the interpretation and use of your estimated equation become suspect. Leaving out a relevant variable, like price from a demand equation, not only prevents you from getting an estimate of the coefficient of price but also usually causes bias in the estimated coefficients of the variables that are in the equation.

The bias caused by leaving a variable out of an equation is called **omitted variable bias** (or, more generally, **specification bias.**) In an equation with more than one independent variable, the coefficient β_k represents the change in the dependent variable Y caused by a one-unit increase in the independent variable X_k, holding constant the other independent variables in the equation. If a variable is omitted, then it is not included as an independent variable, and it is not held constant for the calculation and interpretation of $\hat{\beta}_k$. This omission can cause bias: It can force the expected value of the estimated coefficient away from the true value of the population coefficient.

Thus, omitting a relevant variable is usually evidence that the entire estimated equation is suspect because of the likely bias in the coefficients of the variables that remain in the equation. Let's look at this issue in more detail.

6.1.1 The Consequences of an Omitted Variable

What happens if you omit an important variable from your equation (perhaps because you can't get the data for the variable or didn't even think of the variable in the first place)? The major consequence of omitting a relevant independent variable from an equation is to cause bias in the regression coefficients that remain in the equation. Suppose that the true regression model is

$$Y_i = \beta_0 + \beta_1 X_{1i} + \beta_2 X_{2i} + \epsilon_i \tag{6.1}$$

where ϵ_i is a classical error term. If you omit X_2 from the equation then the equation becomes:

$$Y_i = \beta_0 + \beta_1 X_{1i} + \epsilon_i^* \tag{6.2}$$

where ϵ_i^* equals

$$\epsilon_i^* = \epsilon_i + \beta_2 X_{2i} \tag{6.3}$$

because the stochastic error term includes the effects of any omitted variables, as mentioned in Section 1.2.3. From Equations 6.2 and 6.3, it might seem as though we could get unbiased estimates of β_0 and β_1 even if we left X_2 out of the equation. Unfortunately, this is not the case,[1] because the included coefficients almost surely pick up some of the effect of the omitted variable and therefore will change, causing bias. To see why, take another look at Equations 6.2 and 6.3. The error term ϵ_i^* is not independent of the explanatory variable X_{1i}, as long as X_{1i} and X_{2i} are correlated because if X_{2i} changes, both X_{1i} and ϵ_i^* will change. In other words, if we leave an important variable out of an equation, we violate Classical Assumption III (that the explanatory variables are independent of the error term), unless the omitted variable is uncorrelated with all the included independent variables (which is extremely unlikely). Recall that the correlation between X_1 and X_2 can be measured by the simple correlation coefficient between the two variables (r_{12}) using Equation 5.8.

In general, when there is a violation of one of the Classical Assumptions, the Gauss–Markov Theorem does not hold, and the OLS estimates are not BLUE. Given linear estimators, this means that the estimated coefficients are no longer unbiased or are no longer minimum variance (for all linear unbiased estimators), or both. In such a circumstance, econometricians first deter-

---

1. For this to be true, X_1 and X_2 must be perfectly uncorrelated and $E(\beta_2 X_{2i})$ must equal zero, both of which are extremely unlikely.

mine the exact property (unbiasedness or minimum variance) that no longer holds and then suggest an alternative estimation technique that might, in some sense, be better than OLS.

An omitted variable causes Classical Assumption III to be violated in a way that causes bias. The estimation of Equation 6.2 when Equation 6.1 is the truth will cause bias in the estimates of Equation 6.2. This means that:

$$E(\hat{\beta}_1^*) \neq \beta_1 \tag{6.4}$$

Instead of having an expected value equal to the true β_1, the estimate will compensate for the fact that X_2 is missing from the equation. If X_1 and X_2 are correlated and X_2 is omitted from the equation, then the OLS program will attribute to X_1 variations in Y actually caused by X_2, and a biased estimate will result.

To see how a left-out variable can cause bias, picture a production function that states that output (Y) depends on the amount of labor (X_1) and capital (X_2) used. What would happen if data on capital were unavailable for some reason and X_2 was omitted from the equation? In this case, we would be leaving out the impact of capital on output in our model. This omission would almost surely bias the estimate of the coefficient of labor because it is likely that capital and labor are positively correlated (an increase in capital usually requires at least some labor to utilize it and vice versa). As a result, the OLS program would attribute to labor the increase in output actually caused by capital to the extent that labor and capital were correlated. Thus the bias would be a function of the impact of capital on output (β_2) and the correlation between capital and labor.

To generalize for a model with two independent variables, the expected value of the coefficient of an included variable (X_1) when a relevant variable (X_2) is omitted from the equation equals:

$$E(\beta_1) = \beta_1 + \beta_2 \cdot \alpha_1 \tag{6.5}$$

where α_1 is the slope coefficient of the secondary regression that relates X_2 to X_1:

$$X_{2i} = \alpha_0 + \alpha_1 X_{1i} + u_i \tag{6.6}$$

where u_i is a classical error term. α_1 can be expressed as a function of the correlation between X_1 and X_2, the included and excluded variables, or $f(r_{12})$.

Let's take a look at Equation 6.5. It states that the expected value of the included variable's coefficient is equal to its true value plus the omitted variable's true coefficient times a function of the correlation between the included (in) and omitted (om) variables.[2] Since the expected value of an unbiased estimate equals the true value, the right-hand term in Equation 6.5 measures the omitted variable bias in the equation:

$$\text{Bias} = \beta_2\alpha_1 \quad \text{or} \quad \text{Bias} = \beta_{om} \cdot f(r_{in,om}) \qquad (6.7)$$

In general terms, the bias thus equals β_{om}, the coefficient of the omitted variable, times $f(r_{in,om})$, a function of the correlation between the included and omitted variables.

This bias exists unless:

1. the true coefficient equals zero or
2. the included and omitted variables are uncorrelated.

The term $\beta_{om}f(r_{in,om})$ is the amount of specification bias introduced into the estimate of the coefficient of the included variable by leaving out the omitted variable. Although it's true that there is no bias if the included and excluded variables are uncorrelated, there almost always is some correlation between any two variables in the real world (even if it's just random), and so bias is almost always caused by the omission of a relevant variable.[3]

6.1.2   An Example of Specification Bias

Consider the following equation for the annual consumption of chicken in the United States. (The data for this example are included in Exercise 5; t-scores differ because of rounding.)

$$\hat{Y}_t = 31.5 - 0.73PC_t + 0.11PB_t + 0.23YD_t \qquad (6.8)$$
$$\phantom{\hat{Y}_t = 31.5 -} (0.08) \quad\;\; (0.05) \quad\;\; (0.02)$$
$$t = \quad -9.12 \qquad 2.50 \qquad 14.22$$
$$\overline{R}^2 = .986 \quad n = 44 \text{ (annual 1951–1994)}$$

---

2. Equation 6.5 is a conditional expectation that holds when there are exactly two independent variables, but the more general equation is quite similar.

3. Although the omission of a relevant variable almost always produces bias in the estimators of the coefficients of the included variables, the variances of these estimators are generally lower than they otherwise would be. One method of deciding whether this decreased variance in the distribution of the βs is valuable enough to offset the bias is to compare different estimation techniques with a measure called Mean Square Error (MSE). MSE is equal to the variance plus the square of the bias. The lower the MSE, the better.

where: Y_t = per capita chicken consumption (in pounds) in year t
          PC_t = the price of chicken (in cents per pound) in year t
          PB_t = the price of beef (in cents per pound) in year t
          YD_t = U.S. per capita disposable income (in hundreds of dollars)
          in year t

This equation is a simple demand for chicken equation that includes the prices of chicken and a close substitute (beef) and an income variable. Note that the signs of the estimated coefficients agree with the signs you would have hypothesized before seeing any regression results.

If we estimate this equation without the price of the substitute, we obtain:

$$\hat{Y}_t = 32.9 - 0.70PC_t + 0.27YD_t \qquad (6.9)$$
$$\phantom{\hat{Y}_t = 32.9} (0.08) \qquad (0.01)$$
$$t = -8.33 \qquad 45.91$$
$$\overline{R}^2 = .984 \qquad n = 44 \text{ (annual 1951–1994)}$$

Let's compare Equations 6.8 and 6.9 to see if dropping the beef price variable had an impact on the estimated equations. If you compare the overall fit, for example, you can see that $\overline{R}^2$ fell slightly from .986 to .984 when PB was dropped, exactly what we'd expect to occur when a relevant variable is omitted.

More important, from the point of view of showing that an omitted variable causes bias, let's see if the coefficient estimates of the remaining variables changed. Sure enough, dropping PB caused $\hat{\beta}_{PC}$ to go from -0.73 to -0.70 and caused $\hat{\beta}_{YD}$ to go from 0.23 to 0.27. The direction of this bias, by the way, is considered positive because the biased coefficient of PC (-0.70) is more positive (less negative) than the suspected unbiased one (-0.73) and the biased coefficient of YD (0.27) is more positive than the suspected unbiased one of (0.23).

The fact that the bias is positive could have been guessed before any regressions were run if Equation 6.7 had been used. The specification bias caused by omitting the price of beef is expected[4] to be positive because the expected sign of the coefficient of PB is positive and because the expected correlation between the price of beef and the price of chicken itself is positive:

---

4. It is important to note the distinction between expected bias and any actual observed differences between coefficient estimates. Because of the random nature of the error term (and hence the $\hat{\beta}$s), the change in an estimated coefficient brought about by dropping a relevant variable from the equation will not necessarily be in the expected direction. Biasedness refers to the central tendency of the sampling distribution of the $\hat{\beta}$s, not to every single drawing from that distribution. However, we usually (and justifiably) rely on these general tendencies. Note also that Equation 6.8 has three independent variables whereas Equation 6.7 was derived for use with equations with exactly two. However, Equation 6.7 represents a general tendency that is still applicable.

$$\text{Expected bias in } \hat{\beta}_{PC} = \beta_{PB} \cdot f(r_{PC,PB}) = (+) \cdot (+) = (+)$$

Similarly for YD:

$$\text{Expected bias in } \hat{\beta}_{YD} = \beta_{PB} \cdot f(r_{YD,PB}) = (+) \cdot (+) = (+)$$

Note that both correlation coefficients are anticipated to be (and actually are) positive. To see this, think of the impact of an increase in the price of chicken on the price of beef and then follow through the impact of any increase in income on the price of beef.

To sum, if a relevant variable is left out of a regression equation

1. there is no longer an estimate of the coefficient of that variable in the equation, and
2. the coefficients of the remaining variables are likely to be biased.

Although the amount of the bias might not be very large in some cases (when, for instance, there is little correlation between the included and excluded variables), it is extremely likely that at least a small amount of specification bias will be present in all such situations.

6.1.3 Correcting for an Omitted Variable

In theory, the solution to a problem of specification bias seems easy: Simply add the omitted variable to the equation. Unfortunately, that's more easily said than done, for a couple of reasons.

First, omitted variable bias is hard to detect. As mentioned above, the amount of bias introduced can be small and not immediately detectable. This is especially true when there is no reason to believe that you have misspecified the model. Some indications of specification bias are obvious (such as an estimated coefficient that is significant in the direction opposite from that expected), but others are not so clear. Could you tell from Equation 6.9 alone that a variable was missing? The best indicators of an omitted relevant variable are the theoretical underpinnings of the model itself. What variables *must* be included? What signs do you expect? Do you have any notions about the range into which the coefficient values should fall? Have you accidentally left out a variable that most researchers would agree is important? The best way to avoid omitting an important variable is to invest the time to think carefully through the equation before the data are entered into the computer.

A second source of complexity is the problem of choosing which variable to add to an equation once you decide that it is suffering from omitted variable bias. That is, a researcher faced with a clear case of specification bias (like an estimated $\hat{\beta}$ that is significantly different from zero in the unexpected direction) will often have no clue as to what variable could be causing the problem. Some beginning researchers, when faced with this dilemma, will add all the possible relevant variables to the equation at once, but this process leads to less precise estimates, as will be discussed in the next section. Other beginning researchers will test a number of different variables and keep the one in the equation that does the best statistical job of appearing to reduce the bias (by giving plausible signs and satisfactory t-values). This technique, adding a "left-out" variable to "fix" a strange-looking regression result, is invalid because the variable that best corrects a case of specification bias might do so only by chance rather than by being the true solution to the problem. In such an instance, the "fixed" equation may give superb statistical results for the sample at hand but then do terribly when applied to other samples because it does not describe the characteristics of the true population.

Dropping a variable will not help cure omitted variable bias. If the sign of an estimated coefficient is different from expected, it cannot be changed to the expected direction by dropping a variable that has a t-score lower (in absolute value) than the t-score of the coefficient estimate that has the unexpected sign. Furthermore, the sign in general will not likely change even if the variable to be deleted has a large t-score.[5]

If the estimated coefficient is significantly different from our expectations (either in sign or magnitude), then it is extremely likely that some sort of specification bias exists in our model. Although it is true that a poor sample of data or a poorly theorized expectation may also yield statistically significant unexpected signs or magnitudes, these possibilities sometimes can be eliminated.

If an unexpected result leads you to believe that you have an omitted variable, one way to decide which variable to add to the equation is to use expected bias analysis. **Expected bias** is the likely bias that omitting a particular variable would have caused in the estimated coefficient of one of the included variables. It can be estimated with Equation 6.7:

$$\text{Expected bias} = \beta_{om} \cdot f(r_{in,om}) \tag{6.7}$$

If the sign of the expected bias is the same as the sign of your unexpected result, then the variable might be the source of the apparent bias. If the sign of the expected bias is *not* the same as the sign of your unexpected result, how-

---

5. Ignazio Visco, "On Obtaining the Right Sign of a Coefficient Estimate by Omitting a Variable from the Regression," *Journal of Econometrics*, February 1978, pp. 115–117.

ever, then the variable is extremely unlikely to have caused your unexpected result. Expected bias analysis should be used only when an equation has obvious bias (like a coefficient that is significant in an unexpected direction) and only when you're choosing between theoretically sound potential variables.

As an example of expected bias analysis, let's return to Equation 6.9, the chicken demand equation without the beef price variable. Let's assume that you had expected the coefficient of β_{PC} to be in the range of -1.0 and that you were surprised by the unexpectedly positive coefficient of PC in Equation 6.9. (As you can see by comparing Equations 6.8 and 6.9, your expectation was reasonable, but you can never be sure of this fact in practice.)

This unexpectedly positive result could not have been caused by an omitted variable with negative expected bias but could have been caused by an omitted variable with positive expected bias. One such variable is the price of beef. The expected bias in $\hat{\beta}_{PC}$ due to leaving out PB is positive since both the expected coefficient of PB and the expected correlation between PC and PB are positive:

$$\text{Expected bias in } \hat{\beta}_{PC} = \beta_{PB} \cdot f(r_{PC,PB}) = (+) \cdot (+) = (+)$$

Hence the price of beef is a reasonable candidate to be omitted variable in Equation 6.9.

Although you can never actually observe bias (since you don't know the true β), the use of this technique to screen potential causes of specification bias should reduce the number of regressions run and therefore increase the statistical validity of the results. This technique will work best when only one (or one kind of) variable is omitted from the equation in question. With a number of different kinds of variables omitted simultaneously, the impact on the equation's coefficients is quite hard to specify.

A brief warning: It may be tempting to conduct what might be called "residual analysis" by examining a plot of the residuals in an attempt to find patterns that suggest variables that have been accidentally omitted. A major problem with this approach is that the coefficients of the estimated equation will possibly have some of the effects of the left-out variable already altering their estimated values. Thus, residuals may show a pattern that only vaguely resembles the pattern of the actual omitted variable. The chances are high that the pattern shown in the residuals may lead to the selection of an incorrect variable. In addition, care should be taken to use residual analysis only to choose between theoretically sound candidate variables rather than to generate those candidates.

6.2   Irrelevant Variables

What happens if you include a variable in an equation that doesn't belong there? This case, **irrelevant variables,** is the converse of omitted variables and can be analyzed using the model we developed in Section 6.1. Whereas the omitted variable model has more independent variables in the true model than in the estimated equation, the irrelevant variable model has more independent variables in the estimated equation than in the true one.

The addition of a variable to an equation where it doesn't belong does not cause bias, but it does increase the variances of the estimated coefficients of the included variables.

6.2.1   Impact of Irrelevant Variables

If the true regression specification is

$$Y_i = \beta_0 + \beta_1 X_{1i} + \epsilon_i \tag{6.10}$$

but the researcher for some reason includes an extra variable,

$$Y_i = \beta_0 + \beta_1 X_{1i} + \beta_2 X_{2i} + \epsilon_i^{**} \tag{6.11}$$

the misspecified equation's error term can be seen to be:

$$\epsilon_i^{**} = \epsilon_i - \beta_2 X_{2i} \tag{6.12}$$

Such a mistake will not cause bias if the true coefficient of the extra (or irrelevant) variable is zero. In that case, $\epsilon_i = \epsilon_i^{**}$. That is, $\hat{\beta}_1$ in Equation 6.11 is unbiased when $\beta_2 = 0$.

However, the inclusion of an irrelevant variable will increase the variance of the estimated coefficients, and this increased variance will tend to decrease the absolute magnitude of their t-scores. Also, an irrelevant variable usually will decrease the R^2 (but not the $\bar{R}^2$). In a model of Y on X_1 and X_2, the variance of the OLS estimator of β_1 is:

$$VAR(\hat{\beta}_1) = \frac{\sigma^2}{(1 - r_{12}^2) \cdot \sum(X_1 - \bar{X}_1)^2} \tag{6.13}$$

If the irrelevant variable is not in the equation (or if $r_{12} = 0$), then:

$$VAR(\hat{\beta}_1) = \frac{\sigma^2}{\sum(X_1 - \bar{X}_1)^2} \tag{6.14}$$

Thus, although the irrelevant variable causes no bias, it causes problems for the regression because it reduces the precision of the regression.

To see why this is so, try plugging a nonzero value (between $+1.0$ and -1.0) for r_{12} into Equation 6.13 and note that $VAR(\hat{\beta}_1)$ has increased when compared to Equation 6.14. The equation with an included variable that does not belong in the equation usually has lower t-scores and a lower $\overline{R}^2$ than it otherwise would. The property holds, by the way, only when $r_{12} \neq 0$, but since this is the case in virtually every sample, the conclusion of increased variance due to irrelevant variables is a valid one. Table 6.1 summarizes the consequences of the omitted variable and the included irrelevant variable cases:

TABLE 6.1   EFFECT OF OMITTED VARIABLES AND IRRELEVANT VARIABLES ON THE COEFFICIENT ESTIMATES

Effect on Coefficient Estimates	Omitted Variable	Irrelevant Variable
Bias	Yes*	No
Variance	Decreases*	Increases*

*Unless $r_{12} = 0$.

6.2.2   An Example of an Irrelevant Variable

Let's return to the equation from Section 6.1 for the annual consumption of chicken and see what happens when we add an irrelevant variable to the equation. The original equation was:

$$\hat{Y}_t = 31.5 - 0.73PC_t + 0.11PB_t + 0.23YD_t \qquad (6.8)$$
$$\phantom{\hat{Y}_t = 31.5 -} (0.08) \qquad (0.05) \qquad (0.02)$$
$$t = -9.12 \qquad\quad 2.50 \qquad\quad 14.22$$
$$\overline{R}^2 = .986 \quad n = 44 \text{ (annual 1951–1994)}$$

Suppose you hypothesize that the demand for chicken also depends on R, the interest rate (which, perhaps, confuses the demand for a nondurable good with an equation you saw for a consumer durable). If you now estimate the equation with the interest rate included, you obtain:

$$\hat{Y}_t = 30.0 - 0.73PC_t + 0.12PB_t + 0.22YD_t + 0.17R_t \qquad (6.15)$$
$$\phantom{\hat{Y}_t = 30.0 -} (0.08) \qquad (0.06) \qquad (0.02) \qquad (0.21)$$
$$t = -9.10 \qquad\quad 2.08 \qquad\quad 11.05 \qquad\quad 0.82$$
$$\overline{R}^2 = .985 \quad n = 44 \text{ (annual 1951–1994)}$$

A comparison of Equations 6.8 and 6.15 will make the theory in Section 6.2.1 come to life. First of all, $\overline{R}^2$ has fallen slightly, indicating the reduction in fit adjusted for degrees of freedom. Second, none of the regression coefficients from the original equation changed significantly; compare these results with the larger differences between Equations 6.8 and 6.9. Further, slight increases in the standard errors of the estimated coefficients took place. Finally, the t-score for the potential variable (the interest rate) is very small, indicating that it is not significantly different from zero. Given the theoretical shakiness of the new variable, these results indicate that it is irrelevant and never should have been included in the regression.

6.2.3 Four Important Specification Criteria

We have now discussed at least four valid criteria to help decide whether a given variable belongs in the equation. We think these criteria are so important that we urge beginning researchers to work through them every time a variable is added or subtracted.

1. *Theory:* Is the variable's place in the equation unambiguous and theoretically sound?
2. *t-Test:* Is the variable's estimated coefficient significant in the expected direction?
3. $\overline{R}^2$: Does the overall fit of the equation (adjusted for degrees of freedom) improve when the variable is added to the equation?
4. *Bias:* Do other variables' coefficients change significantly when the variable is added to the equation?

If all these conditions hold, the variable belongs in the equation; if none of them do, the variable is irrelevant and can be safely excluded from the equation. When a typical omitted relevant variable is included in the equation, its inclusion probably will increase $\overline{R}^2$ and change other coefficients. If an irrelevant variable, on the other hand, is included, it will reduce $\overline{R}^2$, have an insignificant t-score, and have little impact on the other variables' coefficients.

In many cases, all four criteria do not agree. It is possible for a variable to have an insignificant t-score that is greater than one, for example. In such a case, it can be shown that $\overline{R}^2$ will go up when the variable is added to the equation and yet the t-score will still be insignificant.

Whenever the four criteria for whether a variable should be included in an equation disagree, the econometrician must use careful judgment and should not rely on a single criterion like $\overline{R}^2$ to determine the specification. Researchers should not misuse this freedom by testing various combinations of variables until they find the results that appear to statistically support the point they want to make. All such decisions are a bit easier when you realize that the single most important determinant of a variable's relevance is its theoretical justification. No amount of statistical evidence should make a theoretical necessity into an "irrelevant" variable. Once in a while, a researcher is forced to leave a theoretically important variable out of an equation for lack of a better alternative; in such cases, the usefulness of the equation is limited.

6.3   An Illustration of the Misuse of Specification Criteria

At times, the four specification criteria outlined in the previous section will lead the researcher to an incorrect conclusion if those criteria are applied blindly to a problem without the proper concern for economic principles or common sense. In particular, a t-score can often be insignificant for reasons other than the presence of an irrelevant variable. Since economic theory is the most important test for including a variable, an example of why a variable should not be dropped from an equation simply because it has an insignificant t-score is in order.

Suppose you believe that the demand for Brazilian coffee in the United States is a negative function of the real price of Brazilian coffee (P_{bc}) and a positive function of both the real price of tea (P_t) and real disposable income in the United States (Y_d).[6] Suppose further that you obtain the data, run the implied regression, and observe the following results:

$$\widehat{COFFEE} = 9.1 + 7.8P_{bc} + 2.4P_t + 0.0035Y_d \qquad (6.16)$$
$$(15.6) \qquad (1.2) \qquad (0.0010)$$
$$t = 0.5 \qquad 2.0 \qquad 3.5$$
$$\overline{R}^2 = .60 \quad n = 25$$

The coefficients of the second and third variables, P_t and Y_d, appear to be fairly significant in the direction you hypothesized, but the first variable, P_{bc}, appears to have an insignificant coefficient with an unexpected sign. If you

---

6. This example was inspired by a similar one concerning Ceylonese tea published in Potluri Rao and Roger LeRoy Miller, *Applied Econometrics* (Belmont, California: Wadsworth, 1971), pp. 38–40. This book is now out of print.

think there is a possibility that the demand for Brazilian coffee is perfectly price inelastic (that is, its coefficient is zero), you might decide to run the same equation without the price variable, obtaining:

$$\widehat{COFFEE} = 9.3 + 2.6P_t + 0.0036Y_d \qquad (6.17)$$
$$(1.0) \quad (0.0009)$$
$$t = 2.6 \quad 4.0$$
$$\overline{R}^2 = .61 \quad n = 25$$

By comparing Equations 6.16 and 6.17, we can apply our four specification criteria for the inclusion of a variable in an equation that were outlined in the previous section:

1. *Theory:* Since the demand for coffee could possibly be perfectly price inelastic, the theory behind dropping the variable seems plausible.
2. *t-Test:* The t-score of the possibly irrelevant variable is 0.5, insignificant at any level.
3. *$\overline{R}^2$:* $\overline{R}^2$ increases when the variable is dropped, indicating that the variable is irrelevant. (Since the t-score is less than one, this is to be expected.)
4. *Bias:* The remaining coefficients change only a small amount when P_{bc} is dropped, suggesting that there is little if any bias caused by excluding the variable.

Based upon this analysis, you might conclude that the demand for Brazilian coffee is indeed perfectly price inelastic and that the variable is therefore irrelevant and should be dropped from the model. As it turns out, this conclusion would be unwarranted. Although the elasticity of demand for coffee in general might be fairly low (actually, the evidence suggests that it is inelastic only over a particular range of prices), it is hard to believe that Brazilian coffee is immune to price competition from other kinds of coffee. Indeed, one would expect quite a bit of sensitivity in the demand for Brazilian coffee with respect to the price of, for example, Colombian coffee. To test this hypothesis, the price of Colombian coffee (P_{cc}) should be added to the original Equation 6.16:

$$\widehat{COFFEE} = 10.0 + 8.0P_{cc} - 5.6P_{bc} + 2.6P_t + 0.0030Y_d \qquad (6.18)$$
$$(4.0) \quad (2.0) \quad (1.3) \quad (0.0010)$$
$$t = 2.0 \quad -2.8 \quad 2.0 \quad 3.0$$
$$\overline{R}^2 = .65 \quad n = 25$$

By comparing Equations 6.16 and 6.18, we can once again apply the four criteria:

1. *Theory:* Both prices should always have been included in the model; their logical justification is quite strong.

2. *t-Test:* The t-score of the new variable, the price of Colombian coffee, is 2.0, significant at most levels.

3. $\overline{R}^2$: $\overline{R}^2$ increases with the addition of the variable, indicating that the variable was an omitted variable.

4. *Bias:* Although two of the coefficients remain virtually unchanged, indicating that the correlations between these variables and the price of Colombian coffee variable are low, the coefficient for the price of Brazilian coffee does change significantly, indicating bias in the original result.

An examination of the bias question will also help us understand Equation 6.7, the equation for bias. Since the expected sign of the coefficient of the omitted variable (P_{cc}) is positive and since the simple correlation coefficient between the two competitive prices ($r_{P_{cc},P_{bc}}$) is also positive, the direction of the expected bias in $\hat{\beta}_{P_{bc}}$ in the estimation of Equation 6.16 is positive. If you compare Equations 6.16 and 6.18, that positive bias can be seen because the coefficient of P_{bc} is $+7.8$ instead of -5.6. The increase from -5.6 to $+7.8$ may be due to the positive bias that results from leaving out P_{cc}.

The moral to be drawn from this example is that theoretical considerations should never be discarded, even in the face of statistical insignificance. If a variable known to be extremely important from a theoretical point of view turns out to be statistically insignificant in a particular sample, that variable should be left in the equation despite the fact that it makes the results look bad.

Don't conclude that the particular path outlined in this example is the correct way to specify an equation. Trying a long string of possible variables until you get the particular one that makes P_{bc} turn negative and significant is not the way to obtain a result that will stand up well to other samples or alternative hypotheses. The original equation should never have been run without the Colombian coffee variable. Instead, the problem should have been analyzed enough so that such errors of omission were unlikely before any regressions were attempted at all. The more thinking that's done before the first regression is run, and the fewer alternative specifications that are estimated, the better the regression results are likely to be.

6.4 Specification Searches

One of the weaknesses of econometrics is that a researcher can potentially manipulate a data set to produce almost *any* results by specifying different regressions until estimates with the desired properties are obtained. Thus, the integrity of all empirical work is potentially open to question.

Although the problem is a difficult one, it makes sense to attempt to minimize the number of equations estimated and to rely on theory rather than statistical fit as much as possible when choosing variables. Theory, not statistical fit, should be the most important criterion for the inclusion of a variable in a regression equation. To do otherwise runs the risk of producing incorrect and/or disbelieved results. We'll try to illustrate this by discussing three of the most commonly used *incorrect* techniques for specifying a regression equation. These techniques produce the best specification only by chance. At worst, they are possibly unethical in that they misrepresent the methods used to obtain the regression results and the significance of those results.

6.4.1 Data Mining

Almost surely the worst way to choose a specification is to simultaneously try a whole series of possible regression formulations and then choose the equation that conforms the most to what the researcher wants the results to look like. In such a situation, the researcher would estimate virtually every possible combination of the various alternative independent variables, and the choice between them would be made on the basis of the results. This practice of simultaneously estimating a number of combinations of independent variables and selecting the best from them ignores the fact that a number of specifications have been examined before the final one. To oversimplify, if you are 95 percent confident that a regression result didn't occur by chance and you run more than 20 regressions, how much confidence can you have in your result? Since you'll tend to keep regressions with high t-scores and discard ones with low t-scores, the reported t-scores overstate the degree of statistical significance of the estimated coefficients.

Furthermore, such "data mining" and "fishing expeditions" to obtain desired statistics for the final regression equation are potentially unethical methods of empirical research. These procedures include using not only many alternative combinations of independent variables but also many functional forms, lag structures, and what are offered as "sophisticated" or "advanced" estimating techniques. "If you just torture the data long enough, they will confess."[7] In other words, if enough alternatives are tried, the chances of

---

7. Thomas Mayer, "Economics as a Hard Science: Realistic Goal or Wishful Thinking?" *Economic Inquiry*, April 1980, p. 175.

obtaining the results desired by the researcher are increased tremendously, but the final result is essentially worthless. The researcher hasn't found any scientific evidence to support the original hypothesis; rather, prior expectations were imposed on the data in a way that is essentially misleading.

6.4.2   Stepwise Regression Procedures

A **stepwise regression** involves the use of a computer program to choose the independent variables to be included in the estimation of a particular equation. The computer program is given a "shopping list" of possible independent variables, and then it builds the equation in steps. It chooses as the first explanatory variable the one that by itself explains the largest amount of the variation of the dependent variable around its mean. It chooses as the second variable the one that adds the most to R^2, given that the first variable is already in the equation. The stepwise procedure continues until the next variable to be added fails to achieve some researcher-specified increase in R^2 (or all the variables are added). The measure of the supposed contribution of each independent variable is the increase in R^2 (which is sometimes called the "R^2 delete") caused by the addition of the variable.

Unfortunately, any correlation among the independent variables (called multicollinearity, which we will take up in more detail in Chapter 8) causes this procedure to be deficient. To the extent that the variables are related, it becomes difficult to tell the impact of one variable from another. As a result, in the presence of multicollinearity, it's impossible to determine unambiguously the individual contribution of each variable enough to say which one is more important and thus should be included first.[8] Even worse, there is no necessity that the particular combination of variables chosen has any theoretical justification or that the coefficients have the expected signs.

Because of these problems, most econometricians avoid stepwise procedures. The major pitfalls are that the coefficients may be biased, the calculated t-values no longer follow the t-distribution, relevant variables may be excluded because of the arbitrary order in which the selection takes place, and

---

8. Some programs compute standardized beta coefficients, which are the estimated coefficients for an equation in which all variables have been standardized by subtracting their means from them and by dividing them by their own standard deviations. The higher the beta of an independent variable is in absolute value, the more important it is thought to be in explaining the movements in the dependent variable. Unfortunately, beta coefficients are deficient in the presence of multicollinearity, as are partial correlation coefficients, which measure the correlation between the dependent variable and a given independent variable holding all other independent variables constant.

the signs of the estimated coefficients at intermediate or final stages of the routine may be different from the expected signs. Using a stepwise procedure is an admission of ignorance concerning which variables should be entered.

6.4.3   Sequential Specification Searches

To their credit, most econometricians avoid data mining and stepwise regressions. Instead, they tend to specify equations by estimating an initial equation and then sequentially dropping or adding variables (or changing functional forms) until a plausible equation is found with "good statistics." Faced with knowing that a few variables are relevant (on the basis of theory) but not knowing whether other additional variables are relevant, inspecting $\overline{R}^2$ and t-tests for all variables for each specification appears to be the generally accepted practice. Indeed, it would be easy to draw from a casual reading of the previous sections the impression that such a sequential specification search is the best way to go about finding the "truth." Instead, as we shall see, there is a vast difference in approach between a sequential specification search and our recommended approach.

The **sequential specification search** technique allows a researcher to estimate an undisclosed number of regressions and then present a final choice (which is based upon an unspecified set of expectations about the signs and significance of the coefficients) as if it were the only specification estimated. Such a method misstates the statistical validity of the regression results for two reasons:

1. The statistical significance of the results is overestimated because the estimations of the previous regressions are ignored.

2. The set of expectations used by the researcher to choose between various regression results is rarely if ever disclosed.[9] Thus the reader has no way of knowing whether or not all the other regression results had opposite signs or insignificant coefficients for the important variables.

Unfortunately, there is no universally accepted way of conducting sequential searches, primarily because the appropriate test at one stage in the procedure depends on which tests were previously conducted, and also because the tests have been very difficult to invent. One possibility is to reduce the degrees of freedom in the "final" equation by one for each alternative specifica-

---

9. As mentioned in Chapter 5, Bayesian regression is a technique for dealing systematically with these prior expectations. For more on this issue, see Edward E. Leamer, *Specification Searches* (New York: Wiley), 1978.

tion attempted. This procedure is far from exact, but it does impose an explicit penalty for specification searches.

More generally, we recommend trying to keep the number of regressions estimated as low as possible; to focus on theoretical considerations when choosing variables, functional forms, and the like; and to document all the various specifications investigated. That is, we recommend combining parsimony (using theory and analysis to limit the number of specifications estimated) with disclosure (reporting all the equations estimated).

There is another side to the story, however. Some researchers feel that the true model will show through if given the chance and that the best statistical results (including signs of coefficients, etc.) are most likely to have come from the true specification. The problem with this philosophy is that the element of chance is ordinarily quite strong in any given application. In addition, reasonable people often disagree as to what the "true" model should look like. As a result, different researchers can look at the same data set and come up with very different "best" equations. Because this can happen, the distinction between good and bad econometrics is not always as clear cut as is implied by the previous paragraphs. As long as researchers have a healthy respect for the dangers inherent in specification searches, they are very likely to proceed in a reasonable way.

The lesson to be learned from this section should be quite clear. Most of the work of specifying an equation should be done before even attempting to estimate the equation on the computer. Since it is unreasonable to expect researchers to be perfect, there will be times when additional specifications must be estimated; however, these new estimates should be thoroughly grounded in theory and explicitly taken into account when testing for significance or summarizing results. In this way, the danger of misleading the reader about the statistical properties of estimates is reduced.

6.4.4 Bias Caused by Relying on the *t*-Test to Choose Variables

In the previous section, we stated that sequential specification searches are likely to mislead researchers about the statistical properties of their results. In particular, the practice of dropping a potential independent variable simply because its t-score indicates that its estimated coefficient is insignificantly different from zero will cause systematic bias in the estimated coefficients (and their t-scores) of the remaining variables.[10]

---

10. For a number of better techniques, including sequential or "pretest" estimators and "Stein-rule" estimators, see George G. Judge, W. E. Griffiths, R. Carter Hill, Helmut Lutkepohl, and Tsoung-Chao Lee, *The Theory and Practice of Econometrics* (New York: Wiley, 1985).

Say the hypothesized model for a particular dependent variable is:

$$Y_i = \beta_0 + \beta_1 X_{1i} + \beta_2 X_{2i} + \epsilon_i \tag{6.19}$$

Assume further that, on the basis of theory, we are certain that X_1 belongs in the equation but that we are not as certain that X_2 belongs. Even though we have stressed four criteria to determine whether X_2 should be included, many inexperienced researchers just use the t-test on $\hat{\beta}_2$ to determine whether X_2 should be included. If this preliminary t-test indicates that $\hat{\beta}_2$ is significantly different from zero, then these researchers leave X_2 in the equation, and they choose Equation 6.19 as their final model. If, however, the t-test does *not* indicate that $\hat{\beta}_2$ is significantly different from zero, then such researchers drop X_2 from the equation and consider Y as a function of X_1.

Two kinds of mistakes can be made using such a system. First, X_2 can sometimes be left in the equation when it does not belong there, but such a mistake does not change the expected value of $\hat{\beta}_1$. Second, X_2 can sometimes be dropped from equation when it belongs, and then the estimated coefficient of X_1 will be biased by the value of the true β_2 to the extent that X_1 and X_2 are correlated. In other words, $\hat{\beta}_1$ will be biased every time X_2 belongs in the equation and is left out, and X_2 will be left out every time that its estimated coefficient is not significantly different from zero. That is, the expected value of $\hat{\beta}_1$ will not equal the true β_1, and we will have systematic bias in our equation

$$E(\hat{\beta}_1) = \beta_1 + \beta_2 \cdot f(r_{X_1, X_2}) \cdot P \neq \beta_1 \tag{6.20}$$

where P indicates the probability of an insignificant t-score. It is also the case that the t-score of $\hat{\beta}_1$ no longer follows the t-distribution. In other words, the t-test is biased by sequential specification searches.

Since most researchers consider a number of different variables before settling on the final model, someone who relies on the t-test alone is likely to encounter this problem systematically.

6.4.5 Scanning and Sensitivity Analysis

Throughout this text, we've encouraged you to estimate as few specifications as possible and to avoid depending on fit alone to choose between those specifications. If you read the current economics literature, however, it won't take you long to find well-known researchers who have estimated five or more specifications and then have listed all their results in an academic journal article. What's going on?

In almost every case, these authors have employed one of the two following techniques:

1. Scanning to develop a testable theory

2. Sensitivity analysis

Scanning involves analyzing a data set not for the purpose of testing a hypothesis but for the purpose of developing a testable theory or hypothesis. A researcher who is scanning will run quite a few different specifications, will select the specifications that fit best, and then will analyze these results in the hopes that they will provide clues to a new theory or hypothesis. As a means for stimulating fresh thinking or influencing thinking about substantive issues, scanning may have even more potential than does classical hypothesis testing.[11]

Be careful, however; before you can "accept" a theory or hypothesis, it should be tested on a *different* data set (or in another context) using the hypothesis testing techniques of this text. A new data set must be used because our typical statistical tests have little meaning if the new hypotheses are tested on the old data set; after all, the researcher knows ahead of time what the results will be! The use of such dual data sets is easiest when there is a plethora of data. This sometimes is the case in cross-sectional research projects but rarely is the case for time-series research.

Sensitivity analysis consists of purposely running a number of alternative specifications to determine whether particular results are *robust* (not statistical flukes). In essence, we're trying to determine how sensitive a particular result is to a change in specification. Researchers who use sensitivity analysis run (and report on) a number of different specifications and tend to discount a result that appears significant in some specifications and insignificant in others. Indeed, the whole purpose of sensitivity analysis is to gain confidence that a particular result is significant in a variety of alternative specifications and is not based on a single specification that has been estimated on only one data set. For a simple example of sensitivity analysis, see Exercise 15 at the end of the chapter.

6.5   Lagged Independent Variables

Virtually all the regressions we've studied so far have been "instantaneous" in nature. In other words, they have included independent and dependent variables from the same time period, as in:

---

11. For an excellent presentation of this argument, see Lawrence H. Summers, "The Scientific Illusion in Empirical Macroeconomics," *Scandinavian Journal of Economics*, 1991, pp. 129–148. For a number of related points of view, see David F. Hendry, Edward E. Leamer, and Dale J. Poirer, *A Conversation on Econometric Methodology*, Institute of Statistics and Decision Sciences, Duke University, 1989, 144 pages.

$$Y_t = \beta_0 + \beta_1 X_{1t} + \beta_2 X_{2t} + \epsilon_t \qquad (6.21)$$

where the subscript t is used to refer to a particular point in time. If all variables have the same subscript, then the equation is instantaneous.

Some beginning researchers, when choosing their independent variables, jump to the mistaken conclusion that all regressions should follow the pattern of Equation 6.21 and contain only variables that come from the same time period. Such a conclusion ignores the fact that not all economic or business situations imply such instantaneous relationships between the dependent and independent variables. In many cases we must allow for the possibility that time might elapse between a change in the independent variable and the resulting change in the dependent variable. The length of this time between cause and effect is called a **lag.** Many econometric equations include one or more *lagged independent variables* like X_{1t-1}, where the subscript $t - 1$ indicates that the observation of X_1 is from the time period previous to time period t, as in the following equation:

$$Y_t = \beta_0 + \beta_1 X_{1t-1} + \beta_2 X_{2t} + \epsilon_t \qquad (6.22)$$

In this equation, X_1 has been lagged by one time period, but the relationship between Y and X_2 is still instantaneous.

For example, think about the process by which the supply of an agricultural product is determined. Since agricultural goods take time to grow, decisions on how many acres to plant or how many eggs to let hatch into egg-producing hens (instead of selling them immediately) must be made months if not years before the product is actually supplied to the consumer. Any change in an agricultural market, such as an increase in the price that the farmer can earn for providing cotton, has a lagged effect on the supply of that product:

$$C_t = f(\overset{+}{PC}_{t-1}, \overset{-}{PF}_t) + \epsilon_t = \beta_0 + \beta_1 PC_{t-1} + \beta_2 PF_t + \epsilon_t \qquad (6.23)$$

where: C_t = the quantity of cotton supplied in year t
  PC_{t-1} = the price of cotton in year $t - 1$
  PF_t = the price of farm labor in year t

Note that this equation hypothesizes a lag between the price of cotton and the production of cotton, but not between the price of farm labor and the production of cotton. It's reasonable to think that if cotton prices change, farmers won't be able to react immediately because it takes a while for cotton to be planted and to grow.

The meaning of the regression coefficient of a lagged variable is not the same as the meaning of the coefficient of an unlagged variable. The estimated coefficient of a lagged X measures the change in *this year's* Y attributed to a one-unit increase in *last year's* X (holding constant the other Xs in the equation). Thus β_1 in Equation 6.23 measures the extra number of units of cotton that would be produced this year as a result of a one-unit increase in last year's price of cotton, holding this year's price of farm labor constant.

If the lag structure is hypothesized to take place over more than one time period, or if a lagged dependent variable is included on the right-hand side of an equation, the question becomes significantly more complex. Such cases, called *distributed lags*, will be dealt with in Chapter 12.

6.6   An Example of Choosing Independent Variables

It's time to get some experience choosing independent variables. After all, every equation so far in the text has come with the specification already determined, but once you've finished this course you'll have to make all such specification decisions on your own. In future chapters, we'll use a technique called "interactive regression learning exercises" to allow you to make your own actual specification choices and get feedback on your choices. To start, though, let's work through a specification together.

To keep things as simple as possible, we'll begin with a topic near and dear to your heart, your GPA! Suppose a friend who attends a small liberal arts college surveys all 25 members of her econometrics class, obtains data on the variables listed below, and asks for your help in choosing a specification:

GPA_i = the cumulative college grade point average on the *i*th student on a four-point scale

$HGPA_i$ = the cumulative high school grade point average of the *i*th student on a four-point scale

$MSAT_i$ = the highest score earned by the *i*th student on the math section of the SAT test (800 maximum)

$VSAT_i$ = the highest score earned by the *i*th student on the verbal section of the SAT test (800 maximum)

SAT_i = $MSAT_i + VSAT_i$

$GREK_i$ = a dummy variable equal to 1 if the *i*th student is a member of a fraternity or sorority, 0 otherwise

HRS_i = the *i*th student's estimate of the average number of hours spent studying per course per week in college

$PRIV_i$ = a dummy variable equal to 1 if the *i*th student graduated from a private high school, 0 otherwise

$JOCK_i$ = a dummy variable equal to 1 if the ith student is or was a member of a varsity intercollegiate athletic team for at least one season, 0 otherwise

$lnEX_i$ = the natural log of the number of full courses that the ith student has completed in college.

Assuming that GPA_i is the dependent variable, which independent variables would you choose? Before you answer, think through the possibilities carefully. What are the expected signs of each of the coefficients? How strong is the theory behind each variable? Which variables seem obviously important? Which variables seem potentially irrelevant or redundant? Are there any other variables that you wish your friend had collected?

To get the most out of this example, you should take the time to *write down* the exact specification that you would run:

$$GPA_i = f(?, ?, ?, ?, ?) + \epsilon$$

It's hard for most beginning econometricians to avoid the temptation of including *all* the above variables in a GPA equation and then dropping any variables that have insignificant t-scores. Even though we mentioned in the previous section that such a specification search procedure will result in biased coefficient estimates, most beginners don't trust their own judgment and tend to include too many variables. With this warning in mind, do you want to make any changes in our proposed specification?

No? OK, let's compare notes. We believe that grades are a function of a student's ability, how hard the student works, and the student's experience taking college courses. Consequently, our specification would be:

$$GPA_i = f(\overset{+}{HGPA_i}, \overset{+}{HRS_i}, \overset{+}{lnEX_i}) + \epsilon$$

We can already hear you complaining! What about SATs, you say? Everyone knows they're important. How about jocks and Greeks? Don't they have lower GPAs? Don't prep schools grade harder and prepare students better than public high schools?

Before we answer, it's important to note that we think of specification choice as choosing which variables to *include,* not which variables to *exclude.* That is, we don't assume automatically that a given variable should be included in an equation simply because we can't think of a good reason for dropping it.

Given that, however, why did we choose the variables we did? First, we think that the best predictor of a student's college GPA is his or her high school GPA. We have a hunch that once you know HGPA, SATs are redundant, at least at a liberal arts college where there are few multiple choice tests. In addition, we're concerned that possible racial and gender bias in the SAT test makes it a questionable measure of academic potential, but we recognize that we could be wrong on this issue.

As for the other variables, we're more confident. For example, we feel that once we know how many hours a week a student spends studying, we couldn't care less what that student does with the rest of his or her time, so JOCK and GREK are superfluous once HRS is included. Finally, while we recognize that some private schools are superb and that some public schools are not, we'd guess that PRIV is irrelevant; it probably has only a minor effect.

If we estimate this specification on the 25 students, we obtain:

$$\widehat{GPA_i} = -0.26 + 0.49HGPA_i + 0.06HRS_i + 0.42lnEX_i \quad (6.24)$$
$$(0.21) \qquad (0.02) \qquad (0.14)$$
$$t = 2.33 \qquad 3.00 \qquad 3.00$$
$$n = 25 \quad \overline{R}^2 = .585 \quad F = 12.3$$

Since we prefer this specification on theoretical grounds, since the overall fit seems reasonable, and since each coefficient meets our expectations in terms of sign, size, and significance, we consider this an acceptable equation. The only circumstance under which we'd consider estimating a second specification would be if we had theoretical reasons to believe that we had omitted a relevant variable. The only variable that might meet this description is SAT_i (which we prefer to the individual MSAT and VSAT):

$$\widehat{GPA_i} = -0.92 + 0.47HGPA_i + 0.05HRS_i \quad (6.25)$$
$$(0.22) \qquad (0.02)$$
$$t = 2.12 \qquad 2.50$$
$$+ 0.44lnEX_i \quad + 0.00060SAT_i$$
$$(0.14) \qquad (0.00064)$$
$$t = 3.12 \qquad 0.93$$
$$n = 25 \quad \overline{R}^2 = .583 \quad F = 9.4$$

Let's use our four specification criteria to compare Equations 6.24 and 6.25:

1. *Theory:* As discussed above, the theoretical validity of SAT tests is a matter of some academic controversy, but they still are one of the most-cited measures of academic potential in this country.

2. t-*Test:* The coefficient of SAT is positive, as we'd expect, but it's not significantly different from zero.

3. $\overline{R}^2$: As you'd expect (since SAT's t-score is under one), $\overline{R}^2$ falls slightly when SAT is added.

4. *Bias:* None of the estimated slope coefficients changes significantly when SAT is added, though some of the t-scores do change because of the increase in the $SE(\hat{\beta})s$ caused by the addition of SAT.

Thus, the statistical criteria support our theoretical contention that SAT is irrelevant.

Finally, it's important to recognize that different researchers could come up with different final equations on this topic. A researcher whose prior expectation was that SAT unambiguously belonged in the equation would have estimated Equation 6.25 and accepted that equation without bothering to estimate Equation 6.24.

6.7   Summary

1. The omission of a variable from an equation will cause bias in the estimates of the remaining coefficients to the extent that the omitted variable is correlated with included variables.

2. The bias to be expected from leaving a variable out of an equation equals the coefficient of the excluded variable times a function of the simple correlation coefficient between the excluded variable and the included variable in question.

3. Including a variable in an equation in which it is actually irrelevant does not cause bias, but it will usually increase the variances of the included variables' estimated coefficients, thus lowering their t-values and lowering $\overline{R}^2$.

4. Four useful criteria for the inclusion of a variable in an equation are:
   a. Theory
   b. *t*-Test
   c. $\overline{R}^2$
   d. Bias

5. Theory, not statistical fit, should be the most important criterion for the inclusion of a variable in a regression equation. To do otherwise runs the risk of producing incorrect and/or disbelieved results. For example, stepwise regression routines will generally give biased esti-

mates and will almost always have test statistics that will not follow the distribution necessary to use standard t-tables.

Exercises

(Answers to even-numbered questions are in Appendix A.)

1. Write the meaning of each of the following terms without referring to the book (or your notes), and compare your definition with the version in the text for each:
   a. omitted variable
   b. irrelevant variable
   c. specification bias
   d. stepwise regression
   e. sequential specification search
   f. specification error
   g. the four specification criteria
   h. expected bias
   i. lagged independent variable

2. For each of the following situations, determine the *sign* (and if possible comment on the likely size) of the expected bias introduced by omitting a variable:
   a. In an equation for the demand for peanut butter, the impact on the coefficient of disposable income of omitting the price of peanut butter variable. (*Hint:* Start by hypothesizing signs.)
   b. In an earnings equation for workers, the impact on the coefficient of experience of omitting the variable for age.
   c. In a production function for airplanes, the impact on the coefficient of labor of omitting the capital variable.
   d. In an equation for daily attendance at outdoor concerts, the impact on the coefficient of the weekend dummy variable (1 = weekend) of omitting a variable that measures the probability of precipitation at concert time.

3. Consider the following annual model of the death rate (per million population) due to coronary heart disease in the United States (Y_t):

$$\hat{Y}_t = 140 + 10.0C_t + 4.0E_t - 1.0M_t$$
$$(2.5) \quad (1.0) \quad (0.5)$$
$$t = 4.0 \quad\quad 4.0 \quad -2.0$$
$$n = 31 \ (1950-1980) \quad \overline{R}^2 = .678$$

where: C_t = per capita cigarette consumption (pounds of to-
bacco) in year t

E_t = per capita consumption of edible saturated fats
(pounds of butter, margarine, and lard) in year t

M_t = per capita consumption of meat (pounds) in year t

a. Create and test appropriate null hypotheses at the 10 percent level.
What, if anything, seems to be wrong with the estimated coefficient
of M?

b. The most likely cause of a coefficient that is significant in the unexpected direction is omitted variable bias. Which of the following
variables could possibly be an omitted variable that is causing $\hat{\beta}_M$'s
unexpected sign? Explain.

B_t = per capita consumption of hard liquor (gallons) in year t

F_t = the average fat content (percentage) of the meat that was
consumed in year t

W_t = per capita consumption of wine and beer (gallons) in year t

R_t = per capita number of miles run in year t

H_t = per capita open-heart surgeries in year t

O_t = per capita amount of oat bran eaten in year t

c. If you had to choose one variable to add to the equation, what
would it be? Explain your answer. (*Hint:* You're not limited to the
variables listed in part b above.)

4. Assume that you've been hired by the surgeon general of the United
States to study the determinants of smoking behavior and that you estimate the following cross-sectional model based on data from 1988
for all 50 states (standard errors in parentheses)[12]:

$$\hat{C}_i = 100 - 9.0E_i + 1.0I_i - 0.04T_i - 3.0V_i + 1.5R_i \quad (6.26)$$
$$\phantom{\hat{C}_i = 100}\;(3.0)\quad(1.0)\quad(0.04)\quad(1.0)\quad(0.5)$$
$$t = -3.0\quad\;\;1.0\quad-1.0\quad-3.0\quad\;\;3.0$$
$$\overline{R}^2 = .50 \quad n = 50 \text{ (states)}$$

where: C_i = the number of cigarettes consumed per day per person in the ith state

---

12. This question is generalized from a number of similar studies, including John A. Bishop
and Jang H. Yoo, "The Impact of the Health Scare, Excise Taxes, and Advertising on Cigarette
Demand and Supply," *Southern Economic Journal*, January 1988, pp. 402–411.

E_i = the average years of education for persons over 21 in the ith state

I_i = the average income in the ith state (thousands of dollars)

T_i = the tax per package of cigarettes in the ith state (cents)

V_i = the number of video ads against smoking aired on the three major networks in the ith state.

R_i = the number of radio ads against smoking aired on the five largest radio networks in the ith state

a. Develop and test (at the 5 percent level) appropriate hypotheses for the coefficients of the variables in this equation.

b. Do you appear to have any irrelevant variables? Do you appear to have any omitted variables? Explain your answer.

c. Let's assume that your answer to part b was yes to both. Which problem is more important to solve first, irrelevant variables or omitted variables? Why?

d. One of the purposes of running the equation was to determine the effectiveness of antismoking advertising on television and radio. What is your conclusion?

e. The surgeon general decides that tax rates are irrelevant to cigarette smoking and orders you to drop them from your equation. Given the following results, use our four specification criteria to decide whether you agree with her conclusion. Carefully explain your reasoning (standard errors in parentheses).

$$\hat{C}_i = 101 - 9.1E_i + 1.0I_i - 3.5V_i + 1.6R_i \qquad (6.27)$$
$$(3.0) \quad (0.9) \quad (1.0) \quad (0.5)$$
$$\overline{R}^2 = .50 \quad n = 50 \text{ (states)}$$

5. The data set in Table 6.2 is the one that was used to estimate the chicken demand examples of Sections 6.1.2 and 6.2.2.

a. Use these data to reproduce the specifications in the chapter. (file-name CHICK6)

b. Find data for the price of another substitute for chicken and add that variable to your version of Equation 6.8. Analyze your results. In particular, apply the four criteria for the inclusion of a variable to determine whether the price of the substitute is an irrelevant or previously was an omitted variable.

6. You have been retained by the "Expressive Expresso" company to help them decide where to build their next "Expressive Expresso" store.

TABLE 6.2 DATA FOR THE CHICKEN DEMAND EQUATION

Year	Y	PC	PB	YD
1951	21.8	25.0	28.7	14.86
1952	22.1	22.1	24.3	15.39
1953	21.9	22.1	16.3	16.11
1954	22.8	16.8	16.0	16.19
1955	21.3	18.6	15.6	17.04
1956	24.4	16.0	14.9	17.87
1957	25.4	13.7	17.2	18.51
1958	28.0	14.0	21.9	18.84
1959	28.7	11.0	22.6	19.68
1960	28.0	12.2	20.4	20.14
1961	30.0	10.1	20.2	20.67
1962	30.0	10.2	21.3	21.56
1963	30.7	10.0	19.9	22.30
1964	31.1	9.2	18.0	23.89
1965	33.4	8.9	19.9	25.47
1966	35.5	9.7	22.2	27.20
1967	36.3	7.9	22.3	28.83
1968	36.4	8.2	23.4	31.02
1969	38.1	9.7	26.2	33.03
1970	40.1	9.1	27.1	35.51
1971	40.1	7.7	29.0	38.12
1972	41.5	9.0	33.5	40.82
1973	39.7	15.1	42.8	45.63
1974	39.6	9.7	35.6	49.42
1975	38.8	9.9	32.3	53.83
1976	41.9	12.9	33.7	58.57
1977	42.7	12.0	34.5	63.84
1978	44.8	12.4	48.5	71.24
1979	48.3	13.9	66.1	78.90
1980	48.4	11.0	62.4	86.97
1981	50.4	11.1	58.6	96.03
1982	51.5	10.3	56.7	101.33
1983	52.6	12.7	55.5	107.77
1984	54.5	15.9	57.3	119.14
1985	56.3	14.8	53.7	125.94
1986	58.1	12.5	52.6	132.13
1987	61.9	11.0	61.1	138.53
1988	63.8	9.2	66.6	148.84
1989	67.5	14.9	69.5	157.74
1990	70.4	9.3	74.6	166.89
1991	73.5	7.1	72.7	171.82
1992	76.8	8.6	71.3	180.32
1993	78.9	10.0	72.6	185.64
1994	80.5	7.6	66.7	192.59

Sources: U.S. Department of Agriculture. *Agricultural Statistics;* U.S. Bureau of the Census. *Historical Statistics of the United States,* U.S. Bureau of the Census. *Statistical Abstract of the United States.*
Note: filename CHICK6

You decide to run a regression on the sales of the 30 existing "Expressive Expresso" stores as a function of the characteristics of the locations they are in and then use the equation to predict the sales at the various locations you are considering for the newest store. You end up estimating (standard errors in parentheses):

$$\hat{Y}_i = 30 + 0.1X_{1i} + 0.01X_{2i} + 10.0X_{3i} + 3.0X_{4i}$$
$$\qquad\quad (0.02)\quad (0.01)\qquad (1.0)\qquad (1.0)$$

where: Y_i = average daily sales (in hundreds of dollars) of the ith store
X_{1i} = the number of cars that pass the ith location per hour
X_{2i} = average income in the area of the ith store
X_{3i} = the number of tables in the ith store
X_{4i} = the number of competing shops in the area of the ith store

a. Hypothesize expected signs, calculate the correct t-scores, and test the significance at the 1 percent level for each of the coefficients.
b. What problems appear to exist in the equation? What evidence of these problems do you have?
c. What suggestions would you make for a possible second run of this admittedly hypothetical equation? (*Hint:* Before recommending the inclusion of a potentially left-out variable, consider whether the exclusion of the variable could possibly have caused any observed bias.)

7. Discuss the topic of specification searches with various members of your econometrics class. What is so wrong with not mentioning previous (probably incorrect) estimates? Why should readers be suspicious when researchers attempt to find results that support their hypotheses? Who would try to do the opposite? Do these concerns have any meaning in the world of business? In particular, if you're not trying to publish a paper, couldn't you use any specification search techniques you want to find the best equation?

8. Suppose you run a regression explaining the number of hamburgers that the campus fast-food store (let's call it "The Cooler") sells per day as a function of the price of their hamburgers (in dollars), the weather (in degrees F), the price of hamburgers at a national chain nearby (also in dollars), and the number of students (in thousands) on campus that day. Assume that The Cooler stays open whether or not

school is in session (for staff, etc.). Unfortunately, a lightning bolt strikes the computer and wipes out all the memory and you cannot tell which independent variable is which! Given the following regression results (standard errors in parentheses):

$$\hat{Y}_i = 10.6 + 28.4X_{1i} + 12.7X_{2i} + 0.61X_{3i} - 5.9X_{4i}$$
$$(2.6) \qquad (6.3) \qquad (0.61) \qquad (5.9)$$
$$\bar{R}^2 = .63 \quad n = 35$$

a. Attempt to identify which result corresponds to which variable.
b. Explain your reasoning for part a above.
c. Develop and test hypotheses about the coefficients assuming that your answer to part a is correct. What suggestions would you have for changes in the equation for a rerun when the computer is back up again?

9. Most of the examples in the text so far have been demand-side equations or production functions, but economists often also have to quantify supply-side equations that are not true production functions. These equations attempt to explain the production of a product (for example, Brazilian coffee) as a function of the price of the product and various other attributes of the market that might have an impact on the total output of growers.
a. What sign would you expect the coefficient of price to have in a supply-side equation? Why?
b. What other variables can you think of that might be important in a supply-side equation?
c. Many agricultural decisions are made months (if not a full year or more) before the results of those decisions appear in the market. How would you adjust your hypothesized equation to take account of these lags?
d. Given all the above, carefully specify the exact equation you would use to attempt to explain Brazilian coffee production. Be sure to hypothesize the expected signs, be specific with respect to lags, and try to make sure you have not omitted an important independent variable.

10. If you think about the previous question, you'll realize that the *same* dependent variable (quantity of Brazilian coffee) can have different expected signs for the coefficient of the *same* independent variable (the price of Brazilian coffee), depending on what other variables are in the regression.

a. How is this possible? That is, how is it possible to expect different signs in demand-side equations from what you would expect in supply-side ones?

b. Given that we will not discuss how to estimate simultaneous equations until Chapter 14, what can be done to avoid the "simultaneity bias" of getting the price coefficient from the demand equation in the supply equation and vice versa?

c. What can you do to systematically ensure that you do not have supply-side variables in your demand equation or demand-side variables in your supply equation?

11. You've been hired by "Indo," the new Indonesian automobile manufacturer, to build a model of U.S. car prices in order to help the company undercut our prices. Allowing Friedmaniac zeal to overwhelm any patriotic urges, you build the following model of the price of 35 different American-made 1996 U.S. sedans (standard errors in parentheses):

$$\text{Model A: } \hat{P}_i = 3.0 + 0.28W_i + 1.2T_i + 5.8C_i + 0.20L_i$$
$$\qquad\qquad (0.07) \quad (0.4) \quad (2.9) \quad (0.20)$$
$$\overline{R}^2 = .92$$

where: P_i = the list price of the ith car (thousands of dollars)
W_i = the weight of the ith car (hundreds of pounds)
T_i = a dummy equal to 1 if the ith car has an automatic transmission, 0 otherwise
C_i = a dummy equal to 1 if the ith car has cruise control, 0 otherwise
L_i = the size of the engine of the ith car (in liters)

a. Your firm's pricing expert hypothesizes positive signs for all the slope coefficients in Model A. Test her expectations at the 95 percent level of confidence.

b. What econometric problems appear to exist in Model A? In particular, does the size of the coefficient of C cause any concern? Why? What could be the problem?

c. You decide to test the possibility that L is an irrelevant variable by dropping it and rerunning the equation, obtaining Model T below. Which model to you prefer? Why? (*Hint:* Be sure to use our four specification criteria.)

d. In answering part c, you surely noticed that the $\overline{R}^2$ figures were identical. Did this surprise you? Why or why not?

$$\text{Model T: } \hat{P} = 18 + 0.29W_i + 1.2T_i + 5.9C_i$$
$$\qquad\qquad (0.07) \quad\;\; (0.03) \;\; (2.9)$$
$$\overline{R}^2 = .92$$

12. Determine the sign (and, if possible, comment on the likely size) of the bias introduced by leaving a variable out of an equation in each of the following cases:
    a. In an annual equation for corn yields per acre (in year t), the impact on the coefficient of rainfall in year t of omitting average temperature that year. (*Hint:* Drought and cold weather both hurt corn yields.)
    b. In an equation for daily attendance at Los Angeles Lakers' home basketball games, the impact on the coefficient of the winning percentage of the opponent (as of the game in question) of omitting a dummy variable that equals 1 if the opponent's team includes a superstar.
    c. In an equation for annual consumption of apples in the United States, the impact on the coefficient of the price of bananas of omitting the price of oranges.
    d. In an equation for student grades on the first midterm in this class, the impact on the coefficient of total hours studied (for the test) of omitting hours slept the night before the test.

13. Suppose that you run a regression to determine whether gender or race has any significant impact on scores on a test of the economic understanding of children.[13] You model the score of the ith student on the test of elementary economics (S_i) as a function of the composite score on the Iowa Tests of Basic Skills of the ith student, a dummy variable equal to 1 if the ith student is female (0 otherwise), the average number of years of education of the parents of the ith student, and a dummy variable equal to 1 if the ith student is nonwhite (0 otherwise). Unfortunately, a rainstorm floods the computer center and makes it impossible to read the part of the computer output that identifies which variable is which. All you know is that the regression results are (standard errors in parentheses):

$$\hat{S}_i = 5.7 - 0.63X_{1i} - 0.22X_{2i} + 0.16X_{3i} + 0.12X_{4i}$$
$$\qquad\;\; (0.63) \qquad (0.88) \qquad (0.08) \qquad (0.01)$$
$$n = 24 \quad \overline{R}^2 = .54$$

---

13. These results have been jiggled to meet the needs of this question, but this research actually was done. See Stephen Buckles and Vera Freeman, "Male-Female Differences in the Stock and Flow of Economic Knowledge," *Review of Economics and Statistics*, May 1983, pp. 355–357.

a. Attempt to identify which result corresponds to which variable. Be specific.
b. Explain the reasoning behind your answer to part a above.
c. Assuming that your answer is correct, create and test appropriate hypotheses (at the 5 percent level) and come to conclusions about the effects of gender and race on the test scores of this particular sample.
d. Did you use a one-tailed or two-tailed test in part c above? Why?

14. William Sander[14] estimated a 50-state cross-sectional model of the farm divorce rate as part of an effort to determine whether the national trend toward more divorces could be attributed in part to increases in the earning ability of women. His equation was (t-scores in parentheses):

$$\hat{Y}_i = -4.1 + 0.003P_i + 0.06L_i - 0.002A_i + 0.76N_i$$
$$\qquad\qquad (3.3) \qquad (1.5) \quad (-0.6) \qquad (13.5)$$

where: Y_i = the farm divorce rate in the ith state
P_i = the population density of the ith state
L_i = the labor force participation of farm women in the ith state
A_i = farm assets held by women in the ith state
N_i = the rural nonfarm divorce rate in that state

a. Develop and test hypotheses about the slope coefficients of Sander's equation at the 5 percent level.
b. What (if any) econometric problems (out of omitted variables and irrelevant variables) appear to exist in this equation? Justify your answer.
c. What one specification change in this equation would you suggest? Be specific.
d. Use our four specification criteria to decide whether you believe L is an irrelevant variable. The equation without L (t-scores again in parentheses) was:

$$\hat{Y}_i = -2.5 + 0.004P_i - 0.004A_i + 0.79N_i$$
$$\qquad\qquad (4.3) \quad (-1.3) \qquad (14.8)$$

(*Hint:* We don't provide $\bar{R}^2$ for these equations, but you can determine whether it went up or down anyway. How?)

14. William Sander, "Women, Work, and Divorce," *The American Economic Review*, June 1985, pp. 519–523.

15. Look back again at Exercise 16 in Chapter 5, the equation on international price discrimination in pharmaceuticals. In that cross-sectional study, Schut and VanBergeijk estimated two equations in addition to the one cited in the exercise.[15] These two equations tested the possibility that CV_i, total volume of consumption of pharmaceuticals in the ith country, and N_i, the population of the ith country, belonged in the original equation, Equation 5.17, repeated here:

$$\hat{P}_i = 38.22 + 1.43GDPN_i - 0.6CVN_i + 7.31PP_i \qquad (5.17)$$
$$\phantom{\hat{P}_i = 38.22 + } (0.21) \qquad\quad (0.22) \qquad (6.12)$$
$$t = \qquad\quad 6.69 \qquad\qquad -2.66 \qquad 1.19$$

$$-15.63DPC_i - 11.38IPC_i$$
$$(6.93) \qquad\quad (7.16)$$
$$t = \qquad -2.25 \qquad\quad -1.59$$

$$n = 32 \text{ (national 1975 data)} \quad \bar{R}^2 = .775 \quad F = 22.35$$

where: P_i = the pharmaceutical price level in the ith country divided by that of the United States

$GDPN_i$ = per capita domestic product in the ith country divided by that of the United States

CVN_i = per capita volume of consumption of pharmaceuticals in the ith country divided by that of the United States

PP_i = a dummy variable equal to 1 if patents for pharmaceutical products are recognized in the ith country and equal to 0 otherwise

DPC_i = a dummy variable equal to 1 if the ith country applied strict price controls and 0 otherwise

IPC_i = a dummy variable equal to 1 if the ith country encouraged price competition and 0 otherwise

a. Using EViews (or your own computer program) and datafile DRUG5 (or Table 5.1), estimate these two equations. That is, estimate:

i. Equation 5.17 with CV_i added, and

ii. Equation 5.17 with N_i added

---

15. Frederick T. Schut and Peter A. G. VanBergeijk, "International Price Discrimination: The Pharmaceutical Industry," *World Development*, 1986, pp. 1141–1150.

b. Use our four specification criteria to determine whether CV and N are irrelevant or omitted variables. (*Hint:* The authors expected that prices would be lower if market size was larger because of possible economies of scale and/or enhanced competition.)

c. Why didn't the authors run Equation 5.17 with *both* CV and N included? (*Hint:* While you can estimate this equation yourself, you don't have to do so to answer the question.)

d. Why do you think that the authors reported all three estimated specifications in their results when they thought that Equation 5.17 was the best?

6.8   Appendix: Additional Specification Criteria

So far in this chapter, we've suggested four criteria for choosing the independent variables (economic theory, $\overline{R}^2$, the *t*-test, and possible bias in the coefficients). Sometimes, however, these criteria don't provide enough information for a researcher to feel confident that a given specification is best. For instance, there can be two different specifications that both have excellent theoretical underpinnings. In such a situation, many econometricians use additional, often more formal, specification criteria to provide comparisons of the properties of the alternative estimated equations.

The use of formal specification criteria is not without problems, however. First, no test, no matter how sophisticated, can "prove" that a particular specification is the true one. The use of specification criteria, therefore, must be tempered with a healthy dose of economic theory and common sense. A second problem is that more than 20 such criteria have been proposed; how do we decide which one(s) to use? Because many of these criteria overlap with one another or have varying levels of complexity, a choice between the alternatives is a matter of personal preference.

In this section, we'll describe the use of three of the most popular specification criteria, J. B. Ramsey's RESET test, Akaike's Information Criterion, and the Schwarz Criterion. Our inclusion of just these techniques does not imply that other tests and criteria are not appropriate or useful. Indeed, the reader will find that most other formal specification criteria have quite a bit in common with at least one of the techniques that we include. We think that you'll be more able to use and understand other formal specification criteria[16] once you've mastered these three.

---

16. In particular, the likelihood ratio test, versions of which will be covered in Section 12.2, can be used as a specification test. For an introductory level summary of six other specification criteria, see Ramu Ramanathan, *Introductory Econometrics* (Fort Worth: Harcourt Brace Jovanovich, 1998, pp. 164–166).

6.8.1   Ramsey's Regression Specification Error Test (RESET)

One of the most-used formal specification tests other than $\bar{R}^2$ is the Ramsey Regression Specification Test (RESET).[17] The **Ramsey RESET test** is a general test that determines the likelihood of an omitted variable or some other specification error by measuring whether the fit of a given equation can be significantly improved by the addition of $\hat{Y}^2$, $\hat{Y}^3$, and $\hat{Y}^4$ terms.

What's the intuition behind RESET? The additional terms act as proxies for any possible (unknown) omitted variables or incorrect functional forms. If the proxies can be shown by the F-test to have improved the overall fit of the original equation, then we have evidence that there is some sort of specification error in our equation. As we'll learn in Chapter 7, the $\hat{Y}^2$, $\hat{Y}^3$, and $\hat{Y}^4$ terms form a *polynomial* functional form. Such a polynomial is a powerful curve-fitting device that has a good chance of acting as a proxy for a specification error if one exists. If there is no specification error, then we'd expect the coefficients of the added terms to be insignificantly different from zero because there is nothing for them to act as a proxy for.

The Ramsey RESET test involves three steps:

1. Estimate the equation to be tested using OLS:

$$\hat{Y}_i = \hat{\beta}_0 + \hat{\beta}_1 X_{1i} + \hat{\beta}_2 X_{2i} \qquad (6.28)$$

2. Take the $\hat{Y}_i$ values from Equation 6.28 and create $\hat{Y}_i^2$, $\hat{Y}_i^3$, and $\hat{Y}_i^4$ terms. Then add these terms to Equation 6.28 as additional explanatory variables and estimate the new equation with OLS:

$$Y_i = \beta_0 + \beta_1 X_{1i} + \beta_2 X_{2i} + \beta_3 \hat{Y}_i^2 + \beta_4 \hat{Y}_i^3 + \beta_5 \hat{Y}_i^4 + \epsilon_i \qquad (6.29)$$

3. Compare the fits of Equations 6.28 and 6.29 using the F-test. If the two equations are significantly different in overall fit, we can conclude that it's likely that equation 6.28 is misspecified.

While the Ramsey RESET test is fairly easy to use, it does little more than signal *when* a major specification error might exist. If you encounter a significant Ramsey RESET test, then you face the daunting task of figuring out exactly *what* the error is! Thus, the test often ends up being more useful in "supporting" (technically, not refuting) a researcher's contention that a given

---

17. J. B. Ramsey, "Tests for Specification Errors in Classical Linear Squares Regression Analysis," *Journal of the Royal Statistical Society*, 1969, pp. 350–371.

specification has no major specification errors than it is in helping find an otherwise undiscovered flaw.[18]

As an example of the Ramsey RESET test, let's return to the chicken demand model of this chapter to see if RESET can detect the known specification error (omitting the price of beef) in Equation 6.9. Step one involves running the original equation without PB.

$$\hat{Y}_t = 32.9 - 0.70PC_t + 0.27YD_t \qquad (6.9)$$
$$(0.08) \qquad (0.01)$$
$$t = -8.33 \qquad 45.91$$
$$\overline{R}^2 = .984 \quad n = 44 \text{ (annual 1951}-1994) \quad RSS = 185.66$$

For step two, we take $\hat{Y}_t$ from Equation 6.9, calculate $\hat{Y}_t^2$, $\hat{Y}_t^3$, and $\hat{Y}_t^4$, and then reestimate Equation 6.9 with the three new terms added in:

$$Y_t = 23.80 - 0.59PC_t + 0.36YD_t + 0.02\hat{Y}_t^2 \qquad (6.30)$$
$$(1.71) \qquad (0.71) \qquad (0.08)$$
$$t = -0.34 \qquad 0.50 \qquad +0.29$$

$$-0.007\hat{Y}_t^3 + 0.000055\hat{Y}_t^4 + e_t$$
$$(0.0011) \quad (0.000054)$$
$$t = -0.68 \qquad +1.02$$
$$\overline{R}^2 = .987 \quad n = 44 \text{ (annual 1951}-1994) \quad RSS = 138.41$$

In step three, we compare the fits of the two equations by using the *F*-test. Specifically, we test the hypothesis that the coefficients of all three of the added terms are equal to zero:

$$H_0: \hat{\beta}_3 = \hat{\beta}_4 = \hat{\beta}_5 = 0$$
$$H_A: \text{otherwise}$$

The appropriate F-statistic to use is one that is presented in more detail in Section 7.7:

$$F = \frac{(RSS_M - RSS)/M}{RSS/(n - K - 1)} \qquad (6.31)$$

---

18. The particular version of the Ramsey RESET test we describe in this section is only one of a number of possible formulations of the test. For example, some researchers delete the $\hat{Y}^4$ term from Equation 6.29. In addition, versions of the Ramsey RESET test are useful in testing for functional form errors (to be described in Chapter 7) and serial correlation (to be described in Chapter 9).

where RSS_M is the residual sum of squares from the restricted equation (Equation 6.9), RSS is the residual sum of squares from the unrestricted equation (Equation 6.30), M is the number of restrictions (3), and $(n - K - 1)$ is the number of degrees of freedom in the unrestricted equation (38):

$$F = \frac{(185.66 - 138.41)/3}{138.41/38} = 4.32$$

The critical F-value to use, 2.86, is found in Statistical Table B-2 at the 5 percent level of significance with 3 numerator and 38 denominator[19] degrees of freedom. Since 17.23 is greater than 2.86, we can reject the null hypothesis that the coefficients of the added variables are jointly zero, allowing us to conclude that there is indeed a specification error in Equation 6.9. Such a conclusion is no surprise, since we know that the price of beef was left out of the equation. Note, however, that the Ramsey RESET test tells us only that a specification error is likely to exist in Equation 6.9; it does not specify the details of that error.

6.8.2 Akaike's Information Criterion and the Schwarz Criterion

A second category of formal specification criteria involves adjusting the summed squared residuals (RSS) by one factor or another to create an index of the fit of an equation. The most popular criterion of this type is $\overline{R}^2$, but a number of interesting alternatives have been proposed.

Akaike's Information Criterion (AIC) and the *Schwarz Criterion* (SC) are methods of comparing alternative specifications by adjusting RSS for the sample size (n) and the number of dependent variables (K).[20] These criteria can be used to augment our four basic specification criteria when we try to decide if the improved fit caused by an additional variable is worth the decreased degrees of freedom and increased complexity caused by the addition. Their equations are:

$$AIC = Log(RSS/n) + 2(K + 1)/n \qquad (6.32)$$

$$SC = Log(RSS/n) + Log(n)(K + 1)/n \qquad (6.33)$$

---

19. Statistical Table B-2 does not list 38 numerator degrees of freedom, so, as mentioned in footnote 15 of Chapter 5, you must interpolate between 30 and 40 numerator degrees of freedom to get the answer. In this case, some researchers would note that the calculated F-value exceeds both critical F-values and wouldn't bother with the interpolation. If you'd like more information about this kind of F-test, see Section 7.7.

20. H. Akaike, "Likelihood of a Model and Information Criteria," *Journal of Econometrics*, 1981, pp. 3–14 and G. Schwarz, "Estimating the Dimension of a Model," *The Annals of Statistics*, 1978, pp. 461–464.

To use AIC and SC, estimate two alternative specifications and calculate AIC and SC for each equation. The lower AIC or SC are, the better the specification. Note that even though the two criteria were developed independently to maximize different object functions, their equations are quite similar. Both criteria tend to penalize the addition of another explanatory variable more than $\overline{R}^2$ does. As a result, AIC and SC will quite often[21] be minimized by an equation with fewer independent variables than the ones that maximize $\overline{R}^2$.

Let's apply Akaike's Information Criterion and the Schwarz Criterion to the same chicken demand example we used for Ramsey's RESET. To see if AIC and/or SC can detect the specification error we already know exists in Equation 6.9 (the omission of the price of beef), we need to calculate AIC and SC for equations with and without the price of beef. The equation with the lower AIC and SC values will, other things being equal, be our preferred specification.

The original chicken demand model, Equation 6.8, was:

$$\hat{Y}_t = 31.5 - 0.73PC_t + 0.11PB_t + 0.23YD_t \qquad (6.8)$$
$$(0.08) \quad (0.05) \quad (0.02)$$
$$t = -9.12 \quad 2.50 \quad 14.22$$
$$\overline{R}^2 = .986 \quad n = 44 \text{ (annual } 1951-1994) \quad RSS = 160.59$$

Plugging the numbers from Equation 6.8 into Equations 6.32 and 6.33, AIC and PC can be seen to be:

$$AIC = Log(160.59/44) + 2(4)/44 = 1.48$$

$$SC = Log(160.59/44) + Log(44)4/44 = 1.64$$

Equation 6.9 (repeated in Section 6.8.1), which omits the price of beef, has an RSS of 185.66 with K = 2. Thus:

$$AIC = Log(185.66/44) + 2(3)/44 = 1.58$$

$$SC = Log(185.66/44) + Log(44)3/44 = 1.70$$

For AIC, 1.48 < 1.58, and for SC, 1.64 < 1.70, so both Akaike's Information

---

21. Using a Monte Carlo study, Judge *et al.* showed that (given specific simplifying assumptions) a specification chosen by maximizing $\overline{R}^2$ is over 50 percent more likely to include an irrelevant variable than is one chosen by minimizing AIC or SC. See George C. Judge, R. Carter Hill, W. E. Griffiths, Helmut Lutkepohl, and Tsoung-Chao Lee, *Introduction to the Theory and Practice of Econometrics* (New York: Wiley, 1988), pp. 849–850. At the same time, minimizing AIC or SC will omit a relevant variable more frequently than will maximizing $\overline{R}^2$.

Criterion and the Schwarz Criterion provide evidence that Equation 6.8 is preferable to Equation 6.9. That is, the price of beef appears to belong in the equation. In practice, these calculations may not be necessary because AIC and SC are automatically calculated by some regression software packages, including EViews.

As it turns out, then, all three new specification criteria indicate the presence of a specification error when we leave the price of beef out of the equation. This result is not surprising, since we purposely left out a theoretically justified variable, but it provides an example of how useful these criteria could be when we're less than sure about the underlying theory.

Note that AIC and SC require the researcher to come up with a particular alternative specification, whereas Ramsey's RESET does not. Such a distinction makes RESET easier to use, but it makes AIC and SC more informative if a specification error is found. Thus our additional specification criteria serve different purposes. RESET is most useful as a general test of the existence of a specification error, whereas AIC and SC are more useful as means of comparing two or more alternative specifications.

Specification: Choosing a Functional Form

Even after you've chosen your independent variables, the job of specifying the equation is not over. The next step is to choose the functional form of the relationship between each independent variable and the dependent variable. Should the equation go through the origin? Do you expect a curve instead of a straight line? Does the effect of a variable peak at some point and then start to decline? An affirmative answer to any of these questions suggests that an equation other than the standard "linear in the variables" model of the previous chapters might be appropriate. Such alternative specifications are important for two reasons: a correct explanatory variable may well appear to be insignificant or to have an unexpected sign if an inappropriate functional form is used, and the consequences of an incorrect functional form for interpretation and forecasting can be severe.

Theoretical considerations usually dictate the form of a regression model. The basic technique involved in deciding on a functional form is to choose the shape that best exemplifies the expected underlying economic or business principles and then to use the mathematical form that produces that shape. To help with that choice, this chapter contains plots of the most commonly used functional forms along with the mathematical equations that correspond to each.

The chapter begins with a brief discussion of the constant term. In particular, we suggest that the constant term should be retained in equations even if theory suggests otherwise, and that estimates of the constant term should not be relied on for inference or analysis. The chapter concludes with a discussion of dummy variables and, in particular, the use of dummy variables to allow the coefficients of independent variables to differ for qualitative conditions (slope dummies).

7.1   The Use and Interpretation of the Constant Term

In the linear regression model, β_0 is the intercept or constant term. It is the expected value of Y when all the explanatory variables (and the error term) equal zero. At times, β_0 is of theoretical importance. Consider, for example, the following cost equation:

$$C_i = \beta_0 + \beta_1 Q_i + \epsilon_i$$

where C_i is the total cost of producing level of output Q_i. The term $\beta_1 Q_i$ represents the total variable cost associated with output level Q_i, and β_0 represents the total fixed cost, defined as the cost when output $Q_i = 0$. Thus, a regression equation might seem useful to a researcher who wanted to determine the relative magnitudes of fixed and variable costs. This would be an example of relying on the constant term for inference.

On the other hand, the product involved might be one for which it is known that there are few if any fixed costs. In such a case, a researcher might want to eliminate the constant term; to do so would conform to the notion of zero fixed costs and would conserve a degree of freedom (which would presumably make the estimate of β_1 more precise). This would be an example of suppressing the constant term.

Neither suppressing the constant term nor relying on it for inference is advisable, however, and reasons for these conclusions are explained in the following sections.

7.1.1   Do Not Suppress the Constant Term

Chapter 4 explained that Assumption II (the error term has an expected value of zero) requires that the constant term absorb any nonzero mean that the observations of the error term might have in a given sample. Thus, suppressing the constant term can lead to a violation of this Classical Assumption. The only time that this assumption would not be violated by leaving out the intercept term is when the mean effect of the unobserved error term (without a constant term) is zero over all the observations.

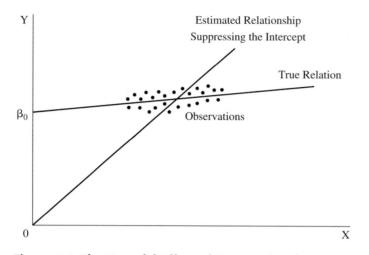

Figure 7.1 The Harmful Effect of Suppressing the Constant Term

If the constant (or intercept) term is suppressed, the estimated regression will go through the origin. Such an effect potentially biases the β̂s and inflates their t-scores. In this particular example, the true slope is close to zero in the range of the sample, but forcing the regression through the origin makes the slope appear to be significantly positive.

The consequence of suppressing the constant term is that the slope coefficient estimates are potentially biased and their t-scores are potentially inflated. This is demonstrated in Figure 7.1. Given the pattern of the X and Y observations, estimating a regression equation with a constant term would likely produce an estimated regression line very similar to the true regression line, which has a constant term (β_0) quite different from zero. The slope of this estimated line is very low, and the t-score of the estimated slope coefficient may be very close to zero, implying that the slope coefficient is statistically insignificant; that is, it does not differ significantly from zero.

However, if the researcher were to suppress the constant term, which implies that the estimated regression line must pass through the origin, then the estimated regression line shown in Figure 7.1 would result. The slope coefficient is now large. That is, it is biased upward compared with the true slope coefficient. Thus, the t-score is biased upward, and it may very well be large enough to indicate that the estimated slope coefficient is statistically significantly positive. Such a conclusion would be incorrect.

It might seem as though it'd make sense to suppress the constant when the true relationship is nonlinear and passes through the origin. However, if this nonlinear relationship were to be approximated by a linear regression line, it would still be important not to suppress the constant term. Over the relevant range of the observations (that is, the sample range), the estimated regression line with the constant suppressed doesn't provide an adequate approximation of the true regression line, compared with an estimated regression equation that includes the constant term. It is a legitimate exercise in applied econometrics to use linear approximations of nonlinear functional forms; suppressing the constant term doesn't permit an accurate approximation over the sample range of observations.

Thus, even though some regression packages allow the constant term to be suppressed (set to zero), the general rule is: *Don't,* even if theory specifically calls for it.

7.1.2   Do Not Rely on Estimates of the Constant Term

It would seem logical that if it's a bad idea to suppress the constant term, then the constant term must be an important analytical tool to use in evaluating the results of the regression. Unfortunately, there are at least two reasons that suggest that the intercept should *not* be relied on for purposes of analysis or inference.

First, the error term is generated, in part, by the omission of a number of marginal independent variables, the mean effect of which is placed in the constant term. The constant term acts as a garbage collector, with an unknown amount of this mean effect being dumped into it. The constant term's estimated coefficient may be different from what it would have been without performing this task, which is done for the sake of the equation as a whole. As a result, it's meaningless to run a t-test on $\hat{\beta}_0$.

Second, the constant term is the value of the dependent variable when all the independent variables and the error term are zero, but the values of variables used for economic analysis are usually positive. Thus, the origin often lies *outside* the range of sample observations (as can be seen in Figure 7.1). Since the constant term is an estimate of Y when the Xs are outside the range of the sample observations, estimates of it are tenuous. Estimating the constant term is like forecasting beyond the range of the sample data, a procedure that inherently contains greater error than within-sample forecasts. For more on this, see Chapter 15.

7.2   Alternative Functional Forms

The choice of a functional form for an equation is a vital part of the specification of that equation. The use of OLS requires that the equation be linear in the coefficients, but there is a wide variety of functional forms that are linear in the coefficients while being nonlinear in the variables. Indeed, in previous chapters we've already used several equations that are linear in the coefficients and nonlinear in the variables, but we've said little about when to use such nonlinear equations. The purpose of the current section is to present the details of the most frequently used functional forms to help the reader develop the ability to choose the correct one when specifying an equation.

The choice of a functional form almost always should be based on the underlying economic or business theory and only rarely on which form provides the best fit. The logical form of the relationship between the dependent variable and the independent variable in question should be compared with the properties of various functional forms, and the one that comes closest to that underlying theory should be chosen. To allow such a comparison, the paragraphs that follow characterize the most frequently used forms in terms of graphs, equations, and examples. In some cases, more than one functional form will be applicable, but usually a choice between alternative functional forms can be made on the basis of the information we'll present.

7.2.1 Linear Form

The linear regression model, used almost exclusively in this text thus far, is based on the assumption that the slope of the relationship between the independent variable and the dependent variable is constant:[1]

$$\frac{\Delta Y}{\Delta X_k} = \beta_k \qquad k = 1, 2, \ldots, K \tag{7.1}$$

The slope is constant, so the **elasticity** of Y with respect to X (the percentage change in the dependent variable caused by a 1 percent increase in the independent variable, holding the other variables in the equation constant) is not constant:

$$\text{Elasticity}_{Y, X_k} = \frac{\Delta Y/Y}{\Delta X_k/X_k} = \frac{\Delta Y}{\Delta X_k} \cdot \frac{X_k}{Y} = \beta_k \frac{X_k}{Y} \tag{7.2}$$

If the hypothesized relationship between Y and X is such that the slope of the relationship can be expected to be constant, then the linear functional form should be used.

Unfortunately, theory frequently predicts only the sign of a relationship and not its functional form. When there is little theory on which to base an

---

1. Throughout this section, the "delta" notation (Δ) will be used instead of the calculus notation to make for easier reading. The specific definition of Δ is "change," and it implies a small change in the variable it is attached to. For example, the term ΔX should be read as "change in X." Since a regression coefficient represents the change in the expected value of Y brought about by a one-unit increase in X (holding constant all other variables in the equation), then $\beta_k = \Delta Y/\Delta X_k$. Those comfortable with calculus should substitute partial derivative signs for Δs.

expected functional form, the linear form should be used until strong evidence that it is inappropriate is found. Unless theory, common sense, or experience justifies using some other functional form, you should use the linear model. Because, in effect, it's being used by default, this model is sometimes referred to as the *default* functional form.

7.2.2 Double-Log Form

The double-log form is the most common functional form that is nonlinear in the variables while still being linear in the coefficients. Indeed, the double-log form is so popular that some researchers use it as their default functional form instead of the linear form. In a **double-log functional form,** the natural log of Y is the dependent variable and the natural log of X is the independent variable:

$$\ln Y = \beta_0 + \beta_1 \ln X_1 + \beta_2 \ln X_2 + \epsilon \tag{7.3}$$

where lnY refers to the natural log of Y, and so on. For a brief review of the meaning of a log, see the boxed feature on pages 204–205.

The double-log form, sometimes called the log-log form, often is used because a researcher has specified that the elasticities of the model are constant and the slopes are not. This is in contrast to the linear model, in which the slopes are constant but the elasticities are not. If an elasticity is assumed to be constant, then:

$$\text{Elasticity}_{Y, X_k} = \frac{\% \, \Delta Y}{\% \, \Delta X_k} = \beta_k = \text{a constant} \tag{7.4}$$

Given the assumption of constant elasticity, the proper form is the **exponential functional form:**

$$Y = e^{\beta_0} X_1^{\beta_1} X_2^{\beta_2} e^{\epsilon} \tag{7.5}$$

where e is the base of the natural logarithm. A logarithmic transformation can be applied to Equation 7.5 by taking the log of both sides of the equation to make it linear in the coefficients. This transformation converts Equation 7.5 into Equation 7.3, the double-log functional form.

In a double-log equation, an individual regression coefficient, for example β_k, can be interpreted as an elasticity because:

$$\beta_k = \frac{\Delta(\ln Y)}{\Delta(\ln X_k)} = \frac{\Delta Y/Y}{\Delta X_k/X_k} = \text{Elasticity}_{Y, X_k} \tag{7.6}$$

Since regression coefficients are constant, the condition that the model have a constant elasticity is met by the double-log equation.

The way to interpret β_k in a double-log equation is that if X_k increases by 1 percent while the other Xs are held constant, then Y will change by β_k percent. Since elasticities are constant, the slopes are now no longer constant.

Figure 7.2 is a graph of the double-log function (ignoring the error term). The panel on the left shows the economic concept of a production function (or an indifference curve). Isoquants from production functions show the

What Is a Log?

What the heck is a log? If e (a constant equal to 2.71828) to the "bth power" produces x, then b is the log of x:

$$b \text{ is the log of x to the base e if:} \quad e^b = x$$

Thus, a **log** (or logarithm) is the exponent to which a given base must be taken in order to produce a specific number. While logs come in more than one variety, we'll use only *natural* logs (logs to the base e) in this text. The symbol for a natural log is "ln," so $\ln(x) = b$ means that $(2.71828)^b = x$ or, more simply,

$$\ln(x) = b \qquad \text{means that} \qquad e^b = x$$

For example, since $e^2 = (2.71828)^2 = 7.389$, we can state that:

$$\ln(7.389) = 2$$

Thus, the natural log of 7.389 is 2! Two is the power of e that produces 7.389. Let's look at some other natural log calculations:

$$
\begin{aligned}
\ln(100) &= 4.605 \\
\ln(1000) &= 6.908 \\
\ln(10000) &= 9.210 \\
\ln(100000) &= 11.513 \\
\ln(1000000) &= 13.816
\end{aligned}
$$

different combinations of factors X_1 and X_2, probably capital and labor, that can be used to produce a given level of output Y. The panel on the right of Figure 7.2 shows the relationship between Y and X_1 that would exist if X_2 were held constant or were not included in the model. Note that the shape of the curve depends on the sign and magnitude of coefficient β_1.

Before using a double-log model, make sure that there are no negative or zero observations in the data set. Since the log of a nonpositive number is undefined, a regression cannot be run. Double-log models should be run

---

Note that as a number goes from 100 to 1,000,000, its natural log goes from 4.605 to only 13.816! Since logs are exponents, even a small change in a log can mean a big change in impact. As a result, logs can be used in econometrics if a researcher wants to reduce the absolute size of the numbers associated with the same actual meaning.

One useful property of natural logs in econometrics is that they make it easier to figure out impacts in percentage terms. If you run a double-log regression, the meaning of a slope coefficient is the percentage change in the dependent variable caused by a one percentage point increase in the independent variable, holding the other independent variables in the equation constant.[2] It's because of this percentage change property that the slope coefficients in a double-log equation are elasticities.

Two other properties of logs will come in handy. First, the natural log of a product of two variables equals the sum of the natural logs of those two variables. Thus,

$$\ln(X \cdot Y) = \ln(X) + \ln(Y)$$

Second, the natural log of a variable that has an exponent equals the exponent times the natural log of the variable:

$$\ln(X^2) = 2 \cdot \ln(X)$$

These two properties combined are what allow us to move from Equation 7.5 in the text to Equation 7.3.

---

2. This is because the derivative of a natural log of X equals dX/X (or $\Delta X/X$), which is the same as percentage change.

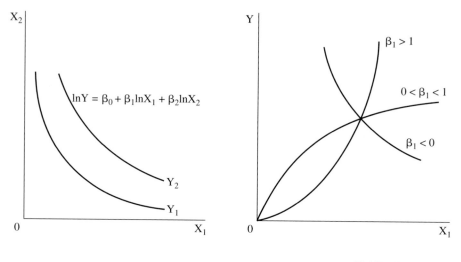

(Holding X_2 constant)

Figure 7.2 Double-Log Functions

Depending on the values of the regression coefficients, the double-log functional form can take on a number of shapes. The left panel shows the use of a double-log function to depict a shape useful in describing the economic concept of a production function (or an indifference curve). The right panel shows various shapes that can be achieved with a double-log function if X_2 is held constant or is not included in the equation.

only when the logged variables take on positive values. Dummy variables, which can take on the value of zero, should not be logged but still can be used in a double-log equation.[3]

7.2.3 Semilog Form

The **semilog functional form** is a variant of the double-log equation in which some but not all of the variables (dependent and independent) are expressed in terms of their natural logs. For example, you might choose to use

---

3. If it is necessary to take the log of a dummy variable, that variable needs to be transformed to avoid the possibility of taking the log of zero. The best way is to redefine the entire dummy variable so that instead of taking on the values of zero and one, it takes on the values of one and e (the base of the natural logarithm). The log of this newly defined dummy then takes on the values of zero and one, and the interpretation of β remains the same as in a linear equation. Such a transformation changes the coefficient value but not the usefulness or theoretical validity of the dummy variable.

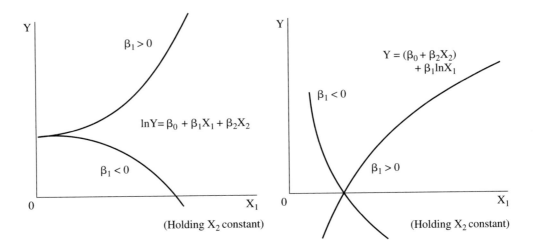

Figure 7.3 Semilog Functions

The semilog functional form on the right (lnX) can be used to depict a situation in which the impact of X_1 on Y is expected to increase at a decreasing rate as X_1 gets bigger as long as β_1 is greater than zero (holding X_2 constant). The semilog functional form on the left (lnY) can be used to depict a situation in which an increase in X_1 causes Y to increase at an increasing rate.

as explanatory variables the logarithms of one or more of the original independent variables as in:

$$Y_i = \beta_0 + \beta_1 \ln X_{1i} + \beta_2 X_{2i} + \epsilon_i \qquad (7.7)$$

In this case, the economic meanings of the two slope coefficients are different, since X_2 is linearly related to Y while X_1 is nonlinearly related to Y.

The right-hand side of Figure 7.3 shows the relationship between Y and X_1 in this kind of semilog equation when X_2 is held constant. Note that if β_1 is greater than zero, the impact of changes in X_1 on Y decreases as X_1 gets bigger. Thus, the semilog functional form should be used when the relationship between X_1 and Y is hypothesized to have this "increasing at a decreasing rate" form.

Applications of the semilog form are quite frequent in economics and business. For example, most consumption functions tend to increase at a decreasing rate past some level of income. These *Engel curves* tend to flatten out because as incomes get higher, a smaller percentage of income goes to consumption and a greater percentage goes to saving. Consumption thus increases at a decreasing rate. If Y is the consumption of an item and X_1 is disposable income (with X_2 standing for all the other independent variables), then the use of the semilog functional form is justified whenever the item's consumption can be expected to tail off as income increases.

For example, recall the chicken consumption Equation 6.8 from the previous chapter.

$$\hat{Y}_t = 31.5 - 0.73PC_t + 0.11PB_t + 0.23YD_t \tag{6.8}$$
$$(0.08) \quad (0.05) \quad (0.02)$$
$$t = \ -9.12 \quad\quad 2.50 \quad\quad 14.22$$
$$\overline{R}^2 = .986 \quad n = 44 \text{ (annual 1951–1994)}$$

If we substitute the log of disposable income (LYD) for disposable income in Equation 6.8, we get:

$$\hat{Y}_t = \ -6.94 - 0.57PC_t + 0.25PB_t + 12.2LYD_t \tag{7.8}$$
$$(0.19) \quad (0.11) \quad (2.81)$$
$$t = \ -3.05 \quad\quad 2.19 \quad\quad 4.35$$
$$\overline{R}^2 = .942 \quad n = 44 \text{ (annual 1951–1994)}$$

In Equation 7.8, the independent variables include the two price variables (PC and PB) and the *log* of disposable income. Equation 7.8 would be appropriate if we hypothesize that as income rises, consumption will increase at a decreasing rate. For other products, perhaps like yachts or summer homes, no such decreasing rate could be hypothesized, and the semilog function would not be appropriate.

Note from Equation 7.7 that various combinations of the functional forms are possible. Thus the form taken by X_1 may be different from the form taken by X_2. In addition, Y may assume yet another different functional form.[4]

Not all semilog functions have the log on the right-hand side of the equation, as in Equation 7.7. The alternative semilog form is to have the log on the left-hand side of the equation. This would mean that the natural log of Y would be a function of unlogged values of the Xs, as in:

$$\ln Y = \beta_0 + \beta_1 X_1 + \beta_2 X_2 + \epsilon \tag{7.9}$$

---

4. One example of such a combination functional form is called the *translog function*. The translog function combines three different functional forms to come up with an equation for estimating various kinds of cost functions. For more on the translog function, see Laurits R. Christensen and William H. Greene, "Economies of Scale in U.S. Electrical Power Generation," *Journal of Political Economy*, August 1976, pp. 655–676.

This model has neither a constant slope nor a constant elasticity, but the co-efficients do have a very useful interpretation. If X_1 increases by one *unit*, then Y will change in *percentage* terms. Specifically, Y will change by $\beta_1 \cdot 100$ percent, holding X_2 constant, for every unit that X_1 increases. The left-hand side of Figure 7.3 shows such a semilog function.

This fact means that the lnY semilog function of Equation 7.9 is perfect for any model in which the dependent variable adjusts in percentage terms to a unit change in an independent variable. The most common economic and business application of Equation 7.9 is in a model of salaries of individuals, where firms often give annual raises in percentage terms. In such a model Y would be the salary of the *i*th employee, and X_1 would be the experience of the *i*th worker. Each year X_1 would increase by one, and β_1 would measure the percentage raises given by the firm. For more on this example of a left-side semilog functional form, see Exercise 4 at the end of the chapter.

Note that we now have two different kinds of semilog functional forms, creating possible confusion. As a result, many econometricians use phrases like "right-side semilog" or "lin-log functional form" to refer to Equation 7.7 while using "left-side semilog" or "log-lin functional form" to refer to Equation 7.9.

7.2.4 Polynomial Form

In most cost functions, the slope of the cost curve changes as output changes. If the slopes of a relationship are expected to depend on the level of the variable itself (for example, change sign as output increases) then a polynomial model should be considered. **Polynomial functional forms** express Y as a function of independent variables, some of which are raised to powers other than one. For example, in a second-degree polynomial (also called a quadratic) equation, at least one independent variable is squared:

$$Y_i = \beta_0 + \beta_1 X_{1i} + \beta_2 (X_{1i})^2 + \beta_3 X_{2i} + \epsilon_i \qquad (7.10)$$

Such a model can indeed produce slopes that change as the independent variables change. The slopes of Y with respect to the Xs in Equation 7.10 are:

$$\frac{\Delta Y}{\Delta X_1} = \beta_1 + 2\beta_2 X_1 \quad \text{and} \quad \frac{\Delta Y}{\Delta X_2} = \beta_3 \qquad (7.11)$$

Note that the first slope depends on the level of X_1 and the second slope is constant. If this were a cost function, with Y being the average cost of produc-

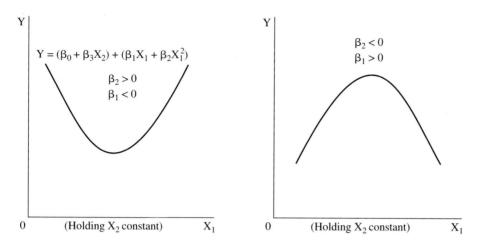

Figure 7.4 Polynomial Functions

Quadratic functional forms (polynomials with squared terms) take on U or inverted U shapes, depending on the values of the coefficients (holding X_2 constant). The left panel shows the shape of a quadratic function that could be used to show a typical cost curve; the right panel allows the description of an impact that rises and then falls (like the impact of age on earnings).

tion and X_1 being the level of output of the firm, then we would expect β_1 to be negative and β_2 to be positive if the firm has the typical U-shaped cost curve depicted in the left half of Figure 7.4.

For another example, consider a model of annual employee earnings as a function of the age of each employee and a number of other measures of productivity such as education. What is the expected impact of age on earnings? As a young worker gets older, his or her earnings will typically increase. Beyond some point, however, an increase in age will not increase earnings by very much at all, and around retirement we expect earnings to start to decrease with age. As a result, a logical relationship between earnings and age might look something like the right half of Figure 7.4; earnings would rise, level off, and then fall as age increased. Such a theoretical relationship could be modeled with a quadratic equation:

$$\text{Earnings}_i = \beta_0 + \beta_1 \text{Age}_i + \beta_2 \text{Age}_i^2 + \cdots + \epsilon_i \qquad (7.12)$$

What would the expected signs of $\hat{\beta}_1$ and $\hat{\beta}_2$ be? As a worker got older, the difference between "Age" and "Age^2" would increase dramatically, because "Age^2" would become quite large. As a result, the coefficient of "Age" would be more important at lower ages than it would be at higher ages. Conversely, the coefficient of "Age^2" would be more important at higher ages. Since you expect the impact of age to rise and fall, you'd thus expect $\hat{\beta}_1$ to be positive and $\hat{\beta}_2$ to be negative (all else being equal). In fact, this is exactly what many researchers in labor economics have observed.

With polynomial regressions, the interpretation of the individual regression coefficients becomes difficult, and the equation may produce unwanted results for particular ranges of X. For example, the slope for a third-degree polynomial can be positive over some range of X, then negative over the next range, and then positive again. Unless such a relationship is called for by theory, it would be inappropriate to use a higher-degree polynomial. Even a second-degree polynomial, as in Equation 7.10, imposes a particular shape (a U shape or its inverse) that might be unreasonable in some cases. For example, review the rain equation in Section 5.5, where it seems obvious that the squared term was added solely to provide a better fit to this admittedly cooked-up equation. To avoid such curve fitting, great care must be taken when using a polynomial regression equation to ensure that the functional form will achieve what is intended by the researcher and no more.

7.2.5 Inverse Form

The **inverse functional form** expresses Y as a function of the reciprocal (or inverse) of one or more of the independent variables (in this case, X_1):

$$Y_i = \beta_0 + \beta_1(1/X_{1i}) + \beta_2 X_{2i} + \epsilon_i \qquad (7.13)$$

The inverse (or reciprocal) functional form should be used when the impact of a particular independent variable is expected to approach zero as that independent variable increases and eventually approaches infinity. To see this, note that as X_1 gets larger, its impact on Y decreases.

In Equation 7.13, X_1 cannot equal zero, since if X_1 equaled zero, dividing it into anything would result in infinite or undefined values. The slopes are:

$$\frac{\Delta Y}{\Delta X_1} = \frac{-\beta_1}{X_1^2} \quad \text{and} \quad \frac{\Delta Y}{\Delta X_2} = \beta_2 \qquad (7.14)$$

The slopes for X_1 fall into two categories, both of which are depicted in Figure 7.5:

1. When β_1 is positive, the slope with respect to X_1 is negative and decreases in absolute value as X_1 increases. As a result, the relationship

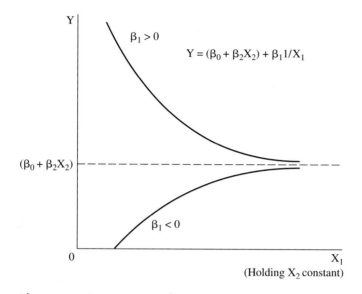

Figure 7.5 Inverse Functions

Inverse (or reciprocal) functional forms allow the impact of an X_1 on Y to approach zero as X_1 increases in size. The inverse function approaches the same value (the asymptote) from the top or bottom depending on the sign of β_1.

between Y and X_1 holding X_2 constant approaches $\beta_0 + \beta_2 X_2$ as X_1 increases (ignoring the error term).

2. When β_1 is negative, the relationship intersects the X_1 axis at $-\beta_1/(\beta_0 + \beta_2 X_2)$ and slopes upward toward the same horizontal line (called an asymptote) that it approaches when β_1 is positive.

Applications of reciprocals or inverses exist in a number of areas in economic theory and the real world. For example, one way to think of the once-popular Phillips curve, a nonlinear relationship between the rate of unemployment and the percentage change in wages, is to posit that the percentage change in wages (W) is negatively related to the rate of unemployment (U), but that past some level of unemployment, further increases in the unemployment rate do not reduce the level of wage increases any further because of institutional or other reasons. Such a hypothesis could be tested with an inverse functional form:

$$W_t = \beta_0 + \beta_1(1/U_t) + \epsilon_t \qquad (7.15)$$

Estimating this equation using OLS gives the following:

$$\hat{W}_t = 0.00679 + 0.1842(1/U_t) \qquad (7.16)$$
$$(0.0590)$$
$$t = 3.20$$
$$R^2 = .397$$

This indicates that W and U are related in a way similar to that hypothesized (as shown in Figure 7.5 when β_1 is positive), but it doesn't provide any evidence that the inverse functional form is the best way to depict this particular theory. For more on this example, see Exercise 5.

7.3   Problems with Incorrect Functional Forms

The best way to choose a functional form for a regression model is to choose a specification that matches the underlying theory of the equation. In a majority of cases, the linear form will be adequate, and for most of the rest, common sense will point out a fairly easy choice from among the alternatives outlined above. Table 7.1 contains a summary of the properties of the various alternative functional forms.

Once in a while, however, a circumstance will arise in which the model is logically nonlinear in the variables, but the exact form of this nonlinearity is hard to specify. In such a case, the linear form is not correct, and yet a choice between the various nonlinear forms cannot be made on the basis of economic theory. Even in these cases, however, it still pays (in terms of understanding the true relationships) to avoid choosing a functional form on the basis of fit alone.

For example, recall the estimated Phillips curve in Equation 7.16. Although the negative relationship between unemployment and inflation (using the percentage increase in wages as a proxy) implied by the Phillips curve suggests a downward-sloping nonlinear curve, there are a number of other functional forms that could produce such a curve. In addition to the inverse relationship that was actually used, the double-log form and various semilog and exponential forms could also give shapes that would fit the hypothesis fairly well. If all the functional forms are so similar, and if theory does not specify exactly which form to use, why should we try to avoid using goodness of fit over the sample to determine which equation to use? This section will highlight two answers to this question:

1. $\overline{R}^2$s are difficult to compare if the dependent variable is transformed.

2. An incorrect functional form may provide a reasonable fit within the sample but have the potential to make large forecast errors when used outside the range of the sample.

TABLE 7.1 SUMMARY OF ALTERNATIVE FUNCTIONAL FORMS

Functional Form	Equation (one X only)	Slope $= \left(\dfrac{\Delta Y}{\Delta X}\right)$	Elasticity $= \left(\dfrac{\Delta Y}{\Delta X} \cdot \dfrac{X}{Y}\right)$
Linear	$Y_i = \beta_0 + \beta_1 X_i + \epsilon_i$	β_1	$\beta_1\left(\dfrac{X_i}{Y_i}\right)$
Double-log	$\ln Y_i = \beta_0 + \beta_1 \ln X_i + \epsilon_i$	$\beta_1\left(\dfrac{Y_i}{X_i}\right)$	β_1
Semilog (lnX)	$Y_i = \beta_0 = \beta_1 \ln X_i + \epsilon_i$	$\beta_1\left(\dfrac{1}{X_i}\right)$	$\beta_1\left(\dfrac{1}{Y_i}\right)$
Semilog (lnY)	$\ln Y_i = \beta_0 + \beta_1 X_i + \epsilon_i$	$\beta_1 Y_i$	$\beta_1 X_i$
Polynomial	$Y_i = \beta_0 + \beta_1 X_i + \beta_2 X_i^2 + \epsilon_i$	$\beta_1 + 2\beta_2 X_i$	$\beta_1\left(\dfrac{X_i}{Y_i}\right) + 2\beta_2\left(\dfrac{X_i^2}{Y_i}\right)$
Inverse	$Y_i = \beta_0 + \beta_1\left(\dfrac{1}{X_i}\right) + \epsilon_i$	$-\beta_1\left(\dfrac{1}{X_i^2}\right)$	$-\beta_1\left(\dfrac{1}{X_i Y_i}\right)$

Note: Slopes and elasticities that include X_i or Y_i are not constant; they vary from point to point, depending on the value of X_i or Y_i. If general slopes or elasticities are desired, $\overline{X}$ and $\overline{Y}$ can be substituted into the equations.

7.3.1 $\overline{R}^2$s Are Difficult to Compare When Y Is Transformed

When the dependent variable is transformed from its linear version, the overall measure of fit, the $\overline{R}^2$, cannot be used for comparing the fit of the nonlinear equation with the original linear one. This problem is not especially important in most cases because the emphasis in applied regression analysis is usually on the coefficient estimates. However, if $\overline{R}^2$s are ever used to compare the fit of two different functional forms, then it becomes crucial that this lack of comparability be remembered. For example, suppose you were trying to compare a linear equation

$$Y = \beta_0 + \beta_1 X_1 + \beta_2 X_2 + \epsilon \tag{7.17}$$

with a semilog version of the same equation (using the version of a semilog function that takes the log of the dependent variable):

$$\ln Y = \beta_0 + \beta_1 X_1 + \beta_2 X_2 + \epsilon \tag{7.18}$$

Notice that the only difference between Equations 7.17 and 7.18 is the functional form of the dependent variable. The reason that the $\overline{R}^2$s of the respective equations cannot be used to compare overall fits of the two equations is that the total sum of squares (TSS) of the dependent variable around its mean is different in the two formulations. That is, the $\overline{R}^2$s are not comparable because the dependent variables are different. There is no reason to expect that different dependent variables will have the identical (or easily comparable) degrees of dispersion around their means. Since the two TSS are different, the $\overline{R}^2$s (or R^2s) will not be comparable.[5]

7.3.2 Incorrect Functional Forms Outside the Range of the Sample

If an incorrect functional form is used, then the probability of mistaken inferences about the true population parameters will increase. Using an incorrect functional form is a kind of specification error that is similar to the omitted variable bias discussed in Section 6.1. Although the characteristics of any specification errors depend on the exact details of the particular situation, there is no reason to expect that coefficient estimates obtained from an incorrect functional form will necessarily be unbiased and have minimum variance. Even if an incorrect functional form provides good statistics within a sample, though, large residuals almost surely will arise when the misspecified equation is used on data that were not part of the sample used to estimate the coefficients.

In general, the extrapolation of a regression equation to data that are outside the range over which the equation was estimated runs increased risks of large forecasting errors and incorrect conclusions about population values.

---

5. One way to get around this problem is to create a "quasi-R^2," an R^2 that allows the comparison of the overall fits of equations with different functional forms by transforming the predicted values of one of the dependent variables into the functional form of the other dependent variable.

This would mean taking the following steps:

1. Estimate Equation 7.18 and create a set of $\widehat{\ln Y}$s for the sample.

2. Transform the $\widehat{\ln Y}$s by taking their antilogs (an antilog reverses the log function: antilog $[\ln Y] = Y$).

3. Calculate quasi-R^2 (or quasi-$\overline{R}^2$) by using the newly calculated antilogs as $\hat{Y}$s to get the residuals needed in the R^2 equation:

$$\text{quasi-}R^2 = 1 - \frac{\sum [Y_i - \text{antilog}(\ln\hat{Y}_i)]^2}{\sum [Y_i - \overline{Y}]^2} \tag{7.19}$$

This quasi-R^2 for Equation 7.18 is directly comparable to the conventional R^2 for Equation 7.17.

This risk is heightened if the regression uses a functional form that is inappropriate for the particular variables being studied; nonlinear functional forms should be used with extreme caution for data outside the range of the sample because nonlinear functional forms by definition change their slopes. It is entirely possible that the slope of a particular nonlinear function could change to an unrealistic value outside the range of the sample even if the form produced reasonable slopes within the sample. Of course, even a linear function could be inappropriate in this way. If the true relationship changed slope outside the sample range, the linear functional form's constant slope would be quite likely to lead to large forecasting errors outside the sample range.

As a result, two functional forms that behave similarly over the range of the sample may behave quite differently outside that range. If the functional form is chosen on the basis of theory, then the researcher can take into account how the equation would act over any range of values, even if some of those values are outside the range of the sample. If functional forms are chosen on the basis of fit, then extrapolating outside the sample becomes tenuous.

Figure 7.6 contains a number of hypothetical examples. As can be seen, some functional forms have the potential to fit quite poorly outside the sample range. Others seem less likely to encounter this problem. Such graphs are meant as examples of what could happen, not as statements of what necessarily will happen, when incorrect functional forms are pushed outside the range of the sample over which they were estimated. Do not conclude from these diagrams that nonlinear functions should be avoided completely. If the true relationship is nonlinear, then the *linear* functional form will make large forecasting errors outside the sample. Instead, the researcher must take the time to think through how the equation will act for values both inside and outside the sample before choosing a functional form to use to estimate the equation. If the theoretically appropriate nonlinear equation appears to work well over the relevant range of possible values, then it should be used without concern over this issue.

7.4 Using Dummy Variables

In Section 3.1 we introduced the concept of a dummy variable, which we defined as one that takes on the values of 0 or 1, depending on a qualitative attribute such as gender. In that section our sole focus was on the use of a dummy variable as an **intercept dummy,** a dummy variable that changes the

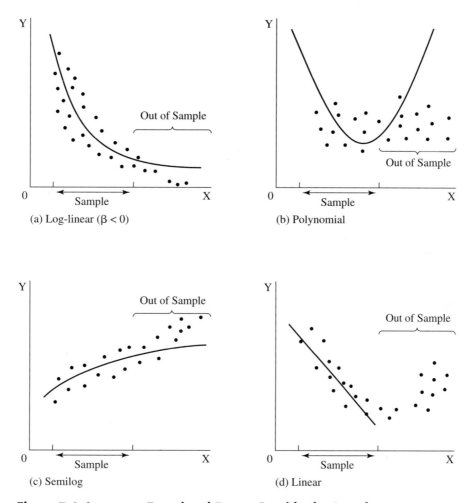

Figure 7.6 Incorrect Functional Forms Outside the Sample Range

If an incorrect form is applied to data outside the range of the sample on which it was estimated, the probability of large mistakes increases. In particular, note how the polynomial
functional form can change slope rapidly outside the sample range (panel b) and that
even a linear form can cause mistakes if the true functional form is nonlinear (panel d).

constant or intercept term, depending on whether the qualitative condition
is met. These take the general form:

$$Y_i = \beta_0 + \beta_1 X_i + \beta_2 D_i + \epsilon_i \qquad (7.20)$$

where $D_i = \begin{cases} 1 \text{ if the } i\text{th observation meets a particular condition} \\ 0 \text{ otherwise} \end{cases}$

As can be seen in Figure 7.7, the intercept dummy does indeed change the intercept depending on the value of D, but the slopes remain constant no matter what value D takes.

Note that in this example only one dummy variable is used even though there were two conditions. This is because one fewer dummy variable is constructed than conditions. The event not explicitly represented by a dummy variable, the **omitted condition,** forms the basis against which the included conditions are compared. Thus, for dual situations only one dummy variable is entered as an independent variable; the coefficient is interpreted as the effect of the included condition relative to the omitted condition.

For an example of the meaning of the coefficient of a dummy variable, let's look at a study of the relationship between fraternity/sorority membership and grade point average (GPA). Most noneconometricians would approach this research problem by calculating the mean grades of fraternity/sorority (so-called Greek) members and comparing them to the mean grades of nonmembers. However, such a technique ignores the possibility that differences in mean grades might be related to characteristics other than Greek membership.

Instead, we'd want to build a regression model that explains college GPA. Independent variables would include not only Greek membership but also other predictors of academic performance such as Scholastic Aptitude Test (SAT) scores and high school grades. Being a member of a social organization is a qualitative variable, however, so we'd have to create a dummy variable to represent fraternity or sorority membership quantitatively in a regression equation:

$$G_i = \begin{cases} 1 & \text{if the } i\text{th student is an active member of} \\ & \text{a fraternity or sorority} \\ 0 & \text{otherwise} \end{cases}$$

If we collect data from all the students in our class and estimate the equation implied above, we obtain:

$$\widehat{CG}_i = 0.37 + 0.81HG_i + 0.00001S_i - 0.38G_i \qquad (7.21)$$
$$\overline{R}^2 = .45 \quad n = 25$$

where: CG_i = the cumulative college GPA (4-point scale) of the ith student
HG_i = the cumulative high school GPA (4-point scale) of the ith student
S_i = the sum of the highest verbal and mathematics SAT scores earned by the ith student (1600 maximum)

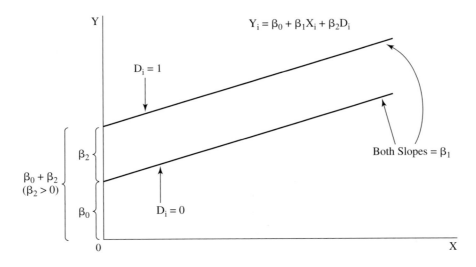

Figure 7.7 An Intercept Dummy

If an intercept dummy $(\beta_2 D_i)$ is added to an equation, a graph of the equation will have different intercepts for the two qualitative conditions specified by the dummy variable. The difference between the two intercepts is β_2. The slopes are constant with respect to the qualitative condition.

The meaning of the estimated coefficient of G_i in Equation 7.21 is very specific. Stop for a second and figure it for yourself. What is it? The estimate that $\hat{\beta}_G = -0.38$ means that, for this sample, the GPA of fraternity/sorority members is 0.38 lower than for nonmembers, holding SATs and high school GPA constant. Thus, Greek members are doing about a third of a grade worse than otherwise might be expected. To understand this example better, try using Equation 7.21 to predict your own GPA; how close does it come?

Before you rush out and quit whatever social organization you're in, however, note that this sample is quite small and that we've surely omitted some important determinants of academic success from the equation. As a result, we shouldn't be too quick to conclude that Greeks are dummies.

To this point, we've used dummy variables to represent just those qualitative variables that have exactly two possibilities (such as gender). What about situations where a qualitative variable has three or more alternatives? For example, what if you're trying to measure the impact of education on salaries in business and you want to distinguish high school graduates from holders of B.A.s and M.B.A.s? The answer certainly isn't to have MBA = 2, BA = 1, and 0 otherwise, because we have no reason to think that the impact of having an M.B.A. is exactly twice that of having a B.A. when compared to having no college degree at all. If not that, then what?

The answer is to create one less dummy variable than there are alternatives and to use each dummy to represent just one of the possible conditions. In the salary case, for example, you'd create two variables, the first equal to 1 if the employee had an M.B.A. (0 otherwise) and the second equal to 1 if the employee's highest degree was a B.A. (and 0 otherwise). As before, the omitted condition is represented by having both dummies equal to zero. This way you can measure the impact of each degree independently, without having to link the impacts of having an M.B.A. and a B.A.

A dummy variable that has only a single observation with a value of one while the rest of the observations are zeroes (or vice versa) is to be avoided unless the variable is required by theory. Such a "one-time dummy" acts merely to eliminate that observation from the data set, improving the fit artificially by setting the dummy's coefficient equal to the residual for that observation. One would obtain exactly the same estimates of the other coefficients if that observation were deleted, but the deletion of an observation is rarely, if ever, appropriate. Finally, dummy variables can be used as *dependent* variables; this possibility is covered in an entire chapter, Chapter 13.

7.5 Slope Dummy Variables

Until now, every independent variable in this text has been multiplied by exactly one other item, the slope coefficient. To see this, take another look at Equation 7.20:

$$Y_i = \beta_0 + \beta_1 X_i + \beta_2 D_i + \epsilon_i \qquad (7.20)$$

In this equation X is multiplied only by β_1, and D is multiplied only by β_2, and there are no other factors involved.

This restriction does not apply to a new kind of variable called an interaction term. An **interaction term** is an independent variable in a regression equation that is the *multiple* of two or more other independent variables. Each interaction term has its own regression coefficient, so the end result is that the interaction term has three or more components, as in $\beta_3 X_i D_i$. Such interaction terms are used when the change in Y with respect to one independent variable (in this case X) depends on the level of another independent variable (in this case D). For an example of the use of interaction terms that do not involve dummy variables, see Exercise 14.

The most frequent application of interaction terms is to create slope dummies. **Slope dummy variables** allow the slope of the relationship between the dependent variable and an independent variable to be different depending on whether the condition specified by a dummy variable is met. This is in contrast to an intercept dummy variable, which changes the intercept, but does not change the slope, when a particular condition is met.

In practice, slope dummy variables have many realistic uses. Slope dummies can be used whenever the impact of an independent variable on the dependent variable is hypothesized to change if some qualitative condition is met. For example, consider a consumption function that is estimated over a time period that includes a major war. Being in a war would surely reduce the marginal propensity to consume, and such a change can be modeled with a slope dummy that takes on one value during war years and the other during nonwar years.

In general, a slope dummy is introduced by adding to the equation a variable that is the multiple of the independent variable that has a slope you want to change and the dummy variable that you want to cause the changed slope. The general form of a slope dummy equation is:

$$Y_i = \beta_0 + \beta_1 X_i + \beta_2 D_i + \beta_3 X_i D_i + \epsilon_i \qquad (7.22)$$

Note the difference between Equations 7.20 and 7.22. Equation 7.22 is the same as Equation 7.20 except that we have added an interaction term in which the dummy variable is multiplied by an independent variable $(\beta_3 X_i D_i)$. In the case of the consumption function, Y would be consumption, X would be disposable income, and D would measure if the *i*th year was a war year. Let's check to make sure that the slope of Y with respect to X does indeed change if D changes:

$$\text{When } D = 0, \quad \Delta Y/\Delta X = \beta_1$$
$$\text{When } D = 1, \quad \Delta Y/\Delta X = (\beta_1 + \beta_3)$$

In essence, the coefficient of X *changes* when the condition specified by D is met. To see this, substitute $D = 0$ and $D = 1$, respectively, into Equation 7.22 and factor out X.

Note that Equation 7.22 includes both a slope dummy and an intercept dummy. It turns out that whenever a slope dummy is used, it's vital to also use an intercept dummy to avoid bias in the estimate of the coefficient of the slope dummy term. Such a specification should be used in all but highly unusual and forced situations. If there are other Xs in an equation, they should not be multiplied by D unless you hypothesize that their slopes change with respect to D as well.

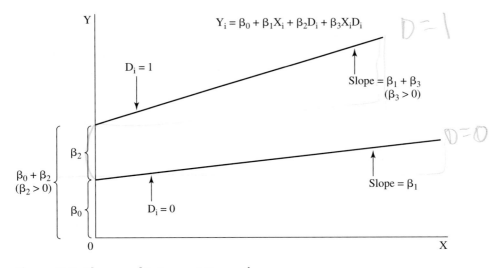

Figure 7.8 Slope and Intercept Dummies

If slope dummy ($\beta_3 X_i D_i$) and intercept dummy ($\beta_2 D_i$) terms are added to an equation, a graph of the equation will have different intercepts *and* different slopes depending on the value of the qualitative condition specified by the dummy variable. The difference between the two intercepts is β_2, whereas the difference between the two slopes is β_3.

Take a look at Figure 7.8, which has both a slope dummy and an intercept dummy. In Figure 7.8 the intercept will be β_0 when $D = 0$ and $\beta_0 + \beta_2$ when $D = 1$. In addition, the slope of Y with respect to X will be β_1 when $D = 0$ and $\beta_1 + \beta_3$ when $D = 1$. As a result, there really are two equations:

$$Y_i = \beta_0 \qquad\qquad + \beta_1 X_i + \epsilon_i \qquad [\text{when } D = 0]$$
$$Y_i = (\beta_0 + \beta_2) + (\beta_1 + \beta_3)X_i + \epsilon_i \qquad [\text{when } D = 1]$$

As can be seen in Figure 7.9, an equation with both a slope and an intercept dummy can take on a number of different shapes depending on the signs and absolute values of the coefficients. As a result, slope dummies can be used to model a wide variety of relationships, but it's necessary to be fairly specific when hypothesizing values of the coefficients of the various dummy terms.

For example, consider the question of earnings differentials between men and women. Although there is little argument that these differentials exist, there is quite a bit of controversy over the extent to which these differentials are caused by sexual discrimination (as opposed to other factors). Suppose you decide to build a model of earnings to get a better view of this controversy. If you hypothesized that men earn more than women on average, then

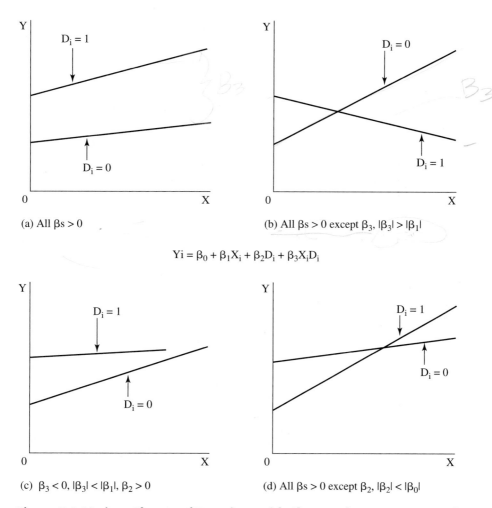

(a) All βs > 0

(b) All βs > 0 except β_3, $|\beta_3| > |\beta_1|$

$$Yi = \beta_0 + \beta_1 X_i + \beta_2 D_i + \beta_3 X_i D_i$$

(c) $\beta_3 < 0$, $|\beta_3| < |\beta_1|$, $\beta_2 > 0$

(d) All βs > 0 except β_2, $|\beta_2| < |\beta_0|$

Figure 7.9 Various Shapes of Equations with Slope and Intercept Dummies

Depending on the values of the coefficients of the slope (β_3) and intercept (β_2) dummies, equations with both slope and intercept dummies in them can take on a number of different shapes. When using such equations it is therefore necessary to be fairly specific when hypothesizing values of the coefficients of the various dummy terms.

you would want to use an intercept dummy variable for gender in an earnings equation that included measures of experience, special skills, education, and so on, as independent variables:

$$\text{Earnings}_i = \beta_0 + \beta_1 D_i + \beta_2 \text{EXP}_i + \cdots + \epsilon_i \qquad (7.23)$$

where: D_i = 1 if the ith worker is male and 0 otherwise
 EXP_i = the years experience of the ith worker
 ϵ_i = a classical error term

In Equation 7.23, $\hat{\beta}_1$ would be an estimate of the average difference between males and females holding constant their experience and the other factors in the equation. Equation 7.23 also forces the impact of increases in experience (and the other factors in the equation) to have the same effect for females as for males because the slopes are the same for both genders.

If you hypothesized that men also increase their earnings more per year of experience than women, then you would include a slope dummy as well as an intercept dummy in such a model:

$$\text{Earnings}_i = \beta_0 + \beta_1 D_i + \beta_2 EXP_i + \beta_3 D_i EXP_i + \cdots + \epsilon_i \qquad (7.24)$$

In Equation 7.24, $\hat{\beta}_3$ would be an estimate of the differential impact of an extra year of experience on earnings between men and women. We could test the possibility of a positive true β_3 by running a one-tailed t-test on $\hat{\beta}_3$. If $\hat{\beta}_3$ were significantly different from zero in a positive direction, then we could reject the null hypothesis of no difference due to gender in the impact of experience on earnings, holding constant the other variables in the equation.[6] Such an equation would be described by panel a in Figure 7.9.

7.6 Summary

1. Do not suppress the constant term even if it appears to be theoretically likely to equal zero. On the other hand, don't rely on estimates of the constant term for inference even if it appears to be statistically significant.

2. The choice of a functional form should be based on the underlying eco-

---

6. Another approach to this problem is to use the Chow test suggested at the very end of Section 7.7 (the appendix on the F-test). To apply the Chow test to the question of earnings differentials between genders, use Equation 7.24 as the unconstrained equation (with all independent variables also having slope dummy formulations) and

$$\text{Earnings}_i = \beta_0 + \beta_1 EXP_i + \cdots + \epsilon_i \qquad (7.25)$$

as the constrained equation for the full data set and for each gender separately. If the F-test shows that the fit of Equation 7.24 is significantly better than the fit of Equation 7.25, then we would reject the null hypothesis of equivalence between the male and female slope coefficients in the earnings equation.

nomic theory to the extent to which theory suggests a shape similar to that provided by a particular functional form. A form that is linear in the variables should be used until a specific hypothesis suggests otherwise.

3. Functional forms that are nonlinear in the variables include the double-log form, the semilog form, the polynomial form, and the inverse form. The double-log form is especially useful if the elasticities involved are expected to be constant. The semilog and inverse forms have the advantage of allowing the effect of an independent variable to tail off as that variable increases. The polynomial form is useful if the slopes are expected to depend on the level of an independent variable, but polynomials of degree higher than two should be avoided unless the underlying theory specifically calls for them.

4. The use of nonlinear functional forms has a number of potential problems. In particular, the $\overline{R}^2$s are difficult to compare if Y has been transformed, and the residuals are potentially large if an incorrect functional form is used for forecasting outside the range of the sample.

5. A slope dummy is a dummy variable that is multiplied by an independent variable to allow the slope of the relationship between the dependent variable and the particular independent variable to change, depending on whether or not a particular condition is met.

Exercises

(Answers to even-numbered exercises in Appendix A.)

1. Write out the meaning of each of the following terms without referring to the book (or your notes), and compare your definition with the version in the text for each:
   a. elasticity
   b. double-log functional form
   c. semilog functional form
   d. polynomial functional form
   e. inverse functional form
   f. slope dummy
   g. natural log
   h. omitted condition

2. For each of the following pairs of dependent (Y) and independent (X) variables, pick the functional form that you think is likely to be ap-

propriate, and then explain your reasoning (assume that all other relevant independent variables are included in the equation):

a. Y = sales of shoes
  X = disposable income
b. Y = the attendance at the Hollywood Bowl outdoor symphony concerts on a given night
  X = whether the orchestra's most famous conductor was scheduled to conduct that night
c. Y = aggregate consumption of goods and services in the United States
  X = aggregate disposable income in the United States
d. Y = the money supply in the United States
  X = the interest rate on Treasury Bills (in a demand function)
e. Y = the average cost of production of a box of pasta
  X = the number of boxes of pasta produced
f. How would your answer to part e change if you knew there was a significant outlier due to a capacity constraint and a rush order one year?

3. Can either (or both) of the following be estimated with OLS? Why?

a. $Y_i = \beta_0 X_{1i}^{\beta_1} X_{2i}^{\beta_2} e^{u_i}$

b. $Y_i = e^{\beta_0} X_{1i}^{\beta_1} X_{2i}^{\beta_2} + u_i$

where u_i is a typical classical error term and e is the base of the natural logarithm.

4. Consider the following estimated semilog equation (standard errors are in parentheses):

$$\widehat{\ln SAL_i} = 8.10 + 0.100 ED_i + 0.110 EXP_i$$
$$(0.025) \qquad (0.050)$$
$$\overline{R}^2 = .48 \qquad n = 28$$

where: $\ln SAL_i$ = the log of the salary of the ith worker
  ED_i = the years of education of the ith worker
  EXP_i = the years of experience of the ith worker

a. Make appropriate hypotheses for signs, calculate t-scores, and test your hypotheses.
b. What is the economic meaning of the constant in this equation?
c. Why do you think a left-side semilog functional form is used in this model? More specifically, what are the slopes of salary with respect to education and experience?

d. Suppose you ran the linear version of this equation and obtained an $\overline{R}^2$ of .46. What can you conclude from this result?

5. The Phillips curve discussed in Section 7.2.5 is a good example of the use of econometrics to develop, refine, and test theory. The curve was originally "discovered" in an empirical study and once was firmly believed to be true. Today, the Phillips curve is not as highly regarded as it used to be, in part because of empirical results. Since data for estimating a Phillips curve are readily available, you can test the validity of the Phillips curve yourself.

a. Search the literature (starting with the *Journal of Economic Literature*) and follow the controversy surrounding the topic of the Phillips curve and its estimation.[7]

b. Review the possible functional forms summarized in Section 7.2. What else besides an inverse function could have been used to estimate the model?

c. Collect data and compare alternative functional forms for the Phillips curve.

d. From the middle 1970s to the early 1980s, a Phillips curve estimated from data on the U.S. economy might have shown a positive slope. What inference should you draw from such an unexpected sign? Why?

6. In an effort to explain regional wage differentials, you collect wage data from 7,338 unskilled workers, divide the country into four regions (Northeast, South, Midwest, and West), and estimate the following equation (standard errors in parentheses):

$$\hat{Y}_i = 4.78 - 0.038E_i - 0.041S_i - 0.048W_i$$
$$\phantom{\hat{Y}_i = 4.78 - } (0.019) \quad (0.010) \quad (0.012)$$
$$\overline{R}^2 = .49 \qquad n = 7{,}338$$

where: Y_i = the hourly wage (in dollars) of the *i*th unskilled worker

E_i = a dummy variable equal to 1 if the *i*th worker lives in the Northeast and 0 otherwise

S_i = a dummy variable equal to 1 if the *i*th worker lives in the South and 0 otherwise

W_i = a dummy variable equal to 1 if the *i*th worker lives in the West and 0 otherwise

---

7. For example, see Nancy Wulwick, "Phillips' Approximate Regression," in Neil de Marchi and Christopher Gilbert, eds., *History and Methodology of Econometrics* (Oxford: Clarendon Press, 1989), pp. 170–188. This book contains many other interesting articles on econometrics.

a. What is the omitted condition in this equation?
b. If you add a dummy variable for the omitted condition to the equation without dropping E_i, S_i, or W_i, what will happen?
c. If you add a dummy variable for the omitted condition to the equation and drop E_i, what will the sign of the new variable's estimated coefficient be?
d. Which of the following three statements is most correct? Least correct? Explain your answer.
   i. The equation explains 49 percent of the variation of Y around its mean with regional variables alone, so there must be quite a bit of wage variation by region.
   ii. The coefficients of the regional variables are virtually identical, so there must not be much wage variation by region.
   iii. The coefficients of the regional variables are quite small compared with the average wage, so there must not be much wage variation by region.
e. If you were going to add one variable to this model, what would it be? Justify your choice.

7. V. N. Murti and V. K. Sastri[8] investigated the production characteristics of various Indian industries, including cotton and sugar. They specified Cobb–Douglas production functions for output (Q) as a double-log function of labor (L) and capital (K)

$$\ln Q_i = \beta_0 + \beta_1 \ln L_i + \beta_2 \ln K_i + \epsilon_i$$

and obtained the following estimates (standard errors in parentheses):

Industry	$\hat{\beta}_0$	$\hat{\beta}_1$	$\hat{\beta}_2$	R^2
Cotton	0.97	0.92 (0.03)	0.12 (0.04)	.98
Sugar	2.70	0.59 (0.14)	0.33 (0.17)	.80

a. Hypothesize and test appropriate null hypotheses at the 5 percent level of significance. (*Hint:* This is much harder than it looks!)

---

8. V. N. Murti and V. K. Sastri, "Production Functions for Indian Industry," *Econometrica*, April 1957, pp. 205–221.

b. Graph the involved relationships. Does a double-log function seem theoretically justified in this case?

c. What are the elasticities of output with respect to labor and capital for each industry?

d. What economic significance does the sum $(\hat{\beta}_1 + \hat{\beta}_2)$ have?

8. Suppose you are studying the rate of growth of income in a country as a function of the rate of growth of capital in that country and of the per capita income of that country. You're using a cross-sectional data set that includes both developed and developing countries. Suppose further that the underlying theory suggests that income growth rates will increase as per capita income increases and then start decreasing past a particular point. Describe how you would model this relationship with each of the following functional forms:

a. a quadratic function

b. a semilog function

c. a slope dummy equation

9. A study of hotel investments in Waikiki estimated this revenue production function:

$$R = AL^{\alpha}K^{\beta}e^{\epsilon}$$

where: R = the annual net revenue of the hotel (in thousands of dollars)

A = a constant term

L = land input (site area in square feet)

K = capital input (construction cost in thousands of dollars)

ϵ = a classical error term

e = the base of the natural log

a. What are your general expectations for the population values of α and β? What are their theoretical interpretations?

b. Create specific null and alternative hypotheses for this equation.

c. Create specific decision rules for the two sets of hypotheses above (5 percent level with 25 degrees of freedom).

d. Calculate the appropriate t-values and run *t*-tests given the following regression result (standard errors in parentheses):

$$\widehat{\ln R} = -0.91750 + 0.273\ln L + 0.733\ln K$$
$$\qquad\qquad\qquad (0.135) \qquad (0.125)$$

Did you reject or "accept" your null hypotheses?

e. Is this result surprising? If you were going to build a Waikiki hotel, what input would you most want to use for investment? Is there an additional piece of information you would need to know before you could answer?

10. William Comanor and Thomas Wilson[9] specified the following regression in their study of advertising's effect on the profit rates of 41 consumer goods firms:

$$PR_i = \beta_0 + \beta_1 ADV_i/SALES_i + \beta_2 \ln CAP_i + \beta_3 \ln ES_i + \beta_4 \ln DG_i + \epsilon_i$$

where: PR_i = the profit rate of the ith firm
ADV_i = the advertising expenditures in the ith firm (in dollars)
$SALES_i$ = the total gross sales of the ith firm (in dollars)
CAP_i = the capital needed to enter the ith firm's market at an efficient size
ES_i = the degree to which economies of scale exist in the ith firm's industry
DG_i = percent growth in sales (demand) of the ith firm over the last 10 years
$\ln$ = natural logarithm
ϵ_i = a classical error term

a. Hypothesize expected signs for each of the slope coefficients.
b. Note that there are two different kinds of nonlinear (in the variables) relationships in this equation. For each independent variable, determine the shape that the chosen functional form implies, and state whether you agree or disagree with this shape. Explain your reasoning in each case.
c. Comanor and Wilson state that the simple correlation coefficient between $ADV_i/SALES_i$ and each of the other independent variables is positive. If one of these remaining variables were omitted, in which direction would $\hat{\beta}_1$ likely be biased?

11. Suggest the appropriate functional forms for the relationships between the following variables. Be sure to explain your reasoning:
a. The age of the ith house in a cross-sectional equation for the sales price of houses in Cooperstown, New York. (*Hint:* Cooperstown is known as a lovely town with a number of elegant historic homes.)

9. William S. Comanor and Thomas A. Wilson, "Advertising, Market Structure and Performance," *Review of Economics and Statistics*, November 1967, p. 432.

b. The price of natural gas in year t in a demand-side time-series equation for the consumption of natural gas in the United States.

c. The income of the *i*th individual in a cross-sectional equation for the number of suits owned by individuals.

d. A dummy variable for being a student (1 = yes) in the equation specified in part c.

e. The number of long-distance telephone calls handled per year in a cross-sectional equation for the marginal cost of a telephone call faced by various competing long-distance telephone carriers.

12. Suppose you've been hired by a union that wants to convince workers in local dry cleaning establishments that joining the union will improve their well-being. As your first assignment, your boss asks you to build a model of wages for dry cleaning workers that measures the impact of union membership on those wages. Your first equation (standard errors in parentheses) is:

$$\hat{W}_i = -11.40 + 0.30A_i - 0.003A_i^2 + 1.00S_i + 1.20U_i$$
$$\quad\quad\quad (0.10)\quad (0.002)\quad (0.20)\quad (1.00)$$
$$n = 34 \quad\quad \overline{R}^2 = .14$$

where: W_i = the hourly wage (in dollars) of the *i*th worker
$\quad\quad\quad$ A_i = the age of the *i*th worker
$\quad\quad\quad$ S_i = the number of years of education of the *i*th worker
$\quad\quad\quad$ U_i = a dummy variable = 1 if the *i*th worker is a union member, 0 otherwise

a. Evaluate the equation. How do $\overline{R}^2$ and the signs and significance of the coefficients compare with your expectations?

b. What is the meaning of the A^2 term? What relationship between A and W does it imply? Why doesn't the inclusion of A and A^2 violate the Classical Assumption of no perfect collinearity between two independent variables?

c. Do you think you should have used the log of W as your dependent variable? Why or why not? (*Hint:* Compare this equation to the one in Exercise 4 above.)

d. Even though we've been told not to analyze the value of the intercept, isn't −$11.40 too low to ignore? What should be done to correct this problem?

e. On the basis of your regression, should the workers be convinced that joining the union will improve their well-being? Why or why not?

13. Your boss manages to use the regression results in Exercise 12 to convince the dry cleaning workers to join your union. About a year later, they go on strike, a strike that turns violent. Now your union is being sued by all the local dry cleaning establishments for some of the revenues lost during the strike. Their claim is that the violence has intimidated replacement workers, thus decreasing production. Your boss doesn't believe that the violence has had a significant impact on production efficiency and asks you to test his hypothesis with a regression. Your results (standard errors in parentheses) are:

$$\widehat{LE}_t = 3.08 + 0.16LQ_t - 0.020A_t - 0.0001V_t$$
$$\phantom{\widehat{LE}_t = 3.08 + } (0.04) \quad\quad (0.010) \quad\quad (0.0008)$$
$$n = 24 \quad\quad \overline{R}^2 = .855$$

where LE_t = the natural log of the efficiency rate (defined as the ratio of actual total output to the goal output in week t)

   LQ_t = the natural log of actual total output in week t
   A_t = the absentee rate (%) during week t
   V_t = the number of incidents of violence during week t

a. Hypothesize signs and develop and test the appropriate hypotheses for the individual estimated coefficients (95 percent level).
b. If the functional form is correct, what does its use suggest about the theoretical elasticity of E with respect to Q compared with the elasticities of E with respect to A and V?
c. On the basis of this result, do you think the court will conclude that the violence had a significant impact on the efficiency rate? Why or why not?
d. What problems appear to exist in this equation? (*Hint:* The problems may be theoretical as well as econometric.) If you could make one change in the specification of this equation, what would it be?

14. Richard Fowles and Peter Loeb studied the interactive effect of drinking and altitude on traffic deaths.[10] The authors hypothesized that drunk driving fatalities are more likely at high altitude than at low al-

10. Richard Fowles and Peter D. Loeb, "The Interactive Effect of Alcohol and Altitude on Traffic Fatalities," *Southern Economic Journal*, July 1992, pp. 108–111. To focus the analysis, we have omitted the coefficients of three other variables (the minimum legal drinking age, the percent of the population between 18 and 24, and the variability of highway driving speeds) that were insignificant in Equations 7.26 and 7.27.

titude because higher elevations diminish the oxygen intake of the brain, increasing the impact of a given amount of alcohol. To test this hypothesis, they used an interaction variable between altitude and beer consumption. They estimated the following cross-sectional model (by state for the continental United States) of the motor vehicle fatality rate (t-scores in parentheses):

$$\hat{F}_i = -3.36 - 0.002B_i + 0.17S_i - 0.31D_i + 0.011B_i^*A_i \quad (7.26)$$
$$(-0.08) \quad (1.85) \ (-1.29) \quad (4.05)$$
$$n = 48 \qquad \overline{R}^2 = .499$$

where: F_i = traffic fatalities per motor vehicle mile driven in the ith state

B_t = per capita consumption of beer (malt beverages) in state i

S_i = average highway driving speed in state i

D_i = a dummy variable equal to 1 if the ith state had a vehicle safety inspection program and 0 otherwise

A_i = the average altitude of metropolitan areas in state i (in thousands)

a. Carefully state and test appropriate hypotheses about the coefficients of B, S, and D at the 5 percent level. Do these results give any indication of econometric problems in the equation? Explain.

b. Think through the interaction variable. What is it measuring? Carefully state the meaning of the coefficient of B*A.

c. Create and test appropriate hypotheses about the coefficient of the interaction variable at the 5 percent level.

d. Note that A_i is included in the equation in the interaction variable but not as an independent variable on its own. If an equation includes an interaction variable, should both components of the interaction be independent variables in the equation as a matter of course? Why or why not? (*Hint:* Recall that with slope dummies, we emphasized that both the intercept dummy term and the slope dummy variable term should be in the equation.)

e. When the authors included A_i in their model, the results were as in Equation 7.27. Which equation do you prefer? Explain your answer.

$$\hat{F}_i = -2.33 - 0.024B_i + 0.14S_i - 0.24D_i - 0.35A_i + 0.023B_i^*A_i \quad (7.27)$$
$$(-0.80) \quad (1.53) \ (-0.96) \ (-1.07) \quad (1.97)$$
$$n = 48 \quad \overline{R}^2 = .501$$

15. Walter Primeaux used slope dummies to help test his hypothesis that publicly owned monopolies tend to advertise less intensively than do duopolies in the electric utility industry.[11] His estimated equation (which also included a number of geographic dummies and a time variable) was (t-scores in parentheses):

$$\hat{Y}_i = 0.15 + 5.0S_i + 0.015G_i + 0.35D_i$$
$$(4.5) \quad (0.4) \quad\quad (2.9)$$
$$- 20.0S_i \cdot D_i + 0.49G_i \cdot D_i$$
$$(-5.0) \quad\quad (2.3)$$
$$\overline{R}^2 = .456 \quad\quad n = 350$$

where: Y_i = advertising and promotional expense (in dollars) per 1,000 residential kilowatt hours (KWH) of the *i*th electric utility

S_i = number of residential customers of the *i*th utility (hundreds of thousands)

G_i = annual percentage growth in residential KWH of the *i*th utility

D_i = a dummy variable equal to 1 if the *i*th utility is a duopoly, 0 if a monopoly

a. Hypothesize and test the relevant null hypotheses with the *t*-test at the 5 percent level of significance. (*Hint:* Note that *both* independent variables have slope dummies.)

b. Assuming that Primeaux's equation is correct, graph the relationship between advertising (Y_i) and size (S_i) for monopolies and for duopolies.

c. Assuming that Primeaux's equation is correct, graph the relationship between advertising and growth (G_i) for monopolies and for duopolies.

16. What attributes make a car accelerate well? If you're like most people, you'd answer that the fastest accelerators are high-powered, light, manual transmission cars with aerodynamic shapes. To test this, use the data in Table 7.2 for 1995 model vehicles to estimate the following equation (standard errors in parentheses)[12]:

11. Walter J. Primeaux, Jr., "An Assessment of the Effects of Competition on Advertising Intensity," *Economic Inquiry*, October 1981, pp. 613–625.

12. The data are from Daniel P. Heraud, *Chilton's Road Report, 1995* (Radnor, PA: Chilton, 1995), and the estimated equations come from an unpublished term paper by Stephanie Ream.

$$\hat{S}_i = 9.22 - 0.79T_i + 7.9E_i + 0.00041P_i - 0.019H_i \qquad (7.28)$$
$$\phantom{\hat{S}_i = 9.22} (0.59) \quad (3.7) \quad (0.0005) \qquad (0.003)$$
$$t = -1.33 \qquad 2.16 \qquad 0.82 \qquad\qquad -7.09$$
$$n = 38 \qquad \overline{R}^2 = .674$$

where: S_i = the number of seconds it takes the *i*th car to accelerate from 0 to 60 miles per hour

T_i = a dummy equal to 1 if the *i*th car has a manual transmission and 0 otherwise

E_i = the coefficient of drag of the *i*th car

P_i = the curb weight (in pounds) of the *i*th car

H_i = the bhp horsepower of the *i*th car

a. Create and test appropriate hypotheses about the slope coefficients
of the equation at the 1 percent level. (*Hint:* The coefficient of drag
is low for a jet airplane and high for a parachute.)

b. What possible econometric problems, out of omitted variables, irrelevant variables, or incorrect functional form, does Equation 7.28
appear to have? Explain.

c. Suppose your next door neighbor is a physics major who tells you
that horsepower can be expressed in terms of the following equation:
H = MDA/S where M = mass, D = distance, A = acceleration,
and S and H are as defined above. Does this change your answer to
part b? How? Why?

d. On the basis of your answer to part c, you decide to change the
functional form of the relationship between S and H to an inverse
because that's the appropriate theoretical relationship between the
two variables. What would the expected sign of the coefficient of
1/H be? Explain.

e. Equation 7.29 shows what happens if you switch your horsepower
functional form to an inverse. Which equation do you prefer?
Why? If Equation 7.28 had a higher $\overline{R}^2$ and higher t-scores, would
that change your answer? Why or why not?

$$\hat{S}_i = -2.16 - 1.59T_i + 7.4E_i + 0.0013P_i + 886(1/H_i) \qquad (7.29)$$
$$\phantom{\hat{S}_i = -2.16} (0.50) \quad (3.2) \quad (0.0005) \quad (102)$$
$$t = -3.15 \qquad 2.28 \qquad 2.64 \qquad 8.66$$
$$n = 38 \qquad \overline{R}^2 = .748$$

f. Since the two equations have different functional forms, can $\overline{R}^2$ be
used to compare the overall fit of the equations? Why or why not?

TABLE 7.2   ACCELERATION TIMES FOR 1995 MODEL VEHICLES

Vehicle	S	T	E	P	H
1. Acura Legend	9.00	0.0	0.34	3571	200
2. BMW 850CSi	6.70	0.0	0.29	4123	322
3. Lexus GS300	9.70	0.0	0.31	3660	220
4. Hyundai Elantra GL	12.50	1.0	0.34	2474	113
5. Jaguar XJS4.0	8.20	1.0	0.38	3805	237
6. Jeep Wrangler S	12.80	1.0	0.65	2943	123
7. Subaru Justy	12.80	1.0	0.39	2004	73
8. Toyota Supra Turbo	5.00	1.0	0.32	3505	320
9. Volkswagen Eurovan GL	14.50	1.0	0.36	3814	110
10. Honda Accord EX-R	8.50	1.0	0.33	3009	145
11. Chevrolet Corvette	5.20	1.0	0.33	3514	405
12. Bugatti EB-110	3.46	1.0	0.29	3571	560
13. Infiniti Q45	7.50	0.0	0.30	4039	278
14. Chrysler Lebaron	11.00	0.0	0.38	1416	141
15. Lincoln Mark III	7.80	0.0	0.33	3765	280
16. Toyota Celica	9.00	1.0	0.32	2579	135
17. Ferrari Testarossa	5.00	1.0	0.32	3344	421
18. Dodge Ram Pick-up	11.50	1.0	0.44	4032	170
19. Audi Quattro A6 S	12.00	0.0	0.29	3671	172
20. Alfa Romeo 164S	7.50	1.0	0.30	3351	200
21. Ford Probe GT	7.90	1.0	0.34	2866	164
22. Buick Riviera	8.00	0.0	0.34	3787	225
23. Oldsmobile Aurora	9.50	0.0	0.32	3966	250
24. Lamborghini Diablo	5.80	1.0	0.30	3737	492
25. Lotus Esprit S4	5.00	1.0	0.32	2976	264
26. Mazda Millenia S	8.20	0.0	0.29	3391	210
27. Mercedes C280	9.00	0.0	0.32	3291	158
28. Eagle Talon ESi	9.50	1.0	0.29	2835	140
29. Dodge Stealth	5.50	1.0	0.33	3792	315
30. Nissan XS	9.00	1.0	0.36	2937	138
31. Volkswagen Corrado	7.00	1.0	0.32	2808	178
32. Volvo 850 Turbo	7.60	1.0	0.32	3278	222
33. Honda Civic DX	9.40	1.0	0.31	2227	102
34. Ford Mustang Cobra	6.80	1.0	0.35	3223	240
35. Dodge Viper RT/10	4.80	1.0	0.55	3488	400
36. Ford Aspire	12.50	1.0	0.36	2004	63
37. Ford Taurus SHO	7.50	1.0	0.32	3307	220
38. Saturn SC2	8.00	1.0	0.31	2359	124

Source: Daniel P. Heraud, *Chilton's Road Report, 1995* (Radnor, PA: Chilton, 1995).

Note: datafile = CARS7

7.7   Appendix: More Uses for the *F*-Test

While the *F*-test is used more commonly to test the overall significance of a regression, it has many other uses. In fact, the *F*-test of overall significance is nothing more than a specialized application of the general *F*-test. This general *F*-test can be used to conduct tests of any (linear) hypothesis that involves more than one coefficient at a time. Such tests should be used whenever the underlying economic theory implies a hypothesis that simultaneously specifies values for more than one coefficient ("joint" or "compound" hypotheses). Interestingly, many of these joint hypotheses involve some of the functional forms presented in this chapter.

The way in which the *F*-test evaluates hypotheses about more than one coefficient at a time is fairly ingenious. The first step is to translate the particular null hypothesis in question into constraints that will be placed on the equation. The resulting constrained equation can be thought of as what the equation would look like if the null hypothesis were correct; you substitute the hypothesized values into the regression equation in order to see what would happen if the equation was constrained to agree with the null hypothesis. As a result, in the *F*-test the null hypothesis always leads to a constrained equation even if this violates our standard practice that the alternative hypothesis contains that which we expect is true.

The second step in an *F*-test is to estimate this constrained equation with OLS and compare the fit of this constrained equation with the fit of the unconstrained equation. If the fits of the constrained equation and the unconstrained equation are not significantly different, the null hypothesis should not be rejected. If the fit of the unconstrained equation is significantly better than that of the constrained equation, then we reject the null hypothesis. The fit of the constrained equation is never superior to the fit of the unconstrained equation, as we'll explain below.

The fits of the equations are compared with a special F-statistic:

$$F = \frac{(RSS_M - RSS)/M}{RSS/(n - K - 1)} \qquad (7.30)$$

where: RSS = residual sum of squares from the unconstrained equation.

RSS_M = residual sum of squares from the constrained equation

M = number of constraints placed on the equation (usually equal to the number of βs eliminated from the unconstrained equation)

$(n - K - 1)$ = degrees of freedom in the unconstrained equation

RSS_M is always greater than or equal to RSS; imposing constraints on the coefficients instead of allowing OLS to select their values can never decrease the summed squared residuals. (Recall that OLS selects that combination of values of the coefficients that minimizes RSS.) At the extreme, if the unconstrained regression yields exactly the same estimated coefficients as does the constrained regression, then the RSS are equal, and the F-statistic is zero. In this case, H_0 is not rejected because the data indicate that the constraints appear to be correct. As the difference between the constrained coefficients and the unconstrained coefficients increases, the data indicate that the null hypothesis is less likely to be true. Thus, when F gets larger than the critical F-value, the hypothesized restrictions specified in the null hypothesis are rejected by the test.

The decision rule for the *F*-test is:

$$\text{Reject} \qquad H_0 \text{ if } F \geq F_c$$
$$\text{Do Not Reject} \quad H_0 \text{ if } F < F_c$$

where F_c is the critical F-value found in the appropriate F-table.

As an example, let's look at a linearized annual Cobb–Douglas production function for the United States:

$$Q_t = \beta_0 + \beta_1 L_t + \beta_2 K_t + \epsilon_t \tag{7.31}$$

where: Q_t = the natural log of total output in the United States in year t
L_t = the natural log of labor input in the United States in year t
K_t = the natural log of capital input in the United States in year t
ϵ_t = a well-behaved stochastic error term

One of the properties of such a double-log equation is that the coefficients of Equation 7.31 can be used to test for constant returns to scale. (Constant returns to scale refers to a situation in which a given percentage increase in inputs translates to exactly that percentage increase in output.) It can be shown that a Cobb–Douglas production function with constant returns to scale is one where β_1 and β_2 add up to exactly one, so the null hypothesis to be tested is:

$$H_0: \beta_1 + \beta_2 = 1$$
$$H_A: \text{otherwise}$$

To test this null hypothesis with the *F*-test, we must run regressions on the unconstrained Equation 7.31 and an equation that is constrained to conform to the null hypothesis. To create such a constrained equation, we solve the null hypothesis for β_2 and substitute it into Equation 7.31, obtaining:

$$Q_t = \beta_0 + \beta_1 L_t + (1 - \beta_1)K_t + \epsilon_t \qquad (7.32)$$
$$= \beta_0 + \beta_1(L_t - K_t) + K_t + \epsilon_t$$

If we move K_t to the left-hand side of the equation, we obtain our constrained equation:

$$(Q_t - K_t) = \beta_0 + \beta_1(L_t - K_t) + \epsilon_t \qquad (7.33)$$

Equation 7.33 is the equation that would hold if our null hypothesis were correct.

To run an *F*-test on our null hypothesis of constant returns to scale, we need to run regressions on the constrained Equation 7.33 and the unconstrained Equation 7.31 and compare the fits of the two equations with the F-ratio from Equation 7.30. If we use annual U.S. data from 1970 through 1993, we obtain an unconstrained equation of:

$$\hat{Q}_t = -38.08 + 1.28L_t + 0.72K_t \qquad (7.34)$$
$$(0.30) \quad (0.05)$$
$$t = \quad 4.24 \quad 13.29$$
$$n = 24 \text{ (annual U.S. data)} \quad \overline{R}^2 = .997 \quad F = 4118.9$$

If we run the constrained equation and substitute the appropriate RSS into Equation 7.30, we obtain F = 16.26. When this F is compared to a 5 percent critical F-value of only 4.32 (for 1 and 21 degrees of freedom) we must reject the null hypothesis that constant returns to scale characterized the U.S. economy in the 1970s and 1980s. The degrees of freedom in the numerator equal one because only one coefficient has been eliminated from the equation by the constraint.

Interestingly, the estimate of $\hat{\beta}_1 + \hat{\beta}_2 = 1.28 + 0.72 = 2.00$ indicates drastically increasing returns to scale. However, since $\beta_1 = 1.28$, and since economic theory suggests that the slope coefficient of a Cobb–Douglas production function should be between zero and one, we should be extremely cautious. There are problems in the equation that need to be resolved before we can feel comfortable with this conclusion.

The *F*-test can be used with null hypotheses and constrained equations that apply to various subsets of the coefficients in the equation. For example, if

$$Y_i = \beta_0 + \beta_1 X_{1i} + \beta_2 X_{2i} + \beta_3 X_{3i} + \epsilon_i$$

then the only way to test a null hypothesis involving two of the slope coefficients (for example, $H_0: \beta_1 = \beta_2$) would be to estimate constrained and unconstrained equations and to compare their fits with the F-test.

An illustration of the use of the F-test to test null hypotheses that involve only a subset of the slope coefficients can be obtained by looking at the problem of testing the significance of seasonal dummies. **Seasonal dummies** are dummy variables that are used to account for seasonal variation in the data in time-series models. In a quarterly model, if:

$$X_{1t} = \begin{cases} 1 \text{ in quarter 1} \\ 0 \text{ otherwise} \end{cases}$$

$$X_{2t} = \begin{cases} 1 \text{ in quarter 2} \\ 0 \text{ otherwise} \end{cases}$$

$$X_{3t} = \begin{cases} 1 \text{ in quarter 3} \\ 0 \text{ otherwise} \end{cases}$$

then:

$$Y_t = \beta_0 + \beta_1 X_{1t} + \beta_2 X_{2t} + \beta_3 X_{3t} + \beta_4 X_{4t} + \epsilon_t \qquad (7.35)$$

where X_4 is a nondummy independent variable and t indexes the quarterly observations. Notice that only three dummy variables are required to represent four seasons. In this formulation β_1 shows the extent to which the expected value of Y in the first quarter differs from its expected value in the fourth quarter, the omitted condition. β_2 and β_3 can be interpreted similarly.

Inclusion of a set of seasonal dummies "deseasonalizes" Y and any independent variables that are not seasonally adjusted. This procedure may be used as long as Y and X_4 are not "seasonally adjusted" prior to estimation. Many researchers avoid the type of seasonal adjustment done prior to estimation because they think it distorts the data in unknown and arbitrary ways, but seasonal dummies have their own limitations such as remaining constant for the entire time period. As a result, there is no unambiguously best approach to deseasonalizing data.

To test the hypothesis of significant seasonality in the data, one must test the hypothesis that all the dummies equal zero simultaneously rather than test the dummies one at a time. In other words, the appropriate test of seasonality in a regression model using seasonal dummies involves the use of the F-test instead of the t-test.

In this case, the null hypothesis is that there is *no* seasonality:

$$H_0: \beta_1 = \beta_2 = \beta_3 = 0$$
$$H_A: H_0 \text{ is not true}$$

The constrained equation would then be $Y = \beta_0 + \beta_4 X_4 + \epsilon$. To determine whether the whole set of seasonal dummies should be included, the fit of the estimated constrained equation would be compared to the fit of the estimated unconstrained equation by using the F-test. Note that this example does indeed use the F-test to test null hypotheses that include only a subset of the slope coefficients.

The exclusion of some seasonal dummies because their estimated coefficients have low t-scores is not recommended. Preferably, testing seasonal dummy coefficients should be done with the F-test instead of with the t-test because seasonality is usually a single compound hypothesis rather than 3 (or 11 with monthly data) individual hypotheses having to do with each quarter (or month). To the extent that a hypothesis is a joint one, it should be tested with the F-test. If the hypothesis of seasonal variation can be summarized into a single dummy variable, then the use of the t-test will cause no problems. Often, where seasonal dummies are unambiguously called for, no hypothesis testing at all is undertaken.

Another common use of the F-test is to test the equivalence of regression coefficients between two sets of data, that is, whether two sets of data contain significantly different regression coefficients for the same theoretical equation. This can be helpful when deciding if it is appropriate to combine two data sets. For example, the null hypothesis may be that the slope coefficients are the same in two samples such as before and after a major war. The concern is whether there has been a major structural shift in the economy from one set of data to the other. This application of the F-test is often referred to as a *Chow test*, and it can be set up by using dummy variables that distinguish between data sets.[13]

A Chow test has four steps:

1. Run identically specified regressions on the two samples of data being tested and note the RSS from the two (RSS_1 and RSS_2).

2. Pool the data from the two samples, run an identically specified regression on the combined sample, and note this equation's RSS (RSS_T).

13. See Gregory C. Chow, "Tests of Equality Between Sets of Coefficients in Two Linear Regressions," *Econometrica*, July 1960, pp. 591–605, or any advanced econometrics textbook for the details of this test.

3. Calculate the following F-statistic:

$$F = \frac{(RSS_T - RSS_1 - RSS_2)/(K + 1)}{(RSS_1 + RSS_2)/(N_1 + N_2 - 2K - 2)}$$ (7.36)

where: K = the number of independent variables
N_1 = the number of observations in sample 1
N_2 = the number of observations in sample 2

4. Reject the null hypothesis that the two sets of regression coefficients are equivalent if $F \geq F_c$, where F_c is the critical F-value for $(K + 1)$ numerator and $(N_1 + N_2 - 2K - 2)$ denominator degrees of freedom.

Multicollinearity

The next three chapters deal with violations of the Classical Assumptions and remedies for those violations. This chapter addresses multicollinearity; the next two chapters are on serial correlation and heteroskedasticity. For each of these three problems, we will attempt to answer the following questions:

1. What is the nature of the problem?
2. What are the consequences of the problem?
3. How is the problem diagnosed?
4. What remedies for the problem are available?

Strictly speaking, **perfect multicollinearity** is the violation of the assumption that no independent variable is a perfect linear function of one or more other independent variables (Classical Assumption VI). Perfect multicollinearity is rare, but severe imperfect multicollinearity (where two or more independent variables are highly correlated in the particular data set being studied), although not violating Classical Assumption VI, still causes substantial problems.

Recall that the coefficient β_k can be thought of as the impact on the dependent variable of a one-unit increase in the independent variable X_k, holding constant the other independent variables in the equation. But if two explanatory variables are significantly related in a particular sample, whenever one changes, the other will tend to change too, and the OLS computer program will find it difficult to distinguish the effects of one variable from the effects of the other. Since the Xs can move together more in one sample than they do in another, the severity of multicollinearity can vary tremendously.

In essence, the more highly correlated two (or more) independent variables are, the more difficult it becomes to accurately estimate the coefficients of the true model. If two variables move identically, then there is no hope of distinguishing between the impacts of the two; but if the variables are only roughly correlated, then we still might be able to estimate the two effects accurately enough for most purposes.

8.1 Perfect versus Imperfect Multicollinearity

8.1.1 Perfect Multicollinearity

Perfect multicollinearity[1] violates Classical Assumption VI, which specifies that no explanatory variable is a perfect linear function of any other explanatory variables. The word *perfect* in this context implies that the variation in one explanatory variable can be *completely* explained by movements in another explanatory variable. Such a perfect linear function between two independent variables would be:

$$X_{1i} = \alpha_0 + \alpha_1 X_{2i} \tag{8.1}$$

where the αs are constants and the Xs are independent variables in:

$$Y_i = \beta_0 + \beta_1 X_{1i} + \beta_2 X_{2i} + \epsilon_i \tag{8.2}$$

Notice that there is no error term in Equation 8.1. This implies that X_1 can be exactly calculated given X_2 and the equation. Examples of such perfect linear relationships would be:

$$X_{1i} = 3X_{2i} \quad \text{or} \quad X_{1i} = 6 + X_{2i} \quad \text{or} \quad X_{1i} = 2 + 4X_{2i} \tag{8.3}$$

Figure 8.1 shows a graph of explanatory variables that are perfectly correlated. As can be seen in Figure 8.1, a perfect linear function has all data

---

1. The word *collinearity* describes a linear correlation between two independent variables, and *multicollinearity* indicates that more than two independent variables are involved. In common usage, multicollinearity is used to apply to both cases, and so we'll typically use that term in this text even though many of the examples and techniques discussed relate, strictly speaking, to collinearity.

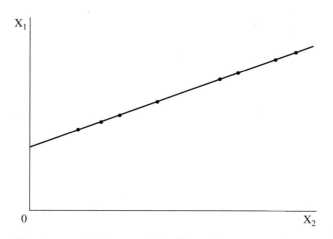

Figure 8.1 Perfect Multicollinearity

With perfect multicollinearity, an independent variable can be completely explained by the movements of one or more other independent variables. Perfect multicollinearity can usually be avoided by careful screening of the independent variables before a regression is run.

points on the same straight line. There is none of the variation that accompanies the data from a typical regression.

Some examples of perfect multicollinearity were briefly mentioned in Section 4.1. Recall what happens when nominal and real interest rates are both included as explanatory variables in an equation. Usually, the relationship between nominal and real interest rates continually changes because the difference between the two, the rate of inflation, is always changing. If the rate of inflation somehow was constant (during extremely strict price controls, for instance), then the difference between the two would be constant, the two would be perfectly linearly related, and perfect multicollinearity would result:

$$\text{in}_t = \text{ir}_t + \text{inf}_t = \text{ir}_t + \alpha \tag{8.4}$$

where: in_t = the nominal (or money) interest rate in time t
ir_t = the real interest rate in time t
inf_t = the rate of inflation in time t
α = the constant rate of inflation

What happens to the estimation of an econometric equation where there is perfect multicollinearity? OLS is incapable of generating estimates of the regression coefficients, and most OLS computer programs will print out an error message in such a situation. Using Equation 8.2 as an example, we theoretically would obtain the following estimated coefficients and standard errors:

$$\hat{\beta}_1 = \text{indeterminate} \qquad SE(\hat{\beta}_1) = \infty \tag{8.5}$$

$$\hat{\beta}_2 = \text{indeterminate} \qquad SE(\hat{\beta}_2) = \infty \tag{8.6}$$

Perfect multicollinearity ruins our ability to estimate the coefficients because the two variables cannot be distinguished. You cannot "hold all the other independent variables in the equation constant" if every time one variable changes, another changes in an identical manner.

Fortunately, instances in which one explanatory variable is a perfect linear function of another are rare. More important, perfect multicollinearity should be fairly easy to discover before a regression is run. You can detect perfect multicollinearity by asking whether one variable equals a multiple of another or if one variable can be derived by adding a constant to another. If so, then one of the variables should be dropped because there is no essential difference between the two.

A special case related to perfect multicollinearity occurs when a variable that is definitionally related to the dependent variable is included as an independent variable in a regression equation. Such a **dominant variable** is by definition so highly correlated with the dependent variable that it completely masks the effects of all other independent variables in the equation. In a sense, this is a case of perfect collinearity between the dependent and an independent variable.

For example, if you include a variable measuring the amount of raw materials used by the shoe industry in a production function for that industry, the raw materials variable would have an extremely high t-score, but otherwise important variables like labor and capital would have quite insignificant t-scores. Why? In essence, if you knew how much leather was used by a shoe factory, you could predict the number of pairs of shoes produced without knowing *anything* about labor or capital. The relationship is definitional, and the dominant variable should be dropped from the equation to get reasonable estimates of the coefficients of the other variables.

A dominant variable involves a tautology; it is defined in such a way that you can calculate the dependent variable from it without any knowledge of the underlying theory. Be careful, though; dominant variables shouldn't be confused with highly significant or important explanatory variables. Instead, they should be recognized as being virtually identical to the dependent variable. While the fit between the two is superb, knowledge of that fit could have been obtained from the definitions of the variables without any econometric estimation.

8.1.2 Imperfect Multicollinearity

Since perfect multicollinearity is fairly easy to avoid, econometricians almost never talk about perfect multicollinearity. Instead, when we use the word multicollinearity, we are really talking about severe imperfect multicollinearity. **Imperfect multicollinearity** can be defined as a linear functional relationship between two or more independent variables that is so strong that it can significantly affect the estimation of the coefficients of the variables.

In other words, imperfect multicollinearity occurs when two (or more) explanatory variables are imperfectly linearly related as in:

$$X_{1i} = \alpha_0 + \alpha_1 X_{2i} + u_i \qquad (8.7)$$

Compare Equation 8.7 to Equation 8.1; notice that Equation 8.7 includes u_i, a stochastic error term. This implies that although the relationship between X_1 and X_2 might be fairly strong, it is not strong enough to allow X_1 to be completely explained by X_2; some unexplained variation still remains. Figure 8.2 shows the graph of two explanatory variables that might be considered imperfectly multicollinear. Notice that although all the observations in the sample are fairly close to the straight line, there is still some variation in X_1 that cannot be explained by X_2.

Imperfect multicollinearity is a strong linear relationship between the explanatory variables. The stronger the relationship between the two (or more) explanatory variables, the more likely it is that they'll be considered significantly multicollinear. Whether explanatory variables are multicollinear in a given equation depends on the theoretical relationship between the variables and on the particular sample chosen. Two variables that might be only slightly related in one sample might be so strongly related in another that they could be considered to be imperfectly multicollinear. In this sense, it is fair to say that multicollinearity is a sample phenomenon as well as a theoretical one. Whether the data are correlated enough to have a significant effect on the estimation of the equation depends on the particular sample drawn, and each sample must be investigated (using, for example, the simple correlation coefficient to measure collinearity) before multicollinearity can be diagnosed. This contrasts with perfect multicollinearity because two variables that are perfectly related probably can be detected on a logical basis. The detection of the multicollinearity will be discussed in more detail in Section 8.3.

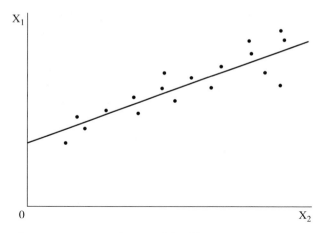

Figure 8.2 Imperfect Multicollinearity

With imperfect multicollinearity, an independent variable is a strong but not perfect linear function of one or more other independent variables. Imperfect multicollinearity varies in degree from sample to sample.

8.2   The Consequences of Multicollinearity

If the multicollinearity in a particular sample is severe, what will happen to estimates calculated from that sample? Since perfect multicollinearity means that the estimation of an equation is impossible, what consequences does significant imperfect multicollinearity imply? The purpose of this section is to explain the consequences of multicollinearity and then to explore some examples of such consequences.

Recall the properties of OLS estimators that might be affected by this or some other econometric problem. In Chapter 4, we stated that the OLS estimators are BLUE (or MvLUE) if the Classical Assumptions hold. This means that OLS estimates can be thought of as being unbiased and having the minimum variance possible for unbiased linear estimators.

8.2.1   What Are the Consequences of Multicollinearity?

The major consequences of multicollinearity are:

1. *Estimates will remain unbiased.* Even if an equation has significant multicollinearity, the estimates of the βs will still be centered around the
   true population βs if all the Classical Assumptions are met for a correctly specified equation.

2. *The variances and standard errors of the estimates will increase.* This is the principal consequence of multicollinearity. Since two or more of the explanatory variables are significantly related, it becomes difficult to precisely identify the separate effects of the multicollinear variables. In essence, we are asking the regression to tell us something about which we have little information. When it becomes hard to distinguish the effect of one variable from the effect of another, then we're much more likely to make large errors in estimating the βs than we were before we encountered multicollinearity. As a result, the estimated coefficients, although still unbiased, now come from distributions with much larger variances and, therefore, standard errors.[2]

To see this, recall the equation for the standard error (the square root of the variance) of an estimated slope coefficient in a multivariate regression model with exactly two independent variables. That equation was Equation 4.10:

$$SE(\hat{\beta}_1) = \sqrt{\frac{\sum e_i^2/(n-3)}{\sum(X_{1i} - \overline{X}_1)^2(1 - r_{12}^2)}} \qquad (4.10)$$

What happens to $SE(\hat{\beta}_1)$, and therefore to the variance, in the face of severe multicollinearity? With multicollinearity, the simple correlation coefficient between X_1 and X_2, r_{12}, will be high. If r_{12} is high, then $(1 - r_{12}^2)$ will be low, causing $SE(\hat{\beta}_2)$ to be high. Thus, multicollinearity causes $SE(\hat{\beta}_1)$ and the variance of the estimated coefficients to be higher than they would be without such correlation.

Figure 8.3 compares a distribution of $\hat{\beta}$s from a sample with severe multicollinearity to one with virtually no correlation between any of the independent variables. Notice that the two distributions have the same mean, indicating that multicollinearity does not cause bias. Also note how much wider the distribution of $\hat{\beta}$ becomes when multicollinearity is severe; this is the result of the increase in the standard error of $\hat{\beta}$ that is caused by multicollinearity.

In particular, with multicollinearity there is a higher probability of obtaining a $\hat{\beta}$ that is dramatically different from the true β. For example, it turns out that multicollinearity increases the likelihood of ob-

---

2. Even though the variances and standard errors are larger with multicollinearity than they are without it, OLS is still BLUE when multicollinearity exists. That is, no other linear unbiased estimation technique can get lower variances than OLS even in the presence of multicollinearity. Thus, although the effect of multicollinearity is to increase the variance of the estimated coefficients, OLS still has the property of minimum variance (these "minimum variances" are just fairly large).

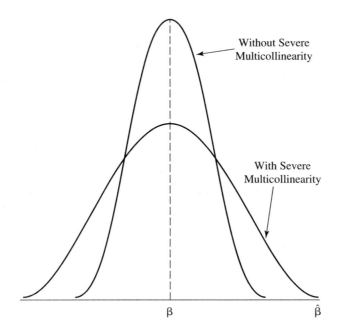

Figure 8.3 Severe Multicollinearity Increases the Variances of the $\hat{\beta}$s

Severe multicollinearity produces a distribution of the $\hat{\beta}$s that is centered around the true β but that has a much wider variance. Thus, the distribution of $\hat{\beta}$s with multicollinearity is much wider than otherwise.

taining an unexpected sign[3] for a coefficient even though, as mentioned above, multicollinearity causes no bias. For more on this, see Exercise 6 at the end of the chapter.

3. *The computed t-scores will fall.* Multicollinearity tends to decrease the t-scores of the estimated coefficients mainly because of the formula for the t-statistic:

$$t_k = \frac{(\hat{\beta}_k - \hat{\beta}_{H_0})}{SE(\hat{\beta}_k)} \qquad (8.8)$$

3. These unexpected signs generally occur because the distribution of the $\hat{\beta}$s with multicollinearity is wider than without it, increasing the chance that a particular observed $\hat{\beta}$ will be on the other side of zero from the true β (have an unexpected sign). More specifically, particular combinations of multicollinear variables can make such unexpected signs occur quite frequently. For instance, if two independent variables both have positive true coefficients and positive simple correlation coefficients with Y in the observed sample, and if the simple correlation coefficient between the independent variables in the sample is higher than either of the two simple correlation coefficients between Y and the Xs, then one of the two slope coefficients is virtually assured of having an unexpected sign.

Notice that this equation is divided by the standard error of the estimated coefficient. Multicollinearity increases the variance, estimated variance, and therefore the standard error of the estimated coefficient. If the standard error increases, then the t-score must fall, as can be seen from Equation 8.8. Not surprisingly, it's quite common to observe low t-scores in equations with severe multicollinearity.

4. *Estimates will become very sensitive to changes in specification.* The addition or deletion of an explanatory variable or of a few observations will often cause major changes in the values of the $\hat{\beta}$s when significant multicollinearity exists. If you drop a variable, even one that appears to be statistically insignificant, the coefficients of the remaining variables in the equation will sometimes change dramatically.

These large changes occur because OLS estimation is sometimes forced to emphasize small differences between variables in order to distinguish the effect of one multicollinear variable from another. Thus even a minor specification change can cause a major change in the attribute on which the computer program had "focused," and the estimated coefficients can change significantly. If two variables are virtually identical throughout most of the sample, the estimation procedure relies on the observations in which the variables move differently in order to distinguish between them. As a result, a specification change that drops a variable that has an unusual value for one of these crucial observations can cause the estimated coefficients of the multicollinear variables to change dramatically.

5. *The overall fit of the equation and the estimation of nonmulticollinear variables will be largely unaffected.* Even though the individual t-scores are often quite low in a multicollinear equation, the overall fit of the equation, as measured by $\overline{R}^2$ or the *F*-test, will not fall much, if at all, in the face of significant multicollinearity. One of the unique consequences of multicollinearity is that the overall level of significance of an equation is affected far less by multicollinearity than are the levels of significance of the individual regression coefficients. Multicollinearity severe enough to substantially lower t-scores does little to increase $\overline{R}^2$ and the F-statistic. Given this, one of the first indications of severe multicollinearity is the combination of a high $\overline{R}^2$ with no statistically significant individual regression coefficients.

Because multicollinearity has little effect on the overall fit of the equation, it will also have little effect on the use of that equation for prediction or forecasting, as long as the independent variables maintain the same pattern of multicollinearity in the forecast period that they demonstrated in the sample.

Similarly, if an explanatory variable in an equation is not multi-collinear (also called orthogonal) with the other variables, then the estimation of its coefficient and standard error usually will not be affected. It's unusual to find an explanatory variable that's totally uncorrelated with any other explanatory variable. If this were to occur, though, then the multicollinearity in the rest of the equation would not change the estimated coefficient or the t-score of the nonmulticollinear variable.

8.2.2 Two Examples of the Consequences of Multicollinearity

To see what severe multicollinearity does to an estimated equation, let's look at a hypothetical example. Suppose you decide to estimate a "student consumption function." After the appropriate preliminary work, you come up with the following hypothesized equation:

$$CO_i = f(\overset{+}{Yd_i}, \overset{+}{LA_i}) + \epsilon_i = \beta_0 + \beta_1 Yd_i + \beta_2 LA_i + \epsilon_i \qquad (8.9)$$

where: CO_i = the annual consumption expenditures of the ith student on items other than tuition and room and board
Yd_i = the annual disposable income (including gifts) of that student
LA_i = the liquid assets (savings, etc.) of the ith student
ϵ_i = a stochastic error term

You then collect a small amount of data from people who are sitting near you in class:

Student	CO_i	Yd_i	LA_i
Mary	$2000	$2500	$25000
Robby	2300	3000	31000
Jim	2800	3500	33000
Giorgio	3800	4000	39000
Colleen	3500	4500	48000
Jennifer	5000	5000	54000
Harwood	4500	5500	55000

Note: filename CONS8

If you run an OLS regression on your data set for Equation 8.9, you obtain:

$$\widehat{CO}_i = -367.83 + 0.5113Yd_i + 0.0427LA_i \qquad (8.10)$$
$$(1.0307) \qquad (0.0942)$$
$$t = 0.496 \qquad 0.453$$
$$\overline{R}^2 = .835$$

On the other hand, if you had consumption as a function of disposable income alone, then you would have obtained:

$$\widehat{CO}_i = -471.43 + 0.9714Yd_i \qquad (8.11)$$
$$(0.157)$$
$$t = 6.187$$
$$\overline{R}^2 = .861$$

Notice from Equations 8.10 and 8.11 that the t-score for disposable income increases more than 10-fold when the liquid assets variable is dropped from the equation. Why does this happen? First of all, the simple correlation coefficient between Yd and LA is quite high: $r_{Yd,LA} = .986$. This high degree of correlation causes the standard errors of the estimated coefficients to be very high when both variables are included. In the case of $\hat{\beta}_{Yd}$, the standard error goes from 0.157 to 1.03! In addition, the coefficient estimate itself changes somewhat. Further, note that the $\overline{R}^2$s of the two equations are quite similar despite the large differences in the significance of the explanatory variables in the two equations. It's quite common for $\overline{R}^2$ to stay virtually unchanged when multicollinear variables are dropped. All of these results are typical of equations with multicollinearity.

Which equation is better? If the liquid assets variable theoretically belongs in the equation, then to drop it will run the risk of omitted variable bias, but to include the variable will mean certain multicollinearity. There is no automatic answer when dealing with multicollinearity. We'll discuss this issue in more detail in Sections 8.4 and 8.5.

A second example of the consequences of multicollinearity is based on actual, rather than hypothetical, data. Suppose you've decided to build a cross-sectional model of the demand for gasoline by state:

$$PCON_i = f(\overset{+}{UHM}_i, \overset{-}{TAX}_i, \overset{+}{REG}_i) + \epsilon_i \qquad (8.12)$$

where: $PCON_i$ = petroleum consumption in the ith state (trillions of BTUs)
UHM_i = urban highway miles within the ith state
TAX_i = the gasoline tax rate in the ith state (cents per gallon)
REG_i = motor vehicle registrations in the ith state (thousands)

A complete listing of the data for this model is contained in Section 10.5, so let's move on to the estimation of Equation 8.12 using a linear functional form (assuming a stochastic error term):

$$\widehat{PCON_i} = 389.6 + 60.8UHM_i - 36.5TAX_i - 0.061REG_i \qquad (8.13)$$

$$\begin{array}{cccc} & (10.3) & (13.2) & (0.043) \\ & t = 5.92 & -2.77 & -1.43 \\ & n = 50 & \overline{R}^2 = .919 \end{array}$$

What's wrong with this equation? The motor vehicle registrations variable has an insignificant coefficient with an unexpected sign, but it's hard to believe that the variable is irrelevant. Is a left-out variable causing bias? It's possible, but adding a variable is unlikely to fix things. Does it help to know that the simple correlation coefficient between REG and UHM is 0.98? Given that, it seems fair to say that one of the two variables is redundant; both variables are really measuring the *size* of the state, so we have multicollinearity.

Notice the impact of the multicollinearity on the equation. The coefficient of a variable such as motor vehicle registrations, which has a very strong theoretical relationship to petroleum consumption, is insignificant and has a sign contrary to our expectations. This is mainly because the multicollinearity has increased the variance of the distribution of the estimated $\hat{\beta}$s.

What would happen if we were to drop one of the multicollinear variables?

$$\widehat{PCON_i} = 551.7 - 53.6TAX_i + 0.186REG_i \qquad (8.14)$$

$$\begin{array}{ccc} & (16.9) & (0.012) \\ & t = -3.18 & 15.88 \\ & n = 50 & \overline{R}^2 = .861 \end{array}$$

Dropping UHM has made REG extremely significant. Why did this occur? The answer is that the standard error of the coefficient of REG has fallen substantially (from 0.043 to 0.012) now that the multicollinearity has been removed from the equation. Also note that the sign of the estimated coefficient has now become positive as hypothesized. The reason is that REG and UHM are virtually indistinguishable from an empirical point of view, and so the OLS program latched onto minor differences between the variables to explain the movements of PCON. Once the multicollinearity was removed, the direct positive relationship between REG and PCON was obvious. Note, however, that the coefficient of the REG variable now measures the effect of both REG and UHM on PCON. Since we've dropped a variable, the remaining coefficient soaks up the effect of the left-out variable.

Either UHM or REG could have been dropped with similar results because the two variables are, in a quantitative sense, virtually identical as indicated by the high simple correlation coefficient between them. In this case, REG was judged to be theoretically superior to UHM. Even though $\overline{R}^2$ fell when UHM was dropped, Equation 8.14 should be considered superior to Equation 8.13. This is an example of the point, first made in Chapter 3, that the fit of the equation is not the most important criterion to be used in determining its overall quality.

8.3   The Detection of Multicollinearity

How do we decide whether an equation has a severe multicollinearity problem? A first step is to recognize that some multicollinearity exists in every equation. It's virtually impossible in a real-world example to find a set of explanatory variables in which the explanatory variables are totally uncorrelated with each other. Our main purpose in this section will be to learn to determine *how much* multicollinearity exists in an equation, not *whether* any multicollinearity exists.

A second key point is that multicollinearity is a sample phenomenon as well as a theoretical one. That is, the severity of multicollinearity in a given equation can change from sample to sample depending on the characteristics of the sample. As a result, the theoretical underpinnings of the equation are not quite as important in the detection of multicollinearity as they are in the detection of an omitted variable or an incorrect functional form. Instead, we tend to rely more on data-oriented techniques to determine the severity of the multicollinearity in a given sample. Of course, we can never ignore the theory behind an equation. The trick is to find variables that are theoretically relevant (for meaningful interpretation) and that are also statistically non-multicollinear (for meaningful inference).

Because multicollinearity is a sample phenomenon, and the level of damage of its impact is a matter of degree, many of the methods used to detect it are informal tests without critical values or levels of significance. Indeed, there are no generally accepted, true statistical tests for multicollinearity. Most researchers develop a general feeling for the severity of multicollinearity in an estimated equation by looking at a number of the characteristics of that equation. Let's examine two of the most-used of those characteristics.

8.3.1   High Simple Correlation Coefficients

One way to detect severe multicollinearity is to examine the simple correlation coefficients between the explanatory variables. If an r is high in absolute value, then we know that these two particular Xs are quite correlated and that multicollinearity is a potential problem. For example, in Equation 8.10, the simple correlation coefficient between disposable income and liquid assets is 0.986. A simple correlation coefficient this high, especially in an equation with only two independent variables, is a certain indication of severe multicollinearity.

How high is high? Some researchers pick an arbitrary number, such as 0.80, and become concerned about multicollinearity any time the absolute value of a simple correlation coefficient exceeds 0.80.

A more systematic method is to test the significance of individual simple correlation coefficients using the *t*-test as described in Equation 5.11 in Section 5.3. (For practice in using this test, see Exercise 10 of Chapter 5.) Unfortunately, the *t*-test on r rejects the null hypothesis that r = 0 for simple correlation coefficients with absolute values well below 0.80. Some researchers avoid this problem by using two-sided tests at the 1 percent level.

Be careful; all tests of simple correlation coefficients as an indication of the extent of multicollinearity share a major limitation if there are more than two explanatory variables. It is quite possible for groups of independent variables, acting together, to cause multicollinearity without any single simple correlation coefficient being high enough to prove that multicollinearity is in fact severe. As a result, tests of simple correlation coefficients must be considered to be sufficient but not necessary tests for multicollinearity. Although a high r does indeed indicate the probability of severe multicollinearity, a low r by no means proves otherwise.[4]

8.3.2 High Variance Inflation Factors (VIFs)

The use of tests to give an indication of the severity of multicollinearity in a particular sample is controversial. Some econometricians reject even the simple indicator described above, mainly because of the limitations cited. Others tend to use a variety of more formal tests.[5]

One measure of the severity of multicollinearity that is easy to use and that is gaining in popularity is the variance inflation factor. The **variance inflation factor (VIF)** is a method of detecting the severity of multicollinearity by

---

4. Most authors criticize the use of simple correlation coefficients to detect multicollinearity in equations with large numbers of explanatory variables, but many researchers continue to do so because a scan of the simple correlation coefficients is a "quick and dirty" way to get a feel for the degree of multicollinearity in an equation.

5. Perhaps the most used of these is the Condition number. For more on the Condition number, which is a single index of the degree of multicollinearity in the overall equation, see D. A. Belsley, E. Kuh, and R. E. Welsch, *Regression Diagnostics, Identifying Influential Data and Sources of Collinearity* (New York: Wiley, 1980), Chapter 3.

looking at the extent to which a given explanatory variable can be explained by all the other explanatory variables in the equation. There is a VIF for each explanatory variable in an equation. The VIF is an estimate of how much multicollinearity has increased the variance of an estimated coefficient. A high VIF indicates that multicollinearity has increased the estimated variance of the estimated coefficient by quite a bit, yielding a decreased t-score.

Suppose you want to use the VIF to attempt to detect multicollinearity in an original equation with k independent variables:

$$Y = \beta_0 + \beta_1 X_1 + \beta_2 X_2 + \cdots + \beta_k X_k + \epsilon$$

Doing so requires calculating k different VIFs, one for each X_i. Calculating the VIF for a given X_i involves three steps:

1. *Run an OLS regression that has X_i as a function of all the other explanatory variables in the equation.* For example, if i = 1, then this equation would be:

$$X_1 = \alpha_1 + \alpha_2 X_2 + \alpha_3 X_3 + \cdots + \alpha_k X_k + v \qquad (8.15)$$

   where v is a typical stochastic error term. Note that X_1 is not included on the right-hand side of Equation 8.15, which is referred to as an auxiliary regression. Thus there are k auxiliary regressions, one for each independent variable in the original equation.

2. *Calculate the variance inflation factor for $\hat{\beta}_i$:*

$$VIF(\hat{\beta}_i) = \frac{1}{(1 - R_i^2)} \qquad (8.16)$$

   where R_i^2 is the coefficient of determination (the unadjusted R^2) of the auxiliary regression in step one. Since there is a separate auxiliary regression for each independent variable in the original equation, there also is an R_i^2 and a $VIF(\hat{\beta}_i)$ for each X_i.

3. *Analyze the degree of multicollinearity by evaluating the size of the $VIF(\hat{\beta}_i)$.* The higher a given variable's VIF, the higher the variance of that variable's estimated coefficient (holding constant the variance of the error term.) Hence, the higher the VIF, the more severe the effects of multicollinearity.

Why will a high VIF indicate multicollinearity? The $\text{VIF}(\hat{\beta}_i)$ can be thought of as the ratio of the estimated variance of $\hat{\beta}_i$ to what the variance would be with no correlation between X_i and the other Xs in the equation. How high is high? An R_i^2 of one, indicating perfect multicollinearity, produces a VIF of infinity, whereas an R_i^2 of zero, indicating no multicollinearity at all, produces a VIF of one. While there is no table of formal critical VIF values, a common rule of thumb is that if $\text{VIF}(\hat{\beta}_i) > 5$, the multicollinearity is severe.

For example, let's return to Equation 8.10 and calculate the VIFs for both independent variables. Both VIFs equal 36, confirming the quite severe multicollinearity we already know exists. It's no coincidence that the VIFs for the two variables are equal. In an equation with exactly two independent variables, the two auxiliary equations will have identical R_i^2s, leading to equal VIFs.[6]

Thus, the VIF is a method of detecting multicollinearity that takes into account all the explanatory variables at once. Some authors and statistical software programs replace the VIF with its reciprocal, $(1 - R_i^2)$, called *tolerance*, or TOL. Whether we calculate VIF or TOL is a matter of personal preference, but either way, the general approach is the most comprehensive multicollinearity detection technique we've discussed in this text.

Unfortunately, there are a couple of problems with using VIFs. First, as mentioned, there is no hard-and-fast VIF decision rule. Second, it's possible to have multicollinear effects in an equation that has no large VIFs. For instance, if the simple correlation coefficient between X_1 and X_2 is 0.88, multicollinear effects are quite likely, and yet the VIF for the equation (assuming no other Xs) is only 4.4.

In essence, then, the VIF is a sufficient but not necessary test for multicollinearity, just like the other test described in this section. Indeed, as is probably obvious to the reader by now, there is no test that allows a researcher to reject the possibility of multicollinearity with any real certainty.

8.4 Remedies for Multicollinearity

What can be done to minimize the consequences of severe multicollinearity? There is no automatic answer to this question because multicollinearity is a phenomenon that could change from sample to sample even for the same

---

6. Another use for the R^2s of these auxiliary equations is to compare them with the overall equation's R^2. If an auxiliary equation's R^2 is higher, it's yet another sign of multicollinearity.

specification of a regression equation. The purpose of this section is to out-line a number of alternative remedies for multicollinearity that might be ap-propriate under certain circumstances.

8.4.1 Do Nothing

The first step to take once severe multicollinearity has been diagnosed is to decide whether anything should be done at all. As we'll see, it turns out that every remedy for multicollinearity has a drawback of some sort, and so it of-ten happens that doing nothing is the correct course of action.

One reason for doing nothing is that multicollinearity in an equation will not always reduce the t-scores enough to make them insignificant or change the $\hat{\beta}$s enough to make them differ from expectations. In other words, the mere existence of multicollinearity does not necessarily mean anything. A remedy for multicollinearity should be considered only if the consequences cause insignificant t-scores or unreliable estimated coefficients. For example, it's possible to observe a simple correlation coefficient of .97 between two ex-planatory variables and yet have each individual t-score be significant. It makes no sense to consider remedial action in such a case, because any rem-edy for multicollinearity would probably cause other problems for the equa-tion. In a sense, multicollinearity is similar to a non-life-threatening human disease that requires general anesthesia to operate on the patient: The risk of the operation should be undertaken only if the disease is causing a signifi-cant problem.

A second reason for doing nothing is that the deletion of a multicollinear variable that belongs in an equation is fairly dangerous because it will cause specification bias. If we drop such a variable, then we are *purposely* creating bias. Given all the effort typically spent avoiding omitted variables, it seems foolhardy to consider running that risk on purpose. As a result, experienced econometricians often will leave multicollinear variables in equations de-spite low t-scores.

The final reason for considering doing nothing to offset multicollinearity is a theoretical one that would apply to all equations. Every time a regression is rerun, we risk encountering a specification that fits because it accidentally works for the particular data set involved, not because it is the truth. The larger the number of experiments, the greater the chances of finding the acci-dental result. In addition, when there is significant multicollinearity in the sample, the odds of strange results increase rapidly because of the sensitivity of the coefficient estimates to slight specification changes. Thus, the case against sequential specification searches outlined in Chapter 6 is even stronger in the face of severe multicollinearity.

To sum, it is often best to leave an equation unadjusted in the face of all but extreme multicollinearity. Such advice might be difficult for beginning researchers to take, however, if they think that it's embarrassing to report that their final regression is one with insignificant t-scores. Compared to the alternatives of possible omitted variable bias or accidentally significant regression results, the low t-scores seem like a minor problem. For an example of "doing nothing" in the face of severe multicollinearity, see Section 8.5.1.

8.4.2   Drop a Redundant Variable

On occasion, the simple solution of dropping one of the multicollinear variables is a good one. For example, some inexperienced researchers include too many variables in their regressions, not wanting to face left-out variable bias. As a result, they often have two or more variables in their equations that are measuring essentially the same thing. In such a case the multicollinear variables are not irrelevant, since any one of them is quite probably theoretically and statistically sound. Instead, the variables might be called **redundant;** only one of them is needed to represent the effect on the dependent variable that all of them currently represent. For example, in an aggregate demand function, it would not make sense to include disposable income and GDP because both are measuring the same thing: income. A bit more subtle is the inference that population and disposable income should not both be included in the same aggregate demand function because, once again, they really are measuring the same thing: the size of the aggregate market. As population rises, so too will income. Dropping these kinds of redundant multicollinear variables is doing nothing more than making up for a specification error; the variables should never have been included in the first place.

To see how this solution would work, let's return to the student consumption function example of Equation 8.10:

$$\widehat{CO}_i = -367.83 + 0.5113Yd_i + 0.0427LA_i \qquad (8.10)$$
$$(1.0307) \qquad (0.0942)$$
$$t = 0.496 \qquad 0.453 \qquad \overline{R}^2 = .835$$

where CO = consumption, Yd = disposable income, and LA = liquid assets. When we first discussed this example, we compared this result to the same equation without the liquid assets variable (also reproduced):

$$\widehat{CO}_i = -471.43 + 0.9714Yd_i \qquad (8.11)$$
$$(0.157)$$
$$t = 6.187 \qquad \overline{R}^2 = .861$$

If we had instead dropped the disposable income variable, we would have obtained:

$$\widehat{CO}_i = -199.44 + 0.08876 LA_i \qquad (8.17)$$
$$(0.01443)$$
$$t = 6.153 \qquad \overline{R}^2 = .860$$

Note that dropping one of the multicollinear variables has eliminated both the multicollinearity between the two explanatory variables and also the low t-score of the coefficient of the remaining variable. By dropping Yd, we were able to increase t_{LA} from 0.453 to 6.153. Since dropping a variable changes the meaning of the remaining coefficient (because the dropped variable is no longer being held constant), such dramatic changes are not unusual. The coefficient of the remaining included variable also now measures almost all of the joint impact on the dependent variable of the multicollinear explanatory variables.

Assuming you want to drop a variable, how do you decide which variable to drop? In cases of severe multicollinearity, it makes no statistical difference which variable is dropped. To see this, compare the $\overline{R}^2$ and the t-score from Equation 8.11 with those in Equation 8.17. Note that they are virtually identical. This is hardly a surprise, since the variables themselves move in virtually identical patterns. As a result, it doesn't make sense to pick the variable to be dropped on the basis of which one gives superior fit or which one is more significant (or has the expected sign) in the original equation. Instead, the theoretical underpinnings of the model should be the basis for such a decision. In the example of the student consumption function, there is more theoretical support for the hypothesis that disposable income determines consumption than there is for the liquid assets hypothesis. Therefore, Equation 8.11 should be preferred to Equation 8.17.

8.4.3 Transform the Multicollinear Variables

On rare occasions, the consequences of multicollinearity are serious enough to warrant the consideration of remedial action when the variables are all extremely important on theoretical grounds. In these cases, neither inaction nor dropping a variable is especially helpful. However, it's sometimes possible to transform the variables in the equation to get rid of at least some of the multicollinearity. The two most common such transformations are to:

1. Form a combination of the multicollinear variables.
2. Transform the equation into first differences.

The technique of forming a **combination** of two or more of the multi-collinear variables consists of creating a new variable that is a function of the multicollinear variables and using the new variable to replace the old ones in the regression equation.

For example, if X_1 and X_2 are highly multicollinear, a new variable, $X_3 = X_1 + X_2$ (or more generally, any linear combination of the two variables like $k_1 X_1 + k_2 X_2$) might be substituted for both of the multicollinear variables in a reestimation of the model. This technique is especially useful if the equation is going to be for forecasting, since the multicollinearity outside the sample might not exist or might not follow the same pattern that it did inside the sample.

A major disadvantage of the technique is that both portions of the combination variable are forced to have the same coefficient in the reestimated equation. For example, if $X_{3i} = X_{1i} + X_{2i}$:

$$Y_i = \beta_0 + \beta_3 X_{3i} + \epsilon_i = \beta_0 + \beta_3(X_{1i} + X_{2i}) + \epsilon_i \qquad (8.18)$$

Care must be taken not to include (in a combination) variables with different expected coefficients (such as different expected signs) or dramatically different mean values (such as different orders of magnitude) without adjusting for these differences by using appropriate constants (ks) in the more general equation $X_3 = k_1 X_1 + k_2 X_2$.

The second kind of transformation to consider as a possible remedy for severe multicollinearity is to switch the functional form of the equation to first differences. A **first difference** is nothing more than the change in a variable from the previous time period to the current time period (which we've referred to as "delta" or Δ). That is, we shall define a first difference as:

$$\Delta X_t = X_t - X_{t-1}$$

If an equation (or some of the variables in an equation) is switched from its normal specification to a first difference specification, it's quite likely that the degree of multicollinearity will be significantly reduced for two reasons. First, any change in the definitions of the variables (except a simple linear change) will change the degree of multicollinearity. Second, multicollinearity takes place most frequently (although certainly not exclusively) in time-series data, in which first differences are far less likely to move steadily upward than are the aggregates from which they are calculated. For example, although GDP might grow only 5 or 6 percent from year to year, the *change in GDP* (or the first difference) could fluctuate severely.

Although the severity of multicollinearity sometimes can be diminished by switching to first differences, changing the functional form of an equation simply to avoid multicollinearity is almost never worth the possible theoretical complications. For example, modeling capital stock is not the same as modeling the change in capital stock, which is investment, even though one equation can be derived from the other. If the basic purpose of running the regression were to model first differences, then the model should have been specified that way in the first place.

Using first differences has one unexpected advantage, however. This involves the concept of a *nonstationary* time series, or a time series that has a significant trend of some sort (for example, a rapidly increasing mean or variance over time). Evidence of multicollinearity in a time series is often evidence that a number of the independent variables are nonstationary. By coincidence, one possible (though inefficient) remedy for nonstationary variables is to convert to first differences, so first differences are possible remedies for *both* multicollinearity and nonstationarity. Thus, beginning econometricians who use first differences to "cure" multicollinearity sometimes are doing the right thing for the wrong reason! We'll discuss nonstationarity in more detail in Chapter 12.

8.4.4 Increase the Size of the Sample

Another way to deal with multicollinearity is to attempt to increase the size of the sample to reduce the degree of multicollinearity. Although such increases may be impossible when limitations of some sort exist, they are useful alternatives to be considered when they are feasible.

The idea behind increasing the size of the sample is that a larger data set (often requiring new data collection) will allow more accurate estimates than a small one, since the large sample normally will reduce somewhat the variance of the estimated coefficients, diminishing the impact of the multicollinearity.

For most economic and business applications, however, this solution isn't feasible. After all, samples typically are drawn by getting all the available data that seem comparable. As a result, new data are generally impossible or quite expensive to find. Going out and generating new data is much easier in an experimental situation than it is when the samples must be generated by the passage of time.

One way to increase the sample is to pool cross-sectional and time-series data. Such a combination of data sources usually consists of the addition of cross-sectional data (typically nonmulticollinear) to multicollinear time-series data, thus potentially reducing the multicollinearity in the total sample. The major problem with this pooling is in the interpretation and use of the estimates that are generated. Unless there is reason to believe that the underlying theoretical model is the same in both settings, the parameter estimates obtained will be some sort of joint functions of the true time-series model and the true cross-sectional model. In general, combining different kinds of data is not recommended as a means of avoiding multicollinearity. In most cases, the unknown interpretation difficulties are worse than the known consequences of the multicollinearity.

8.5   Choosing the Proper Remedy

Of all the remedies listed, how do you go about making a choice? There is no automatic answer to this question; an adjustment for multicollinearity that might be useful in one equation could be inappropriate in another. As a result, all that this section can accomplish is to illustrate general guidelines to follow when attempting to rid an equation of severe multicollinearity.

8.5.1   Why Multicollinearity Often Should Be Left Unadjusted

Our first case provides an example of the idea that multicollinearity is often best left unadjusted. Suppose you work in the marketing department of a hypothetical soft drink company and you build a model of the impact on sales of your firm's advertising:

$$\hat{S}_t = 3080 - 75,000P_t + 4.23A_t - 1.04B_t \qquad (8.19)$$
$$\phantom{\hat{S}_t = 3080} (25,000) \quad (1.06) \quad (0.51)$$
$$\phantom{\hat{S}_t = 3080} t = -3.00 \quad\;\; 3.99 \quad\; -2.04$$
$$\phantom{\hat{S}_t = 3080} \overline{R}^2 = .825 \quad\;\; n = 28$$

where: S_t = sales of the soft drink in year t
P_t = average relative price of the drink in year t
A_t = advertising expenditures for the company in year t
B_t = advertising expenditures for the company's main competitor in year t

Assume that there are no left-out variables. All variables are measured in real dollars; that is, the nominal values are divided, or deflated, by a price index.

On the face of it, this is a reasonable-looking result. Estimated coefficients are significant in the directions implied by the underlying theory, and both the overall fit and the size of the coefficients seem acceptable. Suppose you now were told that advertising in the soft drink industry is cutthroat in nature and that firms tend to match their main competitor's advertising expenditures. This would lead you to suspect that significant multicollinearity was possible. Further suppose that the simple correlation coefficient between the two advertising variables is 0.974.

Such a correlation coefficient is evidence that there is severe multicollinearity in the equation, but there is no reason even to consider doing anything about it, because the coefficients are so powerful that their t-scores remain significant, even in the face of severe multicollinearity. Unless multicollinearity causes problems in the equation, it should be left unadjusted. To change the specification might give us better-looking results, but the adjustment would decrease our chances of obtaining the best possible estimates of the true coefficients. Although it's certainly lucky that there were no major problems due to multicollinearity in this example, that luck is no reason to try to fix something that isn't broken.

When a variable is dropped from an equation, its effect will be absorbed by the other explanatory variables to the extent that they are correlated with the newly omitted variable. It's likely that the remaining multicollinear variable(s) will absorb virtually all the bias, since the variables are highly correlated. This bias may destroy whatever usefulness the estimates had before the variable was dropped.

For example, if a variable, say B, is dropped from the equation to fix the multicollinearity, then the following might occur:

$$\hat{S}_t = 2586 - 78{,}000P_t + 0.52A_t \qquad (8.20)$$
$$(24{,}000) \quad (4.32)$$
$$t = -3.25 \quad 0.12$$
$$\overline{R}^2 = .531 \qquad n = 28$$

What's going on here? The company's advertising coefficient becomes less instead of more significant when one of the multicollinear variables is dropped. To see why, first note that the expected bias on $\hat{\beta}_A$ is negative because the product of the expected sign of the coefficient of B and of the correlation between A and B is negative:

$$\text{Bias} = \beta_B \cdot f(r_{A,B}) = (-) \cdot (+) = - \qquad (8.21)$$

Second, this negative bias is strong enough to decrease the estimated coefficient of A until it is insignificant. Although this problem could have been avoided by using a relative advertising variable (A divided by B, for instance), that formulation would have forced identical absolute coefficients on the two advertising effects. Such identical coefficients will sometimes be theoretically expected or empirically reasonable but, in most cases, these kinds of constraints will force bias onto an equation that previously had none.

This example is simplistic, but its results are typical in cases in which equations are adjusted for multicollinearity by dropping a variable without regard to the effect that the deletion is going to have. The point here is that it's quite often theoretically or operationally unwise to drop a variable from an equation and that multicollinearity in such cases is best left unadjusted.

8.5.2   A More Complete Example of Dealing with Multicollinearity

Finally, let's work through a more complete example of dealing with significant multicollinearity, a model of the annual demand for fish in the United States from 1946 to 1970.[7] Suppose that you decide to try to confirm your idea that the Pope's 1966 decision to allow Catholics to eat meat on non-Lent Fridays caused a shift in the demand function for fish (instead of just changing the days of the week when fish was eaten without changing the total amount of fish consumed). Let's say your hypothesized equation was:

$$F_t = f(\overset{-}{PF_t}, \overset{+}{PB_t}, \overset{+}{Yd_t}, \overset{+}{N_t}, \overset{-}{P_t}) + \epsilon_t \qquad (8.22)$$

where: F_t = average pounds of fish consumed per capita in year t
            PF_t = price index for fish in year t
            PB_t = price index for beef in year t
            Yd_t = real per capita disposable income in year t (in billions of dollars)
            N_t = the number of Catholics in the United States in year t (tens of thousands)
            P_t = a dummy variable equal to 1 after the Pope's 1966 decision and 0 otherwise

and that you chose the following functional form:

$$F_t = \beta_0 + \beta_1 PF_t + \beta_2 PB_t + \beta_3 \ln Yd_t + \beta_4 N_t + \beta_5 P_t + \epsilon_t \qquad (8.23)$$

A few words about this specification are in order. First, note that the method you have chosen to test your hypothesis is an intercept dummy. Since you've

---

7. The data used in this study were obtained from *Historical Statistics of the U.S., Colonial Times to 1970* (Washington, D.C.: U.S. Bureau of the Census, 1975).

TABLE 8.1	DATA FOR THE FISH/POPE EXAMPLE				
Year	**F**	**PF**	**PB**	**N**	**Yd**
1946	12.8	56.0	50.1	24402	1606
1947	12.3	64.3	71.3	25268	1513
1948	13.1	74.1	81.0	26076	1567
1949	12.9	74.5	76.2	26718	1547
1950	13.8	73.1	80.3	27766	1646
1951	13.2	83.4	91.0	28635	1657
1952	13.3	81.3	90.2	29408	1678
1953	13.6	78.2	84.2	30425	1726
1954	13.5	78.7	83.7	31648	1714
1955	12.9	77.1	77.1	32576	1795
1956	12.9	77.0	74.5	33574	1839
1957	12.8	78.0	82.8	34564	1844
1958	13.3	83.4	92.2	36024	1831
1959	13.7	84.9	88.8	39505	1881
1960	13.2	85.0	87.2	40871	1883
1961	13.7	86.9	88.3	42105	1909
1962	13.6	90.5	90.1	42882	1969
1963	13.7	90.3	88.7	43847	2015
1964	13.5	88.2	87.3	44874	2126
1965	13.9	90.8	93.9	45640	2239
1966	13.9	96.7	102.6	46246	2335
1967	13.6	100.0	100.0	46864	2403
1968	14.0	101.6	102.3	47468	2486
1969	14.2	107.2	111.4	47873	2534
1970	14.8	118.0	117.6	47872	2610

Source: *Historical Statistics of the U.S., Colonial Times to 1970* (Washington, D.C.: U.S. Bureau of the Census, 1975).

Note: filename FISH8

stated that you expect this coefficient to be negative, the null hypothesis should be $H_0: \beta_5 \geq 0$. Second, you've chosen a semilog function to relate disposable income to the quantity of fish consumed; this is consistent with the theory that as income rises, the portion of that extra income devoted to the consumption of fish will decrease. Leaving other valid criticisms aside, let's investigate the model and the consequences of multicollinearity for it.

After collecting the data (which are in Table 8.1), you obtain the following OLS estimates:

$$\hat{F}_t = -1.99 + 0.039PF_t - 0.00077PB_t + 1.77\ln Yd_t \quad (8.24)$$
$$(0.031) \quad\quad (0.02020) \quad\quad (1.87)$$
$$t = \quad 1.27 \quad\quad\quad -0.0384 \quad\quad\quad 0.945$$
$$-0.0031N_t - 0.355P_t$$
$$(0.0033) \quad (0.353)$$
$$t = -0.958 \quad\quad -1.01$$
$$\overline{R}^2 = .666 \quad\quad n = 25$$

This result is not encouraging, since you don't have to look at a t-table to know that none of your estimated coefficients is significant. In addition, three of your coefficients have unexpected signs. Your problems could have been caused, for example, by omitted variables (biasing the coefficients), irrelevant variables (not belonging in the equation), or multicollinearity (a good guess, since this is the topic of the current chapter).

Where do you start? If you have confidence in your review of the literature and the theoretical work you did before estimating the equation, a good place would be to see if there are any signs of multicollinearity. Supporting this decision is the $\overline{R}^2$ of .666 (an ominous number in a religious regression), which seems fairly high for such unanimously insignificant t-scores.

One measure of severe multicollinearity is the size of the simple correlation coefficients. Looking at the variables without knowing those statistics, which pairs (or sets) of variables look likely to be significantly correlated? It appears that per capita disposable income and the number of Catholics are quite likely to be highly correlated in virtually any time-series sample from the United States, and both appear to have been included in the equation to measure buying power. Sure enough, the correlation coefficient between N_t and $\ln Yd_t$ is .946.

In addition, it's not unreasonable to think that food prices might move together. Since the prices that we observe are equilibrium prices, supply and demand shocks might affect beef and fish price indices in similar ways. For example, an oil spill that makes fish unmarketable will admittedly raise the price of fish, but that increase will almost surely shift the demand for beef upward, thus increasing the price of beef. Thus it is quite possible for prices of substitutes to tend to move together. As it turns out, the simple correlation coefficient between the two price variables is .958. With multicollinearity of this severity between two variables with opposite expected signs, it is no surprise that the two coefficients "switched signs." As multicollinearity increases, the distribution of the $\hat{\beta}$s widens, and the probability of observing an unexpected sign increases.

The second method of detecting multicollinearity, the size of the variance inflation factors, also indicates severe problems. All the VIFs for Equation 8.24 except VIF_P are well above the VIF > 5 indicator of severe multicollinearity:

$$VIF_{PF} = 43.4$$
$$VIF_{\ln Yd} = 23.3$$
$$VIF_{PB} = 18.9$$
$$VIF_{N} = 18.5$$
$$VIF_{P} = 4.4$$

So, there appears to be significant multicollinearity in the model. What, if anything, should you do about it? Before going on with this section, go back over Equation 8.24 and review not only the estimates but also the underlying theory.

The easiest multicollinearity to cope with is between income and the number of Catholics. Independently, either variable is quite likely to be significant because each represents the increase in the buying power of the market over time. Together, however, they ruin each other's chances because of multicollinearity. As a result, one should be dropped as a *redundant* variable; they should never have been included together in the first place. Given that the logic behind including the number of Catholics in a per capita fish demand equation is fairly weak, you decide to drop N:

$$\hat{F}_t = 7.96 + 0.03PF_t + 0.0047PB_t + 0.36\ln Yd_t - 0.12P_t \qquad (8.25)$$
$$(0.03) \qquad (0.019) \qquad (1.15) \qquad (0.26)$$
$$t = 0.98 \qquad 0.24 \qquad 0.31 \qquad -0.48$$
$$\overline{R}^2 = .667 \qquad n = 25$$

Take a look at Equation 8.25. Have we solved our multicollinearity problem? Dropping N certainly eliminated a redundant variable from Equation 8.24, but Equation 8.25 still has severe multicollinearity as measured by both of our detection techniques. (To confirm this, see Exercise 13.) The remaining multicollinearity appears to involve our price variables. What should we do?

In the case of the prices, we don't have the option of dropping one of the multicollinear variables because both PB and PF are too theoretically important to the model. In such a situation it's worth investigating another of our potential remedies, transforming the variables. For example, one alternative would be to create a transformation of the two price variables by dividing one by the other to form a relative price variable:

$$RP_t = PF_t / PB_t$$

Such a variable would make sense if theory called for keeping both variables in the equation and if the two coefficients could be expected to be close in absolute value but of opposite signs.[8] Choosing to use a relative price variable in effect would be hypothesizing that while consumers might not be sophisticated enough to always consider real prices, they do compare prices of substitutes before making their purchases. For the purpose of discussion, suppose you decide to estimate the latter equation:

$$F_i = f(\overset{-}{RP_i}, \overset{+}{Yd_i}, \overset{-}{P_i}) + \epsilon$$

obtaining

$$\hat{F}_t = -5.17 - 1.93RP_t + 2.71 \ln Yd_t + 0.0052P_t \qquad (8.26)$$
$$\phantom{\hat{F}_t = -5.17 -} (1.43) \qquad (0.66) \qquad (0.2801)$$
$$t = -1.35 \qquad 4.13 \qquad 0.019$$
$$\overline{R}^2 = .588 \qquad n = 25$$

Although these are all questions of judgment, the two changes appear to have worked reasonably well in terms of ridding the equation of much of its severe multicollinearity. (The VIFs, for example, are now all below 3.) More important, once we decide that this specification is good enough, we can now test the hypothesis that was the real reason for the research project. What was the result? If this specification is at all close to the best one, then the null hypothesis of no effect cannot be rejected. For all intents and purposes, it appears that the Pope's decision did not cut down on consumption of fish (the coefficient is quite insignificant).[9]

Finally, notice that someone else might take a completely different approach to alleviating the severe multicollinearity in this sample. There is no obviously correct remedy. Indeed, if you want to be sure that your choice of a

---

8. To see why opposite signs are required, note that an increase in PF will increase RP whereas an increase in PB will decrease it. Unless PF and PB are hypothesized to have opposite effects on the dependent variable, this relative price variable will not work at all. To test your understanding of this point, attempt to figure out the expected sign of the coefficient of RP in this equation before going on with this example. Note, by the way, that a relative price ratio such as RP is a real variable even if PF and PB are not.

9. This is in contrast with the findings of the original empirical work on the issue, Frederick Bell's "The Pope and the Price of Fish," *American Economic Review*, December 1968, pp. 1346–1350. Bell built monthly models of the price of seven different species of fish and determined that the Pope's decision had a significant negative impact on the demand for fish in New England in the first 9 months after the decision. Since our example was misspecified purposely to cause multicollinearity and then specified in part to allow an example of the use of a relative price variable, Equation 8.24 should not be considered to refute Bell's result. It is interesting, however, that none of the specifications considered in constructing this example included a significantly negative coefficient of the dummy variable, so the result is fairly robust.

specification did not influence your inability to reject the null hypothesis about β_P, you might see how sensitive that conclusion is to an alternative approach toward fixing the multicollinearity. (In such a case, both results would have to be part of the research report.)

8.6   Summary

1. Perfect multicollinearity is the violation of the assumption that no explanatory variable is a perfect linear function of other explanatory variable(s). Perfect multicollinearity results in indeterminate estimates of the regression coefficients and infinite standard errors of those estimates.

2. Imperfect multicollinearity, which is what is typically meant when the word "multicollinearity" is used, is a linear relationship between two or more independent variables that is strong enough to significantly affect the estimation of that equation. Multicollinearity is a sample phenomenon as well as a theoretical one. Different samples can exhibit different degrees of multicollinearity.

3. The major consequence of severe multicollinearity is to increase the variances of the estimated regression coefficients and therefore decrease the calculated t-scores of those coefficients. Multicollinearity causes no bias in the estimated coefficients, and it has little effect on the overall significance of the regression or on the estimates of any nonmulticollinear explanatory variables.

4. Severe multicollinearity causes difficulty in the identification of the separate effects of the multicollinear variables in a regression equation. In addition, coefficient estimates become very sensitive to changes in specification in the presence of multicollinearity.

5. Since multicollinearity exists, to one degree or another, in virtually every data set, the question to be asked in detection is how severe the multicollinearity in a particular sample is.

6. Two useful methods for the detection of severe multicollinearity are:
    a. Are the simple correlation coefficients between the explanatory variables high?
    b. Are the variance inflation factors high?

    If either of these answers is yes, then multicollinearity certainly exists, but multicollinearity can also exist even if the answers are no.

7. The four most common remedies for multicollinearity are:
    a. Do nothing (and thus avoid specification bias).
    b. Drop a redundant variable.
    c. Transform the multicollinear variables or the equation.
    d. Increase the size of the sample.

8. Quite often, doing nothing is the best remedy for multicollinearity. If the multicollinearity has not decreased t-scores to the point of insignificance, then no remedy should even be considered. Even if the t-scores are insignificant, remedies should be undertaken cautiously, because all impose costs on the estimation that may be greater than the potential benefit of ridding the equation of multicollinearity.

Exercises

(Answers to even-numbered exercises are in Appendix A.)

1. Write the meaning of each of the following terms without referring to the book (or your notes), and then compare your definition with the version in the text for each:
    a. perfect multicollinearity
    b. severe imperfect multicollinearity
    c. dominant variable
    d. combination variable
    e. first difference
    f. variance inflation factor
    g. redundant variable

2. Beginning researchers quite often believe that they have multicollinearity when they've accidentally included in their equation two or more explanatory variables that basically serve the same purpose or are, in essence, measuring the same thing. Which of the following pairs of variables are likely to include such a redundant variable?
    a. GDP and NDP in a macroeconomic equation of some sort
    b. the price of refrigerators and the price of washing machines in a durable goods demand function
    c. the number of acres harvested and the amount of seed used in an agricultural supply function
    d. long-term interest rates and the money supply in an investment function

3. A researcher once attempted to estimate an asset demand equation that included the following three explanatory variables: current wealth W_t, wealth in the previous quarter W_{t-1}, and the change in wealth $\Delta W_t = W_t - W_{t-1}$. What problem did this researcher encounter? What should have been done to solve this problem?

4. In each of the following situations, determine whether the variable involved is a dominant variable:
   a. games lost in year t in an equation for the number of games won in year t by a baseball team that plays the same number of games each year
   b. number of Woody's restaurants in a model of the total sales of the entire Woody's chain of restaurants
   c. disposable income in an equation for aggregate consumption expenditures
   d. number of tires purchased in an annual model of the number of automobiles produced by a Big Three automaker that does not make its own tires
   e. number of acres planted in an agricultural supply function

5. The formation of linear combinations is an arbitrary process. For example, one possible linear combination between liquid assets and disposable income in Section 8.4.3 could be $X_{3i} = 10(Yd_i) + LA_i$ because the mean of the liquid assets variable is almost exactly 10 times the mean of the disposable income variable. To ensure that one does not overwhelm the other, an adjustment by a factor of 10 makes sense. Other researchers prefer to regress one of the explanatory variables on the other. In this case, we also obtain evidence that a multiple of 10 makes sense:

$$\widehat{LA}_t = -2428.6 + 10.786Yd_t$$
$$(0.8125)$$
$$t = 13.274 \qquad \overline{R}^2 = .967$$

Use this same general technique to form linear combinations of the following variables:
   a. height and weight in Table 1.1 (assume both are explanatory Xs)
   b. P and I from the Woody's data set in Table 3.1
   c. Y and Yd in Table 6.2 (assume both are explanatory Xs)

6. You've been hired by the Dean of Students Office to help reduce damage done to dorms by rowdy students, and your first step is to build a

cross-sectional model of last term's damage to each dorm as a function of the attributes of that dorm:

$$\hat{D}_i = 210 + 733F_i - 0.805S_i + 74.0A_i$$
$$(253) \quad (0.752) \quad (12.4)$$
$$n = 33 \qquad \overline{R}^2 = .84$$

where: D_i = the amount of damage (in dollars) done to the ith dorm last term

F_i = the percentage of the ith dorm residents who are frosh

S_i = the number of students who live in the ith dorm

A_i = the number of incidents involving alcohol that were reported to the Dean of Students Office from the ith dorm last term (incidents involving alcohol may or may not involve damage to the dorm)

a. Hypothesize signs, calculate t-scores, and test hypotheses for this result (5 percent level).

b. What problems (left-out variables, irrelevant variables, or multicollinearity) appear to exist in this equation? Why?

c. Suppose you were now told that the simple correlation coefficient between S_i and A_i was 0.94; would that change your answer? How?

d. Is it possible that the unexpected sign of $\hat{\beta}_S$ could have been caused by multicollinearity? Why?

7. Suppose your friend was modeling the impact of income on consumption in a quarterly model and discovered that income's impact on consumption lasts at least a year. As a result, your friend estimated the following model:

$$C_t = \beta_0 + \beta_1 Yd_t + \beta_2 Yd_{t-1} + \beta_3 Yd_{t-2} + \beta_4 Yd_{t-3} + \epsilon_t$$

a. Would this equation be subject to perfect multicollinearity?

b. Would this equation be subject to imperfect multicollinearity?

c. What, if anything, could be done to rid this equation of any multicollinearity it might have? (One answer to this question, the autoregressive approach to distributed lags, will be covered in Chapter 12.)

8. In 1998, Mark McGwire hit 70 homers to break Roger Maris' old record of 61, and yet McGwire wasn't voted the Most Valuable

Player (MVP) in his league. To try to understand how this happened, you collect the following data on MVP votes, batting average (BA), home runs (HR), and runs batted in (RBI) from the 1998 National League:

Name	Votes (V)	BA	HR	RBI
Sosa	438	.308	66	158
McGwire	272	.299	70	147
Alou	215	.312	38	124
Vaughn	185	.272	50	119
Biggio	163	.325	20	88
Galarraga	147	.305	44	121
Bonds	66	.303	37	122
Jones	56	.313	34	107

Note: filename MVP8

Just as you are about to run the regression, your friend (trying to get back at you for your comments on Exercise 7) warns you that you probably have multicollinearity.

a. What should you do about your friend's warning before running the regression?

b. Run the regression implied above: $V = f(\overset{+}{BA}, \overset{+}{HR}, \overset{+}{RBI}) + \epsilon$ on the data above. What signs of multicollinearity are there?

c. What suggestions would you make for another run of this equation? (If you didn't get a chance to run the equation yourself, refer to Appendix A before answering this part of the question.) In particular, what would you do about multicollinearity?

9. A full-scale regression model for the total annual gross sales in thousands of dollars of J. C. Quarter's durable goods for the last 26 years produces the following result (all measurements are in real dollars—or billions of real dollars). Standard errors are in parentheses:

$$\widehat{SQ}_t = -7.2 + 200.3PC_t - 150.6PQ_t + 20.6Y_t$$
$$\phantom{\widehat{SQ}_t = -7.2 + } (250.1) \quad\ (125.6) \quad\ (40.1)$$

$$- 15.8C_t + 201.1N_t$$
$$(10.6) \quad\ (103.8)$$

where: SQ_t = sales of durable goods at J. C. Quarter's in year t
         PC_t = average price of durables in year t at J. C. Quarter's main competition
         PQ_t = the average price of durables at J. C. Quarter's in year t
         Y_t = U.S. gross domestic product in year t
         C_t = U.S. aggregate consumption in year t
         N_t = the number of J. C. Quarter's stores open in year t

a. Hypothesize signs, calculate t-scores, and test hypotheses for this result (5 percent level).
b. What problems (out of omitted variables, irrelevant variables, and multicollinearity) appear to exist in this equation? Explain.
c. Suppose you were now told that the $\overline{R}^2$ was .821, that $r_{Y,C}$ was .993, and that $r_{PC,PQ}$ was .813. Would this change your answer to the above question? How?
d. What recommendation would you make for a rerun of this equation with different explanatory variables? Why?

10. A cross-sectional regression was run on a sample of 44 states in an effort to understand federal defense spending by state (standard errors in parentheses):

$$\hat{S}_i = -148.0 + 0.841C_i - 0.0115P_i - 0.0078E_i$$
$$\qquad\qquad (0.027) \quad (0.1664) \quad (0.0092)$$

where: S_i = annual spending (millions of dollars) on defense in the ith state
         C_i = contracts (millions of dollars) awarded in the ith state (contracts are often for many years of service) per year
         P_i = annual payroll (millions of dollars) for workers in defense-oriented industries in the ith state
         E_i = the number of civilians employed in defense-oriented industries in the ith state

a. Hypothesize signs, calculate t-scores, and test hypotheses for this result (5 percent level).
b. The VIFs for this equation are all above 20, and those for P and C are above 30. What conclusion does this information allow you to draw?
c. What recommendation would you make for a rerun of this equation with a different specification? Explain your answer.

11. Consider the following regression result paraphrased from a study conducted by the admissions office at the Stanford Business School (standard errors in parentheses):

$$\hat{G}_i = 1.00 + 0.005M_i + 0.20B_i - 0.10A_i + 0.25S_i$$
$$\quad\quad\quad (0.001) \quad (0.20) \quad (0.10) \quad (0.10)$$
$$\overline{R}^2 = 0.20 \quad\quad n = 1000$$

where: G_i = the Stanford Business School GPA of the *i*th student (4 = high)

M_i = the score on the graduate management admission test of the *i*th student (800 = high)

B_i = the number of years of business experience of the *i*th student

A_i = the age of the *i*th student

S_i = dummy equal to 1 if the *i*th student was an economics major and 0 otherwise

a. Theorize the expected signs of all the coefficients (try not to look at the results) and test these expectations with appropriate hypotheses (including choosing a significance level).

b. Do any problems appear to exist in this equation? Explain your answer.

c. How would you react if someone suggested a polynomial functional form for A? Why?

d. What suggestions (if any) would you have for another run of this equation?

12. Calculating VIFs typically involves running sets of auxiliary regressions, one regression for each independent variable in an equation. To get practice with this procedure, calculate the following:

a. the VIFs for N, P, and I from the Woody's data in Table 3.1.

b. the VIFs for PB, PC, and YD from the chicken demand data in Table 6.2 (using Equation 6.8).

c. the VIF for X_1 in an equation where X_1 and X_2 are the only independent variables, given that the VIF for X_2 is 3.8 and n = 28.

d. the VIF for X_1 in an equation where X_1 and X_2 are the only independent variables, given that the simple correlation coefficient between X_1 and X_2 is 0.80 and n = 15.

13. Test Equation 8.25 for multicollinearity using both of our detection techniques. (*Hint:* This involves using the Pope/fish data set, datafile = FISH8).

14. Let's assume that you were hired by the Department of Agriculture to do a cross-sectional study of weekly expenditures for food consumed at home by the ith household (F_i) and that you estimated the following equation (standard errors in parentheses):

$$\hat{F}_i = -10.50 + 2.1Y_i - .04Y_i^2 + 13.0H_i - 2.0A_i$$
$$\phantom{\hat{F}_i = -10.50 + }(0.7) \quad (.05) \quad\;\; (2.0) \quad (2.0)$$
$$\overline{R}^2 = .46 \qquad n = 235$$

where: Y_i = the weekly disposable income of the ith household
H_i = the number of people in the ith household
A_i = the number of children (under 19) in the ith household

a. Create and test appropriate hypotheses at the 10 percent level.
b. Does the functional form of this equation appear reasonable? Isn't the estimated coefficient for Y impossible? (There's no way that people can spend twice their income on food.) Explain your answer.
c. Which econometric problems (omitted variables, irrelevant variables, or multicollinearity) appear to exist in this equation? Explain your answer.
d. Suppose that you were now told that the VIFs for A and H were both between 5 and 10. How does this change your answer to part c above?
e. Would you suggest changing this specification for one final run of this equation? How? Why? What are the possible econometric costs of estimating another specification?

15. Suppose you hear that because of the asymmetry of the human heart, the heartbeat of any individual is a function of the difference between the lengths of that individual's legs rather than of the length of either leg. You decide to collect data and build a regression model to test this hypothesis, but you can't decide which of the following two models to estimate[10]:

$$\text{Model A: } H_i = \alpha_0 + \alpha_1 R_i + \alpha_2 L_i + \epsilon_i$$
$$\text{Model B: } H_i = \beta_0 + \beta_1 R_i + \beta_2(L_i - R_i) + \epsilon_i$$

where: H_i = the heartbeat of the ith cardiac patient
R_i = the length of the ith patient's right leg
L_i = the length of the ith patient's left leg

---

10. Potluri Rao and Roger Miller, *Applied Econometrics* (Belmont, CA: Wadsworth, 1971), p. 48.

a. Model A seems more likely to encounter multicollinearity than does Model B, at least as measured by the simple correlation coefficient. Why? What remedy for this multicollinearity would you recommend?

b. Suppose you estimate a set of coefficients for Model A. Can you calculate estimates of the coefficients of Model B from this information? If so, how? If not, why?

c. What does your answer to part b tell you about which of the two models is more vulnerable to multicollinearity?

d. Suppose you had dropped L_i from Model A because of the high simple correlation coefficient between L_i and R_i. What would this deletion have done to your answers to parts b and c?

16. In 1974 W. Andrews and C. Christenson published a pioneering study of underground coal mine safety in which a major purpose was to figure out the impact of the 1952 Mine Safety Act on mine fatalities.[11] One of the goals of the legislation was to cut down on the high accident rate in small mines. The authors hypothesized that mine fatalities were a function of the level of mine technology, average mine size, and mine safety regulation. Consider the following estimated equation, Equation 8.27 (standard errors in parentheses):

$$\hat{F}_t = 3.49 - 0.023T_t - 0.017S_t - 0.005O_t + 0.028R_t + 0.077W_t$$
$$\quad\quad\;\; (0.005)\quad (0.006)\quad (0.163)\quad (0.107)\quad (0.110)$$
$$\quad\quad t = -4.20\quad\;\; -2.89\quad\;\; -0.03\quad\quad 0.26\quad\quad 0.69$$
$$n = 26\ (\text{annual }1940\text{--}1965)\quad \overline{R}^2 = .665\quad F = 10.9 \quad\quad (8.27)$$

where: F_t = fatal injuries per million man-hours worked in year t
   T_t = percent of year t's output that was mechanically loaded
   S_t = the average number of workers per mine in year t
   O_t = tons of coal produced per man-hour in year t
   R_t = a regulation dummy equal to 1 for 1953–1965 (when the Mine Safety Act was in force) and 0 otherwise
   W_t = a war dummy equal to 1 in 1940–1944 and 0 otherwise

---

11. W. H. Andrews and C. L. Christenson, "Some Economic Factors Affecting Safety in Underground Bituminous Coal Mines," *Southern Economic Journal*, January 1974, pp. 364–376. The idea for the second half of part e of this question came from William F. Lott and Subhash C. Ray, *Applied Econometrics* (Fort Worth: Dryden Press/Harcourt Brace, 1992), p. 63, which is also a good source of additional analysis on this article.

a. Create and test appropriate hypotheses about the individual slope coefficients and the overall significance of this equation at the 5 percent level. (*Hint:* The authors considered T and O, holding S constant, to be alternative measures of mine technology.)

b. The simple correlation coefficients between T, S, and O are all above 0.80, and the three variables' VIFs are all above 8. Is multicollinearity a potential concern in this equation? Why? (*Hint:* "Because this question is in the multicollinearity chapter" is not a complete response!)

c. The authors created TI_t, a linear combination of O and T by using a formula that is different from the procedures outlined in Section 8.4.3 and Exercise 5:

$$TI_t = \left(\frac{T_t}{\overline{T}} + \frac{O_t}{\overline{O}} \right) / 2$$

Is this a reasonable way to combine two variables to avoid the multicollinearity between them? Why or why not?

d. If you drop O_t from the equation, you obtain Equation 8.28 below (standard errors in parentheses). Compare Equations 8.27 and 8.28. Which do you prefer? Why? Do the results indicate that O_t is irrelevant or redundant? Explain.

$$\hat{F}_t = 3.48 - 0.023T_t - 0.017S_t + 0.028R_t + 0.076W_t \quad (8.28)$$
$$\phantom{\hat{F}_t = 3.48} (0.005) \quad (0.004) \quad (0.105) \quad (0.105)$$
$$\phantom{\hat{F}_t = 3.48} t = -4.34 \quad -4.23 \quad 0.27 \quad 0.73$$
$$n = 26 \text{ (annual 1940--1965)} \quad \overline{R}^2 = .681 \quad F = 14.3$$

e. What's your conclusion: Did the 1952 Mine Safety Act save lives? Before you answer, however, make sure that you're satisfied with the functional form of Equation 8.28, which was the equation the authors actually published. In particular, is there any chance that slope dummy variables involving R_t are the appropriate way to test the effectiveness of the Mine Safety Act? (*Hint:* Use the data in Table 8.2, filename MINE8, to estimate the necessary equations.)

f. (optional) The authors also studied the impact of the 1952 Mine Safety Act on per capita *nonfatal* mine injuries in year t (NF_t). Answer parts a through e of this question for the dependent variable NF_t by estimating the necessary equations yourself.

TABLE 8.2	MINE SAFETY DATA					
Year	F	NF	T	S	O	TI
1940	1.70	61.3	35.4	65.1	0.60	55.4
1941	1.36	59.3	40.7	66.4	0.60	59.0
1942	1.43	61.0	45.2	69.3	0.61	62.7
1943	1.41	58.8	48.9	68.3	0.61	65.3
1944	1.25	57.2	52.9	65.0	0.60	67.6
1945	1.17	57.9	56.1	65.0	0.62	70.9
1946	1.14	60.9	58.4	62.4	0.63	73.0
1947	1.28	59.2	60.7	49.9	0.67	76.6
1948	1.19	58.4	64.3	51.0	0.67	79.2
1949	0.98	53.9	67.0	53.4	0.69	82.0
1950	0.96	49.7	69.4	53.4	0.74	86.3
1951	1.22	49.1	73.1	43.3	0.78	91.0
1952	0.94	49.9	75.6	42.8	0.80	93.7
1953	0.94	47.2	79.6	39.2	0.88	100.6
1954	1.07	45.6	84.0	34.5	0.98	108.8
1955	1.02	45.5	84.6	29.1	1.05	112.8
1956	1.09	45.8	84.0	27.4	1.08	113.8
1957	1.27	46.6	84.8	27.8	1.13	117.0
1958	1.27	45.5	84.9	23.2	1.18	119.6
1959	1.02	42.7	86.0	21.8	1.27	125.0
1960	1.25	44.4	86.3	19.7	1.34	128.7
1961	1.35	46.6	86.3	18.9	1.42	132.8
1962	1.31	47.4	85.7	17.9	1.51	136.9
1963	1.22	46.8	85.8	16.9	1.60	141.6
1964	1.07	46.0	87.4	17.8	1.70	147.8
1965	1.23	47.5	89.2	18.2	1.76	152.1

Source: W. H. Andrews and C. L. Christenson, "Some Economic Factors Affecting Safety in Underground Bituminous Coal Mines," *Southern Economic Journal*, January 1974, p. 375.

Note: filename MINE8

8.7   Appendix: The SAT Interactive Regression Learning Exercise

Econometrics is difficult to learn by reading examples, no matter how good they are. Most econometricians, the author included, had trouble understanding how to use econometrics, particularly in the area of specification choice, until they ran their own regression projects. This is because there's an element of econometric understanding that is better learned by *doing* than by reading about what someone else is doing.

Unfortunately, mastering the art of econometrics by running your own regression projects without any feedback is also difficult because it takes quite a while to learn to avoid some fairly simple mistakes. Probably the best way to learn is to work on your own regression project, analyzing your own problems and making your own decisions, but with a more experienced econometrician nearby to give you one-on-one feedback on exactly which of your decisions were inspired and which were flawed (and why).

This section is an attempt to give you an opportunity to make independent specification decisions and to then get feedback on the advantages or disadvantages of those decisions. Using the interactive learning exercise of this section requires neither a computer nor a tutor, although either would certainly be useful. Instead, we have designed an exercise that can be used on its own to help to bridge the gap between the typical econometrics examples (which require no decision making) and the typical econometrics projects (which give little feedback). An additional interactive learning exercise is presented in Chapter 11.

STOP!

To get the most out of the exercise, it's important to follow the instructions carefully. Reading the pages "in order" as with any other example will waste your time, because once you have seen even a few of the results, the benefits to you of making specification decisions will diminish. In addition, you shouldn't look at any of the regression results until you have specified your first equation.

8.7.1 Building a Model of Scholastic Aptitude Test Scores

The dependent variable for this interactive learning exercise is the combined SAT score, math plus verbal, earned by students in the senior class at Arcadia High School. Arcadia is an upper-middle-class suburban community located near Los Angeles, California. Out of a graduating class of about 640, a total of 65 students who had taken the SATs were randomly selected for inclusion in the data set. In cases in which a student had taken the test more than once, the highest score was recorded.

A review of the literature on the SAT shows many more psychological studies and popular press articles than econometric regressions. Many articles have been authored by critics of the SAT, who maintain (among other things) that it is biased against women and minorities. In support of this argument, these critics have pointed to national average scores for women and some minorities, which in recent years have been significantly lower than the national averages for white males. Any reader interested in reviewing a portion of the applicable literature should do so now before continuing on with the section.[12]

If you were going to build a single-equation linear model of SAT scores, what factors would you consider? First, you'd want to include some measures of a student's academic ability. Three such variables are cumulative high school grade point average (GPA) and participation in advanced placement math and English courses (APMATH and APENG). Advanced placement (AP) classes are academically rigorous courses that may help a student do well on the SAT. More important, students are invited to be in AP classes on the basis of academic potential, and students who choose to take AP classes are revealing their interest in academic subjects, both of which bode well for SAT scores. GPAs at Arcadia High School are weighted GPAs; each semester that a student takes an AP class adds one extra point to his or her total grade points. (For example, a semester grade of "A" in an AP math class counts for five grade points as opposed to the conventional four points.)

A second set of important considerations includes qualitative factors that may affect performance on the SAT. Available dummy variables in this category include measures of a student's gender (GEND), ethnicity (RACE), and native language (ESL). All of the students in the sample are either Asian or Caucasian, and RACE is assigned a value of one if a student is Asian. Asian students are a substantial proportion of the student body at Arcadia High. The ESL dummy is given a value of one if English is a student's second language. In addition, studying for the test may be relevant, so a dummy variable indicating whether or not a student has attended an SAT preparation class (PREP) is also included in the data.

To sum, the explanatory variables available for you to choose for your model are:

GPA_i = the weighted GPA of the ith student
$APMATH_i$ = a dummy variable equal to 1 if the ith student has taken AP math, 0 otherwise
$APENG_i$ = a dummy variable equal to 1 if the ith student has taken AP English, 0 otherwise

12. See Jay Ambert, "The SAT," *American Scholar*, Autumn 1982, pp. 535–542, and James Fallows, "The Tests and the 'Brightest': How Fair are the College Boards?" *The Atlantic*, February 1980, pp. 37–48. We are grateful to former Occidental student Bob Sego for his help in preparing this interactive exercise.

AP_i = a dummy variable equal to 1 if the ith student has taken AP math and/or AP English, 0 if the ith student has taken neither

ESL_i = a dummy variable equal to 1 if English is not the ith student's first language, 0 otherwise

$RACE_i$ = a dummy variable equal to 1 if the ith student is Asian, 0 if the student is Caucasian

$GEND_i$ = a dummy variable equal to 1 if the ith student is male, 0 if the student is female

$PREP_i$ = a dummy variable equal to 1 if the ith student has attended a SAT preparation course, 0 otherwise

The data for these variables are presented in Table 8.3.

TABLE 8.3 DATA FOR THE SAT INTERACTIVE LEARNING EXERCISE

SAT	GPA	APMATH	APENG	AP	ESL	GEND	PREP	RACE
1060	3.74	0	1	1	0	0	0	0
740	2.71	0	0	0	0	0	1	0
1070	3.92	0	1	1	0	0	1	0
1070	3.43	0	1	1	0	0	1	0
1330	4.35	1	1	1	0	0	1	0
1220	3.02	0	1	1	0	1	1	0
1130	3.98	1	1	1	1	0	1	0
770	2.94	0	0	0	0	0	1	0
1050	3.49	0	1	1	0	0	1	0
1250	3.87	1	1	1	0	1	1	0
1000	3.49	0	0	0	0	0	1	0
1010	3.24	0	1	1	0	0	1	0
1320	4.22	1	1	1	1	1	0	1
1230	3.61	1	1	1	1	1	1	1
840	2.48	1	0	1	1	1	0	1
940	2.26	1	0	1	1	0	0	1
910	2.32	0	0	0	1	1	1	1
1240	3.89	1	1	1	0	1	1	0
1020	3.67	0	0	0	0	1	0	0
630	2.54	0	0	0	0	0	1	0
850	3.16	0	0	0	0	0	1	0
1300	4.16	1	1	1	1	1	1	0
950	2.94	0	0	0	0	1	1	0
1350	3.79	1	1	1	0	1	1	0
1070	2.56	0	0	0	0	1	0	0

TABLE 8.3 (continued)								
SAT	GPA	APMATH	APENG	AP	ESL	GEND	PREP	RACE
1000	3.00	0	0	0	0	1	1	0
770	2.79	0	0	0	0	0	1	0
1280	3.70	1	0	1	1	0	1	1
590	3.23	0	0	0	1	0	1	1
1060	3.98	1	1	1	1	1	0	1
1050	2.64	1	0	1	0	0	0	0
1220	4.15	1	1	1	1	1	1	1
930	2.73	0	0	0	0	1	1	0
940	3.10	1	1	1	1	0	0	1
980	2.70	0	0	0	1	1	1	1
1280	3.73	1	1	1	0	1	1	0
700	1.64	0	0	0	1	0	1	1
1040	4.03	1	1	1	1	0	1	1
1070	3.24	0	1	1	0	1	1	0
900	3.42	0	0	0	0	1	1	0
1430	4.29	1	1	1	0	1	0	0
1290	3.33	0	0	0	0	1	0	0
1070	3.61	1	0	1	1	0	1	1
1100	3.58	1	1	1	0	0	1	0
1030	3.52	0	1	1	0	0	1	0
1070	2.94	0	0	0	0	1	1	0
1170	3.98	1	1	1	1	1	1	0
1300	3.89	1	1	1	0	1	0	0
1410	4.34	1	1	1	1	0	1	1
1160	3.43	1	1	1	0	1	1	0
1170	3.56	1	1	1	0	0	0	0
1280	4.11	1	1	1	0	0	1	0
1060	3.58	1	1	1	1	0	1	0
1250	3.47	1	1	1	0	1	1	0
1020	2.92	1	0	1	1	1	1	1
1000	4.05	0	1	1	1	0	0	1
1090	3.24	1	1	1	1	1	1	1
1430	4.38	1	1	1	1	0	0	1
860	2.62	1	0	1	1	0	0	1
1050	2.37	0	0	0	0	1	0	0
920	2.77	0	0	0	0	0	1	0
1100	2.54	0	0	0	0	1	1	0
1160	3.55	1	0	1	1	1	1	1
1360	2.98	0	1	1	1	0	1	0
970	3.64	1	1	1	0	0	1	0

Note: filename SAT8

Now:

1. Hypothesize expected signs for each of these variables in an equation for the SAT score of the *i*th student. Examine each variable carefully; what is the theoretical content of your hypothesis?

2. Choose carefully the best set of explanatory variables. Start off by including GPA, APMATH, and APENG; what other variables do you think should be specified? Don't simply include all the variables, intending to drop the insignificant ones. Instead, think through the problem carefully and find the best possible equation.

Once you've specified your equation, you're ready to move to Section 8.7.2. Keep following the instructions in the exercise until you have specified your equation completely. You may take some time to think over the questions contained in Section 8.7.2 or take a break, but when you return to the interactive exercise make sure to go back to the exact point from which you left rather than starting all over again. To the extent you can do it, try to avoid looking at the hints until after you've completed the entire project. The hints are there to help you if you get stuck, not to allow you to check every decision you make.

One final bit of advice: each regression result is accompanied by a series of questions. Take the time to answer all these questions, in writing if possible. Rushing through this interactive exercise will lessen its effectiveness.

8.7.2 The SAT Score Interactive Regression Exercise

To start, choose the specification you'd like to estimate, find the regression run number[13] of that specification in the following list, and then turn to that regression. Note that the simple correlation coefficient matrix for this data set is in Table 8.4 just before the results begin.

All the equations include SAT as the dependent variable and GPA, APMATH, and APENG as explanatory variables. Find the combination of explanatory variables (from ESL, GEND, PREP, and RACE) that you wish to include and go to the indicated regression:

---

13. All the regression results appear exactly as they are produced by the EViews regression package.

None of them, go to regression run 8.1
ESL only, go to regression run 8.2
GEND only, go to regression run 8.3
PREP only, go to regression run 8.4
RACE only, go to regression run 8.5
ESL and GEND, go to regression run 8.6
ESL and PREP, go to regression run 8.7
ESL and RACE, go to regression run 8.8
GEND and PREP, go to regression run 8.9
GEND and RACE, go to regression run 8.10
PREP and RACE, go to regression run 8.11
ESL, GEND, and PREP, go to regression run 8.12
ESL, GEND, and RACE, go to regression run 8.13
ESL, PREP, and RACE, go to regression run 8.14
GEND, PREP, and RACE, go to regression run 8.15
All four, go to regression run 8.16

TABLE 8.4   MEANS, STANDARD DEVIATIONS, AND SIMPLE CORRELATION COEFFICIENTS FOR THE SAT INTERACTIVE REGRESSION LEARNING EXERCISE

Means, Standard Deviations, and Correlations
Sample Range: 1–65

Variable	Mean	Standard Deviation
SAT	1075.538	191.3605
GPA	3.362308	0.612739
APMATH	0.523077	0.503354
APENG	0.553846	0.500961
AP	0.676923	0.471291
ESL	0.400000	0.493710
GEND	0.492308	0.503831
PREP	0.738462	0.442893
RACE	0.323077	0.471291

	Correlation Coeff		Correlation Coeff
APMATH,GPA	0.497	GPA,SAT	0.678
APENG,SAT	0.608	APMATH,SAT	0.512
APENG,APMATH	0.444	APENG,GPA	0.709
AP,SAT	0.579	AP,GPA	0.585
AP,APMATH	0.723	AP,APENG	0.769
ESL,GPA	0.071	ESL,SAT	0.024
ESL,APENG	0.037	ESL,APMATH	0.402
GEND,GPA	−0.008	ESL,AP	0.295
GEND,APENG	−0.044	GEND,SAT	0.293
GEND,ESL	−0.050	GEND,APMATH	0.077
PREP,SAT	−0.100	GEND,AP	−0.109
PREP,APMATH	−0.147	PREP,GPA	0.001
PREP,AP	−0.111	PREP,APENG	0.029
PREP,GEND	−0.044	PREP,ESL	−0.085
RACE,SAT	−0.085	RACE,GPA	−0.025
RACE,APMATH	0.330	RACE,APENG	−0.107
RACE,AP	0.195	RACE,ESL	0.846
RACE,GEND	−0.022	RACE,PREP	−0.187

Regression Run 8.1

```
Dependent Variable: SAT
Method: Least Squares
Date: 02/29/00   Time: 15:05
Sample: 1 65
Included observations: 65
```

Variable	Coefficient	Std. Error	t-Statistic	Prob.
C	545.2537	117.8141	4.628086	0.0000
GPA	131.8512	40.86212	3.226735	0.0020
APMATH	78.60445	39.13018	2.008793	0.0490
APENG	82.77424	48.40687	1.709969	0.0924

R-squared	0.524341	Mean dependent var	1075.538
Adjusted R-squared	0.500948	S.D. dependent var	191.3605
S.E. of regression	135.1840	Akaike info criterion	12.71071
Sum squared resid	1114757.	Schwarz criterion	12.84452
Log likelihood	-409.0982	F-statistic	22.41440
Durbin-Watson stat	1.998585	Prob(F-statistic)	0.000000

Answer each of the following questions for the above regression run.

   a. Evaluate this result with respect to its economic meaning, overall fit, and the signs and significance of the individual coefficients.

   b. What econometric problems (out of omitted variables, irrelevant variables, or multicollinearity) does this regression have? Why? If you need feedback on your answer, see hint 2 in the material on this chapter in Appendix A.

   c. Which of the following statements comes closest to your recommendation for further action to be taken in the estimation of this equation?

      i.   No further specification changes are advisable (go to Section 8.7.3).

      ii. I would like to add ESL to the equation (go to run 8.2).

      iii. I would like to add GEND to the equation (go to run 8.3).

      iv. I would like to add PREP to the equation (go to run 8.4).

      v.   I would like to add RACE to the equation (go to run 8.5).

If you need feedback on your answer, see hint 6 in the material on this chapter in Appendix A.

Regression Run 8.2

Dependent Variable: SAT
Method: Least Squares
Date: 02/29/00   Time: 15:06
Sample: 1 65
Included observations: 65

Variable	Coefficient	Std. Error	t-Statistic	Prob.
C	566.7551	118.6016	4.778644	0.0000
GPA	128.3402	40.78800	3.146519	0.0026
APMATH	101.5886	43.19023	2.352121	0.0220
APENG	77.30713	48.40462	1.597102	0.1155
ESL	-46.72721	37.88203	-1.233493	0.2222

R-squared	0.536105	Mean dependent var	1075.538
Adjusted R-squared	0.505179	S.D. dependent var	191.3605
S.E. of regression	134.6098	Akaike info criterion	12.71644
Sum squared resid	1087187.	Schwarz criterion	12.88370
Log likelihood	-408.2843	F-statistic	17.33489
Durbin-Watson stat	2.027210	Prob(F-statistic)	0.000000

Answer each of the following questions for the above regression run.

a. Evaluate this result with respect to its economic meaning, overall fit, and the signs and significance of the individual coefficients.

b. What econometric problems (out of omitted variables, irrelevant variables, or multicollinearity) does this regression have? Why? If you need feedback on your answer, see hint 3 in the material on this chapter in Appendix A.

c. Which of the following statements comes closest to your recommendation for further action to be taken in the estimation of this equation?

    i. No further specification changes are advisable (go to Section 8.7.3).

    ii. I would like to drop ESL from the equation (go to run 8.1).

    iii. I would like to add GEND to the equation (go to run 8.6).

    iv. I would like to add RACE to the equation (go to run 8.8).

    v. I would like to add PREP to the equation (go to run 8.7).

If you need feedback on your answer, see hint 6 in the material on this chapter in Appendix A.

Regression Run 8.3

```
Dependent Variable: SAT
Method: Least Squares
Date: 02/29/00   Time: 15:07
Sample: 1 65
Included observations: 65
```

Variable	Coefficient	Std. Error	t-Statistic	Prob.
C	491.8225	108.5429	4.531135	0.0000
GPA	131.5798	37.29970	3.527638	0.0008
APMATH	65.04046	35.91313	1.811049	0.0751
APENG	94.10841	44.29652	2.124510	0.0378
GEND	112.0465	30.82961	3.634379	0.0006

R-squared	0.610162	Mean dependent var	1075.538
Adjusted R-squared	0.584173	S.D. dependent var	191.3605
S.E. of regression	123.3982	Akaike info criterion	12.54251
Sum squared resid	913626.4	Schwarz criterion	12.70977
Log likelihood	-402.6317	F-statistic	23.47754
Durbin-Watson stat	2.104997	Prob(F-statistic)	0.000000

Answer each of the following questions for the above regression run.

a. Evaluate this result with respect to its economic meaning, overall fit, and the signs and significance of the individual coefficients.

b. What econometric problems (out of omitted variables, irrelevant variables, or multicollinearity) does this regression have? Why? If you need feedback on your answer, see hint 5 in the material on this chapter in Appendix A.

c. Which of the following statements comes closest to your recommendation for further action to be taken in the estimation of this equation?

   i. No further specification changes are advisable (go to Section 8.7.3).

   ii. I would like to add ESL to the equation (go to run 8.6).

   iii. I would like to add PREP to the equation (go to run 8.9).

   iv. I would like to add RACE to the equation (go to run 8.10).

If you need feedback on your answer, see hint 19 in the material on this chapter in Appendix A.

Regression Run 8.4

Dependent Variable: SAT
Method: Least Squares
Date: 02/29/00   Time: 15:07
Sample: 1 65
Included observations: 65

Variable	Coefficient	Std. Error	t-Statistic	Prob.
C	569.2532	121.1058	4.700463	0.0000
GPA	132.7666	40.94846	3.242287	0.0019
APMATH	72.29444	39.84456	1.814412	0.0746
APENG	85.68562	48.60529	1.762887	0.0830
PREP	-34.38129	38.88201	-0.884247	0.3801

R-squared	0.530460	Mean dependent var	1075.538
Adjusted R-squared	0.499157	S.D. dependent var	191.3605
S.E. of regression	135.4263	Akaike info criterion	12.72854
Sum squared resid	1100417.	Schwarz criterion	12.89580
Log likelihood	-408.6774	F-statistic	16.94616
Durbin-Watson stat	1.976378	Prob(F-statistic)	0.000000

Answer each of the following questions for the above regression run.

a. Evaluate this result with respect to its economic meaning, overall fit, and the signs and significance of the individual coefficients.

b. What econometric problems (out of omitted variables, irrelevant variables, or multicollinearity) does this regression have? Why? If you need feedback on your answer, see hint 8 in the material on this chapter in Appendix A.

c. Which of the following statements comes closest to your recommendation for further action to be taken in the estimation of this equation?

i. No further specification changes are advisable (go to Section 8.7.3).

ii. I would like to drop PREP from the equation (go to run 8.1).

iii. I would like to add ESL to the equation (go to run 8.7).

iv. I would like to add GEND to the equation (go to run 8.9).

v. I would like to replace APMATH and APENG with AP, a linear combination of the two variables (go to run 8.17).

If you need feedback on your answer, see hint 12 in the material on this chapter in Appendix A.

Regression Run 8.5

```
Dependent Variable: SAT
Method: Least Squares
Date: 02/29/00   Time: 15:08
Sample: 1 65
Included observations: 65
```

Variable	Coefficient	Std. Error	t-Statistic	Prob.
C	570.8148	117.7382	4.848172	0.0000
GPA	128.2798	40.48924	3.168244	0.0024
APMATH	106.2137	42.71559	2.486533	0.0157
APENG	67.42362	48.92704	1.378044	0.1733
RACE	-60.33471	39.47330	-1.528494	0.1316

R-squared	0.542168	Mean dependent var	1075.538
Adjusted R-squared	0.511646	S.D. dependent var	191.3605
S.E. of regression	133.7271	Akaike info criterion	12.70328
Sum squared resid	1072977.	Schwarz criterion	12.87054
Log likelihood	-407.8567	F-statistic	17.76314
Durbin-Watson stat	2.033014	Prob(F-statistic)	0.000000

Answer each of the following questions for the above regression run.

a. Evaluate this result with respect to its economic meaning, overall fit, and the signs and significance of the individual coefficients.

b. What econometric problems (out of omitted variables, irrelevant variables, or multicollinearity) does this regression have? Why? If you need feedback on your answer, see hint 3 in the material on this chapter in Appendix A.

c. Which of the following statements comes closest to your recommendation for further action to be taken in the estimation of this equation?

  i.   No further specification changes are advisable (go to Section 8.7.3).

  ii. I would like to drop RACE from the equation (go to run 8.1).

  iii. I would like to add ESL to the equation (go to run 8.8).

  iv. I would like to add GEND to the equation (go to run 8.10).

  v.   I would like to add PREP to the equation (go to run 8.11).

If you need feedback on your answer, see hint 14 in the material on this chapter in Appendix A.

Regression Run 8.6

Dependent Variable: SAT
Method: Least Squares
Date: 02/29/00   Time: 15:08
Sample: 1 65
Included observations: 65

Variable	Coefficient	Std. Error	t-Statistic	Prob.
C	508.8237	110.0355	4.624179	0.0000
GPA	129.0595	37.41416	3.449484	0.0010
APMATH	81.97538	40.00950	2.048898	0.0449
APENG	89.84960	44.54376	2.017109	0.0482
ESL	-33.64469	34.94751	-0.962721	0.3396
GEND	108.8598	31.02552	3.508717	0.0009

R-squared	0.616191	Mean dependent var	1075.538
Adjusted R-squared	0.583665	S.D. dependent var	191.3605
S.E. of regression	123.4735	Akaike info criterion	12.55770
Sum squared resid	899496.2	Schwarz criterion	12.75841
Log likelihood	-402.1251	F-statistic	18.94449
Durbin-Watson stat	2.142956	Prob(F-statistic)	0.000000

Answer each of the following questions for the above regression run.

a. Evaluate this result with respect to its economic meaning, overall fit, and the signs and significance of the individual coefficients.

b. What econometric problems (out of omitted variables, irrelevant variables, or multicollinearity) does this regression have? Why? If you need feedback on your answer, see hint 7 in the material on this chapter in Appendix A.

c. Which of the following statements comes closest to your recommendation for further action to be taken in the estimation of this equation?

   i. No further specification changes are advisable (go to Section 8.7.3).

   ii. I would like to drop ESL from the equation (go to run 8.3).

   iii. I would like to add PREP to the equation (go to run 8.12).

   iv. I would like to add RACE to the equation (go to run 8.13).

If you need feedback on your answer, see hint 4 in the material on this chapter in Appendix A.

Regression Run 8.7

```
Dependent Variable: SAT
Method: Least Squares
Date: 02/29/00   Time: 15:09
Sample: 1 65
Included observations: 65
```

Variable	Coefficient	Std. Error	t-Statistic	Prob.
C	591.2047	121.8609	4.851472	0.0000
GPA	129.2439	40.86539	3.162673	0.0025
APMATH	95.35163	43.81128	2.176417	0.0335
APENG	80.21916	48.58978	1.650947	0.1041
ESL	-47.03944	37.94402	-1.239706	0.2200
PREP	-34.82031	38.71083	-0.899498	0.3720

R-squared	0.542380	Mean dependent var	1075.538
Adjusted R-squared	0.503599	S.D. dependent var	191.3605
S.E. of regression	134.8244	Akaike info criterion	12.73359
Sum squared resid	1072480.	Schwarz criterion	12.93430
Log likelihood	-407.8417	F-statistic	13.98561
Durbin-Watson stat	2.008613	Prob(F-statistic)	0.000000

Answer each of the following questions for the above regression run.

a. Evaluate this result with respect to its economic meaning, overall fit, and the signs and significance of the individual coefficients.

b. What econometric problems (out of omitted variables, irrelevant variables, or multicollinearity) does this regression have? Why? If you need feedback on your answer, see hint 8 in the material on this chapter in Appendix A.

c. Which of the following statements comes closest to your recommendation for further action to be taken in the estimation of this equation?

   i. No further specification changes are advisable (go to Section 8.7.3).

   ii. I would like to drop ESL from the equation (go to run 8.4).

   iii. I would like to drop PREP from the equation (go to run 8.2).

   iv. I would like to add GEND to the equation (go to run 8.12).

   v. I would like to add RACE to the equation (go to run 8.14).

If you need feedback on your answer, see hint 18 in the material on this chapter in Appendix A.

Regression Run 8.8

	Dependent Variable: SAT			
	Method: Least Squares			
	Date: 02/29/00 Time: 15:10			
	Sample: 1 65			
	Included observations: 65			

Variable	Coefficient	Std. Error	t-Statistic	Prob.
C	570.6367	118.8985	4.799359	0.0000
GPA	128.3251	40.86223	3.140434	0.0026
APMATH	106.0310	43.55940	2.434170	0.0180
APENG	67.23015	49.81328	1.349643	0.1823
ESL	1.885689	66.79448	0.028231	0.9776
RACE	-61.96231	70.05962	-0.884423	0.3801

R-squared	0.542175	Mean dependent var	1075.538
Adjusted R-squared	0.503376	S.D. dependent var	191.3605
S.E. of regression	134.8548	Akaike info criterion	12.73404
Sum squared resid	1072962.	Schwarz criterion	12.93475
Log likelihood	-407.8563	F-statistic	13.97402
Durbin-Watson stat	2.032924	Prob(F-statistic)	0.000000

Answer each of the following questions for the above regression run.

a. Evaluate this result with respect to its economic meaning, overall fit, and the signs and significance of the individual coefficients.

b. What econometric problems (out of omitted variables, irrelevant variables, or multicollinearity) does this regression have? Why? If you need feedback on your answer, see hint 9 in the material on this chapter in Appendix A.

c. Which of the following statements comes closest to your recommendation for further action to be taken in the estimation of this equation?

   i. No further specification changes are advisable (go to Section 8.7.3).

   ii. I would like to drop ESL from the equation (go to run 8.5).

   iii. I would like to drop RACE from the equation (go to run 8.2).

   iv. I would like to add GEND to the equation (go to run 8.13).

   v. I would like to add PREP to the equation (go to run 8.14).

If you need feedback on your answer, see hint 15 in the material on this chapter in Appendix A.

Regression Run 8.9

Dependent Variable: SAT
Method: Least Squares
Date: 02/29/00   Time: 15:11
Sample: 1 65
Included observations: 65

Variable	Coefficient	Std. Error	t-Statistic	Prob.
C	513.9945	111.6115	4.605210	0.0000
GPA	132.4152	37.38088	3.542326	0.0008
APMATH	59.37168	36.54919	1.624432	0.1096
APENG	96.69438	44.47540	2.174109	0.0337
GEND	111.3943	30.89564	3.605501	0.0006
PREP	-31.31762	35.50451	-0.882074	0.3813

R-squared	0.615236	Mean dependent var	1075.538
Adjusted R-squared	0.582629	S.D. dependent var	191.3605
S.E. of regression	123.6270	Akaike info criterion	12.56018
Sum squared resid	901734.9	Schwarz criterion	12.76089
Log likelihood	-402.2059	F-statistic	18.86816
Durbin-Watson stat	2.065021	Prob(F-statistic)	0.000000

Answer each of the following questions for the above regression run.

a. Evaluate this result with respect to its economic meaning, overall fit, and the signs and significance of the individual coefficients.

b. What econometric problems (out of omitted variables, irrelevant variables, or multicollinearity) does this regression have? Why? If you need feedback on your answer, see hint 8 in the material on this chapter in Appendix A.

c. Which of the following statements comes closest to your recommendation for further action to be taken in the estimation of this equation?

   i.   No further specification changes are advisable (go to Section 8.7.3).

   ii. I would like to drop PREP from the equation (go to run 8.3).

   iii. I would like to add ESL to the equation (go to run 8.12).

   iv. I would like to add RACE to the equation (go to run 8.15).

If you need feedback on your answer, see hint 17 in the material on this chapter in Appendix A.

Regression Run 8.10

| Dependent Variable: SAT |
| Method: Least Squares |
| Date: 02/29/00   Time: 15:11 |
| Sample: 1 65 |
| Included observations: 65 |

Variable	Coefficient	Std. Error	t-Statistic	Prob.
C	514.5822	109.0157	4.720259	0.0000
GPA	128.6381	37.08886	3.468376	0.0010
APMATH	88.26401	39.45591	2.237029	0.0291
APENG	81.07941	44.98391	1.802409	0.0766
GEND	108.5953	30.70716	3.536482	0.0008
RACE	-49.83756	36.27973	-1.373703	0.1747

R-squared	0.622244	Mean dependent var	1075.538
Adjusted R-squared	0.590231	S.D. dependent var	191.3605
S.E. of regression	122.4960	Akaike info criterion	12.54180
Sum squared resid	885310.6	Schwarz criterion	12.74251
Log likelihood	-401.6085	F-statistic	19.43712
Durbin-Watson stat	2.148211	Prob(F-statistic)	0.000000

Answer each of the following questions for the above regression run.

a. Evaluate this result with respect to its economic meaning, overall fit, and the signs and significance of the individual coefficients.

b. What econometric problems (out of omitted variables, irrelevant variables, or multicollinearity) does this regression have? Why? If you need feedback on your answer, see hint 10 in the material on this chapter in Appendix A.

c. Which of the following statements comes closest to your recommendation for further action to be taken in the estimation of this equation?

   i.   No further specification changes are advisable (go to Section 8.7.3).

   ii. I would like to drop RACE from the equation (go to run 8.3).

   iii. I would like to add ESL to the equation (go to run 8.13).

   iv. I would like to add PREP to the equation (go to run 8.15).

If you need feedback on your answer, see hint 4 in the material on this chapter in Appendix A.

Regression Run 8.11

Dependent Variable: SAT
Method: Least Squares
Date: 02/29/00   Time: 15:12
Sample: 1 65
Included observations: 65

Variable	Coefficient	Std. Error	t-Statistic	Prob.
C	602.4718	121.0769	4.975943	0.0000
GPA	129.0898	40.43172	3.192785	0.0023
APMATH	100.8919	42.92558	2.350391	0.0221
APENG	69.65070	48.89190	1.424586	0.1595
PREP	-42.14969	38.62038	-1.091385	0.2795
RACE	-65.60984	39.70586	-1.652397	0.1038

R-squared	0.551228	Mean dependent var	1075.538
Adjusted R-squared	0.513197	S.D. dependent var	191.3605
S.E. of regression	133.5147	Akaike info criterion	12.71407
Sum squared resid	1051744.	Schwarz criterion	12.91478
Log likelihood	-407.2071	F-statistic	14.49400
Durbin-Watson stat	2.020544	Prob(F-statistic)	0.000000

Answer each of the following questions for the above regression run.

a. Evaluate this result with respect to its economic meaning, overall fit, and the signs and significance of the individual coefficients.

b. What econometric problems (out of omitted variables, irrelevant variables, or multicollinearity) does this regression have? Why? If you need feedback on your answer, see hint 8 in the material on this chapter in Appendix A.

c. Which of the following statements comes closest to your recommendation for further action to be taken in the estimation of this equation?

   i. No further specification changes are advisable (go to Section 8.7.3).

   ii. I would like to drop PREP from the equation (go to run 8.5).

   iii. I would like to drop RACE from the equation (go to run 8.4).

   iv. I would like to add GEND to the equation (go to run 8.15).

   v. I would like to replace APMATH and APENG with AP, a linear combination of the two variables (go to run 8.18).

If you need feedback on your answer, see hint 18 in the material on this chapter in Appendix A.

Regression Run 8.12

```
Dependent Variable: SAT
Method: Least Squares
Date: 02/29/00   Time: 15:14
Sample: 1 65
Included observations: 65
```

Variable	Coefficient	Std. Error	t-Statistic	Prob.
C	531.4692	113.1041	4.698939	0.0000
GPA	129.8782	37.48974	3.464368	0.0010
APMATH	76.41832	40.55854	1.884149	0.0646
APENG	92.42253	44.71331	2.067002	0.0432
ESL	-34.01275	35.01006	-0.971513	0.3353
GEND	108.1642	31.08865	3.479219	0.0010
PREP	-31.72391	35.52388	-0.893030	0.3755

R-squared	0.621397	Mean dependent var	1075.538
Adjusted R-squared	0.582231	S.D. dependent var	191.3605
S.E. of regression	123.6859	Akaike info criterion	12.57481
Sum squared resid	887295.9	Schwarz criterion	12.80897
Log likelihood	-401.6813	F-statistic	15.86581
Durbin-Watson stat	2.106229	Prob(F-statistic)	0.000000

Answer each of the following questions for the above regression run.

a. Evaluate this result with respect to its economic meaning, overall fit, and the signs and significance of the individual coefficients.

b. What econometric problems (out of omitted variables, irrelevant variables, or multicollinearity) does this regression have? Why? If you need feedback on your answer, see hint 8 in the material on this chapter in Appendix A.

c. Which of the following statements comes closest to your recommendation for further action to be taken in the estimation of this equation?

   i. No further specification changes are advisable (go to Section 8.7.3).

   ii. I would like to drop ESL from the equation (go to run 8.9).

   iii. I would like to drop PREP from the equation (go to run 8.6).

   iv. I would like to add RACE to the equation (go to run 8.16).

If you need feedback on your answer, see hint 17 in the material on this chapter in Appendix A.

Regression Run 8.13

```
Dependent Variable: SAT
Method: Least Squares
Date: 02/29/00   Time: 15:14
Sample: 1 65
Included observations: 65
```

Variable	Coefficient	Std. Error	t-Statistic	Prob.
C	512.6796	110.0966	4.656635	0.0000
GPA	129.0460	37.41213	3.449311	0.0011
APMATH	86.52973	40.26408	2.149055	0.0358
APENG	79.42187	45.73811	1.736449	0.0878
ESL	16.88299	61.30223	0.275406	0.7840
GEND	109.1893	31.02557	3.519333	0.0008
RACE	-64.35243	64.14694	-1.003204	0.3199

R-squared	0.622738	Mean dependent var	1075.538
Adjusted R-squared	0.583711	S.D. dependent var	191.3605
S.E. of regression	123.4668	Akaike info criterion	12.57126
Sum squared resid	884154.4	Schwarz criterion	12.80543
Log likelihood	-401.5660	F-statistic	15.95653
Durbin-Watson stat	2.143234	Prob(F-statistic)	0.000000

Answer each of the following questions for the above regression run.

a. Evaluate this result with respect to its economic meaning, overall fit, and the signs and significance of the individual coefficients.

b. What econometric problems (out of omitted variables, irrelevant variables, or multicollinearity) does this regression have? Why? If you need feedback on your answer, see hint 9 in the material on this chapter in Appendix A.

c. Which of the following statements comes closest to your recommendation for further action to be taken in the estimation of this equation?

   i.   No further specification changes are advisable (go to Section 8.7.3).

   ii. I would like to drop ESL from the equation (go to run 8.10).

   iii. I would like to drop RACE from the equation (go to run 8.6).

   iv. I would like to add PREP to the equation (go to run 8.16).

If you need feedback on your answer, see hint 15 in the material on this chapter in Appendix A.

Regression Run 8.14

```
Dependent Variable: SAT
Method: Least Squares
Date: 02/29/00   Time: 15:15
Sample: 1 65
Included observations: 65
```

Variable	Coefficient	Std. Error	t-Statistic	Prob.
C	602.1427	122.0822	4.932274	0.0000
GPA	129.4491	40.80133	3.172669	0.0024
APMATH	99.37976	43.89816	2.263871	0.0273
APENG	68.29405	49.73286	1.373218	0.1750
ESL	13.89708	67.55991	0.205700	0.8377
PREP	-43.45964	39.45502	-1.101498	0.2752
RACE	-77.76882	71.39042	-1.089345	0.2805

R-squared	0.551556	Mean dependent var	1075.538
Adjusted R-squared	0.505165	S.D. dependent var	191.3605
S.E. of regression	134.6116	Akaike info criterion	12.74411
Sum squared resid	1050977.	Schwarz criterion	12.97827
Log likelihood	-407.1834	F-statistic	11.88933
Durbin-Watson stat	2.020634	Prob(F-statistic)	0.000000

Answer each of the following questions for the above regression run.

a. Evaluate this result with respect to its economic meaning, overall fit, and the signs and significance of the individual coefficients.

b. What econometric problems (out of omitted variables, irrelevant variables, or multicollinearity) does this regression have? Why? If you need feedback on your answer, see hint 9 in the material on this chapter in Appendix A.

c. Which of the following statements comes closest to your recommendation for further action to be taken in the estimation of this equation?

   i. No further specification changes are advisable (go to Section 8.7.3).

   ii. I would like to drop ESL from the equation (go to run 8.11).

   iii. I would like to drop PREP from the equation (go to run 8.8).

   iv. I would like to add GEND to the equation (go to run 8.16).

   v. I would like to replace APMATH and APENG with AP, a linear combination of the two variables (go to run 8.19).

If you need feedback on your answer, see hint 15 in the material on this chapter in Appendix A.

Regression Run 8.15

```
Dependent Variable: SAT
Method: Least Squares
Date: 02/29/00   Time: 15:15
Sample: 1 65
Included observations: 65
```

Variable	Coefficient	Std. Error	t-Statistic	Prob.
C	543.6309	112.2128	4.844641	0.0000
GPA	129.3628	37.04936	3.491632	0.0009
APMATH	83.66463	39.64091	2.110563	0.0391
APENG	82.94048	44.96213	1.844674	0.0702
GEND	107.4700	30.68735	3.502094	0.0009
PREP	-37.90098	35.41026	-1.070339	0.2889
RACE	-54.68974	36.51752	-1.497630	0.1397

R-squared	0.629561	Mean dependent var	1075.538
Adjusted R-squared	0.591240	S.D. dependent var	191.3605
S.E. of regression	122.3451	Akaike info criterion	12.55301
Sum squared resid	868162.5	Schwarz criterion	12.78717
Log likelihood	-400.9728	F-statistic	16.42852
Durbin-Watson stat	2.114836	Prob(F-statistic)	0.000000

Answer each of the following questions for the above regression run.

a. Evaluate this result with respect to its economic meaning, overall fit, and the signs and significance of the individual coefficients.

b. What econometric problems (out of omitted variables, irrelevant variables, or multicollinearity) does this regression have? Why? If you need feedback on your answer, see hint 8 in the material on this chapter in Appendix A.

c. Which of the following statements comes closest to your recommendation for further action to be taken in the estimation of this equation?

   i. No further specification changes are advisable (go to Section 8.7.3).

   ii. I would like to drop PREP from the equation (go to run 8.10).

   iii. I would like to drop RACE from the equation (go to run 8.9).

   iv. I would like to add ESL to the equation (go to run 8.16).

If you need feedback on your answer, see hint 17 in the material on this chapter in Appendix A.

Regression Run 8.16

Dependent Variable: SAT
Method: Least Squares
Date: 02/29/00   Time: 15:16
Sample: 1 65
Included observations: 65

Variable	Coefficient	Std. Error	t-Statistic	Prob.
C	542.4723	113.0203	4.799777	0.0000
GPA	130.0882	37.34094	3.483794	0.0010
APMATH	80.47642	40.53608	1.985303	0.0519
APENG	80.32262	45.64401	1.759762	0.0838
ESL	27.96510	61.95989	0.451342	0.6535
GEND	108.3766	30.96543	3.499924	0.0009
PREP	-40.50116	36.11828	-1.121348	0.2668
RACE	-79.06514	65.33603	-1.210131	0.2312

R-squared	0.630880	Mean dependent var	1075.538
Adjusted R-squared	0.585550	S.D. dependent var	191.3605
S.E. of regression	123.1937	Akaike info criterion	12.58021
Sum squared resid	865070.9	Schwarz criterion	12.84783
Log likelihood	-400.8568	F-statistic	13.91736
Durbin-Watson stat	2.106524	Prob(F-statistic)	0.000000

Answer each of the following questions for the above regression run.

a. Evaluate this result with respect to its economic meaning, overall fit, and the signs and significance of the individual coefficients.

b. What econometric problems (out of omitted variables, irrelevant variables, or multicollinearity) does this regression have? Why? If you need feedback on your answer, see hint 9 in the material on this chapter in Appendix A.

c. Which of the following statements comes closest to your recommendation for further action to be taken in the estimation of this equation?

   i.   No further specification changes are advisable (go to Section 8.7.3).

   ii. I would like to drop ESL from the equation (go to run 8.15).

   iii. I would like to drop PREP from the equation (go to run 8.13).

   iv. I would like to drop RACE from the equation (go to run 8.12).

If you need feedback on your answer, see hint 15 in the material on this chapter in Appendix A.

Regression Run 8.17

```
Dependent Variable: SAT
Method: Least Squares
Date: 02/29/00   Time: 15:17
Sample: 1 65
Included observations: 65
```

Variable	Coefficient	Std. Error	t-Statistic	Prob.
C	475.7963	104.7275	4.543185	0.0000
GPA	163.4716	34.41783	4.749619	0.0000
AP	107.7460	45.02942	2.392790	0.0198
PREP	-30.92277	38.84976	-0.795958	0.4291

R-squared	0.516299	Mean dependent var	1075.538
Adjusted R-squared	0.492511	S.D. dependent var	191.3605
S.E. of regression	136.3219	Akaike info criterion	12.72748
Sum squared resid	1133604.	Schwarz criterion	12.86129
Log likelihood	-409.6431	F-statistic	21.70368
Durbin-Watson stat	1.912398	Prob(F-statistic)	0.000000

Answer each of the following questions for the above regression run.

a. Evaluate this result with respect to its economic meaning, overall fit, and the signs and significance of the individual coefficients.

b. What econometric problems (out of omitted variables, irrelevant variables, or multicollinearity) does this regression have? Why? If you need feedback on your answer, see hint 11 in the material on this chapter in Appendix A.

c. Which of the following statements comes closest to your recommendation for further action to be taken in the estimation of this equation?

   i. No further specification changes are advisable (go to Section 8.7.3).

   ii. I would like to drop PREP from the equation (go to run 8.20).

   iii. I would like to add RACE to the equation (go to run 8.18).

   iv. I would like to replace the AP combination variable with APMATH and APENG (go to run 8.4).

If you need feedback on your answer, see hint 16 in the material on this chapter in Appendix A.

Regression Run 8.18

Dependent Variable: SAT
Method: Least Squares
Date: 02/29/00   Time: 15:17
Sample: 1 65
Included observations: 65

Variable	Coefficient	Std. Error	t-Statistic	Prob.
C	522.4920	107.1073	4.878210	0.0000
GPA	154.0768	34.42039	4.476323	0.0000
AP	125.9048	45.75812	2.751529	0.0078
PREP	-41.06153	38.80679	-1.058102	0.2943
RACE	-61.63421	37.41938	-1.647120	0.1048

R-squared	0.537225	Mean dependent var	1075.538
Adjusted R-squared	0.506373	S.D. dependent var	191.3605
S.E. of regression	134.4472	Akaike info criterion	12.71402
Sum squared resid	1084563.	Schwarz criterion	12.88128
Log likelihood	-408.2058	F-statistic	17.41313
Durbin-Watson stat	1.887634	Prob(F-statistic)	0.000000

Answer each of the following questions for the above regression run.

a. Evaluate this result with respect to its economic meaning, overall fit, and the signs and significance of the individual coefficients.

b. What econometric problems (out of omitted variables, irrelevant variables, or multicollinearity) does this regression have? Why? If you need feedback on your answer, see hint 11 in the material on this chapter in Appendix A.

c. Which of the following statements comes closest to your recommendation for further action to be taken in the estimation of this equation?

   i. No further specification changes are advisable (go to Section 8.7.3).

   ii. I would like to drop RACE from the equation (go to run 8.17).

   iii. I would like to add ESL to the equation (go to run 8.19).

   iv. I would like to replace the AP combination variable with APMATH and APENG (go to run 8.11).

If you need feedback on your answer, see hint 16 in the material on this chapter in Appendix A.

Regression Run 8.19

Dependent Variable: SAT
Method: Least Squares
Date: 02/29/00   Time: 15:18
Sample: 1 65
Included observations: 65

Variable	Coefficient	Std. Error	t-Statistic	Prob.
C	524.8762	108.0514	4.857655	0.0000
GPA	153.7341	34.67841	4.433136	0.0000
AP	122.3201	47.01130	2.601930	0.0117
ESL	26.00898	67.33954	0.386236	0.7007
PREP	-43.55594	39.61488	-1.099484	0.2760
RACE	-84.43699	70.04203	-1.205519	0.2328

R-squared	0.538392	Mean dependent var	1075.538
Adjusted R-squared	0.499272	S.D. dependent var	191.3605
S.E. of regression	135.4107	Akaike info criterion	12.74227
Sum squared resid	1081828.	Schwarz criterion	12.94298
Log likelihood	-408.1237	F-statistic	13.76280
Durbin-Watson stat	1.894863	Prob(F-statistic)	0.000000

Answer each of the following questions for the above regression run.

a. Evaluate this result with respect to its economic meaning, overall fit, and the signs and significance of the individual coefficients.

b. What econometric problems (out of omitted variables, irrelevant variables, or multicollinearity) does this regression have? Why? If you need feedback on your answer, see hint 11 in the material on this chapter in Appendix A.

c. Which of the following statements comes closest to your recommendation for further action to be taken in the estimation of this equation?

 i. No further specification changes are advisable (go to Section 8.7.3).

 ii. I would like to drop ESL from the equation (go to run 8.18).

 iii. I would like to replace the AP combination variable with APMATH and APENG (go to run 8.14).

If you need feedback on your answer, see hint 16 in the material on this chapter in Appendix A.

Regression Run 8.20

Dependent Variable: SAT				
Method: Least Squares				
Date: 02/29/00 Time: 15:19				
Sample: 1 65				
Included observations: 65				
Variable	Coefficient	Std. Error	t-Statistic	Prob.
C	457.2010	101.7863	4.491773	0.0000
GPA	161.2106	34.19889	4.713912	0.0000
AP	112.7129	44.46296	2.534985	0.0138
R-squared	0.511276	Mean dependent var		1075.538
Adjusted R-squared	0.495510	S.D. dependent var		191.3605
S.E. of regression	135.9185	Akaike info criterion		12.70704
Sum squared resid	1145378.	Schwarz criterion		12.80740
Log likelihood	-409.9789	F-statistic		32.43043
Durbin-Watson stat	1.917047	Prob(F-statistic)		0.000000

Answer each of the following questions for the above regression run.

a. Evaluate this result with respect to its economic meaning, overall fit, and the signs and significance of the individual coefficients.

b. What econometric problems (out of omitted variables, irrelevant variables, or multicollinearity) does this regression have? Why? If you need feedback on your answer, see hint 13 in the material on this chapter in Appendix A.

c. Which of the following statements comes closest to your recommendation for further action to be taken in the estimation of this equation?

   i. No further specification changes are advisable (go to Section 8.7.3).

   ii. I would like to add PREP to the equation (go to run 8.17).

   iii. I would like to replace the AP combination variable with APMATH and APENG (go to run 8.1).

If you need feedback on your answer, see hint 13 in the material on this chapter in Appendix A.

8.7.3 Evaluating the Results from Your Interactive Exercise

Congratulations! If you've reached this section, you must have found a specification that met your theoretical and econometric goals. Which one did you pick? Our experience is that most beginning econometricians end up with either regression run 8.3, 8.6, or 8.10, but only after looking at three or more regression results (or a hint or two) before settling on that choice.

In contrast, we've found that most experienced econometricians gravitate to regression run 8.6, usually after inspecting, at most, one other specification. What lessons can we learn from this difference?

1. *Learn that a variable isn't irrelevant simply because its t-score is low.* In our opinion, ESL belongs in the equation for strong theoretical reasons, and a slightly insignificant t-score in the expected direction isn't enough evidence to get us to rethink the underlying theory.

2. *Learn to spot redundant (multicollinear) variables.* ESL and RACE wouldn't normally be redundant, but in this high school, with its particular ethnic diversity, they are. Once one is included in the equation, the other shouldn't even be considered.

3. *Learn to spot false variables.* At first glance, PREP is a tempting variable to include because prep courses almost surely improve the SAT scores of the students who choose to take them. The problem is that a student's decision to take a prep course isn't independent of his or her previous SAT scores (or expected scores). We trust the judgment of students who feel a need for a prep course, and we think that all the course will do is bring them up to the level of their peers who didn't feel they needed a course. As a result, we wouldn't expect a significant effect in either direction.

If you enjoyed and learned from this interactive regression learning exercise, you'll be interested to know that there is another in Chapter 11. Good luck!

Serial Correlation

In the next two chapters we'll investigate the final component of the specification of a regression equation—choosing the correct form of the stochastic error term. Our first topic, serial correlation, is the violation of Classical Assumption IV that different observations of the error term are uncorrelated with each other. Serial correlation, also called autocorrelation, can exist in any research study in which the order of the observations has some meaning. It therefore occurs most frequently in time-series data sets. In essence, serial correlation implies that the error term from one time period depends in some systematic way on error terms from other time periods. Since time-series data are used in many applications of econometrics, it's important to understand serial correlation and its consequences for OLS estimators.

The approach of this chapter to the problem of serial correlation will be similar to that used in the previous chapter. We'll attempt to answer the same four questions:

1. What is the nature of the problem?
2. What are the consequences of the problem?
3. How is the problem diagnosed?
4. What remedies for the problem are available?

9.1   Pure versus Impure Serial Correlation

9.1.1   Pure Serial Correlation

Pure serial correlation occurs when Classical Assumption IV, which assumes uncorrelated observations of the error term, is violated in a *correctly specified* equation. Assumption IV implies that:

$$E(r_{\epsilon_i \epsilon_j}) = 0 \qquad (i \neq j)$$

If the expected value of the simple correlation coefficient between any two observations of the error term is not equal to zero, then the error term is said to be serially correlated. When econometricians use the term serial correlation without any modifier, they are referring to pure serial correlation.

The most commonly assumed kind of serial correlation is **first-order serial correlation,** in which the current observation of the error term is a function of the previous observation of the error term:

$$\epsilon_t = \rho \epsilon_{t-1} + u_t \qquad (9.1)$$

where: ϵ = the error term of the equation in question
ρ = the parameter depicting the functional relationship between observations of the error term
u = a classical (nonserially correlated) error term

The functional form in Equation 9.1 is called a first-order Markov scheme, and the new symbol, ρ (rho, pronounced "row"), is called the **first-order autocorrelation coefficient.** For this kind of serial correlation, all that is needed is for the value of one observation of the error term to directly affect the value of the next observation of the error term.

The magnitude of ρ indicates the strength of the serial correlation in an equation. If ρ is zero, then there is no serial correlation (because ϵ would equal u, a classical error term). As ρ approaches one in absolute value, the value of the previous observation of the error term becomes more important in determining the current value of ϵ_t, and a high degree of serial correlation exists. For ρ to be greater than one in absolute value is unreasonable because it implies that the error term has a tendency to continually increase in absolute value over time ("explode"). As a result of the above, we can state that:

$$-1 < \rho < +1 \qquad (9.2)$$

The sign of ρ indicates the nature of the serial correlation in an equation. A positive value for ρ implies that the error term tends to have the same sign from one time period to the next. This is called **positive serial correlation**. Such a tendency means that if ϵ_t happens by chance to take on a large value in one time period, subsequent observations would tend to retain a portion of this original large value and would have the same sign as the original. For example, in time-series models, a large external shock to an economy in one period may linger on for several time periods. If this occurs now and then, the error term will tend to be positive for a number of observations, then negative for several more, and then back again.

Figure 9.1 shows two different examples of positive serial correlation. The error term observations plotted in Figure 9.1 are arranged in chronological order, with the first observation being the first period for which data are available, the second being the second, and so on. To see the difference between error terms with and without positive serial correlation, compare the patterns in Figure 9.1 with the depiction of no serial correlation ($\rho = 0$) in Figure 9.2.

A negative value of ρ implies that the error term has a tendency to switch signs from negative to positive and back again in consecutive observations. This is called **negative serial correlation** and implies that there is some sort of cycle (like a pendulum) behind the drawing of stochastic disturbances. Figure 9.3 shows two different examples of negative serial correlation. For instance, negative serial correlation might exist in the error term of an equation that is in first differences because *changes* in a variable often follow a cyclical pattern. In most time-series applications, however, negative pure serial correlation is much less likely than positive pure serial correlation. As a result, most econometricians analyzing pure serial correlation concern themselves primarily with positive serial correlation.

Serial correlation can take on many forms other than first-order serial correlation. For example, in a quarterly model, the current quarter's error term observation may be functionally related to the observation of the error term from the same quarter in the previous year. This is called seasonally based serial correlation:

$$\epsilon_t = \rho\epsilon_{t-4} + u_t$$

Similarly, it is possible that the error term in an equation might be a function of more than one previous observation of the error term:

$$\epsilon_t = \rho_1\epsilon_{t-1} + \rho_2\epsilon_{t-2} + u_t$$

Such a formulation is called *second-order* serial correlation. Higher-order expressions are similarly formed, but the justifications for assuming these

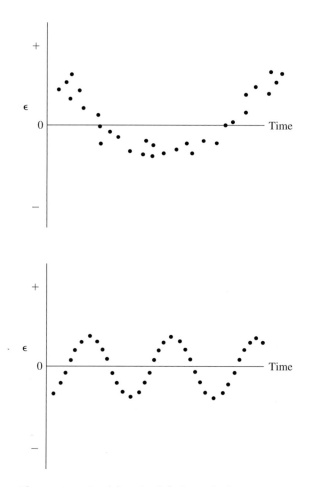

Figure 9.1 Positive Serial Correlation

With positive first-order serial correlation, the current observation of the error term tends to have the same sign as the previous observation of the error term. An example of positive serial correlation would be external shocks to an economy that take more than one time period to completely work through the system.

higher-order forms are usually weaker than the justification for the second-order form, which itself is not always all that strong.

9.1.2   Impure Serial Correlation

By **impure serial correlation** we mean serial correlation that is caused by a specification error such as an omitted variable or an incorrect functional

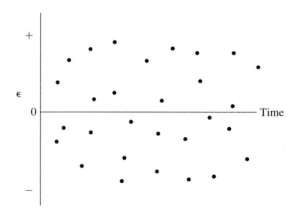

Figure 9.2 No Serial Correlation

With no serial correlation, different observations of the error term are completely uncorrelated with each other. Such error terms would conform to Classical Assumption IV.

form. While pure serial correlation is caused by the underlying distribution of the error term of the true specification of an equation (which cannot be changed by the researcher), impure serial correlation is caused by a specification error that often can be corrected.

How is it possible for a specification error to cause serial correlation? Recall that the error term can be thought of as the effect of omitted variables, nonlinearities, measurement errors, and pure stochastic disturbances on the dependent variable. This means, for example, that if we omit a relevant variable or use the wrong functional form, then the portion of that omitted effect that cannot be represented by the included explanatory variables must be absorbed by the error term. The error term for an incorrectly specified equation thus includes a portion of the effect of any omitted variables and/or a portion of the effect of the difference between the proper functional form and the one chosen by the researcher. This new error term might be serially correlated even if the true one is not. If this is the case, the serial correlation has been caused by the researcher's choice of a specification and not by the pure error term associated with the correct specification.

As we'll see in Section 9.4, the proper remedy for serial correlation depends on whether the serial correlation is likely to be pure or impure. Not surprisingly, the best remedy for impure serial correlation usually is to attempt to find the omitted variable (or at least a good proxy) or the correct functional form for the equation. As a result, most econometricians try to make sure they have the best specification possible before they spend too much time worrying about pure serial correlation.

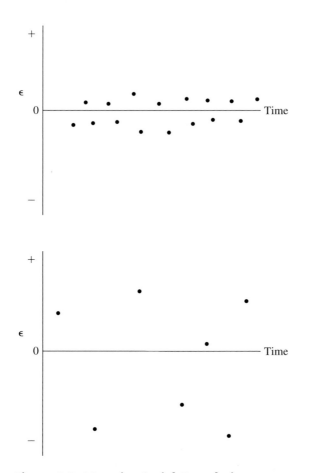

Figure 9.3 Negative Serial Correlation

With negative first-order serial correlation, the current observation of the error term tends to have the opposite sign from the previous observation of the error term. In most time-series applications, negative serial correlation is much less likely than positive serial correlation.

To see how a left-out variable can cause the error term to be serially correlated, suppose that the true equation is:

$$Y_t = \beta_0 + \beta_1 X_{1t} + \beta_2 X_{2t} + \epsilon_t$$

where ϵ_t is a classical error term. As shown in Section 6.1, if X_2 is accidentally omitted from the equation (or if data for X_2 are unavailable), then:

$$Y_t = \beta_0 + \beta_1 X_{1t} + e_t^* \qquad \text{where } \epsilon_t^* = \beta_2 X_{2t} + \epsilon_t \qquad (9.3)$$

Thus, the error term being used in the omitted variable case is not the classical error term ϵ. Instead, it's also a function of one of the independent variables, X_2. As a result, the new error term, ϵ^*, can be serially correlated even if the true error term ϵ, is not. In particular, the new error term ϵ^* will tend to be serially correlated when:

1. X_2 itself is serially correlated (this is quite likely in a time series) *and*
2. the size of ϵ is small compared to the size[1] of $\beta_2\overline{X}_2$.

These tendencies hold even if there are a number of included and/or omitted variables.

Note that while the error term ϵ^* appears to have a nonzero mean, this will not actually occur since the OLS estimate of the constant term, $\hat{\beta}_0^*$, will adjust to offset this problem. Second, since impure serial correlation implies a specification error such as an omitted variable, impure serial correlation is likely to be associated with biased coefficient estimates. Both the bias and the impure serial correlation will disappear if the specification error is corrected.

An example of how an omitted variable might cause serial correlation in the error term of an incorrectly specified equation involves the fish-demand equation of Section 8.5:

$$F_t = \beta_0 + \beta_1 RP_t + \beta_2 \ln Yd_t + \beta_3 D_t + \epsilon_t \tag{9.4}$$

where: F_t = per capita pounds of fish consumed in year t
RP_t = the price of fish relative to beef in year t
Yd_t = real per capita disposable income in year t
D_t = a dummy variable equal to 0 in years before the Pope's decision and 1 thereafter
ϵ_t = a classical (nonserially correlated) error term

Assume that Equation 9.4 is the "correct" specification. What would happen to this equation if disposable income, Yd, were omitted?

$$F_t = \beta_0 + \beta_1 RP_t + \beta_3 D_t + \epsilon_t^* \tag{9.5}$$

---

1. If typical values of ϵ are significantly larger in absolute value than $\beta_2\overline{X}_2$, then even a serially correlated omitted variable (X_2) will not change ϵ very much. In addition, recall that the omitted variable, X_2, will cause bias in the estimate of β_1, depending on the correlation between the two Xs. If $\hat{\beta}_1$ is biased because of the omission of X_2, then a portion of the $\beta_2\overline{X}_2$ effect must have been absorbed by $\hat{\beta}_1$ and will not end up in the residuals. As a result, tests for serial correlation based on those residuals may give incorrect readings. Just as important, such residuals may leave misleading clues as to possible specification errors. This is only one of many reasons why an analysis of the residuals should not be the only procedure used to determine the nature of possible specification errors.

The most obvious effect would be that the estimated coefficients of RP and D would be biased, depending on the correlation of RP and D with Yd. A secondary effect would be that the error term would now include a large portion of the left-out effect of disposable income on the consumption of fish. That is, ϵ_t^* would be a function of $\epsilon_t + \beta_2 \ln Yd_t$. It's reasonable to expect that disposable income (and therefore its log) might follow a fairly serially correlated pattern:

$$\ln Yd_t = f(\ln Yd_{t-1}) + u_t \qquad (9.6)$$

Why is this likely? Observe Figure 9.4, which plots the log of U.S. disposable income over time. Note that the continual rise of disposable income over time makes it (and its log) act in a serially correlated or autoregressive manner. But if disposable income is serially correlated (and if its impact is not small relative to ϵ) then ϵ^* is likely to also be serially correlated, which can be expressed as:

$$\epsilon_t^* = \rho \epsilon_{t-1}^* + u_t$$

where ρ is the coefficient of serial correlation and u is a classical error term. This example has shown that it is indeed possible for an omitted variable to

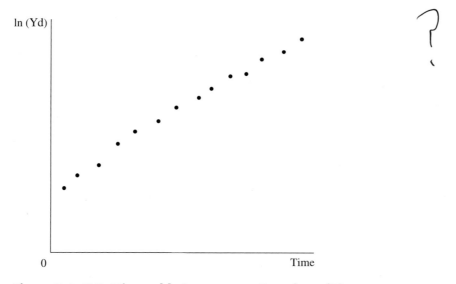

Figure 9.4 U.S. Disposable Income as a Function of Time

U.S. disposable income (and most other national aggregates) tends to increase steadily over time. As a result, such variables are serially correlated (or autocorrelated), and the omission of such a variable from an equation could potentially introduce impure serial correlation into the error term of that equation.

introduce "impure" serial correlation into an equation. For more on this example, see Exercise 10.

Another common kind of impure serial correlation is that caused by an incorrect functional form. Here, the choice of the wrong functional form can cause the error term to be serially correlated. Let's suppose that the true equation is polynomial in nature:

$$Y_t = \beta_0 + \beta X_{1t} + \beta_2 X_{1t}^2 + \epsilon_t \tag{9.7}$$

but that instead a linear regression is run:

$$Y_t = \alpha_0 + \alpha_1 X_{1t} + \epsilon_t^* \tag{9.8}$$

The new error term ϵ^* is now a function of the true error term ϵ and of the differences between the linear and the polynomial functional forms. As can be seen in Figure 9.5, these differences often follow fairly autoregressive patterns. That is, positive differences tend to be followed by positive differences, and negative differences tend to be followed by negative differences. As a result, using a linear functional form when a nonlinear one is appropriate will usually result in positive impure serial correlation. For a more complete example of impure serial correlation caused by an incorrect functional form, see Exercise 14.

9.2   The Consequences of Serial Correlation

The consequences of serial correlation are quite different in nature from the consequences of the problems discussed so far in this text. Omitted variables, irrelevant variables, and multicollinearity all have fairly recognizable external symptoms. Each problem changes the estimated coefficients and standard errors in a particular way, and an examination of these changes (and the underlying theory) often provides enough information for the problem to be detected. As we shall see, serial correlation is more likely to have internal symptoms; it affects the estimated equation in a way that is not easily observable from an examination of just the results themselves.

There are three major consequences of serial correlation:

1. Pure serial correlation does not cause bias in the coefficient estimates.

2. Serial correlation increases the variances of the $\hat{\beta}$ distributions.[2]

---

2. This holds as long as the serial correlation is positive, as is typically the case in economic examples. In addition, if the regression includes a lagged dependent variable as an independent variable, then the problems worsen significantly. For more on this topic (called distributed lags), see Chapter 12.

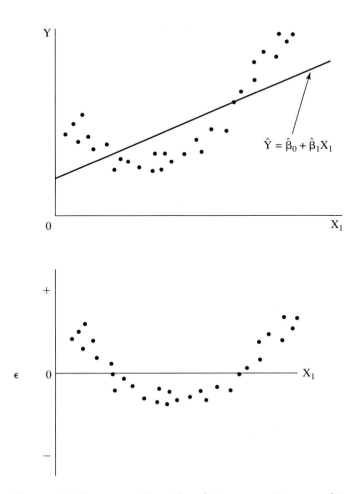

Figure 9.5 Incorrect Functional Form as a Source of Impure Serial Correlation

The use of an incorrect functional form tends to group positive and negative residuals together, causing positive impure serial correlation.

3. Serial correlation causes OLS to underestimate the standard errors of the coefficients.

Let's now go on to explain these consequences in more detail and to then work through a hypothetical example of how a serially correlated error term affects the estimation of an equation. In the process we will focus mainly on positive pure first-order serial correlation because it's the kind of autocorrelation most frequently assumed in economic analysis.

9.2.1   An Overview of the Consequences of Serial Correlation

The existence of serial correlation in the error term of an equation violates Classical Assumption IV, and the estimation of the equation with OLS has at least three consequences:

1. *Pure serial correlation does not cause bias in the coefficient estimates.* Recall that the most important property of the OLS estimation technique is that it is minimum variance for the class of linear unbiased estimators. If the errors are serially correlated, one of the assumptions of the Gauss–Markov Theorem is violated, but this violation does not cause the coefficient estimates to be biased. Suppose that the error term of the following equation:

$$Y_t = \beta_0 + \beta_1 X_{1t} + \beta_2 X_{2t} + \epsilon_t \tag{9.9}$$

is known to have pure first-order serial correlation:

$$\epsilon_t = \rho \epsilon_{t-1} + u_t \tag{9.10}$$

where u_t is a classical (nonserially correlated) error term.

   If Equation 9.9 is correctly specified and is estimated with OLS, then the estimates of the coefficients of the equation obtained from the OLS estimation will be unbiased. That is,

$$E(\hat{\beta}_1) = \beta_1 \quad \text{and} \quad E(\hat{\beta}_2) = \beta_2$$

   Pure serial correlation introduces no bias into the estimation procedure. This conclusion doesn't depend on whether the serial correlation is positive or negative or first order. If the serial correlation is impure, however, bias may be introduced by the use of an incorrect specification.

   This lack of bias does not necessarily mean that the OLS estimates of the coefficients of a serially correlated equation will be close to the true coefficient values; the single estimate observed in practice can come from a wide range of possible values. In addition, the standard errors of these estimates will typically be increased by the serial correlation. This increase will raise the probability that a $\hat{\beta}$ will differ significantly from the true β value. What unbiased means in this case is that the distribution of the $\hat{\beta}$s is still centered around the true β.

2. *Serial correlation increases the variances of the $\hat{\beta}$ distributions.* Although the violation of Classical Assumption IV causes no bias, it does affect the

other main conclusion of the Gauss–Markov Theorem, that of minimum variance. In particular, we cannot prove that the distribution of the OLS $\hat{\beta}$s is minimum variance when Assumption IV is violated. As a result, if the error term is serially correlated, then OLS no longer provides minimum variance estimates of the coefficients.

The serially correlated error term causes the dependent variable to fluctuate in a way that the OLS estimation procedure attributes to the independent variables. Thus, OLS is more likely to misestimate the true β in the face of serial correlation. On balance, the $\hat{\beta}$s are still unbiased because overestimates are just as likely as underestimates; however, these errors increase the variance of the distribution of the estimates, increasing the amount that any given estimate is likely to differ from the true β. Indeed, it can be shown that if the error term is distributed as in Equation 9.10, then the variance of the $\hat{\beta}$s is a function of ρ. The larger the absolute value of ρ, the larger the variance of the $\hat{\beta}$s.

The effect of serial correlation on the distribution of the coefficient estimates is shown in Figure 9.6, which shows that the distribution of $\hat{\beta}$s from a serially correlated equation is centered around the true β but is much wider than the distribution from an equation without serial correlation.

3. *Serial correlation causes OLS to underestimate the standard errors of the coefficients.* With serial correlation, the typical OLS formula for the standard error doesn't apply anymore and yields values that tend to underestimate the true standard deviation. As a result, serial correlation increases the standard deviations of the estimated coefficients, but it does so in a way that is masked by the OLS estimates.

OLS tends to underestimate the standard errors of the coefficients of serially correlated equations because serial correlation usually results in a pattern of observations that allows a better fit than the actual non-serially correlated observations would justify. This better fit results in underestimates not only of the standard errors of the $\hat{\beta}$s but also of the standard error of the residuals, so t-scores, the F-score, and $\overline{R}^2$ all can be overestimates if you have uncorrected serial correlation.

In particular, the tendency of OLS to underestimate the SE($\hat{\beta}$)s in the face of serial correlation will cause it to overestimate the t-scores of the estimated coefficients since:

$$t = \frac{(\hat{\beta} - \beta_{H_0})}{SE(\hat{\beta})} \qquad (9.11)$$

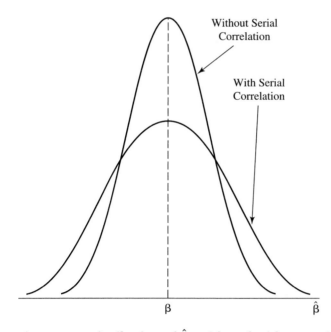

Figure 9.6 Distribution of $\hat{\beta}$s with and without Serial Correlation

The distribution of $\hat{\beta}$s from a serially correlated equation is centered around the true β, but it is often much wider than the distribution from an equation without serial correlation because serial correlation increases the variances of the $\hat{\beta}$ distributions. Unfortunately, OLS underestimates these variances, masking this effect.

If a too low $SE(\hat{\beta})$ causes a high t-score for a particular coefficient, then it becomes more likely that we will reject a null hypothesis ($\beta = 0$) when it's true. In a sense, then, OLS misleads the researcher about the significance of a particular result. Serial correlation not only increases the standard deviations but also causes mistaken conclusions by making it difficult for OLS to capture this increase.

9.2.2   An Example of the Consequences of Serial Correlation

Error terms can never be observed, so we can't examine an existing "real world" data set and be sure what kind of serial correlation, if any, exists. Examples of serial correlation therefore are always clouded by lack of knowledge about the true degree of serial correlation in the error terms. Let's look at a hypothetical example of serial correlation and its effects on OLS estimates. After we've explored this hypothetical example, we'll be able to deal with real world situations much better.

Suppose you're studying the relationship between the real interest rate and the budget deficit. You read the literature on the topic, finding many theoretical articles mostly in favor (at least until recently) of such a link but finding no empirical studies that show a direct, significant, positive relationship between the deficit and real interest rates in the United States.[3]

After some mainly Keynesian consideration, you decide to specify the following equation:

$$r_t = f(\overset{+}{D_t}, \overset{-}{M_t}) + \epsilon_t = \beta_0 + \beta_D D_t + \beta_M M_t + \epsilon_t \qquad (9.12)$$

where: r_t = the short-term real interest rate in year t
D_t = the budget deficit in year t (percent of GDP)
M_t = the nominal money growth rate in year t
ϵ_t = a classical error term

You then estimate Equation 9.12 on annual U.S. data:

$$\hat{r}_t = 0.050 + 0.008D_t - 0.002M_t \qquad (9.13)$$
$$(0.002) \quad (0.001)$$
$$t = 4.00 \quad -2.00 \quad \overline{R}^2 = .60$$

You're excited because it appears that you've shown that the deficit is a significant positive factor in the determination of short-term real interest rates. You worry, however, that serial correlation might invalidate your results. Your concern is in part due to the possibility that many of the involved relationships might take at least a year to work through the macroeconomy. This would mean that shocks to the system would work their way through slowly, causing positive first-order serial correlation. In addition, it seems likely that any omitted variables (of which there could be many in such a simplistic equation) in a time series would have some autocorrelated pattern over time, causing impure serial correlation.

---

3. See, for example, Martin S. Feldstein and Otto Eckstein, "The Fundamental Determinants of the Interest Rate," *Review of Economics and Statistics*, November 1970, pp. 363–375, or Gregory P. Hoelscher, "Federal Borrowing and Short-Term Interest Rates," *Southern Economic Journal*, October 1983, pp. 319–333.

Since your concern is with the estimated coefficient and standard error of the deficit variable, let's take a look at the consequences of serial correlation for your hypothetical results (with respect to D):

A. With no serial correlation:

$\hat{\beta}_D$ = 0.008

$SE(\hat{\beta}_D)$ = 0.002

t-score = 4.00

With no serial correlation, valid inferences about the statistical significance of $\hat{\beta}$ can be drawn from Equation 9.13's t-scores. Unfortunately, if the error term is serially correlated, we will not attain these results.

B. With serial correlation but a correct estimate of the standard error:

$\hat{\beta}_D$ = 0.008

$SE^*(\hat{\beta}_D)$ = 0.006

t-score = 1.33

With serial correlation, the standard deviation increases, and a correct estimate of it $[SE^*(\hat{\beta}_D)]$ would decrease the t-score. This is the result that would be printed out if your computer program estimated "correct" $SE(\hat{\beta})$s and t-scores.

C. With serial correlation and the OLS underestimate of the standard error:

$\hat{\beta}_D$ = 0.008

$SE(\hat{\beta}_D)$ = 0.003

t-score = 2.66

OLS will underestimate the standard error, giving an unrealistically high t-score. This is the result that will actually be printed out by the OLS computer program. It masks what should be a decreased t-score.

In a real case of serial correlation, the OLS printout would look like result C not result B. In this hypothetical example, however, we've been able to do what can never be done in an actual regression. That is, we have separated the increase in the standard deviation due to serial correlation from the simultaneous underestimate of that standard deviation by OLS. As a result, we can see that the OLS result (t = 2.66) is not a good indication of the actual significance of a particular coefficient in the face of serial correlation (t = 1.33). To decide what to do, it's clear that we need to be able to test for the existence of serial correlation.

9.3   The Durbin–Watson *d* Test

While the first step in detecting serial correlation often is observing a pattern in the residuals like that in Figure 9.1, the test for serial correlation that is most widely used is the Durbin–Watson *d* test.

9.3.1 The Durbin–Watson d Statistic

The **Durbin–Watson d statistic** is used to determine if there is first-order serial correlation in the error term of an equation by examining the *residuals* of
a particular estimation of that equation.[4] It's important to use the Durbin–
Watson d statistic only when the assumptions that underlie its derivation are met:

1. The regression model includes an intercept term.
2. The serial correlation is first-order in nature:

$$\epsilon_t = \rho\epsilon_{t-1} + u_t$$

   where ρ is the coefficient of serial correlation and u is a classical (nonserially correlated) error term.
3. The regression model does not include a lagged dependent variable
   (discussed in Chapter 12) as an independent variable.[5]

The equation for the *Durbin–Watson d statistic* for T observations is:

$$d = \sum_{2}^{T} (e_t - e_{t-1})^2 \Big/ \sum_{1}^{T} e_t^2 \qquad (9.14)$$

where the e_ts are the OLS residuals. Note that the numerator has one fewer
observation than the denominator because an observation must be used to
calculate e_{t-1}. The Durbin–Watson d statistic equals zero if there is extreme
positive serial correlation, two if there is no serial correlation, and four if
there is extreme negative serial correlation. To see this, put appropriate residual values into Equation 9.14 for these cases:

1. Extreme Positive Serial Correlation: d = 0

   In this case, $e_t = e_{t-1}$, so $(e_t - e_{t-1}) = 0$ and d = 0.

---

4. J. Durbin and G. S. Watson, "Testing for Serial Correlation in Least-Squares Regression," *Biometrika*, 1951, pp. 159–177. The second most-used test, the Lagrange Multiplier test, is presented in Chapter 12.

5. In such a circumstance, the Durbin–Watson d is biased toward 2, but the Durbin *h* test or
other tests can be used instead; see Section 12.2.

2. Extreme Negative Serial Correlation: $d \approx 4$

   In this case, $e_t = -e_{t-1}$, and $(e_t - e_{t-1}) = (2e_t)$. Substituting into Equation 9.14, we obtain $d = \sum (2e_t)^2 / \sum (e_t)^2$ and $d \approx 4$.

3. No Serial Correlation: $d \approx 2$

   When there is no serial correlation, the mean of the distribution of d is equal to two.[6] That is, if there is no serial correlation, $d \approx 2$.

9.3.2   Using the Durbin–Watson d Test

The Durbin–Watson d test is unusual in two respects. First, econometricians almost never test the one-sided null hypothesis that there is negative serial correlation in the residuals because negative serial correlation, as mentioned above, is quite difficult to explain theoretically in economic or business analysis. Its existence often means that impure serial correlation has been caused by some error of specification.

Second, the Durbin–Watson test is sometimes inconclusive. Whereas previously explained decision rules always have had only "acceptance" regions and rejection regions, the Durbin–Watson test has a third possibility, called the inconclusive region.[7] We'll discuss what to do when the test is inconclusive in Section 9.4.

With these exceptions, the use of the Durbin–Watson d test is quite similar to the use of the t- and F-tests. To test for positive serial correlation, the following steps are required:

1. Obtain the OLS residuals from the equation to be tested and calculate the d statistic by using Equation 9.14.

2. Determine the sample size and the number of explanatory variables and then consult Statistical Tables B-4, B-5, or B-6 in Appendix B to find the upper critical d value, d_U, and the lower critical d value, d_L, respectively. Instructions for the use of these tables are also in that appendix.

---

6. To see this, multiply out the numerator of Equation 9.14, obtaining

$$d = \left[\sum_{2}^{T} e_t^2 - 2 \sum_{2}^{T} (e_t e_{t-1}) + \sum_{2}^{T} e_{t-1}^2 \right] \Big/ \sum_{1}^{T} e_t^2 \approx \left[\sum_{2}^{T} e_t^2 + \sum_{2}^{T} e_{t-1}^2 \right] \Big/ \sum_{1}^{T} e_t^2 \approx 2$$

If there is no serial correlation, then e_t and e_{t-1} are not related, and, on average, $\sum (e_t e_{t-1}) = 0$.

7. This inconclusive region is troubling, but the development of exact Durbin–Watson tests may eliminate this problem in the near future. See William H. Greene, *Econometric Analysis* (New York: Macmillan, 1990), pp. 449–452. Some computer programs, including recent versions of SHAZAM, allow the user the option of calculating an exact Durbin–Watson probability (of first-order serial correlation).

3. Given the null hypothesis of no positive serial correlation and a one-sided alternative hypothesis:

$$H_0: \rho \leq 0 \qquad \text{(no positive serial correlation)}$$
$$H_A: \rho > 0 \qquad \text{(positive serial correlation)}$$

the appropriate decision rule is:

$$
\begin{aligned}
&\text{if } d < d_L & \text{Reject } H_0 \\
&\text{if } d > d_U & \text{Do Not Reject } H_0 \\
&\text{if } d_L \leq d \leq d_U & \text{Inconclusive}
\end{aligned}
$$

In some circumstances, particularly first differenced equations, a two-sided d test will be appropriate. In such a case, steps 1 and 2 above are still used, but step 3 is now:

Given the null hypothesis of no serial correlation and a two-sided alternative hypothesis:

$$H_0: \rho = 0 \qquad \text{(no serial correlation)}$$
$$H_A: \rho \neq 0 \qquad \text{(serial correlation)}$$

the appropriate decision rule is:

$$
\begin{aligned}
&\text{if } d < d_L & \text{Reject } H_0 \\
&\text{if } d > 4 - d_L & \text{Reject } H_0 \\
&\text{if } 4 - d_U > d > d_U & \text{Do Not Reject } H_0 \\
&\text{otherwise} & \text{Inconclusive}
\end{aligned}
$$

9.3.3 Examples of the Use of the Durbin–Watson d Statistic

Let's work through some applications of the Durbin–Watson test. First, turn to Statistical Tables B-4, B-5, and B-6. Note that the upper and lower critical d values (d_U and d_L) depend on the number of explanatory variables (do not count the constant term), the sample size, and the level of significance of the test.

Now set up a one-sided 95 percent confidence test for a regression with three explanatory variables and 25 observations. As can be seen from the 5 percent table (B-4), the critical d values are $d_L = 1.12$ and $d_U = 1.66$. As a result, if the hypotheses are:

$$H_0: \rho \leq 0 \quad \text{(no positive serial correlation)}$$
$$H_A: \rho > 0 \quad \text{(positive serial correlation)}$$

the appropriate decision rule is:

$$
\begin{array}{ll}
\text{if } d < 1.12 & \text{Reject } H_0 \\
\text{if } d > 1.66 & \text{Do Not Reject } H_0 \\
\text{if } 1.12 \leq d \leq 1.66 & \text{Inconclusive}
\end{array}
$$

A computed d statistic of 1.78, for example, would indicate that there is no evidence of positive serial correlation, a value of 1.28 would be inconclusive, and a value of 0.60 would imply positive serial correlation. Figure 9.7 provides a graph of the "acceptance," rejection, and inconclusive regions for this example.

For a more familiar example, we return to the chicken demand model of Equation 6.8. As can be confirmed with the data provided in Table 6.2, the Durbin–Watson statistic from Equation 6.8 is 0.98. Is that cause to be concerned about serial correlation? What would be the result of a one-sided 95 percent test of the null hypothesis of no positive serial correlation? Our first step would be to consult Statistical Table B-4. In that table, with k' (the number of explanatory variables, K) equal to 3 and n (the number of observations) equal to 44 (using 45), we would find the critical d values $d_L = 1.38$ and $d_U = 1.67$.

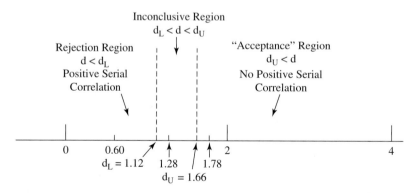

Figure 9.7 An Example of a One-Sided Durbin–Watson d Test

In a one-sided Durbin–Watson test for positive serial correlation, only values of d significantly below 2 cause the null hypothesis of no positive serial correlation to be rejected. In this example, a d of 1.78 would indicate no positive serial correlation, a d of 0.60 would indicate positive serial correlation, and a d of 1.28 would be inconclusive.

The decision rule would thus be:

$$\text{if } d < 1.38 \qquad \text{Reject } H_0$$
$$\text{if } d > 1.67 \qquad \text{Do Not Reject } H_0$$
$$\text{if } 1.38 \leq d \leq 1.67 \qquad \text{Inconclusive}$$

Since 0.98 is less than the critical lower limit of the d statistic, we would reject the null hypothesis of no positive serial correlation, and we would have to decide how to cope with that serial correlation.

9.4   Generalized Least Squares

Suppose that the Durbin–Watson d statistic detects serial correlation in the residuals of your equation. Is there a remedy? Some students suggest reordering the observations of Y and the Xs to avoid serial correlation. They think that if this time's error term appears to be affected by last time's error term, why not reorder the data randomly to get rid of the problem? The answer is that the reordering of the data does not get rid of the serial correlation; it just makes the problem harder to detect. If $\epsilon_2 = f(\epsilon_1)$ and we reorder the data, then the error term observations are still related to each other, but they now no longer follow each other, and it becomes almost impossible to discover the serial correlation. Interestingly, reordering the data changes the Durbin–Watson d statistic but does not change the estimates of the coefficients or their standard errors at all.[8]

Instead, the place to start in correcting a serial correlation problem is to look carefully at the specification of the equation for possible errors that might be causing impure serial correlation. Is the functional form correct? Are you sure that there are no omitted variables? In particular, are there specification errors that might have some pattern over time that could have introduced impure serial correlation into the residuals? Only after the specification of the equation has been reviewed carefully should the possibility of an adjustment for pure serial correlation be considered.

It's worth noting that if one or more of the variables increases or decreases steadily over time, as is often the case, or if the data set is logically reordered (say, according to the magnitude of one of the variables), then the Durbin–Watson statistic can help detect impure serial correlation. A signifi-

---

8. This can be proven mathematically, but it is usually more instructive to estimate a regression yourself, change the order of the observations, and then reestimate the regression. See Exercise 3 at the end of the chapter.

cant Durbin–Watson statistic can easily be caused by an omitted variable or an incorrect functional form. In such circumstances, the Durbin–Watson test does not distinguish between pure and impure serial correlation, but the detection of negative serial correlation is often a strong hint that the serial correlation is impure. If you conclude that you have pure serial correlation, then the appropriate response is to consider the application of Generalized Least Squares.

9.4.1 What Is Generalized Least Squares?

Generalized least squares (GLS) is a method of ridding an equation of pure first-order serial correlation and in the process restoring the minimum variance property to its estimation. GLS starts with an equation that does not meet the Classical Assumptions (due in this case to the pure serial correlation in the error term) and transforms it into one (Equation 9.19) that does meet those assumptions.

At this point, you could skip directly to Equation 9.19, but it's easier to understand the GLS estimator if you examine the transformation from which it comes. Start with an equation that has first-order serial correlation:

$$Y_t = \beta_0 + \beta_1 X_{1t} + \epsilon_t \tag{9.15}$$

which, if $\epsilon_t = \rho \epsilon_{t-1} + u_t$ (due to pure serial correlation) also equals:

$$Y_t = \beta_0 + \beta_1 X_{1t} + \rho \epsilon_{t-1} + u_t \tag{9.16}$$

where ϵ is the serially correlated error term, ρ is the coefficient of serial correlation, and u is a classical (nonserially correlated) error term.

If we could get the $\rho \epsilon_{t-1}$ term out of Equation 9.16, the serial correlation would be gone because the remaining portion of the error term (u_t) has no serial correlation in it. To rid $\rho \epsilon_{t-1}$ from Equation 9.16, multiply Equation 9.15 by ρ and then lag the new equation by one time period, obtaining

$$\rho Y_{t-1} = \rho \beta_0 + \rho \beta_1 X_{1t-1} + \rho \epsilon_{t-1} \tag{9.17}$$

Notice that we now have an equation with a $\rho \epsilon_{t-1}$ term in it. If we now subtract Equation 9.17 from Equation 9.16, the equivalent equation that remains no longer contains the serially correlated component of the error term:

$$Y_t - \rho Y_{t-1} = \beta_0(1 - \rho) + \beta_1(X_{1t} - \rho X_{1t-1}) + u_t \tag{9.18}$$

Equation 9.18 can be rewritten as:

$$Y_t^* = \beta_0^* + \beta_1 X_{1t}^* + u_t \qquad (9.19)$$

where: $\qquad Y_t^* = Y_t - \rho Y_{t-1}$ $\qquad\qquad\qquad\qquad\qquad$ (9.20)
$\qquad\qquad X_{1t}^* = X_{1t} - \rho X_{1t-1}$
$\qquad\qquad \beta_0^* = \beta_0 - \rho \beta_0$

Equation 9.18 is called a Generalized Least Squares (or "quasi-differenced") version of Equation 9.16. Notice that:

1. The error term is not serially correlated. As a result, OLS estimation of Equation 9.18 will be minimum variance.

2. The slope coefficient β_1 is the same as the slope coefficient of the original serially correlated equation, Equation 9.15. Thus GLS estimates have the same economic meaning as OLS estimates.

3. The dependent variable has changed compared to that in Equation 9.15. As mentioned in Section 7.3, this means that the GLS $\overline{R}^2$ is not directly comparable to the OLS $\overline{R}^2$.

4. To forecast with GLS, adjustments like those discussed in Section 15.2 are required.

9.4.2 Estimating Generalized Least Squares Equations

If all we need to do to rid Equation 9.16 of pure serial correlation is to estimate Equation 9.18, why is there a whole long section on estimating such GLS equations?

The answer is that Generalized Least Squares equations are tricky to estimate. To see why, take another look at Equation 9.18. Notice that it includes ρ and that we rarely know the true ρ. Thus, we need to estimate ρ in addition to β_0 and β_1. Unfortunately, this cannot be done using OLS (even if we shift the ρY_{t-1} term to the right side of the equation) because β_0 and β_1 are multiplied by ρ. Equation 9.18 is nonlinear in the coefficients! Luckily, there are a number of alternative solutions to this problem. The two most popular ways of estimating GLS equations are the Cochrane–Orcutt method and the AR(1) method.

The Cochrane–Orcutt method[9] is a two-step iterative technique that first produces an estimate of ρ and then estimates the GLS equation using that $\hat{\rho}$. These two steps are:

---

9. D. Cochrane and G. H. Orcutt, "Application of Least Squares Regression Containing Autocorrelated Error Terms," *Journal of the American Statistical Association,* 1949, pp. 32–61. EViews does not provide Cochrane–Orcutt estimates, but many other econometric software packages do.

Step 1: Estimate ρ by running a regression based on the residuals of the equation suspected of having serial correlation:

$$e_t = \rho e_{t-1} + u_t \tag{9.21}$$

where the e_ts are the OLS residuals from the equation suspected of having pure serial correlation and u is a well-behaved error term.

Step 2: Use this $\hat{\rho}$ to estimate the GLS equation by substituting $\hat{\rho}$ into Equation 9.18 and using OLS to estimate Equation 9.18 with the adjusted data.

These two steps are repeated (iterated) until further iteration results in little change in $\hat{\rho}$. Once $\hat{\rho}$ has converged (usually in just a few iterations), the results of this last estimate of step 2 are printed out (often with a listing of all the intermediate $\hat{\rho}$s computed in the process).

Let's examine an application of the Cochrane–Orcutt method to the chicken demand example that was found to have positive serial correlation in the previous section. Recall that we estimated the per capita demand for chicken as a function of the price of chicken, the price of beef, and disposable income with Equation 6.8:

$$\hat{Y}_t = 31.5 - 0.73PC_t + 0.11PB_t + 0.23YD_t \tag{6.8}$$
$$\phantom{\hat{Y}_t = 31.5 - }(0.08) \quad\ (0.05) \quad\ (0.02)$$
$$\phantom{\hat{Y}_t = 31.5 - }t = -9.12 \quad\ 2.50 \quad\ 14.22$$
$$\overline{R}^2 = .986 \quad n = 44 \text{ (annual 1951–1994)} \quad DW = 0.98$$

Note that we have added the Durbin–Watson d statistic to the documentation with the notation DW. All future time-series results will include the DW statistic, but cross-sectional documentation of the DW is not required unless the observations are ordered in some meaningful manner.

If equation 6.8 is reestimated with the Cochrane–Orcutt approach to GLS, we obtain:

$$\hat{Y}_t = 28.1 - 0.11PC_t + 0.09PB_t + 0.24YD_t \tag{9.22}$$
$$\phantom{\hat{Y}_t = 28.1 - }(0.08) \quad\ (0.04) \quad\ (0.03)$$
$$\phantom{\hat{Y}_t = 28.1 - }t = -1.30 \quad\ 2.12 \quad\ 8.04$$
$$\overline{R}^2 = .986 \quad n = 43 \text{ (annual 1951–1994)} \quad \hat{\rho} = 0.93$$

Let's compare these two results. First, note that the $\hat{\rho}$ used in Equation 9.22 is

0.93. That means that Y was actually run as $Y_t^* = Y_t - 0.93Y_{t-1}$, PC as $PC_t^* = PC_t - 0.93PC_{t-1}$, etc. Second, note that even though serial correlation causes no bias in the estimates of the βs, the GLS estimates of the slope coefficients are different from the OLS ones. Just because two estimates have the same expected values does not mean that they will be identical.

Note that $\hat{\rho}$ replaces DW in the documentation of GLS estimates since the DW of Equation 9.22 is not strictly comparable with non-GLS DWs (it is biased toward 2). Also note that the estimated model typically is presented in the format of Equation 9.19 without the asterisks attached to the transformed Y* and X* variables. Finally, note that the sample size of this regression is 43 (n − 1) because the first observation has to be used to create the lagged values for the calculation of the quasi-differenced variables in Equation 9.20.

The second way to estimate GLS equations is **the AR(1) Method,** which is a step-one process that estimates $\hat{\rho}$, $\hat{\beta}_0$, and $\hat{\beta}_1$ simultaneously.[10] In essence, the AR(1) method estimates Equation 9.18 all at once by using iterative nonlinear regression techniques that are well beyond the scope of this chapter. Although the AR(1) technique is more complicated, it has a number of advantages. First, the regression is on the entire data set, whereas Cochrane–Orcutt is forced to use up the first observation creating the quasi-differenced variables. Second, AR(1) tends to have better-behaved $SE(\hat{\beta})$s than does Cochrane–Orcutt. Interestingly, the estimates of the slope coefficients tend to be identical (depending on the convergence characteristics of the two software packages).

To compare AR(1) with Cochrane–Orcutt as alternative methods of estimating GLS equations, let's return to the chicken demand equation and estimate the equation using the AR(1) method:

$$\hat{Y}_t = 26.7 - 0.11PC_t + 0.09PB_t + 0.24YD_t \qquad (9.23)$$
$$(0.08) \quad (0.04) \quad (0.03)$$
$$t = -1.29 \quad 2.06 \quad 9.13$$
$$\overline{R}^2 = .995 \quad n = 43 \text{ (annual 1951–1994)} \quad \hat{\rho} = 0.90$$

Compare Equation 9.23 with Equation 9.22. Note that the estimated slope coefficients are indeed identical but that the $SE(\hat{\beta})$s differ slightly, causing different t-scores. This is because of the improved properties of the AR(1)

---

10. To run GLS with EViews, simply add "AR(1)" to the equation as if it were an independent variable. The resulting equation is a GLS estimate where $\hat{\rho}$ will appear as the estimated coefficient of the variable AR(1).

standard errors. Which equation is better? Since the only difference between the two equations is that the AR(1) standard error estimates are superior, our recommendation is to use AR(1) procedures as long as your computer can support such nonlinear regression. This issue is hardly settled, however, because Cochrane–Orcutt remains more popular than AR(1), and because an alternative to GLS, to be described in Section 9.4.3, is also gaining support.

9.4.3 Why Generalized Least Squares Shouldn't Automatically Be Used

There are a number of reasons why GLS should not be applied every time that the Durbin–Watson test indicates the likelihood of serial correlation in the residuals of an equation. Because of these reasons, it's our strong recommendation to avoid the use of GLS when the Durbin–Watson test is inconclusive.

1. *The significant DW may be caused by impure serial correlation.* When autocorrelation is detected, the cause may be an omitted variable or a poor choice of functional form. In such a case, the best solution is to find the missing variable or the proper form. Even if these easy answers cannot be found, the application of GLS to the misspecified equation is not necessarily superior to OLS. Impure serial correlation justifies using GLS only when the cause is an omitted variable that is at least reasonably correlated with one of the included variables. In this case, if the left-out variable cannot be found, GLS will reduce the bias somewhat, because the procedure proxies for the autocorrelated portion of the omitted variable. In cases of uncorrelated omitted variables or improper functional form, it can be shown that OLS is superior to GLS for estimating an incorrectly specified equation. In all cases, of course, the best course of action is to use the correct specification.

2. *The consequences of the serial correlation may be minor.* GLS works well if $\hat{\rho}$ is close to the actual ρ, but $\hat{\rho}$ is biased in small samples, potentially causing estimation problems. Since pure serial correlation causes no bias, it's possible that the harm done to the equation by the serial correlation may be less than the damage done by attempting to fix that problem with a biased $\hat{\rho}$. In particular, when coefficient estimates seem theoretically reasonable, and when the t-scores of the various coefficients are not being relied on for the retention of independent variables, the harm caused by serial correlation may be minor.

3. *Newey–West standard errors could be used.* Not all corrections for pure serial correlation involve Generalized Least Squares. The **Newey–West**

technique directly adjusts the SE($\hat{\beta}$)s to take account of serial correlation without changing the $\hat{\beta}$s themselves in any way.[11] The logic behind Newey–West standard errors is powerful: if serial correlation does not cause bias but does impact the standard errors, then it makes sense to adjust the estimated equation in a way that changes the SE($\hat{\beta}$)s but not the $\hat{\beta}$s. Newey–West standard errors currently are estimated by only a small percentage of applied econometricians, but it seems likely that their use will increase over time.

9.5 Summary

1. Serial correlation, or autocorrelation, is the violation of Classical Assumption IV that the observations of the error term are uncorrelated with each other. Usually, econometricians focus on first-order serial correlation, in which the current observation of the error term is assumed to be a function of the previous observation of the error term and a nonserially correlated error term (u):

$$\epsilon_t = \rho\epsilon_{t-1} + u_t \qquad -1 < \rho < 1$$

where ρ is "rho," the coefficient of serial correction.

2. Pure serial correlation is serial correlation that is a function of the error term of the correctly specified regression equation. Impure serial correlation is caused by specification errors such as an omitted variable or an incorrect functional form. While impure serial correlation can be positive $(0 < \rho < 1)$ or negative $(-1 < \rho < 0)$, pure serial correlation in economics or business situations is almost always positive.

3. The major consequence of serial correlation is an increase in the variances of the $\hat{\beta}$ distributions that is masked by an underestimation of those variances (and the standard errors) by OLS. Pure serial correlation does not cause bias in the estimates of the βs.

4. The most commonly used method of detecting first-order serial correlation is the Durbin–Watson d test, which uses the residuals of an esti-

---

11. W. K. Newey and K. D. West, "A Simple, Positive Semi-Definite Heteroskedasticity and Autocorrelation Consistent Covariance Matrix," *Econometrica*, 1987, pp. 703–708. Newey-West standard errors are similar in concept to SE*($\hat{\beta}_D$) on page 324. For a slightly longer discussion of a similar topic, see the discussion of heteroskedasticity-corrected standard errors in Section 10.4.

mated regression to test the possibility of serial correlation in the error terms. A d value of 0 indicates extreme positive serial correlation, a d value of 2 indicates no serial correlation, and a d value of 4 indicates extreme negative serial correlation.

5. The first step in ridding an equation of serial correlation is to check for possible specification errors. Only once the possibility of impure serial correlation has been reduced to a minimum should remedies for pure serial correlation be considered.

6. Generalized Least Squares (GLS) is a method of transforming an equation to rid it of pure first-order serial correlation. The use of GLS requires the estimation of ρ. GLS should not be automatically applied every time the Durbin–Watson test indicates the possibility of serial correlation in an equation.

Exercises

(Answers to even-numbered exercises are in Appendix A.)

1. Write the meaning of each of the following terms without referring to the book (or your notes), and compare your definition with the version in the text for each:
    a. impure serial correlation
    b. first-order serial correlation
    c. first-order autocorrelation coefficient
    d. Durbin–Watson d statistic
    e. Generalized Least Squares
    f. positive serial correlation

2. Use Statistical Tables B-4, B-5, and B-6 to test for serial correlation given the following Durbin–Watson d statistics for serial correlation.
    a. $d = 0.81$, $k' = 3$, $n = 21$,   5 percent, one-sided positive test
    b. $d = 3.48$, $k' = 2$, $n = 15$,   1 percent, one-sided positive test
    c. $d = 1.56$, $k' = 5$, $n = 30$,   2.5 percent, one-sided positive test
    d. $d = 2.84$, $k' = 4$, $n = 35$,   5 percent, two-sided test
    e. $d = 1.75$, $k' = 1$, $n = 45$,   5 percent, one-sided positive test
    f. $d = 0.91$, $k' = 2$, $n = 28$,   2 percent, two-sided test
    g. $d = 1.03$, $k' = 6$, $n = 26$,   5 percent, one-sided positive test

3. Recall from Section 9.4 that switching the order of a data set will not change its coefficient estimates. A revised order will change the Durbin–Watson statistic, however. To see both these points, run re-

gressions ($HS = \beta_0 + \beta_1 P + \epsilon$) and compare the coefficient estimates and DW d statistics for this data set:

Year	Housing Starts	Population
1	9090	2200
2	8942	2222
3	9755	2244
4	10327	2289
5	10513	2290

in the following three orders (in terms of year):
a. 1, 2, 3, 4, 5
b. 5, 4, 3, 2, 1
c. 2, 4, 3, 5, 1

4. After GLS has been run on an equation, the $\hat{\beta}$s are still good estimates of the original (nontransformed) equation except for the constant term:
   a. What must be done to the estimate of the constant term generated by GLS to compare it with the one estimated by OLS?
   b. Why is such an adjustment necessary?
   c. Return to Equation 9.23 and calculate the $\hat{\beta}_0$ that would be comparable to the one in Equation 6.8.
   d. The two estimates are different. Why? Does such a difference concern you?

5. Carefully distinguish between the following concepts:
   a. positive and negative serial correlation
   b. pure and impure serial correlation
   c. serially correlated observations of the error term and serially correlated residuals
   d. the Cochrane–Orcutt method and the AR(1) method

6. In Statistical Table B-4, column $k' = 5$, d_U is greater than 2 for the five smallest sample sizes in the table. What does it mean if $d_U > 2$?

7. Recall the example of the relationship between the short-term real interest rate and the budget deficit discussed at the end of Section 9.2. The hypothetical results in that section were extrapolated from a cross-sectional study by M. Hutchinson and D. Pyle[12] that found at

---

12. M. M. Hutchinson and D. H. Pyle, "The Real Interest Rate/Budget Deficit Link: International Evidence, 1973–82," *Federal Reserve Bank of San Francisco Economic Review*, Fall 1984, pp. 26–35.

least some evidence of such a link in a sample that pools annual time-series and cross-sectional data from six countries.

a. Suppose you were told that the Durbin–Watson d from their best regression was 0.81. Test this DW for indications of serial correlation ($n = 70$, $k' = 4$, 95 percent one-sided test for positive serial correlation).

b. Based on this result, would you conclude that serial correlation existed in their study? Why or why not? (*Hint:* The six countries were the United Kingdom, France, Japan, Canada, Italy, and the United States; assume that the order of the data was United Kingdom 1973–82, followed by France 1973–82, etc.)

c. How would you use GLS to correct for serial correlation in this case?

8. Suppose the data in a time-series study were entered in reverse chronological order. Would this change in any way the testing or adjusting for serial correlation? How? In particular:

a. What happens to the Durbin–Watson statistic's ability to detect serial correlation if the order is reversed?

b. What happens to the GLS method's ability to adjust for serial correlation if the order is reversed?

c. What is the intuitive economic explanation of reverse serial correlation?

9. Suppose that a plotting of the residuals of a regression with respect to time indicates a significant outlier in the residuals. (Be careful here, this is not an outlier in the original data but is an outlier in the *residuals* of a regression.)

a. How could such an outlier occur? What does it mean?

b. Is the Durbin–Watson d statistic applicable in the presence of such an outlier? Why or why not?

10. Recall the discussion of impure serial correlation caused by leaving out the log of disposable income variable from the fish demand equation of the previous chapter (see Equations 8.26 and 9.4–9.6).

a. Return to that data set and estimate Equation 9.5; that is, leave out the $\ln Yd$ variable and estimate:

$$F = \beta_0 + \beta_1 RP_t + \beta_3 D_t + \epsilon_t^*$$

(If you do not have access to a computer, or if you do not have time to estimate the equation yourself, look up the result in the answer to this question in Appendix A and then attempt to do the rest of the question on your own.)

b. Analyze the results. In particular, test the coefficients for 5 percent statistical significance, test for serial correlation, and decide whether or not the result confirms our original expectation that the Pope's decision did indeed decrease per capita fish consumption.

c. How would you have gone about analyzing this problem if you had not known that the omission of the lnYd variable was the cause? In particular, how would you have determined whether the potential serial correlation was pure or impure?

11. Your friend is just finishing a study of attendance at Los Angeles Laker regular season home basketball games when she hears that you've read a chapter on serial correlation and asks your advice. Before running the equation on last season's data, she "reviewed the literature" by interviewing a number of basketball fans. She found out that fans like to watch winning teams. In addition, she learned that while some fans like to watch games throughout the season, others are most interested in games played late in the season. Her estimated equation (standard errors in parentheses) was:

$$\hat{A}_t = 14123 + 20L_t + 2600P_t + 900W_t$$
$$\qquad\qquad (500)\quad (1000)\quad (300)$$
$$DW = 0.85 \qquad n = 40 \qquad \overline{R}^2 = .46$$

where: A_t = the attendance at game t
L_t = the winning percentage (games won divided by games played) of the Lakers before game t
P_t = the winning percentage before game t of the Lakers' opponent in that game
W_t = a dummy variable equal to one if game t was on Friday, Saturday, or Sunday, 0 otherwise

a. Test for serial correlation using the Durbin–Watson d test at the 5 percent level.

b. Make and test appropriate hypotheses about the slope coefficients at the 1 percent level.

c. Compare the size and significance of the estimated coefficient of L with that for P. Is this difference surprising? Is L an irrelevant variable? Explain your answer.

d. If serial correlation exists, would you expect it to be pure or impure serial correlation? Why?

e. Your friend omitted the first game of the year from the sample because the first game is always a sellout and because neither team
had a winning percentage yet. Was this a good decision?

12. In Section 2.2.3, we considered an equation for U.S. per capita consumption of beef for the years 1960–1987 that was kept simple for
the purpose of that chapter. A more complete specification of the
equation estimated on the same data produces:

$$\hat{B}_t = -330.3 + 49.1 \ln Y_t - 0.34PB_t + 0.33PP_t - 15.4D_t \qquad (9.24)$$
$$\phantom{\hat{B}_t = -330.3 +} (7.4) \qquad (0.13) \qquad (0.12) \qquad (4.1)$$
$$\phantom{\hat{B}_t = -330.3} t = 6.6 \qquad -2.6 \qquad 2.7 \qquad -3.7$$
$$\phantom{\hat{B}_t = -3} \overline{R}^2 = .700 \qquad n = 28 \qquad DW = 0.94$$

where: B_t = the annual per capita pounds of beef consumed in
the United States in year t

$\ln Y$ = the log of real per capita disposable income in the
United States in 1982 dollars

PB   = average annualized real wholesale price of beef (in
cents per pound)

PP   = average annualized real wholesale price of pork (in
cents per pound)

D   = a dummy variable equal to 1 for years after 1981, 0
otherwise (an attempt to capture the increased consumer awareness of the health dangers of red meat)

a. Develop and test your own hypotheses with respect to the individual estimated slope coefficients.
b. Test for serial correlation in Equation 9.24 using the Durbin–
Watson d test at the 5 percent level.
c. What econometric problem(s) (if any) does Equation 9.24 appear
to have? What remedy would you suggest?
d. You take your own advice, and apply GLS to Equation 9.24, obtaining:

$$\hat{B}_t = -193.3 + 35.2 \ln Y_t - 0.38PB_t + 0.10PP_t - 5.7D_t \qquad (9.25)$$
$$\phantom{\hat{B}_t = -193.3 +} (14.1) \qquad (0.10) \qquad (0.09) \qquad (3.9)$$
$$\phantom{\hat{B}_t = -193.3} t = 2.5 \qquad -3.7 \qquad 1.1 \qquad -1.5$$
$$\phantom{\hat{B}_t = -1} \overline{R}^2 = .857 \qquad n = 28 \qquad \hat{\rho} = 0.82$$

Compare Equations 9.24 and 9.25. Which do you prefer? Why?

13. You're hired by Farmer Vin, a famous producer of bacon and ham, to
test the possibility that feeding pigs at night allows them to grow

faster than feeding them during the day. You take 200 pigs (from newborn piglets to extremely old porkers) and randomly assign them to feeding only during the day or feeding only at night and, after six months, end up with the following (admittedly very hypothetical) equation:

$$\hat{W}_i = 12 + 3.5G_i + 7.0D_i - 0.25F_i$$
$$\phantom{\hat{W}_i = 12 + }(1.0) \quad (1.0) \quad (0.10)$$
$$t = 3.5 \quad\quad 7.0 \quad\quad -2.5$$
$$\overline{R}^2 = .70 \quad\quad n = 200 \quad\quad DW = 0.50$$

where: W_i = the percentage weight gain of the ith pig
   G_i = a dummy variable equal to 1 if the ith pig is a male, 0 otherwise
   D_i = a dummy variable equal to 1 if the ith pig was fed only at night, 0 if only during the day
   F_i = the amount of food (pounds) eaten per day by the ith pig

a. Test for serial correlation at the 5 percent level in this equation.

b. What econometric problems appear to exist in this equation? (*Hint:* Be sure to make and test appropriate hypotheses about the slope coefficients.)

c. The goal of your experiment is to determine whether feeding at night represents a significant improvement over feeding during the day. What can you conclude?

d. The observations are ordered from the youngest pig to the oldest pig. Does this information change any of your answers to the previous parts of this question? Is this ordering a mistake? Explain your answer.

14. In a 1988 article, Josef Brada and Ronald Graves built an interesting model of defense spending in the Soviet Union just before the breakup of that nation.[13] The authors felt sure that Soviet defense spending was a function of U.S. defense spending and Soviet GNP but were less sure about whether defense spending also was a function of the ratio of Soviet nuclear warheads to U.S. nuclear warheads. Using a

13. Josef C. Brada and Ronald L. Graves, "The Slowdown in Soviet Defense Expenditures," *Southern Economic Journal*, April 1988, pp. 969–984. In addition to the variables used in this exercise, Brada and Graves also provide data for SFP_t, the rate of Soviet factor productivity in year t, which we include in Table 9.1 because we suggest exercises using SFP in the instructor's manual.

double-log functional form, the authors estimated a number of alternative specifications, including (standard errors in parentheses):

$$\widehat{\ln SDH_t} = -1.99 + 0.056\ln USD_t + 0.969\ln SY_t + 0.057\ln SP_t$$
$$\phantom{\widehat{\ln SDH_t} = -1.99 +}\ (0.074)\qquad\ (0.065)\qquad\ (0.032)$$
$$\phantom{\widehat{\ln SDH_t} = -1.99 +}\ t = 0.76\qquad\quad 14.98\qquad\quad 1.80$$
$$n = 25 \text{ (annual 1960–1984)}\quad \overline{R}^2 = .979 \quad DW = 0.49 \qquad (9.26)$$

$$\widehat{\ln SDH_t} = -2.88 + 0.105\ln USD_t + 1.066\ln SY_t \qquad\qquad (9.27)$$
$$\phantom{\widehat{\ln SDH_t} = -2.88 +}\ (0.073)\qquad\quad (0.038)$$
$$\phantom{\widehat{\ln SDH_t} = -2.88 +}\ t = 1.44\qquad\qquad 28.09$$
$$n = 25 \text{ (annual 1960–1984)}\quad \overline{R}^2 = .977 \quad DW = 0.43$$

where: SDH_t = the CIA's "high" estimate of Soviet defense expenditures in year t (billions of 1970 rubles)

USD_t = U.S. defense expenditures in year t (billions of 1980 dollars)

SY_t = Soviet GNP in year t (billions of 1970 rubles)

SP_t = the ratio of the number of USSR nuclear warheads (NR_t) to the number of U.S. nuclear warheads (NU_t) in year t

a. The authors expected positive signs for all the slope coefficients of both equations. Test these hypotheses at the 5 percent level.
b. Use our four specification criteria to determine whether SP is an irrelevant variable. Explain your reasoning.
c. Test both equations for positive first-order serial correlation. Does the high probability of serial correlation cause you to reconsider your answer to part b? Explain.
d. Someone might argue that because the DW statistic improved when lnSP was added, that the serial correlation was impure and that GLS was not called for. Do you agree with this conclusion? Why or why not?
e. If we run a GLS version of Equation 9.26, we get Equation 9.28. Does this result cause you to reconsider your answer to part b? Explain:

$$\widehat{\ln SDH_t} = 3.55 + 0.108\ln USD_t + 0.137\ln SY_t - 0.0008\ln SP_t \qquad (9.28)$$
$$\phantom{\widehat{\ln SDH_t} = 3.55 +}\ (0.067)\qquad\quad (0.214)\qquad\quad (0.027)$$
$$\phantom{\widehat{\ln SDH_t} = 3.55 +}\ t = 1.61\qquad\qquad 0.64\qquad\quad -0.03$$
$$n = 25 \text{ (annual 1960–1984)}\quad \overline{R}^2 = .994 \quad \hat{\rho} = 0.96$$

15. Let's return to the model of Soviet defense spending of the previous exercise. Throughout that exercise, the dependent variable is the CIA's high estimate of Soviet defense spending (SDH), but the authors also provide a "low" CIA estimate as well (SDL). Using the data from Table 9.1 or datafile DEFEND9 and either EViews or your computer's regression program, answer all parts of Exercise 14 with lnSDL as the dependent variable instead of lnSDH. That is, estimate versions of Equations 9.26 through 9.28 with lnSDL as the dependent variable and then use your estimates to determine the answer to each part of Exercise 14 for the new dependent variable. Does your evaluation of the authors' conclusions change when you use this dependent variable? Why or why not?

TABLE 9.1   DATA ON SOVIET DEFENSE SPENDING

Year	SDH	SDL	USD	SY	SFP	NR	NU
1960	31	23	200.54	232.3	7.03	415	1,734
1961	34	26	204.12	245.3	6.07	445	1,846
1962	38	29	207.72	254.5	3.90	485	1,942
1963	39	31	206.98	251.7	2.97	531	2,070
1964	42	34	207.41	279.4	1.40	580	2,910
1965	43	35	185.42	296.8	1.87	598	4,110
1966	44	36	203.19	311.9	4.10	674	4,198
1967	47	39	241.27	326.3	4.90	1,058	4,338
1968	50	42	260.91	346.0	4.07	1,270	4,134
1969	52	43	254.62	355.9	2.87	1,662	4,026
1970	53	44	228.19	383.3	4.43	2,047	5,074
1971	54	45	203.80	398.2	3.77	3,199	6,282
1972	56	46	189.41	405.7	2.87	2,298	7,100
1973	58	48	169.27	435.2	3.87	2,430	8,164
1974	62	51	156.81	452.2	4.30	2,534	8,522
1975	65	53	155.59	459.8	6.33	2,614	9,170
1976	69	56	169.91	481.8	0.63	3,219	9,518
1977	70	56	170.94	497.4	2.23	4,345	9,806
1978	72	57	154.12	514.2	1.03	5,097	9,950
1979	75	59	156.80	516.1	0.17	6,336	9,945
1980	79	62	160.67	524.7	0.27	7,451	9,668
1981	83	63	169.55	536.1	0.47	7,793	9,628
1982	84	64	185.31	547.0	0.07	8,031	10,124
1983	88	66	201.83	567.5	1.50	8,730	10,201
1984	90	67	211.35	578.9	1.63	9,146	10,630

Source: Josef C. Brada and Ronald L. Graves, "The Slowdown in Soviet Defense Expenditures," *Southern Economic Journal*, April 1988, p. 974.

Note: filename DEFEND9

16. As an example of impure serial correlation caused by an incorrect functional form, let's return to the equation for the percentage of putts made (P_i) as a function of the length of the putt in feet (L_i) that we discussed originally in Exercise 6 in Chapter 1. The complete documentation of that equation is

$$\hat{P}_i = 83.6 - 4.1L_i \tag{9.29}$$
$$(0.4)$$
$$t = -10.6$$
$$n = 19 \qquad \overline{R}^2 = .861 \qquad DW = 0.48$$

a. Test Equation 9.29 for serial correlation using the Durbin–Watson d test at the 1 percent level.

b. Why might the linear functional form be inappropriate for this study? Explain your answer.

c. If we now re-estimate Equation 9.29 using a double-log functional form, we obtain:

$$\widehat{\ln P}_i = 5.50 - 0.92\ln L_i \tag{9.30}$$
$$(0.07)$$
$$t = -13.0$$
$$n = 19 \qquad \overline{R}^2 = .903 \qquad DW = 1.22$$

Test Equation 9.30 for serial correlation using the Durbin–Watson d test at the 1 percent level.

d. Compare Equations 9.29 and 9.30. Which equation do you prefer? Why?

Heteroskedasticity

Heteroskedasticity is the violation of Classical Assumption V, which states that the observations of the error term are drawn from a distribution that has a constant variance.[1] The assumption of constant variances for different observations of the error term (homoskedasticity) is not always realistic. For example, in a model explaining heights, compare a one-inch error in measuring the height of a basketball player with a one-inch error in measuring the height of a mouse. It's likely that error term observations associated with the height of a basketball player would come from distributions with larger variances than those associated with the height of a mouse. As we'll see, the distinction between heteroskedasticity and homoskedasticity is important because OLS, when applied to heteroskedastic models, is no longer the minimum variance estimator (it still is unbiased, however).

In general, heteroskedasticity is more likely to take place in cross-sectional models than in time-series models. This focus on cross-sectional models is not to say that heteroskedasticity in time-series models is impossible, though.

---

1. Various authors spell this "heteroscedasticity, but Huston McCulloch appears to settle this controversy in favor of "heteroskedasticity" because of the word's Greek origin. See J. Huston McCulloch, "On Heteros*edasticity," *Econometrica*, March 1985, p. 483. Although heteroskedasticity is a difficult word to spell, at least it's an impressive comeback when parents ask, "What'd you learn for all that money?"

Within this context, we'll attempt to answer the same four questions for heteroskedasticity that we answered for multicollinearity and serial correlation in the previous two chapters:

1. What is the nature of the problem?
2. What are the consequences of the problem?
3. How is the problem diagnosed?
4. What remedies for the problem are available?

10.1 Pure versus Impure Heteroskedasticity

Heteroskedasticity, like serial correlation, can be divided into pure and impure versions. Pure heteroskedasticity is caused by the error term of the correctly specified equation; impure heteroskedasticity is caused by a specification error such as an omitted variable.

10.1.1 Pure Heteroskedasticity

Pure heteroskedasticity refers to heteroskedasticity that is a function of the error term of a correctly specified regression equation. As with serial correlation, use of the word "heteroskedasticity" without any modifier (like pure or impure) implies *pure* heteroskedasticity.

Such **pure heteroskedasticity** occurs when Classical Assumption V, which assumes that the variance of the error term is constant, is violated in a correctly specified equation. Assumption V assumes that:

$$VAR(\epsilon_i) = \sigma^2 \qquad \text{a constant} \qquad (i = 1, 2, \ldots, n) \qquad (10.1)$$

If this assumption is met, all the observations of the error term can be thought of as being drawn from the same distribution: a distribution with a mean of zero and a variance of σ^2. This σ^2 does not change for different observations of the error term; this property is called homoskedasticity. A homoskedastic error term distribution is pictured in the top half of Figure 10.1; note that the variance of the distribution is constant (even though individual observations drawn from that sample will vary quite a bit).

With heteroskedasticity, this error term variance is not constant; instead, the variance of the distribution of the error term depends on exactly which observation is being discussed:

$$VAR(\epsilon_i) = \sigma_i^2 \qquad (i = 1, 2, \ldots, n) \qquad (10.2)$$

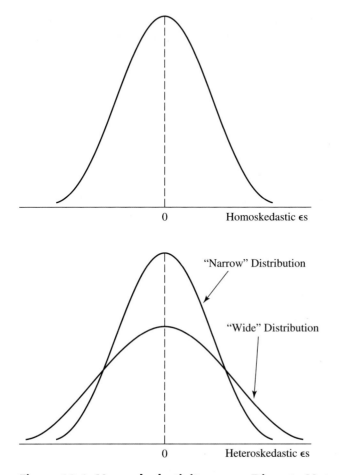

Figure 10.1 Homoskedasticity versus Discrete Heteroskedasticity

In homoskedasticity the distribution of the error term has a constant variance, so the observations are continually drawn from the same distribution (shown in the top panel). In the simplest heteroskedastic case, discrete heteroskedasticity, there would be two different error term variances and, therefore, two different distributions (one wider than the other, as in the bottom panel) from which the observations of the error term could be drawn.

Note that the only difference between Equation 10.1 and Equation 10.2 is the subscript "i" attached to σ^2, which implies that instead of being constant over all the observations, a heteroskedastic error term's variance can change depending on the observation (hence the subscript).

Heteroskedasticity often occurs in data sets in which there is a wide disparity between the largest and smallest observed values. The larger the disparity

between the size of observations in a sample, the larger the likelihood that the error term observations associated with them will have different variances and therefore be heteroskedastic. That is, we'd expect that the error term distribution for very large observations might have a large variance, but the error term distribution for small observations might have a small variance.

In cross-sectional data sets, it's easy to get such a large range between the highest and lowest values of the variables. Recall that in cross-sectional models, the observations are all from the same time period (a given month or year, for example) but are from different entities (individuals, states, or countries, for example). The difference between the size of California's labor force and Rhode Island's, for instance, is quite large (comparable in percentage terms to the difference between the heights of a basketball player and a mouse). Since cross-sectional models often include observations of widely different sizes in the same sample (cross-state studies of the United States usually include California and Rhode Island as individual observations, for example), heteroskedasticity is hard to avoid if economic topics are going to be studied cross sectionally.

Another way to visualize pure heteroskedasticity is to picture a world in which some of the observations of the error term are drawn from much wider distributions than are others. The simplest situation would be that the observations of the error term could be grouped into just two different distributions, "wide" and "narrow." We'll call this simple version of the problem *discrete heteroskedasticity*. Here, both distributions would be centered around zero, but one would have a larger variance than the other, as indicated in the bottom half of Figure 10.1. Note the difference between the two halves of the figure. With homoskedasticity, all the error term observations come from the same distribution; with heteroskedasticity, they come from different distributions.

Heteroskedasticity takes on many more complex forms. In fact, the number of different models of heteroskedasticity is virtually limitless, and an analysis of even a small percentage of these alternatives would be a huge task. Instead, we'd like to address the general principles of heteroskedasticity by focusing on the most frequently specified model of pure heteroskedasticity, just as we focused on pure, positive, first-order serial correlation in the previous chapter. However, don't let this focus mislead you into concluding that econometricians are concerned only with one kind of heteroskedasticity.

In this model of heteroskedasticity, the variance of the error term is related to an exogenous variable Z_i. For a typical regression equation:

$$Y_i = \beta_0 + \beta_1 X_{1i} + \beta_2 X_{2i} + \epsilon_i \qquad (10.3)$$

the variance of the otherwise classical error term ϵ might be equal to:

$$VAR(\epsilon_i) = \sigma^2 Z_i^2 \qquad (10.4)$$

where Z may or may not be one of the Xs in the equation. The variable Z is called a **proportionality factor** because the variance of the error term changes proportionally to the square of Z_i. The higher the value of Z_i, the higher the variance of the distribution of the ith observation of the error term. There would be n different distributions, one for each observation, from which the observations of the error term could be drawn depending on the number of different values that Z takes. To see what homoskedastic and heteroskedastic distributions of the error term look like with respect to Z, examine Figures 10.2 and 10.3. Note that the heteroskedastic distribution gets wider as Z increases but that the homoskedastic distribution maintains the same width no matter what value Z takes.

What is an example of a proportionality factor Z? How is it possible for an exogenous variable such as Z to change the whole distribution of an error term? Think about a function that relates the consumption of a household to its income. The expenditures of a low income household are not likely to be as variable in absolute value as the expenditures of a high income one because a 10 percent change in spending for a high income family involves a lot more money than a 10 percent change for a low income one. In addition, the proportion of the low income budget that must be spent on necessities is much higher than that of the high income budget. In such a case, the Y_i factor would be consumption expenditures and the proportionality factor, Z, would be household income. As household income rose, so too would the variance of the error term of an equation built to explain expenditures. The error term distributions would look something like those in Figure 10.3, where the Z in Figure 10.3 is household income, one of the independent variables in the function.

This example helps emphasize that heteroskedasticity is likely to occur in cross-sectional models because of the large variation in the size of the dependent variable involved. An exogenous disturbance that might seem huge to a low income household could seem miniscule to a high income one, for instance.

Heteroskedasticity can occur in at least two situations other than a cross-sectional data set with a large amount of variation in the size of the dependent variable:

1. Heteroskedasticity can occur in a time-series model with a significant amount of change in the dependent variable. If you were modeling sales of VCRs from 1970 to 1999, it's quite possible that you would

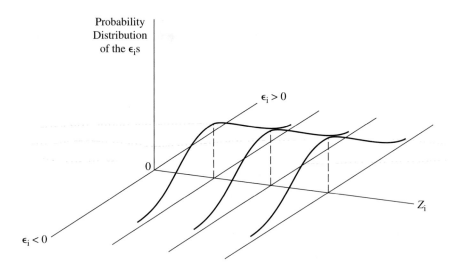

Figure 10.2 A Homoskedastic Error Term with Respect to Z_i

If an error term is homoskedastic with respect to Z_i, the variance of the distribution of the error term is the same (constant) no matter what the value of Z_1 is: $VAR(\epsilon_i) = \sigma^2$.

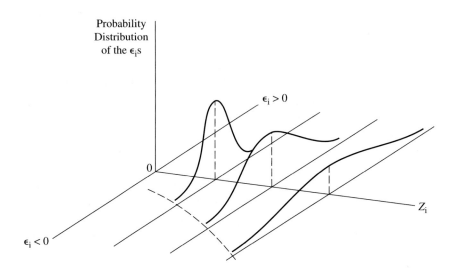

Figure 10.3 A Heteroskedastic Error Term with Respect to Z_i

If an error term is heteroskedastic with respect to Z_i, the variance of the distribution of the error term changes systematically as a function of Z_i. In this example, the variance is an increasing function of Z_i, as in $VAR(\epsilon_i) = \sigma^2 Z_i^2$.

have a heteroskedastic error term. As the phenomenal growth of the industry took place, the variance of the error term probably increased as well. Such a possibility is unlikely in time series that have low rates of change, however.

2. Heteroskedasticity can occur in any model, time series or cross sectional, where the quality of data collection changes dramatically within the sample. As data collection techniques get better, the variance of the error term should fall because measurement errors are included in the error term. As measurement errors decrease in size, so should the variance of the error term. For more on this topic (called "errors in the variables"), see Section 14.6.

10.1.2 Impure Heteroskedasticity

Heteroskedasticity that is caused by an error in specification, such as an omitted variable, is referred to as **impure heteroskedasticity**. Although improper functional form is less likely to cause impure heteroskedasticity than it is to cause impure serial correlation, the two concepts are similar in most other ways.

An omitted variable can cause a heteroskedastic error term because the portion of the omitted effect not represented by one of the included explanatory variables must be absorbed by the error term. If this effect has a heteroskedastic component, the error term of the misspecified equation might be heteroskedastic even if the error term of the true equation is not. This distinction is important because with impure heteroskedasticity the correct remedy is to find the omitted variable and include it in the regression. It's therefore important to be sure that your specification is correct before trying to detect or remedy pure heteroskedasticity.[2]

For example, consider a cross-sectional study of the 1999 imports of a number of variously sized nations. For simplicity, assume that the best model of a nation's imports in such a cross-sectional setting includes a positive function of its GDP and a positive function of the relative price ratio (including the impact of exchange rates) between it and the rest of the world. In such a case, the "true" model would look like:

$$M_i = f(\overset{+}{GDP}, \overset{+}{PR}) + \epsilon_i = \beta_0 + \beta_1 GDP_i + \beta_2 PR_i + \epsilon_i \qquad (10.5)$$

---

2. If this paragraph sounds vaguely familiar, that's because our discussion of impure heteroskedasticity parallels our discussion of impure serial correlation.

where: M_i = the imports (in dollars) of the ith nation
GDP_i = the Gross Domestic Product (in dollars) of the ith nation
PR_i = the ratio of the domestic price of normally traded goods
(converted to dollars by the exchange rate) to the world
price of those goods (measured in dollars) for the ith
nation
ϵ_i = a classical error term

Now suppose that the equation is run without GDP. Since GDP is left out, the equation would become:

$$M_i = \beta_0 + \beta_2 PR_i + \epsilon_i^* \qquad (10.6)$$

where the error term of the misspecified equation, ϵ_i^*, is a function of the omitted variable (GDP) and a nonheteroskedasic error term ϵ:

$$\epsilon_i^* = \epsilon_i + \beta_1 GDP_i \qquad (10.7)$$

To the extent that the relative price ratio does not act as a proxy for GDP, the error term has to incorporate the effects of the omitted variable. If this new effect has a larger variance for larger values of GDP, which seems likely, the new error term, ϵ_i^*, is heteroskedastic. The impact of such an effect also depends on the size of the $\beta_1 \overline{GDP}$ component compared with the absolute value of the typical ϵ component. The larger the omitted variable portion of ϵ_i^*, the more likely it is to have impure heteroskedasticity. In such a case, the error term observations, ϵ_i^*, when plotted with respect to GDP_i, appear as in Figure 10.4. As can be seen, the larger the GDP, the larger the variance of the error term.

10.2 The Consequences of Heteroskedasticity

If the error term of your equation is known to be heteroskedastic, what does that mean for the estimation of your coefficients? If the error term of an equation is heteroskedastic, there are three major consequences[3]:

1. *Pure heteroskedasticity does not cause bias in the coefficient estimates.* Even if the error term of an equation is known to be purely heteroskedastic,

---

3. It turns out that the consequences of heteroskedasticity are almost identical in general framework to those of serial correlation, though the two problems are quite different.

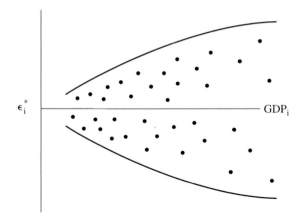

ϵ_i^* GDP$_i$

Figure 10.4 Impure Heteroskedasticity Caused by the Omission of GDP

Impure heteroskedasticity is a nonconstant variance of the distribution of the error term that is caused by an incorrect specification. In this case, the omission of GDP from the equation has forced the error term to incorporate the impact of GDP, causing the distribution of the error term to be wider (higher variance) for large values of GDP than for small ones.

that heteroskedasticity will not cause bias in the OLS estimates of the coefficients. This is true because with pure heteroskedasticity, none of the independent variables is correlated with the error term. As a result, we can say that an otherwise correctly specified equation that has pure heteroskedasticity still has the property that:

$$E(\hat{\beta}) = \beta \qquad \text{for all } \beta\text{s}$$

Lack of bias does not guarantee "accurate" coefficient estimates, especially since heteroskedasticity increases the variance of the estimates, but the distribution of the estimates is still centered around the true β. Equations with impure heteroskedasticity caused by an omitted variable, of course, will have possible specification bias.

2. *Heteroskedasticity increases the variances of the $\hat{\beta}$ distributions.* Pure heteroskedasticity causes no bias in the estimates of the OLS coefficients, but it does affect the minimum-variance property. If the error term of an equation is heteroskedastic with respect to a proportionality factor Z:

$$VAR(\epsilon_i) = \sigma^2 Z_i^2 \qquad (10.8)$$

then the minimum-variance portion of the Gauss–Markov Theorem cannot be proven because there are other linear unbiased estimators that have smaller variances. This is because the heteroskedastic error term causes the dependent variable to fluctuate in a way that the OLS estimation procedure attributes to the independent variables. Thus, OLS is more likely to misestimate the true β in the face of heteroskedasticity. On balance, the $\hat{\beta}$s are still unbiased because overestimates are just as likely as underestimates; however, these errors increase the variance of the distribution of the estimates, increasing the amount that any given estimate is likely to differ from the true β. (See Figure 10.5.)

3. *Heteroskedasticity causes OLS to tend to underestimate the variances (and standard errors) of the coefficients.* Heteroskedasticity turns out to increase the variances of the $\hat{\beta}$s in a way that is masked by the OLS estimates of them, and OLS nearly always underestimates those variances.[4] As a result, neither the t-statistic nor the F-statistic can be relied on in the face of uncorrected heteroskedasticity. In practice, OLS usually ends up with higher t-scores than would be obtained if the error terms were homoskedastic, sometimes leading researchers to reject null hypotheses that shouldn't be rejected.

Why does heteroskedasticity cause this particular pattern of consequences? As Z and the variance of the distribution of the error term increase, so does the probability of drawing a large (in absolute value) observation of the error term. If the pattern of these large observations happens to be positive when one of the independent variables is substantially above average, the OLS $\hat{\beta}$ for that variable will tend to be greater than it would have been otherwise. On the other hand, if the pattern of these large error term observations accidentally happens to be negative when one of the Xs is substantially above average, then the OLS $\hat{\beta}$ for that variable will tend to be less than it would have been. Since the error term is still assumed to be independent of all the explanatory variables, overestimates are just as likely as underestimates, and the

---

4. Actually, the OLS estimates of the variance and the standard error of the coefficient estimates $\hat{\beta}_k$ are biased, and the bias is negative as long as σ_i^2 and $(X_{ki} - \overline{X}_k)^2$ are positively correlated. The $SE(\hat{\beta})$s will be underestimated as long as an increase in X is related to an increase in the variance of the error terms. In economic examples, such a positive correlation would almost always be expected in cases in which a sizable correlation is likely to exist. For some variables, no correlation at all might exist, but a negative correlation would occur quite infrequently. As a result, the statement that OLS underestimates the variances, although a simplification, is almost always true.

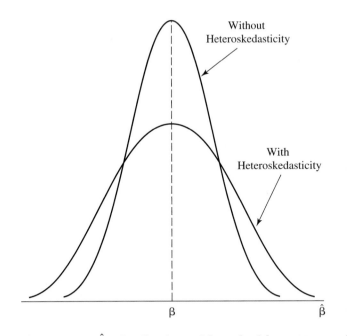

Figure 10.5 $\hat{\beta}$ Distribution with and without Heteroskedasticity

Heteroskedasticity increases the variance of the βs, widening the β distribution. It does not cause bias, however, so the $\hat{\beta}$ distribution is centered around the true β whether or not there is heteroskedasticity.

OLS estimator is still unbiased in the face of heteroskedasticity. The heteroskedasticity has caused the $\hat{\beta}$s to be farther from the true value, however, and so the variance of the distribution of the $\hat{\beta}$s has increased.

For example, the real interest rate/budget deficit study of Section 9.2.2 could just as well be a hypothetical example of the consequences of heteroskedasticity. The OLS-estimated t-scores are too high, leading to potential mistakes of inference whenever t-tests are used in heteroskedastic equations. Before we can get rid of heteroskedasticity, however, we must detect it.

10.3 Testing for Heteroskedasticity

Econometricians do not all use the same test for heteroskedasticity because heteroskedasticity takes a number of different forms, and its precise manifestation in a given equation is almost never known. The "Z_i proportionality factor" approach of this chapter, for example, is only one of many specifications of the form of heteroskedasticity. As a result, there is no universally agreed upon method of testing for heteroskedasticity; econometrics textbooks list as many as eight different methods of such testing.

Because of this wide variety, we'll describe the use of two different tests for heteroskedasticity. Our primary focus will be on the *Park test*, because it tests precisely the functional form that we use in this chapter to illustrate the problem of pure heteroskedasticity, and the *White test*, which is more generally used than the Park test. No test for heteroskedasticity can "prove" that heteroskedasticity exists in an equation, though, so the best we can do is to get a general indication of its likelihood.

There's no need to run a heteroskedasticity test for every specification estimated, however, so before using any test, it's a good idea to ask the following preliminary questions:

1. Are there any obvious specification errors? If the estimated equation is suspected of having an omitted variable or is about to be rerun for some other specification reason, a test for heteroskedasticity should be delayed until the specification is as good as possible.

2. Is the subject of the research often afflicted with heteroskedasticity? Not only are cross-sectional studies the most likely source of heteroskedasticity, but some cross-sectional studies (with large variations in the size of the dependent variable, for instance) are more susceptible to heteroskedasticity than others.

3. Finally, does a graph of the residuals show any evidence of heteroskedasticity? It sometimes saves time to plot the residuals with respect to a potential Z proportionality factor. In such cases, the graphs can often show that heteroskedasticity is or is not likely without a test. Figure 10.4 shows an example of what to look for: an expanding (or contracting) *range* of the residuals.

10.3.1 The Park Test

How do we test for pure heteroskedasticity of the form that we assumed in the previous section? That form, as we outlined in the previous section, is:

$$\text{VAR}(\epsilon_i) = \sigma^2 Z_i^2$$

where: ϵ = the error term of the equation being estimated
σ^2 = the variance of the homoskedastic error term
Z = the proportionality factor

The **Park test**[5] is a formal procedure that attempts to test the residuals for this heteroskedasticity in a manner similar to the way that the Durbin–Watson d statistic tests residuals for serial correlation. The Park test has three basic steps. First, the regression equation is estimated by OLS and the residuals are calculated. Second, the log of the squared residuals is used as the dependent variable of an equation whose sole explanatory variable is the log of the proportionality factor Z. Finally, the results of the second regression are tested to see if there is any evidence of heteroskedasticity.

If there is reason to suspect heteroskedasticity, it's appropriate to run a Park test. Since the Park test is not run automatically by computer regression packages, you should know how to run the test yourself:

1. *Obtain the residuals of the estimated regression equation.* The first step is to estimate the equation with OLS and then find the residuals from their estimation:

$$e_i = Y_i - \hat{Y}_i = Y_i - \hat{\beta}_0 - \hat{\beta}_1 X_{1i} - \hat{\beta}_2 X_{2i} \qquad (10.9)$$

These residuals, which are printed out by most computer regression packages, are the same ones used to calculate the Durbin–Watson d statistic to test for serial correlation.

2. *Use these residuals to form the dependent variable in a second regression.* In particular, the Park test suggests that you run the following double-log regression:

$$\ln(e_i^2) = \alpha_0 + \alpha_1 \ln Z_i + u_i \qquad (10.10)$$

where: e_i = the residual from the *i*th observation from Equation 10.9

Z_i = your best choice as to the possible proportionality factor (Z)

u_i = a classical (homoskedastic) error term[6]

---

5. R. E. Park, "Estimation with Heteroskedastic Error Terms," *Econometrica*, October 1966, p. 888.

6. One criticism of the Park test is that this error term is not necessarily homoskedastic. See S. M. Goldfeld and R. E. Quandt, *Nonlinear Methods in Econometrics* (Amsterdam: North-Holland Publishing Company, 1972), pp. 93–94.

3. *Test the significance of the coefficient of Z in Equation 10.10 with a t-test.* The last step is to use the t-statistic to test the significance of $\ln Z$ in explaining $\ln(e^2)$ in Equation 10.10. If the coefficient of Z is significantly different from zero, this is evidence of heteroskedastic patterns in the residuals with respect to Z; otherwise, heteroskedasticity related to this particular Z is not supported by the evidence in these residuals. However, it's impossible to prove that a particular equation's error terms are homoskedastic.

The Park test is not always easy to use. Its major problem is the identification of the proportionality factor Z. Although Z is often an explanatory variable in the original regression equation, there is no guarantee of that. A particular Z should be chosen for your Park test only after investigating the type of potential heteroskedasticity in your equation.[7] A good Z is a variable that seems likely to vary with the variance of the error term.

For example, in a cross-sectional model of countries or states, a good Z would be one that measured the size of the observation relative to the dependent variable in question. For a dependent variable such as gallons of gasoline consumed, the number of registered drivers or automobiles might be a better measure of size than the population. Although it's difficult to identity the best Z for a particular equation, it's often easier to distinguish good Zs from bad Zs. In the gasoline consumption equation, for example, a bad Z might be the speed limit in the state because, while the speed limit might be important in determining how much gasoline is used, it is unlikely to "cause" any heteroskedasticity. This is because the speed limit in a state does not vary in size in the same way that gasoline consumption does. The states likely to have large error term variances are not also likely to have high speed limits. For more on this fairly thorny issue, see Exercise 2 at the end of the chapter.

10.3.2 An Example of the Use of the Park Test

Let's return to the Woody's Restaurants example of Section 3.2 and test for heteroskedasticity in the residuals of Equation 3.4. Recall that regression explained the number of customers, as measured by the check volume (Y) at a

---

7. Some econometricians have suggested using the Park test for insight into the form of the heteroskedasticity. If $VAR(\epsilon_i) = \sigma^2 Z_i^2$, then $\ln(e_i^2)$ should be equal to $\alpha_0 + 2\ln Z_i$ plus an error term. Thus the estimate of the coefficient of $\ln Z$ in the Park test indicates whether the proportionality factor should be squared or raised to some other power. For more on this and its implications for deciding which form to use to adjust for heteroskedasticity, see R. S. Pindyck and D. L. Rubinfeld, *Econometric Models and Econometric Forecasts* (New York: McGraw-Hill, 1998), pp. 148–152.

cross section of 33 different Woody's restaurants as a function of the number of nearby competitors (N), the nearby population (P), and the average household income of the local area (I):

$$\hat{Y}_i = 102{,}192 - 9075N_i + 0.355P_i + 1.288I_i \qquad (3.7)$$
$$(2053) \quad (0.073) \quad (0.543)$$
$$t = -4.42 \quad 4.88 \quad 2.37$$
$$n = 33 \quad \overline{R}^2 = .579 \quad F = 15.65$$

This equation is cross sectional, so heteroskedasticity is a theoretical possibility. However, the dependent variable does not change much in size from restaurant to restaurant, so heteroskedasticity is not likely to be a major problem. As a result, the assumption of a constant variance of the error term (homoskedasticity) seems reasonable.

To judge whether this tentative conclusion is correct, let's use the Park test to see if the residuals from Equation 3.7 give any indication of heteroskedasticity.

1. *Calculate the residuals.* First, obtain the residuals from the equation you want to test. In the Woody's example, these residuals have already been calculated. They're at the end of Section 3.2.

2. *Use these residuals as the dependent variable in a second regression.* Run a regression with the log of the squared residual as the dependent variable as a function of the log of the suspected proportionality factor Z as first outlined in Equation 10.10:

$$\ln(e_i^2) = \alpha_0 + \alpha_1 \ln Z_i + u_i \qquad (10.10)$$

It's possible that no Z exists, but if one does, it seems likely that it would somehow be related to the size of the market that the particular Woody's restaurant serves. Since larger error term variances might exist in more heavily populated areas, population (P) is a reasonable choice as a Z to try in our Park test. Any other variable related to the size of the market or of the particular restaurant would also be a reasonable possibility.

If the logged and squared residuals from Equation 3.7 are regressed as a function of the log of P, we obtain:

$$\widehat{\ln(e_i^2)} = 21.05 - 0.2865 \ln P_i \qquad (10.11)$$
$$(0.6263)$$
$$t = -0.457$$
$$n = 33 \quad R^2 = .0067 \quad F = 0.209$$

3. *Test the significance of $\hat{\alpha}_1$ in Equation 10.10.* As can be seen from the calculated t-score, there is virtually no measurable relationship between the squared residuals of Equation 3.7 and population. The calculated t-score of -0.457 is quite a bit smaller in absolute value than 2.750, the critical t-value (from Statistical Table B-1) for a two-tailed, one percent test. As a result, we would not be able to reject the null hypothesis of homoskedasticity[8]:

$$H_0: \alpha_1 = 0$$
$$H_A: \alpha_1 \; 2 \; 0$$

For more practice in the use of the Park test, see Exercise 4 at the end of the chapter.

10.3.3 The White Test

Unfortunately, to use the Park test we must know Z_i, the variable suspected of being proportional to the possible heteroskedasticity. Quite often, however, we may want to test the possibility that more than one proportionality factor is involved simultaneously. Less frequently, we might not be able to decide which of a number of possible Z factors to test. In either of these situations, it's unadvisable to run a series of Park tests (one for each possible proportionality factor). Instead, it is appropriate to use the White test, one of a family of such tests.[9]

Like the Park test, the **White test**[10] approaches the detection of heteroskedasticity by running a regression with the squared residuals as the dependent variable. This time, though, the right-hand side of the secondary

---

8. Recall that not being able to reject the null hypothesis of homoskedasticity doesn't prove that the error terms are homoskedastic. In addition, note that *this* Park test says nothing about *other* proportionality factors or other forms of heteroskedasticity. Although heteroskedasticity of any kind is unlikely in this example because of the nature of the dependent variable, it's possible to find homoskedasticity with respect to one proportionality factor (or form) but heteroskedasticity with respect to some other proportionality factor (or form). Careful thinking is necessary before a potential Z can be chosen. Running a Park test on every conceivable variable would do little but increase the chance of Type I Error (rejecting the null hypothesis of homoskedasticity when it's true).

9. These are a general group of tests based on the Lagrange Multiplier (LM). For more on LM tests, see Section 12.2.

10. Halbert White, "A Heteroskedasticity-Consistent Covariance Matrix Estimator and a Direct Test for Heteroskedasticity," *Econometrica*, 1980, pp. 817–838.

equation includes all the original independent variables, the squares of all the original independent variables, and the cross products of all the original independent variables with each other. The White test thus has the distinct advantage of not assuming any particular form of heteroskedasticity. As a result, it's rapidly gaining support as the best[11] test yet devised to apply to all types of heteroskedasticity.

To run a White test:

1. Obtain the residuals of the estimated regression equation. This first step is identical to the first step in the Park test.

2. Use these residuals (squared) as the dependent variable in a second equation that includes as explanatory variables each X from the original equation, the square of each X, and the product of each X times every other X. For example, if the original equation's independent variables are X_1, X_2, and X_3, the appropriate White test equation is:

$$
\begin{aligned}
(e_i)^2 = \alpha_0 &+ \alpha_1 X_{1i} + \alpha_2 X_{2i} + \alpha_3 X_{3i} + \alpha_4 X_{1i}^2 \\
&+ \alpha_5 X_{2i}^2 + \alpha_6 X_{3i}^2 + \alpha_7 X_{1i} X_{2i} + \alpha_8 X_{1i} X_{3i} \qquad (10.12)\\
&+ \alpha_9 X_{2i} X_{3i} + u_i
\end{aligned}
$$

3. Test the overall significance of Equation 10.12 with the chi-square test. The appropriate test statistic here is nR^2, or the sample size (n) times the coefficient of determination (the unadjusted R^2) of Equation 10.12. This test statistic has a chi-square distribution with degrees of freedom equal to the number of slope coefficients in Equation 10.12. If nR^2 is larger than the critical chi-square value found in Statistical Table B-8, then we reject the null hypothesis and conclude that it's likely that we have heteroskedasticity. If nR^2 is less than the critical chi-square value, then we cannot reject the null hypothesis of homoskedasticity.

---

11. For time-series data, the best test is Engle's Autoregressive Conditional Heteroskedasticity (ARCH) test. An ARCH model considers the variance of the current observation of the error to be a function of (to be conditional on) the variances of previous time periods' error term observations. Thus, testing for heteroskedasticity consists of measuring the fit of an equation that specifies e_t^2 as a function of e_{t-1}^2, e_{t-2}^2, e_{t-3}^2, etc. See Robert F. Engle, "Autoregressive Conditional Heteroskedasticity with Estimates of Variance of United Kingdom Inflation," *Econometrica*, July 1982, pp. 987–1007.

The White test can be thought of as a generalized Park test, since the White test includes a variety of possible proportionality factors, but the Park test includes just one. In fact, if there is exactly one independent variable in the equation and if that variable is an appropriate proportionality factor, the White and Park tests are identical except that the Park test uses a double-log functional form.[12]

One problem with the White test is that, in some situations, the secondary equation cannot be estimated because it has negative degrees of freedom. This can happen when the original equation has such a small sample size and/or so many variables that the secondary equation has more independent variables (including the squared and cross-product terms) than observations. Sometimes the difficulty can be avoided if there are dummy independent variables in the original equation because we must drop the squares of all dummies from Equation 10.12 (since $0^2 = 0$ and $1^2 = 1$, they're perfectly collinear). For practice in the use of the White test, see Exercises 7 and 8.

10.4 Remedies for Heteroskedasticity

The first thing to do if the Park test or the White test indicates the possibility of heteroskedasticity is to examine the equation carefully for specification errors. Although you should never include an explanatory variable simply because a test indicates the possibility of heteroskedasticity, you ought to rigorously think through the specification of the equation. If this rethinking allows you to discover a variable that should have been in the regression from the beginning, then that variable should be added to the equation. However, if there are no obvious specification errors, the heteroskedasticity is probably pure in nature, and one of the remedies described in this section should be considered:

1. Weighted Least Squares

2. Heteroskedasticity-Corrected Standard Errors

3. Redefining the Variables

---

12. Technically, the White test is a power series expansion that provides a nonparametric fit to any function of the independent variables. Many econometric software packages, including EViews, allow a researcher to run the White test at the click of a mouse, but this option is not available for the Park test because the researcher must choose a proportionality factor Z before a Park test can be run.

10.4.1 Weighted Least Squares

Take an equation with pure heteroskedasticity caused by a proportionality factor Z:

$$Y_i = \beta_0 + \beta_1 X_{1i} + \beta_2 X_{2i} + \epsilon_i \qquad (10.13)$$

where the variance of the error term, instead of being constant, is

$$VAR(\epsilon_i) = \sigma_i^2 = \sigma^2 Z_i^2 \qquad (10.14)$$

where σ^2 is the constant variance of a classical (homoskedastic) error term u_i and Z_i is the proportionality factor. Given that pure heteroskedasticity exists, then Equation 10.13 can be shown to be equal to[13]:

$$Y_i = \beta_0 + \beta_1 X_{1i} + \beta_2 X_{2i} + Z_i u_i \qquad (10.15)$$

The error term in Equation 10.15, $Z_i u_i$, is heteroskedastic because $\sigma^2 Z_i^2$, its variance, is not constant.

How could we adjust Equation 10.15 to make the error term homoskedastic? That is, what should be done to $Z_i u_i$ to make it turn into u_i? The easiest method is to divide the entire equation through by the proportionality factor Z_i, resulting in an error term, u_i, that has a constant variance σ^2. The new equation satisfies the Classical Assumptions, and a regression run on this new equation would no longer be expected to have heteroskedasticity.

This general remedy to heteroskedasticity is called Weighted Least Squares (WLS), which is actually a version of GLS. **Weighted Least Squares** involves dividing Equation 10.15 through by whatever will make the error term homoskedastic and then rerunning the regression on the transformed variables. Given the commonly assumed form of heteroskedasticity in Equation 10.14, this means that the technique consists of three steps:

1. Dividing Equation 10.15 through the proportionality factor Z, obtaining:

$$Y_i/Z_i = \beta_0/Z_i + \beta_1 X_{1i}/Z_i + \beta_2 X_{2i}/Z_i + u_i \qquad (10.16)$$

The error term of Equation 10.16 is now u_i, which is homoskedastic.

---

13. The key is to show that the error term $Z_i u_i$ has a variance equal to $\sigma^2 Z_i^2$. For more, see Exercise 6.

2. Recalculate the data for the variables to conform to Equation 10.16.

3. Estimate Equation 10.16 with OLS.

This third step in Weighted Least Squares, the estimation of the transformed equation, is fairly tricky, because the exact details of how to complete this regression depend on whether the proportionality factor Z is also an explanatory variable in Equation 10.13. If Z is not an explanatory variable in Equation 10.13, then the regression to be run in step 3 might seem to be:

$$Y_i/Z_i = \beta_0/Z_i + \beta_1 X_{1i}/Z_i + \beta_2 X_{2i}/Z_i + u_i \qquad (10.17)$$

Note, however, that this equation has no constant term. Most OLS computer packages can run such a regression only if the equation is forced through the origin by specifically suppressing the intercept with an instruction to the computer.

As pointed out in Section 7.1, however, the omission of the constant term forces the constant effect of omitted variables, nonlinearities, and measurement error into the other coefficient estimates. To avoid having these constant term elements forced into the slope coefficient estimates, one alternative approach to Equation 10.17 is to add a constant term before the transformed equation is estimated.[14] Consequently, when Z is not identical to one of the Xs in the original equation, then we suggest that the following specification be run as step 3 in Weighted Least Squares:

$$Y_i/Z_i = \alpha_0 + \beta_0/Z_i + \beta_1 X_{1i}/Z_i + \beta_2 X_{2i}/Z_i + u_i \qquad (10.18)$$

If Z *is* an explanatory variable in Equation 10.13, then no constant term need be added because one already exists. Look again at Equation 10.17. If Z = X_1 (or, similarly, if Z = X_2), then one of the slope coefficients becomes the constant term in the transformed equation because $X_1/Z = 1$:

$$Y_i/Z_i = \beta_0/Z_i + \beta_1 + \beta_2 X_{2i}/Z_i + u_i \qquad (10.19)$$

If this form of Weighted Least Squares is used, however, coefficients obtained from an estimation of Equation 10.19 must be interpreted very carefully. Notice that β_1 is now the intercept term of Equation 10.19 even though it is a slope coefficient in Equation 10.13 and that β_0 is a slope coefficient in Equation 10.19, even though it is the intercept in Equation 10.13. As a result, a researcher interested in an estimate of the coefficient of X_1 in Equation 10.13 would have to examine the intercept of Equation 10.19, and a researcher in-

---

14. The suggestion of adding a constant term is also made by Potluri Rao and Roger LeRoy Miller, *Applied Econometrics* (Belmont, California: Wadsworth, 1971), p. 121, and others. Some authors prefer not to add a constant because Equation 10.18 becomes more difficult to interpret.

terested in an estimate of the intercept term of Equation 10.13 would have to examine the coefficient of $1/Z_i$ in Equation 10.19. The computer will print out $\hat{\beta}_0$ as a "slope coefficient" and $\hat{\beta}_1$ as a "constant term" when in reality they are estimates of the opposite coefficients in the original Equation 10.13.

There are three other major problems with using Weighted Least Squares:

1. The job of identifying the proportionality factor Z is, as has been pointed out, quite difficult.

2. The functional form that relates the Z factor to the variance of the error term of the original equation may not be our assumed squared function of Equation 10.14. When some other functional relationship is involved, a different transformation is required. For more on these advanced transformations, see Exercise 12.

3. Sometimes Weighted Least Squares is applied to an equation with impure heteroskedasticity. In such cases, it can be shown that the WLS estimates reduce somewhat the bias from an omitted variable, but the estimates are inferior to those obtained from the correctly specified equation.

10.4.2 Heteroskedasticity-Corrected Standard Errors

The most popular remedy for heteroskedasticity is heteroskedasticity-corrected standard errors, which take a completely different approach to the problem. It focuses on improving the estimation of the $SE(\hat{\beta})$s without changing the estimates of the slope coefficients. The logic behind this approach is powerful. Since heteroskedasticity causes problems with the $SE(\hat{\beta})$s but not with the $\hat{\beta}$s, it makes sense to improve the estimation of the $SE(\hat{\beta})$s in a way that doesn't alter the estimates of the slope coefficients. This differs from our other two remedies because both WLS and reformulating the equation affect the $\hat{\beta}$s as well as the $SE(\hat{\beta})$s.

Thus, **heteroskedasticity-corrected (HC) standard errors** are $SE(\hat{\beta})$s that have been calculated specifically to avoid the consequences of heteroskedasticity.[15] The HC procedure yields an estimator of the standard errors that,

---

15. For a linear regression model with one independent variable in which both X and Y are measured as deviations from the mean, the HC estimator of the variance of the estimated slope coefficient is

$$\frac{\sum\limits_{t=1}^{T} X_t^2 e_t^2}{\left(\sum\limits_{t=1}^{T} X_t^2\right)^2},$$

where e_t is the OLS residual for observation t.

while they are biased, are generally more accurate than uncorrected standard errors for large samples in the face of heteroskedasticity. As a result, the HC SE($\hat{\beta}$)s can be used in *t*-tests and other hypothesis tests in most samples without the errors of inference potentially caused by heteroskedasticity. Typically, the HC SE($\hat{\beta}$)s are greater than the OLS SE($\hat{\beta}$)s, thus producing lower t-scores and decreasing the probability that a given estimated coefficient will be significantly different from zero. The technique was suggested by Halbert White in the same article in which he proposed the White test for heteroskedasticity.[16]

There are a few problems with using heteroskedasticity-corrected standard errors. First, as mentioned, the technique works best in large samples. Second, details of the calculation of the HC SE($\hat{\beta}$)s are beyond the scope of this text and imply a model that is substantially more general than the basic theoretical construct, $VAR(\epsilon_i) = \sigma^2 Z_i^2$, of this chapter. In addition, not all computer regression software packages calculate heteroskedasticity-corrected standard errors.

10.4.3 Redefining the Variables

Another approach to ridding an equation of heteroskedasticity is to go back to the basic underlying theory of the equation and redefine the variables in a way that avoids heteroskedasticity. A redefinition of the variables often is useful in allowing the estimated equation to focus more on the behavioral aspects of the relationship. Such a rethinking is a difficult and discouraging process because it appears to dismiss all the work already done. However, once the theoretical work has been reviewed, the alternative approaches that are discovered are often exciting in that they offer possible ways to avoid problems that had previously seemed insurmountable.

In some cases, the only redefinition that's needed to rid an equation of heteroskedasticity is to switch from a linear functional form to a double-log functional form. The double-log form has inherently less variation than the linear form, so it's less likely to encounter heteroskedasticity. In addition, there are many research topics for which the double-log form is just as theoretically logical as the linear form. This is especially true if the linear form was chosen by default, as is often the case.

---

16. Halbert White, "A Heteroskedasticity-Consistent Covariance Matrix Estimator and a Direct Test of Heteroskedasticity," *Econometrica*, 1980, pp. 817–838. Most authors refer to this method as HCCM, for heteroskedasticity-consistent covariance matrix. Note that Newey–West standard errors, introduced in Section 9.4, also can be used as HC standard errors. Indeed, some econometric software packages, including EViews, provide a choice between the White and Newey–West procedures. Unless otherwise noted, however, HC standard errors should be assumed to be of the White variety.

In other situations, it might be necessary to completely rethink the research project in terms of its underlying theory. For example, consider a cross-sectional model of the total expenditures by the governments of different cities. Logical explanatory variables to consider in such an analysis are the aggregate income, the population, and the average wage in each city. The larger the total income of a city's residents and businesses, for example, the larger the city government's expenditures (see Figure 10.6). In this case, it's not very enlightening to know that the larger cities have larger incomes and larger expenditures (in absolute magnitude) than the smaller ones.

Fitting a regression line to such data (see the line in Figure 10.6) also gives undue weight to the larger cities because they would otherwise give rise to large squared residuals. That is, since OLS minimizes the summed squared residuals, and since the residuals from the large cities are likely to be large due simply to the size of the city, the regression estimation will be especially sensitive to the residuals from the larger cities. This is often called "spurious correlation" due to size.

In addition, the residuals may indicate heteroskedasticity. The remedy for this kind of heteroskedasticity is not to automatically use Weighted Least

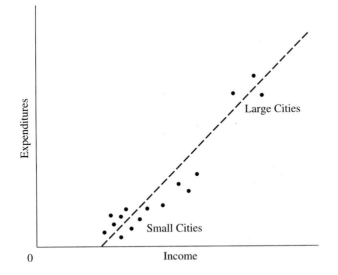

Figure 10.6 An Aggregate City Expenditures Function

If city expenditures are explained in an aggregate model, the larger cities play a major role in the determination of the coefficient values. Note how the slope would be somewhat lower without the heavy influence of the larger cities. In addition, heteroskedasticity is a potential problem in an aggregate model because the wide range of sizes of the dependent variable makes different error term variances more likely.

Squares, however, nor is it to throw out the observations from large cities. It makes sense to consider reformulating the model in a way that will discount the scale factor (the size of the cities) and emphasize the underlying behavior. In this case, per capita expenditures would be a logical dependent variable. Such a transformation is shown in Figure 10.7. This form of the equation places New York and Los Angeles on the same scale as, say, Pasadena or New Brunswick and thus gives them the same weight in estimation. If an explanatory variable happened not to be a function of the size of the city, however, it would not need to be adjusted to per capita terms. If the equation included the average wage of city workers, for example, that wage would not be divided through by population in the transformed equation.

Note that this transformation is similar in some ways to Weighted Least Squares, since many variables have been divided by population. The differences are that there is no term equal to the reciprocal of population (as there is in Weighted Least Squares) and that not all explanatory variables are divided by population. For the original equation,

$$EXP_i = \beta_0 + \beta_1 POP_i + \beta_2 INC_i + \beta_3 WAGE_i + \epsilon_i \qquad (10.20)$$

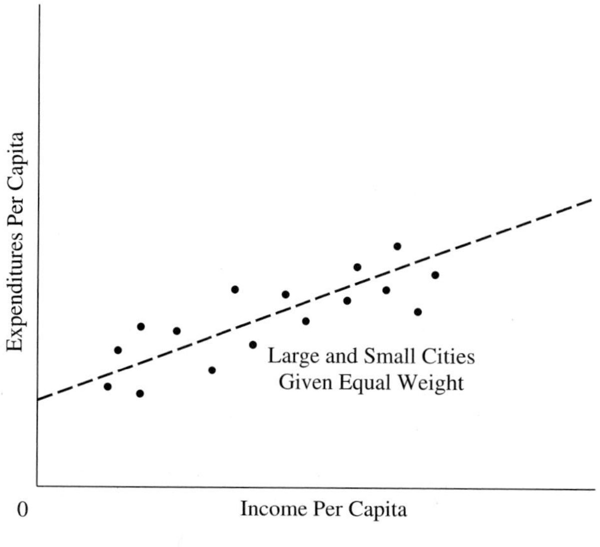

Figure 10.7 A per Capita City Expenditures Function

If city expenditures are explained in a per capita model, then large and small cities have equal weights. In addition, heteroskedasticity is less likely, because the dependent variable does not vary over a wide range of sizes.

the Weighted Least Squares version would be:

$$EXP_i/POP_i = \beta_1 + \beta_0/POP_i + \beta_2 INC_i/POP_i \qquad (10.21)$$
$$+ \beta_3 WAGE_i/POP_i + u_i$$

and the directly transformed equation would be

$$EXP_i/POP_i = \alpha_0 + \alpha_1 INC_i/POP_i + \alpha_2 WAGE_i + u_i \qquad (10.22)$$

where EXP_i refers to expenditures, INC_i refers to income, $WAGE_i$ refers to the average wage, and POP_i refers to the population of the *i*th city. As can be seen, the Weighted Least Squares Equation 10.21 divides through the entire equation by population, but the theoretically transformed one divides only expenditures and income by population. While the directly transformed Equation 10.22 does indeed solve any potential heteroskedasticity in the model, such a solution should be considered incidental to the benefits of rethinking the equation in a way that focuses on the basic behavior being examined.

Note that it's possible that the *reformulated* Equation 10.22 could have heteroskedasticity; the error variances might be larger for the observations having the larger per capita values for income and expenditures than they are for smaller per capita values. Thus, it is legitimate to suspect and test for heteroskedasticity even in this transformed model. Such heteroskedasticity in the transformed equation is unlikely, however, because there will be little of the variation in size normally associated with heteroskedasticity.

A thoughtful transformation of the variables that corrects for heteroskedasticity and at the same time avoids the spurious correlation due to size may sometimes be the best approach to solving these problems. Note, however, that unlike with Weighted Least Squares, not every variable in the equation is treated the same. Each variable in a cross-sectional model must be examined for possible transformations that will yield a meaningful and properly interpreted regression equation.

10.5 A More Complete Example

Let's work through a more complete example that involves a cross-sectional data set and heteroskedasticity. In the mid-1970s, the U.S. Department of Energy attempted to allocate gasoline to regions, states, and even individual retailers on the basis of past usage, changing demographics, and other factors. Underlying these allocations must have been some sort of model of the usage of petroleum by state (or region) as a function of a number of factors. It seems likely that such a cross-sectional model, if ever estimated, would have had to cope with the problem of heteroskedasticity.

In a model where the dependent variable is petroleum consumption by state, possible explanatory variables include functions of the size of the state (such as the number of miles of roadway, the number of motor vehicle registrations, or the population) and variables that are *not* functions of the size of the state (such as the gasoline tax *rate* or the speed limit). Since there is little to be gained by including more than one variable that measures the size of the state (because such an addition would be theoretically redundant and likely to cause needless multicollinearity), and since the speed limit was the same for all states (it would be a useful variable in a time-series model, however) a reasonable model to consider might be:

$$PCON_i = f(\overset{+}{REG}, \overset{-}{TAX}) + \epsilon_i = \beta_0 + \beta_1 REG_i + \beta_2 TAX_i + \epsilon_i \qquad (10.23)$$

where: $PCON_i$ = petroleum consumption in the ith state (millions of BTUs)
REG_i = motor vehicle registrations in the ith state (thousands)
TAX_i = the gasoline tax rate in the ith state (cents per gallon)
ϵ_i = a classical error term

The more cars registered in a state, we would think, the more petroleum consumed; a high tax rate on gasoline would decrease aggregate gasoline purchases in that state. If we now collect the data from that era for this example (see Table 10.1) we can estimate Equation 10.23, obtaining

$$\widehat{PCON_i} = 551.7 + 0.1861 REG_i - 53.59 TAX_i \qquad (10.24)$$
$$(0.0117) \qquad (16.86)$$
$$t = 15.88 \qquad -3.18$$
$$\overline{R}^2 = .861 \qquad n = 50$$

This equation seems to have no problems; the coefficients are significant in the hypothesized directions, and the overall equation is statistically significant. No Durbin–Watson d statistic is shown because there is no "natural" order of the observations to test for serial correlation (if you're curious, the DW for the order in Table 10.1 is 2.20). Given the discussion in the previous sections, let's investigate the possibility of heteroskedasticity caused by variation in the size of the states.

TABLE 10.1 DATA FOR THE PETROLEUM CONSUMPTION EXAMPLE

PCON	UHM	TAX	REG	POP	e	STATE
270	2.2	9	743	1136	62.335	Maine
122	2.4	14	774	948	176.52	New Hampshire
58	0.7	11	351	520	30.481	Vermont
821	20.6	9.9	3750	5750	101.87	Massachusetts
98	3.6	13	586	953	133.92	Rhode Island
450	10.1	11	2258	3126	67.527	Connecticut
1819	36.4	8	8235	17567	163.24	New York
1229	22.2	8	4917	7427	190.83	New Jersey
1200	27.9	11	6725	11879	−13.924	Pennsylvania
1205	29.2	11.7	7636	10772	−140.98	Ohio
650	17.6	11.1	3884	5482	−29.764	Indiana
1198	30.3	7.5	7242	11466	−299.72	Illinois
760	25.1	13	6250	9116	−258.33	Michigan
460	13.8	13	3162	4745	16.446	Wisconsin
503	13.0	13	3278	4133	37.855	Minnesota
371	8.1	13	2346	2906	79.330	Iowa
571	13.9	7	3412	4942	−240.63	Missouri
136	1.6	8	653	672	−108.50	North Dakota
109	1.6	13	615	694	139.52	South Dakota
203	4.3	13.9	1215	1589	170.08	Nebraska
349	8.4	8	2061	2408	−157.58	Kansas
118	1.4	11	415	600	78.568	Delaware
487	9.8	13.5	2893	4270	120.31	Maryland
628	12.4	11	3705	5485	−23.806	Virginia
192	2.9	10.5	1142	1961	−9.5451	West Virginia
642	17.1	12	4583	6019	−119.64	North Carolina
320	7.1	13	1975	3227	97.385	South Carolina
677	15.6	7.5	3916	5648	−201.65	Georgia
1459	28.5	8	8335	10466	−215.37	Florida
434	6.9	10	2615	3692	−68.513	Kentucky
482	11.9	9	3381	4656	−216.68	Tennessee
457	13.7	11	3039	3941	−70.842	Alabama
325	6.3	9	1593	2569	−40.877	Mississippi
300	7.4	9.5	1481	2307	−18.235	Arkansas
1417	10.1	8	2800	4383	772.87	Louisiana
451	11.4	6.58	2780	3226	−265.51	Oklahoma
3572	59.9	5	11388	15329	1168.6	Texas
131	2.3	9	758	805	−79.457	Montana
105	2.2	7.5	873	977	−207.25	Idaho
163	1.5	8	508	509	−54.515	Wyoming
323	9.2	9	2502	3071	−212.07	Colorado
192	4.4	11	1193	1367	7.7577	New Mexico
291	8.9	10	2216	2892	−137.25	Arizona
169	5.0	11	1038	1571	13.608	Utah
133	2.4	12	710	876	92.250	Nevada
562	14.8	12	3237	4276	50.895	Washington
364	8.4	8	2075	2668	−145.18	Oregon
2840	62.5	9	17130	24697	−417.81	California
155	1.2	8	319	444	−27.336	Alaska
214	1.3	8.5	586	997	8.7623	Hawaii

Source: *1985 Statistical Abstract* (U.S. Department of Commerce), except the residual.
Note: Data File = GAS10

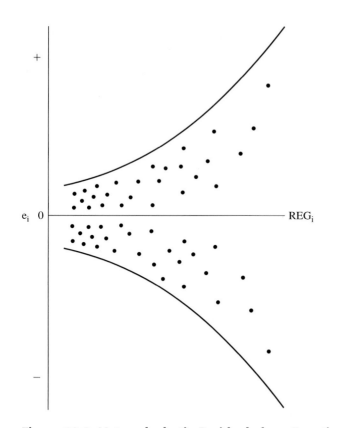

Figure 10.8 Heteroskedastic Residuals from Equation 10.24

If the residuals from Equation 10.24 and Table 10.1 are plotted with respect to Motor Vehicle Registrations (REG) by state, they appear to follow a wider distribution for large values of REG than for small values of REG. Such a pattern is preliminary evidence of heteroskedasticity that should be tested more formally with a test like the Park test.

To test this possibility, we obtain the residuals from Equation 10.24, which are listed in Table 10.1, and run a Park test on them. Before we can run a Park test, we must decide what possible proportionality factor Z to investigate.

Almost any variable related to market size would be appropriate, but motor vehicle registrations (REG) is certainly a reasonable choice. Note that to run a Park test with the gasoline tax rate (TAX) as the proportionality factor Z would be a mistake, since there is little evidence that the rate varies significantly with the size of the state. Total tax receipts, on the other hand, would be a possible alternative to REG. To see what the residuals look like if plotted against REG, see Figure 10.8; note that the residuals do indeed look potentially heteroskedastic. The next step would be to run a Park test:

$$\ln(e_i^2) = \alpha_0 + \alpha_1 \ln REG_i + u_i \qquad (10.25)$$

where e_i is the residual for the ith state from Equation 10.24, and u_i is a classical (homoskedastic) error term.

If we run this Park test regression, we obtain:

$$\widehat{\ln(e_i^2)} = 1.650 + 0.952 \ln REG_i \qquad (10.26)$$
$$(0.308)$$
$$t = 3.09$$
$$\overline{R}^2 = .148 \qquad n = 50 \qquad F = 9.533$$

Since the critical t-value for a 99 percent two-tailed t-test is about 2.7 (interpolated) in Statistical Table B-1, we can reject the null hypothesis of homoskedasticity because the appropriate decision rule is:

Reject H_0: $\alpha = 0$ if $|t_{PARK}| > 2.7$
Do Not Reject H_0:   if $|t_{PARK}| \leq 2.7$

Since there appears to be heteroskedasticity in the residuals of Equation 10.24, what should we do? First we think through the specification of the equation in search of an omitted variable. While there are a number of possible ones for this equation, it turns out that all of the ones we tried involve either significant multicollinearity (as shown in Chapter 8) or do not cure the heteroskedasticity.

As a result, we'll reestimate Equation 10.23 with Weighted Least Squares, using REG as the proportionality factor Z:

$$PCON_i/REG_i = \beta_0/REG_i + \beta_1 + \beta_2 TAX_i/REG_i + u_i \qquad (10.27)$$

which results in the following estimates[17]:

$$\widehat{PCON_i/REG_i} = 218.54/REG_i + 0.168 - 17.389 TAX_i/REG_i \qquad (10.28)$$
$$(0.014) \quad (4.682)$$
$$t = 12.27 \quad -3.71$$
$$\overline{R}^2 = .333 \qquad n = 50$$

---

17. Note that we've divided the equation through by REG_i. This assumes that the error term $\epsilon_i = Z_i u_i$. The coefficient of lnREG in the Park test is approximately one, which is evidence that the appropriate functional form may be $\epsilon_i = u_i \sqrt{Z}$, but such a transformation should not be adopted simply on the basis of the Park test coefficient alone. If the underlying theory gives evidence in support of such a change, which is not the case in this example, then we would divide the equation through by the square root of Z_i. For more on this, reread footnote 7.

Compare this result carefully with Equation 10.24. Note that:

1. The coefficient of the reciprocal of REG in Equation 10.28 is really an estimate of the intercept of Equation 10.24, and therefore no t-test is conducted even though the OLS regression program will indicate that it is a slope coefficient.

2. What appears to be the intercept of Equation 10.28 is an estimate of the coefficient of REG in Equation 10.24. Note that this particular estimate is quite close in magnitude and significance to the original results in Equation 10.24.

3. The t-score of the coefficient of the proportionality factor, REG, is lower in the Weighted Least Squares estimate than it is in the potentially heteroskedastic Equation 10.24. The overall fit is also worse, but this has no particular importance because the dependent variables are different in the two equations.

However, as mentioned in Section 10.4.3, an alternative is to rethink the purpose of the regression and reformulate the variables of the equation to try to avoid heteroskedasticity resulting from spurious correlation due to size. If we were to rethink Equation 10.23, we might decide to attempt to explain per capita petroleum consumption, coming up with:

$$PCON_i/POP_i = \beta_0 + \beta_1 REG_i/POP_i + \beta_2 TAX_i + \epsilon_i \quad (10.29)$$

where POP_i is the population of the ith state in thousands of people.

We've reformulated the equation in a way similar to Weighted Least Squares, but we now have an equation that can stand on its own from a theoretical point of view. If we estimate Equation 10.29, we obtain:

$$\widehat{PCON_i/POP_i} = 0.168 + 0.1082 REG_i/POP_i - 0.0103 TAX_i \quad (10.30)$$
$$(0.0716) \qquad\qquad (0.0035)$$
$$t = 1.51 \qquad\qquad -2.95$$
$$\overline{R}^2 = .165 \qquad n = 50$$

If we compare Equation 10.30 with Equations 10.28 and 10.24, we see that this approach is not necessarily better but quite different. The statistical properties of Equation 10.30, though not directly comparable to the other equations, do not appear as strong as they ought to be, but this is not necessarily an important factor.

Which is better, the unadjusted potentially heteroskedastic equation, the one derived from Weighted Least Squares, or the reformulated one? It depends on the purposes of your research. If your goal is to determine the impact of tax rates on gasoline consumption, all three models give virtually the same results in terms of the sign and significance of the coefficient, but the latter two models avoid the heteroskedasticity. If your goal is to allocate petroleum in aggregate amounts to states, then the original equation may be just fine. In most cases of severe heteroskedasticity, some remedial action is necessary, but whether Weighted Least Squares or a reformulation is called for depends on the particular equation in question. We generally find that if reformulation makes intuitive sense, it's usually the best remedy to apply, since it more easily avoids the arbitrary process of choosing a Z.

Finally, let's apply the most popular of our remedies, heteroskedasticity-corrected standard errors, to this example. If we start with Equation 10.23 and use White's suggested method for estimating $SE(\hat{\beta})$s that are minimum variance (for large samples) in the face of heteroskedasticity, we obtain:

$$\widehat{PCON_i} = 551.7 + 0.186REG_i - 53.59TAX_i \qquad (10.31)$$
$$(0.022) \qquad (23.90)$$
$$t = 8.64 \qquad -2.24$$
$$\overline{R}^2 = .86 \qquad n = 50$$

Compare Equation 10.31 with Equation 10.24. Note that the slope coefficients are identical, as you'd expect. Also note that the HC $SE(\hat{\beta})$s are higher than the OLS $SE(\hat{\beta})$s, as is usually but not necessarily the case. While the resulting t-scores are lower, they are still significantly different from zero in the direction we expected, making Equation 10.31 very appealing indeed.

Is the heteroskedasticity-corrected standard error approach the best one for this example? Most beginning researchers would say yes, because Equation 10.31 has a better overall fit, better t-scores, and easier interpretation than do Equations 10.30 and 10.28. Unfortunately, most experienced researchers wouldn't be so sure, in part because the sample size of 50 makes it unlikely that the large sample properties of HC estimation hold in this case. Finally, if t-scores are not being used to test hypotheses or retain variables, as is true in this example, it's not at all clear that any sort of remedy for heteroskedasticity is even necessary.

10.6 Summary

1. Heteroskedasticity is the violation of Classical Assumption V that the observations of the error term are drawn from a distribution with a

constant variance. Homoskedastic error term observations are drawn from a distribution that has a constant variance for all observations, and heteroskedastic error term observations are drawn from distributions whose variances differ from different observations. Heteroskedasticity occurs most frequently in cross-sectional data sets.

2. The variance of a heteroskedastic error term is not equal to σ^2, a constant. Instead, it equals σ_i^2, where the subscript i indicates that the variance can change from observation to observation. Many different kinds of heteroskedasticity are possible, but a common model is one in which the variance changes systematically as a function of some other variable, a proportionality factor Z:

$$VAR(\epsilon_i) = \sigma^2 Z_i^2$$

The proportionality factor Z is usually a variable related in some way to the size or accuracy of the dependent variable.

3. Pure heteroskedasticity is a function of the error term of the correctly specified regression equation. Impure heteroskedasticity is caused by a specification error such as an omitted variable.

4. The major consequence of heteroskedasticity is an increase in the variance of the $\hat{\beta}$s that is masked by an underestimation of the standard errors by OLS. As a result, OLS tends to overestimate t-scores in the face of heteroskedasticity, sometimes leading to errors of inference. Pure heteroskedasticity does not cause bias in the estimates of the $\hat{\beta}$s themselves.

5. Many tests use the residuals of an equation to test for the possibility of heteroskedasticity in the error terms. The Park test uses a function of these residuals as the dependent variable of a second regression whose explanatory variable is a function of the suspected proportionality factor Z:

$$\ln(e_i^2) = \alpha_0 + \alpha_1 \ln Z_i + u_i$$

If $\hat{\alpha}_1$ is significantly different from zero, then we reject the null hypothesis of homoskedasticity.

6. The first step in correcting heteroskedasticity is to check for an omitted variable that might be causing impure heteroskedasticity. If the specification is as good as possible, then solutions such as Weighted Least Squares or HC standard errors should be considered.

Exercises

(Answers to even-numbered exercises are in Appendix A.)

1. Write the meaning of each of the following terms without referring to the book (or your notes), and compare your definition with the version in the text for each.
   a. impure heteroskedasticity
   b. proportionality factor Z
   c. the Park test
   d. Weighted Least Squares
   e. the White test
   f. heteroskedasticity-corrected standard errors

2. In the common model of heteroskedasticity $(\mathrm{VAR}(\epsilon_i) = \sigma^2 Z_i^2)$, one of the major difficulties is choosing a proportionality factor (Z). In each of the following equations, separate the listed explanatory variables into those that are likely or unlikely to be proportionality factors.
   a. The number of economics majors in a cross section of various sized colleges and universities as a function of the number of undergraduates attending a school, the number of required courses in that school's economics major, the average GPA in the major, and the number of economics professors there.
   b. GDP in a cross section of various countries as a function of the aggregate gross investment in a nation, the percentage growth of its money supply, the maximum marginal tax rate on capital gains there, and its population.
   c. The demand for carrots in a time-series model of the United States as a function of the real price of carrots, U.S. disposable income, U.S. per capita disposable income, population, the percentage error in carrot sales measurement, and the real price of celery.

3. Of all the econometric problems we've encountered, heteroskedasticity is the one that seems the most difficult to understand. Close your book and attempt to write an explanation of heteroskedasticity in your own words. Be sure to include a diagram in your description.

4. Use the Park test to test the null hypothesis of homoskedasticity in each of the following situations (1 percent level of significance):
   a. The calculated t-score of your suspected proportionality factor Z is 3.561 from a Park test regression with 25 degrees of freedom.
   b. The following residuals and values for the potential Z. (*Hint:* This requires the use of a regression.)

Observation	Residual	Proportionality Factor Z
1	3.147	120
2	9.394	240
3	−2.344	900
4	−1.034	50
5	5.678	600
6	2.113	20
7	−4.356	200

c. How would your answer to the above change if the seventh observation of Z was minus 200? How would you even take the log of Z?

5. A. Ando and F. Modigliani collected the following data on the income and consumption of non-self-employed homeowners[18]:

Income Bracket ($)	Average Income ($)	Average Consumption ($)
0–999	556	2760
1000–1999	1622	1930
2000–2999	2664	2740
3000–3999	3587	3515
4000–4999	4535	4350
5000–5999	5538	5320
6000–7499	6585	6250
7500–9999	8582	7460
10000–above	14033	11500

a. Run a regression to explain average consumption as a function of average income.
b. Use the Park test to test the residuals from the equation you ran in part a for heteroskedasticity, using income as the potential proportionality factor Z (1 percent).
c. If there is only one explanatory variable, what does the equation for Weighted Least Squares look like? Does running Weighted Least Squares have any effect on the estimation? Why or why not?
d. If the Park test run in part b above shows evidence of heteroskedasticity, then what, if anything, should be done about it?

18. Albert Ando and Franco Modigliani, "The 'Permanent Income' and 'Life Cycle' Hypotheses of Saving Behavior: Comparisons and Tests," in I. Friend and R. Jones, eds. *Consumption and Saving*, Vol. II., 1960, p. 154.

6. Show that Equation 10.15 is true by showing that the variance of an error term that equals a classical error term multiplied times a proportionality factor Z is that shown in Equation 10.14. That is, show that if $\epsilon_i = u_i Z_i$, then $VAR(\epsilon_i) = \sigma^2 Z_i^2$ if $VAR(u_i) = \sigma^2$ (a constant). (*Hint:* Start with the definition of a variance and then calculate the variance for an error term $Z_i u_i$.)

7. The best way to feel comfortable with the White test for heteroskedasticity is to apply the test to a set of residuals to which we've already applied the Park test. Run a White test on the residuals from the Woody's example in Table 3.1 at the 1 percent level. Be sure to compare your answer with the Park test result in Section 10.3.2.

8. As further practice, run a 1 percent White test on the residuals from the state gasoline model (Equation 10.24) in Table 10.1. Be sure to compare your answer with the Park test result in Section 10.5.

9. What makes a college library great? While quality of holdings and ease of use are important, the simplest measure of the quality of a library is the number of books it holds. Suppose you've been hired by the Annual American Research on the Number of Books project (AARON) to build a model of the number of books in a cross section of 60 U.S. university and college libraries. After researching the literature, you estimate (standard errors in parentheses):

$$\widehat{VOL}_i = -1842 + 0.038STU_i + 1.73FAC_i + 1.83SAT_i \qquad (10.32)$$
$$\phantom{\widehat{VOL}_i = -1842 +} (0.026) \qquad (0.44) \qquad (0.82)$$
$$\phantom{\widehat{VOL}_i = -1842 +} t = 1.45 \qquad 3.91 \qquad 2.23$$
$$\phantom{\widehat{VOL}_i = -1842 +} \overline{R}^2 = .81 \qquad n = 60$$

where: VOL_i = thousands of books in the ith school's library
STU_i = the number of students in the ith school
FAC_i = the number of faculty in the ith school
SAT_i = the average SATs of students in the ith school

a. The simple correlation coefficient between STU and FAC is 0.93, a Park test on the residuals of Equation 10.32 produces a t-score of 3.50, and the Durbin–Watson d for the equation is 1.91. Given this information, what econometric problems appear to exist in this equation? Explain. Which problem do you think you should attempt to correct first? Why?

b. You decide to create a linear combination of students and faculty ($TOT_i = 10FAC_i + STU_i$) and to rerun Equation 10.32, obtaining Equation 10.33 below. Which equation do you prefer? Explain your reasoning.

$$\widehat{VOL_i} = -1704 + 0.087TOT_i + 1.69SAT_i \qquad (10.33)$$
$$(0.007) \qquad (0.84)$$
$$t = 12.87 \qquad 2.02$$
$$\overline{R}^2 = .80 \qquad n = 60 \qquad DW = 1.85$$

c. Use the data in Table 10.2 (filename BOOKS10) to test for heteroskedasticity in the residuals of Equation 10.33 using the Park test and/or the White test (depending on the tests typically used in your class).

d. If you run Weighted Least Squares (WLS) (using TOT as your proportionality factor) on Equation 10.33, you get Equation 10.34, but take a look at it! Why don't we provide a t-score for the coefficient

TABLE 10.2 DATA ON COLEGE AND UNIVERSITY LIBRARY HOLDINGS				
Observation	VOL	FAC	STU	SAT
1	11.5	5	58	850
2	200.0	138	2454	954
3	70.0	44	573	874
4	100.0	98	2172	941
5	7000.0	1651	31123	1185
6	70.0	26	295	874
7	125.0	35	1131	902
8	2200.0	1278	22571	1048
9	400.0	365	6554	960
10	110.0	47	793	930
11	6000.0	1650	36330	1142
12	58.4	39	522	800
13	212.0	69	1041	1060
14	400.0	57	1059	1000
15	1888.0	896	16411	1150
16	486.0	125	1678	1170
17	439.0	135	2529	1100
18	1900.0	653	19082	1080
19	155.0	114	3523	1026

TABLE 10.2 (continued)				
Observation	VOL	FAC	STU	SAT
20	6.9	11	207	873
21	509.0	346	6781	1097
22	180.0	25	147	990
23	53.0	21	214	920
24	100.0	44	764	900
25	30.0	18	176	1176
26	157.0	99	3682	930
27	475.0	223	5665	1037
28	613.6	384	4411	960
29	483.6	141	3341	860
30	2500.0	2021	41528	1086
31	142.0	66	1251	1030
32	210.0	73	1036	1000
33	20.0	10	120	1070
34	150.0	94	2344	858
35	300.0	195	2400	1180
36	233.5	70	1416	910
37	235.0	165	4148	1001
38	460.7	316	9738	980
39	1632.0	355	5578	1060
40	93.0	30	505	930
41	263.0	185	3724	1124
42	144.5	101	2387	945
43	770.0	148	1900	1190
44	1700.0	960	16750	1057
45	1100.0	284	2833	1310
46	1900.0	905	15762	1090
47	60.0	55	875	848
48	1200.0	445	6603	1060
49	1600.0	623	14727	1120
50	1289.0	412	11179	1230
51	1666.0	1607	9251	883
52	15.0	26	608	800
53	160.0	48	656	1010
54	200.0	281	3892	980
55	263.0	195	2987	1070
56	487.0	275	5148	1060
57	3300.0	867	11240	1260
58	145.0	37	569	843
59	205.0	28	628	980
60	7377.0	2606	34055	1160

Note: filename BOOKS10

of the inverse of TOT? Why didn't WLS work very well? What alternative remedy would you suggest?

$$\widehat{VOL/TOT_i} = 0.089 - 63.6\,(1/TOT_t) + 0.079SAT_i/TOT_i$$
$$\qquad\qquad (0.010) \qquad\qquad\qquad (0.057)$$
$$\qquad\quad t = 8.57 \qquad\qquad\qquad\quad 1.39$$
$$\qquad\quad \overline{R}^2 = .02 \qquad n = 60 \qquad DW = 1.89 \qquad (10.34)$$

e. Start from the equation you prefer (between 10.32 and 10.33) and use the data in Table 10.2 to correct for heteroskedasticity using some method other than WLS (*Hint:* You might reformulate the equation or calculate HC SE($\hat{\beta}$)s.)

10. Consider the following double-log equation (standard errors in parentheses)[19]:

$$\hat{Y}_i = 0.442X_{1i} + 0.092X_{2i} + 0.045X_{3i} + 0.259X_{4i}$$
$$\quad (0.058) \qquad (0.042) \qquad (0.014) \qquad (0.034)$$
$$\qquad\qquad R^2 = .620 \qquad n = 430$$

where: Y_i = the log of the gross value of agricultural output (in drachmas) of the *i*th Greek farm in a given year
        X_{1i} = the log of farmer workdays in a year on the *i*th farm
        X_{2i} = the log of the amount of land on the *i*th farm (in stremmata, equal to a quarter of an acre)
        X_{3i} = the log of the value of the plant and equipment (plus operating expenses for plant and equipment) on the *i*th farm that year (in drachmas)
        X_{4i} = the log of the value of livestock (including trees) plus operating expenses on livestock (in drachmas) in the *i*th farm that year

a. Create hypotheses about the signs of the various coefficients and then calculate the t-scores to test those hypotheses at the 5 percent level of significance.

b. Suppose you were now told that the Park test, using X_1 as a potential proportionality factor Z, indicated the likelihood of heteroskedasticity in the residuals of this equation. Is it likely that there

19. Adapted from Pan A. Yotopoulos and Jeffrey B. Nugent, *Economics of Development* (New York: Harper & Row, 1976), p. 82. No estimate of the intercept was reported.

actually is a heteroskedasticity in such a double-log equation? Why or why not?

c. Is there a logical reformulation of the equation that might rid the model of heteroskedasticity?

d. If you decided to apply Weighted Least Squares to the equation, what equation would you estimate?

11. Consider the following estimated regression equation for average annual hours worked (per capita) for young (16–21 years) black men in 94 standard metropolitan statistical areas (standard errors in parentheses):

$$\hat{B}_i = 300.0 + 0.50W_i - 7.5U_i - 18.3\ln P_i$$
$$\quad\quad\quad\;(0.05)\quad\;(7.5)\quad\;(6.1)$$
$$DW = 2.00 \quad\quad n = 94 \quad\quad \overline{R}^2 = .64$$

where: B_i = average annual hours worked (per capita) by young (age 16 to 21) black men in the ith city

W_i = average annual hours worked by young white men in the ith city

U_i = black unemployment rate in the ith city

$\ln P_i$ = natural log of the black population of the ith city

a. Develop and test (5 percent level) your own hypotheses with respect to the individual estimated slope coefficients.

b. How would you respond to the claim that an estimated coefficient of W that is far less than one is proof that racial discrimination exists in the labor markets in this country?

c. Since this is a cross-sectional model, is it reasonable to worry about heteroskedasticity? What variable would you choose as a possible Z? Explain your choice.

d. Suppose you ran a Park test with respect to your chosen Z and found a t-score of 1.91. Does this support or refute your answer to part c above? (*Hint:* Be sure to complete the Park test.)

e. Suppose you were asked to make one change in the specification of this equation. What would you suggest? Explain your choice.

12. Given the most commonly used functional form for the relationship between the proportionality factor Z and the error term ($\epsilon_i = Z_i u_i$ where u_i is a homoskedastic error term), we can derive the appropriate Weighted Least Squares equation of:

$$Y \!>\! Z_i = \beta_0 \!>\! Z_i + \beta_1 + \beta_2 X_{2i} \!>\! Z_i + u_i$$

when $Z = X_1$, an explanatory variable already in the equation. This is accomplished by dividing the equation by the precise value (Z_i) necessary to make the error term homoskedastic in nature. Find the appropriate Weighted Least Squares equations to be used in the following situations:

a. $\epsilon_i = u_i\sqrt{Z_i}$ where $Z = X_1$, an explanatory variable already in the equation.

b. $\epsilon_i = u_iZ_i$ where $Z = X_3$, a variable not in the equation

c. $\epsilon_i = u_i\hat{Y}_i$, where $\hat{Y}_i$ is the estimated value of the dependent variable obtained from the regression equation

13. R. Bucklin, R. Caves, and A. Lo estimated the following double-log model to explain the yearly circulation of metropolitan newspapers (standard errors in parentheses)[20]:

$$\hat{C}_i = -8.2 - 0.56P_i + 0.90I_i + 0.76Q_i + 0.27A_i + 0.08S_i - 0.77T_i$$
$$\phantom{\hat{C}_i = -8.2 -} (0.58) \quad (0.14) \quad (0.21) \quad (0.14) \quad (0.05) \quad (0.27)$$
$$n = 50$$

where: C_i = yearly circulation of the *i*th newspaper

P_i = the weighted average single copy price of the *i*th newspaper

I_i = the total disposable income of the metropolitan area of the *i*th newspaper

Q_i = the number of personnel in editorial positions for the *i*th newspaper

A_i = the volume of retail advertising in the *i*th newspaper

S_i = amount of competition from suburban dailies in the *i*th newspaper's region

T_i = the number of television stations in the *i*th newspaper's region

(All variables are in logarithmic form.)

a. Hypothesize signs and run *t*-tests on each of the individual slope coefficients.

---

20. R. E. Bucklin, R. E. Caves, and A. W. Lo, "Games of Survival in the U.S. Newspaper Industry," *Applied Economics*, May 1989, pp. 631–650. Note that the Park test results are hypothetical and that the equation was originally estimated with Two-Stage Least Squares (to be discussed in Chapter 14). These facts don't change the equation's usefulness as an exercise in this chapter.

b. Does heteroskedasticity seem theoretically likely? Test for hetero-skedasticity at the 99 percent level assuming that a Park test with I_i as Z produces a t-score of 3.13.

c. Given your responses to parts a and b above, what econometric problems (out of omitted variables, irrelevant variables, incorrect functional form, multicollinearity, serial correlation, and hetero-skedasticity) appear to exist in this equation?

d. If you could suggest just one change in the specification of this equation, what would that change be? Carefully explain your answer.

14. Think back to the Farmer Vin pig growing equation of Exercise 13 in Chapter 9:

$$\hat{W}_i = 12 + 3.5G_i + 7.0D_i - 0.25F_i \qquad (10.35)$$
$$\phantom{\hat{W}_i = 12 + }(1.0) \quad (1.0) \quad (0.10)$$
$$\phantom{\hat{W}_i = 12 + } t = 3.5 \qquad 7.0 \qquad -2.5$$
$$\overline{R}^2 = .70 \qquad n = 200 \qquad DW = 0.50$$

where: W_i = the percentage weight gain of the *i*th pig during the six-month experiment

G_i = a dummy variable equal to 1 if the *i*th pig is a male, 0 otherwise

D_i = a dummy variable equal to 1 if the *i*th pig was fed only at night, 0 if the *i*th pig was fed only during the day

F_i = the amount of food (pounds) eaten per day by the *i*th pig

It turns out that this study was estimated originally with the dependent variable equal to "pounds gained by the *i*th pig," but a Park test showed severe heteroskedasticity. (Recall that the sample pigs ranged all the way from pink piglets to ponderous porkers.) The dependent variable was converted to percentage terms in an effort to "rethink the equation" and eliminate the heteroskedasticity. Equation 10.35 was the result.

a. How theoretically likely is it that there is heteroskedasticity in the revised equation, Equation 10.35? Explain your answer.

b. Suppose that you run a Park test on the residuals of Equation 10.35 and a find a t-score of -6.31 (using the weight of the *i*th pig as the potential proportionality factor). Do you have heteroskedasticity?

c. The t-score from your Park test in part b above is negative, and yet we've never discussed "negative" or "positive" heteroskedasticity.

What importance, if any, would you attach to the *sign* of the estimated slope coefficient in this Park test?

d. You appear to have heteroskedasticity in both the original and the revised versions of your equation. What should you do? Explain.

15. Let's investigate the possibility of heteroskedasticity in time-series data by looking at a model of the black market for U.S. dollars in Brazil that was studied by R. Dornbusch and C. Pechman.[21] In particular, the authors wanted to know if the Demsetz-Bagehot bid-ask theory, previously tested on cross-sectional data from the United States, could be extended to time-series data outside the United States.[22] They estimated the following model on monthly data from Brazil for March 1979 through December 1983:

$$S_t = f(\overset{+}{I_t}, \overset{+}{V_t}) + \epsilon_t = \beta_0 + \beta_1 I_t + \beta_2 \ln(1 + V_t) + \epsilon_t \qquad (10.36)$$

where: S_t = the average daily spread between the bid and asking prices for the U.S. dollar on the Brazilian black market in month t

I_t = the average interest rate in month t

V_t = the variance of the daily premium between the black market rate and the official exchange rate for the dollar in month t

a. Use the authors' data in Table 10.3 (filename BID10) to estimate Equation 10.36 and test the residuals for positive first-order serial correlation.

b. If serial correlation appears to exist, reestimate Equation 10.36 using GLS. Do the coefficient estimates change? Which equation do you prefer? Why?

c. The authors noted that S nearly doubled in size during their sample period. Does this make you concerned about the possibility of heteroskedasticity? Why or why not?

---

21. Rudiger Dornbusch and Clarice Pechman, "The Bid-Ask Spread in the Black Market for Dollars in Brazil," *Journal of Money, Credit and Banking*, November 1985, pp. 517–520. The data for this study were not published with the original article but are on the data diskette that accompanies William F. Lott and Subhash C. Ray, *Applied Econometrics: Problems with Data Sets* (Fort Worth: Dryden/Harcourt Brace, 1992). The analytical approach of this question also comes from Lott and Ray, pp. 169–173, and we appreciate permission to use their work.

22. For a review of this literature at the time of Dornbusch and Pechman's research, see Kalman Cohen et al., "Market Makers and the Market Spread: A Review of the Recent Literature," *Journal of Financial and Quantitative Studies*, November 1979, pp. 813–835.

d. Test the residuals of Equation 10.36 for heteroskedasticity using the Park test or the White test. (*Hint:* A possible proportionality factor is a time-trend variable that equals 1 for March 1979 and that increases by one for each following month.)

e. Test the residuals of your GLS version of Equation 10.36 for heteroskedasticity using the Park test or the White test. Did running GLS change the possibility of heteroskedasticity?

f. What remedy would you suggest for any heteroskedasticity that might exist in such a time-series model? Be specific.

TABLE 10.3 DATA ON THE BRAZILIAN BLACK MARKET FOR DOLLARS			
Month	S	I	V
1979:03	2.248	4.15	20.580
1979:04	2.849	4.04	12.450
1979:05	2.938	2.68	21.230
1979:06	2.418	2.81	26.300
1979:07	2.921	1.92	22.600
1979:08	2.587	2.37	18.750
1979:09	2.312	3.59	20.040
1979:10	2.658	2.03	31.110
1979:11	2.262	2.41	29.040
1979:12	4.056	4.09	20.590
1980:01	3.131	3.28	11.770
1980:02	3.404	2.89	7.900
1980:03	2.835	3.44	6.150
1980:04	3.309	2.43	6.780
1980:05	3.042	2.13	8.550
1980:06	3.417	2.94	13.380
1980:07	2.929	3.19	11.870
1980:08	3.821	3.26	15.560
1980:09	2.753	3.98	24.560
1980:10	2.633	3.69	21.110
1980:11	2.608	4.43	15.000
1980:12	2.168	5.86	7.480
1981:01	2.273	4.36	2.820
1981:02	1.892	5.66	1.540
1981:03	2.283	4.60	1.520
1981:04	2.597	4.42	4.930
1981:05	2.522	5.41	10.790
1981:06	2.865	4.63	17.160
1981:07	4.206	5.46	30.590
1981:08	2.708	5.88	23.900

(*continued*)

TABLE 10.3 (continued)			
Month	S	I	V
1981:09	2.324	5.52	20.620
1981:10	2.736	6.07	18.900
1981:11	3.277	5.48	26.790
1981:12	3.194	6.79	29.640
1982:01	3.473	5.46	32.870
1982:02	2.798	6.20	30.660
1982:03	3.703	6.19	40.740
1982:04	3.574	6.06	48.040
1982:05	3.484	6.26	33.510
1982:06	2.726	6.27	23.650
1982:07	4.430	6.89	37.080
1982:08	4.158	7.55	51.260
1982:09	5.633	6.93	60.450
1982:10	5.103	8.14	83.980
1982:11	3.691	7.80	69.490
1982:12	3.952	9.61	68.030
1983:01	3.583	7.01	85.630
1983:02	4.459	7.94	77.060
1983:03	6.893	10.06	71.490
1983:04	5.129	11.82	51.520
1983:05	4.171	11.18	43.660
1983:06	5.047	10.92	59.500
1983:07	8.434	11.72	61.070
1983:08	5.143	9.54	75.380
1983:09	3.980	9.78	72.205
1983:10	4.340	9.91	59.258
1983:11	4.330	9.61	38.860
1983:12	4.350	10.09	33.380

Source: William F. Lott and Subhash C. Ray, *Applied Econometrics: Problems with Data Sets* (Fort Worth: Dryden/Harcourt Brace, 1992). (data diskette)

Note: filename BID10

CHAPTER 11

A Regression User's Handbook

The real-world problems that a regression user encounters are not as neatly labeled and compartmentalized as the previous 10 chapters might imply. Instead, researchers must consider all the possible difficulties in an equation in order to decide which specification and estimation techniques to use. As a result, it's useful to have summaries of the definitions, problems, solutions, and statistical tests that are central to basic single-equation linear regression models. The first two sections of this chapter contain such summaries; although you should certainly read these now, we also hope that you'll benefit from using them as a reference whenever you're undertaking econometric research.

The next two sections focus on how to carry out your own regression project. How might you choose a topic? Where can you go to collect data? What should your research report contain? Although there is no agreed-upon format that all researchers must follow, we still have quite a few practical hints that will make your first independent research project a lot more rewarding.

Unfortunately, no matter how superbly planned or well thought-out your project might be, it's very unusual for a beginning researcher's regression to be "perfect" the first time out. Something always goes wrong!

When this happens, econometrics becomes an art. The core of the problem is that we never know what the true model is. There's a fine line between curve fitting and searching for the truth by formulating and estimating alternative specifications or using alternative estimating techniques. Some regression results may very well be strictly a product of chance, because the researchers might have experimented with a number of models and estimators until they obtained the results that came closest to what they wanted; such an approach is unscientific. On the other hand, it would be foolhardy to go to the opposite extreme and ignore obvious estimation or specification errors in a first regression run; that would also be unscientific. The last three sections of this chapter help beginning researchers strike a balance between these two positions by providing advice on econometric ethics and by giving some hands-on regression experience. The interactive regression exercise in Section 11.7 is a "half-way house" between reading someone else's regression results (and having no input) and doing one's own regression analysis (and getting no feedback). We strongly encourage the reader to take the exercise seriously and work through the example rather than just read it.

11.1 A Regression User's Checklist

Table 11.1 contains a list of the items that a researcher checks when reviewing the output from a computer regression package. Not every item in the checklist will be produced by your computer package, and not every item in your computer output will be in the checklist, but the checklist can be a very useful reference. In most cases, a quick glance at the checklist will remind you of the text sections that deal with the item, but if this is not the case, the fairly minimal explanation in the checklist should *not* be relied on to cover everything needed for complete analysis and judgment. Instead, you should look up the item in the index. In addition, note that the actions in the right-hand column are merely suggestions. The circumstances of each individual research project are much more reliable guides than any dogmatic list of actions.

There are two ways to use the checklist. First, you can refer to it as a "glossary of packaged computer output terms" when you encounter something in your regression result that you don't understand. Second, you can work your way through the checklist in order, finding the items in your computer output and marking them. As with the Regression User's Guide (Table 11.2), the use of the Regression User's Checklist will be most helpful for beginning researchers, but we also find ourselves referring back to it once in a while even after years of experience.

Be careful. All simplified tables, like the two in this chapter, must trade completeness for ease of use. As a result, strict adherence to a set of rules is not recommended even if the rules come from one of our tables. Someone

TABLE 11.1 REGRESSION USER'S CHECKLIST

Symbol	Checkpoint	Reference	Decision
X, Y	Data observations	Check for errors, especially outliers, in the data. Spot check transformations of variables. Check means, maximums, and minimums.	Correct any errors. If the quality of the data is poor, may want to avoid regression analysis or use just OLS.
df	Degrees of freedom	$n - K - 1 > 0$ n = number of observations K = number of explanatory variables	If $n - K - 1 \leq 0$, equation cannot be estimated, and if the degrees of freedom are low, precision is low. In such a case, try to include more observations.
$\hat{\beta}$	Estimated coefficient	Compare signs and magnitudes to expected values.	If they are unexpected, respecify model if appropriate or assess other statistics for possible correct procedures.
t	t-statistic $$t_k = \frac{\hat{\beta}_k - \beta_{H_0}}{SE(\hat{\beta}_k)}$$ or $$t_k = \frac{\hat{\beta}_k}{SE(\hat{\beta}_k)}$$ for computer-supplied t-scores or whenever $\beta_{H_0} = 0$	Two-sided test: $H_0: \beta_k = \beta_{H_0}$ $H_A: \beta_k \neq \beta_{H_0}$ One-sided test: $H_0: \beta_k \leq \beta_{H_0}$ $H_A: \beta_k > \beta_{H_0}$ β_{H_0}, the hypothesized β, is supplied by the researcher, and is often zero.	Reject H_0 if $\|t_k\| > t_c$ and if the estimate is of the expected sign. t_c is the critical value of α level of significance and $n - K - 1$ degrees of freedom.
R^2	Coefficient of determination	Measures the degree of overall fit of the model to the data	A guide to the overall fit.
$\overline{R}^2$	R^2 adjusted for degrees of freedom	Same as R^2. Also attempts to show the contribution of an additional explanatory variable.	One indication that an explanatory variable is irrelevant is if the $\overline{R}^2$ falls when it is included.

(*continued*)

TABLE 11.1 (continued)

Symbol	Checkpoint	Reference	Decision
F	F-statistic	To test $H_0: \beta_1 = \beta_2 = \ldots = \beta_k = 0$ $H_A: H_0$ not true Calculate special F-statistic to test joint hypotheses.	Reject H_0 if $F \geq F_c$, the critical value for α level of significance and K numerator and $n - K - 1$ denominator d.f.
DW	Durbin–Watson d statistic	Tests: $H_0: p \leq 0$ $H_A: p > 0$ For positive serial correlation	Reject H_0 if DW $< d_L$. Inconclusive if $d_L \leq$ DW $\leq d_U$. (d_L and d_U are critical DW values.)
e_i	Residual	Check for transcription errors. Check for heteroskedasticity by examining the pattern of the residuals.	Correct the data. May take appropriate corrective action, but test first.
SEE	Standard error of the equation	An estimate of σ. Compare with $\bar{Y}$ for a measure of overall fit.	A guide to the overall fit.
TSS	Total sum of squares	$TSS = \sum_i (Y_i - \bar{Y})^2$	Used to compute F, R^2, and $\bar{R}^2$.
RSS	Residual sum of squares	$RSS = \sum_i (Y_i - \hat{Y}_i)^2$	Same as above. Also used in hypothesis testing.
$SE(\hat{\beta}_k)$	Standard error of $\hat{\beta}_k$	Used in t-statistic.	A guide to statistical significance.
$\hat{p}$	Estimated first-order autocorrelation coefficient	Usually provided by an autoregressive routine.	If negative, implies a specification error.
r_{12}	Simple correlation coefficient between X_1 and X_2	Used to detect collinearity.	Suspect severe multicollinearity if *t*-test shows r_{12} is significant.
VIF	Variance inflation factor	Used to detect multicollinearity.	Suspect severe multicollinearity if VF > 5.

who understands the purpose of the research, the exact definitions of the variables, and the problems in the data is much more likely to make a correct judgment than is someone equipped with a set of rules created to apply to a wide variety of possible applications.

11.2 A Regression User's Guide

Table 11.2 contains a brief summary of the major econometric maladies discussed so far in this text. For each econometric problem, we list:

1. Its nature.
2. Its consequences for OLS estimation.
3. How to detect it.
4. How to attempt to get rid of it.

How might you use the guide? If an estimated equation has a particular problem, such as a significant unexpected sign for a coefficient estimate or a correct but insignificant coefficient estimate, a quick glance at the guide can give some idea of what econometric problems might be causing that symptom. Both multicollinearity and irrelevant variables can cause regression coefficients to have insignificant t-scores, for example, and someone who remembered only one of these potential causes might take the wrong correction action. After some practice, the use of this guide will decrease until it eventually will seem fairly limiting and simplistic. Until then, however, our experience is that those about to undertake their first econometric research can benefit by referring to this guide.

11.3 Running Your Own Regression Project

We believe that econometrics is best learned by doing, not by reading books, listening to lectures, or taking tests. To us, learning the art of econometrics has more in common with learning to fly a plane or learning to play golf than it does with learning about history or literature. In fact, we developed the interactive exercises of this chapter and Chapter 8 precisely because of our confidence in learning by doing.

Although interactive exercises are a good bridge between textbook examples and running your own regressions, they don't go far enough. You still need to "get your hands dirty." We think that you should run your own regression project before you finish reading this book even if you're not re-

TABLE 11.2 A REGRESSION USER'S GUIDE

What Can Go Wrong?	What Are the Consequences?	How Can It Be Detected?	How Can It Be Corrected?
Omitted Variable			
The omission of a relevant independent variable	Bias in the coefficient estimates (the $\hat{\beta}$s) of the included Xs.	Theory, significant unexpected signs, or surprisingly poor fits.	Include the left-out variable or a proxy.
Irrelevant Variable			
The inclusion of a variable that does not belong in the equation	Decreased precision in the form of higher standard errors and lower t-scores.	1. Theory 2. t-test on $\hat{\beta}$ 3. $\overline{R}^2$ 4. Impact on other coefficients if X is dropped	Delete the variable if its inclusion is not required by the underlying theory.
Incorrect Functional Form			
The functional form is inappropriate	Biased and inconsistent estimates, poor fit, and difficult interpretation.	Examine the theory carefully; think about the relationship between X and Y.	Transform the variable or the equation to a different functional form.
Multicollinearity			
Some of the independent variables are (imperfectly) correlated	No biased $\hat{\beta}$s, but estimates of the separate effects of the Xs are not reliable, i.e., high SEs (and low t-scores).	No universally accepted rule or test is available. Use the t-test on r_{12} or the VIF test.	Drop redundant variables, but to drop others might introduce bias. A combination variable may be useful, but often doing nothing is best.
Serial Correlation			
Observations of the error term are correlated, as in: $\epsilon_t = \rho\epsilon_{t-1} + u_t$	No biased $\hat{\beta}$s, but the variances of the $\hat{\beta}$s increase (and t-scores fall) in a way not captured by OLS.	Use Durbin–Watson d test; if significantly less than 2, positive serial correlation exists.	If impure, add the omitted variable or change the functional form. Otherwise, consider Generalized Least Squares.
Heteroskedasticity			
The variance of the error term is not constant for all observations, as in: $VAR(\epsilon_i) = \sigma^2 Z_i^2$	Same as for serial correlation.	Plot the spread of contraction of the residuals (against one of the Xs, for example) or use the Park or White tests.	If impure, add the omitted variable. Otherwise, run a Weighted Least Squares or use HC standard errors.

quired to do so. We're not alone. Some professors substitute a research project for the final exam as their class's comprehensive learning experience.

Running your own regression project has three major components:

1. Choosing a topic.
2. Applying the six steps in regression analysis to that topic.
3. Writing your research report.

The first and third of these components are the topics of this section. The second component is covered in Chapter 3 except for data collection, which we cover in Section 11.4.

11.3.1 Choosing a Topic

The purpose of an econometric research project is to use regression analysis to build the best explanatory equation for a particular dependent variable for a particular sample. Often, though, the hardest part is getting started. How can you choose a good topic?

There are at least three keys to choosing a topic. First, try to pick a field that you find interesting and/or that you know something about. If you enjoy working on your project, the hours involved will seem to fly by. In addition, if you know something about your subject, you'll be more likely to make correct specification choices and/or to notice subtle indications of data errors or theoretical problems. A second key is to make sure that data are readily available with a reasonable sample (we suggest at least 25 observations). Nothing is more frustrating than searching through data source after data source in search of numbers for your dependent variable or one of your independent variables, so before you lock yourself into a topic, see if the data are there. The final key is to make sure that there is some substance to your topic. Try to avoid topics that are purely descriptive or virtually tautological in nature. Instead, look for topics that include a hypothesis or two that you'd like to test.

Perhaps the best place to look for ideas for topics is to review your textbooks and notes from previous economics classes or to look over the examples and exercises of the first 10 chapters of this book. Often, you can take an idea from a previous study and update the data to see if the idea can be applied in a different context. Other times, reading an example will spark an idea about a similar or related study that you'd be interested in doing. Don't feel that your topic has to contain an original hypothesis or equation. On your first or second project, it's more important to get used to the econometrics than it is to create a publishable masterpiece.

Another way to find a topic is to read through issues of economics journals, looking for article topics that you find interesting and that might be possible to model. Although this is an excellent way to get ideas, it's also frustrating, because most current articles use econometric techniques that go beyond those that we've covered so far in this text. As a result, it's often difficult to compare your results to those in the article.

If you get stuck for a topic, go directly to the data sources themselves. That is, instead of thinking of a topic and then seeing if the data are available, look over what data are available and see if they help generate ideas for topics. Quite often, a reference will have data not only for a dependent variable but also for most of the relevant independent variables all in one place, minimizing time spent collecting data.

Once you pick a topic, don't rush out and run your first regression. Remember, the more time you spend reviewing the literature and analyzing your expectations on a topic, the better the econometric analysis and, ultimately, your research report will be. Speaking of your research report . . .

11.3.2 Writing Your Research Report

Once you've finished your research, it's important to write a report on your results so that others can benefit from what you found out (or didn't find out) or so that you can get feedback on your econometric techniques from someone else. Most good research reports have a number of elements in common:

a. A brief introduction that defines the dependent variable and states the goals of the research.

b. A short review of relevant previous literature and research.

c. An explanation of the specification of the equation (model). This should include explaining why particular independent variables and functional forms were chosen as well as stating the expected signs of (or other hypotheses about) the slope coefficients.

d. A description of the data (including generated variables), data sources, and any irregularities with the data.

e. A presentation of each estimated specification, using our standard documentation format. If you estimate more than one specification, be sure to explain which one is best (and why).

f. A careful analysis of the regression results that includes a discussion of any econometric problems encountered and complete documentation of all equations estimated and all tests run. (Beginning researchers are well advised to test for every possible econometric problem; with experience, you'll learn to focus on the most likely difficulties.)

g. A short summary/conclusion that includes any policy recommendations or suggestions for further research.

h. A bibliography.

i. An appendix that includes all data, all regression runs, and all relevant computer output. Do this carefully; readers appreciate a well-organized and labeled appendix.

We think that the easiest way to write such a research report is to keep a research journal as you go along. In this journal, you can keep track of *a priori* hypotheses, regression results, statistical tests, different specifications you considered, and theoretical analyses of what you thought was going on in your equation. You'll find that when it comes time to write your research report, this journal will almost write your paper for you! The alternative to keeping a journal is to wait until you've finished all your econometric work before starting to write your research report, but this runs the risk of forgetting the thought process that led you to make a particular decision (or some other important item).

11.4 Economic Data

Before any quantitative analysis can be done, the data must be collected, organized, and entered into a computer. Usually, this is a time-consuming and frustrating task because of the difficulty of finding data, the existence of definitional differences between theoretical variables and their empirical counterparts, and the high probability of data entry errors or data transmission errors. In general, though, time spent thinking about and collecting the data is well spent, since a researcher who knows the data sources and definitions is much less likely to make mistakes using or interpreting regressions run on that data.

11.4.1 What Data to Look For

Before you settle on a research topic, it's good advice to make sure that data for your dependent variable and all relevant independent variables are available. However, checking for data availability means deciding what specific variables you want to study. Half of the time that beginning researchers spend collecting data is wasted by looking for the wrong variables in the wrong places. A few minutes thinking about what data to look for will save hours of frustration later.

For example, if the dependent variable is the quantity of television sets demanded per year, then most independent variables should be measured annually as well. It would be inappropriate and possibly misleading to define the price of TVs as the price from a particular month. An average of prices over the year (usually weighted by the number of TVs sold per month) would be more meaningful. If the dependent variable includes all TV sets sold regardless of brand, then the price would appropriately be an aggregate based on prices of all brands. Calculating such aggregate variables, however, is not straightforward. Researchers typically make their best efforts to compute the respective aggregate variables and then acknowledge that problems still remain. For example, if the price data for all the various brands are not available, a researcher may be forced to compromise and use the prices of one or a few of the major brands as a substitute for the proper aggregate price.

Another issue is suggested by the TV example. Over the years of the sample, it's likely that the market shares of particular kinds of TV sets have changed. For example, 21-inch color TV sets might have made up a majority of the market in one decade, but 19-inch black and white sets might have been the favorite 20 years before. In cases where the composition of the market share, the size, or the quality of the various brands have changed over time, it would make little sense to measure the dependent variable as the number of TV sets because a "TV set" from one year has little in common with a "TV set" from another. The approach usually taken to deal with this problem is to measure the variable in dollar terms, under the assumption that value encompasses size and quality. Thus, we would work with the dollar sales of TVs rather than the number of sets sold.

A third issue, whether to use nominal or real variables, usually depends on the underlying theory of the research topic. Nominal (or money) variables are measured in current dollars and thus include increases caused by inflation. If theory implies that inflation should be filtered out, then it's best to state the variables in real (constant dollar) terms by selecting an appropriate price deflator, such as the Consumer Price Index, and adjusting the money (or nominal) value by it.

As an example, the appropriate price index for Gross Domestic Product is called the GDP deflator. Real GDP is calculated by multiplying nominal GDP by the ratio of the GDP deflator from the base year to the GDP deflator from the current year:

Real GDP = nominal GDP × (base GDP deflator/current GDP deflator)

In 1994, U.S. nominal GDP was $6891 billion and the GDP deflator 127.0 (for a base year of 1987 = 100), so real GDP was[1]:

---

1. *1995 Economic Report of the President*, pp. 274–278.

$$\text{Real GDP} = \$6891 \cdot (100/127.0) = \$5426 \text{ billion}$$

That is, the goods and services produced in 1994 were worth $6891 billion if 1994 dollars were used but were worth only $5426 billion if 1987 prices were used.

Fourth, recall that all economic data are either time series or cross sectional in nature. Since time-series data are for the same economic entity from different time periods, whereas cross-sectional data are from the same time period but for different economic entities, the appropriate definitions of the variables depend on whether the sample is a time series or a cross section.

To understand this, consider the TV set example once again. A time-series model might study the sales of TV sets in the United States from 1960 to 1998, and a cross-sectional model might study the sales of TV sets by state for 1998. The time-series data set would have 39 observations, each of which would refer to a particular year. In contrast, the cross-sectional model data set would have 50 observations, each of which would refer to a particular state. A variable that might be appropriate for the time-series model might be completely inappropriate for the cross-sectional model and vice versa; at the very least, it would have to be measured differently. National advertising in a particular year would be appropriate for the time-series model, for example, while advertising in or near each particular state would make more sense for the cross-sectional one.

Finally, learn to be a critical reader of the descriptions of variables in econometric research. For instance, most readers breezed right through Equation 2.10 on the demand for beef (and the accompanying data in Table 2.2) without asking some vital questions. Where did the data originate? Are prices and income measured in nominal or real terms? Is the price of beef wholesale or retail? A careful reader would want to know the answers to these questions before analyzing the results of Equation 2.10. (For the record, Yd measures real income, P measures real wholesale prices, and the data come from various issues of *Agricultural Statistics*, published in Washington, D.C., by the U.S. Department of Agriculture.)

11.4.2 Where to Look for Economic Data

Although some researchers generate their own data through surveys or other techniques, the vast majority of regressions are run on publicly available data. The best sources for such data are government publications and machine-readable data files. In fact, the U.S. government has been called the most thorough statistics-collecting agency in history.

Excellent government publications include the annual *Statistical Abstract of the U.S.*, the annual *Economic Report of the President*, the *Handbook of Labor*

Statistics, and *Historical Statistics of the U.S.* (published in 1975). One of the best places to start with U.S. data is the annual *Census Catalog and Guide,* which provides overviews and abstracts of data sources and various statistical products as well as details on how to obtain each item.[2] Also quite valuable is the Bureau of Labor Statistics (BLS) *Customer Service Guide,* which provides details of BLS program areas, products, and on-line access.[3]

Consistent international data are harder to come by, but the United Nations publishes a number of compilations of figures. The best of these are the *U.N. Statistical Yearbook* and the *U.N. Yearbook of National Account Statistics.*

Recently, more and more researchers have started using on-line computer databases to find data instead of plowing through stacks of printed volumes. These on-line databases, available through most college and university libraries, contain complete series on literally thousands of possible variables. For example, one database, "U.S. Econ.," contains more than 25,000 time-series variables for the U.S. economy. The *Directory of Online Databases* (New York: Quadra/Elsevier, 1995) contains a complete listing of all available on-line databases. Two of the most useful of these are the "Economic Literature Index," which is an on-line summary of the *Journal of Economic Literature,* and "Dialog," which provides on-line access to a large number of data sets at a lower cost than many alternatives.

Finally, a huge variety of data is available on the Internet. The best guides to the data available in this rapidly changing world are "Resources For Economists on the Internet," Economagic, and WebEC.[4] Links to these sites and other good sources of data are on the text's website <www.awl.com/studenmund>.

11.4.3 Missing Data

Suppose the data aren't there? What happens if you choose the perfect variable and look in all the right sources and can't find the data?

The answer to this question depends on how much data are missing. If a few observations have incomplete data in a cross-sectional study, you usually

---

2. To obtain this guide, write the Superintendent of Documents, Government Printing Office, Washington, D.C., 20402-9325, or call 202-783-9325 and ask for stock/catalog #C3-163/3.

3. The BLS maintains a 24-hour data hot line (including information on how to order data) at 202-606-7828.

4. On the Web, the resources location is http://econwpa.wustl.edu/EconFAQ.html. You can also access the guide via e-mail by putting GET ECON.FAQ in the subject line of a message to econ-wp@econwpa.wustl.edu. The Economagic location is http://www.economagic.com/. The WebEC location is http://rfe.wustl.edu/Data/index.html.

can afford to drop these observations from the sample. If the incomplete data are from a time series, you can sometimes estimate the missing value by interpolating (taking the mean of adjacent values). Similarly, if one variable is available only annually in an otherwise quarterly model, you may want to consider quarterly interpolations of that variable. In either case, interpolation can be justified only if the variable moves in a slow and smooth manner. Extreme caution should always be exercised when "creating" data in such a way (and full documentation is required).

If no data exist for a theoretically relevant variable, then the problem worsens significantly. Omitting a relevant variable runs the risk of biased coefficient estimates, as we learned in Chapter 6. After all, how can you hold a variable constant if it's not included in the equation? In such cases, most researchers resort to the use of proxy variables.

Proxy variables can sometimes substitute for theoretically desired variables when data on variables are missing. For example, the value of net investment is a variable that is not measured directly in a number of countries. As a result, a researcher might use the value of gross investment as a proxy, the assumption being that the value of gross investment is directly proportional to the value of net investment. This proportionality (which is similar to a change in units) is required because the regression analyzes the relationship between changes among variables, rather than the absolute levels of the variables.

In general, a proxy variable is a "good" proxy when its movements correspond relatively well to movements in the theoretically correct variable. Since the latter is unobservable whenever a proxy must be used, there is usually no easy way to examine a proxy's "goodness" directly. Instead, the researcher must document as well as possible why the proxy is likely to be a good or bad one. Poor proxies and variables with large measurement errors constitute "bad" data, but the degree to which the data are bad is a matter of judgment by the individual researcher.

11.5 The Ethical Econometrician

One conclusion that a casual reader of this book might draw from the large number of specifications we include is that we encourage the estimation of numerous regression results as a way of insuring the discovery of these best possible estimates.

Nothing could be further from the truth!

As every reader of this book should know by now, our opinion is that the best models are those on which much care has been spent to develop the theoretical underpinnings and only a short time is spent pursuing alternative estimations of that equation. Many econometricians, ourselves included, would hope to be able to estimate only *one* specification of an equation for each data set. Econometricians are fallible and our data are sometimes imperfect, however, so it is unusual for a first attempt at estimation to be totally problem free. As a result, two or even more regressions are often necessary to rid an estimation of fairly simple difficulties that perhaps could have been avoided in a world of perfect foresight.

Unfortunately, a beginning researcher usually has little motivation to stop running regressions until he or she likes the way the result looks. If running another regression provides a result with a better fit, why shouldn't one more specification be tested?

The reason is a compelling one. Every time an extra regression is run and a specification choice is made on the basis of fit or statistical significance, the chances of making a mistake of inference increase dramatically. This can happen in at least two ways:

1. If you consistently drop a variable when its coefficient is insignificant but keep it when it is significant, it can be shown, as discussed in Section 6.4, that you bias your estimates of the coefficients of the equation and of the t-scores.

2. If you choose to use a lag structure, or a functional form or an estimation procedure other than OLS, on the basis of fit rather than on the basis of previously theorized hypotheses, you run the risk that your equation will work poorly when it's applied to data outside your sample. If you restructure your equation to work well on one data set, you might decrease the chance of it working well on another.

What might be thought of as ethical econometrics is also in reality good econometrics. That is, the real reason to avoid running too many different specifications is that the fewer regressions you run, the more reliable and more consistently trustworthy are your results. The instance in which professional ethics come into play is when a number of changes are made (different variables, lag structures, functional forms, estimation procedures, data sets, dropped outliers, and so on), but the regression results are presented to colleagues, clients, editors, or journals as if the final and best equation had been the first and only one estimated. Our recommendation is that all estimated equations be reported even if footnotes or an appendix have to be added to the documentation.

We think that there are two reasonable goals for econometricians when estimating models:

1. Run as few different specifications as possible while still attempting to avoid the major econometric problems.[5]

2. Report honestly the number and type of different specifications estimated so that readers of the research can evaluate how much weight to give to your results.

Therefore, the art of econometrics boils down to attempting to find the best possible equation in the fewest possible number of regression runs. Only careful thinking and reading before estimating first regression can bring this about. An ethical econometrician is honest and complete in reporting the different specifications and/or data sets used.

11.6 Summary

1. Table 11.1 contains a listing of terms that should be checked when reviewing the output from a computer regression package.

2. Table 11.2 contains a summary of the nature, consequences, detection, and correction procedures for the various econometric problems covered so far in this text. A review of this table is a good way to prepare for the first few attempts at applied regression analysis.

3. The art of econometrics involves finding the best possible equation in the fewest possible number of regression runs. The only way to do this is to spend quite a bit of time thinking through the underlying principles of every research project before the first regression is run.

4. An ethical econometrician is always honest and complete in reporting all the different regressions estimated and/or data sets used before the final results were chosen.

11.7 Appendix: The Housing Price Interactive Exercise

This interactive regression learning exercise is somewhat different from the previous one in Section 8.7. Our goal is still to bridge the gap between textbook and computer, but we feel that if you completed the previous interac-

---

5. The only exceptions to our recommendation to run as few specifications as possible are scanning and sensitivity analysis, described in Section 6.4.5.

tive exercise you should be ready to do the computer work on your own.[6] As a result, this interactive exercise will provide you with a short literature review and the data, but you'll be asked to calculate your own estimates. Feedback on your specification choices will once again be found in the hints in Appendix A.

Since the only difference between this interactive exercise and the first one is that this one requires you to estimate your chosen specification(s) with the computer, our guidelines for interactive exercises will apply:

1. Take the time to look over a portion of the reading list before choosing a specification.

2. Try to estimate as few regression runs as possible.

3. Avoid looking at the hints until after you've reached what you think is your best specification.

We believe that the benefits you get from an interactive exercise are directly proportional to the effort you put into it. If you have to delay this exercise until you have the time and energy to do your best, that's probably a good idea.

11.7.1 Building a Hedonic Model of Housing Prices

In the next section, we're going to ask you to specify the independent variables and functional form for an equation whose dependent variable is the price of a house in Southern California. Before making these choices, it's vital to review the housing price literature and to think through the theory behind such models. Such a review is especially important in this case because the model we'll be building will be *hedonic* in nature.

What is a hedonic model? Recall that in Section 1.5 we estimated an equation for the price of a house as a function of the size of that house. Such a model is called **hedonic** because it uses measures of the quality of a product as independent variables instead of measures of the market for that product (like quantity demanded, income, etc.). Hedonic models are most useful when the product being analyzed is heterogeneous in nature because we need to analyze what causes products to be different and therefore to have different prices. With a homogeneous product, hedonic models are virtually useless.

---

6. If you have not completed the interactive exercise in Section 8.7, we urge you to do so before beginning this one. Instructors interested in additional interactive exercises can find them in our instructor's manual and on the text's internet site <www.awlonline.com/studenmund>.

Perhaps the most-cited early hedonic housing price study is that of G. Grether and P. Mieszkowski.[7] Grether and Mieszkowski collected a 7-year data set and built a number of linear models of housing price using different combinations of variables. They included square feet of space, the number of bathrooms, and the number of rooms, although the latter turned out to be insignificant. They also included lot size and the age of the house as variables, specifying a quadratic function for the age variable. Most innovatively, they used several slope dummies in order to capture the interaction effects of various combinations of variables (like a hardwood floors dummy times the size of the house).

Peter Linneman[8] estimated a housing price model on data from Los Angeles, Chicago, and the entire United States. His goal was to create a model that worked for the two individual cities and then to apply it to the nation to test the hypothesis of a national housing market. Linneman did not include any lot characteristics, nor did he use any interaction variables. His only measures of the size of the living space were the number of bathrooms and the number of nonbathrooms. Except for an age variable, the rest of the independent variables were dummies describing quality characteristics of the house and neighborhood. Although many of the dummy variables were quite fickle, the coefficients of age, number of bathrooms, and the number of nonbathrooms were relatively stable and significant. Central air conditioning had a negative, insignificant coefficient for the Los Angeles regression.

K. Ihlanfeldt and J. Martinez-Vasquez[9] investigated sample bias in various methods of obtaining house price data and concluded that the house's sales price is the least biased of all measures. Unfortunately, they went on to estimate an equation by starting with a large number of variables and then dropping all those that had t-scores below one, almost surely introducing bias into their equation.

---

7. G. M. Grether and Peter Mieszkowski, "Determinants of Real Estate Values," *Journal of Urban Economics*, April 1974, pp. 127–146. Another classic article of the same era is J. Kain and J. Quigley, "Measuring the Value of Housing Quality," *Journal of American Statistical Association*, June 1970.

8. Peter Linneman, "Some Empirical Results on the Nature of Hedonic Price Functions for the Urban Housing Market," *Journal of Urban Economics*, July 1980, pp. 47–68.

9. Keith Ihlanfeldt and Jorge Martinez-Vasquez, "Alternate Value Estimates of Owner-Occupied Housing: Evidence on Sample Selection Bias and Systematic Errors," *Journal of Urban Economics*, November 1986, pp. 356–369. Also see Eric Cassel and Robert Mendelsohn, "The Choice of Functional Forms for Hedonic Price Equations: Comment," *Journal of Urban Economics*, September 1985, pp. 135–142.

Finally, Allen Goodman[10] added some innovative variables to an estimate on a national data set. He included measures of specific problems like rats, cracks in the plaster, holes in the floors, plumbing breakdowns, and the level of property taxes. Although the property tax variable showed the capitalization of low property taxes, as would be expected, the rats variable was insignificant, and the cracks variable's coefficient asserted that cracks significantly increase the value of a house.

11.7.2 The Housing Price Interactive Exercise

Now that we've reviewed at least a portion of the literature, it's time to build your own model. Recall that in Section 1.5, we built a simple model of the price of a house as a function of the size of that house, Equation 1.23:

$$\hat{P}_i = 40.0 + 0.138S_i \qquad (1.23)$$

where: P_i = the price (in thousands of dollars) of the ith house
S_i = the size (in square feet) of the ith house

Equation 1.23 was estimated on a sample of 43 houses that were purchased in the same Southern California town (Monrovia) within a few weeks of each other. It turns out that we have a number of additional independent variables for the data set we used to estimate Equation 1.23. Also available are:

N_i = the quality of the neighborhood of the ith house (1 = best, 4 = worst) as rated by two local real estate agents
A_i = the age of the ith house in years
BE_i = the number of bedrooms in the ith house
BA_i = the number of bathrooms in the ith house
CA_i = a dummy variable equal to 1 if the ith house has central air conditioning, 0 otherwise
SP_i = a dummy variable equal to 1 if the ith house has a pool, 0 otherwise
Y_i = the size of the yard around the ith house (in square feet)

Read through the list of variables again, developing your own analyses of the theory behind each variable. What are the expected signs of the coefficients?

---

10. Allen C. Goodman, "An Econometric Model of Housing Price, Permanent Income, Tenure Choice, and Housing Demand," *Journal of Urban Economics*, May 1988, pp. 327–353.

Which variables seem potentially redundant? Which variables *must* you include?

In addition, there are a number of functional form modifications that can be made. For example, you might consider a quadratic polynomial for age, as Grether and Mieszkowski did, or you might consider creating slope dummies such as SP·S or CA·S. Finally, you might consider interactive variables that involve the neighborhood proxy variable such as N·S or N·BA. What hypotheses would each of these imply?

Develop your specification carefully. Think through each variable and/or functional form decision, and take the time to write out your expectations for the sign and size of each coefficient. Don't take the attitude that you should include *every* possible variable and functional form modification and then drop the insignificant ones. Instead, try to design the best possible hedonic model of housing prices you can the first time around.

Once you've chosen a specification, estimate your equation, using the data in Table 11.3 (page 408), and analyze the result.

1. Test your hypotheses for each coefficient with the *t*-test. Pay special attention to any functional form modifications.

2. Test the overall significance of the equation with the *F*-test.

3. Decide what econometric problems exist in the equation, testing, if appropriate, for multicollinearity, serial correlation, or heteroskedasticity.

4. Decide whether to accept your first specification as the best one or to make a modification in your equation and estimate again. Make sure you avoid the temptation to estimate an additional specification "just to see what it looks like."

Once you've decided to make no further changes, you're finished—congratulations! Now turn to the hints for Section 11.7.2 in Appendix A for feedback on your choices.

TABLE 11.3 DATA FOR THE HOUSING PRICE INTERACTIVE EXERCISE

P	S	N	A	BE	BA	CA	SP	Y
107	736	4	39	2	1	0	0	3364
133	720	3	63	2	1	0	0	1780
141	768	2	66	2	1	0	0	6532
165	929	3	41	3	1	0	0	2747
170	1080	2	44	3	1	0	0	5520
173	942	2	65	2	1	0	0	6808
182	1000	2	40	3	1	0	0	6100
200	1472	1	66	3	2	0	0	5328
220	1200	1.5	69	3	1	0	0	5850
226	1302	2	49	3	2	0	0	5298
260	2109	2	37	3	2	1	0	3691
275	1528	1	41	2	2	0	0	5860
280	1421	1	41	3	2	0	1	6679
289	1753	1	1	3	2	1	0	2304
295	1528	1	32	3	2	0	0	6292
300	1643	1	29	3	2	0	1	7127
310	1675	1	63	3	2	0	0	9025
315	1714	1	38	3	2	1	0	6466
350	2150	2	75	4	2	0	0	14825
365	2206	1	28	4	2.5	1	0	8147
503	3269	1	5	4	2.5	1	0	10045
135	936	4	75	2	1	0	0	5054
147	728	3	40	2	1	0	0	1922
165	1014	3	26	2	1	0	0	6416
175	1661	3	27	3	2	1	0	4939
190	1248	2	42	3	1	0	0	7952
191	1834	3.5	40	3	2	0	1	6710
195	989	2	41	3	1	0	0	5911
205	1232	1	43	2	2	0	0	4618
210	1017	1	38	2	1	0	0	5083
215	1216	2	77	2	1	0	0	6834
228	1447	2	44	2	2	0	0	4143
242	1974	1.5	65	4	2	0	1	5499
250	1600	1.5	63	3	2	1	0	4050
250	1168	1.5	63	3	1	0	1	5182
255	1478	1	50	3	2	0	0	4122
255	1756	2	36	3	2	0	1	6420
265	1542	2	38	3	2	0	0	6833
265	1633	1	32	4	2	0	1	7117
275	1500	1	42	2	2	1	0	7406
285	1734	1	62	3	2	0	1	8583
365	1900	1	42	3	2	1	0	19580
397	2468	1	10	4	2.5	1	0	6086

Note: filename HOUSE11

PART III

EXTENSIONS OF THE BASIC

REGRESSION MODEL

CHAPTER 12

Time-Series Models

When we're working with time-series data, complications sometimes arise that simply can't happen with cross-sectional data. Most of these complications relate to the order of the observations; after all, order matters quite a bit in time-series data but doesn't matter much (if at all) in cross-sectional data. Thus, the purpose of this chapter is to provide an introduction to a number of interesting models that have been designed to cope with and take advantage of the special properties of time-series data.

The most important of these topics is distributed lags, the concept that the impact of an independent variable can be spread out over a number of time periods instead of being limited to the current time period. Consider, for example, the impact of advertising on sales. Many analysts believe that people remember advertising for more than one time period, so advertising affects sales in the future as well as in the current time period. As a result, models of sales should include current *and lagged* values of advertising, thus distributing the impact of advertising over a number of different lags. We'll learn about Koyck distributed lag models and we'll also investigate the problems that serial correlation causes in distributed lag models.

The chapter concludes with a brief introduction to a topic called nonstationarity. If variables have significant trends over time, they are said to be nonstationary, and it turns out that nonstationary variables have the potential to inflate t-scores and measures of overall fit in an equation.

12.1 Koyck Distributed Lag Models

12.1.1 Distributed Lag Models

Ever since we introduced the idea of lags in Section 6.5, we've used lagged independent variables whenever we've expected X to affect Y after a period of time. For example, if the underlying theory has suggested that X_1 affects Y with a one-time-period lag (but X_2 has an instantaneous impact on Y) we've used equations like:

$$Y_t = \beta_0 + \beta_1 X_{1t-1} + \beta_2 X_{2t} + \epsilon_t \qquad (12.1)$$

Such lags are called simple lags, and the estimation of β_1 with OLS is no more difficult than the estimation of the coefficients of nonlagged equations, except for possible impure serial correlation if the lag is misspecified. Remember, however, that the coefficients of such equations should be interpreted carefully. For example, β_2 in Equation 12.1 measures the effect of a one-unit increase in this time's X_2 on this time's Y holding *last time's* X_1 constant.

A case more complicated than this simple lag model occurs when the impact of an independent variable is expected to be spread out over a number of time periods. For example, suppose we're interested in studying the impact of a change in the money supply on GDP. Theoretical and empirical studies have provided evidence that because of rigidities in the marketplace, it takes time for the economy to react completely to a change in the money supply. Some of the effect on GDP will take place in the first quarter, some more in the second quarter, and so on. In such a case, the appropriate econometric model would be a distributed lag model:

$$Y_t = a_0 + \beta_0 X_t + \beta_1 X_{t-1} + \beta_2 X_{t-2} + \cdots + \beta_p X_{t-p} + \epsilon_t \qquad (12.2)$$

A **distributed lag model** explains the current value of Y as a function of current and past values of X, thus "distributing" the impact of X over a number of time periods. Take a careful look at Equation 12.2. The coefficients β_0, β_1, and β_2 through β_p measure the effects of the various lagged values of X on the current value of Y. In most economic applications, including our money supply example, we'd expect the impact of X on Y to decrease as the length of the lag (indicated by the subscript of the β) increases. That is, although β_0 might be larger or smaller than β_1, we certainly would expect either β_0 or β_1 to be larger in absolute value than β_6 or β_7.

Unfortunately, the estimation of Equation 12.2 with OLS causes a number of problems:

1. The various lagged values of X are likely to be severely multicollinear, making coefficient estimates imprecise.

2. In large part because of this multicollinearity, there is no guarantee that the estimated βs will follow the smoothly declining pattern that economic theory would suggest. Instead, it's quite typical for the estimated coefficients of Equation 12.2 to follow a fairly irregular pattern, for example:

$$\hat{\beta}_0 = 0.26 \quad \hat{\beta}_1 = 0.07 \quad \hat{\beta}_2 = 0.17 \quad \hat{\beta}_3 = -0.03 \quad \hat{\beta}_4 = 0.08$$

3. The degrees of freedom tend to decrease, sometimes substantially, for two reasons. First, we have to estimate a coefficient for each lagged X, thus increasing K and lowering the degrees of freedom $(n - K - 1)$. Second, unless data for lagged Xs outside the sample are available, we have to decrease the sample size by one for each lagged X we calculate, thus lowering the number of observations, n, and therefore the degrees of freedom.

As a result of these problems with OLS estimation of functions like Equation 12.2, called ad hoc distributed lag equations, it's standard practice to use a simplifying assumption to avoid these problems. The most commonly used simplification is the Koyck model.

12.1.2 What Are Koyck Lags?

A **Koyck distributed lag model** is one that assumes that the coefficients of the lagged variables decrease in a geometric fashion the longer the lag:[1]

$$\beta_i = \beta_0 \lambda^i \tag{12.3}$$

where i is the length of the lag, 1, 2, . . . , p and $0 < \lambda < 1$. For example, $\beta_3 = \beta_0 \lambda^3$.

If we substitute Equation 12.3 into Equation 12.2 for each coefficient and factor out β_0, we obtain

$$Y_t = a_0 + \beta_0(X_t + \lambda X_{t-1} + \lambda^2 X_{t-2} + \lambda^3 X_{t-3} + \cdots) + \epsilon_t \tag{12.4}$$

---

1. L. M. Koyck, *Distributed Lags and Investment Analysis* (Amsterdam: North-Holland Publishing Company, 1954).

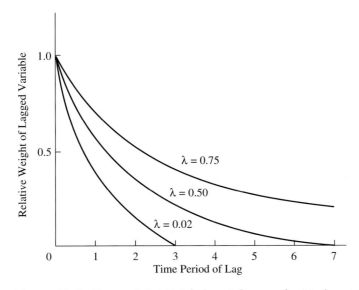

Figure 12.1 Geometric Weighting Schemes for Various Koyck Lag Models

No matter what λ is used, a Koyck distributed lag model has the impact of the independent variable declining as the length of the lag increases.

Since we have assumed that λ is between zero and one, λ to the $(n + 1)$th power is smaller than λ to the nth power. As a result, each successive lagged term has a smaller coefficient than the previous term.[2] For example, if $\lambda = 0.2$, then Equation 12.4 becomes:

$$Y_t = a_0 + \beta_0(X_t + 0.2X_{t-1} + 0.04X_{t-2} + 0.008X_{t-3} + \cdots) + \epsilon_t \tag{12.5}$$

because $(0.2)^1 = 0.2$, $(0.2)^2 = 0.04$, and so on. As can be seen in Figure 12.1, each successive lagged value does indeed have relatively less weight in determining the current value of Y.

---

2. One distributed lag model in which the coefficient need not follow this pattern is the Almon polynomial distributed lag model, an estimation procedure for distributed lags that allows the coefficients of the lagged independent variables to follow a variety of continuous patterns as the length of the lag increases. Although coefficients from a simple Koyck model are limited to a steadily decreasing pattern (Figure 12.1), the Almon model can allow coefficients to first increase and then decrease or to change direction more than once. See Shirley Almon, "The Distributed Lag Between Capital Appropriations and Expenditures," *Econometrica*, 1965, pp. 178–196.

How can we estimate Equation 12.4? As it stands, the equation is nonlinear in the coefficients and can't be estimated with OLS. However, with some manipulation, Equation 12.4 can be transformed into an equivalent equation that is linear in the coefficients α_0, β_0, and λ. To see this, multiply both sides of Equation 12.4 by λ and lag it once (that is, substitute $t - 1$ for t in every instance that it appears):

$$\lambda Y_{t-1} = \lambda a_0 + \beta_0(\lambda X_{t-1} + \lambda^2 X_{t-2} + \lambda^3 X_{t-3} + \cdots) + \lambda \epsilon_{t-1} \qquad (12.6)$$

Now subtract the resulting equation (Equation 12.6) from Equation 12.4 and rewrite, producing:

$$Y_t = \alpha_0 + \beta_0 X_t + \lambda Y_{t-1} + u_t \qquad (12.7)$$

where $u_t = \epsilon_t - \lambda \epsilon_{t-1}$ and where $\alpha_0 = a_0 - \lambda a_0$ (still a constant). Compare Equation 12.7 with Equation 12.4; the Koyck transformation has changed a distributed lag equation into an equation with a lagged dependent variable, often called an *autoregressive* equation.

This equation (Equation 12.7) then becomes the estimating equation. OLS can be applied to Equation 12.7 as long as the sample is large enough. How large is "large enough?" Our recommendation, based more on experience than proof, is to aim for a sample size of at least 50 observations.[3] The smaller the sample, the more likely you are to encounter bias. Samples below 25 in size should be avoided entirely, in part because of bias and in part because hypothesis testing becomes untrustworthy.

Koyck distributed lag models have other potentially serious problems. If the original error term ϵ_t satisfies all the Classical Assumptions, then the error term in the Koyck model, u_t, is almost sure to be serially correlated. In addition, OLS estimation of Equation 12.7 is biased no matter how large the sample. These problems will be discussed in Section 12.2. Also, the presence of a lagged dependent variable as an independent variable forces every other independent variable in the equation to be related to the dependent variable by a declining geometric (Kyock) distributed lag function.

As an example of this latter problem, suppose that we want to build a model of Y that includes a distributed lag of X_1 and also includes X_2 as an unlagged independent variable. Suppose further that we use the following equation:

---

3. If u_t is well behaved, OLS estimation of Equation 12.7 can be shown to have desirable properties for extremely large samples, but not enough is known about the small sample properties of this model to issue firm sample size guidelines. See H. Doran and W. Griffiths, "Inconsistency of the OLS Estimator of the Partial-Adjustment-Adaptive Expectations Model," *Journal of Econometrics*, 1978, pp. 133–146.

$$Y_t = \alpha_0 + \beta_0 X_{1t} + \lambda Y_{t-1} + \beta_1 X_{2t} + u_t \qquad (12.8)$$

The use of the λY_{t-1} term forces both X_1 *and* X_2 to have Koyck distributed lag patterns with respect to Y. Thus, if we don't expect X_2 to have lagged effects on Y, a Koyck function is not an appropriate model in this case unless the equation is specifically adjusted to offset this problem.

12.1.3 An Example of Koyck Distributed Lags

As an example of a Koyck distributed lag model, let's look at an aggregate consumption function from a macroeconomic equilibrium GDP model. Many economists argue that, in such a model, consumption is not just an instantaneous function of income. Instead, they maintain that current purchases of goods and services (CO_t) are influenced by past levels of disposable income (YD_{t-1}, YD_{t-2}, etc.) as well as current levels of disposable income (YD_t):

$$CO_t = f(\overset{+}{YD_t}, \overset{+}{YD_{t-1}}, \overset{+}{YD_{t-2}}, \text{etc.}) + u_t \qquad (12.9)$$

Such an equation fits well with simple models of consumption, but it only makes sense if the weights given past levels of income decrease as the length of the lag increases. That is, we would expect the coefficient of YD_{t-2} to be less than the coefficient of YD_{t-1}, and so on.

As a result, most econometricians would model Equation 12.9 with a Koyck distributed lag equation:

$$CO_t = \alpha_0 + \beta_0 YD_t + \lambda CO_{t-1} + u_t \qquad (12.10)$$

This equation not only fits a simple model of aggregate consumption, but it also is quite close to that suggested by Milton Friedman for his permanent income hypothesis.[4] In that hypothesis, Friedman suggested that consumption was based not on current income but instead on the consumer's perception of lifetime income. Consequently, changes in transitory income wouldn't affect consumption. Since it's reasonable to hypothesize that perceptions of permanent income are based on past levels of income, the simple Koyck consumption model and the more sophisticated permanent income model have similar equations.

---

4. Milton Friedman, *A Theory of the Consumption Function* (Princeton, N.J.: Princeton University Press/National Bureau of Economic Research, 1957). It's interesting to note, however, that Friedman's original function did not include a constant term because of the nature of his derivation of permanent income.

To estimate Equation 12.10, we use data from Section 14.3, where we will build a small macro model of the U.S. economy from 1964 through 1994. The OLS estimates of Equation 12.10 for this data set are (standard errors in parentheses):

$$\widehat{CO}_t = -38.11 + 0.52YD_t + 0.46CO_{t-1} \qquad (12.11)$$
$$\phantom{\widehat{CO}_t = -38.11 + } (0.12) \qquad (0.12)$$
$$\phantom{\widehat{CO}_t = -38.11 + } t = 4.44 \qquad 3.74$$
$$\bar{R}^2 = .998 \qquad n = 31 \qquad \text{(annual 1964–1994)}$$

One way to analyze the coefficients of this equation is to convert the estimates back into the format of Equation 12.9 by using the Koyck distributed lag definitions of the individual coefficients, Equation 12.3:

$$\beta_i = \beta_0 \lambda^i \qquad (12.3)$$

If we substitute $\beta_0 = 0.52$ and $\lambda = 0.46$ into Equation 12.3 for $i = 1$, we obtain $\beta_1 = \beta_0 \lambda^1 = (0.52)(0.46)^1 = 0.24$. If we continue this process, it turns out that Equation 12.11 is equivalent to[5]:

$$\widehat{CO}_t = -70.57 + 0.52YD_t + 0.24YD_{t-1} + 0.11YD_{t-2} \qquad (12.12)$$
$$+ 0.05YD_{t-3} + \cdots$$

As can be seen, the coefficients of YD in Equation 12.12 do indeed smoothly decline as we'd expect in a Koyck distributed lag equation.

To compare this estimate with an OLS estimate of the same equation without the Koyck lag format, we'd need to estimate an ad hoc distributed lag equation with the same number of lagged variables:

$$CO_t = \alpha_0 + \beta_0 YD_t + \beta_1 YD_{t-1} + \beta_2 YD_{t-2} + \beta_3 YD_{t-3} + \epsilon_t \qquad (12.13)$$

As expected, the coefficients of the ad hoc estimate do not follow the same smoothly declining pattern:

$$\widehat{CO}_t = -152.8 + 0.93YD_t + 0.10YD_{t-1} - 0.05YD_{t-2} - 0.03YD_{t-3}$$
$$(12.14)$$

---

5. Note that the constant term equals $\hat{\alpha}_0/(1 - \hat{\lambda})$.

How do the coefficients of Equation 12.14 look? As the lag increases, the coefficients of YD decrease sharply, actually going negative for t − 2 and t − 3. Neither economic theory nor common sense leads us to expect this pattern. Such a poor result is due to the severe multicollinearity between the lagged Xs. Most econometricians therefore estimate distributed lag models with a lagged dependent variable simplification scheme like the Koyck function in Equation 12.10.

An interesting interpretation of the results in Equation 12.11 concerns the long-run multiplier implied by the model. The long-run multiplier measures the total impact of a change in income on consumption after all the lagged effects have been felt. An estimate of the long-run multiplier can be obtained from Equation 12.11 by calculating $\hat{\beta}_0[1/(1 - \hat{\lambda})]$, which in this case equals $0.52[1/(1 - 0.46)]$ or 0.96. A sample of this size is likely to encounter small sample bias, however, so we shouldn't overanalyze the results. For more on this data set and the other equations in the model, see Section 14.3. For more on testing and adjusting distributed lag equations like Equation 12.11 for serial correlation, let's move on to the next section.

12.2 Serial Correlation and Koyck Distributed Lags

Perhaps the most serious drawback of Koyck lags is the high probability of serial correlation. Equations with a lagged dependent variable are more likely to encounter serial correlation than are other equations. To understand why, take a look at a typical Koyck error term from Equation 12.7:

$$u_t = \epsilon_t - \lambda\epsilon_{t-1}$$

Do you see the problem? This time's error term (u_t) is a moving average of ϵ_t, so ϵ_{t-1} affects both u_t and u_{t-1}. Since u_t and u_{t-1} are affected by the same variable, (ϵ_{t-1}), they're almost sure to be correlated, violating Classical Assumption IV.[6]

Compounding this, the consequences, detection, and remedies for serial correlation that we discussed in Chapter 9 are all either incorrect or need to be modified in the presence of a lagged dependent variable. Since all Koyck distributed lag models include a lagged dependent variable, a discussion of serial correlation in Koyck models is critical to an understanding of distributed lags.

---

6. More formally, if we start with $u_t = \epsilon_t - \lambda\epsilon_{t-1}$, lag this equation one time period, solve for ϵ_{t-1}, and then substitute back into the original definition of u_t, we obtain: $u_t = \epsilon_t - \lambda u_{t-1} - \lambda^2\epsilon_{t-2}$. In other words, this time's error term u_t is a function of last time's error term, u_{t-1}.

12.2.1 Serial Correlation Causes Bias in Koyck Lag Models

In Section 9.2, we stated that pure serial correlation does not cause bias in the estimates of the coefficients. Unfortunately, the use of a Koyck distributed lag model changes all that. More specifically, if an equation that contains a lagged dependent variable as an independent variable has a serially correlated error term, then OLS estimates of the coefficients of that equation will be biased, even in large samples.

To see where this bias comes from, let's look at an equation with a lagged dependent variable and a serially correlated error term of the type $(u_t = \epsilon_t - \lambda\epsilon_{t-1}$, called a moving average) found in Koyck distributed lag equations:

$$Y_t = \alpha_0 + \beta_0 X_t + \lambda \overset{\uparrow}{Y}_{t-1} + \epsilon_t - \lambda \overset{\uparrow}{\epsilon}_{t-1} \qquad (12.15)$$

Let's also look at Equation 12.15 lagged one time period:

$$\overset{\uparrow}{Y}_{t-1} = \alpha_0 + \beta_0 X_{t-1} + \lambda Y_{t-2} + \overset{\uparrow}{\epsilon}_{t-1} - \lambda\epsilon_{t-2} \qquad (12.16)$$

What happens when last time period's error term (ϵ_{t-1}) is positive? In Equation 12.16, the positive ϵ_{t-1} causes Y_{t-1} to be larger than it would have been otherwise (these changes are marked by upward pointing arrows).

Take a look at the right-hand side of Equation 12.15. Every time ϵ_{t-1} is positive, Y_{t-1} will be larger than otherwise. Thus, the two variables are correlated and, therefore, so are u_t and Y_{t-1}. Such a situation violates Classical Assumption III that the error term is not correlated with any of the explanatory variables. What happens if ϵ_{t-1} is negative? In this case, Y_{t-1} will be lower than it would have been otherwise, so they're still correlated.

The consequences of this correlation include biased estimates, in particular of the coefficient λ. In essence, the uncorrected serial correlation acts like an omitted variable (ϵ_{t-1}). Since an omitted variable causes bias whenever it is correlated with one of the included independent variables, and since ϵ_{t-1} is correlated with Y_{t-1}, the combination of a lagged dependent variable and serial correlation causes bias in the coefficient estimates.[7]

Serial correlation in a Koyck lag model also causes estimates of the standard errors of the estimated coefficients and the residuals to be biased. The

---

7. The reason that pure serial correlation doesn't cause bias in the coefficient estimates of equations that don't include a lagged dependent variable is that the "omitted variable" ϵ_{t-1} isn't correlated with any of the included independent variables.

former bias means that hypothesis testing is invalid, even for large samples. The latter bias means that tests based on the residuals, like the Durbin–Watson *d* test, are potentially invalid.

12.2.2 Testing Koyck Lag Models for Serial Correlation

Until now, we've relied on the Durbin–Watson *d* test of Section 9.3 to test for serial correlation, but, as mentioned above, the Durbin–Watson d is potentially invalid for an equation that contains a lagged dependent variable as an independent variable. This is because the biased residuals described in the previous paragraph cause the DW d statistic to be biased toward 2. This bias toward 2 means that the Durbin–Watson test sometimes fails to detect the presence of serial correlation in a Koyck (or similar) lag model.[8]

The most-used alternative is **Durbin's h test**,[9] which is a large-sample method of adjusting the Durbin–Watson d statistic to test for first-order serial correlation in the presence of a lagged dependent variable. The equation for Durbin's h statistic is:

$$h = (1 - 0.5 \cdot d) \sqrt{\frac{n}{(1 - n \cdot [S_\lambda^2])}} \tag{12.17}$$

where: d = the Durbin–Watson statistic
  n = the sample size
  S_λ^2 = the square of the estimated standard error of $\hat{\lambda}$, the estimated coefficient of Y_{t-1}

Durbin's h is normally distributed, so a 95 percent two-tailed test implies a critical z-value of 1.96. Therefore, the decision rule is:

If the absolute value of h is greater than 1.96, reject the null hypothesis of no first-order serial correlation.

If the absolute value of h is less than 1.96, do not reject the null hypothesis of no first-order serial correlation.

As an example, let's test our Koyck distributed lag aggregate consumption function, Equation 12.11, for serial correlation:

---

8. The opposite is not a problem. A Durbin–Watson *d* test that indicates serial correlation in the presence of a lagged dependent variable, despite the bias toward 2, is an even stronger affirmation of serial correlation.

9. J. Durbin, "Testing for Serial Correlation in Least Squares Regression When Some of the Regressors Are Lagged Dependent Variables," *Econometrica*, 1970, pp. 410–421.

$$\widehat{CO}_{t-1} = -38.11 + 0.52YD_t + 0.46CO_{t-1} \qquad (12.11)$$
$$(0.12) \qquad (0.12)$$
$$t = 4.44 \qquad 3.74$$
$$\overline{R}^2 = .998 \qquad n = 31 \qquad DW = 0.89$$

Substituting into Equation 12.17, we obtain:

$$h = (1 - 0.5 \cdot 0.89)\sqrt{\frac{31}{[1 - 31(0.12)^2]}} = 4.15 \qquad (12.18)$$

Since $4.15 > 1.96$, we can reject the null hypothesis of no first-order serial correlation and conclude that, as expected, there is indeed significant serial correlation in our consumption function.

Durbin's h test has at least two problems, however. First, the test statistic is undefined in certain circumstances (when $n \cdot [S_\lambda^2] \geq 1$) because the value under the square root sign in Equation 12.17 is negative. Second, Durbin's h test cannot be used if the model in question has more than one lagged dependent variable or if the serial correlation being tested for isn't first order in nature. Although some researchers adjust Durbin's h in these situations, a more satisfactory solution would be to find a test that avoids these two problems altogether while working just as well in the simple case.

One such test is the Lagrange Multiplier test. The **Lagrange Multiplier (LM) test** is a method that can be used to test for serial correlation in the presence of a lagged dependent variable by analyzing how well the lagged residuals explain the residuals of the original equation (in an equation that includes all the explanatory variables of the original model). If the lagged residuals are significant in explaining this time's residuals (as shown by the chi-square test), then we can reject the null hypothesis of no serial correlation. The Lagrange Multiplier test also is useful as a specification test and as a test for heteroskedasticity and other econometric problems.[10]

Using the Lagrange Multiplier to test for serial correlation for a typical Koyck model involves three steps:

1. Obtain the residuals from the estimated equation:

$$e_t = Y_t - \hat{Y}_t = Y_t - \hat{\alpha}_0 - \hat{\beta}_0 X_{1t} - \hat{\lambda} Y_{t-1} \qquad (12.19)$$

---

10. For example, some readers may remember that the White test of Section 10.3.3 is a Lagrange Multiplier test. For a survey of the various uses to which Lagrange Multiplier tests can be put and a discussion of the LM test's relationship to the Wald and Likelihood Ratio tests, see Robert F. Engle, "Wald, Likelihood Ratio, and Lagrange Multiplier Tests in Econometrics," in Z. Griliches and M. D. Intriligator, eds., *Handbook of Econometrics*, Volume II (Amsterdam: Elsevier Science Publishers, 1984).

2. Use these residuals as the dependent variable in an auxiliary equation that includes as independent variables all those on the right-hand side of the original equation as well as the lagged residuals:

$$e_t = a_0 + a_1 X_t + a_2 Y_{t-1} + a_3 e_{t-1} + u_t \qquad (12.20)$$

3. Estimate Equation 12.20 using OLS and then test the null hypothesis that $a_3 = 0$ with the following test statistic:

$$LM = n \cdot R^2 \qquad (12.21)$$

where n is the sample size and R^2 is the unadjusted coefficient of determination, both of the auxiliary equation, Equation 12.20. For large samples, LM has a chi-square distribution with degrees of freedom equal to the number of restrictions in the null hypothesis (in this case, one). If LM is greater than the critical chi-square value from Statistical Table B-8, then we reject the null hypothesis that $a_3 = 0$ and conclude that there is indeed serial correlation in the original equation.

To run an LM test for second-order or higher-order serial correlation, add lagged residuals (e_{t-2} for second order, e_{t-2} and e_{t-3} for third order) to the auxiliary equation, Equation 12.20. This latter change makes the null hypothesis $a_3 = a_4 = a_5 = 0$. Such a null hypothesis raises the degrees of freedom in the chi-square test to three because we have imposed three restrictions on the equation (three coefficients are jointly set equal to zero). To run an LM test with more than one lagged dependent variable, add the lagged variables (Y_{t-2}, Y_{t-3}, etc.) to the original equation. For practice with the LM test, see Exercise 6; for practice with testing for higher-order serial correlation, see Exercise 7.

12.2.3 Correcting for Serial Correlation in Koyck Models

There are three strategies for attempting to rid a Koyck lag model (or a similar model) of serial correlation: improving the specification, instrumental variables, and modified GLS.

The first strategy is to consider the possibility that the serial correlation could be impure, caused by either omitting a relevant variable or by failing to capture the actual distributed lag pattern accurately. Unfortunately, finding an omitted variable or an improved lag structure is easier said than done, as we've seen in previous chapters. Because of the dangers of sequential specification searches, this option should be considered only if an alternative specification exists that has a theoretically sound justification.

The second strategy, called instrumental variables, consists of substituting a proxy (an "instrument") for Y_{t-1} in the original equation, thus eliminating the correlation between Y_{t-1} and u_t. Although using an instrument is a reasonable option that is straightforward in principle, it's not always easy to find a proxy that retains the distributed lag nature of the original equation. For a more complete discussion of instrumental variables, see Section 14.3.

The final solution to serial correlation in Koyck models (or in models with lagged dependent variables and similar error term structures) is to use an iterative maximum likelihood technique to estimate the components of the serial correlation and then to transform the original equation so that the serial correlation has been eliminated. This technique, which is similar to the GLS procedure outlined in Section 9.4, is not without its complications. In particular, the sample needs to be large, the standard errors of the estimated coefficients potentially need to be adjusted, and the estimation techniques are flawed under some circumstances.[11] In essence, serial correlation causes bias in Koyck distributed lag models, but ridding the equation of that serial correlation is not an easy task.

12.3 Granger Causality

One application of ad hoc distributed lag models is to test the direction of causality in economic relationships. Such a test is useful when we know that two variables are related but we don't know which variable causes the other to move. For example, most economists believe that increases in the money supply stimulate GDP, but others feel that increases in GDP eventually lead the monetary authorities to increase the money supply. Who's right?

One approach to such a question of indeterminate causality is to theorize that the two variables are determined simultaneously. We'll address the estimation of simultaneous equation models in Chapter 14. A second approach to the problem is to test for what is called "Granger causality."

How can we claim to be able to test for causality? After all, didn't we say in Chapter 1 that even though most economic relationships are causal in nature, regression analysis cannot prove such causality? The answer is that we don't actually test for theoretical causality; instead, we test for Granger causality.

---

11. For more on these complications, see A. C. Harvey, *The Econometric Analysis of Time Series* (New York: Wiley, 1981), and R. Betancourt and H. Kelejian, "Lagged Endogenous Variables and Cochrane-Orcutt Procedure," *Econometrica*, 1981, pp. 1073–1078.

Granger causality, or precedence, is a circumstance in which one time-series variable consistently and predictably changes before another variable does.[12] If one variable precedes ("Granger causes") another, we still can't be sure that the first variable "causes" the other to change, but we can be fairly sure that the opposite is not the case.

To see this, suppose event A always happens before event B. It's unlikely that B is the cause of A, isn't it? After all, how often does an event that will happen in the future cause an event that has already happened? In such a situation, we can reject the hypothesis that event B causes event A with a fairly high level of confidence.

On the other hand, we still have not shown that event A "causes" B. Proving that people carry umbrellas around before it rains doesn't prove that carrying the umbrellas actually causes the rain. All we've shown is that one event preceded or, more specifically, "Granger-caused" the other. Granger causality is important because it allows us to analyze which variable precedes or "leads" the other, and, as we shall see, such leading variables are extremely useful for forecasting purposes. Despite the value of Granger causality, however, we shouldn't let ourselves be lured into thinking that it allows us to prove economic causality in any rigorous way.

There are a number of different tests for Granger causality, and all the various methods involve distributed lag models in one way or another.[13] Our preference is to use an expanded version of a test originally developed by Granger. Granger suggested that to see if B Granger-caused Y, we should run:

$$Y_t = f(Y_{t-1}, Y_{t-2}, \ldots, Y_{t-p}, B_{t-1}, B_{t-2}, \ldots, B_{t-p}) + \epsilon_t \qquad (12.22)$$

and test the null hypothesis that the coefficients of the lagged Bs jointly equal zero. If we can reject this null hypothesis using the F-test, then we have evidence that B Granger-causes Y. Note that if $p = 1$, Equation 12.22 is similar to a Koyck distributed lag model.

---

12. See C. W. J. Granger, "Investigating Causal Relations by Econometric Models and Cross-Spectral Methods," *Econometrica*, 1969, pp. 24–36.

13. Perhaps the most famous of these tests is the Sims test: Christopher A. Sims, "Money, Causality, and Income," *American Economic Review*, 1972, pp. 540–552. Unfortunately, the Sims test has some problems, especially its inability to deal with serially correlated future values of independent variables. See John Geweke, R. Meese, and W. Dent, "Comparing Alternative Tests of Causality in Temporal Systems," *Journal of Econometrics*, 1982, pp. 161–194, and Rodney Jacobs, Edward Leamer, and Michael Ward, "Difficulties with Testing for Causation," *Economic Inquiry*, 1979, pp. 401–413.

For a number of reasons, we recommend running two Granger tests, one in each direction. That is, run Equation 12.22 and also run:

$$B_t = f(Y_{t-1}, Y_{t-2}, \ldots, Y_{t-p}, B_{t-1}, B_{t-2}, \ldots, B_{t-p}) + \epsilon_t \qquad (12.23)$$

testing for Granger causality in both directions. If the *F*-test is significant for Equation 12.22 but not for Equation 12.23, then we can conclude that B Granger-causes Y. For practice with this dual version of the Granger test, see Exercise 8.

12.4   Spurious Correlation and Nonstationarity

One problem with time-series data is that independent variables can appear to be more significant than they actually are if they have the same underlying trend as the dependent variable. In a country with rampant inflation, for example, almost any nominal variable will appear to be highly correlated with all other nominal variables. Why? Nominal variables are unadjusted for inflation, so every nominal variable will have a powerful inflationary component. This inflationary component will usually outweigh any real causal relationship, causing nominal variables to appear to be correlated even if they aren't.

Such a problem is an example of **spurious correlation,** a strong relationship between two or more variables that is caused by a statistical fluke or by the nature of the specification of the variables, not by a real underlying causal relationship. If you run a regression in which the dependent variable and one or more independent variables are spuriously correlated, the result is a *spurious regression,* and the t-scores and overall fit of such spurious regressions are likely to be overstated and untrustworthy.

There are many causes of spurious correlation. In a cross-sectional data set, for example, spurious correlation can be caused by dividing the dependent variable and one independent variable by a third variable that varies considerably more than do the first two. The focus of this section, however, will be on time-series data and in particular on spurious correlation caused by nonstationary time series.

12.4.1 Stationary and Nonstationary Time Series

A *stationary* time series is one whose basic properties don't change over time. In contrast, a nonstationary variable has some sort of upward or downward trend. For instance, a nominal aggregate variable for an inflationary country is very likely to be nonstationary but a real per capita version of the same variable in the same country might be stationary.

More formally, a time-series variable, X_t, is **stationary** if:

1. the mean of X_t is constant over time,
2. the variance of X_t is constant over time, and
3. the simple correlation coefficient between X_t and X_{t-k} (also called an autocorrelation function) depends on the length of the lag (k) but on no other variable (for all k).[14]

If one or more of these three properties is not met, then X_t is **nonstationary.** If a series is nonstationary, that problem is often referred to as **nonstationarity.**

Before going on, let's discuss two concepts. First, the autocorrelation functions (ACFs) mentioned in property number 3 are not as forbidding as they might seem at first glance. To calculate an autocorrelation function of lag k, compute the simple correlation coefficient between X_t and X_{t-k} over the $n - k$ such pairs in the data set:

$$ACF(k) = \frac{\sum (X_t - \bar{X})(X_{t-k} - \bar{X})}{\sum (X_t - \bar{X})^2} \qquad (12.24)$$

For practice with autocorrelation functions, see Exercise 10 at the end of the chapter. Second, although our definition of a stationary series focuses on stationary and nonstationary *variables,* it's important to note that *error terms* (and, therefore, residuals) can also be nonstationary. In fact, we've already had experience with a nonstationary error term. Most cases of heteroskedasticity in time-series data involve an error term with a variance that increases with each time period. Thus, a heteroskedastic error term is also nonstationary!

The major consequence of nonstationarity for regression analysis is spurious correlation that inflates $\bar{R}^2$ and the t-scores of the nonstationary independent variables. This occurs because the regression estimation procedure attributes to the nonstationary X_t changes in Y_t that were actually caused by some factor (trend, for example) that also affects X_t. Thus, the variables move together because of the nonstationarity, increasing $\bar{R}^2$ and the relevant t-scores. This is especially important in macroeconometrics, and the literature is dominated by articles that examine various macroeconomic series for signs of nonstationarity.[15]

---

14. There are a number of different kinds of stationarity. The particular definition we use here is a simplification of the most frequently cited definition, referred to by various authors as a weak, wide-sense, or covariance stationarity.

15. See, for example, C. R. Nelson and C. I. Plosser, "Trends and Random Walks in Macroeconomic Time Series: Some Evidence and Implication," *Journal of Monetary Economics,* 1982, pp. 169–182, and J. Campbell and N. G. Mankiw, "Permanent and Transitory Components in Macroeconomic Fluctuations," *American Economic Review,* May 1987, pp. 111–117.

12.4.2 Testing for Nonstationarity

How can you tell if a time series is nonstationary? There are at least three ways. The first and easiest test is to visually examine the data. For many time series, a quick glance at the data (or a diagram of the data) will tell you that the mean of a variable is increasing dramatically over time and that the series is nonstationary.

A second, more careful, test is to see if the ACFs for a variable tend to zero as k (the length of the lag) increases, using the *t*-test of r described in Chapter 5, to see if the ACF is significantly different from 0. If the ACFs tend to zero fairly quickly, the variable is stationary, but if they don't, the variable is nonstationary. For practice in this kind of testing, see Exercise 10.

The third and most popular method of testing for nonstationarity is the **Dickey–Fuller test,** which examines the hypothesis that the variable in question has a unit root and, as a result, is likely to benefit from being expressed in first-difference form.[16] To run a Dickey–Fuller test, estimate the following equation:

$$\Delta Y_t = (Y_t - Y_{t-1}) = \beta_0 + \beta_1 Y_{t-1} + \epsilon_t \qquad (12.25)$$

and run a one-sided *t*-test on the hypothesis that $\beta_1 = 0$.

$$H_0: \beta_1 = 0$$
$$H_A: \beta_1 < 0$$

If $\hat{\beta}_1$ is significantly less than 0, then we can reject the null hypothesis of non-stationarity. On the other hand, recall from Chapter 5 that if we're *not* able to reject the null hypothesis, we still have not "proven" that Y is nonstationary.

Be careful, however. The standard t-table does not apply to Dickey–Fuller tests; Table 12.1 lists asymptotic $(n \to \infty)$ values for t_c. For smaller samples, critical t-values are about 60 percent higher (in absolute value) than those in

---

16. D. A. Dickey and W. A. Fuller, "Distribution of the Estimators for Autoregressive Time-Series with a Unit Root," *Journal of the American Statistical Association*, 1979, pp. 427–431. The Dickey–Fuller test comes in a variety of forms, including an augmented test to use in cases of a serially correlated error term. The phrase "unit root" refers to the possibility that $\beta_1 = 1$ in $Y_t = \beta_0 + \beta_1 Y_{t-1} + \epsilon_t$. If β_1 exactly equals 1, Y_t can be characterized by a random walk process, where the change in Y is assumed to be drawn from a distribution with a mean of zero. This process is inherently nonstationary. For more on unit roots, see John Y. Campbell and Pierre Peron, "Pitfalls and Opportunities: What Macroeconomists Should Know About Unit Roots," *NBER Macroeconomics Annual* (Cambridge: MIT Press, 1991), pp. 141–219.

TABLE 12.1 ASYMPTOTIC CRITICAL VALUES FOR THE DICKEY–FULLER TEST

One-Sided Significance Level:	.01	.025	.05	.10
t_c	3.43	3.12	2.86	2.57

Statistical Table B-1. For example, a 2.5 percent one-sided t-test of $\hat{\beta}_1$ from Equation 12.25 with 50 degrees of freedom has a critical t-value of 3.22, compared to 2.01 for a standard t-test.[17] For practice in running Dickey–Fuller tests, see Exercise 11.

12.4.3 Adjusting for Nonstationarity

If one of our three tests reveals nonstationarity, what should we do? Some authors attempt to "detrend" an equation by including a time-trend variable ($t = 1, 2, \ldots, T$) as an independent variable in the regression, but we urge you not to do so for a number of reasons.[18]

Instead, if it's necessary to rid a series of nonstationarity, the traditional practice has been to take a first difference:

$$\Delta Y_t = Y_t - Y_{t-1} \qquad (12.26)$$

and use ΔY_t in place of Y_t in the equation. With economic data, taking a first difference usually is enough to convert a nonstationary series to a stationary one, but it's a good habit to test ΔY_t just to make sure. Unfortunately, there are major disadvantages to using first differences to correct for nonstationarity. The two most important of these drawbacks are that using first differences (a) changes the inherent theoretical meaning of the differenced variable, and (b) discards information about the long-run trend in that variable. As a result, first differences should not be used without weighing the costs and benefits of that shift.

---

17. For adjusted critical t-values for the Dickey–Fuller test, including those in Table 12.1, see J. G. MacKinnon, "Critical Values of Cointegration Tests," in Rob Engle and C. W. J. Granger, eds., *Long-Run Economic Relationships: Readings in Cointegration* (New York: Oxford University Press, 1991), Chapter 13.

18. See C. R. Nelson and H. Kang, "Pitfalls in the Use of Time as an Explanatory Variable in Regression," *Journal of Business and Economic Statistics*, January 1984, pp. 73–82. An exception to this recommendation is that if both a unit root *and* a time trend are present, it's important to include the time trend as an independent variable when constructing a test statistic for a unit root.

An important alternative to using first differences to correct for nonstationarity is a concept called *cointegration*. **Cointegration** consists of matching up the degree of nonstationarity of the variables in an equation in a way that makes the residuals of the equation stationary and rids the equation of any spurious regression results.[19]

Consider, for example, the following equation:

$$Y_t = \beta_0 + \beta_1 X_t + \epsilon_t \tag{12.27}$$

Suppose that both Y_t and X_t are nonstationary to the same degree; that is, suppose that ΔY_t and ΔX_t are both stationary. In such a situation there's a reasonable possibility that the nonstationarity in the two variables will "cancel each other out," leaving Equation 12.27 as a whole free of nonstationarity. An OLS estimate of Equation 12.27 would not be spurious, given such a situation.

How can you tell if any nonstationarity in an equation is cointegrated? The answer is to test the residuals of the equation for stationarity, using, say, the Dickey–Fuller test. If the residuals are stationary, then we have evidence that the nonstationary variables in the equation are on the same wavelength and that first differences are not necessary. In our example, this would mean estimating Equation 12.27, solving for the residual e_t:

$$e_t = \hat{Y}_t - \hat{\beta}_0 - \hat{\beta}_1 X_t \tag{12.28}$$

and running a test for nonstationarity on e_t. Once again, however, the standard t-values do not apply to this application. Instead, adjusted critical t-values developed by Engle and Granger should be used.[20] The values in Statistical Table B-1 are only slightly lower than these adjusted critical t-values, however, so they can be used as rough estimates of the more accurate figures.

12.5 Summary

1. A distributed lag model explains the current value of Y as a function of current and past values of X, thus "distributing" the impact of X over a number of lagged time periods. OLS estimation of distributed lag equations without any constraints (ad hoc distributed lags) en-

19. For more on cointegration, see B. Bhaskara Rau, ed., *Cointegration for the Applied Economist* (New York: St. Martin's Press, 1994).

20. Rob Engle and C. W. J. Granger, "Co-integration and Error Correction: Representation, Estimation and Testing," *Econometrica*, 1987, pp. 251–276.

counters problems with multicollinearity, degrees of freedom, and a noncontinuous pattern of coefficients over time.

2. A Koyck distributed lag model avoids these problems by assuming that the coefficients of the lagged independent variables decrease in a geometric fashion the longer the lag ($\beta_i = \beta_0 \lambda^i$), where i is the length of the lag and $0 < \lambda < 1$. Given this, the Koyck distributed lag equation can be simplified to:

$$Y_t = \alpha_0 + \beta_0 X_t + \lambda Y_{t-1} + u_t$$

where $u_t = \epsilon_t - \lambda\epsilon_{t-1}$ and where Y_{t-1} is a lagged dependent variable. Thus, the use of a lagged dependent variable as an independent variable usually implies a Koyck distributed lag model.

3. In small samples, OLS estimates of a Koyck distributed lag model (or a similar model) are biased and have unreliable hypothesis testing properties. Even in large samples, OLS will produce biased estimates of the coefficients of a Koyck (or similar) model if the error term is serially correlated.

4. In a Koyck lag (or similar) model, the Durbin–Watson d test sometimes can fail to detect the presence of serial correlation because d is biased toward 2. The most-used alternative is Durbin's h test, even though the Lagrange Multiplier test has similar properties and is more generally applicable.

5. Granger causality, or precedence, is a circumstance in which one time-series variable consistently and predictably changes before another variable does. If one variable precedes (Granger-causes) another, we still can't be sure that the first variable "causes" the other to change, but we can be fairly sure that the opposite is not the case.

6. A nonstationary series is one that exhibits a significant trend (for example in its mean or variance) over time. If the dependent variable and at least one independent variable are nonstationary, a regression is likely to encounter spurious correlation that inflates R^2 and the t-scores of the nonstationary independent variable(s).

7. Nonstationarity can be detected using a number of tests, including visual inspection of the data and the Dickey–Fuller test. The most-used remedy for nonstationarity is converting the series to first differences, but this solution changes the theoretical underpinnings and long-term trend in the series.

Exercises

(Answers to even-numbered exercises are in Appendix A.)

1. Write the meaning of each of the following terms without referring to
    the book (or your notes), and then compare your definition with the
    version in the text for each:
    a. Koyck distributed lag model
    b. ad hoc distributed lag model
    c. Durbin's h test
    d. Lagrange Multiplier (LM) test
    e. nonstationary series
    f. Dickey–Fuller test
    g. autocorrelation function (ACF)
    h. cointegration

2. Calculate and graph the pattern of the impact of a lagged X on Y as
    the lag increases for each of the following estimated Koyck distributed
    lag equations.
    a. $Y_t = 13.0 + 12.0X_t + 0.04Y_{t-1}$
    b. $Y_t = 13.0 + 12.0X_t + 0.08Y_{t-1}$
    c. $Y_t = 13.0 + 12.0X_t + 2.0Y_{t-1}$
    d. $Y_t = 13.0 + 12.0X_t - 0.4Y_{t-1}$
    e. Look over your graphs for parts c and d. What λ restriction do they
       combine to show the wisdom of?

3. Consider the following equation aimed at estimating the demand for
    real cash balances in Mexico (standard errors in parentheses):

    $$\widehat{lnM_t} = 2.00 - 0.10lnR_t + 0.70lnY_t + 0.60lnM_{t-1}$$
    $$\phantom{\widehat{lnM_t} = 2.00 - } (0.10) \qquad (0.35) \qquad (0.10)$$
    $$\overline{R}^2 = .90 \qquad DW = 1.80 \qquad n = 26$$

    where: M_t = the money stock in year t (millions of pesos)
    R_t = the long-term interest rate in year t (percent)
    Y_t = the real GNP in year t (millions of pesos)

    a. What economic relationship between Y and M is implied by the
       equation?
    b. How are Y and R similar in terms of their relationship to M?
    c. Test for serial correlation in this equation.
    d. Now suppose you learn that the estimated standard error of the es-
       timated coefficient of lnM_{t-1} is actually 0.30. How does this
       change your answer to part c above?

4. Consider the following equation for the determination of wages in the United Kingdom (standard error in parentheses)[21]:

$$\widehat{W}_t = 8.562 + 0.364P_t + 0.004P_{t-1} - 2.56U_t$$
$$(0.080) \quad (0.072) \quad\quad (0.658)$$
$$\overline{R}^2 = .87 \quad\quad n = 19$$

where: W_t = wages and salaries per employee in year t
P_t = the price level in year t
U_t = the unemployment in year t

a. Develop and test your own hypotheses with respect to the individual slope coefficients at the 90 percent level.
b. Discuss the theoretical validity of P_{t-1} and how your opinion of that validity has been changed by its statistical significance. Should P_{t-1} be dropped from the equation? Why or why not?
c. If P_{t-1} is dropped from the equation, the general functional form of the equation changes radically? Why?

5. You've been hired to determine the impact of advertising on gross sales revenue for "Four Musketeers" candy bars. Four Musketeers has the same price and more or less the same ingredients as competing candy bars, so it seems likely that only advertising affects sales. You decide to build a distributed lag model of sales as a function of advertising, but you're not sure whether an ad hoc or a Koyck distributed lag model is more appropriate.

   Using data on Four Musketeers candy bars from Table 12.2, estimate both of the following distributed lag equations from 1976–2000 and compare the lag structures implied by the estimated coefficients (*Hint:* Be careful to use the correct sample.):
   a. an ad hoc distributed lag model (4 lags)
   b. a Koyck distributed lag model

6. Test for serial correlation in the estimated Koyck lag equation you got as your answer to Exercise 5b by using:
   a. Durbin's *h* test
   b. The Lagrange Multiplier test

7. Suppose you're building a Koyck distributed lag model and are concerned with the possibility that serial correlation, instead of being first order, is second order: $u_t = f(u_{t-1}, u_{t-2})$.

---

21. *Prices and Earnings in 1951–1969: An Econometric Assessment,* United Kingdom Department of Employment, 1971, p. 35.

TABLE 12.2 DATA FOR THE FOUR MUSKETEERS EXERCISE

Year	Sales	Advertising
1972	*	30
1973	*	35
1974	*	36
1975	320	39
1976	360	40
1977	390	45
1978	400	50
1979	410	50
1980	400	50
1981	450	53
1982	470	55
1983	500	60
1984	500	60
1985	490	60
1986	580	65
1987	600	70
1988	700	70
1989	790	60
1990	730	60
1991	720	60
1992	800	70
1993	820	80
1994	830	80
1995	890	80
1996	900	80
1997	850	75
1998	840	75
1999	850	75
2000	850	75

Note: filename MOUSE12

    a. What is the theoretical meaning of such second-order serial correlation?

    b. Carefully write out the formula for the Lagrange Multiplier auxiliary equation (similar to Equation 12.20) that you would have to estimate to test such a possibility. How many degrees of freedom would there be in such a Lagrange Multiplier test?

    c. Test for second-order serial correlation in the estimated Koyck lag equation you got as your answer to Exercise 5b above.

8. Most economists consider investment and output to be jointly (simultaneously) determined. One test of this simultaneity would be to

see whether one of the variables could be shown to Granger-cause the other. Take the data set from the small macroeconomic model in Table 14.1 and test the possibility that investment (I) Granger-causes GDP (Y) (or vice versa) with a two-sided Granger test with four lagged Xs.

9. Some farmers were interested in predicting inches of growth of corn as a function of rainfall on a monthly basis, so they collected data from the growing season and estimated an equation of the following form:

$$G_t = \beta_0 + \beta_1 R_t + \beta_2 G_{t-1} + \epsilon_t$$

where: G_t = inches of growth of corn in month t
         R_t = inches of rain in month t
         ϵ_t = a normally distributed classical error term

Although the farmers expected a negative sign for β_2 (they felt that since corn can only grow so much, if it grows a lot in one month, it won't grow much in the next month), they got a positive estimate instead. What suggestions would you have for this problem?

10. Calculate the following autocorrelation functions (ACFs) using the data from the small macroeconomic model in Table 14.1 and then determine which of the variables, if any, you think are nonstationary. Explain your answer. [*Hint:* To calculate the ACFs on EViews, bring up the data, create the appropriate lagged versions of each variable (remembering to adjust for the smaller sample size), and then have the computer calculate the simple correlation coefficient between the variable and itself lagged k times.]
    a. Y   (GDP), using ACFs with k = 2 and k = 6
    b. r   (the interest rate), using ACFs with k = 2 and k = 6
    c. CO (consumption), using ACFs with k = 2 and k = 6
    d. I   (investment), using ACFs with k = 2 and k = 6

11. Run 2.5 percent Dickey–Fuller tests (of the form in Equation 12.25) for the following variables using the data from the small macroeconomic model in Table 14.1 and determine which variables, if any, you think are nonstationary. (*Hint:* Use 3.22 as your critical t-value.)
    a. Y   (GDP)
    b. r   (the interest rate)
    c. CO (consumption)
    d. I   (investment)

CHAPTER 13

Dummy Dependent Variable Techniques

Until now, our discussion of dummy variables has been restricted to dummy independent variables. However, there are many important research topics for which the *dependent* variable is appropriately treated as a dummy, equal only to zero or one.

In particular, researchers analyzing consumer choice often must cope with dummy dependent variables (also called qualitative dependent variables). For example, how do high school students decide whether to go to college? What distinguishes Pepsi drinkers from Coke drinkers? How can we convince people to commute using public transportation instead of driving? For an econometric study of these topics, or of any topic that involves a *discrete* choice of some sort, the dependent variable is typically a dummy variable.

In the first two sections of this chapter, we'll present two frequently used ways to estimate equations that have dummy dependent variables: the linear probability method and the binomial logit model. In the last section, we'll briefly discuss two other useful dummy dependent variable techniques: the binomial probit model and the multinomial logit model.

13.1   The Linear Probability Model

13.1.1 What Is a Linear Probability Model?

The most obvious way to estimate a model with a dummy dependent variable is to run OLS on a typical linear econometric equation. A **linear proba-**

bility model is just that, a linear-in-the-coefficients equation used to explain a dummy dependent variable:

$$D_i = \beta_0 + \beta_1 X_{1i} + \beta_2 X_{2i} + \epsilon_i \qquad (13.1)$$

where D_i is a dummy variable and the Xs, βs, and ϵ are typical independent variables, regression coefficients, and an error term, respectively.

For example, suppose you're interested in understanding why some state legislatures voted to ratify the Equal Rights Amendment (ERA) to the Constitution and others did not. In such a model, the appropriate dependent variable would be a dummy, for example D_i equal to one if the ith state ratified the ERA and equal to zero otherwise. If we hypothesize that states with a high percentage of females and a low percentage of Republicans would be likely to have approved the amendment, then a linear probability model of ERA voting by state would be:

$$D_i = \beta_0 + \beta_1 F_i + \beta_2 R_i + \epsilon_i$$

where: $\quad D_i$ = 1 if the ith state ratified the ERA, 0 otherwise
$\qquad\quad F_i$ = females as a percent of the ith state's population
$\qquad\quad R_i$ = Republicans as a percent of the ith state's registered voters

The term *linear probability model* comes from the fact that the right-hand side of the equation is linear, while the expected value of the left side is a probability. Let's discuss more thoroughly the concept that this equation measures a probability. It can be shown that the expected value of D_i equals the probability that D_i will equal one.[1] If we define P_i as the probability that D_i equals one, then this is the same as saying that the expected value of D_i equals P_i. Since Equation 13.1 specifies this choice as a function of X_{1i}, X_{2i}, this can be formally stated as:

$$E[D_i | X_{1i}, X_{2i}] = P_i \qquad (13.2)$$

We can never observe the probability P_i, however, because it reflects the state of mind of a decision maker *before* a discrete choice is made. After a choice is made, we can observe only the outcome of that choice, and so the dependent

---

1. The expected value of a variable equals the sum of the products of each of the possible values the variable can take times the probability of that value occurring. If P_i is defined as the probability that D_i will equal one, then the probability that D_i will equal zero is $(1 - P_i)$, since D_i can take on only two values. Thus, the expected value of $D_i = P_i \cdot 1 + (1 - P_i) \cdot 0 = P_i$, the probability that D_i equals one.

variable D_i can take on the values of only zero or one. Thus, even though the expected value (P_i) can be anywhere from zero to one, we can only observe the two extremes (0 and 1) in our dependent variable (D_i).

13.1.2 Problems with the Linear Probability Model

Unfortunately, the use of OLS to estimate the coefficients of an equation with a dummy dependent variable encounters four major problems:

1. *The error term is not normally distributed.* Because the dependent variable takes on only two values, the error term is binomial, and Classical Assumption VII is violated. This flaw makes hypothesis testing unreliable.

2. *The error term is inherently heteroskedastic.* The variance of ϵ_i equals $P_i \cdot (1 - P_i)$, where P_i is the probability that D_i equals 1. Since P_i can vary from observation to observation, so too can the variance of ϵ_i. Thus the variance of ϵ_i is not constant, and Classical Assumption V is violated.

3. *$\overline{R}^2$ is not an accurate measure of overall fit.* For models with a dummy dependent variable, $\overline{R}^2$ tells us very little about how well the model explains the choices of the decision makers. To see why, take a look at Figure 13.1. D_i can equal only 1 or 0, but $\hat{D}_i$ must move in a continuous fashion from one extreme to the other. This means that $\hat{D}_i$ is likely to be quite different from D_i for some range of X_i. Thus, $\overline{R}^2$ is likely to be much lower than 1 even if the model actually does an exceptional job of explaining the choices involved. As a result, $\overline{R}^2$ (or R^2) should not be relied on as a measure of the overall fit of a model with a dummy dependent variable.

4. *$\hat{D}_i$ is not bounded by 0 and 1.* Since the expected value of D_i is a probability, we'd expect $\hat{D}_i$ to be limited to a range of 0 to 1. After all, the prediction that a probability equals 2.6 (or -2.6, for that matter) is almost meaningless. However, take another look at Equation 13.1. Depending on the values of the Xs and the $\hat{\beta}$s, the right-hand side might well be outside the meaningful range. For instance, if all the Xs and $\hat{\beta}$s in Equation 13.1 equal 2.0, then $\hat{D}_i$ equals 10.0, substantially greater than 1.0.

Luckily, there are potential solutions to the first three problems cited above. First, the nonnormality problem can be ignored in coefficient estimation

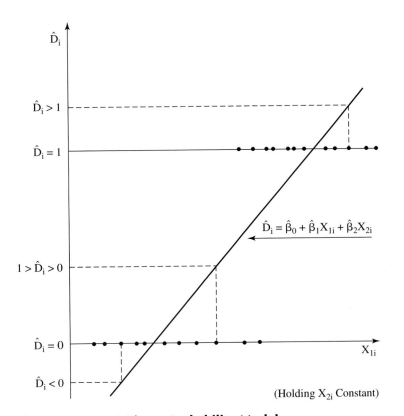

Figure 13.1   A Linear Probability Model

In a linear probability model, all the observed D_is equal either zero or one but $\hat{D}_i$ moves linearly from one extreme to the other. As a result, $\bar{R}^2$ is often quite low even if the model does an excellent job of explaining the decision maker's choice. In addition, exceptionally large or small values of X_{1i} (holding X_{2i} constant), can produce values of $\hat{D}_i$ outside the meaningful range of zero to one.

because Classical Assumption VII is not used to prove the Gauss–Markov Theorem.

Second, a solution to the heteroskedasticity problem is to use Weighted Least Squares. Recall that we know that the variance of ϵ_i equals $P_i \cdot (1 - P_i)$. As shown in Chapter 10, if we were to divide the equation through by $\sqrt{P_i \cdot (1 - P_i)}$, then the variance of the error term would no longer be heteroskedastic. Although we don't know the actual value of P_i, we do know that P_i equals the expected value of D_i. Thus, if we estimate Equation 13.1 and obtain $\hat{D}_i$, we can use $\hat{D}_i$ as an estimate of P_i. To run Weighted Least Squares, we'd then calculate:

estimate of p

$$Z_i = \sqrt{\hat{D}_i \cdot (1 - \hat{D}_i)} \tag{13.3}$$

divide Equation 13.1 by Z_i, and estimate the new equation with OLS.[2]

Third, an alternative to $\overline{R}^2$ is R_p^2, the percentage of the observations in the sample that a particular estimated equation explains correctly. To use this approach, consider a $\hat{D}_i \geq .5$ to predict that $D_i = 1$ and a $\hat{D}_i < .5$ to predict that $D_i = 0$, compare this prediction with the actual D_i, and then compute:

how likely people outside 0 or 1

$$R_p^2 = \frac{\text{number of observations "predicted" correctly}}{\text{total number of observations (n)}} \tag{13.4}$$

Since R_p^2 is not used universally, we'll calculate and discuss both $\overline{R}^2$ and R_p^2 throughout this chapter.

For most researchers, therefore, the major difficulty with the linear probability model is the unboundedness of the predicted D_is. Take another look at Figure 13.1 for a graphical interpretation of the situation. Because of the linear relationship between the X_is and $\hat{D}_i$, $\hat{D}_i$ can fall well outside the relevant range of 0 to 1. Using the linear probability model, despite this unboundedness problem, may not cause insurmountable difficulties. In particular, the signs and general significance levels of the estimated coefficients of the linear probability model are often similar to those of the alternatives we will discuss later in this chapter.

One simplistic way to get around the unboundedness problem is to assign $\hat{D}_i = 1.0$ to all values of $\hat{D}_i$ above one and $\hat{D}_i = 0.0$ to all negative values. This approach copes with the problem by ignoring it, since an observation for which the linear probability model predicts a probability of 2.0 has been judged to be more likely to be equal to 1.0 than an observation for which the model predicts a 1.0, and yet they are lumped together. What is needed is a systematic method of forcing the $\hat{D}_i$s to range from 0 to 1 in a smooth and meaningful fashion. We'll present such a method, the binomial logit, in Section 13.2.

13.1.3 An Example of a Linear Probability Model

Before moving on to investigate the logit, however, let's take a look at an example of a linear probability model: a disaggregate study of the labor force participation of women.

---

2. Note that when $\hat{D}_i$ is quite close to 0 or 1, $\hat{D}_i \cdot (1 - \hat{D}_i)$ is extremely small and X_i/Z_i is huge. Also note that when $\hat{D}_i$ is outside the 0–1 range, $\hat{D}_i \cdot (1 - \hat{D}_i)$ is negative and Z_i is undefined. See R. G. McGilvray, "Estimating the Linear Probability Function," *Econometrica*, 1970, pp. 775–776. Some researchers arbitrarily drop all such observations to avoid the resulting estimation problems. We think that a better alternative is to impose an arbitrary floor, say 0.02, on $\hat{D}_i \cdot (1 - \hat{D}_i)$. Either way, WLS is not efficient.

A person is defined as being in the labor force if she either has a job or is actively looking for a job. Thus, a disaggregate (cross-sectional by person) study of women's labor force participation is appropriately modeled with a dummy dependent variable:

$$D_i = 1 \text{ if the } i\text{th woman has or is looking for a job,}$$
$$0 \text{ otherwise (not in the labor force)}$$

A review of the literature[3] reveals that there are many potentially relevant independent variables. Two of the most important are the marital status and the number of years of schooling of the woman. The expected signs for the coefficients of these variables are fairly straightforward, since a woman who is unmarried and well educated is much more likely to be in the labor force than her opposite:

$$D_i = f(\overset{-}{M_i}, \overset{+}{S_i}) + \epsilon_i$$

where: M_i = 1 if the ith woman is married and 0 otherwise
S_i = the number of years of schooling of the ith woman

The data are presented in Table 13.1. The sample size is limited to 30 in order to make it easier for readers to estimate this example on their own. Unfortunately, such a small sample will make hypothesis testing fairly unreliable. Table 13.1 also includes the age of the ith woman for use in Exercises 8 and 9. Another typically used variable, O_i = other income available to the ith woman, is not available for this sample, introducing possible omitted variable bias.

If we choose a linear functional form for both independent variables, we've got a linear probability model:

$$D_i = \beta_0 + \beta_1 M_i + \beta_2 S_i + \epsilon_i \tag{13.5}$$

where ϵ_i is an inherently heteroskedastic error term with variance = $P_i \cdot (1 - P_i)$. If we now estimate Equation 13.5 with the data on the labor force participation of women from Table 13.1, we obtain (standard errors in parentheses):

3. See James P. Smith and Michael P. Ward, "Time-Series Growth in the Female Labor Force," *Journal of Labor Economics*, 1985, pp. 559–590. Smith and Ward include a number of estimated logits in their work.

TABLE 13.1 DATA ON THE LABOR FORCE PARTICIPATION OF WOMEN

Observation #	D_i	M_i	A_i	S_i	$\hat{D}_i$	$\hat{D}_i(1 - \hat{D}_i)$	Z_i
1	1.0	0.0	31.0	16.0	1.20	0.020	0.141
2	1.0	1.0	34.0	14.0	0.63	0.231	0.481
3	1.0	1.0	41.0	16.0	0.82	0.146	0.382
4	0.0	0.0	67.0	9.0	0.55	0.247	0.497
5	1.0	0.0	25.0	12.0	0.83	0.139	0.374
6	0.0	1.0	58.0	12.0	0.45	0.247	0.497
7	1.0	0.0	45.0	14.0	1.01	0.020	0.141
8	1.0	0.0	55.0	10.0	0.64	0.228	0.478
9	0.0	0.0	43.0	12.0	0.83	0.139	0.374
10	1.0	0.0	55.0	8.0	0.45	0.248	0.498
11	1.0	0.0	25.0	11.0	0.73	0.192	0.439
12	1.0	0.0	41.0	14.0	1.01	0.020	0.141
13	0.0	1.0	62.0	12.0	0.45	0.247	0.497
14	1.0	1.0	51.0	13.0	0.54	0.248	0.498
15	0.0	1.0	39.0	9.0	0.17	0.141	0.376
16	1.0	0.0	35.0	10.0	0.64	0.228	0.478
17	1.0	1.0	40.0	14.0	0.63	0.231	0.481
18	0.0	1.0	43.0	10.0	0.26	0.194	0.440
19	0.0	1.0	37.0	12.0	0.45	0.247	0.497
20	1.0	0.0	27.0	13.0	0.92	0.069	0.263
21	1.0	0.0	28.0	14.0	1.01	0.020	0.141
22	1.0	1.0	48.0	12.0	0.45	0.247	0.497
23	0.0	1.0	66.0	7.0	−0.01	0.020	0.141
24	0.0	1.0	44.0	11.0	0.35	0.229	0.479
25	0.0	1.0	21.0	12.0	0.45	0.247	0.497
26	1.0	1.0	40.0	10.0	0.26	0.194	0.440
27	1.0	0.0	41.0	15.0	1.11	0.020	0.141
28	0.0	1.0	23.0	10.0	0.26	0.194	0.440
29	0.0	1.0	31.0	11.0	0.35	0.229	0.479
30	1.0	1.0	44.0	12.0	0.45	0.247	0.497

Note: $\hat{D}_i(1 - \hat{D}_i)$ has been set equal to 0.02 for all values of $\hat{D}_i$ less than 0.02 or greater than 0.98.
filename WOMEN13 (In this datafile D is represented by J.)

$$\hat{D}_i = -0.28 - 0.38M_i + 0.09S_i \tag{13.6}$$
$$(0.15) \quad (0.03)$$
$$n = 30 \quad \overline{R}^2 = .32 \quad R_p^2 = .80$$

How do these results look? At first glance, they look terrific. Despite the small
sample and the possible bias due to omitting O_i, both independent variables
have estimated coefficients that are significant in the expected direction. In

addition, the $\overline{R}^2$ of .32 is fairly high for a linear probability model (since D_i equals only 0 or 1, it's almost impossible to get a $\overline{R}^2$ much higher than .70). Further evidence of good fit is the fairly high R_p^2 of .80, meaning that 80 percent of the choices were predicted "correctly" by Equation 13.6.

We need to be careful when we interpret the estimated coefficients in Equation 13.6, however. The slope coefficient in a linear probability model represents the change in the probability that D_i equals one caused by a one-unit increase in the independent variable (holding the other independent variables constant). Viewed in this context, do the estimated coefficients still make economic sense? The answer is yes: the probability of a woman participating in the labor force falls by 38 percent if she is married (holding constant her schooling). In addition, each year of schooling increases the probability of labor force participation by 9 percent (holding constant marital status).

However, Equation 13.6 is far from perfect. Recall that the error term is inherently heteroskedastic, that hypothesis testing is unreliable in such a small sample, that $\overline{R}^2$ is not an accurate measure of fit, and that one or more relevant variables have been omitted. While we can do nothing about some of these problems, there is a solution to the heteroskedasticity problem: Weighted Least Squares (WLS).

To use WLS, we take the $\hat{D}_i$ from Equation 13.6 and calculate $Z_i = \sqrt{\hat{D}_i \cdot (1 - \hat{D}_i)}$, as in Equation 13.3 [taking care to impose a floor of 0.02 on $\hat{D}_i \cdot (1 - \hat{D}_i)$ as suggested in footnote 2.] We then divide Equation 13.5 through by Z_i, obtaining:

$$D_i/Z_i = \alpha_0 + \beta_0(1/Z_i) = \beta_1 M_i/Z_i + \beta_2 S_i/Z_i + u_i \qquad (13.7)$$

where u_i is a nonheteroskedastic error term $= \epsilon_i/Z_i$. Note that since Z_i is not an independent variable in Equation 13.6, we have chosen to add α_0, a constant term, to Equation 13.7 to avoid violating Classical Assumption II (as discussed in Chapter 9). If we now estimate Equation 13.7 with OLS, we obtain:

$$\widehat{D_i/Z_i} = 0.18 - 0.21(1/Z_i) - 0.39M_i/Z_i + 0.08S_i/Z_i \qquad (13.8)$$
$$(0.15) \qquad (0.02)$$
$$n = 30 \qquad \overline{R}^2 = .86 \qquad R_p^2 = .83$$

Let's compare Equations 13.8 and 13.6. Surprisingly, the estimated standard errors of the estimated coefficients are almost identical in the two equations, indicating that at least for this sample the impact of the heteroskedasticity is minimal. The high $\overline{R}^2$ comes about in part because dividing the entire equation by the same number (Z_i) causes some spurious correlation, especially when some of the Z_i values are quite small. As evidence, note that R_p^2 is only slightly higher in Equation 13.8 than in Equation 13.6 even though $\overline{R}^2$ jumped from .32 to .86.

To make it easier for the reader to reproduce the WLS procedure, the values for $\hat{D}_i \cdot (1 - \hat{D}_i)$ and Z_i have been included in Table 13.1. Also included are the $\hat{D}_i$s from Equation 13.6; note that $\hat{D}_i$ is indeed often outside the meaningful range of 0 and 1, causing most of the problems cited earlier. To attack this problem of the unboundedness of $\hat{D}_i$, however, we need a new estimation technique, so let's take a look at one.

13.2 The Binomial Logit Model

To avoid the possibility that a prediction of D_i might be outside the probability interval of 0 to 1, we no longer model D_i directly. Instead, we model the ratio $D_i/(1 - D_i)$. This ratio is the likelihood, or odds,[4] of obtaining a successful outcome $(D_i = 1)$. If we take the log of this ratio, we have the left side of the equation that has become the standard approach to dummy dependent variable analysis: the binomial logit.

13.2.1 What Is the Binomial Logit?

The **binomial logit** is an estimation technique for equations with dummy dependent variables that avoids the unboundedness problem of the linear probability model by using a variant of the cumulative logistic function:

$$\ln\left(\frac{D_i}{[1 - D_i]}\right) = \beta_0 + \beta_1 X_{1i} + \beta_2 X_{2i} + \epsilon_i \tag{13.9}$$

where D_i is a dummy variable. The expected value of D_i continues to be P_i, the probability that the *i*th person will make the choice described by $D_i = 1$. Consequently, the dependent variable of Equation 13.9 can be thought of as the log of the odds that the choice in question will be made.

How does the logit avoid the unboundedness problem of the linear probability model? It turns out that *both* sides of Equation 13.9 are unbounded. To see this, note that if $D_i = 1$, then the left-side of Equation 13.9 becomes:

---

4. *Odds* refer to the ratio of the number of times a choice will be made divided by the number of times it will not. In today's world, odds are used most frequently with respect to sporting events, such as horse races, on which bets are made.

$$\ln\left(\frac{D_i}{[1 - D_i]}\right) = \ln\left(\frac{1}{0}\right) = \infty \tag{13.10}$$

Similarly, if $D_i = 0$:

$$\ln\left(\frac{D_i}{[1 - D_i]}\right) = \ln\left(\frac{0}{1}\right) = -\infty \tag{13.11}$$

because the log of zero approaches negative infinity.

Are the $\hat{D}_i$s produced by a logit now limited by zero and one? The answer is yes, but to see why we need to solve Equation 13.9 for D_i. It can be shown[5] that Equation 13.9 is equivalent to:

$$D_i = \frac{1}{1 + e^{-[\beta_0 + \beta_1 X_{1i} + \beta_2 X_{2i} + \epsilon_i]}} \tag{13.12}$$

Take a close look at Equation 13.12. What is the largest that $\hat{D}_i$ can be? Well, if $\hat{\beta}_0 + \hat{\beta}_1 X_{1i} + \hat{\beta}_2 X_{2i}$ equals infinity, then:

$$\hat{D}_i = \frac{1}{1 + e^{-\infty}} = \frac{1}{1} = 1 \tag{13.13}$$

because e to the minus infinity equals zero. What's the smallest that $\hat{D}_i$ can be? If $\hat{\beta}_0 + \hat{\beta}_1 X_{1i} + \hat{\beta}_2 X_{2i}$ equals minus infinity, then:

$$\hat{D}_i = \frac{1}{1 + e^{\infty}} = \frac{1}{\infty} = 0 \tag{13.14}$$

Thus, $\hat{D}_i$ is bounded by one and zero. As can be seen in Figure 13.2, $\hat{D}_i$ approaches one and zero very slowly (asymptotically). The binomial logit model therefore avoids the major problem that the linear probability model encounters in dealing with dummy dependent variables. In addition, the logit is quite satisfying to most researchers because it turns out that real-world data often are described well by S-shape patterns like that in Figure 13.2.

Logits cannot be estimated using OLS. Instead, we use **maximum likelihood,** an iterative estimation technique that is especially useful for equations that are nonlinear in the coefficients. Maximum likelihood (ML) estimation is inherently different from least squares in that it chooses coefficient esti-

---

5. Those interested in this proof should see Exercise 4.

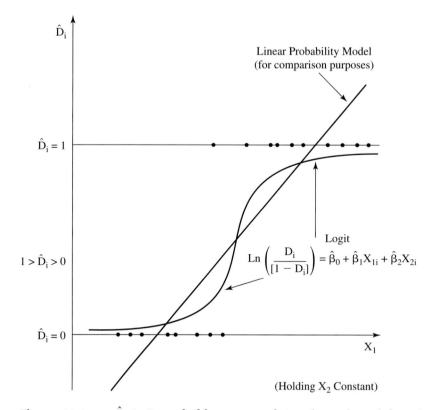

Figure 13.2 $\hat{D}_i$ Is Bounded by Zero and One in a Binomial Logit Model

In a binomial logit model, $\hat{D}_i$ is nonlinearly related to X_1, so even exceptionally large or small values of X_{1i}, holding X_{2i} constant, will not produce values of $\hat{D}_i$ outside the meaningful range of zero to one.

mates that *maximize the likelihood* of the sample data set being observed.[6] Interestingly, OLS and ML estimates are not necessarily different; for a linear equation that meets the Classical Assumptions (including the normality assumption), ML estimates are identical to the OLS ones.

One of the reasons that maximum likelihood is used is that ML has a number of desirable large sample properties; ML is consistent and asymptotically efficient (unbiased and minimum variance for large samples). With very

6. Actually, the ML program chooses coefficient estimates that maximize the log of the probability (or likelihood) of observing the particular set of values of the dependent variable in the sample $(Y_1, Y_2, \ldots, Y_n)$ for a given set of Xs. For more on maximum likelihood, see Robert S. Pindyck and Daniel L. Rubinfeld, *Economic Models and Economic Forecasts* (New York: McGraw-Hill, 1998), pp. 51–53 and 329–330.

large samples, ML has the added advantage of producing normally distributed coefficient estimates, allowing the use of typical hypothesis testing techniques. As a result, sample sizes for logits should be substantially larger than for linear regressions. Some researchers aim for samples of 500 or more.

It's also important to make sure that a logit sample contains a reasonable representation of both alternative choices. For instance, if 98 percent of a sample chooses alternative A and 2 percent chooses B, a random sample of 500 would have only 10 observations that choose B. In such a situation, our estimated coefficients would be overly reliant on the characteristics of those 10 observations. A better technique would be to disproportionately sample from those who choose B. It turns out that using different sampling rates for subgroups within the sample does not cause bias in the slope coefficients of a logit model,[7] even though it might do so in a linear regression.

The maximum likelihood computer program is applied to a logit that has been solved for D_i (Equation 13.12), not to a logit solved for the log of the odds (Equation 13.9). This distinction is necessary because, as shown earlier, the left-hand side of Equation 13.9 can be observed only as infinity and negative infinity. Such infinite values make calculations quite difficult.

Once the binomial logit has been estimated, hypothesis testing and econometric analysis can be undertaken in much the same way as for linear equations. When interpreting coefficients, however, be careful to recall that they represent the impact of a one-unit increase in the independent variable in question, holding the other explanatory variables constant, on the log of the odds of a given choice, not on the probability itself (as was the case with the linear probability model).

For instance, β_1 in Equation 13.9 measures the impact of a one-unit increase in X_1 on the log of the odds of a given choice, holding X_2 constant. As a result, the absolute sizes of estimated logit coefficients tend to be quite different from the absolute sizes of estimated linear probability model coefficients for the same variables. Interestingly, as mentioned above, the signs and significance levels of the estimated coefficients from the two models often are similar.

Measuring the overall fit, however, is not quite as straightforward. Recall from Chapter 7 that since the functional form of the dependent variable has been changed, $\overline{R}^2$ cannot be used to compare the fit of a logit with an otherwise comparable linear probability model. One way around this difficulty is to use the quasi-R^2 approach of Chapter 7 (a nonlinear estimate of R^2) to com-

---

7. The constant term, however, needs to be adjusted. Multiply $\hat{\beta}_0$ by $[\ln(p_1) - \ln(p_2)]$, where p_1 is the proportion of the observations chosen if $D_i = 1$ and p_2 is the proportion of the observations chosen if $D_i = 0$. See G. S. Maddala, *Limited-Dependent and Qualitative Variables in Econometrics* (Cambridge: Cambridge University Press, 1983), pp. 90–91.

pare the two fits. However, this quasi-R^2 shares the general faults inherent in using $\overline{R}^2$ with equations with dummy dependent variables. A better approach might be to use the percentage of correct predictions, R_p^2, from Equation 13.4.

To allow a fairly simple comparison between the logit and the linear probability model, let's estimate a logit on the same women's labor force participation data that we used in the previous section. The OLS estimate of that model, Equation 13.6, was:

$$\hat{D}_i = -0.28 - 0.38M_i + 0.09S_i \qquad (13.6)$$
$$(0.15) \qquad (0.03)$$
$$n = 30 \qquad \overline{R}^2 = .32 \qquad R_p^2 = .80$$

where: D_i = 1 if the ith woman is in the labor force, 0 otherwise
M_i = 1 if the ith woman is married, 0 otherwise
S_i = the number of years of schooling of the ith woman

If we estimate a logit on the same data (from Table 13.1) and the same independent variables, we obtain[8]:

$$\ln\left(\frac{\hat{D}_i}{[1 - D_i]}\right) = -5.89 - 2.59M_i + 0.69S_i \qquad (13.15)$$
$$(1.18) \qquad (0.31)$$
$$t = -2.19 \qquad 2.19$$
$$n = 30 \qquad R_p^2 = .80 \qquad \text{iterations} = 5$$

Let's compare Equations 13.6 and 13.15. As expected, the signs and general significance of the slope coefficients are the same. Note, however, that the actual sizes of the coefficients are quite different because the dependent variable is different. The coefficient of M changes from −0.38 to −2.59! Despite these differences, the overall fits are roughly comparable, especially after taking account of the different dependent variables and estimation techniques. In this example, then, the two estimation procedures differ mainly in that the logit does not produce $\hat{D}_i$s outside the range of zero and one.

However, if the size of the sample in this example is too small for a linear probability model, it certainly is too small for a logit, making any in-depth analysis of Equation 13.15 problematic. Instead, we're better off finding an example with a much larger sample.

---

8. Equation 13.15 has the log of the odds as its dependent variable, but the maximum likelihood computer estimation program that produces the β estimates uses a functional form with D_i as the dependent variable (similar to Equation 13.12).

13.2.2 An Example of the Use of the Binomial Logit

For a more complete example of the binomial digit, let's look at a model of the probability of passing the California State Department of Motor Vehicles drivers' license test. To obtain a license, each driver must past a written and a behind-the-wheel test. Even though the tests are scored from 0 to 100, all that matters is that you pass and get your license.

Since the test requires some boning up on traffic and safety laws, driving students have to decide how much time to spend studying. If they don't study enough, they waste time because they have to retake the test. If they study too much, however, they also waste time, because there's no bonus for scoring above the minimum, especially since there is no evidence that doing well on the test has much to do with driving well after the test (this, of course, might be worth its own econometric study).

Recently, two students decided to collect data on test takers in order to build an equation explaining whether someone passed the Department of Motor Vehicles test. They hoped that the model, and in particular the estimated coefficient of study time, would help them decide how much time to spend studying for the test. (Of course, it took more time to collect the data and run the model than it would have taken to memorize the entire traffic code, but that's another story.)

After reviewing the literature, choosing variables, and hypothesizing signs, the students realized that the appropriate functional form was a binomial logit because their dependent variable was a dummy variable:

$$D_i = \begin{cases} 1 \text{ if the } i\text{th test taker passed the test on the first try} \\ 0 \text{ if the } i\text{th test taker failed the test on the first try} \end{cases}$$

Their hypothesized equation was:

$$D_i = f(\overset{+}{A_i}, \overset{+}{H_i}, \overset{+}{E_i}, \overset{+}{C_i}) + \epsilon_i$$

where: A_i = the age of the ith test taker

H_i = the number of hours the ith test taker studied (usually less than one hour!)

E_i = a dummy variable equal to 1 if the ith test taker's primary language is English, 0 otherwise

C_i = a dummy variable equal to 1 if the ith test taker has any college experience, 0 otherwise

After collecting data from 480 test takers, the students estimated the following equation:

$$\ln\left(\frac{\overset{\frown}{D_i}}{[1 - D_i]}\right) = -1.18 + 0.011A_i + 2.70H_i + 1.62E_i + 3.97C_i$$
$$ (0.009) \quad (0.54) \quad (0.34) \quad (0.99)$$
$$ t = 1.23 \quad\ 4.97 \quad\ 4.65 \quad\ 4.00$$
$$n = 480 \quad R_p^2 = .74 \quad \text{iterations} = 5 \qquad (13.16)$$

Note how similar these results look to a typical linear regression result. All the estimated coefficients have the expected signs, and all but one are significantly different from zero. Remember, though, that the coefficient estimates have different meanings than in a linear regression model. For example, 2.70 is the impact of an extra hour of studying on the log of the odds of passing the test, holding constant the other three independent variables. Note that R_p^2 is .74, indicating that the equation correctly "predicted" almost three quarters of the sample based on nothing but the four variables in Equation 13.16.

And what about the two students? Did the equation help them? How much did they end up deciding to study? They found that given their ages, their college experience, and their English-speaking backgrounds, the expected value of $\hat{D}_i$ for each of them was quite high, even if H_i was set equal to zero. So what did they actually do? They studied for a half hour "just to be on the safe side" and passed with flying colors, having devoted more time to passing the test than anyone else in the history of the state.

13.3 Other Dummy Dependent Variable Techniques

Although the binomial logit is the most frequently used estimation technique for equations with dummy dependent variables, it's by no means the only one. In this section, we'll mention two alternatives, the binomial probit and the multinomial logit, that are useful in particular circumstances. Our main goal is to briefly describe these estimation techniques, not to cover them in any detail.[9]

---

9. For more, see G. S. Maddala, *Limited Dependent Variables and Qualitative Variables in Econometrics* (Cambridge: Cambridge University Press, 1983) and T. Amemiya, "Qualitative Response Models: A Survey," *Journal of Economic Literature*, 1981, pp. 1483–1536. These surveys also cover additional techniques, like the Tobit model, that are useful with bounded dependent variables or other special situations.

13.3.1 The Binomal Probit Model

The **binomial probit model** is an estimation technique for equations with dummy dependent variables that avoids the unboundedness problem of the linear probability model by using a variant of the cumulative normal distribution.

$$P_i = \frac{1}{\sqrt{2\pi}} \int_{-\infty}^{Z_i} e^{-s^2/2} \, ds \qquad (13.17)$$

where: P_i = the probability that the dummy variable $D_i = 1$
$Z_i = \beta_0 + \beta_1 X_{1i} + \beta_2 X_{2i}$
s = a standardized normal variable

As different as this probit looks from the logit that we examined in the previous section, it can be rewritten to look quite familiar:

$$Z_i = F^{-1}(P_i) = \beta_0 + \beta_1 X_{1i} + \beta_2 X_{2i} \qquad (13.18)$$

where F^{-1} is the inverse of the normal cumulative distribution function. Probit models typically are estimated by applying maximum likelihood techniques to the model in the form of Equation 13.17, but the results often are presented in the format of Equation 13.18.

The fact that both the logit and the probit are cumulative distributive functions means that the two have similar properties. For example, a graph of the probit looks almost exactly like the logit in Figure 13.2. In addition, the probit has the same requirement of a fairly large sample before hypothesis testing becomes meaningful. Finally, $\overline{R}^2$ continues to be of questionable value as a measure of overall fit.

From a researcher's point of view, the biggest differences between the two models are that the probit is based on the cumulative normal distribution and that the probit estimation procedure uses more computer time than does the logit. Since the probit is similar to the logit and is more expensive to run, why would you ever estimate one? The answer is that since the probit is based on the normal distribution, it's quite theoretically appealing (because many economic variables are normally distributed). With extremely large samples, this advantage falls away, since maximum likelihood procedures can be shown to be asymptotically normal under fairly general conditions.

For an example of a probit, let's estimate one on the same women's labor force participation data we used in the previous logit and linear probability examples (standard errors in parentheses):

$$\hat{Z}_i = \widehat{F^{-1}(P_i)} = -3.44 - 1.44M_i + 0.40S_i \qquad (13.19)$$
$$(0.62) \qquad (0.17)$$
$$n = 30 \qquad R_p^2 = .80 \qquad \text{iterations} = 5$$

Compare this result with Equation 13.15 from the previous section. Note that except for a slight difference in the scale of the coefficients, the logit and probit models provide virtually identical results in this example.

13.3.2 The Multinomial Logit Model

In many cases, there are more than two qualitative choices available. In some cities, for instance, a commuter has a choice of car, bus, or subway for the trip to work. How could we build and estimate a model of choosing from more than two different alternatives?

One answer is to hypothesize that choices are made sequentially and to model a multichoice decision as a series of binary decisions. For example, we might hypothesize that the commuter would first decide whether or not to drive to work, and we could build a binary model of car versus public transportation. For those commuters who choose public transportation, the next step would be to choose whether to take the bus or the subway, and we could build a second binary model of that choice. This method, called a **sequential binary logit,** is cumbersome and at times unrealistic, but it does allow a researcher to use a binary technique to model an inherently multichoice decision.

If a decision between multiple alternatives is truly made simultaneously, a better approach is to build a multinomial logit model of the decision. A **multinomial logit model** is an extension of the binomial logit technique that allows several discrete alternatives to be considered at the same time. If there are n different alternatives, we need $n - 1$ dummy variables to describe the choice, with each dummy equalling one only when that particular alternative is chosen. For example, D_{1i} would equal one if the ith person chose alternative number 1 and would equal zero otherwise. As before, the probability that D_{1i} is equal to one, P_{1i}, cannot be observed.

In a multinomial logit, one alternative is selected as the "base" alternative, and then each other possible choice is compared to this base alternative with a logit equation. A key distinction is that the dependent variable of these equations is the log of the odds of the ith alternative being chosen *compared to the base alternative:*

$$\ln\!\left(\frac{P_{1i}}{P_{bi}}\right)$$

where: P_{1i} = the probability of the ith person choosing the first alternative

P_{bi} = the probability of the ith person choosing the base alternative

If there are n alternatives, there should be n $-$ 1 different logit equations in the multinomial logit model system, because the coefficients of the last equation can be calculated from the coefficients of the first n $-$ 1 equations. (If you know that A/C = 6 and B/C = 2, then you can calculate that A/B = 3.) For example, if n = 3, as in the commuter-work-trip example cited above, and the base alternative is taking the bus, then a multinomial logit model would have a system of two equations:

$$\ln\left(\frac{P_{si}}{P_{bi}}\right) = \alpha_0 + \alpha_1 X_{1i} + \alpha_2 X_{2i} \qquad (13.20)$$

$$\ln\left(\frac{P_{ci}}{P_{bi}}\right) = \beta_0 + \beta_1 X_{1i} + \beta_2 X_{3i} \qquad (13.21)$$

where s = subway, c = car, and b = bus.

The definitions of the independent variables (and therefore the meanings of their coefficients) are unusual in a multinomial logit. Some of the Xs are characteristics of the decision maker (like the income of the ith commuter). The coefficients of these variables represent the *difference* between the impact of income on the probability of choosing one mode and the impact of income on the probability of choosing the base mode. For example, in Equation 13.20, if X_1 is income, the coefficient α_1 is the impact of an extra dollar of income on the probability of taking the subway to work *minus* the impact of an extra dollar of income on the probability of taking the bus to work (holding X_2 constant).

Xs that aren't characteristics of the decision maker are usually characteristics of the alternative (like travel time for one of the possible modes of travel). A variable that measures a characteristic of an alternative in a multinomial logit model should be *defined* as the difference between the characteristics for the two modes. For example, if the second independent variable in our model is travel time to work, X_2 should be defined as the travel time to work by subway *minus* the travel time to work by bus. The coefficients of such characteristics of the alternatives measure the impact of a unit of time on the ratio of the probabilities (holding X_1 constant). For practice with the meanings of the independent variables and their coefficients in a multinomial logit model, see Exercise 11.

The multinomial logit system has all the basic properties of the binomial logit but with two additional complications in estimation. First, Equations

13.20 and 13.21 are estimated simultaneously,[10] so the iterative nonlinear maximum likelihood procedure used to estimate the system is more costly than for the binomial logit. Second, the relationship between the error terms in the equations (ϵ_{si} and ϵ_{ci}) must be strictly accounted for by using a GLS procedure, a factor that also complicates the estimation procedure.[11]

13.4 Summary

1. A linear probability model is a linear-in-the-coefficients equation used to explain a dummy dependent variable (D_i). The expected value of D_i is the probability that D_i equals one (P_i).

2. The estimation of a linear probability model with OLS encounters four major problems:
   a. The error term is not normally distributed.
   b. The error term is inherently heteroskedastic.
   c. $\overline{R}^2$ is not an accurate measure of overall fit.
   d. The expected value of D_i is not limited by 0 and 1.

3. When measuring the overall fit of equations with dummy dependent variables, an alternative to $\overline{R}^2$ is R_p^2, the percentage of the observations in the sample that a particular estimated equation would have explained correctly.

4. The binomial logit is an estimation technique for equations with dummy dependent variables that avoids the unboundedness problem of the linear probability model by using a variant of the cumulative logistic function:

$$\ln\left(\frac{D_i}{[1 - D_i]}\right) = \beta_0 + \beta_1 X_{1i} + \beta_2 X_{2i} + \epsilon_i$$

5. The binomial logit is best estimated using the maximum likelihood technique and a large sample. A slope coefficient from a logit measures the impact of a one-unit increase of the independent variable in

---

10. As with the binomial logit, the maximum likelihood computer package doesn't estimate these precise equations. Instead, it estimates versions of Equations 13.20 and 13.21 that are similar to Equation 13.12.

11. For an interesting and yet accessible example of the estimation of a multinomial logit model, see Kang H. Park and Peter M. Kerr, "Determinants of Academic Performance: A Multinomial Logit Approach," *The Journal of Economic Education*, 1990, pp. 101–111.

question (holding the other explanatory variables constant) on the log of the odds of a given choice.

6. The binomial probit model is an estimation technique for equations with dummy dependent variables that uses the cumulative normal distribution function. The binomial probit has properties quite similar to the binomial logit except that it takes more computer time to estimate than a logit and is based on the normal distribution.

7. The multinomial logit model is an extension of the binomial logit that allows more than two discrete alternatives to be considered simultaneously. One alternative is chosen as a base alternative, and then each other possible choice is compared to that base alternative with a logit equation.

Exercises

(Answers to even-numbered exercises are in Appendix A.)

1. Write the meaning of each of the following terms without referring to the book (or your notes), and compare your definition with the version in the text for each:
   a. linear probability model
   b. R_p^2
   c. binomial logit model
   d. log of the odds
   e. binomial probit model
   f. sequential binary model
   g. multinomial logit model

2. On graph paper, plot each of the following linear probability models. For what range of X_1 is $1 < \hat{D}_i$? How about $\hat{D}_i < 0$?
   a. $\hat{D}_i = 0.3 + 0.1X_i$
   b. $\hat{D}_i = 3.0 - 0.2X_i$
   c. $\hat{D}_i = -1.0 + 0.3X_i$

3. Bond ratings are letter ratings (Aaa = best) assigned to firms that issue debt. These ratings measure the quality of the firm from the point of view of the likelihood of repayment of the bond. Suppose you've been hired by an arbitrage house that wants to predict *Moody's Bond Ratings* before they're published in order to buy bonds whose ratings are going to improve. In particular, suppose your firm wants to distin-

guish between A-rated bonds (high quality) and B-rated bonds (medium quality) and has collected a data set of 200 bonds with which to estimate a model. As you arrive on the job, your boss is about to buy bonds based on the results of the following model (standard errors in parentheses):

$$\hat{Y}_i = 0.70 + 0.05P_i + 0.05PV_i - 0.020D_i$$
$$(0.05) \quad (0.02) \quad (0.002)$$
$$\overline{R}^2 = .69 \quad DW = 0.50 \quad n = 200$$

where:
Y_i = 1 if the rating of the *i*th bond = A, 0 otherwise
P_i = the profit rate of the firm that issues the *i*th bond
PV_i = the standard deviation of P_i over the last 5 years
D_i = the ratio of debt to total capitalization of the firm that issued the *i*th bond

a. What econometric problems, if any, exist in this equation?
b. What suggestions would you have for a rerun of this equation with a different specification?
c. Suppose that your boss rejects your suggestions, saying, "This is the real world, and I'm sure that my model will forecast bond ratings just as well as yours will." How would you respond? (*Hint:* Saying, "Okay, boss, you win," is sure to keep your job for you, but it won't get much credit on this question.)

4. Show that the logistic function, $D = 1/(1 + e^{-Z})$, is indeed equivalent to the binomial logit model, $\ln[D/(1 - D)] = Z$, where $Z = \beta_0 + \beta_1 X_1 + \beta_2 X_2 + \epsilon$.

5. Plot each of the following binomial logit models. For what range of X_i is $1 < D_i$? How about $D_i < 0$? (*Hint:* When you finish, compare your answers to those for Exercise 2 above.)
a. $\ln[D_i/(1 - D_i)] = 0.3 + 0.1X_i$
b. $\ln[D_i/(1 - D_i)] = 3.0 - 0.2X_i$
c. $\ln[D_i/(1 - D_i)] = -1.0 + 0.3X_i$

6. R. Amatya[12] estimated the following logit model of birth control for 1,145 continuously married women aged 35 to 44 in Nepal:

---

12. Ramesh Amatya, "Supply-Demand Analysis of Differences in Contraceptive Use in Seven Asian Nations, Late 1970s" (paper presented at the Annual Meetings of the Western Economic Association, 1988, Los Angeles).

$$\ln\left(\overbrace{\frac{D_i}{[1 - D_i]}}\right) = -4.47 + 2.03WN_i + 1.45ME_i$$

$$\underset{t = 5.64}{(0.36)} \quad \underset{10.36}{(0.14)}$$

where: D_i = 1 if the *i*th woman has ever used a recognized form of birth control, 0 otherwise

          WN_i = 1 if the *i*th woman wants no more children, 0 otherwise

          ME_i = number of methods of birth control known to the *i*th woman

a. Explain the theoretical meaning of the coefficients for WN and ME. How would your answer differ if this were a linear probability model?

b. Do the signs, sizes, and significance of the estimated slope coefficients meet your expectations? Why or why not?

c. What is the theoretical significance of the constant term in this equation?

d. If you could make one change in the specification of this equation, what would it be? Explain your reasoning.

7. What happens if we define a dummy dependent variable over a range other than zero to one? For example, suppose that in the research cited above, Amatya had defined D_i as being equal to 2 if the *i*th woman had ever used birth control and zero otherwise.

a. What would happen to the size and theoretical meaning of the estimated logit coefficients? Would they stay the same? Would they change? (If so, how?)

b. How would your answers to part a above change if Amatya had estimated a linear probability model instead of a binomial logit?

8. Return to our data on women's labor force participation and consider the possibility of adding A_i, the age of the *i*th woman, to the equation. Be careful when you develop your expected sign and functional form because the expected impact of age on labor force participation is difficult to pin down. For instance, some women drop out of the labor force when they get married, but others continue working even while they're raising their children. Still others work until they get married, stay at home to have children, and then return to the work force once the children reach school age. Malcolm Cohen et al., for example, found the age of a woman to be relatively unimportant in

determining labor force participation, except for women who were 65 and older and were likely to have retired.[13] The net result for our model is that age appears to be a theoretically irrelevant variable. A possible exception, however, is a dummy variable equal to one if the ith woman is 65 or over and zero otherwise.

a. Look over the data set in Table 13.1. What problems do you see with adding an independent variable equal to one if the ith woman is 65 or older and zero otherwise?

b. If you go ahead and add the dummy implied above to Equation 13.15 and reestimate the model, you obtain the equation below. Which equation do you prefer, Equation 13.15 or the one below? Explain your answer.

$$\overwidehat{\ln\left(\frac{D_i}{[1 - D_i]}\right)} = -5.89 - 2.59M_i + 0.69S_i - 0.03AD_i$$
$$(1.18) \quad (0.31) \quad (0.30)$$
$$t = -2.19 \quad 2.19 \quad -0.01$$
$$n = 30 \quad R_p^2 = .80 \quad \text{iterations} = 5$$

where: $AD_i = 1$ if the age of the ith woman is > 65, 0 otherwise

9. To get practice in actually estimating your own linear probability, logit, and probit equations, test the possibility that age (A_i) is actually a relevant variable in our women's labor force participation model. That is, take the data from Table 13.1 and estimate each of the following equations. Then use our specification criteria to compare your equation with the parallel version in the text (without A_i). Explain why you do or do not think that age is a relevant variable.

a. the linear probability model D = f(M,A,S)
b. the logit D = f(M,A,S)
c. the probit D=f(M,A,S)

10. An article published in a book edited by A. Kouskoulaf and B. Lytle[14] presents coefficients from an estimated logit model of the choice between the car and public transportation for the trip to work in Boston. All three public transportation modes in Boston (bus, subway, and train, of which train is the most preferred) were lumped together as a

---

13. Malcolm Cohen, Samuel A. Rea, Jr. and Robert I. Lerman, *A Micro Model of Labor Supply* (Washington, D.C.: U.S. Bureau of Labor Statistics, 1970), p. 212.

14. "The Use of the Multinomial Logit in Transportation Analysis," in A. Kouskoulaf and B. Lytle, eds. *Urban Housing and Transportation* (Detroit: Wayne State University, 1975), pp. 87–90.

single alternative to the car in a binomial logit model. The dependent variable was the log of the odds of taking public transportation for the trip to work, so the first coefficient implies that as income rises, the log of the odds of taking public transportation falls, and so on.

Independent Variable	Coefficient
Family income (9 categories with 1 = low and 9 = high)	−0.12
Number employed in the family	−1.09
Out-of-pocket costs (cents)	−3.16
Wait time (tenths of minutes)	0.18
Walk time (tenths of minutes)	−0.03
In-vehicle travel time (tenths of minutes)	−0.01

The last four variables are defined as the difference between the value of the variable for taking public transportation and its value for taking the car.

a. Do the signs of the estimated coefficients agree with your prior expectations? Which one(s) differ?

b. The transportation literature hypothesizes that people would rather spend time traveling in a vehicle than waiting for or walking to that vehicle. Do the sizes of the estimated coefficients of time support this hypothesis?

c. Since trains run relatively infrequently, the researchers set wait time for train riders fairly high. Most trains run on known schedules, however, so the average commuter learns that schedule and attempts to hold down wait time. Does this fact explain any of the unusual results indicated in your answers to parts a and b above?

11. Suppose that you want to build a multinomial logit model of how students choose which college to attend. For the sake of simplicity, let's assume that there are only four colleges to choose from: your college (c), the state university (u), the local junior college (j), and the nearby private liberal arts college (a). Further assume that everyone agrees that the important variables in such a model are the family income (Y) of each student, the average SAT scores of each college (SAT), and the tuition (T) of each college.

a. How many equations should there be in such a multinomial logit system?

b. If your college is the base, write out the definition of the dependent variable for each equation.

c. Carefully write out the definitions of all the independent variables in each equation.

d. Carefully write out the meanings of all the slope coefficients in each equation.

12. The two most-used forms of home mortgages are fixed rate mortgages, in which the interest rate is fixed over the life of the loan, and adjustable rate mortgages, in which the interest rate can go up or down depending on changes in the rate of U.S. Treasury bills (or another market interest rate). Since adjustable rate mortgages carry a risk of higher rates in the long run, they usually have a lower initial interest rate than do fixed rate mortgages. In 1987, U. Dhillon, J. Schilling, and C. Sirmans studied how borrowers chose between fixed and adjustable rate mortgages as a function of a number of financial and personal variables for a sample of 78 home buyers.[15] Although Dhillon et al. didn't estimate a logit, we can do so using their data (presented in Table 13.2):

$$\hat{A}_i' = -3.72 + 0.90F_i - 0.71M_i - 4.11Y_i \qquad (13.22)$$
$$(0.49) \quad (0.30) \quad (1.90)$$
$$t = 1.86 \quad -2.33 \quad -2.16$$

$$-0.52P_i - 0.24T_i + 0.15N_i$$
$$(0.43) \quad (1.04) \quad (0.08)$$
$$t = -1.22 \quad -0.23 \quad 1.91$$
$$R_P^2 = .78 \qquad n = 78$$

where: $A_i' = \ln[A_i/(1 - A_i)]$, where $A_i = 1$ if the *i*th borrower chose an adjustable rate mortgage and 0 if they chose a fixed rate mortgage.

F_i = the fixed interest rate available to the *i*th borrower

M_i = the interest premium (over the Treasury rate) on the adjustable rate available to the *i*th borrower

Y_i = the 10-year Treasury interest rate minus the 1-year Treasury rate on the day of the *i*th loan

P_i = the points (borrowing cost) on an adjustable mortgage divided by the points on a fixed mortgage available to the *i*th borrower

---

15. Upinder Dhillon, James Shilling, and C. F. Sirmans, "Choosing Between Fixed and Adjustable Rate Mortgages," *Journal of Money, Credit and Banking,* February 1987, pp. 260–267. The data set does not include all of Dhillon et al.'s variables, so we can't exactly replicate their results.

TABLE 13.2 DATA ON FIXED RATE VS. ADJUSTABLE RATE MORTGAGES

Obs	A	F	M	Y	P	T	N	S
1	1.0	13.62	1.50	1.38	2.33	1.50	7.558	22.0
2	1.0	13.62	1.50	1.38	2.33	1.50	7.558	22.0
3	1.0	13.62	1.50	1.38	2.33	1.50	7.558	22.0
4	1.0	13.62	1.50	1.38	2.33	1.50	7.556	22.0
5	1.0	14.00	5.50	1.38	1.75	1.00	7.821	16.0
6	1.0	14.00	4.75	1.38	1.75	1.00	8.014	16.0
7	1.0	14.00	4.75	1.38	1.75	1.00	8.014	16.0
8	1.0	13.62	1.50	1.38	2.33	1.50	7.558	22.0
9	1.0	13.50	2.40	1.59	1.00	1.00	17.860	16.0
10	1.0	13.75	2.44	1.45	2.00	0.67	9.100	19.0
11	1.0	14.00	2.45	1.64	1.00	1.00	2.419	16.0
12	1.0	14.00	2.45	1.64	1.00	1.00	2.419	16.0
13	1.0	13.50	2.40	1.59	1.00	1.00	17.860	16.0
14	1.0	14.00	0.35	1.64	1.25	0.67	5.620	17.0
15	1.0	13.90	3.04	1.50	2.03	1.00	12.404	20.0
16	1.0	13.75	2.33	1.45	2.50	1.00	7.558	22.0
17	1.0	13.75	2.33	1.45	2.50	1.00	7.558	22.0
18	1.0	13.75	2.33	1.45	2.50	1.00	7.558	22.0
19	1.0	13.75	2.33	1.45	2.50	1.00	7.558	22.0
20	1.0	13.75	2.33	1.45	2.50	1.00	7.558	22.0
21	1.0	13.75	2.33	1.45	2.50	1.00	7.558	22.0
22	0.0	13.50	2.40	1.59	1.00	1.00	17.860	16.0
23	0.0	13.88	0.35	2.04	0.83	1.00	4.260	21.0
24	0.0	13.88	0.35	2.04	0.83	1.00	4.260	21.0
25	0.0	13.88	0.35	2.04	0.83	1.00	4.260	21.0
26	0.0	13.50	2.40	1.59	1.00	1.00	17.860	16.0
27	0.0	13.50	3.86	1.60	0.74	0.42	1.977	16.0
28	0.0	12.38	2.73	1.40	1.66	0.85	1.110	18.0
29	0.0	12.13	3.36	1.60	1.66	0.85	0.118	17.0
30	0.0	12.25	3.36	1.60	1.66	0.85	0.885	16.0
31	0.0	12.38	3.36	1.60	1.66	0.85	0.358	13.0
32	0.0	12.38	3.36	1.60	1.66	0.85	0.457	16.0
33	0.0	12.25	3.36	1.60	1.66	0.85	0.573	14.0
34	0.0	12.40	3.36	1.60	1.66	0.85	0.352	12.0
35	0.0	12.50	2.10	1.77	0.00	1.00	0.610	13.0
36	0.0	13.00	3.61	1.69	1.81	1.00	0.733	17.0
37	0.0	13.25	3.61	1.69	4.34	1.00	13.572	16.0
38	0.0	12.25	2.60	1.59	2.55	0.93	0.481	16.0
39	0.0	13.00	2.40	1.59	2.00	1.00	0.170	9.0
40	0.0	12.50	2.60	1.59	1.27	0.93	0.462	12.0
41	0.0	12.50	2.60	1.59	2.55	0.93	0.419	18.0

(*continued*)

TABLE 13.2 (continued)								
Obs	A	F	M	Y	P	T	N	S
42	0.0	12.50	2.60	1.59	1.27	0.93	3.198	24.0
43	0.0	13.00	3.86	1.60	1.48	1.69	3.426	17.0
44	0.0	12.50	2.60	1.59	2.55	0.93	1.676	14.0
45	0.0	13.25	3.86	1.60	1.48	1.27	0.066	6.0
46	0.0	12.50	2.60	1.59	1.09	0.93	0.186	18.0
47	0.0	12.75	3.86	1.60	1.48	0.85	0.721	20.0
48	0.0	12.13	3.36	1.60	1.66	0.85	0.369	16.0
49	0.0	12.75	3.86	1.60	1.48	0.85	0.211	16.0
50	0.0	12.25	2.73	1.40	1.24	0.85	0.420	12.0
51	0.0	12.75	2.60	1.59	0.76	0.93	1.000	15.0
52	0.0	13.25	2.08	1.50	0.97	1.42	0.792	14.0
53	0.0	13.90	3.04	1.50	2.03	1.00	0.261	12.0
54	0.0	12.25	2.60	1.59	0.69	0.93	0.745	14.0
55	0.0	12.75	2.08	1.50	0.49	0.95	0.107	16.0
56	0.0	13.90	3.04	1.50	2.03	1.00	0.884	18.0
57	0.0	12.60	3.36	1.60	1.66	0.85	0.598	16.0
58	0.0	14.00	2.45	1.64	1.00	1.00	0.443	25.0
59	0.0	13.70	2.08	1.50	0.97	2.38	0.797	16.0
60	0.0	13.80	3.04	1.50	2.03	1.00	0.241	16.0
61	0.0	13.75	1.04	1.45	0.67	1.00	2.662	17.0
62	0.0	13.62	1.50	1.38	2.33	1.50	1.237	14.0
63	0.0	14.00	2.40	1.59	1.50	1.00	0.322	11.0
64	0.0	13.00	2.40	1.59	2.00	1.00	0.116	12.0
65	0.0	13.37	0.35	2.04	1.67	1.00	0.405	12.0
66	0.0	13.50	0.35	2.04	1.67	1.50	0.268	12.0
67	0.0	14.00	0.35	2.04	1.67	1.50	3.534	16.0
68	1.0	11.77	1.90	1.88	0.46	1.13	0.435	12.0
69	1.0	11.76	1.75	1.74	0.45	1.11	0.314	16.0
70	1.0	14.00	1.66	1.74	0.50	1.50	0.441	12.0
71	1.0	12.84	0.85	2.03	0.00	1.20	0.360	12.0
72	1.0	13.75	−0.90	1.45	1.00	1.00	−0.056	17.0
73	1.0	12.50	0.95	1.77	0.67	1.00	0.182	12.0
74	1.0	12.50	−0.25	1.77	1.00	1.00	0.253	12.0
75	1.0	13.75	1.04	1.45	0.67	1.00	0.707	15.0
76	1.0	13.75	0.35	2.04	1.67	1.00	0.122	16.0
77	1.0	14.50	2.10	1.77	0.00	1.00	0.336	17.0
78	1.0	14.00	1.10	1.74	0.00	1.50	0.090	15.0

Source: Upinder Dhillon, James Shilling, and C. F. Sirmans, "Choosing Between Fixed and Adjustable Rate Mortgages," *Journal of Money, Credit and Banking,* February 1987, pp. 260–267 as published on the data disk that accompanies William F. Lott and Subhash C. Ray, *Applied Econometrics: Problems with Data Sets* (Fort Worth: Dryden/Harcourt Brace, 1992), pp. 189–195. We appreciate their permission to use these data.
Note: filename MORT13

T_i = the ratio of the adjustable rate maturity (in years) to the fixed rate maturity available to the ith borrower

N_i = the net worth of the ith borrower

a. Create and test appropriate hypotheses concerning the slope coefficients at the 5 percent level. (*Hint:* The underlying theory leads us to expect that β_Y and β_T will be negative, and there are sound theoretical arguments in both directions for β_N.)

b. Using the data in Table 13.2 (datafile MORT13) estimate a linear probability model version of Equation 13.22. Are the estimated coefficients different from the logit ones in sign or significance? How?

c. Using your estimated linear probability model from part b, calculate predicted values for the dependent variable for all 78 observations. How many are outside the 0–1 range? What is your R_p^2?

d. Given your answers to parts b and c, which version do you prefer, the logit or the linear probability model? Explain your answer.

e. The application of the "efficient markets" hypothesis to this model implies that the nonfinancial characteristics of the home buyer should have little to do with their choice between a fixed and adjustable rate mortgage. To test this possibility, add S_i, the number of years of schooling of the ith borrower, to Equation 13.22 and estimate the new specification as a linear probability model *and* (if your software supports it) a logit. You'd expect that the more years of schooling, the more likely someone would be to understand and take a chance on an adjustable mortgage. Do your results support this hypothesis? Explain.

Simultaneous Equations

Unfortunately, the single-equation models we've covered to date ignore much of the interdependence that characterizes the modern world. Most econometric applications are inherently interdependent or simultaneous in nature, and the best approach to understanding this simultaneity is to explicitly acknowledge it with feedback loops in our models. This means specifying and estimating simultaneous equations systems instead of looking at just one equation at a time.

The most important models in economics and business are simultaneous in nature. Supply and demand, for example, is obviously simultaneous. To study the demand for chicken without also looking at the supply of chicken is to take a chance on missing important linkages and thus making significant mistakes. Virtually all the major approaches to macroeconomics, from Keynesian aggregate demand models to rational expectations schemes, are inherently simultaneous. Even models that appear to be inherently single equation in nature often turn out to be much more simultaneous than you might think. The price of housing, for instance, is dramatically affected by the level of economic activity, the prevailing rate of interest in alternative assets, and a number of other simultaneously determined variables.

All this wouldn't mean much to econometricians if it weren't for the fact that the estimation of simultaneous equations systems with OLS causes a number of difficulties that aren't encountered with single equations. Most important, Classical Assumption III, which states that all explanatory variables should be uncorrelated with the error term, is violated in simultaneous models. Mainly because of this, OLS coefficient estimates are biased in simultaneous models. As a result, an alternative estimation procedure called Two-Stage Least Squares is usually employed in such models instead of OLS.

You're probably wondering why we've waited until now to discuss simultaneous equations if they're so important in economics and if OLS encounters bias when estimating them. The answer is that the simultaneous estimation of an equation changes every time the specification of any equation in the entire system is changed, so a researcher must be well equipped to deal with specification problems like those of the previous eight chapters. As a result, it does not make sense to learn how to estimate a simultaneous system until you are fairly adept at estimating a single equation.

14.1   Structural and Reduced-Form Equations

Before we can study the problems encountered in the estimation of simultaneous equations, we need to introduce a few concepts. Readers well versed in the subject are encouraged to skip to Section 14.1.2.

14.1.1 The Nature of Simultaneous Equations Systems

Which came first, the chicken or the egg? This question is impossible to answer satisfactorily because chickens and eggs are **jointly determined;** there is a two-way causal relationship between the variables. The more eggs you have, the more chickens you'll get, but the more chickens you have, the more eggs you'll get.[1] More realistically, the economic world is full of the kind of *feedback effects and dual causality* that require the application of simultaneous equations. Besides the supply and demand and simple macroeconomic model examples mentioned above, we could talk about the dual causality of population size and food supply, the joint determination of wages and prices, or the interaction between foreign exchange rates and international trade and capital flows. In a typical econometric equation:

$$Y_t = \beta_0 + \beta_1 X_{1t} + \beta_2 X_{2t} + \epsilon_t \qquad (14.1)$$

a simultaneous system is one in which Y clearly has an effect on at least one of the Xs in addition to the effect that the Xs have on Y.

---

1. This also depends on how hungry you are, which is a function of how hard you're working, which depends on how many chickens you have to take care of. (Although this chicken/egg example is simultaneous in an annual model, it would not be truly simultaneous in a quarterly or monthly model because of the time lags involved.)

Such topics are usually modeled by distinguishing between variables that are simultaneously determined (the Ys, called **endogenous variables**) and those that are not (the Xs, called **exogenous variables**):

$$Y_{1t} = \alpha_0 + \alpha_1 Y_{2t} + \alpha_2 X_{1t} + \alpha_3 X_{2t} + \epsilon_{1t} \qquad (14.2)$$

$$Y_{2t} = \beta_0 + \beta_1 Y_{1t} + \beta_2 X_{3t} + \beta_3 X_{2t} + \epsilon_{2t} \qquad (14.3)$$

For example, Y_1 and Y_2 might be the quantity and price of chicken (respectively), X_1 the income of the consumers, X_2 the price of beef (beef is a substitute for chicken in both consumption and production), and X_3 the price of chicken feed. With these definitions, Equation 14.2 would characterize the behavior of consumers of chickens and Equation 14.3 the behavior of suppliers of chickens. These behavioral equations are also called *structural equations.* **Structural equations** characterize the underlying economic theory behind each endogenous variable by expressing it in terms of both endogenous and exogenous variables. Researchers must view them as an entire system in order to see all the feedback loops involved. For example, the Ys are jointly determined, so a change in Y_1 will cause a change in Y_2, which will in turn cause Y_1 to change *again.* Contrast this feedback with a change in X_1, which will not eventually loop back and cause X_1 to change again. The αs and the βs in the equation are *structural coefficients,* and hypotheses should be made about their signs just as we did with the regression coefficients of single equations.

Note that a variable is endogenous because it is jointly determined, not just because it appears in both equations. That is, X_2, which is the price of beef but could be another factor beyond our control, is in both equations but is still exogenous in nature because it is not simultaneously determined within the chicken market. In a large general equilibrium model of the entire economy, however, such a price variable would also likely be endogenous. How do you decide whether a particular variable should be endogenous or exogenous? Some variables are almost always exogenous (the weather, for example), but most others can be considered either endogenous or exogenous, depending on the number and characteristics of the other equations in the system. Thus, the distinction between endogenous and exogenous variables usually depends on how the researcher defines the scope of the research project.

Sometimes, lagged endogenous variables appear in simultaneous systems, usually when the equations involved are distributed lag equations (described in Chapter 12). To avoid confusion, **predetermined variables** are defined to include all exogenous and lagged endogenous variables. "Predetermined" implies that exogenous and lagged endogenous variables are determined outside the system of specified equations or prior to the current period. Endogenous variables that are not lagged are not predetermined, because they are jointly determined by the system in the current time period. Therefore, econometricians tend to speak in terms of endogenous and predetermined variables when discussing simultaneous equations systems.

Let's look at the specification of a simple supply and demand model, say for the "cola" soft-drink industry:

$$Q_{Dt} = \alpha_0 + \alpha_1 P_t + \alpha_2 X_{1t} + \alpha_3 X_{2t} + \epsilon_{Dt} \qquad (14.4)$$

$$Q_{St} = \beta_0 + \beta_1 P_t + \beta_2 X_{3t} + \epsilon_{St} \qquad (14.5)$$

$$Q_{St} = Q_{Dt} \quad \text{(equilibrium condition)}$$

where: Q_{Dt} = the quantity of cola demanded in time period t
Q_{St} = the quantity of cola supplied in time period t
P_t = the price of cola in time period t
X_{1t} = dollars of advertising for cola in time period t
X_{2t} = another "demand-side" exogenous variable (e.g., income or the prices or advertising of other drinks)
X_{3t} = a "supply-side" exogenous variable (e.g. the price of artificial flavors or other factors of production)
ϵ_t = classical error terms (each equation has its own error term, subscripted "D" and "S" for demand and supply)

In this case, price and quantity are simultaneously determined, but price, one of the endogenous variables, is not on the left side of any of the equations. It's incorrect to assume automatically that the endogenous variables are those that appear on the left side of at least one equation; in this case, we could have just as easily written Equation 14.5 with price on the left side and quantity supplied on the right side, as we did in the chicken example in Equations 14.2 and 14.3. Although the estimated coefficients would be different, the underlying relations would not. Note also that there must be as many equations as there are endogenous variables. In this case, the three endogenous variables are Q_D, Q_S, and P.

What would be the expected signs for the coefficients of the price variables in Equations 14.4 and 14.5? We'd expect price to enter negatively in the demand equation but to enter positively in the supply equation. The higher the price, after all, the less quantity will be demanded, but the more quantity will be supplied. These signs would result in the typical supply and demand diagram (Figure 14.1) that we're all used to. Look at Equations 14.4 and 14.5

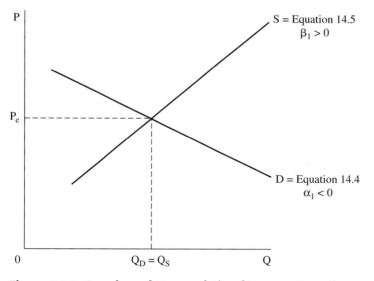

Figure 14.1 Supply and Demand Simultaneous Equations

An example of simultaneous equations that jointly determine two endogenous variables is the supply and demand for a product. In this case, Equation 14.4, the downward-sloping demand function, and Equation 14.5, the upward-sloping supply function, intersect at the equilibrium price and quantity for this market.

again, however, and note that they would be identical but for the different predetermined variables. What would happen if we accidentally put a supply-side predetermined variable in the demand equation or vice versa? We'd have a very difficult time identifying which equation was which, and the expected signs for the coefficients of the endogenous variable P would become ambiguous. As a result, we must take care when specifying the structural equations in a system.

14.1.2 Simultaneous Systems Violate Classical Assumption III

Recall from Chapter 4 that Classical Assumption III states that the error term and each explanatory variable must be uncorrelated with each other. If there is such a correlation, then the OLS regression estimation program is likely to attribute to the particular explanatory variable any variations in the dependent variable that are actually being caused by variations in the error term. The result will be biased estimates.

To see why simultaneous equations violate the assumption of independence between the error term and the explanatory variables, look again at a simultaneous system, Equations 14.2 and 14.3 (repeated with directional errors):

$$\overset{\uparrow}{Y_{1t}} = \alpha_0 + \alpha_1 \overset{\uparrow}{Y_{2t}} + \alpha_2 X_{1t} + \alpha_3 X_{2t} + \overset{\uparrow}{\epsilon_{1t}} \qquad (14.2)$$

$$\overset{\uparrow}{Y_{2t}} = \beta_0 + \beta_1 \overset{\uparrow}{Y_{1t}} + \beta_2 X_{3t} + \beta_3 X_{2t} + \epsilon_{2t} \qquad (14.3)$$

Let's work through the system and see what happens when one of the error terms increases, holding everything else in the equations constant:

1. If ϵ_1 increases in a particular time period, Y_1 will also increase due to Equation 14.2.
2. If Y_1 increases, Y_2 will also rise[2] due to Equation 14.3.
3. But if Y_2 increases in Equation 14.3, it also increases in Equation 14.2 where it is an explanatory variable.

Thus, an increase in the error term of an equation causes an increase in an explanatory variable in the same equation: If ϵ_1 increases, Y_1 increases, and then Y_2 increases, violating the assumption of independence between the error term and the explanatory variables.

This is not an isolated result that depends on the particular equations involved. Indeed, as you'll find in Exercise 3, this result works for other error terms, equations, and simultaneous systems. All that is required for the violation of Classical Assumption III is that there be endogenous variables that are jointly determined in a system of simultaneous equations.

14.1.3 Reduced-Form Equations

An alternative way of expressing a simultaneous equations system is through the use of **reduced-form equations**, equations that express a particular endogenous variable solely in terms of an error term and all the predetermined (exogenous plus lagged endogenous) variables in the simultaneous system.

The reduced-form equations for the structural Equations 14.2 and 14.3 would thus be:

---

2. This assumes that β_1 is positive. If β_1 is negative, Y_2 will decrease and there will be a negative correlation between ϵ_1 and Y_2, but this negative correlation will still violate Classical Assumption III. Also note that both Equations 14.2 and 14.3 could have Y_{1t} on the left side; if two variables are jointly determined, it doesn't matter which variable is considered dependent and which explanatory, because they are actually mutually dependent. We used this kind of simultaneous system in the cola model portrayed in Equations 14.4 and 14.5.

$$Y_{1t} = \pi_0 + \pi_1 X_{1t} + \pi_2 X_{2t} + \pi_3 X_{3t} + v_{1t} \qquad (14.6)$$

$$Y_{2t} = \pi_4 + \pi_5 X_{1t} + \pi_6 X_{2t} + \pi_7 X_{3t} + v_{2t} \qquad (14.7)$$

where the vs are stochastic error terms and the πs are called **reduced-form coefficients** because they are the coefficients of the predetermined variables in the reduced-form equations. Note that each equation includes only one endogenous variable, the dependent variable, and that each equation has exactly the same set of predetermined variables. The reduced-form coefficients, such as π_1 and π_5, are known as **impact multipliers** because they measure the impact on the endogenous variable of a one-unit increase in the value of the predetermined variable, after allowing for the feedback effects from the entire simultaneous system.

There are least four reasons for using reduced-form equations:

1. Since the reduced-form equations have no inherent simultaneity, they do not violate Classical Assumption III. Therefore, they can be estimated with OLS without encountering the problems discussed in this chapter.

2. The reduced-form coefficients estimated in this way can sometimes be mathematically manipulated to allow the estimation of the structural coefficients. That is, estimates of the πs of Equations 14.6 and 14.7 can be used to solve for the αs and βs of Equations 14.2 and 14.3. This method of calculating estimates of the structural coefficients from estimates of the reduced-form coefficients is called **Indirect Least Squares** (ILS). Unfortunately, ILS turns out to be useful only in very limited situations. For more on ILS, see Exercise 4.

3. The interpretation of the reduced-form coefficients as impact multipliers means that they have economic meaning and useful applications of their own. For example, if you wanted to compare a government spending increase with a tax cut in terms of the per dollar impact in the first year, estimates of the impact multipliers (reduced-form coefficients or πs) would allow such a comparison.

4. Perhaps most importantly, reduced-form equations play a crucial role in the estimation technique most frequently used for simultaneous equations. This technique, Two-Stage Least Squares, will be explained in Section 14.3.

To conclude, let's return to the cola supply and demand model and specify the reduced-form equations for that model. (To test yourself, flip back to Equations 14.4 and 14.5 and see if you can get the right answer before going on.) Since the equilibrium conditions forces Q_D to be equal to Q_S, we need only two reduced-form equations:

$$Q_t = \pi_0 + \pi_1 X_{1t} + \pi_2 X_{2t} + \pi_3 X_{3t} + v_{1t} \qquad (14.8)$$

$$P_t = \pi_4 + \pi_5 X_{1t} + \pi_6 X_{2t} + \pi_7 X_{3t} + v_{2t} \qquad (14.9)$$

Even though P never appears on the left side of a structural equation, it's an endogenous variable and should be treated as such.

14.2 The Bias of Ordinary Least Squares (OLS)

All the Classical Assumptions must be met for OLS estimates to be BLUE; when an assumption is violated, we must determine which of the properties no longer holds. It turns out that applying OLS directly to the structural equations of a simultaneous system, called *Direct Least Squares*, produces biased estimates of the coefficients. Such bias is called simultaneous equations bias or simultaneity bias.

14.2.1 Understanding Simultaneity Bias

Simultaneity bias refers to the fact that in a simultaneous system, the expected values of the OLS-estimated structural coefficients ($\hat{\beta}$s) are not equal to the true βs. We are therefore faced with the problem that in a simultaneous system:

$$E(\hat{\beta}) \neq \beta \qquad (14.10)$$

Why does this simultaneity bias exist? Recall from Section 14.1.2 that in simultaneous equations systems, the error terms (the ϵs) tend to be correlated with the endogenous variables (the Ys) whenever the Ys appear as explanatory variables. Let's follow through what this correlation means (assuming positive coefficients for simplicity) in typical structural equations like 14.11 and 14.12:

$$Y_{1t} = \beta_0 + \beta_1 Y_{2t} + \beta_2 X_t + \epsilon_{1t} \qquad (14.11)$$

$$Y_{2t} = \alpha_0 + \alpha_1 Y_{1t} + \alpha_2 Z_t + \epsilon_{2t} \qquad (14.12)$$

Since we cannot observe the error term (ϵ_1) and don't know when ϵ_{1t} is above average, it will appear as if every time Y_1 is above average, so too is Y_2. As a result, the OLS estimation program will tend to attribute increases in Y_1 caused by the error term ϵ_1 to Y_2, thus typically overestimating β_1. This overestimation is simultaneity bias. If the error term is abnormally negative, Y_{1t} is less than it would have been otherwise, causing Y_{2t} to be less than it would have been otherwise, and the computer program will attribute the decrease in Y_1 to Y_2, once again causing us to overestimate β_1 (that is, induce upward bias).

Recall that the causation between Y_1 and Y_2 runs in both directions because the two variables are interdependent. As a result, β_1, when estimated by OLS, can no longer be interpreted as the impact of Y_2 on Y_1, holding X constant. Instead, $\hat{\beta}_1$ now measures some mix of the effects of the two endogenous variables on each other! In addition, consider β_2. It's supposed to be the effect of X on Y_1 holding Y_2 constant, but how can we expect Y_2 to be held constant when a change in Y_1 takes place? As a result, there is potential bias in all the estimated coefficients in a simultaneous system.

What does this bias look like? It's possible to derive an equation[3] for the expected value of the regression coefficients in a simultaneous system that is estimated by OLS. This equation shows that as long as the error term and any of the explanatory variables in the equation are correlated, then the coefficient estimates will be biased. In addition, it also shows that the bias will have the same sign as the correlation between the error term and the endogenous variable that appears as an explanatory variable in that error term's equation. Since that correlation is usually positive in economic and business examples, so is the bias of OLS. The violation of Classical Assumption III will almost always mean bias in the estimation of β_1. In addition, this bias will usually be positive in economic applications, although the direction of the bias in any given situation will depend on the specific details of the structural equations and the model's underlying theory.

This does not mean that every coefficient from a simultaneous system estimated with OLS will be a bad approximation of the true population coefficient; indeed, most researchers use OLS to estimate equations in simultaneous systems under a number of circumstances. Instead, it's vital at least to consider an alternative to OLS whenever simultaneous equations systems are being estimated. Before we investigate the alternative estimation technique most frequently used (Two-Stage Least Squares), let's look at an example of simultaneity bias.

---

3. For Equation 14.11, the expected value of $\hat{\beta}$ simplifies to:

$$E(\hat{\beta}_1) = \beta_1 + E[\Sigma(Y_{2t} - \bar{Y}_2)(\epsilon_{1t})/\Sigma(Y_{2t} - \bar{Y}_2)^2]$$

In a nonsimultaneous equation, where Y_2 and ϵ_1 are not correlated, the expected value of $\hat{\beta}_1$ equals the true β_1 because the expected value of the term $\Sigma(Y_{2t} - \bar{Y}_2)(\epsilon_{1t})$ is zero. If Y_2 and ϵ_1 are positively correlated, as would be true in most simultaneous systems in economics, then the expected value of $\hat{\beta}_1$ is greater than the true β_1 because the expected value of $\Sigma(Y_{2t} - \bar{Y}_2)(\epsilon_{1t})$ is positive. In the less likely case that Y_2 and ϵ_1 are negatively correlated, the expected value of $\hat{\beta}_1$ is less than the true β_1.

14.2.2 An Example of Simultaneity Bias

To show how the application of OLS to simultaneous equations estimation causes bias, we generated an example of such biased estimates. Since it's impossible to know whether any bias exists unless you also know the true βs, we picked a set of coefficients to be arbitrarily considered true, stochastically generated data sets based on these coefficients, and obtained repeated OLS estimates of these coefficients from the generated data sets. The expected value of these estimates turned out to be quite different from the true coefficient values, thus exemplifying the bias in OLS estimates of coefficients in simultaneous systems.

We used a supply and demand model as the basis for our example:

$$Q_t = \beta_0 + \beta_1 P_t + \beta_2 X_t + \epsilon_{Dt} \tag{14.13}$$

$$Q_t = \alpha_0 + \alpha_1 P_t + \alpha_2 Z_t + \epsilon_{St} \tag{14.14}$$

where: Q_t = the quantity demanded and supplied in time period t
P_t = the price in time period t
X_t = a "demand-side" exogenous variable, such as income
Z_t = a "supply-side" exogenous variable, such as weather
ϵ_t = classical error terms (different for each equation)

The first step was to choose a set of true coefficient values that corresponded to our expectations for this model:

$$\beta_1 = -1 \qquad \beta_2 = +1 \qquad \alpha_1 = +1 \qquad \alpha_2 = +1$$

In other words, we have a negative relationship between price and quantity demanded, a positive relationship between price and quantity supplied, and positive relationships between the exogenous variables and their respective dependent variables.

The next step was to randomly generate a number of data sets based on the true values. This also meant specifying some other characteristics of the data[4] before generating the different data sets (5,000 in this case).

The final step was to apply OLS to the generated data sets and to calculate the estimated coefficients of the demand equation (14.13). (Similar results

---

4. Other assumptions included a normal distribution for the current term, $\beta_0 = 0$, $\alpha_0 = 0$, $\sigma_S^2 = 3$, $\sigma_D^2 = 2$, $r_{xz}^2 = 0.4$, and n = 20. In addition, it was assumed that the error terms of the two equations were not correlated. This is another example of a Monte Carlo experiment.

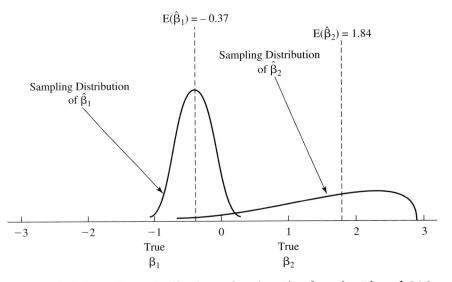

Figure 14.2 Sampling Distributions Showing Simultaneity Bias of OLS Estimates

In the experiment in Section 14.2.2, simultaneity bias is evident in the distribution of the estimates of β_1, which had a mean value of -0.37 compared with a true value of -1.00, and in the estimates of β_2, which had a mean value of 1.84 compared with a true value of 1.00.

were obtained for the supply equation.) The arithmetic means of the results for the 5,000 regressions were:

$$\hat{Q}_{Dt} = \hat{\beta}_0 - 0.37P_t + 1.84X_t \qquad (14.15)$$

In other words, the expected value of $\hat{\beta}_1$ should have been -1.00, but instead it was -0.37; the expected value of $\hat{\beta}_2$ should have been $+1.00$, but instead it was 1.84:

$$E(\hat{\beta}_1) = -0.37 \neq -1.00$$

$$E(\hat{\beta}_2) = 1.84 \neq 1.00$$

This is simultaneity bias! As the diagram of the sampling distributions of the $\hat{\beta}$s in Figure 14.2 shows, the OLS estimates of β_1 were almost never very close to -1.00, and the OLS estimates of β_2 were distributed over a wide range of values.

The biased estimation in this example did not cause incorrect *signs* for the majority of the estimates, but any kind of bias is worth avoiding if it is at all possible. The most frequently used method of reducing simultaneity bias is a technique called Two-Stage Least Squares (2SLS).

14.3 Two-Stage Least Squares (2SLS)

Although there are a number of econometric estimation techniques available that help mitigate the bias inherent in the application of OLS to simultaneous equations systems, the most frequently used alternative to OLS is called Two-Stage Least Squares (2SLS).

14.3.1 What Is Two-Stage Least Squares?

OLS encounters bias in the estimation of simultaneous equations mainly because such equations violate Classical Assumption III, so one solution to the problem is to explore ways to avoid violating that assumption. We could do this if we could find a variable that is:

1. a good proxy for the endogenous variable, and
2. uncorrelated with the error term.

If we then substitute this new variable for the endogenous variable where it appears as an explanatory variable, our new explanatory variable will be uncorrelated with the error term, and Classical Assumption III will be met.

That is, consider Equation 14.16 in the following system:

$$Y_{1t} = \beta_0 + \beta_1 Y_{2t} + \beta_2 X_t + \epsilon_{1t} \qquad (14.16)$$

$$Y_{2t} = \alpha_0 + \alpha_2 Y_{1t} + \alpha_2 Z_t + \epsilon_{2t} \qquad (14.17)$$

If we could find a variable that was highly correlated with Y_2 but that was uncorrelated with ϵ_1, then we could substitute this new variable for Y_2 on the right side of Equation 14.16, and we'd conform to Classical Assumption III. This new variable is called an *instrumental variable*. An **instrumental variable** replaces an endogenous variable (when it is an explanatory variable); it is a good proxy for the endogenous variable and is independent of the error term.

Since there is no joint causality between the instrumental variable and any endogenous variable, the use of the instrumental variable avoids the violation of Classical Assumption III. The job of finding such a variable is another story, though. How do we go about finding variables with these qualifications? For simultaneous equations systems, 2SLS provides an approximate answer.

Two-Stage Least Squares (2SLS) is a method of systematically creating instrumental variables to replace the endogenous variables where they appear as explanatory variables in simultaneous equations systems. 2SLS does this by running a regression on the reduced form of the right-side endogenous variables in need of replacement and then using the $\hat{Y}$s (or fitted values) from those reduced-form regressions as the instrumental variables. More specifically, the two-step procedure consists of:

> **STAGE ONE:** *Run OLS on the reduced-form equations for each of the endogenous variables that appear as explanatory variables in the structural equations in the system.*

Since the predetermined (exogenous plus lagged endogenous) variables are uncorrelated with the reduced-form error term, the OLS estimates of the reduced-form coefficients (the $\hat{\pi}$s) are unbiased. These $\hat{\pi}$s can then be used to calculate estimates of the endogenous variables[5]:

$$\hat{Y}_{1t} = \hat{\pi}_0 + \hat{\pi}_1 X_t + \hat{\pi}_2 Z_t \tag{14.18}$$

$$\hat{Y}_{2t} = \hat{\pi}_3 + \hat{\pi}_4 X_t + \hat{\pi}_5 Z_t \tag{14.19}$$

These $\hat{Y}$s are used as proxies in the structural equations of the simultaneous system.

> **STAGE TWO:** *Substitute the reduced form $\hat{Y}$s for the Ys that appear on the right side (only) of the structural equations, and then estimate these revised structural equations with OLS.*

That is, stage two consists of estimating the following equations with OLS:

$$Y_{1t} = \beta_0 = \beta_1 \hat{Y}_{2t} + \beta_2 X_t + u_{1t} \tag{14.20}$$

$$Y_{2t} = \alpha_0 + \alpha_2 \hat{Y}_{1t} + \alpha_2 Z_t + u_{2t} \tag{14.21}$$

Note that the dependent variables are still the original endogenous variables and that the substitutions are only for the endogenous variables where they appear on the right-hand side of the structural equations.

---

5. Because the πs are not uncorrelated with the ϵs, this procedure produces only approximate instrumental variables that provide consistent (for large samples), but biased (for small samples), estimates of the coefficients of the structural equation (the $\hat{\beta}$s).

If second-stage equations such as Equations 14.20 and 14.21 are estimated with OLS, the SE($\hat{\beta}$)s will be incorrect, so be sure to use your computer's 2SLS estimation procedure.[6]

This description of 2SLS can be generalized to m different simultaneous structural equations. Each reduced-form equation has as explanatory variables every predetermined variable in the entire system of equations. The OLS estimates of the reduced-form equations are used to compute the estimated values of all the endogenous variables that appear as explanatory variables in the m structural equations. After substituting these fitted values for the original values of the endogenous independent variables, OLS is applied to each stochastic equation in the set of structural equations.

14.3.2 The Properties of Two-Stage Least Squares

1. *2SLS estimates are still biased in small samples.* For small samples, the expected value of a $\hat{\beta}$ produced by 2SLS is still not equal to the true β,[7] but as the sample size gets larger, the expected value of the $\hat{\beta}$ approaches the true β. As the sample size gets bigger, the variances of both the OLS and the 2SLS estimates decrease. OLS estimates become very precise estimates of the wrong number, and 2SLS estimates become very precise estimates of the correct number. As a result, the larger the sample size, the better a technique 2SLS is.

   To illustrate, let's look again at the example of Section 14.2. The 2SLS estimate of β_1 was -1.25. This estimate is biased, but it's much closer to the truth ($\beta_1 = -1.00$) than is the OLS estimate of -0.37. We then returned to that example and expanded the data set from 5,000 different samples of size 20 each to 5,000 different samples of 50 observations each. As expected, the average $\hat{\beta}_1$ for 2SLS moved from -1.25 to -1.06 compared to the true value of -1.00. By contrast, the OLS average estimate went from -0.37 to -0.44. Such results are typical; large sample sizes will produce unbiased estimates for 2SLS but biased estimates for OLS.

2. *The bias in 2SLS for small samples typically is of the opposite sign of the bias in OLS.* Recall that the bias in OLS typically was positive, indicating

---

6. Most econometric software packages, including EViews, offer such a 2SLS option. For more on this issue, see Exercise 9 and footnote 11 of this chapter.

7. This bias is caused by remaining correlation between the $\hat{Y}$s produced by the first-stage reduced-form regressions and the ϵs. The effect of the correlation tends to decrease as the sample size increases. Even for small samples, though, it's worth noting that the expected bias due to 2SLS usually is smaller than the expected bias due to OLS.

that a $\hat{\beta}$ produced by OLS for a simultaneous system is likely to be greater than the true β. For 2SLS, the expected bias is negative, and thus a $\hat{\beta}$ produced by 2SLS is likely to be less than the true β. For any given set of data, the 2SLS estimate can be larger than the OLS estimate, but it can be shown that the majority of 2SLS estimates are likely to be less than the corresponding OLS estimates. For large samples, there is little bias in 2SLS.

Return to the example of Section 14.2. Compared to the true value of -1.00 for β_1, the small sample 2SLS average estimate was -1.25, as mentioned above. This means that the 2SLS estimates showed negative bias. The OLS estimates, on the other hand, averaged -0.37; since -0.37 is more positive than -1.00, the OLS estimates exhibited positive bias. Thus, the observed bias due to OLS was opposite the observed bias due to 2SLS, as is generally the case.

3. *If the fit of the reduced-form equation is quite poor, then 2SLS will not work very well.* Recall that the instrumental variable is supposed to be a good proxy for the endogenous variable. To the extent that the fit (as measured by $\overline{R}^2$) of the reduced-form equation is poor, then the instrumental variable is no longer highly correlated with the original endogenous variable, and there is no reason to expect 2SLS to be effective. As the $\overline{R}^2$ of the reduced-form equation increases, the usefulness of the 2SLS will increase.

4. *If the predetermined variables are highly correlated, 2SLS will not work very well.* The first stage of 2SLS includes explanatory variables from different structural equations in the same reduced-form equation. As a result, severe multicollinearity between explanatory variables from different structural equations is possible in the reduced-form equations. When this happens, a $\hat{Y}$ produced by a reduced-form equation can be highly correlated with the exogenous variables in the structural equation. Consequently, the second stage of 2SLS will also show a high degree of multicollinearity, and the variances of the estimated coefficients will be high. Thus, the higher the simple correlation coefficient between predetermined variables (or the higher the variance inflation factors), the less precise 2SLS estimates will be.

5. *The use of the t-test for hypothesis testing is far more accurate using 2SLS estimators than it is using OLS estimators.* The t-test is not exact for the 2SLS estimators, but it is accurate enough in most circumstances. By contrast, the biasedness of OLS estimators in simultaneous systems implies that its t-statistics are not accurate enough to be relied upon for

testing purposes.[8] This means that it may be appropriate to use 2SLS even when the predetermined variables are highly correlated.

On balance, then, 2SLS will almost always be a better estimator of the coefficients of a simultaneous system than OLS will be. The major exception to this general rule is when the fit of the reduced-form equation in question is quite poor for a small sample.

14.3.3 An Example of Two-Stage Least Squares

Let's work through an example of the application of 2SLS to a naive linear Keynesian macroeconomic model of the U.S. economy. We'll specify the following system:

$$Y_t = C_t + I_t + G_t + NX_t \qquad (14.22)$$

$$CO_t = \beta_0 + \beta_1 YD_t + \beta_2 CO_{t-1} + \epsilon_{1t} \qquad (14.23)$$

$$YD_t = Y_t - T_t \qquad (14.24)$$

$$I_t = \beta_3 + \beta_4 Y_t + \beta_5 r_{t-1} + \epsilon_{2t} \qquad (14.25)$$

$$r_t = \beta_6 + \beta_7 Y_t + \beta_8 M_t + \epsilon_{3t} \qquad (14.26)$$

where: Y_t = Gross Domestic Product (GDP) in year t
CO_t = total personal consumption in year t
I_t = total gross private domestic investment in year t
G_t = government purchases of goods and services in year t
NX_t = net exports of goods and services (exports minus imports) in year t
T_t = taxes (actually equal to taxes, depreciation, corporate profits, government transfers, and other adjustments necessary to convert GDP to disposable income) in year t
r_t = the interest rate (yield on commercial paper) in year t
M_t = the money supply (narrowly defined) in year t
YD_t = disposable income in year t

---

8. In our experiments, OLS estimators rejected the correct null hypothesis more than eight times as often as would have been expected from an unbiased procedure. In contrast, the 2SLS estimators were found to reject a correct null hypothesis only twice as frequently as would have been expected.

All variables are in real terms (measured in billions of 1987 dollars) except the interest rate variable, which is measured in nominal percent. The date for this example are from 1964 through 1994 and are presented in Table 14.1.

Equations 14.22 through 14.26 are the structural equations of the system, but only equations 14.23, 14.25, and 14.26 are stochastic (behavioral) and need to be estimated. The other two are identities.

TABLE 14.1 DATA FOR THE SMALL MACROMODEL

Year	r	YD	M	Y	CO	I	G
1963	3.55	na	na	na	1341.9	na	na
1964	3.97	1562.2	160.3	2340.6	1417.2	371.8	549.1
1965	4.38	1653.5	167.9	2470.5	1497.0	413.0	566.9
1966	5.55	1734.3	172.0	2616.2	1573.8	438.0	622.4
1967	5.10	1811.4	183.3	2685.2	1622.4	418.6	667.9
1968	5.90	1886.8	197.4	2796.9	1707.5	440.1	686.8
1969	7.83	1947.4	203.9	2873.0	1771.2	461.3	682.0
1970	7.71	2025.3	214.4	2873.9	1813.5	429.7	665.8
1971	5.11	2099.9	228.3	2955.9	1873.7	475.7	652.4
1972	4.73	2186.2	249.2	3107.1	1978.4	532.2	653.0
1973	8.15	2334.1	262.8	3268.6	2066.7	591.7	644.2
1974	9.84	2317.0	274.3	3248.1	2053.8	543.0	655.4
1975	6.32	2355.4	287.5	3221.7	2097.5	437.6	663.5
1976	5.34	2440.9	306.3	3380.8	2207.3	520.6	659.2
1977	5.61	2512.6	331.1	3533.3	2296.6	600.4	664.1
1978	7.99	2638.4	358.2	3703.5	2391.8	664.6	677.0
1979	10.91	2710.1	382.5	3796.8	2448.4	669.7	689.3
1980	12.29	2733.6	408.5	3776.3	2447.1	594.4	704.2
1981	14.76	2795.8	436.3	3834.1	2476.9	631.1	713.2
1982	11.89	2820.4	474.3	3760.3	2503.7	540.5	723.6
1983	8.89	2893.6	521.0	3906.6	2619.4	599.5	743.8
1984	10.16	3080.1	552.1	4148.5	2746.1	757.5	766.9
1985	8.01	3162.1	619.9	4279.8	2865.8	745.9	813.4
1986	6.39	3261.9	724.5	4404.5	2969.1	735.1	855.4
1987	6.85	3289.5	750.1	4539.9	3052.2	749.3	881.5
1988	7.68	3404.3	787.4	4718.6	3162.4	773.4	886.8
1989	8.80	3464.9	794.7	4838.0	3223.3	784.0	904.4
1990	7.95	3524.5	826.4	4897.3	3272.6	746.8	932.6
1991	5.85	3538.5	897.7	4867.6	3259.4	683.8	944.0
1992	3.80	3648.1	1024.8	4979.3	3349.5	725.3	936.9
1993	3.30	3704.1	1128.4	5134.5	3458.7	819.9	929.8
1994	4.93	3835.4	1147.6	5342.3	3578.5	955.5	922.5

Source: *The Economic Report of the President, 1995.* Note that T and NX can be calculated using Equations 14.22 and 14.24.

Note: filename MACRO14

Stop for a second and look at the system; which variables are endogenous? Which are predetermined? The endogenous variables are those that are jointly determined by the system, namely, Y_t, CO_t, YD_t, and I_t. To see why these four variables are simultaneously determined, note that if you change one of them and follow this change through the system, the change will get back to the original causal variable. For instance, if I_t goes up for some reason, that will cause Y_t to go up, which will feed right back into I_t again. They're simultaneously determined.

What about interest rates? Is r_t an endogenous variable? The surprising answer is that, strictly speaking, r_t is *not* endogenous in this system because r_{t-1} (not r_t) appears in the investment equation and r_t appears only once in the entire system. Thus, there is no simultaneous feedback through the interest rate in this simple model. Because there is no simultaneity, there is no simultaneity bias, and OLS can be used to estimate Equation 14.26. In essence, Equation 14.26 is not in the simultaneous system.[9]

Given this answer, which are the predetermined variables? If Equation 14.26 isn't in the simultaneous system, then the predetermined variables are G_t, NX_t, T_t, CO_{t-1}, and r_{t-1} (but not M_t!). To sum, the simultaneous system has four structural equations, four endogenous variables, and five predetermined variables.

What is the economic content of the stochastic structural equations? The consumption function, Equation 14.23, is a Koyck distributed lag consumption function of the kind we discussed in Chapter 12. We discussed this exact equation in Section 12.1, going so far as to estimate Equation 14.23 with OLS on data from Table 14.1, and the reader is encouraged to reread that analysis.

The investment function, Equation 14.25, includes simplified multiplier and cost of capital components. The multiplier term β_4 measures the stimulus to investment that is generated by an increase in GDP. In a Keynesian model, β_4 thus would be expected to be positive. On the other hand, the higher the cost of capital, the less investment we'd expect to be undertaken (holding multiplier effects constant), mainly because the expected rate of return on marginal capital investments is no longer sufficient to cover the higher cost of capital. Thus β_5 is expected to be negative. It takes time to plan

---

9. Although this sentence is technically correct, it overstates the case. In particular, there are a couple of circumstances in which an econometrician might want to consider Equation 14.26 to be part of the simultaneous system for theoretical reasons. Such possibilities include GLS models and models where the error terms from various equations are thought to be correlated. For our naive Keynesian model with a lagged interest rate effect, however, the equation is not in the simultaneous system.

and start up investment projects, though, so the interest rate is lagged one year.[10]

The interest rate equation is a liquidity preference function solved for the interest rate under the assumption of equilibrium in the money market. In such a situation, an increase in GDP with the money supply held constant would increase the transactions demand for money, pushing up interest rates, so we'd expect β_7 to be positive. If the money supply increased with GDP held constant, we'd expect interest rates to fall, so β_8 should be negative. Recall that a naive Keynesian model has constant prices by assumption.

We're now ready to apply 2SLS to our model.

Stage One: Even though there are four endogenous variables, only two of them appear on the right-hand side of stochastic equations, so only two reduced-form equations need to be estimated to apply 2SLS. These reduced-form equations are estimated automatically by all 2SLS computer estimation programs, but it's instructive to take a look at one anyway:

$$\widehat{YD}_t = 511.6 - 0.55G_t - 0.63NX_t - 0.34T_t + 1.24CO_{t-1} - 2.03r_{t-1}$$
$$(0.20) \quad (0.16) \quad (0.19) \quad (0.06) \quad (4.09)$$
$$t = -2.73 \quad -3.82 \quad -1.84 \quad 21.39 \quad -0.50$$
$$n = 31 \quad \bar{R}^2 = .997 \quad DW = 2.09 \quad (14.27)$$

This reduced form has an excellent overall fit but is almost surely suffering from severe multicollinearity. Note that we don't test any hypotheses on reduced forms, nor do we consider dropping a variable (like r_{t-1}) that is statistically and theoretically irrelevant. The whole purpose of stage one of 2SLS is not to generate meaningful reduced-form estimated equations but rather to generate useful instruments ($\hat{Y}$s) to use as substitutes for endogenous variables in the second stage. To do that, we calculate the $\hat{Y}_t$s and $\widehat{YD}_t$s for all 31 observations by plugging the actual values of all 5 predetermined variables into reduced-form equations like Equation 14.27.

Stage Two: We then substitute these $\hat{Y}_t$s, and $\widehat{YD}_t$s, for the endogenous variables where they appear on the right sides of Equations 14.23 and 14.25. For

---

10. This investment equation is a simplified mix of the accelerator and the neoclassical theories of the investment function. The former emphasizes that changes in the level of output are the key determinant of investment, and the latter emphasizes that user cost of capital (the opportunity cost that the firm incurs as a consequence of owning an asset) is the key. For an introduction to the determinants of consumption and investment, see any intermediate macroeconomics textbook.

example, the $\widehat{YD}_t$ from Equation 14.27 would be substituted into Equation 14.23, resulting in:

$$CO_t = \beta_0 + \beta_1\widehat{YD}_t + \beta_2CO_{t-1} + \epsilon_{1t} \qquad (14.28)$$

If we use OLS to estimate Equation 14.28 and the other second-stage equations given the data in Table 14.1, we obtain the following 2SLS[11] results:

$$\widehat{CO}_t = -24.73 + 0.44\widehat{YD}_t + 0.54CO_{t-1} \qquad (14.29)$$
$$(0.15) \qquad (0.16)$$
$$t = 2.87 \qquad 3.31$$
$$n = 31 \qquad \overline{R}^2 = .998 \qquad DW = 0.98$$

$$\hat{I}_t = 33.90 + 0.164\hat{Y}_t - 5.62r_{t-1} \qquad (14.30)$$
$$(0.010) \qquad (3.11)$$
$$t = 16.51 \qquad -1.81$$
$$n = 31 \qquad \overline{R}^2 = .901 \qquad DW = 0.97$$

If we had estimated these equations with OLS alone instead of with 2SLS, we would have obtained:

$$\widehat{CO}_t = -38.11 + 0.52YD_t + 0.46CO_{t-1} \qquad (14.31)$$
$$(0.12) \qquad (0.12)$$
$$t = 4.44 \qquad 3.74$$
$$n = 31 \qquad \overline{R}^2 = .998 \qquad DW = 0.89$$

$$\hat{I}_t = 32.95 + 0.164Y_t - 5.64r_{t-1} \qquad (14.32)$$
$$(0.010) \qquad (3.11)$$
$$t = 16.55 \qquad -1.81$$
$$n = 31 \qquad \overline{R}^2 = .901 \qquad DW = 0.97$$

---

11. A few notes about 2SLS estimation and this model are in order. The 2SLS estimates in Equations 14.29 and 14.30 are correct, but if you were to estimate those equations with OLS (using as instruments $\hat{Y}$s and $\widehat{YD}$s generated as in Equation 14.27) you would obtain the same coefficient estimates but a different set of estimates of the standard errors (and t-scores). This difference comes about because running OLS on the second stage alone ignores the fact that the first stage was run at all. To get accurate estimated standard errors and t-scores, the estimation should be done on a complete 2SLS program. Finally, note that M is not predetermined (exogenous) because the equation in which it appears is not part of the simultaneous system.

In both cases, we estimate Equation 14.26 with OLS, obtaining:

$$\hat{r}_t = -13.06 + 0.0087Y_t - 0.025M_t \qquad (14.33)$$
$$(0.0016) \quad (0.005)$$
$$t = 5.31 \qquad -5.33$$
$$n = 31 \qquad \overline{R}^2 = .471 \qquad DW = 0.66$$

Let's compare the OLS and 2SLS results. First, there doesn't seem to be much difference between them. If OLS is biased, how could this occur? When the fit of the stage-one reduced-form equations is excellent, as in Equation 14.27, then Y and $\hat{Y}$ are virtually identical, and the second stage of 2SLS is quite similar to the OLS estimate. Second, we'd expect positive bias in the OLS estimation and smaller negative bias in the 2SLS estimation, but the differences between OLS and 2SLS appear to be in the expected direction only about half the time. This might have been caused by the extreme multicollinearity in the 2SLS estimations as well as by the superb fit of the reduced forms mentioned above.

Also, take a look at the Durbin–Watson statistics. DW is well below the d_L of 1.30 (one-sided 5 percent significance, $n = 31$, $k' = 2$) in all the equations despite DW's bias toward 2 in the consumption equation (because it's a Koyck distributed lag). Consequently, positive serial correlation is likely to exist in the residuals of all three equations. Since the interest rate equation (Equation 14.33) was estimated with OLS, we can apply GLS to that equation:

$$\hat{r}_t = -15.57 + 0.0095Y_t - 0.027M_t \qquad (14.34)$$
$$(0.0030) \quad (0.008)$$
$$t = 3.10 \qquad -3.49$$
$$n = 30 \qquad \overline{R}^2 = .684 \qquad \hat{\rho} = 0.67$$

Applying GLS to the two 2SLS-estimated equations is more tricky, however, especially because, as mentioned in Section 12.2, serial correlation causes bias in an equation with a lagged dependent variable, as in the consumption function. One solution to this problem, running GLS *and* 2SLS, is discussed in Exercise 12.

Finally, what about nonstationarity? We learned in Chapter 12 that time-series models like these have the potential to be spurious in the face of non-stationarity. Are any of these regressions spurious? Well, as you can guess from looking at the data (or as you know if you did Exercise 11 in Chapter 12), quite a few of the series in this model are, indeed, nonstationary. Luckily, the interest rate is stationary, so Equations 14.33 and 14.34 are not a concern. In addition, it turns out that the consumption function is reasonably cointe-grated (see Exercise 15 of this chapter), so Equations 14.29 and 14.31 proba-bly can stand as estimated. Unfortunately, the investment equation suffers from nonstationarity that almost surely results in an inflated t-score for GDP and a low t-score for r_{t-1} (because it is stationary when all the other variables in the equation are nonstationary). In fact, most macromodels encounter sim-ilar problems with the significance (and sometimes the sign) of the interest rate variable in investment equations, at least partially because of the nonsta-tionarity of the other variables in the equation. Given the tools covered so far in this text, however, there is little we can do to improve the situation.

These caveats aside, this model has provided us with a complete example of the use of 2SLS to estimate a simultaneous system. However, the applica-tion of 2SLS requires that the equation being estimated be "identified," so before we can conclude our study of simultaneous equations, we need to ad-dress the problem of identification.

14.4 The Identification Problem

Two-Stage Least Squares cannot be applied to an equation unless that equa-tion is *identified*. Before estimating any equation in a simultaneous system, the researcher must address the identification problem. Once an equation is found to be identified, then it can be estimated with 2SLS, but if an equation is not identified (*underidentified*), then 2SLS cannot be used no matter how large the sample. It's important to point out that an equation being identified (and therefore capable of being estimated with 2SLS) does not ensure that the resulting 2SLS estimates will be good ones. The question being asked is not how good the 2SLS estimates will be but whether the 2SLS estimates can be obtained at all.

14.4.1 What Is the Identification Problem?

Identification is a precondition for the appplication of 2SLS to equations in simultaneous systems; a structural equation is identified only when enough of the system's predetermined variables are omitted from the equation in question to allow that equation to be distinguished from all the others in the system. Note that one equation in a simultaneous system might be identified and another might not.

How could we have equations that we could not identify? To see how, let's consider a supply and demand simultaneous system in which only price and quantity are specified:

$$Q_{Dt} = \alpha_0 + \alpha_1 P_t + \epsilon_{Dt} \quad \text{(demand)} \qquad (14.35)$$

$$Q_{St} = \beta_0 + \beta_1 P_t + \epsilon_{St} \quad \text{(supply)} \qquad (14.36)$$

where: $Q_{Dt} = Q_{St}$

Although we've labeled one equation as the demand equation and the other as the supply equation, the computer will not be able to identify them from the data because the right-side and the left-side variables are exactly the same in both equations; without some predetermined variables included to distinguish between these two equations, it would be impossible to distinguish supply from demand.

What if we added a predetermined variable to one of the equations, say the supply equation? Then, Equation 14.36 would become:

$$Q_{St} = \beta_0 + \beta_1 P_t + \beta_2 Z_t + \epsilon_{St} \qquad (14.37)$$

In such a circumstance, every time Z changed, the supply curve would shift, but the demand curve would not, so that eventually we would be able to collect a good picture of what the demand curve looked like.

Figure 14.3 demonstrates this. Given four different values of Z, we get four different supply curves, each of which intersects with the constant demand curve at a different equilibrium price and quantity (intersections 1–4). These equilibria are the data that we would be able to observe in the real world and

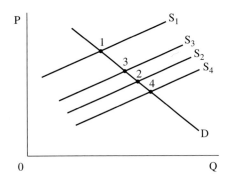

Figure 14.3 A Shifting Supply Curve Allows the Identification of the Demand Curve

If the supply curve shifts but the demand curve does not, then we move along the demand curve, allowing us to identify and estimate the demand curve (but not the supply curve).

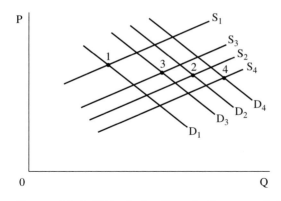

Figure 14.4 If Both the Supply Curve and the Demand Curve Shift, Neither Curve Is Identified

If both the supply curve and the demand curve shift in response to the same variable, then we move from one equilibrium to another, and the resulting data points identify neither curve. To allow such an identification, at least one exogenous factor must cause one curve to shift while allowing the other to remain constant.

are all that we could feed into the computer. As a result, we would be able to identify the demand curve because we left out at least one predetermined variable; when this predetermined variable changed, but the demand curve didn't, the supply curve shifted so that quantity demanded moved along the demand curve and we gathered enough information to estimate the coefficients of the demand curve. The supply curve, on the other hand, remains as much a mystery as ever because its shifts give us no clue whatsoever about its shape. In essence, the demand curve was identified by the predetermined variable that was included in the system but excluded from the demand equation. The supply curve is not identified because there is no such excluded predetermined variable for it.

Even if we added Z to the demand curve as well, that would not identify the supply curve. In fact, if we had Z in both equations, the two would be identical again, and although both would shift when Z changed, those shifts would give us no information about either curve! As illustrated in Figure 14.4, the observed equilibrium prices and quantities would be almost random intersections describing neither the demand nor the supply curve. That is, the shifts in the supply curve are the same as before, but now the demand curve also shifts with Z. In this case, it's not possible to identify either the demand curve or the supply curve.[12]

12. An exception would be if you knew the relative magnitudes of the true coefficients of Z in the two equations, but such knowledge is unlikely.

The way to identify both curves is to have at least one predetermined variable in each equation that is not in the other, as in:

$$Q_{Dt} = \alpha_0 + \alpha_1 P_t + \alpha_2 X_t + \epsilon_{Dt} \qquad (14.38)$$

$$Q_{St} = \beta_0 + \beta_1 P_t + \beta_2 Z_t + \epsilon_{St} \qquad (14.39)$$

Now when Z changes, the supply curve shifts, and we can identify the demand curves from the data on equilibrium prices and quantities. When X changes, the demand curve shifts, and we can identify the supply curve from the data. Of course, if X and Z are highly correlated, we still have problems of estimation, as mentioned in the previous section.

To sum, identification is a precondition for the application of 2SLS to equations in simultaneous systems. A structural equation is identified only when the predetermined variables are arranged within the system so as to allow us to use the observed equilibrium points to distinguish the shape of the equation in question. Most systems are quite a bit more complicated than the ones above, however, so econometricians need a general method by which to determine whether equations are identified. The method typically used is the *order condition* of identification.

14.4.2 The Order Condition of Identification

The **order condition** is a systematic method of determining whether a particular equation in a simultaneous system has the potential to be identified. If an equation can meet the order condition, then it is identified in all but a very small number of cases. We thus say that the order condition is a necessary but not sufficient condition of identification.[13]

What is the order condition? Recall that we have used the phrases endogenous and predetermined to refer to the two kinds of variables in a simultaneous system. Endogenous variables are those that are jointly determined in the system in the current time period. Predetermined variables are exogenous variables plus any lagged endogenous variables that might be in the model. For each equation in the system, we need to determine:

---

13. A sufficient condition for an equation to be identified is called the *rank condition,* but most researchers examine just the order condition before estimating an equation with 2SLS. These researchers let the computer estimation procedure tell them whether the rank condition has been met (by its ability to apply 2SLS to the equation). Those interested in the rank condition are encouraged to consult an advanced econometrics text.

1. The number of predetermined (exogenous plus lagged endogenous) variables in the entire simultaneous system.

2. The number of slope coefficients estimated in the equation in question.

> **THE ORDER CONDITION:** *A necessary condition for an equation to be identified is that the number of predetermined (exogenous plus lagged endogenous) variables in the system be greater than or equal to the number of slope coefficients in the equation of interest.*

In equation form, a structural equation meets the order condition[14] if:

The number of predetermined variables $\geq$ The number of slope coefficients
(in the simultaneous system)   (in the equation)

14.4.3 Two Examples of the Application of the Order Condition

Let's apply the order condition to some of the simultaneous equations systems encountered in this chapter. For example, consider once again the cola supply and demand model of Section 14.1.1:

$$Q_{Dt} = \alpha_0 + \alpha_1 P_t + \alpha_2 X_{1t} + \alpha_3 X_{2t} + \epsilon_{Dt} \qquad (14.4)$$

$$Q_{St} = \beta_0 + \beta_1 P_t + \beta_2 X_{3t} + \epsilon_{St} \qquad (14.5)$$

$$Q_{St} = Q_{Dt}$$

Equation 14.4 is identified by the order condition because the number of predetermined variables in the system (three, X_1, X_2, and X_3) is equal to the number of slope coefficients in the equation (three, α_1, α_2, and α_3). This particular result (equality) implies that Equation 14.4 is *exactly identified* by the order condition. Equation 14.5 is also identified by the order condition because there still are three predetermined variables in the system, but there are only two slope coefficients in the equation; this condition implies that Equation 14.5 is *overidentified*. 2SLS can be applied to equations that are

---

14. A more popular but harder to remember way of stating this condition is that the number of predetermined variables in the system that are excluded from the equation must be greater than or equal to the number of endogenous variables included in the equation minus one.

identified (which includes exactly identified and overidentified), but not to equations that are underidentified.

A more complicated example is the small macroeconomic model of Section 14.3.3:

$$Y_t = CO_t + I_t + G_t + NX_t \tag{14.22}$$

$$CO_t = \beta_0 + \beta_1 YD_t + \beta_2 CO_{t-1} + \epsilon_{1t} \tag{14.23}$$

$$YD_t = Y_t - T_t \tag{14.24}$$

$$I_t = \beta_3 + \beta_4 Y_t + \beta_5 r_{t-1} + \epsilon_{2t} \tag{14.25}$$

As we've noted, there are five predetermined variables (exogenous plus lagged endogenous) in this system (G_t, NX_t, T_t, CO_{t-1}, and r_{t-1}). Equation 14.23 has two slope coefficients (β_1 and β_2), so this equation is overidentified ($5 > 2$) and meets the order condition of identification. As the reader can verify, Equation 14.25 also turns out to be overidentified. Since the 2SLS computer program did indeed come up with estimates of the βs in the model, we knew this already. Note that Equations 14.22 and 14.24 are identities and are not estimated, so we're not concerned with their identification properties.

14.5   Summary

1. Most economic and business models are inherently simultaneous because of the dual causality, feedback loops, or joint determination of particular variables. These simultaneously determined variables are called endogenous, and nonsimultaneously determined variables are called exogenous.

2. A structural equation characterizes the theory underlying a particular variable and is the kind of equation we have used to date in this text. A reduced-form equation expresses a particular endogenous variable solely in terms of an error term and all the predetermined (exogenous and lagged endogenous) variables in the simultaneous system.

3. Simultaneous equations models violate the Classical Assumption of independence between the error term and the explanatory variables because of the feedback effects of the endogenous variables. For example, an unusually high observation of an equation's error term works through the simultaneous system and eventually causes a high

value for the endogenous variables that appear as explanatory variables in the equation in question, thus violating the assumption of no correlation (Classical Assumption III).

4. If OLS is applied to the coefficients of a simultaneous system, the resulting estimates are biased and inconsistent. This occurs mainly because of the violation of Classical Assumption III; the OLS regression package attributes to explanatory variables changes in the dependent variable actually caused by the error term (with which the explanatory variables are correlated).

5. Two-Stage Least Squares is a method of decreasing the amount of bias in the estimation of simultaneous equations systems. It works by systematically using the reduced-form equations of the system to create proxies for the endogenous variables that are independent of the error terms (called instrumental variables). It then runs OLS on the structural equations of the system with the instrumental variables replacing the endogenous variables where they appear as explanatory variables.

6. Two-Stage Least Squares estimates are biased (with a sign opposite that of the OLS bias) but consistent (becoming more unbiased and closer to zero variance as the sample size gets larger). If the fit of the reduced-form equations is poor or if the predetermined variables are highly correlated, then 2SLS will not work very well. The larger the sample size, the better it is to use 2SLS.

7. 2SLS cannot be applied to an equation that's not identified. A necessary (but not sufficient) requirement for identification is the order condition, which requires that the number of predetermined variables in the system be greater than or equal to the number of slope coefficients in the equation of interest. Sufficiency is usually determined by the ability of 2SLS to estimate the coefficients.

Exercises

(Answers to even-numbered exercises are in Appendix A.)

1. Write the meaning of each of the following terms without referring to the book (or your notes), and compare your definition with the version in the text for each:
   a. endogenous variables
   b. predetermined variables

c. structural equations

d. reduced-form equations

e. simultaneity bias

f. Two-Stage Least Squares

g. identification

h. order condition for identification

2.   The word *recursive* is used to describe an equation that has an impact on a simultaneous system without any feedback from the system to the equation. Which of the equations in the following systems are simultaneous, and which are recursive? Be sure to specify which variables are endogenous and which are predetermined:

a. $Y_{1t} = f(Y_{2t}, X_{1t}, X_{2t-1})$

$Y_{2t} = f(Y_{3t}, X_{3t}, X_{4t}$

$Y_{3t} = f(T_{1t}, X_{1t-1}, X_{4t-1})$

b. $Z_t = g(X_t, Y_t, H_t)$

$X_t = g(Z_t, P_{t-1})$

$H_t = g(Z_t, B_t, C_t, D_t)$

c. $Y_t = f(Y_{2t}, X_{1t}, X_{2t})$

$Y_{2t} = f(Y_{3t}, X_{5t})$

3.   Section 14.1.2 works through Equations 14.2 and 14.3 to show the violation of Classical Assumption III by an unexpected increase in ϵ_1. Show the violation of Classical Assumption III by working through the following examples:

a. a decrease in ϵ_2 in Equation 14.3

b. an increase in ϵ_D in Equation 14.4

c. an increase in ϵ_1 in Equation 14.23

4.   As mentioned in Section 14.1.3, Indirect Least Squares (ILS) is a method of calculating the coefficients of the structural equations directly from the coefficients of the reduced-form equations without a second-stage regression. This technique, which requires that the equations be exactly identified, can be used because the coefficients of the structural equations can be expressed in terms of the coefficients of the reduced-form equations. These expressions can be derived by solving the structural equations for one of the endogenous variables in terms of the predetermined variables and then substituting.

a. Return to Equations 14.4 and 14.5 and confirm that the reduced-form equations for that system are Equations 14.8 and 14.9.

b. By mathematically manipulating the equations, express the coefficients of Equation 14.4 in terms of the πs of the reduced-form equations.

c. What disadvantages does ILS have? Why isn't it used frequently?

d. Think through the application of ILS to an overidentified equation. What problem would that estimation encounter?

5. Section 14.2.1 makes the statement that the correlation between the ϵs and the Ys (where they appear as explanatory variables) is usually positive in economics. To see if this is true, investigate the sign of the error term/explanatory variable correlation in the following cases:

a. the three examples in Exercise 3 above

b. the more general case of all the equations in a typical supply and demand model (for instance, the model for cola in Section 14.1)

c. the more general case of all the equations in a simple macroeconomic model (for instance, the small macroeconomic model in Section 14.3.3)

6. Determine the identification properties of the following equations. In particular, be sure to note the number of predetermined variables in the system, the number of slope coefficients in the equation, and whether the equation is underidentified, overidentified, or exactly identified.

a. Equations 14.2–14.3

b. Equations 14.13–14.14

c. part a of Exercise 2 above (assume all equations are stochastic)

d. part b of Exercise 2 above (assume all equations are stochastic)

7. Determine the identification properties of the following equations. In particular, be sure to note the number of predetermined variables in the system, the number of slope coefficients in the equation, and whether the equation is underidentified, overidentified, or exactly identified. (Assume all equations are stochastic unless specified otherwise.)

a. $A_t = f(B_t, C_t, D_t)$
   $B_t = f(A_t, C_t)$

b. $Y_{1t} = f(Y_{2t}, X_{1t}, X_{2t}, X_{3t})$
   $Y_{2t} = f(X_{2t})$
   $X_{2t} = f(Y_{1t}, X_{4t}, X_{3t})$

c. $C_t = f(Y_t)$
   $I_t = f(Y_t, R_t, E_t, D_t)$
   $R_t = f(M_t, R_{t-1}, Y_t - Y_{t-1})$
   $Y_t = C_t + I_t + G_t$ (nonstochastic)

8. Return to the supply and demand example for cola in Section 14.1 and explain exactly how 2SLS would estimate the αs and βs of Equations 14.4 and 14.5. Write out the equations to be estimated in both stages, and indicate precisely what, if any, substitutions would be made in the second stage.

9. As an exercise to gain familiarity with the 2SLS program on your computer, take the data provided for the simple Keynesian model in Section 14.3.3, and:
    a. Estimate the investment function with OLS.
    b. Estimate the reduced form for Y with OLS.
    c. Substitute the $\hat{Y}$ from your reduced form into the investment function and run the second stage yourself with OLS.
    d. Estimate the investment function with your computer's 2SLS program (if there is one) and compare the results with those obtained in part c above.

10. Suppose that one of your friends recently estimated a simultaneous equation research project and found the OLS results to be virtually identical to the 2SLS results. How would you respond if he or she said "What a waste of time! I shouldn't have bothered with 2SLS in the first place! Besides, this proves that there wasn't any bias in my model anyway."
    a. What is the value of 2SLS in such a case?
    b. Does the similarity between the 2SLS and OLS estimates indicate a lack of bias?

11. Think over the problem of building a model for the supply of and demand for labor (measured in hours worked) as a function of the wage and other variables.
    a. Completely specify labor supply and labor demand equations and hypothesize the expected signs of the coefficients of your variables.
    b. Is this system simultaneous or not? That is, is there likely to be feedback between the wage and hours demanded and supplied? Why or why not?
    c. Is your system likely to encounter biased estimates? Why?
    d. What sort of estimation procedure would you use to obtain your coefficient estimates? (*Hint:* Be sure to determine the identification properties of your equations.)

12. Let's analyze the problem of serial correlation in simultaneous models. For instance, recall that in our small macroeconomic model, the 2SLS version of the consumption function, Equation 14.29, was:

$$\widehat{CO}_t = -24.73 + 0.44\widehat{YD}_t + 0.54CO_{t-1} \qquad (14.29)$$
$$(0.15) \qquad (0.16)$$
$$t = 2.87 \qquad 3.31$$
$$n = 31 \qquad \overline{R}^2 = .998 \qquad DW = 0.98$$

where C is consumption and YD is disposable income.

a. Test Equation 14.29 to confirm that we do indeed have a serial correlation problem. (*Hint:* This should seem familiar.)

b. Equation 14.29 will encounter both simultaneity bias and bias due to serial correlation with a lagged endogenous variable. If you could solve only one of these two problems, which would you choose? Why? (*Hint:* Compare Equation 14.29 with the OLS version of the consumption function, Equation 14.31.)

c. Suppose you wanted to solve both problems? Can you think of a way to adjust for both serial correlation and simultaneity bias at the same time? Would it make more sense to run GLS first and then 2SLS, or would you rather run 2SLS first and then GLS? Could they be run simultaneously?

13. Suppose that a fad for oats (resulting from the announcement of the health benefits of oat bran) has made you toy with the idea of becoming a broker in the oat market. Before spending your money, you decide to build a simple model of supply and demand (identical to those in Sections 14.1 and 14.2) of the market for oats:

$$Q_{Dt} = \beta_0 + \beta_1 P_t + \beta_2 YD_t + \epsilon_{Dt}$$
$$Q_{St} = \alpha_0 + \alpha_1 P_t + \alpha_2 W_t + \epsilon_{St}$$
$$Q_{Dt} = Q_{St}$$

where: Q_{Dt} = the quantity of oats demanded in time period t
Q_{St} = the quantity of oats supplied in time period t
P_t = the price of oats in time period t
W_t = average oat-farmer wages in time period t
YD_t = disposable income in time period t

a. You notice that no left-hand-side variable appears on the right side of either of your stochastic simultaneous equations. Does this mean that OLS estimation will encounter no simultaneity bias? Why or why not?

b. You expect that when P_t goes up, Q_{Dt} will fall. Does this mean that if you encounter simultaneity bias in the demand equation, it will be negative instead of the positive bias we typically associate with OLS estimation of simultaneous equations? Explain your answer.

c. Carefully outline how you would apply 2SLS to this system. How many equations (including reduced forms) would you have to estimate? Specify precisely which variables would be in each equation.

d. Given the following hypothetical data,[15] estimate OLS and 2SLS versions of your oat supply and demand equations.

e. Compare your OLS and 2SLS estimates. How do they compare with your prior expectations? Which equation do you prefer? Why?

Year	Q	P	W	YD
1	50	10	100	15
2	54	12	102	12
3	65	9	105	11
4	84	15	107	17
5	75	14	110	19
6	85	15	111	30
7	90	16	111	28
8	60	14	113	25
9	40	17	117	23
10	70	19	120	35

Note: datafile = OATS14

14. Simultaneous equations make sense in cross-sectional as well as time-series applications. For example, James Ragan[16] examined the effects of unemployment insurance (hereafter UI) eligibility standards on unemployment rates and the rate at which workers quit their jobs. Ragan used a pooled data set that contained observations from a number of different states from four different years (requirements for UI eligibility differ by state). His results are as follows (t-scores in parentheses):

$$\widehat{QU_i} = 7.00 + 0.089UR_i - 0.063UN_i - 2.83RE_i - 0.032MX_i$$
$$(0.10) \quad (-0.63) \quad (-1.98) \quad (-0.73)$$
$$+ 0.003IL_i - 0.25QM_i + \cdots$$
$$(0.01) \quad (-0.52)$$

---

15. These data are from the excellent course materials that Professors Bruce Gensemer and James Keeler prepared to supplement the use of this text at Kenyon College.

16. James F. Ragan, Jr., "The Voluntary Leaver Provisions of Unemployment Insurance and Their Effect on Quit and Unemployment Rates," *Southern Economic Journal*, July 1984, pp. 135–146.

$$\widehat{UR_i} = -0.54 + 0.44QU_i + 0.13UN_i + 0.049MX_i$$
$$\quad\quad (1.01) \quad\quad (3.29) \quad\quad (1.71)$$
$$+ 0.56IL_i \quad + 0.63QM_i + \cdots$$
$$(2.03) \quad\quad (2.05)$$

where: QU_i = the quit rate (quits per 100 employees) in the ith state

UR_i = the unemployment rate in the ith state

UN_i = union membership as a percentage of nonagricultural employment in the ith state

RE_i = average hourly earnings in the ith state relative to the average hourly earnings for the United States

IL_i = dummy variable equal to 1 if workers in the ith state are eligible for UI if they are forced to quit a job because of illness, 0 otherwise

QM_i = dummy variable equal to 1 if the ith state maintains full UI benefits for the quitter (rather than lowering benefits), 0 otherwise

MX_i = maximum weekly UI benefits relative to average hourly earnings in the ith state

a. Hypothesize the expected signs for the coefficients of each of the explanatory variables in the system. Use economic theory to justify your answers. Which estimated coefficients are different from your expectations?

b. Ragan felt that these two equations would encounter simultaneity bias if they were estimated with OLS. Do you agree? Explain your answer. (*Hint:* Start by deciding which variables are endogenous and why.)

c. The actual equations included a number of variables not documented above, but the only predetermined variable in the system that was included in the QU equation but not the UR equation was RE. What does this information tell you about the identification properties of the QU equation? The UR equation?

d. What are the implications of the lack of significance of the endogenous variables where they appear on the right-hand side of the equations?

e. What, if any, policy recommendations do these results suggest?

15. Return to the consumption function of the small macromodel of Section 14.3.3 and consider again the issue of cointegration as a possible solution to the problem of nonstationarity.

a. Which of the variables in the equation are nonstationary? (*Hint:* See Exercises 10 and 11 in Chapter 12.)

b. Test the possibility that Equation 14.31 is cointegrated. That is, test the hypothesis that the residuals of Equation 14.31 are stationary. (*Hint:* Use the ACF test and/or the Dickey–Fuller test.)

c. Equation 14.31 is a Koyck distributed lag equation. Do you think that this makes it more or less likely that the equation is cointegrated?

d. Equation 14.31 is the OLS estimate of the consumption function. Would your approach be any different if you were going to test the 2SLS estimate for cointegration? How? Why?

Appendix 14.6: Errors in the Variables

Until now, we have implicitly assumed that our data were measured accurately. That is, although the stochastic error term was defined as including measurement error, we never explicitly discussed what the existence of such measurement error did to the coefficient estimates. Unfortunately, in the real world, errors of measurement are common. Mismeasurement might result from the data being based on a sample, as are almost all national aggregate statistics, or simply because the data were reported incorrectly. Whatever the cause, these **errors in the variables** are mistakes in the measurement of the dependent and/or one or more of the independent variables that are large enough to have potential impacts on the estimation of the coefficients. Such errors in the variables might be better called "measurement errors in the data." We will tackle this subject by first examining errors in the dependent variable and then moving on to look at the more serious problem of errors in an independent variable. We assume a single equation model. The reason we have included this section here is that errors in explanatory variables give rise to biased OLS estimates very similar to simultaneity bias.

14.6.1 Measurement Errors in the Data for the Dependent Variable

Suppose that the true regression model is

$$Y_i = \beta_0 + \beta_1 X_i + \epsilon_i \tag{14.40}$$

and further suppose that the dependent variable, Y_i, is measured incorrectly, so that Y_i^* is observed instead of Y_i, where

$$Y_i^* = Y_i + v_i \qquad (14.41)$$

and where v_i is an error of measurement that has all the properties of a classical error term. What does this mismeasurement do to the estimation of Equation 14.40?

To see what happens when $Y_i^* = Y_i + v_i$, let's add v_i to both sides of Equation 14.40, obtaining

$$Y_i + v_i = \beta_0 + \beta_1 X_i + \epsilon_i + v_i \qquad (14.42)$$

which is the same as

$$Y_i^* = \beta_0 + \beta_1 X_i + \epsilon_i^* \qquad (14.43)$$

where $\epsilon_i^* = (\epsilon_i + v_i)$. That is, we estimate Equation 14.43 when in reality we want to estimate Equation 14.40. Take another look at Equation 14.43. When v_i changes, both the dependent variable and the error term ϵ_i^* move together. This is no cause for alarm, however, since the dependent variable is always correlated with the error term. Although the extra movement will increase the variability of Y and therefore be likely to decrease the overall statistical fit of the equation, an error of measurement in the dependent variable does not cause any bias in the estimates of the βs.

14.6.2 Measurement Errors in the Data for an Independent Variable

This is not the case when the mismeasurement is in the data for one or more of the independent variables. Unfortunately, such errors in the independent variables cause bias that is quite similar in nature (and in remedy) to simultaneity bias. To see this, once again suppose that the true regression model is Equation 14.40:

$$Y_i = \beta_0 + \beta_1 X_i + \epsilon_i \qquad (14.40)$$

and now suppose that the independent variable, X_i, is measured incorrectly, so that X_i^* is observed instead of X_i, where

$$X_i^* = X_i + u_i \qquad (14.44)$$

and where u_i is an error of measurement just like v_i above. To see what this mismeasurement does to the estimation of Equation 14.40, let's add the term $0 = (\beta_1 u_i - \beta_1 u_i)$ to Equation 14.40, obtaining

$$Y_i = \beta_0 + \beta_1 X_i + \epsilon_i + (\beta_1 u_i - \beta_1 u_i) \qquad (14.45)$$

which can be rewritten as

$$Y_i = \beta_0 + \beta_1(X_i + u_i) + (\epsilon_i - \beta_1 u_i) \qquad (14.46)$$

or

$$Y_i = \beta_0 + \beta_1 X_i^* + \epsilon_i^{**} \qquad (14.47)$$

where $\epsilon_i^{**} = (\epsilon_i - \beta_1 u_i)$. In this case, we estimate Equation 14.47 when we should be trying to estimate Equation 14.40. Notice what happens to Equation 14.47 when u_i changes, however. When u_i changes, the stochastic error term ϵ_i^{**} and the independent variable X_i^* move in opposite directions; they are correlated. Such a correlation is a direct violation of Classical Assumption III in a way that is remarkably similar to the violation (described in Section 14.1) of the same assumption in simultaneous equations. Not surprisingly, this violation causes the same problem, bias, for errors-in-the-variables models that it causes for simultaneous equations. That is, because of the measurement error in the independent variable, the OLS estimates of the coefficients of Equation 14.47 are *biased.*

A frequently used technique to rid an equation of the bias caused by measurement errors in the data for one or more of the independent variables is to use an *instrumental variable,* the same technique used to alleviate simultaneity bias. A proxy for X is chosen that is highly correlated with X but is uncorrelated with ϵ. Recall that 2SLS is an instrumental variables technique. Such techniques are applied only rarely to errors in the variables problems, however, because although we may suspect that there are errors in the variables, it's unusual to know positively that they exist, and it's difficult to find an instrumental variable that satisfies both conditions. As a result, X* is about as good a proxy for X as we usually can find, and no action is taken. If the mismeasurement in X were known to be large, however, some remedy would be required.

To sum, an error of measurement in one or more of the independent variables will cause the error term of Equation 14.47 to be correlated with the independent variable, causing bias analogous to simultaneity bias.[17]

---

17. If errors exist in the data for the dependent variable and one or more of the independent variables, then both decreased overall statistical fit and bias in the estimated coefficients will result.

Forecasting

Of the uses of econometrics outlined in Chapter 1, we have discussed forecasting the least. Accurate forecasting is vital to successful planning, so it's the primary goal of many business and governmental uses of econometrics. For example, manufacturing firms need sales forecasts, banks need interest rate forecasts, and governments need unemployment and inflation rate forecasts.

To many business and government leaders, the words *econometrics* and *forecasting* mean the same thing. Such a simplification gives econometrics a bad name because some consulting econometricians overestimate their ability to produce accurate forecasts, resulting in unrealistic claims and unhappy clients. Some of their clients would probably applaud the nineteenth century New York law (luckily unenforced but apparently also unrepealed) that provides that persons "pretending to forecast the future" shall be liable to a $250 fine and/or six months in prison.[1] Although many econometricians might wish that such consultants would call themselves "futurists" or "soothsayers," it's impossible to ignore the importance of econometrics in forecasting in today's world.

The ways in which the prediction of future events is accomplished are quite varied. At one extreme, some forecasters use models with hundreds of equations.[2] At the other extreme, quite accurate forecasts can be created with nothing more than a good imagination and a healthy dose of self-confidence.

---

1. Section 899 of the N.Y. State Criminal Code: the law does not apply to "ecclesiastical bodies acting in good faith and without personal fees."

2. For an interesting comparison of such models, see Ray C. Fair and Robert J. Shiller, "Comparing Information in Forecasts from Econometric Models," *American Economic Review*, June 1990, pp. 375–389.

Unfortunately, it's unrealistic to think we can cover even a small portion of the topic of forecasting in one short chapter. Indeed, there are a number of excellent books and journals on this subject alone.[3] Instead, this chapter is meant to be a brief introduction to the use of econometrics in forecasting. We will begin by using simple linear equations and then move on to investigate a few more complex forecasting situations. The chapter concludes with an introduction to a technique, called ARIMA, that calculates forecasts entirely from past movements of the dependent variable without the use of any independent variables at all.

15.1 What Is Forecasting?

In general, forecasting is the act of predicting the future; in econometrics, **forecasting** is the estimation of the expected value of a dependent variable for observations that are not part of the same data set. In most forecasts, the values being predicted are for time periods in the future, but cross-sectional predictions of values for countries or people not in the sample are also common. To simplify terminology, the words prediction and forecast will be used interchangeably in this chapter. (Some authors limit the use of the word forecast to out-of-sample prediction for a time series.)

We've already encountered an example of a forecasting equation. Think back to the weight/height example of Section 1.3 and recall that the purpose of that model was to guess the weight of a male customer based on his height. In that example, the first step in building a forecast was to estimate Equation 1.21:

$$\text{Estimated weight}_i = 103.4 + 6.38 \cdot \text{Height}_i \text{ (inches over five feet)} \qquad (1.21)$$

That is, we estimated that a customer's weight on average equaled a base of 103.4 pounds plus 6.38 pounds for each inch over 5 feet. To actually make the prediction, all we had to do was to substitute the height of the individual whose weight we were trying to predict into the estimated equation. For a male who is 6'1" tall, for example, we'd calculate:

---

3. See, for example, C. W. J. Granger, *Forecasting in Business and Economics* (New York: Academic Press, 1980), the *Journal of Business Forecasting*, Elia Kacapvr, *Economic Forecasting: The State of the Art* (Armonk: M. E. Sharpe, 1996), and Francis X. Diebold, *Elements of Forecasting* (Cincinati: South Western, 2001). .

$$\text{Predicted weight} = 103.4 + 6.38 \cdot (13 \text{ inches over five feet}) \qquad (15.1)$$

or

$$103.4 + 82.9 = 186.3 \text{ pounds.}$$

The weight-guessing equation is a specific example of using a single linear equation to predict or forecast. Our use of such an equation to make a forecast can be summarized into two steps:

1. *Specify and estimate an equation that has as its dependent variable the item that we wish to forecast.* We obtain a forecasting equation by specifying and estimating an equation for the variable we want to predict:

$$\hat{Y}_t = \hat{\beta}_0 + \hat{\beta}_1 X_{1t} + \hat{\beta}_2 X_{2t} \qquad (t = 1, 2, \ldots, T) \qquad (15.2)$$

   Such specification and estimation have been the topics of the first 14 chapters of this book. The use of $(t = 1, 2, \ldots, T)$ to denote the sample size is fairly standard for time-series forecasts (t stands for "time").

2. *Obtain values for each of the independent variables for the observations for which we want a forecast and substitute them into our forecasting equation.* To calculate a forecast for Equation 15.2, this would mean finding values for period $T + 1$ (for a sample of size T) for X_1 and X_2 and substituting them into the equation:

$$\hat{Y}_{T+1} = \hat{\beta}_0 + \hat{\beta}_1 X_{1T+1} + \hat{\beta}_2 X_{2T+1} \qquad (15.3)$$

   What is the meaning of this $\hat{Y}_{T+1}$? It is a prediction of the value that Y will take in observation $T + 1$ (outside the sample) based upon our values of X_{1T+1} and X_{2T+1} and based upon the particular specification and estimation that produced Equation 15.2.

To understand these steps more clearly, let's look at two applications of this forecasting approach.

Forecasting Chicken Consumption: Let's return to the chicken demand model, Equation 6.8 of Section 6.1, to see how well that equation forecasts aggregate per capita chicken consumption:

$$\hat{Y}_t = 31.5 - 0.73 PC_t + 0.11 PB_t + 0.23 YD_t \qquad (6.8)$$
$$\phantom{\hat{Y}_t = 31.5} (0.08) \quad\;\; (0.05) \quad\;\; (0.02)$$
$$\phantom{\hat{Y}_t = 31.} t = -9.12 \qquad 2.50 \qquad 14.22$$
$$\bar{R}^2 = .986 \qquad n = 44 \text{ (annual } 1951-1994) \qquad DW = 0.98$$

where: Y   = pounds of chicken consumption per capita
          PC and PB = the prices of chicken and beef, respectively, per
                      pound
          YD   = per capita U.S. disposable income

To forecast with this model, we would obtain values for the three independent variables and substitute them into Equation 6.8. For example, in 1995, the actual PC was 6.5, the actual PB was 61.8, and the actual YD was 200.62, giving us:

$$\hat{Y}_{95} = 31.5 - 0.73(6.5) + 0.11(61.8) + 0.23(200.62) = 79.7 \qquad (15.4)$$

Continuing on through 1997, we end up with[4]:

Year	Forecast	Actual	Percent Error
1995	79.7	80.3	0.7
1996	81.0	81.9	1.1
1997	82.6	83.7	1.3

How does the model do? Well, forecasting accuracy, like beauty, is in the eyes of the beholder, but this equation tends to do a superb job of forecasting chicken demand (see Figure 15.1).

Forecasting Stock Prices: Some students react to the previous example by wanting to build a model to forecast stock prices and make a killing on the stock market. "If we could predict the price of a stock three years from now to within one percent," they reason, "we'd know which stocks to buy." To see how such a forecast might work, let's look at a simplified model of the quarterly price of a particular individual stock, that of the J. L. Kellogg Company (maker of breakfast cereals and other products):

$$\widehat{PK}_t = -7.80 + 0.0096DJA_t + 2.68KEG_t + 16.18DIV_t + 4.84BVPS_t$$
$$\phantom{\widehat{PK}_t = -7.80 + } (0.0024) \quad (2.83) \quad (22.70) \quad (1.47)$$
$$t = 3.91 \qquad 0.95 \qquad 0.71 \qquad 3.29$$
$$\overline{R}^2 = .95 \quad n = 35 \quad DW = 1.88 \qquad (15.5)$$

---

4. The rest of the actual values are PC: 1996 = 6.7, 1997 = 7.7; PB: 1996 = 58.7, 1997 = 63.1; YD: 1996 = 208.50, 1997 = 216.31. Many software packages, including EViews, have forecasting modules that will allow you to calculate forecasts using equations like Equation 15.4 automatically. If you use that module, you'll note the forecasts differ slightly because we rounded the coefficient estimates, but EViews did not.

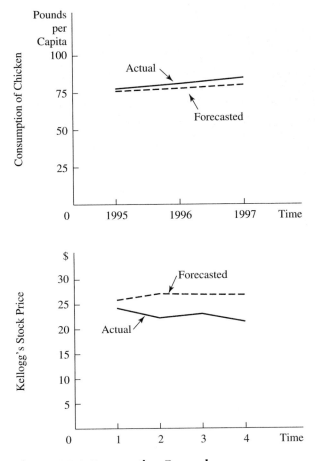

Figure 15.1 Forecasting Examples

In the chicken consumption example, the equation underforecasted slightly. For the stock price model, even actual values for the independent variables and an excellent fit within the sample could not produce an accurate forecast.

where: PK_t = the dollar price of Kellogg's stock in quarter t
         DJA_t = the Dow-Jones industrial average in quarter t
         KEG_t = Kellogg's earnings growth (percent change in annual earnings over the previous five years)
         DIV_t = Kellogg's declared dividends (in dollars) that quarter
         $BVPS_t$ = per-share book value of the Kellogg corporation that quarter

The signs of the estimated coefficients all agree with those hypothesized before the regression was run, $\overline{R}^2$ indicates a good overall fit, and the Durbin–Watson d statistic indicates that the hypothesis of no positive serial correlation cannot be rejected. The low t-scores for KEG and DIV are caused by multicollinearity (r = .985), but both variables are left in the equation because of their theoretical importance. Note also that most of the variables in the equation are nonstationary, surely causing some of the good fit.

To forecast with Equation 15.5, we collected actual values for all of the independent variables for the next four quarters and substituted them into the right side of the equation, obtaining:

Quarter	Foreast	Actual	Percent Error
1	$26.32	$24.38	8.0
2	27.37	22.38	22.3
3	27.19	23.00	18.2
4	27.13	21.88	24.0

How did our forecasting model do? Even though the $\overline{R}^2$ within the sample was .95, even though we used actual values for the independent variables, and even thought we forecasted only four quarters beyond our sample, the model was something like 20 percent off. If we had decided to buy Kellogg's stock based on our forecast, we'd have *lost* money! Since other attempts to forecast stock prices have also encountered difficulties, this doesn't seem a reasonable use for econometric forecasting. Individual stock prices (and many other items) are simply too variable and depend on too many nonquantifiable items to consistently forecast accurately, even if the forecasting equation has an excellent fit! The reason for this apparent contradiction is that equations that worked in the past may or may not work well in the future.

15.2 More Complex Forecasting Problems

The forecasts generated above are unrealistically simple, however, and most actual forecasting involves one or more additional questions. For example:

1. *Unknown Xs:* It's unrealistic to expect always to know the values for the independent variables outside the sample. For instance, we'll almost never know what the Dow-Jones industrial average will be in the future when we are making forecasts of the price of a given stock, and yet we assumed that knowledge when making our Kellogg price forecasts.

What happens when we don't know the values of the independent variables for the forecast period?

2. *Serial Correlation:* If there is serial correlation involved, the forecasting equation may be estimated with GLS. How should predictions be adjusted when forecasting equations are estimated with GLS?

3. *Confidence Intervals:* All the forecasts above were single values, but such single values are almost never exactly right. Wouldn't it be more helpful if we forecasted an interval within which we were confident that the actual value would fall a certain percentage of the time? How can we develop these confidence intervals?

4. *Simultaneous Equations Models:* As we saw in Chapter 14, many economic and business equations are part of simultaneous models. How can we use an independent variable to forecast a dependent variable when we know that a change in value of the dependent variable will change, in turn, the value of the independent variable that we used to make the forecast?

Even a few questions like these should be enough to convince you that forecasting involves issues that are more complex than implied by Section 15.1.

15.2.1 Conditional Forecasting (Unknown X Values for the Forecast Period)

A forecast in which all values of the independent variables are known with certainty can be called an **unconditional forecast,** but, as mentioned above, the situations in which one can make such unconditional forecasts are rare. More likely, we will have to make a **conditional forecast,** for which actual values of one or more of the independent variables are *not* known. We are forced to obtain forecasts for the independent variables before we can use our equation to forecast the dependent variable, making our forecast of Y conditional on our forecast of the Xs.

One key to an accurate conditional forecast is accurate forecasting of the independent variables. If the forecasts of the independent variables are unbiased, using a conditional forecast will not introduce bias into the forecast of the dependent variable. Anything but a perfect forecast of the independent variables will contain some amount of forecast error, however, and so the expected error variance associated with conditional forecasting typically will be larger than that associated with unconditional forecasting. Thus, one should try to find unbiased, minimum variance forecasts of the independent variables when using conditional forecasting.

To get good forecasts of the independent variables, take the forecastability of potential independent variables into consideration when making specification choices. For instance, when you choose which of two redundant variables to include in an equation to be used for forecasting, you should choose the one that is easier to forecast accurately. When you can, you should choose an independent variable that is regularly forecasted by someone else (an econometric forecasting firm, for example) so that you don't have to forecast X yourself.

The careful selection of independent variables can sometimes help you avoid the need for conditional forecasting in the first place. This opportunity can arise when the dependent variable can be expressed as a function of leading indicators. A **leading indicator** is an independent variable the movements of which anticipate movements in the dependent variable. The best known leading indicator, the Index of Leading Economic Indicators, is produced each month.

For instance, the impact of interest rates on investment typically is not felt until two or three quarters after interest rates have changed. To see this, let's look at the investment function of the small macroeconomic model of Section 14.3.3:

$$I_t = \beta_0 + \beta_1 Y_t + \beta_2 r_{t-1} + \epsilon_t \tag{15.6}$$

where I equals gross investment, Y equals GDP, and r equals the interest rate. In this equation, actual values of r can be used to help forecast I_{T+1}. Note, however, that to predict I_{T+2}, we need to forecast r. Thus, leading indicators like r help avoid conditional forecasting for only a time period or two. For long-range predictions, a conditional forecast is usually necessary.

15.2.2 Forecasting with Serially Correlated Error Terms

Recall from Chapter 9 that pure first-order serial correlation implies that the current observation of the error term ϵ_t is affected by the previous error term and an autocorrelation coefficient, ρ:

$$\epsilon_t = \rho \epsilon_{t-1} + u_t$$

where u_t is a non-serially-correlated error term. Also recall that when serial correlation is severe, one remedy is to run Generalized Least Squares (GLS) as noted in Equation 9.18:

$$Y_t - \rho Y_{t-1} = \beta_0(1 - \rho) + \beta_1(X_t - \rho X_{t-1}) + u_t \tag{9.18}$$

Unfortunately, whenever the use of GLS is required to rid an equation of pure first-order serial correlation, the procedures used to forecast with that equation become a bit more complex. To see why this is necessary, note that if Equation 9.18 is estimated, the dependent variable will be:

$$Y_t^* = Y_t - \hat{\rho}Y_{t-1} \tag{15.7}$$

Thus, if a GLS equation is used for forecasting, it will produce predictions of Y_{T+1}^* rather than of Y_{T+1}. Such predictions thus will be of the wrong variable.

If forecasts are to be made with a GLS equation, Equation 9.18 should first be solved for Y_t before forecasting is attempted:

$$Y_t = \rho Y_{t-1} + \beta_0(1 - \rho) + \beta_1(X_t - \rho X_{t-1}) + u_t \tag{15.8}$$

We now can forecast with Equation 15.8 as we would with any other. If we substitute $T + 1$ for t (to forecast time period $T + 1$) and insert estimates for the coefficients, ρs and Xs into the right side of the equation, we obtain:

$$\hat{Y}_{T+1} = \hat{\rho}Y_T + \hat{\beta}_0(1 - \hat{\rho}) + \hat{\beta}_1(\hat{X}_{T+1} - \hat{\rho}X_T) \tag{15.9}$$

Equation 15.9 thus should be used for forecasting when an equation has been estimated with GLS to correct for serial correlation.

We now turn to an example of such forecasting with serially correlated error terms. In particular, recall from Chapter 9 that the Durbin-Watson statistic of the chicken demand equation used as an example in Section 15.1 was 0.98, indicating significant positive first-order serial correlation. As a result, we estimated the chicken demand equation with GLS, obtaining Equation 9.22:

$$\hat{Y}_t = 26.7 - 0.11PC_t + 0.09PB_t + 0.24YD_t \tag{9.22}$$
$$(0.08) \qquad (0.04) \qquad (0.03)$$
$$t = -1.29 \qquad 2.06 \qquad 9.13$$
$$\overline{R}^2 = .994 \qquad n = 43 \text{ (annual 1951–1994)} \qquad \hat{\rho} = 0.90$$

Since Equation 9.22 was estimated with GLS, Y is actually Y_t^*, which equals $(Y_t - \hat{\rho}Y_{t-1})$, PC_t is actually PC_t^*, which equals $PC_t - \hat{\rho}PC_{t-1}$, and so on. Thus, to forecast with Equation 9.22, we have to convert it to the form of Equation 15.9, or:

$$\hat{Y}_{T+1} = 0.90Y_T + 26.80(1 - 0.90) - 0.11(PC_{T+1} - 0.90PC_T) \tag{15.10}$$
$$+ 0.09(PB_{T+1} - 0.90PB_T) + 0.24(YD_{T+1} - 0.90YD_T)$$

Substituting the actual values for the independent variables into Equation 15.10, we obtain:

Year	Forecast	Actual	Percent Error
1995	81.9	80.3	2.0
1996	81.8	81.9	0.1
1997	84.0	83.7	0.4

Compare this forecast to that of Equation 15.4. Note that taking serial correlation into consideration has improved the forecast dramatically in two of the three years. Indeed, GLS often will provide superior forecasting performances to OLS in the presence of serial correlation.

Whether to use GLS is not the topic of this section, however. Instead the point is that if GLS is used to estimate the coefficients of an equation, then Equation 15.9 must be used to forecast with the GLS estimates.

15.2.3 Forecasting Confidence Intervals

Until now, the emphasis in this text has been on obtaining point (or single value) estimates. This has been true whether we have been estimating coefficient values or estimating forecasts. Recall, though, that a point estimate is only one of a whole range of such estimates that could have been obtained from different samples (for coefficient estimates) or different independent variable values or coefficients (for forecasts). The usefulness of such point estimates is improved if we can also generate some idea of the variability of our forecasts. The measure of variability typically used is the *confidence interval*, which was defined in Section 5.2.4 as the range of values within which the actual value of the item being estimated is likely to fall some percentage of the time (called the level of confidence). This is the easiest way to warn forecast users that a sampling distribution exists.

Suppose you are trying to decide how many hot dogs to order for your city's July Fourth fireworks show and that the best point forecast is that you'll sell 24,000 hot dogs. How many hot dogs should you order? If you order 24,000, you're likely to run out about half the time! This is because a point forecast is usually the mean of the distribution of possible sales figures; you will sell more than 24,000 about as frequently as less than 24,000. It would be easier to decide how many dogs to order if you also had a confidence interval that told you the range within which hot dog sales would fall 95 percent of the time. This is because the usefulness of the 24,000 hot dog forecast changes dramatically depending on the confidence interval; an interval of

22,000 to 26,000 would pin down the likely sales, but an interval of 4,000 to 44,000 would leave you virtually in the dark about what to do.[5]

The same techniques we use to test hypotheses can also be adapted to create confidence intervals. Given a point forecast, $\hat{Y}_{T+1}$, all we need to generate a confidence interval around that forecast are t_c, the critical t-value (for the desired level of confidence), and S_F, the estimated standard error of the forecast:

$$\text{Confidence interval} = \hat{Y}_{T+1} \pm S_F t_c \qquad (15.11)$$

or, equivalently,

$$\hat{Y}_{T+1} - S_F t_c \leq Y_{T+1} \leq \hat{Y}_{T+1} + S_F t_c \qquad (15.12)$$

The critical t-value, t_c, can be found in Statistical Table B-1 (for a two-tailed test with $T - K - 1$ degrees of freedom). The standard error of the forecast, S_F, for an equation with just one independent variable, equals the square root of the forecast error variance:

$$S_F = \sqrt{s^2 \left[1 + 1/T + (\hat{X}_{T+1} - \overline{X})^2 / \sum_{t=1}^{T} (X_t - \overline{X})^2 \right]} \qquad (15.13)$$

where s^2 = the estimated variance of the error term
  T = the number of observations in the sample
  $\hat{X}_{T+1}$ = the forecasted value of the single independent variable
  $\overline{X}$ = the arithmetic mean of the observed Xs in the sample.[6]

Note that Equation 15.13 implies that the forecast error variance decreases the larger the sample, the more X varies within the sample, and the closer $\hat{X}$ is

---

5. The decision as to how many hot dogs to order would also depend on the costs of having the wrong number. These may not be the same per hot dog for overestimates as they are for underestimates. For example, if you don't order enough, then you lose the entire retail price of the hot dog minus the wholesale price of the dog (and bun) because your other costs, like hiring employees and building hot dog stands, are essentially fixed. On the other hand, if you order too many, you lose the wholesale cost of the dog and bun minus whatever salvage price you might be able to get for day-old buns, etc. As a result, the right number to order would depend on your profit margin and the importance of nonreturnable inputs in your total cost picture.

6. Equation 15.13 is valid whether Y_t is in the sample period or outside the sample period, but it applies only to point forecasts of individual Y_ts. If a confidence interval for the expected value of Y, $E(Y_t)$, is desired, then the correct equation to use is:

$$S_F = \sqrt{s^2 [1/T + (\hat{X}_{T+1} - \overline{X})^2 / \sum (X_t - \overline{X})^2]}$$

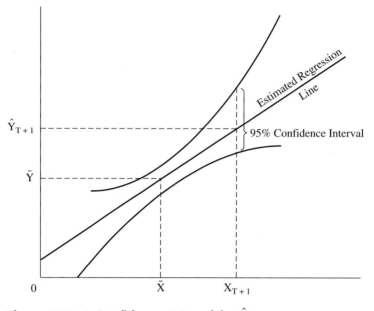

Figure 15.2 A Confidence Interval for $\hat{Y}_{T+1}$

A 95 percent confidence interval for $\hat{Y}_{T+1}$ includes the range of values within which the actual Y_{T+1} will fall 95 percent of the time. Note that the confidence interval widens as X_{T+1} differs more from its within-sample mean, $\overline{X}$.

to its within-sample mean. An important implication is that the farther the X used to forecast Y is from the within-sample mean of the Xs, the wider the confidence interval around the $\hat{Y}$ is going to be. This can be seen in Figure 15.2, in which the confidence interval actually gets wider as $\hat{X}_{T+1}$ is farther from $\overline{X}$. Since forecasting outside the sample range is common, researchers should be aware of this phenomenon. Also note that Equation 15.13 is for unconditional forecasting. If there is any forecast error in $\hat{X}_{T+1}$, then the confidence interval is larger and more complicated to calculate.

As mentioned above, Equation 15.13 assumes that there is only one independent variable; the equation to be used with more than one variable is similar but more complicated. Some researchers who must deal with more than one independent variable avoid this complexity by ignoring Equation 15.13 and estimating a confidence interval equal to $\hat{Y}_{T+1} \pm st_c$, where s is the standard error of the equation. Compare this shortcut with Equation 15.13; note that the shortcut confidence interval will work well for large samples and $\hat{X}$s near the within-sample means but will provide only a rough estimate of the confidence interval in other cases. At a minimum in such cases,

Equation 15.13 should be modified with a $(\hat{X}_{T+1} - \overline{X})^2/\sum(X_t - \overline{X})^2$ term for each X.

Let's look at an example of building a forecast confidence interval by returning to the weight/height example. In particular, let's create a 95 percent confidence interval around the forecast for a 6'1" male calculated in Equation 15.1 (repeated for convenience):

$$\text{Predicted weight}_i = 103.4 + 6.38 \cdot (13 \text{ inches over five feet}) \qquad (15.1)$$

for a predicted weight of $103.4 + 82.9$ or 186.3 pounds. To calculate a 95 percent confidence interval around this prediction, we substitute Equation 15.13 into Equation 15.11, obtaining a confidence interval of:

$$186.3 \pm \left(\sqrt{s^2\left[1 + 1/T + (\hat{X}_{T+1} - \overline{X})^2/\sum_{t=1}^{T}(X_t - \overline{X})^2\right]} \right)t_c \qquad (15.14)$$

We then substitute the actual figures into Equation 15.14. From the data set for the example, we find that $T = 20$, the mean $X = 10.35$, the summed square deviations of X around its mean is 92.50, and $s^2 = 65.05$. From Statistical Table B-1, we obtain the 95 percent, two-tailed critical t-value for 18 degrees of freedom of 2.101. If we now combine this with the information that our $\hat{X}$ is 13, we obtain:

$$186.3 \pm \left(\sqrt{65.05[1 + 1/20 + (13.0 - 10.35)^2/92.50]} \right)t_c \qquad (15.15)$$

$$186.3 \pm 8.558(2.101) = 186.3 \pm 18.0 \qquad (15.16)$$

In other words, our 95 percent confidence interval for a 6'1" college-age male is from 168.3 to 204.3 pounds. Ask around; are 19 out of 20 of your male friends that tall within that range?

15.2.4 Forecasting with Simultaneous Equations Systems

As we learned in Chapter 14, most economic and business models are actually simultaneous in nature; for example, the investment equation used in Section 15.2.1 was estimated with 2SLS as a part of our simultaneous macromodel in Chapter 14. Since GDP is one of the independent variables in the investment equation, when investment rises, so will GDP, causing a feedback effect that is not captured if we just forecast with a single equation. How should forecasting be done in the context of a simultaneous model? There are two approaches to answering this question, depending on whether there are lagged endogenous variables on the right side of any of the equations in the system.

If there are no lagged endogenous variables in the system, then the reduced-form equation for the particular endogenous variable can be used for forecasting because it represents the simultaneous solution of the system for the endogenous variable being forecasted. Since the reduced-form equation is the endogenous variable expressed entirely in terms of the predetermined variables in the system, it allows the forecasting of the endogenous variable without any feedback or simultaneity impacts. This result explains why some researchers forecast potentially simultaneous dependent variables with single equations that appear to combine supply-side and demand-side predetermined variables; they are actually using modified reduced-form equations to make their forecasts.

If there are lagged endogenous variables in the system, then the approach must be altered to take into account the dynamic interaction caused by the lagged endogenous variables. For simple models, this sometimes can be done by substituting for the lagged endogenous variables where they appear in the reduced-form equations. If such a manipulation is difficult, however, then a technique called simulation analysis can be used. *Simulation* involves forecasting for the first postsample period by using the reduced-form equations to forecast all endogenous variables where they appear in the reduced-form equations. The forecast for the second postsample period, however, uses the endogenous variable *forecasts* from the last period as lagged values for any endogenous variables that have one-period lags while continuing to use sample values for endogenous variables that have lags of two or more periods. This process continues until all forecasting is done with reduced-form equations that use as data for lagged endogenous variables the forecasts from previous time periods. Although such dynamic analyses are beyond the scope of this chapter, they're important to remember when considering forecasting with a simultaneous system.[7]

15.3 ARIMA Models

The forecasting techniques of the previous two sections are applications of familiar regression models. We use linear regression equations to forecast the dependent variable by plugging likely values of the independent variables into the estimated equations and calculating a predicted value of Y; this bases

---

7. For more on this topic, see pp. 723–731 in Jan Kmenta, *Elements of Econometrics* (New York: Macmillan, 1985), or chapters 12–14 in Robert S. Pindyck and Daniel L. Rubinfeld, *Econometric Models and Economic Forecasts* (New York: McGraw-Hill, 1998).

the prediction of the dependent variable on the independent variables (and on their estimated coefficients).

ARIMA is an increasingly popular forecasting technique that completely ignores independent variables in making forecasts. **ARIMA** is a highly refined curve-fitting device that uses current and past values of the dependent variable to produce often accurate short-term forecasts of that variable. Examples of such forecasts are stock market price predictions created by brokerage analysts (called "chartists" or "technicians") based entirely on past patterns of movement of the stock prices.

Any forecasting technique that ignores independent variables also essentially ignores all potential underlying theories except those that hypothesize repeating patterns in the variable under study. Since we have emphasized the advantages of developing the theoretical underpinnings of particular equations before estimating them, why would we advocate using ARIMA? The answer is that the use of ARIMA is appropriate when little or nothing is known about the dependent variable being forecasted, when the independent variables known to be important really cannot be forecasted effectively, or when all that is needed is a one or two-period forecast. In these cases, ARIMA has the potential to provide short-term forecasts that are superior to more theoretically satisfying regression models. In addition, ARIMA can sometimes produce better explanations of the residuals from an existing regression equation (in particular, one with known omitted variables or other problems). In other circumstances, the use of ARIMA is not recommended. This introduction to ARIMA is intentionally brief; a more complete coverage of the topic can be obtained from a number of other sources.[8]

The ARIMA approach combines two different specifications (called *processes*) into one equation. The first specification is an *autoregressive* process (hence the AR in ARIMA), and the second specification is a *moving average* (hence the MA).

An **autoregressive process** expresses a dependent variable Y_t as a function of past values of the dependent variable, as in:

$$Y_t = f(Y_{t-1}, Y_{t-2}, \ldots, Y_{t-p}) \qquad (15.17)$$

where Y_t is the variable being forecasted and p is the number of past values used. This equation is similar to the serial correlation error term function of

---

8. See, for example, T. M. O'Donovan, *Short-Term Forecasting* (New York: Wiley, 1983); C. W. J. Granger and Paul Newbold, *Forecasting Economic Time Series* (New York: Academic Press, 1997); Walter Vandaele, *Applied Time Series and Box-Jenkins Models* (New York: Academic Press, 1983); and chapters 15–19 in Robert S. Pindyck and Daniel L. Rubinfeld, *Econometric Models and Economic Forecasts* (New York: McGraw-Hill, 1998).

Chapter 9 and to the distributed lag equation of Chapter 12. Since there are p different lagged values of Y in this equation, it is often referred to as a "pth-order" autoregressive process.

A **moving-average process** expresses a dependent variable Y_t as a function of past values of the error term, as in:

$$Y_t = f(\epsilon_{t-1}, \epsilon_{t-2}, \ldots, \epsilon_{t-q}) \tag{15.18}$$

where ϵ_t is the error term associated with Y_t and q is the number of past values of the error term used. Such a function is a moving average of past error terms that can be added to the mean of Y to obtain a moving average of past values of Y. Such an equation would be a qth-order moving-average process.

To create an ARIMA model, we begin with an econometric equation with no independent variables ($Y_t = \beta_0 + \epsilon_t$) and add to it both the autoregressive and moving-average processes:

autoregressive process

$$Y_t = \beta_0 + \overbrace{\theta_1 Y_{t-1} + \theta_2 Y_{t-2} + \cdots + \theta_p Y_{t-p}} + \epsilon_t \tag{15.19}$$
$$\underbrace{+ \phi_1 \epsilon_{t-1} + \phi_2 \epsilon_{t-2} + \cdots + \phi_q \epsilon_{t-q}}$$

moving-average process

where the θs and the ϕs are the coefficients of the autoregressive and moving-average processes, respectively.

Before this equation can be applied to a time series, however, it must be assumed that the time series is *stationary,* as defined in Section 12.4. If a series is nonstationary, then steps must be taken to convert the series into a stationary one before the ARIMA technique can be applied. For example, a nonstationary series can often be converted into a stationary one by taking the first difference of the variable in question:

$$Y_t^* = \Delta Y_t = Y_t - Y_{t-1} \tag{15.20}$$

If the first differences do not produce a stationary series, then first differences of this first-differenced series can be taken. The resulting series is a second-difference transformation:

$$Y_t^{**} = (\Delta Y_t^*) = Y_t^* - Y_{t-1}^* = \Delta Y_t - \Delta Y_{t-1} \tag{15.21}$$

In general, successive differences are taken until the series is stationary. The number of differences required to be taken before a series becomes stationary is denoted with the letter d. For example, suppose that GDP is increasing by a fairly consistent amount each year. A plot of GDP with respect to time would depict a nonstationary series, but a plot of the first differences of GDP might depict a fairly stationary series. In such a case, d would be equal to one because one first difference was necessary to convert the nonstationary series into a stationary one.

The dependent variable in Equation 15.19 must be stationary, so the Y in that equation may be Y, Y*, or even Y**, depending on the variable in question.[9] If a forecast of Y* or Y** is made, then it must be converted back into Y terms before its use; for example, if d = 1, then

$$\hat{Y}_{T+1} = Y_T + \hat{Y}^*_{T+1} \tag{15.22}$$

This conversion process is similar to integration in mathematics, so the "I" in ARIMA stands for "integrated." ARIMA thus stands for *AutoRegressive Integrated Moving Average*. (If the original series is stationary and d therefore equals 0, this is sometimes shortened to ARMA.)

As a shorthand, an ARIMA model with p, d, and q specified is usually denoted as ARIMA (p,d,q) with the specific integers chosen inserted for p, d, and q, as in ARIMA (2,1,1). ARIMA (2,1,1) would indicate a model with two autoregressive terms, one first difference, and one moving-average term:

$$\text{ARIMA}(2,1,1): Y^*_t = \beta_0 + \theta_1 Y^*_{t-1} + \theta_2 Y^*_{t-2} + \epsilon_t + \phi_1 \epsilon_{t-1} \tag{15.23}$$

where $Y^*_t = Y_t - Y_{t-1}$.

15.4   Summary

1. Forecasting is the estimation of the expected value of a dependent variable for observations that are not part of the sample data set. Forecasts are generated (via regressions) by estimating an equation for the

---

9. If Y in Equation 15.19 is Y*, then β_0 represents the coefficient of the linear trend in the original series, and if Y is Y**, the β_0 represents the coefficient of the second-difference trend in the original series. In such cases, for example Equation 15.23, it's not always necessary that β_0 be in the model.

dependent variable to be forecasted, and substituting values for each of the independent variables (for the observations to be forecasted) into the equation.

2.   An excellent fit within the sample period for a forecasting equation does not guarantee that the equation will forecast well outside the sample period.

3.   A forecast in which all the values of the independent variables are known with certainty is called an unconditional forecast, but if one or more of the independent variables have to be forecasted, it is a conditional forecast. Conditional forecasting introduces no bias into the prediction of Y (as long as the X forecasts are unbiased), but increased forecast error variance is virtually unavoidable with conditional forecasting.

4.   If the coefficients of an equation have been estimated with GLS (to correct for pure first-order serial correlation), then the forecasting equation is:

$$\hat{Y}_{T+1} = \hat{\rho}Y_T = \hat{\beta}_0(1 - \hat{\rho}) + \hat{\beta}_1(X_{T+1} - \hat{\rho}X_T)$$

where ρ is the coefficient of autocorrelation, rho.

5.   Forecasts are often more useful if they are accompanied by a confidence interval, which is a range within which the actual value of the dependent variable should fall a given percentage of the time (the level of confidence). This is:

$$\hat{Y}_{T+1} \pm S_F t_c$$

where S_F is the estimated standard error of the forecast and t_c is the critical two-tailed t-value for the desired level of confidence.

6.   ARIMA is a highly refined curve-fitting technique that uses current and past values of the dependent variable (and only the dependent variable) to produce often accurate short-term forecasts of that variable. The first step in using ARIMA is to make the dependent variable series stationary by taking d first differences until the resulting transformed variable has a constant mean and variance. The ARIMA(p,d,q) approach then combines an autoregressive process (with $\theta_1 Y_{t-1}$ terms) of order p with a moving-average process (with $\phi_1 \epsilon_{t-1}$ terms) of order q to explain the dth differenced dependent variable.

Exercises

(Answers to even-numbered exercises are in Appendix A.)

1. Write the meaning of each of the following terms without referring to the book (or your notes), and compare your definition with the version in the text for each:
    a. conditional forecast
    b. leading indicator
    c. confidence interval
    d. autoregressive process
    e. moving-average process
    f. ARIMA(p,d,q)

2. Calculate the following unconditional forecasts:
    a. Bond prices given the simplified equation in Exercise 9 in Chapter 1 and the following data for the federal funds rate: 5.82, 5.04, 5.54, 7.93.
    b. The expected level of check volume at three possible future sites for new Woody's restaurants, given Equation 3.7 and the following data. If you could only build one new eatery, in which of these three sites would you build (all else equal)?

Site	Composition	Population	Income
Richburgh	6	58,000	38,000
Nowheresville	1	14,000	27,000
Slick City	9	190,000	15,000

    c. Per capita consumption of fish in the United States for 1971–1974 given Equation 8.26 and the following data:

Year	PF	PB	Yd
1971	130.2	116.7	2679
1972	141.9	129.2	2767
1973	162.8	161.1	2934
1974	187.7	164.1	2871

    (*Hint:* Reread Section 8.5.2 before attempting this forecast.)

3. To understand the difficulty of conditional forecasting, use Equation 1.21 to forecast the weights of the next three males you see, using your *estimates* of their heights. (Ask for actual values after finishing.)

4. Calculate 95 percent confidence interval forecasts for the following:
    a. the weight of a male who is 5′9″ tall. (*Hint:* Modify Equation 15.15.)
    b. next month's sales of ice cream cones at the Campus Cooler given an expected price of 60 cents per cone and:

$$\hat{C}_t = 2,000 - 20.0P_t \qquad \overline{R}^2 = .80$$
$$(5.0) \qquad\qquad T = 30$$
$$t = -4.0 \qquad\qquad \overline{P} = 50$$

where: C_t = the number of ice cream cones sold in month t
         P_t = the price of the Cooler's ice cream cones (in cents) in month t
         $s^2 = 25,000$ and $\sum(P_t - \overline{P})^2 = 1000$

5. Build your own (non-ARIMA) forecasting model from scratch: pick a dependent variable, specify your equation, hypothesize signs, find a data set, estimate your model (leaving a couple of the most current observations out of the sample), and forecast your dependent variable. Now comes the "fun" of comparing your forecast with the actual Ys. How did you do?

6. For each of the following series, calculate and plot Y_t, $Y_t^* = \Delta Y_t$, and $Y_t^{**} = \Delta Y_t^*$, describe the stationarity properties of the series, and choose an appropriate value for d.
    a. 2, 3, 4, 5, 6, 7, 8, 9, 10, 11, 12, 13
    b. 2, 2, 3, 4, 5, 6, 8, 10, 12, 15, 19, 24
    c. 2, 3, 6, 3, 4, 2, 3, 5, 1, 4, 4, 6

7. Take the three Y_t^* series you calculated as part of your answer to Exercise 6 above and check to see if they are correct by calculating backward and seeing if you can derive the original three Y_t series from your three Y_t^* series. (*Hint:* Equation 15.22 can be adapted for this "integration" purpose.)

8. Suppose you have been given two different ARIMA(1,0,0) fitted time-series models of the variable Y_t:

$$\text{Model A: } Y_t = 15.0 + 0.5Y_{t-1} + \epsilon_t$$
$$\text{Model T: } Y_t = 45.0 - 0.5Y_{t-1} + \epsilon_t$$

where ϵ_t is a normally distributed error term with mean zero and standard deviation equal to one.

a. The final observation in the sample (time period 96) is $Y_{96} = 31$. Determine forecasts for periods 97, 98, and 99 for both models.

b. Suppose you now find out that the actual Y_{97} was equal to 33. Revise your forecasts for periods 98 and 99 to take the new information into account.

c. Based on the fitted time series and your two forecasts, which model (model A or model T) do you expect to exhibit smoother behavior? Explain your reasoning.

9. Suppose you have been given an ARIMA(1,0,1) fitted time-series model:

$$Y_t = 0.0 + 1.0Y_{t-1} + \epsilon_t - 0.5\epsilon_{t-1}$$

where ϵ_t is a normally distributed error term with mean zero and standard deviation equal to one and where T = 99, $Y_{99} = 27$, and where $\hat{Y}_{99} = 27.5$.

a. Calculate e_{99}.

b. Calculate forecasts for Y_{100}, Y_{101}, and Y_{102}. (*Hint:* Use your answer to part a.)

10. You've been hired to forecast *Sports Illustrated* subscriptions (S) using the following function of GDP (Y) and a classical error term (ϵ):

$$S_t = \beta_0 + \beta_1 Y_t + \beta_2 S_{t-1} + \epsilon_t$$

Explain how you would forecast (out two time periods) with this equation in the following cases:

a. If future sales of Y are known. (*Hint:* Be sure to comment on the functional form of this relationship.)

b. If future values of Y are unknown and *Sports Illustrated* subscriptions are small in comparison to GDP.

c. If *Sports Illustrated* subscriptions are about half of GDP (obviously a sports-lover's heaven!) and all other components of GDP are known to be stochastic functions of time.

Statistical Principles

This chapter* reviews the basic statistical principles that underlie the specification and estimation of econometric models. We start by discussing some simple yet powerful tools for describing data. Then we examine some models that can be used to describe where data come from. The third section looks at how samples can be taken from populations. The fourth and fifth sections explain how a sample can be used to draw inferences about the population from which it came.

16.1   Describing Data

It is very difficult to analyze substantial amounts of data merely by looking at numbers. What sense could we make of pages and pages of a computer printout showing the gender and height of every student at your school? Instead, most researchers use some simple summary statistics to help understand and interpret data.

16.1.1 Median

The most familiar descriptive statistics are *measures of location* that describe the center of the data, without telling us whether the data are tightly clus-

---

* Written by Gary Smith of Pomona College. Gary is also the author of *Statistical Reasoning* (McGraw Hill, 1998).

TABLE 16.1 INCOME IN SMALLAND	
Income (dollars)	**Number of Persons**
5,000	2
10,000	1
30,000	1
40,000	1
50,000	1
60,000	1
1,000,000	1

tered in this center or greatly dispersed. Our first measure is quite literally the center of the data: The **median** is the middle value when the data are arranged in numerical order from the smallest value to the largest value. We can find the median by putting the data in numerical order and then, starting at each end of the data, counting inward. When our two counts meet in the middle, we have located the median. For example, the Smalland income data in Table 16.1 can be arranged as follows:

5,000 5,000 10,000 **30,000 40,000** 50,000 60,000 1,000,000

Because there are an even number of observations (eight), we split the difference between the two middle observations, 30,000 and 40,000, giving a median of 35,000. This is the center of the income data, in that half of the people earned less than 35,000 dollars and half earned more than 35,000 dollars.

When there is an odd number of observations, there is a single middle observation. For example, without the $1,000,000, the median falls to $30,000:

5,000   5,000   10,000   **30,000**   40,000   50,000   60,000

Technically, some of the observations to the right or the left of the median may be equal to the median. Thus, strictly speaking, we should say that at least half of the values are smaller than or equal to the median and at least half are larger than or equal to the median. In popular usage, people generally just say that half of the values are smaller than the median and half are larger than the median.

Let's look at a different set of data. Each February, *Money* magazine shows the performance records of thousands of mutual funds during the preceding calendar year. Table 16.2 shows the 1997 and 1998 annual returns for a random sample of 25 stock mutual funds. To find the median return for these 25 funds in 1997, we can arrange the returns in numerical order and then,

TABLE 16.2 ANNUAL PERCENTAGE RETURNS FOR 25 STOCK MUTUAL FUNDS

	1997	1998
Alliance Strategic Balanced B	10.8	17.2
American Century Equity Growth	36.1	24.1
American Funds Fundamental Investors	26.7	15.0
Bernstein International Value	9.3	10.1
Cohen & Steers Realty Shares	21.2	−20.3
Fidelity Overseas	10.9	12.4
Fidelity Small Cap	27.3	−11.6
Fidelity Adviser Balanced T	22.3	14.1
First Omaha Equity	19.2	14.2
Franklin Calif Growth I	15.7	8.8
Guardian Baillie International A	11.0	18.3
Leuthold Core Investment	17.2	9.7
Merrill Lynch Capital B	20.2	3.7
Nations Emerging Growth Inv. A	20.5	−1.7
Nicholas-Applegate Growth Equity A	17.3	10.5
Parnassas	29.7	−1.8
Phoenix Worldwide Opportunities A	14.1	29.6
Pioneer Capital Growth A	17.5	−8.0
Pioneer Mid-Cap A	7.2	5.3
Putnam Asset Allocation: Conservative A	11.8	8.3
Schwab Analytics	31.8	26.5
Star Relative Value	32.2	17.9
State Street Capital A	6.3	8.7
Templeton Global Small Company I	4.2	−13.3
T. Rowe Price European Stock	17.0	25.5

Source: "Major Stock Funds," *Money*, February 1999, pp. 86–122.

counting in 13 observations from either end, find the median value to be 17.3 percent:

4.2 6.3 7.2 ... 15.7 17.0 17.2 **17.3** 17.5 19.2 20.2 ... 31.8 32.2 36.1

Try a similar analysis of the 1998 data by yourself. Do you agree that the median return in 1998 is 10.1 percent?

16.1.2 Mean

The **mean** is the simple arithmetic average value of the data: the mean of n observations $X_1, X_2, ..., X_n$ is the sum of these n values, divided by n:

$$\text{Mean} = \frac{X_1 + X_2 + \cdots + X_n}{n} \qquad (16.1)$$

The mean is often written as $\overline{X}$, or X with a bar over it (which can be pronounced "X-bar") and we can use the shorthand notation

$$\overline{X} = \frac{\Sigma X_i}{n}$$

The Greek letter Σ (upper case "sigma") indicates that the values of X_i should be added up.

For the hypothetical Smalland incomes in Table 16.1, we add up the eight values and divide by eight:

$$\overline{X} = \frac{5,000 + 5,000 + 10,000 + 30,000 + 40,000 + 50,000 + 60,000 + 1,000,000}{8}$$
$$= \frac{1,200,000}{8}$$
$$= 150,000$$

For the 25 stock mutual fund returns for 1997 shown in Table 16.2, we add up the 25 values and divide by 25:

$$\overline{X} = \frac{10.8 + 36.1 + \cdots + 17.0}{25} = 18.30$$

An average return of 18.30 percent sounds pretty impressive, but it's put into perspective by the fact that the 1997 return on the S&P 500 index of stock prices was 33.4 percent! In 1998, the S&P 500 return was 28.1 percent, whereas the average return for these 25 mutual funds was 8.93 percent:

$$\overline{X} = \frac{17.2 + 24.1 + \cdots + 25.5}{25} = 8.93$$

Is this disappointing record indicative of the performance of the mutual fund industry as a whole? How much confidence can we have in the average return for 25 mutual funds as a measure of the average return for all mutual funds? Later in this chapter, we will see how to draw statistical inferences from such evidence. (The answer turns out to be that even though this sample seems small, these data provide very persuasive evidence that mutual funds, on average, do not do as well as the overall stock market; any stock-selecting prowess they have is more than offset by their management fees and other expenses.)

The mean is the balance point of the data in that the cumulative distance from the mean of those observations above the mean is equal to the cumula-

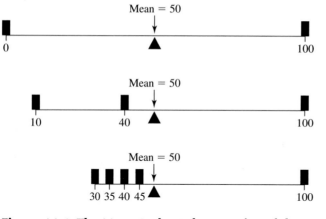

Figure 16.1 The Mean Is the Balance Point of the Data

tive distance from the mean of those observations below the mean. Figure 16.1 gives three examples, each with a mean of 50. In the first case, there are two observations, 0 and 100; the mean of 50 is the balance point in that one observation 50 above the mean is balanced by the other observation 50 below the mean. In the second case, the observation that is 50 above the mean is balanced by one observation 10 below the mean and another observation 40 below the mean. In the third case, the observation that is 50 above the mean is balanced by observations that are 5, 10, 15, and 20 below the mean.

Notice in this third case that the one observation at 100 pulls the mean above the other four observations so that there will be enough observations slightly below the mean to balance out the one observation that is far above the mean. In the same way, the one person in Table 16.1 who earns a million dollars pulls the mean up to $150,000, which is above the income levels of all seven other Smallanders. You should not automatically interpret the mean as the typical value.

The mean income tells us how much each person would earn if total income were equally divided among the people. It need not be the case that half the people earn more than the mean income and half earn less. As in Smalland, the mean can be affected greatly by a few extreme observations. It is for this reason that the U.S. Census Bureau reports both the mean and median household income. In 1992 the mean household income in the United States was $39,020 whereas the median was $30,786. The mean was pulled above the median by a relatively small number of people with relatively high incomes.

The millionaire in Smalland is an **outlier**, in that this value is very different from the other observations. When there are outliers, the mean may give a misleading description of the center of the data. An embarrassing illustration of this principle sometimes occurs when an error is made in transcribing data. In July of 1986, for example, the Joint Economic Committee of Congress issued a report based on data compiled by researchers at the University of Michigan. The report estimated that the share of the nation's wealth owned by the richest 0.5 percent of U.S. families had increased from 25 percent in 1963 to 35 percent in 1983. Newspapers nationwide reported the story with "Rich Get Richer" headlines. Some skeptics in Washington started poking through the numbers, rechecking the calculations, and discovered that the reported increase was due almost entirely to the erroneous recording of one family's wealth as $200,000,000 rather than $2,000,000, an error that raised the mean wealth of the rich people who had been surveyed by nearly 50 percent. Somewhere along the line, someone typed two extra zeros and temporarily misled the nation.

For some questions, the mean clearly provides the most appropriate answer. Whether a household will save money over the course of a year depends on its mean monthly income and expenses. A farm's total crop depends on the mean yield per acre. The total amount of cereal a company needs to fill a million boxes depends on the mean net weight. For other questions, the median may be more appropriate.

A comparison of the mean and median can be illustrated by the income data shown in Table 16.3. What are the median and mean incomes? Because there are nine people, we count in five from either end and find the median income to be $30,000. To find the mean, we add up the nine incomes and divide by nine. This, too, is $30,000. The mean equals the median in this case because the data are symmetrical. To see this, look at Figure 16.2, which is a histogram of the data. A **histogram** is a diagram in which the relative frequency of the observations in each interval is shown by the height of the bar spanning the interval (for equal intervals). An inspection of the histogram in Figure 16.2 allows us to confirm that the data are indeed symmetrical. Each observation above $30,000 is balanced by a corresponding observation equally far below $30,000.

TABLE 16.3 SYMMETRICAL INCOME DATA	
Income (dollars)	Number of Persons
10,000	1
20,000	2
30,000	3
40,000	2
50,000	1

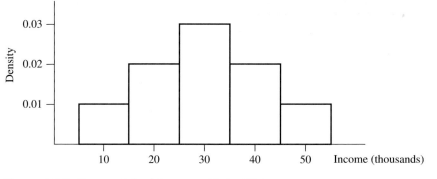

Figure 16.2 Symmetrical Income Data Histogram

This example illustrates the general principle that if a set of data is symmetrical, the median and mean coincide. Conversely, if the data are asymmetrical or skewed, the mean and median will generally not coincide. If the mean and median differ, we need to bear in mind what each measures and use the statistic that is most appropriate for our purposes. The median is the middle value and the mean is the arithmetic average.

16.1.3 Variance and Standard Deviation

The mean is, by far, the most commonly reported summary statistic. However, an average does not tell us the underlying variation in the data, which may be of great interest. When your instructor hands back your midterm examinations, you naturally will be interested not only in how you did, but how the class as a whole did. If the instructor announces that the mean score is 80, you probably will also like to know something about the spread (or variation) in the data. Did most students get scores of around 80? Or did some do substantially better and some much worse? It would be useful to have a simple statistic that gauges the variation, so that we can compare the spread of these data to that of other data. Are the midterm scores more spread out than the homework scores, or than the midterm scores in other sections or in other years? Are the incomes in one country more compact or more dispersed than in other countries, or in this country during other historical periods?

Fortunately, we can supplement the mean (or median) with summary statistics that provide information about the spread or variation in the data. It might seem appealing to compute the average deviation from the mean by subtracting the mean from each observation, adding up each of these devia-

TABLE 16.4 MEASURING THE VARIATION IN DATA

Income (thousands)	Deviation from Mean	Squared Deviation
5	−145	21,025
5	−145	21,025
10	−140	19,600
30	−120	14,400
40	−110	12,100
50	−100	10,000
60	−90	8,100
1,000	850	722,500
Sum	0	828,750
Average	0	118,392.86

Note: The average squared deviation was calculated by dividing by 8 − 1 = 7.

tions from the mean, and then dividing by the number of observations. However, as can be seen by looking at the Smalland income data in Table 16.4, the average deviation from the mean is zero, which is hardly a useful statistic. In fact, because the mean is the balance point of any set of data, *the average deviation from the mean is always zero*, and it tells us nothing at all about the size of the deviations.

To eliminate this offsetting of positive and negative deviations, we can square each deviation, since the squares of positive and negative deviations are both positive. The **variance** of a sample of n observations $X_1, X_2, \ldots, X_n$ is the average squared deviation of these observations about their mean:

$$\text{Variance} = \frac{(X_1 - \bar{X})^2 + (X_2 - \bar{X})^2 + \cdots + (X_n - \bar{X})^2}{n - 1} \quad (16.2)$$

The **standard deviation** s is the square root of the variance, $s = \sqrt{\text{variance}}$.

Notice that the variance of a set of data is calculated by dividing the sum of the squared deviations by n − 1, rather than n. It can be shown mathematically that if the variance in a random sample is used to estimate the variance of the population from which these data came, this estimate will, on average, be too low if we divide by n, but will, on average, be correct if we divide by n − 1.

Because each deviation is squared, the variance has a scale that is much larger than the underlying data. The standard deviation, in contrast, has the same units and scale as the original data. With the exception of this scale difference, the variance and standard deviation are equivalent measures of the dispersion in a set of data. A data set that has a higher variance than another data set also has a higher standard deviation.

The variance and standard deviation are strongly affected by outliers because of the squaring of deviations from the mean. An alternative measure of the spread of the data is the *interquartile range*, which is the range encompassed by the middle half of the data. Even though the interquartile range is more resistant to outliers than is the standard deviation, the standard deviation is generally used to gauge the variation in a set of data because of its mathematical tractability and importance in probability and statistics.

Let's look again at the mutual fund returns in Table 16.2. From just staring at the numbers, it is difficult to tell whether there was more dispersion in the 1997 or 1998 returns. The standard deviations answer this question:

$$1997: \quad \text{Mean} = \frac{10.8 + 36.1 + \cdots + 17.0}{25} = 18.30$$

$$\text{Variance} = \frac{[10.8 - (18.30)]^2 + \cdots + [17.0 - (18.30)]^2}{25 - 1} = 74.5833$$

$$\text{Standard deviation} = \sqrt{74.5833} = 8.64$$

$$1998: \quad \text{Mean} = \frac{17.2 + 24.1 + \cdots + 25.5}{25} = 8.93$$

$$\text{Variance} = \frac{(17.2 - 8.93)^2 + \cdots + (25.5 - 8.93)^2}{25 - 1} = 162.9546$$

$$\text{Standard deviation} = \sqrt{162.9546} = 12.77$$

A comparison of the 8.64 and 12.77 percent standard deviations indicates that there was more variation among these fund returns in 1998 than in 1997.

The interpretation of the standard deviation is not as easy as is the interpretation of the mean. The 18.30 percent average return in 1997 implies that if you had invested an equal amount in each of these 25 funds, your average return would have been 18.30 percent. But what does the 8.64 percent standard deviation mean? A famous theorem and two rules of thumb provide guidance. The remarkable theorem, *Chebyshev's inequality*, states that in any set of data at least $1 - 1/k^2$ of the data are within k standard deviations of the mean.[1] Using k = 2, at least $1 - 1/2^2 = 3/4$ of the data are within two standard deviations of the mean. The two rules of thumb are that in those cases in which the data have the normal distribution's bell shape, roughly two-thirds of the data are within one standard deviation of the mean and approximately 95 percent are within two standard deviations. Table 16.5 shows

---

1. This works as long as k > 1.

TABLE 16.5 THE NUMBER OF MUTUAL FUND RETURNS WITHIN 1 AND 2 STANDARD DEVIATIONS OF THE MEAN		
	1997	**1998**
Mean	18.30	8.93
Standard deviation	8.64	12.77
Mean plus or minus 1 standard deviation	9.66 to 26.94	3.84 to 21.70
Fraction of data within 1 standard deviation	17/25 = 0.68	15/25 = 0.60
Mean plus or minus 2 standard deviations	1.02 to 35.58	−16.61 to 34.77
Fraction of data within 2 standard deviations	24/25 = 0.96	24/25 = 0.96

that, overall, 64 percent (32 of 50) of these mutual fund returns are within one standard deviation of the mean and 96 percent (48 of 50) are within two standard deviations.

16.2 Probability Distributions

Although the mean and standard deviation help describe a set of data, they don't do much to help us draw valid statistical inferences from the data. To make such inferences, we often use probability models to describe where the data come from—for example, a medical test that is correct or incorrect, a surveyed person who supports or opposes a particular candidate, an SAT score that is above or below 700. In this section, we will first see how probabilities can be used to quantify uncertainty and to help us explain and interpret empirical data.

16.2.1 Probability

When we say that a flipped coin has a 0.5 probability of landing with its heads side up, we mean that if this coin were to be flipped an interminable number of times, we anticipate that it will land heads about half the time. More generally, if an event has a probability P of occurring, then the fraction of the times that it occurs in the very long run will be very close to P. Obviously, a probability cannot be negative or larger than one.

A **random variable** X is a variable whose numerical value is determined by chance, the outcome of a random phenomenon.[2] A *discrete random variable,*

---

2. To be mathematically precise, statisticians often use upper-case and lower-case notation to distinguish between a random variable, which can take on different values, and the actual values that happen to occur. Upper-case notation is used throughout this book for simplicity and convenience.

the subject of this section, <u>has a countable number of possible values, such as 0, 1, and 2; in the next section, we will consider</u> *continuous* <u>random variables,</u> such as time and distance, which can take on any value in an interval. All of the discrete random variables that we will examine have a finite number of outcomes, though there are other discrete variables with an infinite number of countable values. For example, if X is equal to the number of times that a coin will be flipped before a heads is obtained, there is no upper limit on the value of X; nonetheless, X is a discrete variable because its values are obtained by counting. Measures of time and distance, in contrast, are continuous variables; between any two possible values, such as 4.7 and 4.8, there are other possible values, such as 4.75 and 4.76.

A **probability distribution** P[X_i] for a discrete random variable X assigns probabilities to the possible values X_1, X_2, and so on. For example, when a fair six-sided die is rolled, there are six equally likely outcomes, each with a 1/6 probability of occurring. Figure 16.3 shows this probability distribution.

Probability distributions are scaled so that the total area inside the rectangles is equal to 1. A probability distribution looks like a data histogram, but it is conceptually different since it refers to the probabilities of various outcomes occurring, rather than the actual frequencies with which they happen to occur in a particular set of experiments. A probability distribution and data histogram are related by the fact that in the long run, the observed frequencies will be very close to the theoretical probabilities.

To illustrate this relationship, we rolled a six-sided die 1000 times. Figure 16.4 shows a data histogram of the results after 100 rolls and after 1000 rolls.

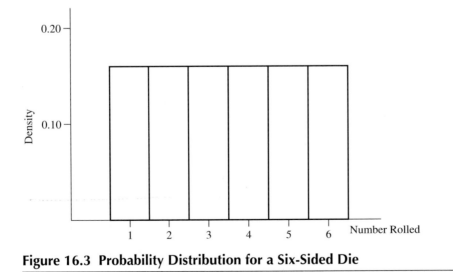

Figure 16.3 Probability Distribution for a Six-Sided Die

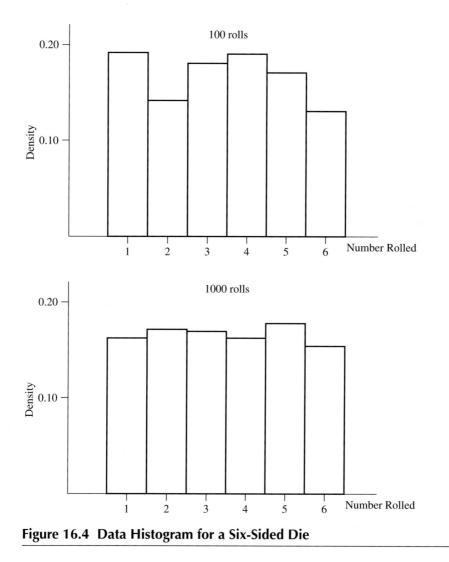

Figure 16.4 Data Histogram for a Six-Sided Die

As the number of rolls increases, the data histogram looks increasingly like the probability distribution in Figure 16.3.

We can think of the probability distribution as describing what our data would look like if the experiment were repeated an infinite number of times. If we roll a six-sided die many, many times, we expect each number to appear about one-sixth of the time; if we roll a die once, each number has a 1/6 probability of appearing. A probability distribution can be thought of as the population from which a single experiment is a random draw.

16.2.2 Mean, Variance, and Standard Deviation

A complete probability distribution can be displayed in a table or graph. Sometimes, a few simple numbers can summarize effectively the important characteristics of a probability distribution. The **expected value** (or **mean**) of a discrete random variable X is

$$\mu = E[X] = \sum_i X_i P[X_i] \tag{16.3}$$

The Greek symbol μ (pronounced "mew") and the notation $E[X]$ denotes the expected value of the random variable X. The summation sign $\sum$ means that we multiply each possible value of the random variable by its associated probability and then add up these products $X_i P[X_i]$.

Suppose, for example, that X is equal to the number obtained when a single fair six-sided die is rolled and we want to find the expected value of X.

1. Determine the possible outcomes (the possible values of X). Here, there are six possible values: 1, 2, 3, 4, 5, 6.

2. Determine the probability of each possible outcome. Here, each of the six possible outcomes has a 1/6 probability.

3. As shown in Equation 16.3, the expected value is equal to the sum of the possible outcomes multiplied by their respective probabilities:

$$\mu = 1\left(\frac{1}{6}\right) + 2\left(\frac{1}{6}\right) + 3\left(\frac{1}{6}\right) + 4\left(\frac{1}{6}\right) + 5\left(\frac{1}{6}\right) + 6\left(\frac{1}{6}\right)$$
$$= 3.5$$

The expected value is not the most likely value of X: the expected value of a dice roll is 3.5, but you will never roll a 3.5. The expected value should be interpreted as the anticipated long-run average value of X. If, in accord with their probabilities, the six die sides come up equally often, the average value of X will be 3.5.

Here's a very different example. In 1998 there were two million 20-year-old nonsmokers in the United States, of whom 1,200 died that year. These data provide an estimate of the probability P that a 20-year-old nonsmoker will die within a year: $P = 1{,}200/2{,}000{,}000 = 0.0006$. An insurance company can use this 0.0006 estimated probability to calculate the expected value of the payoff for a one-year $100,000 life insurance policy for a 20-year-old nonsmoker:

$$\mu = \$100{,}000(0.0006) + \$0(1 - 0.0006) = \$60$$

If its probability estimate is accurate, an insurance company can anticipate paying, on average, $60 per policy.

In 1998, the cost for one company's $100,000 one-year life insurance policy for a 20-year-old nonsmoker was $117—roughly twice the expected value of the payoff. If, as anticipated, a fraction 0.0006 of the insured 20-year-old nonsmokers die, the company will collect $117 per policy and pay out, on average, $60 per policy. Roughly half of the money that the insurance company receives will be paid to beneficiaries and half will be retained by the company to cover administrative expenses and provide a profit. This 50 percent benefit-to-premium ratio is representative of many insurance policies.

Pascal and other early probability theorists used probabilities to calculate the expected value of various games of chance and determine which were the most profitable. They assumed that a rational person would choose the course of action with the highest expected value. This expected-value criterion is appealing for gambles that are repeated over and over. It makes good sense to look at the long-run average when there is a long run to average over. Casinos, state lotteries, and insurance companies are very interested in the expected values on the repetitive gambles they offer, because anything with a negative expected value will almost certainly be unprofitable in the long run.

However, an expected-value criterion is often inappropriate. State lotteries have a positive expected value for the state and, because their gain is our loss, a negative expected value for people who buy lottery tickets. Those who buy lottery tickets are not maximizing expected value. Insurance policies give insurance companies a positive expected value and insurance buyers a negative expected value. People who buy insurance are not maximizing expected value either. Diversified investments provide yet another example. An expected-value maximizer should invest everything in the single asset with the highest expected value. Individuals and financial institutions that hold dozens or thousands of assets must not be maximizing expected value.

The primary inadequacy of expected-value maximization is that it neglects risk—how certain or uncertain a situation is. An expected value maximizer considers a sure $1 million and a 1 percent chance at $100 million equally attractive because each has an expected value of $1 million. If these alternatives were offered over and over, there would be little difference in the long run because the payoffs from each would almost certainly average close to $1 million per play. But if you get only one chance at this game, the outcome may differ considerably from its expected value, a difference ignored by an expected-value calculation. Much of the uncertainty we face is unique, not repetitive, and the possible divergence between the actual outcome and its expected value is properly described as risk.

To measure the extent to which the outcomes may differ from the expected value, we can use the **variance** of a discrete random variable X:

$$\sigma^2 = E[(X - \mu)^2] = \sum_i (X_i - \mu)^2 P[X_i] \qquad (16.4)$$

The **standard deviation** σ is the square root of the variance. (The Greek symbol σ is pronounced "sigma.")

The interpretation of the variance is best understood by dissecting Equation 16.4. The variance is the expected value of $(X - \mu)^2$; that is, the anticipated long-run average value of the squared deviations of the possible values of X from its expected value μ.

The variance and standard deviation are probability-weighted measures of the dispersion of the possible outcomes about their expected value. The standard deviation is usually easier to interpret than the variance because it has the same units (for example, dollars) as X and μ, whereas the units for the variance are squared (for example, dollars-squared). A compact probability distribution has a low standard deviation; a spread-out probability distribution has a high standard deviation.

Consider again a random variable X equal to the number obtained when a single six-sided die is rolled.

1. Determine the expected value of X, here 3.5.

2. For each possible value of X, determine the size of the squared deviation from the expected value μ

Die Outcome X_i	Deviation $X_i - \mu$	Squared Deviation $(X_i - \mu)^2$
1	−2.5	6.25
2	−1.5	2.25
3	−0.5	0.25
4	0.5	0.25
5	1.5	2.25
6	2.5	6.25

3. As shown in Equation 16.4, the variance is equal to the sum of the squared deviations of X_i from μ, multiplied by their respective probabilities:

$$\sigma^2 = (1 - 3.5)^2\left(\frac{1}{6}\right) + (2 - 3.5)^2\left(\frac{1}{6}\right) + \cdots + (6 - 3.5)^2\left(\frac{1}{6}\right)$$
$$= 6.25\left(\frac{1}{6}\right) + 2.25\left(\frac{1}{6}\right) + \cdots + 6.25\left(\frac{1}{6}\right)$$
$$= 2.9167$$

4. The standard deviation is equal to the square root of the variance; here,

$$\sigma = \sqrt{2.9167} = 1.71$$

16.2.3 Continuous Random Variables

Our examples to this point have involved *discrete* random variables, where we can count the number of possible outcomes. The coin can be heads or tails; the die can be 1, 2, 3, 4, 5, or 6. Other random variables can take on a continuum of values. For these *continuous* random variables, the outcome can be any value in a given interval.

For example, Figure 16.5 shows a spinner for randomly selecting a point on a circle. We can imagine that this is a clean, well-balanced device in which each point on the circle is equally likely to be picked. How many possible outcomes are there? How many points are there on the circle? In theory, there are an uncountable infinity of points in that between any two points on the circle, there are still more points.

Weight, height, and time are other examples of continuous variables. Even though we might say that Sarah Cunningham is 19 years old, a person's age can, in theory, be specified with infinite precision. Instead of saying that she is 19 or 20, we could say that she is 19 and a half, or 19 years and 7 months, or 19 years, 220 days, and 10 hours. With continuous variables, we can specify finer and finer gradations within any interval.

How can we specify probabilities when there are an uncountable number of possible outcomes? In Figure 16.5, each point on the circle is equally likely and a point surely will be selected; but if we give each point a positive

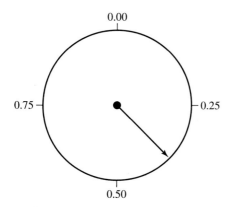

Figure 16.5 Pick a Number, Any Number

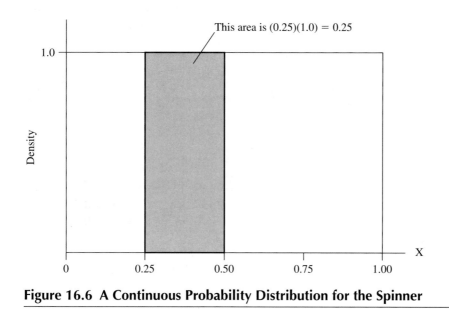

Figure 16.6 A Continuous Probability Distribution for the Spinner

probability P, the sum of this uncountable number of probabilities will be infinity, not one. Mathematicians handle this vexing situation of an uncountable number of possible outcomes by assigning probabilities to *intervals* of outcomes, rather than to individual outcomes. For example, the probability that the spinner will stop between 0.25 and 0.50 is 1/4.

We can display these interval probabilities by using a continuous **probability density curve**, as in Figure 16.6, in which the probability that the outcome is in a specified interval is given by the corresponding area under the curve. The shaded area shows the probability that the spinner will stop between 0.25 and 0.50. This rectangular area is (base)(height) = (0.25)(1.0) = 1/4. What is the probability that the spinner will stop between 0 and 1? This probability is the entire area under the curve: (base)(height) = (1)(1.0) = 1. In fact, the height of the probability density curve, 1.0, was derived from the requirement that the total probability must be 1. If the numbers on our spinner went from 0 to 12, like a clock, the height of the probability density curve would have to be 1/12 for the total area to be (base)(height) = (12)(1/12) = 1.

The smooth density curve for a continuous random variable is analogous to the jagged probability distribution for a discrete random variable. The population mean and the standard deviation consequently have the same interpretation. The population mean is the anticipated long-run average value of the outcomes; the standard deviation measures the extent to which the outcomes are likely to differ from the mean. The population mean is at the center of a symmetrical density function; in Figure 16.6, for example, the mean is 0.5. More generally, however, the mean and standard deviation of a continuous random variable cannot be calculated without using calculus.

16.2.4 Standardized Variables

Many random variables are the cumulative result of a sequence of random events. For instance, a random variable giving the sum of the numbers when eight dice are rolled can be viewed as the cumulative result of eight separate random events. The percentage change in a stock's price over a 12-month period is the cumulative result of a large number of random events during that interval. A person's height at 11 years of age is the cumulative result of a great many random events, some hereditary and some having to do with diet, health, and exercise.

These three different examples—dice rolls, stock price changes, and height—involve very different units of measurement: number, percent, and inches. However, in the eighteenth and nineteenth centuries, researchers discovered that when variables are *standardized*, in a particular way that will soon be explained, their histograms are often virtually identical! This remarkable similarity is perhaps the most important discovery in the long history of probability and statistics.

We have seen that the mean and standard deviation are two important tools for describing probability distributions. One appealing way to standardize variables is to transform them so that they have the same mean and the same standard deviation. This reshaping is easily done in the statistical beauty parlor. To standardize a random variable X, we subtract its mean μ and then divide by its standard deviation σ:

$$Z = \frac{X - \mu}{\sigma}$$

No matter what the initial units of X, the **standardized random variable** Z has a mean of 0 and a standard deviation of 1.

The standardized variable Z measures how many standard deviations X is above or below its mean. If X is equal to its mean, Z is equal to 0. If X is one standard deviation above its mean, Z is equal to 1. If X is two standard deviations below its mean, Z is equal to -2.

For example, if we look at the height of a randomly selected U.S. woman between the ages of 25 and 34, we can consider this height to be a random variable X drawn from a population with a mean of 66 inches and a standard deviation of 2.5 inches. Here are the standardized Z-values corresponding to five different values of X:

X (inches)	Z = (X − 66)/2.5 (standard deviations)
61.0	−2
63.5	−1
66.0	0
68.5	+1
71.0	+2

Instead of saying that a woman is 71 inches tall (which is useful for some purposes, such as clothing sizes), we can say that her height is two standard deviations above the mean (which is useful for other purposes, such as comparing her height with the heights of other women).

Another reason for standardizing variables is that it is difficult to compare the shapes of distributions when they have different means and/or standard deviations. Figure 16.3 showed the probability distribution for a single six-sided die. Now suppose that we want to examine the three probability distributions for a random variable X equal to the sum of the numbers obtained when rolling 2, 10, and 100 standard six-sided dice. If we work with the nonstandardized variable X, each probability distribution has a different mean and standard deviation. With one dice roll, the mean is 3.5 and the standard deviation is 1.7; with 100 dice rolls, the mean is 350 and the standard deviation is 17. By converting these variables to standardized Z values that have the same mean (zero) and the same standard deviation (one), we can focus our attention on the shapes of these probability distributions without being distracted by their location and spread. The results of this standardization are in Figure 16.7, which shows that as the number of dice increases, the probability distribution becomes increasingly shaped like a bell.

Figure 16.8 shows the same pattern using the number of "heads" that result from 10, 100, and 1000 coin flips: the probability distribution becomes increasingly bell shaped as the number of trials increases. (Because the number of equally likely outcomes is larger with a die than with a coin, fewer trials are needed for dice rolls to become bell shaped.) Comparing Figures 16.7 and 16.8, the standardized probability distributions for 100 dice rolls and 1000 coin flips are virtually indistinguishable. When we cumulate a large number of independent uncertain events, either dice rolls or coin flips, the same bell-shaped probability distribution emerges! You can imagine the excitement that mathematicians must have felt when they first discovered this remarkable regularity. They were analyzing situations that not only were governed by unpredictable chance but were also very dissimilar (a six-sided die and a two-sided coin), and yet a regular pattern emerged.

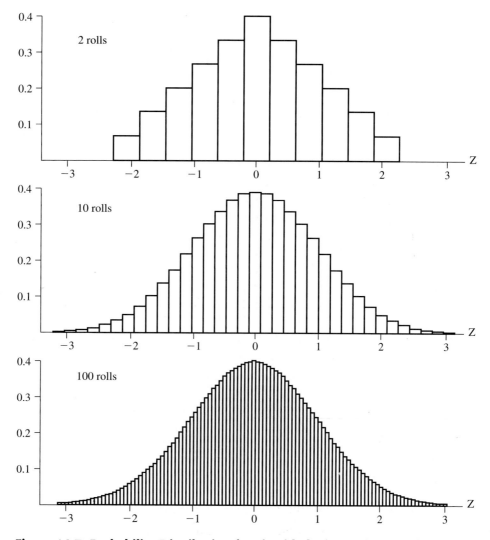

Figure 16.7 Probability Distribution for Six-Sided Dice, Using Standardized Z

No wonder Sir Francis Galton called this phenomenon a "wonderful form of cosmic order."

16.2.5 The Normal Distribution

Karl Gauss (1777–1855) applied the normal distribution to measurements of the shape of the earth and the movements of planets. His work was so extensive and influential that the normal distribution is often called the

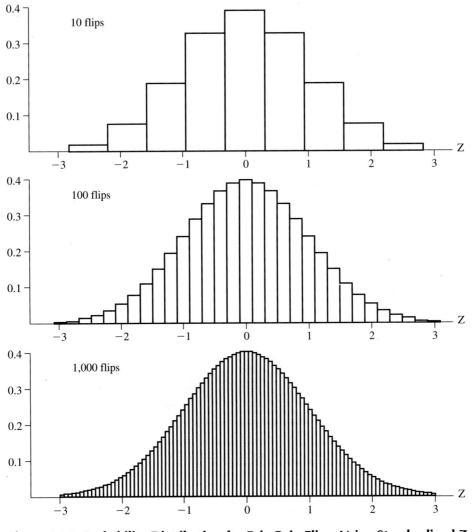

Figure 16.8 Probability Distribution for Fair Coin Flips, Using Standardized Z

Gaussian distribution. Others, following in his footsteps, applied the normal distribution to all sorts of physical and social data. They found that empirical data often conform to a normal distribution, and they proved that many specific probability distributions converge to a normal distribution when they are cumulated. In the 1930s, mathematicians proved that this convergence is true for a very broad range of probability distributions. This theorem is one of the most famous mathematical theorems: the **central limit theorem** states that if Z is a standardized sum of n independent, identically distributed (discrete or continuous) random variables with a finite, nonzero standard deviation, then the probability distribution of Z approaches the normal distribution as n increases.

As remarkable as it is, the central limit theorem would be of little practical value if the normal curve emerged only when the sample size n is extremely large. The normal distribution is important because it so often appears even when n is quite small. Look again at the case of n = 2 dice rolls in Figure 16.7 and n = 10 coin flips in Figure 16.8; for most purposes, a normal curve would be a satisfactory approximation of these probability distributions. If the underlying distribution is reasonably smooth and symmetrical (as with dice rolls and coin flips) the approach to a normal curve is very rapid and values of n larger than 20 or 30 are sufficient for the normal distribution to provide an acceptable approximation. A very asymmetrical distribution, such as a 0.99 probability of success and 0.01 probability of failure, requires a much larger number of trials.

The central limit theorem is remarkably robust in that even if its assumptions aren't exactly true, the normal distribution is still a pretty good approximation. A normal distribution appears when we examine the weights of humans, dogs, and tomatoes. The lengths of thumbs, widths of shoulders, and breadths of skulls are all normally distributed. Scores on IQ, SAT, and GRE tests are normally distributed. So are the number of kernels on ears of corn, ridges on scallop shells, hairs on cats, and leaves on trees. If some phenomenon is the cumulative result of a great many separate influences, then the normal distribution may be a very useful approximation.

This is why the normal distribution is so popular and the central limit theorem so celebrated. However, don't be lulled into thinking that probabilities always follow the normal curve. These examples are approximately, but not perfectly, normal and there are many phenomena whose probability distributions are not normal at all. Our purpose is not to persuade you that there is only one probability distribution, but to explain why many phenomena are well described by the normal distribution.

The density curve for the normal distribution is graphed in Figure 16.9. The probability that the value of Z will be in a specified interval is given by the corresponding area under this curve. However, there is no simple formula for computing areas under a normal curve. These areas can be determined from complex numerical procedures, but nobody wants to do these computations every time a normal probability is needed. Instead, they consult statistical software or a table, such as Table B–7 in Appendix B, that shows the normal probabilities for hundreds of values of Z.

The following three rules of thumb can help us estimate probabilities for normally distributed random variables without consulting Table B–7:

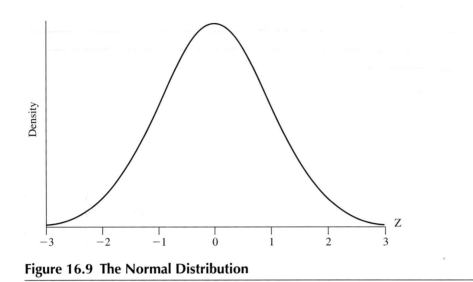

Figure 16.9 The Normal Distribution

$$P[-1 < Z < 1] = 0.6826$$
$$P[-2 < Z < 2] = 0.9544$$
$$P[-3 < Z < 3] = 0.9973$$

A normally distributed random variable has about a 68 percent (roughly two-thirds) chance of being within one standard deviation of its mean, a 95 percent chance of being within two standard deviations of its mean, and better than a 99.7 percent chance of being within three standard deviations of its mean. Turning these around, a normally distributed random variable has less than a 0.3 percent chance of being more than three standard deviations from its mean, roughly a 5 percent chance of being more than two standard deviations from its mean, and a 32 percent chance of being more than one standard deviation from its mean.

For example, there are a number of tests designed to measure a person's IQ (intelligence quotient), reflecting an accurate memory and the ability to reason logically and clearly. Because an individual's score on an IQ test depends on a very large number of hereditary and environmental factors, the central limit theorem explains why IQ scores are approximately normally distributed. One of the most widely used tests today is the Wechsler Adult Intelligence Scale, which has a mean IQ of 100 and a standard deviation of 15. About half the people tested score above 100 and about half score below 100. Our one-standard-deviation rule of thumb implies that about 32 percent of the population will score more than 15 points away from 100: 16 percent above 115 and 16 percent below 85. Our two-standard-deviations rule implies that about 5 percent of the population will score more than 30 points away from 100: 2.5 percent above 130 and 2.5 percent below 70.

16.3 Sampling

The previous sections were concerned with summarizing data. Now we focus on the actual production or collection of empirical data. To draw useful statistical inferences, we must exercise care in gathering the data that will be used to make these inferences. The entire group of items that interests us is called the **population**. The part of this population that we actually observe is called a **sample**. Statistical inference involves using the sample to draw conclusions about the characteristics of the population from which the sample came. In a medical experiment, for example, the population consists of all persons who might use this medication; the sample is the group of people used to test the medication; a possible statistical inference is that people who take the medication tend, on average, to live longer than people who don't.

We use samples to draw inferences about the population because it is often impractical to scrutinize the entire population. If we burn every light bulb that a manufacturer produces to see how long each bulb lasts, all we will have is a large electricity bill and a lot of burnt-out light bulbs. Many tests are not this destructive but are simply too expensive to apply to the entire population. Instead, we sample. A light-bulb manufacturer tests a sample of its bulbs. A software company tests a sample of its disks. Medications and opinion polls are administered to a sample of people because it is too expensive to test or survey everyone.

16.3.1 Selection Bias

Any sample that differs systematically from the population that it is intended to represent is called a *biased sample*. Because a biased sample is unrepresentative of the population, it gives a distorted picture of the population and may lead to unwarranted conclusions. One of the most common causes of biased samples is **selection bias**, which occurs when the selection of the sample systematically excludes or underrepresents certain groups. Selection bias often happens when we use a *convenience sample* consisting of data that are easily collected.

If we are trying to estimate how often people get colds and have a friend who can give us medical records from an elementary school, this is a convenience sample with selection bias. If our intended population is people of all ages, we should not use samples that systematically exclude certain ages. Similarly, the medical records from a prison, military base, or nursing home are convenience samples with selection bias. Military personnel are in better physical health than those living in nursing homes, and both differ systematically from the population as a whole.

Self-selection bias can occur when we examine data for a group of people who have chosen to be in that group. For example, the accident records of people who buy collision insurance may be unrepresentative of the population as a whole; maybe they buy insurance because they know that they are accident prone. The physical fitness of joggers may provide a biased estimates of the benefits of jogging; most of those who choose to run regularly may be more physically fit than the general population, even before they began running.

16.3.2 Survivor Bias

Retrospective studies look at past data for a contemporaneously selected sample; for example, an examination of the lifetime medical records of 65-year-olds. A *prospective* study, in contrast, selects a sample and then tracks the members over time. Retrospective studies are notoriously unreliable, and not just because of faulty memories and lost data. When we choose a sample from a current population in order to draw inferences about a past population, we necessarily exclude members of the past population who are no longer around—an exclusion that causes **survivor bias**, in that we only look at the survivors. If we examine the medical records of 65 year olds in order to identify the causes of health problems, we overlook those who died before reaching 65 years of age and consequently omit data on some fatal health problems. Survivor bias is a form of selection bias in that the use of retrospective data excludes part of the relevant population.

Here's another example. Stock market studies sometimes examine historical data for companies that have been selected randomly from the New York Stock Exchange (NYSE). If we restrict our analysis to companies currently listed on the NYSE, our data will be subject to survivor bias because we will ignore companies that were listed in the past, but have subsequently gone bankrupt. If we want to estimate the average return for an investment in NYSE stocks over the past 50 years, and do not consider the stock of any company that went bankrupt, we will overestimate the average return.

16.3.3 Nonresponse Bias

The systematic refusal of some groups to participate in an experiment or to respond to a poll is called **nonresponse bias**. A study is naturally more suspect the fewer the people who bother to respond. In the 1940s, the makers of

Ipana Tooth Paste boasted that a national survey had found that "Twice as many dentists personally use Ipana Tooth Paste as any other dentifrice preparation. In a recent nationwide survey, more dentists said they recommended Ipana for their patients' daily use than the next two dentifrices combined."[3] The Federal Trade Commission banned this ad after it learned that less than 1 percent of the dentists surveyed had named the brand of toothpaste they used and that even fewer had named a brand recommended for their patients.[4]

16.3.4 The Power of Random Selection

Suppose that we want to estimate the average income of people in our hometown. We could attempt to put together a representative sample by wandering around town and carefully selecting people who appear to be "typical," but if we did, we would probably ignore the very rich and the very poor, and end up with a sample that has far less variation than does the population. Our sample would probably be biased, because those we exclude for being "above average" and those we exclude for being "below average" are unlikely to balance each other out perfectly. Worst of all, these biases would depend, in unknowable ways, on our undoubtedly mistaken perception of the "typical" person. We might also be influenced by our preconceived notions of the results we hope to obtain. If we intend to show that these residents are, on average, better off than the citizens of another town, this intention may well influence the people we choose to interview.

How do we actually make random selections? Returning to our income study, suppose that we were to interview every registered voter. This would be a large sample, but it would have selection bias if there are systematic income differences between those who are and are not registered to vote. Similarly, shoppers at a certain store, owners of certain cars, or members of certain clubs might not be representative of the town as a whole.

Ideally, we would choose a procedure that is equivalent to the following: put each resident's name on a slip of paper, drop these slips into a box, mix thoroughly, and pick names out randomly, just as cards are dealt from a well-shuffled deck. Each person, whether rich or poor, has an equal chance of inclusion in our sample. In practice, instead of putting pieces of paper into a box, random sampling is usually done through some sort of numerical identification combined with the random selection of numbers.

---

3. Earl W. Kintner, *A Primer on the Law of Deceptive Practices* (New York: Macmillan, 1971), p. 153.

4. *Ibid.*

16.4 Estimation

Sampling provides an economical way to estimate the characteristics of a large population. Samples are used to estimate the amount of cholesterol in a person's body, the average acidity of a farmer's soil, and the number of fish in a lake. Production samples are used to estimate the fraction of a company's products that are defective, and marketing samples are used to estimate how many people will buy a new product. The federal government uses samples to estimate the unemployment rate and the rate of inflation. Public opinion polls are used to predict the winners of elections and to estimate the fraction of the population that agrees with certain positions.

In each case, sample data are used to estimate a population value. But exactly how should the data be used to make these estimates? And how much confidence can we have in estimates that are based on a small sample from a large population? In this section we will answer these questions.

16.4.1 Estimation

Earlier in this chapter, we looked at the 1998 returns from a random sample of 25 mutual funds. Let's now see how these data could be used to estimate the average returns for all mutual funds in 1998. First, some terminology. The population mean μ is a *parameter* whose value is unknown but can be estimated. A sample statistic, such as the sample mean, that is used to estimate the value of a population parameter is called an *estimator*. The specific value of the estimator that is obtained in a particular sample is an *estimate*.

How seriously can we take an estimate of the average return for thousands of mutual funds when our estimate is based on just 25 funds? We know that if we were to take another random sample, we would almost certainly not select the same 25 funds and consequently would get a somewhat different sample mean. Because our samples are chosen randomly, *sampling variation* will cause the sample mean to vary from sample to sample, sometimes being larger than the population mean and sometimes lower. How much faith can we place in the mean of one small sample? Let's find out.

16.4.2 Sampling Distributions

The sample mean is a random variable that depends on which particular observations happen to be selected for the random sample. The difference between the value of one particular sample mean and the average of the means of all possible samples of this size is known as the **sampling error**. Sampling error is not due to a poorly designed experiment or sloppy procedure. It is the inevitable result of the fact that the observations in our sample are chosen by chance. In contrast, **systematic errors** or biases cause the sample means to differ, on average, from the population parameter we are trying to estimate.

In practice, we take one sample, calculate the sample mean, and use this value as an estimate of the population mean. It is tempting to regard this number as definitive. That temptation should be resisted. Our particular sample is just one of many samples that might have been selected; other samples would yield somewhat different sample means. We cannot say whether a particular sample mean is above or below the population mean because we don't know the value of the population mean. But we can use probabilities to deduce how likely it is that a sample will be selected whose mean is close to the population mean.

The **sampling distribution** of a statistic, such as the sample mean, is the probability distribution or density curve that describes the population of all possible values of this statistic. It can be shown mathematically that if the individual observations are drawn from a normal distribution, then the sampling distribution for the sample mean is also normal. Even if the population does not have a normal distribution, the sampling distribution of the sample mean will approach a normal distribution as the sample size increases. Here's why. Each observation in a random sample is an independent random variable drawn from the same population. The sample mean is the sum of these n outcomes, divided by n. Except for the unimportant division by n, these are the same assumptions in the central limit theorem! Therefore the sampling distribution for the mean of a random sample from any population approaches a normal distribution as n increases.

Thus, the sampling distribution for the mean of a reasonably sized random sample is bell shaped. The only caution is that the sample be large enough for the central limit theorem to work its magic. With something like mutual fund returns, which are themselves approximately normally distributed, a sample of 10 observations is large enough. If the underlying distribution is not normal, but roughly symmetrical, a sample of size 20 or 30 is generally sufficient for the normal distribution to be appropriate.

It is important to recognize the difference between the probability distribution for a single value of X and the sampling distribution for the sample mean. Figure 16.10 shows the sampling distribution for the mean of samples of size 5 and 10 taken from a uniform distribution in which each number from 1 to 9 has the same probability of being selected. When we select a random sample, some of the outcomes most likely will be above 5 and some below, thereby giving a sample mean that is, in most cases, not far from 5. It is unlikely that the mean of a reasonably large sample will be far from 5 be-

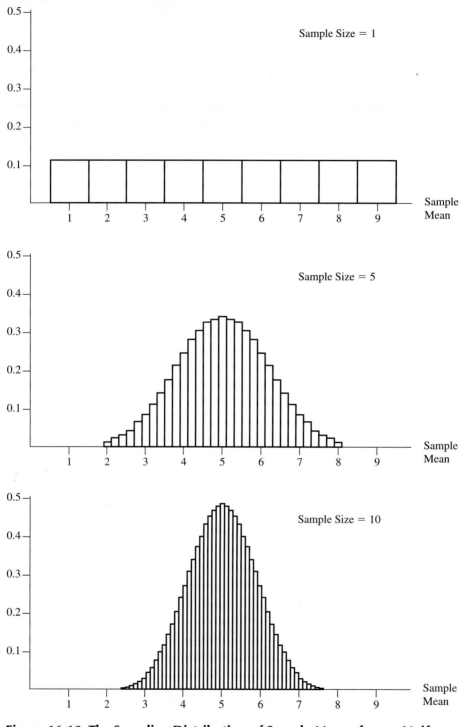

Figure 16.10 The Sampling Distribution of Sample Means from a Uniform Distribution

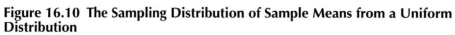

cause, for this to occur, the individual outcomes in the sample must repeatedly be on one side of the population mean. The damping effects of averaging many outcomes give the sampling distribution for the sample mean a symmetrical bell shape.

In addition to the general shape of the sampling distribution, we need to know how its mean and standard deviation are related to the mean μ and standard deviation σ of the population from which the individual observations are drawn. It can be shown mathematically that this sampling distribution has a mean equal to μ and a standard deviation equal to σ divided by the square root of the sample size n:

$$\text{Mean of } \overline{X} = \mu$$
$$\text{Standard deviation of } \overline{X} = \frac{\sigma}{\sqrt{n}} \tag{16.5}$$

16.4.3 The Mean of the Sampling Distribution

Although we can never know with certainty exactly how close a particular sample mean is to the unknown population mean, we can use the mean and standard deviation of the sampling distribution to gauge the reliability of the sample mean as an estimator of the population mean. A sample statistic is an **unbiased estimator** of a population parameter if the mean of the sampling distribution of this statistic is equal to the value of the population parameter. Because the mean of the sampling distribution of the sample mean is μ, the sample mean is an unbiased estimator of the population mean.

Unbiased estimators have considerable appeal. It would be discomforting to use an estimator that one knows to be systematically too high or too low. A statistician who uses unbiased estimators can anticipate estimation errors that, over a lifetime, average close to zero. Of course, average performance is not the only thing that counts. A British Lord Justice once summarized his career by saying that "When I was a young man practicing at the bar, I lost a great many cases I should have won. As I got along, I won a great many cases I ought to have lost; so on the whole justice was done." The conscientious statistician should be concerned with not only how good the estimates are on average, but also how accurate they are in particular cases.

16.4.4 The Standard Deviation of the Sampling Distribution

One way of gauging the accuracy of an estimator is with its standard deviation. If an estimator has a large standard deviation, there is a substantial probability that the estimate will be far from its mean. If an estimator has a small standard deviation, there is a high probability that the estimate will be close to its mean.

Equation 16.5 states that the standard deviation of the sampling distribution for the sample mean is equal to σ divided by the square root of the sample size, n. As the number of observations increases, the standard deviation of the sampling distribution declines. To understand this phenomenon, remember that the standard deviation is a measure of the uncertainty of the outcome. With a large sample, it is extremely unlikely that all of the observations will be far above the mean of the sampling distribution, and equally improbable that all of the observations will be far below the mean. Instead, it is almost certain that some of the observations will be above the mean and some below, and that the average will be close to the mean of the sampling distribution.

16.4.5 The t-Distribution

The standard deviation of the sampling distribution depends on the value of population standard deviation σ, a parameter that is unknown but can be estimated. The most natural estimator of σ, the standard deviation of the population, is s, the standard deviation of the sample data from this population. The formula for the sample variance was given earlier in Equation 16.2, and the standard deviation s is the square root of the variance.

When the standard deviation of an estimator, such as the sample mean, is itself estimated from the data, this estimated standard deviation is called the estimator's *standard error.* The standard error of the sample mean is calculated by replacing the unknown parameter s in Equation 16.5 with its estimate σ:

$$\text{standard error of } \overline{X} = s/\sqrt{n}$$

The need to estimate the standard deviation creates another source of uncertainty in gauging the reliability of the sample mean as an estimator of the population mean.

In 1908, W. S. Gosset figured out how to handle this increased uncertainty when the data are drawn from a normal distribution. Gosset was a statistician employed by the Irish brewery Guinness, which encouraged statistical research but not publication. Because of the importance of his findings, he was able to persuade Guinness to allow his work to be published under the pseudonym "Student" and his calculations became known as the **Student's t-distribution**.

When the mean of a sample from a normal distribution is standardized by subtracting the mean μ of its sampling distribution and dividing by the standard deviation $\sigma/\sqrt{n}$ of its sampling distribution, the resulting Z variable

$$Z = \frac{\overline{X} - \mu}{\sigma/\sqrt{n}}$$

has a normal distribution. Gosset determined the sampling distribution of the variable that is created when the mean of a sample from a normal distribution is standardized by subtracting μ and dividing by its standard error:

$$t = \frac{\overline{X} - \mu}{s/\sqrt{n}} \tag{16.6}$$

The exact distribution of t depends on the sample size, because as the sample size increases, we are increasingly confident of the accuracy of the estimated standard deviation. For an infinite sample, the estimate s will equal the actual value σ, and the distributions of t and Z coincide. With a small sample, s may be either larger or smaller than σ and the distribution of t is consequently more dispersed than the distribution of Z.

Table B–1 in Appendix B shows some probabilities for various t-distributions that are identified by the number of **degrees of freedom**:

$$\begin{array}{ccc} \text{degrees of} \\ \text{freedom} \end{array} = \begin{array}{c} \text{number of} \\ \text{observations} \end{array} - \begin{array}{c} \text{number of parameters that} \\ \text{must be estimated beforehand} \end{array}$$

Here, we calculate s by using n observations and one estimated parameter (the sample mean); therefore, there are $n - 1$ degrees of freedom.

There is another way to think about degrees of freedom that is more closely related to the name itself. We calculate s from n squared deviations about the sample mean. However, we saw earlier in this chapter that the sum of the deviations about the sample mean is always zero. Thus if we know the values of $n - 1$ of these deviations, we know the value of the last deviation, too. Only $n - 1$ deviations are freely determined by the sample.

16.4.6 Confidence Intervals

Now we are ready to use the t-distribution and the standard error of the sample mean to measure the reliability of our estimate of the population mean. If we specify a probability, such as $\alpha = 0.05$, we can use Table B–1 to find the t value t* such that there is a probability $\alpha/2$ that the value of t will exceed t*, a probability $\alpha/2$ that the value of t will be less than $-t^*$, and a probability $1 - \alpha$ that the value of t will be in the interval $-t^*$ to t*:

$$1 - \alpha = P[-t^* < t < t^*]$$

Using Equation 16.6 and rearranging,

$$1 - \alpha = P\left[\mu - t^*\frac{s}{\sqrt{n}} < \overline{X} < \mu + t^*\frac{s}{\sqrt{n}}\right]$$

We can rephrase this probability computation to show the confidence that we have in using the sample mean to estimate the population mean. If there is a $1 - \alpha$ probability that the sample mean will turn out to be within t^* standard errors of the population mean μ, then there is a $1 - \alpha$ probability that the interval from

$$\overline{X} - t^*\left(\frac{s}{\sqrt{n}}\right) \quad \text{to} \quad \overline{X} + t^*\left(\frac{s}{\sqrt{n}}\right)$$

will include the value of μ. Such an interval is called a **confidence interval** and the $1 - \alpha$ probability is the interval's **confidence level**. The shorthand formula for a $1 - \alpha$ percent confidence interval for the population mean μ is

$$1 - \alpha \text{ confidence interval for } \mu: \overline{X} \pm t^*\left(\frac{s}{\sqrt{n}}\right) \qquad (16.7)$$

There is a 0.95 probability that the sample mean $\overline{X}$ will be between $\mu - t^*$ (standard error of $\overline{X}$) and $\mu + t^*$ (standard error of $\overline{X}$), in which case the interval $\overline{X} - t^*$ (standard error of $\overline{X}$) to $\overline{X} + t^*$ (standard error of $\overline{X}$) will encompass μ. There is a 0.05 probability that the sample mean will, by the luck of the draw, turn out to be more than t^* (standard error of $\overline{X}$) from the population mean μ, and that the confidence interval will consequently not include μ.

Gosset derived the t-distribution by assuming that the sample data are taken from a normal distribution. Subsequent research has shown that because of the power of the central limit theorem, confidence intervals based on the t-distribution are remarkably accurate even if the underlying data are not normally distributed, as long as we have at least 15 observations from a roughly symmetrical distribution or at least 30 observations from a clearly asymmetrical distribution.[5] A histogram can be used for a rough symmetry

5. E. S. Pearson and N. W. Please, "Relation Between the Shape of Population Distribution and the Robustness of Four Simple Test Statistics," *Biometrika*, 1975, 62, pp. 223–241; Harry O. Poston, "The Robustness of the One-Sample t-test Over the Pearson System," *Journal of Statistical Computation and Simulation*, 1979, pp. 133–149.

check. Ninety-five percent confidence levels are standard, but there is no compelling reason why we can't use others.

Let's use the 1998 mutual fund data in Table 16.2 to construct a 95 percent confidence interval and a 99 percent confidence interval for the average return for all stock mutual funds in 1998. The sample mean is 8.93 and the standard deviation is 12.7654. The sample size is 25 and there are consequently $25 - 1 = 24$ degrees of freedom. Table B-1 shows that there is a 0.05 probability that the absolute value of t will exceed $t^* = 2.064$ and a 0.01 probability that it will exceed $t^* = 2.797$. Thus,

$$\text{95\% confidence interval for } \mu = 8.93 \pm 2.064\left(\frac{12.7654}{\sqrt{25}}\right) = 8.93 \pm 5.27$$

$$\text{99\% confidence interval for } \mu = 8.93 \pm 2.797\left(\frac{12.7654}{\sqrt{25}}\right) = 8.93 \pm 7.14$$

The actual value of the mean return for all stock mutual funds in 1998 was 12 percent, which is inside both of these confidence intervals.

Notice that it is the sample mean that varies from sample to sample, not the population mean. A 95 percent confidence interval for μ is interpreted as follows: "There is a 0.95 probability that the sample mean will turn out to be sufficiently close to μ so that my confidence interval includes μ. There is a 0.05 probability that the sample mean will happen to be so far from μ that my confidence interval does not include μ." The 0.95 probability refers to the chances that random sampling will result in an interval that includes the fixed parameter μ, not the probability that random sampling will give a value of μ that is inside a fixed confidence interval.

The general procedure for determining a confidence interval for a population mean is summarized here:

1. Calculate the sample mean.
2. Calculate the standard error of the sample mean by dividing the sample standard deviation s by the square root of the sample size n.
3. Select a confidence level (such as 95 percent) and look in Table B–1 with $n - 1$ degrees of freedom to determine the t-value t^* that corresponds to this probability.
4. A confidence interval for the population mean is equal to the sample mean plus or minus t^* standard errors of the sample mean:

$$\text{Confidence interval for } \mu = \overline{X} \pm t^* \text{ (standard error of } \overline{X})$$

$$= \overline{X} \pm t^*\left(\frac{s}{\sqrt{n}}\right)$$

16.4.7 Sampling from Finite Populations

A very interesting characteristic of a confidence interval is that it does not depend on the size of the population. At first glance, this conclusion may seem surprising. If we are trying to estimate a characteristic of a large population, then there is a natural tendency to believe that a large sample is needed. If there are 25 million items in the population, a sample of 25 includes only one out of every million. How can we possibly obtain a reliable estimate with a sample that looks at only one out of every million items?

A moment's reflection reveals why a confidence interval doesn't depend on whether the population consists of one thousand or one billion items. The chances that the luck of the draw will yield a sample whose mean differs substantially from the population mean depends on the size of the sample and the chances of selecting items that are far from the population mean, not on how many items there are in the population.

16.5   Hypothesis Tests

We've seen how sample data can be used to estimate the value of a population parameter, such as μ, and determine a confidence interval that gauges the precision of this estimate. Now we will see how sample data can be used to support or refute theories about the value of μ; for example, whether mutual funds, on average, beat the market.

16.5.1 A General Framework for Hypothesis Tests

Statistical tests are not as definitive as mathematical proofs, because sample data are subject to sampling error. There is always a chance, however small, that a new sample will discredit a previously confirmed theory. We cannot be absolutely certain of the average return of all mutual funds until we actually calculate it using data for every single fund.

Most theories are potentially vulnerable to reassessment because there never is a final tabulation of all possible data. New experiments and fresh observations continually provide new evidence—data that generally reaffirm previous studies, but occasionally create doubt or even reverse conclusions that were once thought firmly established. Theories are especially fragile in the humanities and social sciences, where there are few data and it is difficult to control for extraneous influences. In the 1960s, economists believed that there was a simple inverse relationship between a nation's unemployment rate and its rate of inflation: when unemployment goes up, inflation goes down. In the 1970s, unemployment and inflation both went up, and economists decided that they had overlooked other important influences, including inflation expectations.

If we can never be absolutely sure that a theory is true or false, the next best thing might seem to be to make probability statements, such as, "Based on the available data, there is a 0.90 probability that this theory is true." However, a theory isn't true 90 percent of the time; it's either true or it isn't. As a result, statistics has followed another route. Instead of estimating the probability that a theory is true, based on our observed data, statisticians calculate the reverse probability—that we would observe such data if the theory were true. An understanding of this distinction is crucial to an understanding of the meaning and limitations of hypothesis tests. Hypothesis tests are a proof by statistical contradiction. We calculate the probability of the observed outcome, or a more usual outcome, if the theory were true. If this probability is low, then the data are not consistent with the theory and therefore reject it, what Thomas Huxley called "the great tragedy of science—the slaying of a beautiful hypothesis by an ugly fact." This is a proof by statistical contradiction: because these data are unlikely to occur if the theory were true, we reject the theory. Of course, we can never be 100 percent certain, because unlikely events sometimes do happen. Notice, too, that for a theory not to be rejected, it need only be consistent with the data. This is a relatively weak conclusion, because many other theories may also be consistent with the data.

16.5.2 The Null and Alternative Hypotheses

To make these general ideas more concrete, we will consider the performance of stock mutual funds. Our *research question* is how mutual funds perform, on average, compared with the overall stock market, as measured by the Standard & Poor's index of the stocks of 500 prominent companies. For a proof by statistical contradiction, we make an assumption, called the **null hypothesis** (or H_0), about the population from which the sample is drawn. Typically, the null hypothesis is a "straw assumption" that we anticipate rejecting.

Here, our research question suggests the natural null hypothesis that in any given year, the average return for the entire population of mutual funds is equal to the S&P 500 return. Although we may have initiated this study because we believe that mutual funds systematically underperform or outperform the market, the way to demonstrate this by statistical contradiction is to see if the evidence rejects the straw hypothesis that their average return is equal to the market return. We will analyze mutual fund performance in 1998 data, when the S&P 500 return was 28.1 percent. Thus our null hypothesis is $\mu = 28.1$.

The **alternative hypothesis** (usually written as H_A or H_1) describes the population if the null hypothesis is not true. Here, the natural alternative hypothesis is that the population mean is not equal to 28.1:

$$H_0: \quad \mu = 28.1$$
$$H_A: \quad \mu \neq 28.1$$

This alternative hypothesis is our research question, stated in terms of the value of the population parameter μ. Here the alternative hypothesis is *two sided*, because (even though we might have a hunch about how the study will turn out) we are reluctant to rule out beforehand the possibility that the population mean may be either lower or higher than the value specified by the null hypothesis. If, before seeing the data, we could rule out one of these possibilities, the alternative hypothesis would be *one sided*. If, for example, we were convinced beforehand that the average mutual fund return could not possibly be greater than the S&P 500 return, the one-sided alternative hypothesis would be $H_A: \mu < 28.1$.

16.5.3 The Test Statistic and Statistical Significance

Once we have specified the null and alternative hypotheses, we collect and examine our sample data. Table 16.2 shows the 1998 returns for a random sample of 25 mutual funds. As we are concerned with the value of μ, the population mean return, we calculate the mean of our random sample—because this is what we would use to estimate the value of the population mean. The estimator that is used to test the null hypothesis is called the **test statistic**.

The sample mean for these 25 mutual funds is 8.928 percent, and the standard deviation is 12.765 percent. Does this 8.928 percent average return provide persuasive evidence that the average mutual fund return in 1998 was less than 28.1 percent, or can it be explained by the inevitable variation in the means of small samples drawn from a population with a standard deviation estimated to be 12.765 percent?

As explained earlier in this chapter, the sampling distribution for the mean of a random sample from a population with a mean μ and a standard deviation σ has a mean μ and a standard deviation equal to σ divided by the square root of the sample size. Even if the individual observations are not normally distributed, a sample of size 25 should be sufficient to appeal to the central limit theorem. Thus the Z-statistic

$$Z = \frac{\overline{X} - \mu}{\sigma / \sqrt{n}}$$

has a normal distribution. The replacement of the unknown standard deviation σ with the estimated value s gives this t-statistic:

$$t = \frac{\overline{X} - \mu}{s/\sqrt{n}}$$

which has a t distribution with $n - 1$ degrees of freedom.

Figure 16.11 shows the sample distribution of the t-statistic if the null hypothesis is true. The t-value measures how many standard errors the sample mean is from the value of the population mean if the null hypothesis is true. If $t = 0$, the sample mean is equal to the null hypothesis value of the population mean and consequently provides no evidence whatsoever against the null hypothesis. The farther the t-value is from zero (either positive or negative), the farther the sample mean is from the null hypothesis value and the greater is the evidence against the null hypothesis.

How far is far enough to be statistically persuasive? Researchers often report that their results either are or are not **statistically significant** at a specified level, such as 5 percent. What this cryptic phrase means is that the probability that the value of the test statistic would be so far from its expected value were the null hypothesis true is less than this specified *significance level*. An observed difference that is too large to be attributed plausibly to chance alone is statistically significant in the sense that its statistical improbability persuades us to reject the null hypothesis.

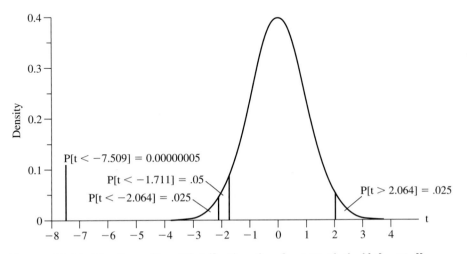

Figure 16.11 The Sampling Distribution for the t-Statistic if the Null Hypothesis Is True

For our mutual fund example, Table B–1 tells us that with n − 1 = 25 − 1 = 24 degrees of freedom, there is a 0.025 probability that the t-value will be less than −2.064 and a 0.025 probability that the t-value will be larger than 2.064. These plus-or-minus 2.064 cutoffs for statistical significance are called the test's *critical values*. A t-value outside this range is sufficient, at the 5 percent level, to reject the null hypothesis that the average return for all mutual funds in 1998 was 28.1 percent.

Notice that because our alternative hypothesis is two sided, we look at t-values that are far from 0 in either direction. If our alternative hypothesis were $H_A: \mu < 28.1$, then we reject the null hypothesis only if the sample mean is sufficiently far below 28.1 to give a sufficiently negative t-value. If the sample mean turns out to be far above 28.1, giving a large positive t-value, we must conclude that an improbable fluke happened. If we say beforehand that μ cannot possibly be above 28.1, we cannot change our mind after seeing the data! If we are willing to be persuaded by the data, then we must initially allow the alternative hypothesis to be two sided.

If, fully aware of this implicit commitment, we are nonetheless convinced that the alternative hypothesis is one sided, then we use only a single critical value (a *one-tail test*). Table B–1 tells us that with 24 degrees of freedom, there is a 0.05 probability that the t-value will be less than −1.711; this is consequently the critical value for the one-sided alternative hypothesis $H_A: \mu < 28.1$.

In our mutual fund example, the t value is −7.509:

$$t = \frac{\overline{X} - \mu}{s/\sqrt{n}}$$

$$= \frac{8.928 - 28.1}{12.765/\sqrt{25}}$$

$$= -7.509$$

This t-value is far greater in absolute value than the −2.064 critical value and therefore rejects the null hypothesis that the average return for all mutual funds in 1998 was 28.1 percent.

16.5.4 P-Values

To measure the extent to which our sample mean of 8.928 provides persuasive evidence against the null hypothesis, we can calculate the probability that the t-value would be so far from 0 if the null hypothesis were true. We don't calculate the probability that t will be exactly equal to −7.509. The probability that a continuous variable like t will equal any single number is zero. Instead, we determine the probability that t will be so far (or farther) from zero: $P[t \leq -7.509] = 0.00000005$.

The **P-value** for a test of a null hypothesis about the population mean is the probability, if the null hypothesis is in fact true, that a random sample of this size would yield a sample mean that is this far (or farther) from the value of the population mean assumed by the null hypothesis. A small P-value casts doubt on the null hypothesis.

The P-value can be obtained from statistical software using the t-distribution and is exactly correct if the data come from a normal distribution and, because of the power of the central limit theorem, is an excellent approximation if we have at least 15 observations from a generally symmetrical distribution, or at least 30 observations from a very asymmetrical distribution.

In calculating the P-value, we must take into account whether the alternative hypothesis is one sided or two sided. For a one-sided alternative hypothesis, the P-value is the probability that the sample mean would be so far to one side of the null hypothesis population mean. For a two-sided alternative hypothesis, the P-value is the probability that the test statistic would be so far, *in either direction*, from the null hypothesis population mean. In our mutual fund example, we report the probability that the sample mean will be 7.509 standard errors or more, in either direction, from 28.1. Because the normal distribution is symmetrical, we double the 0.00000005 probability calculated above and report the *two-sided P-value* as $2(0.00000005) = 0.0000001$.

Because this probability is so slight, sampling error is an unconvincing explanation for why the average return in our sample is less than 28.1. A t-value of -7.509 is too improbable to be explained plausibly by the luck of the draw. We have shown, by statistical contradiction, that the average mutual fund return in 1998 was not 28.1 percent.

16.5.5 Using Confidence Intervals

Confidence intervals provide a useful alternative method of reporting the results of a two-sided statistical test. A null hypothesis will be rejected by a two-sided hypothesis test if and only if its value lies outside a corresponding confidence interval. We can illustrate this equivalence by considering our test of the null hypothesis that the average mutual fund return was 28.1 percent in 1998.

This null hypothesis will be rejected at the 5 percent level if the two-sided P-value is less than 0.05, which requires the sample mean to be more than 2.064 standard errors from 28.1 percent. A 95 percent confidence interval for

μ includes all values that are within 2.064 standard errors of the sample mean. Therefore, a hypothesis test can be conducted by using the sample data to construct a confidence interval and seeing whether the parameter value specified by the null hypothesis is inside this interval.

The additional information provided by a confidence interval is a sense of the practical importance of the difference between the parameter value assumed by the null hypothesis and the value of the estimator. If we just report that the P-value is 0.0000001 or that we "found a statistically significant difference at the 5 percent level," readers will not know the actual value of the estimator. In addition to the P-value, we should report a confidence interval.

For our mutual fund example, we saw earlier in this chapter that a 95 percent confidence interval is:

$$95\% \text{ confidence interval for } \mu = 8.93 \pm 2.064\left(\frac{12.7654}{\sqrt{25}}\right) = 8.93 \pm 5.27$$

As anticipated, the value 28.1 is not inside this confidence interval. Further, we see that the distance of this confidence interval from 28.1 is of considerable practical importance to investors.

The observation that any value inside a 95 confidence interval would not be rejected at the 5 percent level if tested as a null hypothesis reinforces our earlier remark that not rejecting a null hypothesis is a rather weak conclusion. Not rejecting a null hypothesis is not at all the same as proving the null hypothesis to be true. An unrejected null hypothesis is but one of many parameter values that is consistent with the data. Thus we must be careful to say "the data do not reject the null hypothesis," rather than "the data prove the null hypothesis to be true."

16.5.6 Is It Important?

In testing hypotheses, it is easy to be confused by the distinction between statistical significance and practical importance. A statistically significant result may be of little practical importance. Conversely, a researcher may find a potentially very important result that does not happen to be statistically significant.

Consider the question of whether men or women are more likely to be right handed. A sample of 6,672 people found that 90 percent of the men and 92 percent of the women were right handed. This difference is statistically significant, but unimportant. Or consider the conclusion of two economists studying the effect of inflation on election outcomes. They estimated that the inflation issue increased the Republican vote in the 1976 election by 7 percentage points, plus or minus 10 percentage points. Because 0 is inside this interval, they concluded that "in fact, and contrary to widely held views, inflation has no impact on voting behavior."[6] That is not at all what their data show. The fact that they cannot rule out 0 does not prove that 0 is the correct value. Their 95 percent confidence interval does include 0, but it also includes everything from −3 percent to +17 percent. Their best estimate is 7 percent, plus or minus 10 percent, and 7 percent is more than enough to swing most elections one way or another. This result is not statistically significant, but it might be important.

16.5.7 An Overview of Hypothesis Testing

We can summarize our general procedure as follows.

1. Specify the null hypothesis and whether the alternative hypothesis is one sided or two sided.

2. Use the sample data to estimate the value of the population parameter whose value is specified by the null hypothesis.

3. If this sample statistic is approximately normally distributed, calculate the t-value, which measures how many standard errors the estimate is from the null hypothesis:

$$t = \frac{\text{Observed statistic} - \text{Null hypothesis parameter value}}{\text{Standard error of statistic}}$$

For testing a null hypothesis about the value of the population mean, we use the sample mean as our test statistic and calculate this t value:

$$t = \frac{\overline{X} - \mu}{s/\sqrt{n}}$$

4. Determine the critical values of t corresponding to the test's selected significance level, and see if the t-value for this sample is outside this range.

5. Report a confidence interval in order to assess the practical importance of the results.

---

6. F. Arcelus and A. H. Meltzer, "The Effect of Aggregate Economic Variables on Congressional Elections," *American Political Science Review*, 1975, 69, pp. 1232–1239.

16.6 Summary

1. Descriptive statistics can often be used to summarize a set of data. The median and mean describe the center of the data, around which the other values are spread. Outliers, values that are very different from the other observations, can pull the mean substantially above or below the median. In comparison to the mean, the median is more robust or resistant to outliers.

2. The variance or standard deviation can be used to gauge the spread or variation in the data about its mean. The variance is the average squared deviation of the observations about their mean. The standard deviation is the square root of the variance.

3. The probability that the value of a continuous random variable will be in a specified interval is shown by the corresponding area under a probability density curve. The expected value of a random variable is the anticipated long-run average value of the outcomes. The standard deviation measures the extent to which the outcomes may differ from the expected value; a large standard deviation indicates a great deal of uncertainty, as the outcomes are likely to be far from the expected value.

4. A (discrete or continuous) random variable X is standardized by subtracting its mean μ and then dividing by the standard deviation σ:

$$Z = (x - \mu)/\sigma$$

which has a mean of zero and a standard deviation of one. The central limit theorem explains why so many random variables are approximately normally distributed.

5. A population is the entire group of items that interests us; a sample is the part of the population that we actually observe. Statistical inference is used to make inferences about the population from which the sample came. Deliberate attempts to construct representative samples are unwise; instead, statisticians recommend that data be based on a random sample. A selection bias occurs when some members of the population are systematically excluded or underrepresented in the group from which the sample is taken.

6. If a random variable X is normally distributed with a mean μ and standard deviation σ, then the sampling distribution for the mean of

a random sample of n observations is a normal distribution with a mean μ and a standard deviation equal to σ divided by the square root of the sample size n. Even if the underlying distribution is not normal, a sufficiently large sample will ensure that the sampling distribution of the sample mean is approximately normal.

7. The sample mean is an unbiased estimator of μ, and a confidence interval can be used to gauge the degree of sampling error:

$$\text{Confidence interval for } \mu = \overline{X} \pm t^* \text{ (standard error of } \overline{X}) = \overline{X} \pm t^* \left(\frac{s}{\sqrt{n}} \right)$$

where s is the sample standard deviation, n is the sample size, and t^* is given by a t-distribution with n − 1 degrees of freedom.

8. To conduct a hypothesis test, we specify the null and alternative hypotheses and then use the sample data to estimate the population parameter whose value is specified by the null hypothesis. For testing a null hypothesis about the value of the population mean, we use the sample mean as our test statistic and calculate this t-value:

$$t = \frac{\overline{X} - \mu}{s/\sqrt{n}}$$

The critical t-values for a specified significance level, such as 5 percent or 1 percent, are given by the t-distribution with n − 1 degrees of freedom. Alternatively, we can determine the P-value.

Exercises

(Answers to even-numbered exercises are in Appendix A)

1. Write the meaning of each of the following terms without referring to the book (or your notes), and compare your definition with the version in the text for each.
    a. median
    b. mean
    c. histogram
    d. variance
    e. standard deviation
    f. random variable

g. probability distribution
h. standardized random variable
i. sample
j. sampling distribution
k. degrees of freedom

2. A researcher is analyzing data on the financial wealth of 100 professors at a small liberal arts college. The values of their wealth range from $400 to $400,000, with a mean of $40,000, and a median of $25,000. However, when entering these data into a statistics software package, the researcher mistakenly enters $4,000,000 for the person with $400,000 wealth. How much does this error affect the mean and median?

3. A stock's price–earnings (P/E) ratio is the per-share price of its stock divided by the company's annual profit per share. The P/E ratio for the stock market as a whole is used by some analysts as a measure of whether stocks are cheap or expensive, in comparison with other historical periods. Here are some annual P/E ratios for the New York Stock Exchange (NYSE):

Year	P/E	Year	P/E
1970	15.5	1979	7.4
1971	18.5	1980	7.9
1972	18.2	1981	8.4
1973	14.0	1982	8.6
1974	8.6	1983	12.5
1975	10.9	1984	10.0
1976	11.2	1985	12.3
1977	9.3	1986	16.4
1978	8.3		

Calculate the mean and standard deviation. In August 1987 the market's price–earnings ratio was 23. Was this P/E value more than one standard deviation above the mean P/E for 1970–1986? Was it more than two standard deviations above the mean?

4. Which has a higher expected value and which has a higher standard deviation: a standard six-sided die or a four-sided die with the numbers 1 through 4 printed on the sides? Explain your reasoning, without doing any calculations.

5. A nationwide test has a mean of 75 and a standard deviation of 10. Convert the following raw scores to standardized Z values: X = 94, 75, and 67. What raw score corresponds to Z = 1.5?

6. A woman wrote to Dear Abby, saying that she had been pregnant for 310 days before giving birth.[7] Completed pregnancies are normally distributed with a mean of 266 days and a standard deviation of 16 days. Use Table B–7 to determine the probability that a completed pregnancy lasts at least 270 days. At least 310 days.

7. The heights of U.S. females between the age of 25 and 34 are approximately normally distributed with a mean of 66 inches and a standard deviation of 2.5 inches. What fraction of the U.S. female population in this age bracket is taller than 70 inches, the height of the average adult U.S. male of this age?

8. Explain why you think that high-school seniors who take the Scholastic Aptitude Test (SAT) are not a random sample of all high-school seniors. If we were to compare the 50 states, do you think that a state's average SAT score tends to increase or decrease as the fraction of the state's seniors who take the SAT increases?

9. American Express and the French tourist office sponsored a survey that found that most visitors to France do not consider the French to be especially unfriendly.[8] The sample consisted of "1,000 Americans who have visited France more than once for pleasure over the past two years." Why is this survey biased?

10. The first American to win the Nobel prize in physics was Albert Michelson (1852–1931), who was given the award in 1907 for developing and using optical precision instruments. His October 12–November 14, 1882 measurements of the speed of light in air (in kilometers per second) were as follows[9]:

299,883 299,796 299,611 299,781 299,774 299,696 299,748 299,809

299,816 299,682 299,599 299,578 299,820 299,573 299,797 299,723

299,778 299,711 300,051 299,796 299,772 299,748 299,851

---

7. Hartold Jacobs, *Mathematics: A Human Endeavor* (San Francisco: W. H. Freeman), 1982, p. 570.

8. Cynthia Crossen, "Studies Galore Support Products and Positions, But Are They Reliable?," *The Wall Street Journal*, November 14, 1991.

9. S. M. Stigler, "Do Robust Estimators Work With Real Data?," *Annals of Statistics*, 1977, pp. 1055–1078.

Assuming that these measurements were a random sample from a normal distribution, does a 99 percent confidence interval include the value 299,710.5 that is now accepted as the speed of light?

11. A *Wall Street Journal* (July 6, 1987) poll asked 35 economic forecasters to predict the interest rate on 3-month Treasury bills in June 1988. These 35 forecasts had a mean of 6.19 and a variance of 0.47. Assuming these to be a random sample, give a 95 percent confidence interval for the mean prediction of all economic forecasters and then explain why each of these interpretations is or is not correct:
    a. There is a 0.95 probability that the actual Treasury-bill rate on June 1988 will be in this interval.
    b. Approximately 95 percent of the predictions of all economic forecasters are in this interval.

12. The earlobe test was introduced in a letter to the prestigious *New England Journal of Medicine*, in which Dr. Sanders Frank reported that 20 of his male patients with creases in their earlobes had many of the risk factors (such as high cholesterol levels, high blood pressure, and heavy cigarette usage) associated with heart disease. For instance, the average cholesterol level for his patients with noticeable earlobe creases was 257 (mg per 100 ml), compared to an average of 215 with a standard deviation of 10 for healthy middle-aged men. If these 20 patients were a random sample from a population with a mean of 215 and a standard deviation of 10, what is the probability their average cholesterol level would be 257 or higher? Explain why these 20 patients may, in fact, not be a random sample.

13. A researcher examined the admissions to a mental health clinic's emergency room on days when the moon was full.[10] For the 12 days with full moons from August 1971 through July 1972, the number of people admitted were

    5   13   14   12   6   9   13   16   25   13   14   20

    Calculate the t-value for a test of the null hypothesis that these data are a random sample from a normal distribution with a population mean equal to 11.2, the average number of admissions on other days.

---

10. Sheldon Blackman and Don Catalina, "The Moon and the Emergency Room," *Perceptual and Motor Skills*, 1973, 37, pp. 624–626.

14. Use the 1997 data in Table 16.2 to determine the t-value for a test of the null hypothesis that these data were drawn from a population with a mean of 33.4 percent, the return on the S&P 500 index that year.

15. A treatment group was given a cold vaccine while the control group received a placebo. Doctors then recorded the fraction of each group that caught a cold and calculated the two-sided P-value to be 0.08. Explain why you either agree or disagree with each of the interpretations of these results:

    a. "There is an 8 percent probability that this cold vaccine works."

    b. "If a randomly selected person takes this vaccine, the chances of getting sick fall by about 8 percent."

    c. "These data do not show a statistically significant effect at the 5 percent level; therefore, we are 95 percent certain that this vaccine doesn't work."

Answers to Even-Numbered Exercises

Chapter One

1-2. There are four steps to running your first regression on EViews:

    a. Install EViews: Insert the EViews CD-ROM into your computer, open it (by going to the D: drive portion of the "my computer" section of Windows) and then click on "install EViews to disc." If you respond "next" or "yes" when requested, you should eventually get a "successfully installed" message.

    b. Start EViews: Return to the D: drive portion of the "my computer" section of Windows, open EViews (this might require clicking on "EViews 3.1"), and then click on "run."

    c. Open the datafile: In order, click on "file," "open," and "workfile." Then browse to the CD-ROM, select the folder "Studenmund," and click on "HTWT1" and "OK."

    d. Run the regression: Type in "LS Y C X" on the top line of EViews, making sure to leave spaces between the variable names. (LS stands for least squares and C stands for constant.) Then hit "enter," and the regression result will appear on the screen.

1-4. **a.** Customers number 3, 4, and 20; no.

    b. Weight is determined by more than just height.

    c. People who decide to play the weight-guessing game may feel they have a weight that is hard to guess.

1-6. **a.** The coefficient of L_i represents the change in the percentage chance of making a putt when the length of the putt increases by one foot. In this case, the percentage chance of making the putt decreases by 4.1 for each foot longer the putt is.

    b. 42.6 percent, yes; 79.5 percent, no (too low); −18.9 percent, no (negative!).

    c. One problem is that the theoretical relationship between the length of the putt and the percentage of putts made is almost surely nonlinear in the variables; we'll discuss models appropriate to this problem in Chapter 7. A second problem is that the actual dependent variable is limited by zero and one but the regression estimate is not; we'll discuss models appropriate to this problem in Chapter 13.

d. The equations are identical. To convert one to the other, you need to know that $\hat{P}_i = P_i - e_i$, which is true because $e_i = P_i - \hat{P}_i$ (or more generally, $e_i = Y_i - \hat{Y}_i$).

1-8. **a.** β_Y is the change in S caused by a one-unit increase in Y, holding G constant, and β_G is the change in S caused by a one-unit increase in G, holding Y constant.

b. $+,\ -$

c. Yes. Richer states spend at least some of their extra money on education, but states with rapidly growing student populations find it difficult to increase spending at the same rate as the student population, causing spending *per student* to fall, especially if you hold the wealth of the state constant.

d. $\hat{S}_i = -183 + 0.1422Y_i - 59.26G_i$. Note that $59.26 \cdot 10 = 5926 \cdot 0.10$, so nothing in the equation has changed except the scale of the coefficient of G.

1-10. **a.** 19.8: A \$1 billion increase in GDP will be associated with an increase of \$19.80 in the average price of a new house. 7406.6: Technically, the constant term equals the value of the dependent variable when all the independent variables equal zero, but in most cases (as in this one) such a definition has little economic meaning. As we'll learn in Chapters 4 and 7, estimates of the constant term should not be relied on for inference.

b. It doesn't matter what letters we use as symbols for the dependent and independent variables.

c. You could measure both P_t and Y_t in real terms by dividing each observation by the GDP deflator (or the CPI) for that year (and multiplying by 100).

d. The price of houses is determined by the forces of supply and demand, and we won't discuss the estimation of simultaneous equations until Chapter 14. In a demand-oriented sense, GDP is probably measuring buying power, which is better represented by disposable income. In a supply-oriented sense, GDP might be standing for costs like wages and the price of materials.

1-12. Linear in the coefficients: a, b, c.
Linear in neither: d, e.

Linear in the variables: none (c is linear in the logs of the variables but is not linear in the variables themselves. For a quick review of logs, see the boxed feature in Chapter 7.)

Chapter Two

2-2. **a.** 71.
 b. 84.
 c. 213, yes.
 d. 155, yes.

2-4. **a.** $\hat{\beta}_1 = -0.5477$, $\hat{\beta}_0 = 12.289$.
 b. $R^2 = .465$, $\overline{R}^2 = .398$.
 c. Income $= 12.289 - 0.5477(8) = 7.907$.

2-6. **a.** Positive; both going to class and doing problem sets should improve a student's grade.
 b. Yes.
 c. $0.04*1.74 > 0.02*0.60$, so going to class pays off more.
 d. $0.02*1.74 < 0.10*0.60$, so doing problem sets pays off more. Since the units of variables can differ dramatically, coefficient size does not measure importance. (If all variables are measured identically in a properly specified equation, then the size of the coefficient is indeed one measure of importance.)
 e. $R^2 = .33$ means that the equation has explained 33 percent of the variation of G around its mean.
 f. The equation is incomplete because it ignores student ability (among other things). Adding student GPA (or test scores) would certainly raise R^2 and $\overline{R}^2$.

2-8. **a.** Yes.
 b. at first glance, perhaps, but see below.
 c. Three dissertations, since $(489 \times 3 = \$1467) > (\$230)$ or $(120 \times 2 = \$204)$.
 d. The coefficient of D seems to be too high; perhaps it is absorbing the impact of an independent variable that has been omitted from the regression. For example, students may choose a dissertation adviser on the basis of reputation, a variable not in the equation.

2-10. **a.** V_i: positive.
 H_i: negative (although some would argue that in a world of per-

fect information, drivers would take fewer risks if they knew the state had few hospitals).

C_i: ambiguous because a high rate of driving citations could indicate risky driving (raising fatalities) *or* zealous police citation policies (reducing risky driving and therefore fatalities).

b. No, because the coefficient differences are small and the data will differ from year to year. We'd be more concerned if the coefficients differed by orders of magnitude or changed sign.

c. Since the equation for 1982 has similar degrees of freedom and a much lower $\bar{R}^2$, no calculation is needed to know that the equation for 1981 has a higher R^2. Just to be sure, we calculated R^2 and obtained .652 for 1981 and .565 for 1982.

2-12. a. $\partial \sum (e_i^2)/\partial \hat{\beta}_0 = 2 \sum (Y_i - \hat{\beta}_0 - \hat{\beta}_1 X_i)(-1)$
$\partial \sum (e_i^2)/\partial \hat{\beta}_1 = 2 \sum (Y_i - \hat{\beta}_0 - \hat{\beta}_1 X_i)(-\hat{\beta}_1 X_i)$

b. $0 = -2 \sum (Y_i - \hat{\beta}_0 - \hat{\beta}_1 X_i)$
$0 = -2\hat{\beta}_1 \sum (Y_i - \hat{\beta}_0 - \hat{\beta}_1 X_i)(X_1)$ or, rearranging:

$$\sum Y_i = n\hat{\beta}_0 + \hat{\beta}_1 \sum X_i$$
$$\sum Y_i X_i = \hat{\beta}_0 \sum X_i + \hat{\beta}_1 \sum X_i^2$$

These are the normal equations.

c. To get $\hat{\beta}_1$, solve the first normal equation for $\hat{\beta}_0$, obtaining $\hat{\beta}_0 = (\sum Y_i - \beta_1 \sum X_i)/n$ and substitute this value in for $\hat{\beta}_0$ where it appears in the second normal equation, obtaining $\sum Y_i X_i = (\sum Y_i - \hat{\beta}_1 \sum X_i)(\sum X_i)/n + \hat{\beta}_1 \sum X_i^2$, which becomes $\hat{\beta}_1 = (n\sum Y_i X_i - \sum Y_i \sum X_i)/[n\sum X_i^2 - (\sum X_i)^2]$. With some algebraic manipulation (in part using the fact that $\sum X_i = n\bar{X}$), this simplifies to Equation 2.6.

d. To get Equation 2.7, solve the first normal equation for $\hat{\beta}_0$, using $\bar{X} = \sum X_i/n$.

Chapter Three

3.2. a. $D = 1$ if graduate student, and $D = 0$ if undergraduate.

b. Yes, for example E = how many exercises (such as this) the student did.

c. If D is defined as in answer a, then its coefficient's sign would be expected to be positive. If D is defined as 0 if graduate student, 1 if undergraduate, then the expected sign would be negative.

    d. A coefficient with value of .5 indicates that, all else equal, a graduate student would be expected to earn half a grade point higher than an undergraduate. If there were only graduate students or only undergraduates in class, the coefficient of D could not be estimated.

3-4.   **a.** There are many possible omitted explanatory variables; for example, the number of parking spaces near the restaurant.

3-6.   **a.** New P = Old P/1000, so $\hat{\beta}$ goes from 0.3547 to 354.7.
      b. 320.
      c. No.

3-8.   **a.** A male student's GRE subject score in Economics is likely to be 39.7 points higher than a female's, holding constant their GPA and SATs.
      b. This result is evidence of, but not proof of, bias. If we were sure that we had the best possible specification (the topic of Chapter 6) and if this result turned out to be statistically significant (the topic of Chapter 5), and if we were able to reproduce this result in other samples, we'd be much closer to a "proof." Even then, there still would be a possibility that some factor other than bias was the cause of these results.
      c. Possible variables include the number of upper division economics courses taken, the number of mathematics classes taken, and dummy variables measuring whether the student had taken econometrics or international economics (two fields frequently covered in the test). It's vital that any suggested variable be cross-sectional by student, however.
      d. The equation would become $\widehat{GRE_i} = 212.1 - 39.7G_i + 78.9GPA_i + 0.203SATM_i + 0.110SATV_i$.

3-10.   **a.** All positive except for the coefficient of F_i, which in today's male-dominated movie industry probably has a negative expected sign.
      b. Arnold, because \$500,000 < (\$4,000,000 − \$3,027,000).
      c. Yes, since 200 × 15.4 = \$3,080,000 > \$1,200,000.
      d. Yes, since \$1,770,000 > \$1,000,000.
      e. Yes, the unexpected sign of the coefficient of B_i.

Chapter Four

4-2.   Pair "c" clearly violates Assumption VI, and pair "a" might violate it for some samples.

4-4. **a.** Most experienced econometricians would prefer an unbiased nonminimum variance estimate.
b. Yes; an unbiased estimate with an extremely large variance has a high probability of being far from the true value. In such a case, a slightly biased estimate with a very small variance would be better.
c. The most frequently used possibility is to minimize the mean square error (MSE), which is the sum of the expected variance plus the square of any expected bias.

4-6. $Z_i = (X_i - \mu)/\sigma = (1.0 - 0.0)/\sqrt{0.5} = 1.414$; for this Z_i, Table B-7 gives 0.0787, which is the probability of observing an X greater than +1. To also include the probability of an X less than -1, we need to double 0.0787, obtaining a final answer of 0.1574.

4-8. We know that: $\sum e_i^2 = \sum (Y_i - \hat{Y}_i)^2 = \sum (Y_i - \hat{\beta}_0 - \hat{\beta}_i X_i)^2$. To find the minimum, differentiate $\sum e_i^2$ with respect to $\hat{\beta}_0$ and $\hat{\beta}_1$ and set each derivative equal to zero (these are the "normal equations"):

$$\delta(\textstyle\sum e_i^2)/\delta\hat{\beta}_0 = -2[\sum (Y_i - \hat{\beta}_0 - \hat{\beta}_1 X_i)] = 0$$
$$\text{or } \textstyle\sum Y_i = n(\hat{\beta}_0) + \hat{\beta}_1(\sum X_i)$$
$$\delta(\textstyle\sum e_i^2)/\hat{\beta}_1 = -2[\sum (Y_i - \hat{\beta}_0 - \hat{\beta}_1 X_i)X_i] = 0$$
$$\text{or } \textstyle\sum Y_i X_i = \hat{\beta}_0(\sum X_i) + \hat{\beta}_1(\sum X_i^2)$$

Solve the two equations simultaneously and rearrange:

$$\hat{\beta}_1 = [n(\textstyle\sum Y_i X_i) - \sum Y_i X_i]/[n(\sum X_i^2) - (\sum X_i)^2]$$
$$= \textstyle\sum (X_i - \overline{X})(Y_i - Y)/\sum (X_i - \overline{X})^2 = \sum x_i y_i/\sum x_i^2$$

where $x_i = (X_i - \overline{X})$ and $y_i = (Y_i - \overline{Y})$.

$$\hat{\beta}_0 = [\textstyle\sum X_i^2 \sum Y_i - \sum X_i \sum X_i Y_i]/[n(\sum X_i^2) - (\sum X_i)^2] = \overline{Y} - \hat{\beta}_1\overline{X}$$

To prove linearity:

$$\hat{\beta}_1 = \textstyle\sum x_i y_i/\sum x_i^2 = \sum x_i(Y_i - \overline{Y})/\sum x_i^2$$
$$= \textstyle\sum x_i Y_i/\sum x_i^2 - \sum x_i(\overline{Y})/\sum x_i^2$$
$$= \textstyle\sum x_i(Y_i)/\sum x_i^2 - \overline{Y}\sum x_i/\sum x_i^2$$
$$= \textstyle\sum x_i(Y_i)/\sum x_i^2 \text{ since } \sum x_i = 0$$
$$= \textstyle\sum k_i Y_i \text{ where } k_i = x_i/\sum x_i^2$$

$\hat{\beta}_1$ is a linear function of Y, since this is how a linear function is defined. It is also a linear function of the βs and ϵ, which is the basic

interpretation of linearity. $\hat{\beta}_1 = \beta_0 g\, k_i + \beta_1 g\, k_i x_i + g\, k_i \epsilon_i$.
$\hat{\beta}_0 = \bar{Y} - \hat{\beta}_1(\bar{X})$ where $\bar{Y} = \hat{\beta}_0 + \hat{\beta}_1(\bar{X})$, which is also a linear equation.

To prove unbiasedness:
$$\hat{\beta}_1 = g\, k_i Y_i = g\, k_i(\beta_0 + \beta_1 X_i + \epsilon_i)$$
$$= g\, k_i \beta_0 + g\, k_i \beta_1 X_i + g\, k_i \epsilon_i$$

Since $k_i = x_i {>} g\, x_i^2 = (X_i - \bar{X}) {>} g\, (X_i - \bar{X})^2$,
then $g\, k_i = 0$, $g\, k_i^2 = 1 {>} g\, x_i^2$, $g\, k_i x_i = g\, k_i X_i = 1$.
So, $\hat{\beta}_1 = \beta_1 + g\, k_i \epsilon_i$ and given the assumptions of ϵ_i,
$E(\hat{\beta}_i) = \beta_1 + g\, k_i E(\epsilon_i) = \beta_1$, proving $\hat{\beta}_1$ is unbiased.

To prove minimum variance (of all linear unbiased estimators): $\hat{\beta}_1 = g\, k_i Y_i$. Since $k_i = x_i {>} g\, x_i^2 = (X_i - \bar{X}) {>} g\, (X_i - \bar{X})^2$, $\hat{\beta}_1$ is a weighted average of the Ys, and the k_i are the weights. To write an expression for any linear estimator, substitute w_i for k_i, which are also weights but not necessarily equal to k_i:

$$\beta_1^* = g\, w_i Y_i, \text{ so } E(\beta_1^*) = g\, x_i E(Y_i) = g\, w_i(\beta_0 + \beta_1 X_i)$$
$$= \beta_0 g\, w_i + \beta_1 g\, w_i X_i$$

In order for β_1^* to be unbiased, $g\, w_i = 0$ and $g\, w_i X_i = 1$. The variable of β_1^*:

$$VAR(\beta_1^*) = VAR\, g\, w_i Y_i = g\, w_i\, VAR\, Y_i = \sigma^2\, g\, w_i^2$$
$$\{VAR\, (Y_i) = VAR\, (\epsilon_i) = \sigma^2 g$$
$$= \sigma^2 g\, (w_i - x_i {>} g\, x_i^2 + x_i {>} g\, x_i^2)^2$$
$$= \sigma^2 g\, (w_i - x_i {>} g\, x_i^2 + x_i {>} g\, x_i^2)^2$$
$$= \sigma^2 g\, (w_i - x_i {>} g\, x_i^2)^2 + \sigma^2 g\, x_i {>} (g\, x_i^2)^2$$
$$+ 2\sigma^2 g\, (w_i - x_i {>} g\, x_i^2)$$
$$= \sigma^2 g\, (w_i - x_i {>} g\, x_i^2)^2 + \sigma^2 {>} (g\, x_i^2)$$

The last term in this equation is a constant, so the variance of β_1^* can be minimized only by manipulating the first term. The first term is minimized only by letting $w_i = x_i {>} g\, x_i^2$, then:

$$VAR(\beta_1^*) = \sigma^2 {>} g\, x_i^2 = VAR\, (\hat{\beta}_1).$$

When the least-squares weights, k_i, equal w_i, the variance of the linear estimator β_1 is equal to the variance of the least-squares estimator, $\hat{\beta}_1$. When they are not equal, $VAR(\beta_1^*) > VAR(\hat{\beta}_1)$ Q.E.D.

Chapter Five

5-2. **a.** $H_0: \beta_1 \leq 0, H_A: \beta_1 > 0$
b. $H_0: \beta_1 \geq 0, H_A: \beta_1 < 0; H_0: \beta_2 \leq 0, H_A: \beta_2 > 0;$
$H_0: \beta_3 \leq 0, H_A: \beta_3 > 0$ (The hypothesis for β_3 assumes that it is never too hot to go jogging.)
c. $H_0: \beta_1 \leq 0, H_A: \beta_1 > 0; H_0: \beta_2 \leq 0, H_A: \beta_2 > 0;$
$H_0: \beta_3 \geq 0, H_A: \beta_3 < 0$ (The hypothesis for β_3 assumes you're not breaking the speed limit.)
d. $H_0: \beta_G = 0; H_A: \beta_G \neq 0$ (G for grunt.)

5-4. **a.** $t_c = 1.363$; reject H_0 for β_1, cannot reject H_0 for β_2 and β_3.
b. $t_c = 1.318$; reject H_0 for β_1, cannot reject H_0 for β_2 an β_3.
c. $t_c = 3.143$; cannot reject the null hypothesis for β_1, β_2, and β_3.

5-6. **a.** $t_2 = (200 - 160)/25.0 = 1.6$; $t_c = 2.052$; therefore cannot reject H_0. (Notice the violation of the principle that the null contains that which we do not expect.)
b. $t_3 = 2.37$; $t_c = 2.756$; therefore cannot reject the null hypothesis.
c. $t_2 = 5.6$; $t_c = 2.447$; therefore reject H_0 if it is formulated as in the exercise, but this poses a problem because the original hypothesized sign of the coefficient was negative. Thus, the alternative hypothesis ought to have been stated: $H_A: \beta_2 < 0$, and H_0 cannot be rejected.

5-8. **a.** $F = [R^2/(K)]/[(1 - R^2)/(n - K - 1)]$.
b. F is a statistical measure of fit but R^2 is a qualitative measure; printing both saves the reader time and avoids (human) computation errors.

5-10. **a.** $t = 8.509$; with $t_c = 1.746$, reject H_0 of no collinearity.
b. $t = 16.703$; with $t_c = 2.060$, reject H_0.
c. $t = 3.215$; with $t_c = 3.365$, cannot reject H_0 of no collinearity.
d. $t = -7.237$; with $t_c = -1.303$, reject H_0.
e. $t = 3.213$; with $t_c = 2.048$, reject H_0.

5-12. $F = 52.07$; the estimated equation is significant since $52.07 > 4.41$, the critical F-value at the 5 percent level.

5-14. **a.** T: H_0: $\beta_T \leq 0$, H_A: $\beta_T > 0$. Reject H_0 since $|+5.57| > 1.711$ and $+5.57$ has the sign of H_A.

P: H_0: $\beta_P \geq 0$, H_A: $\beta_P < 0$. Reject H_0 since $|-2.35| > 1.711$ and -2.35 has the sign of H_A.

A: H_0: $\beta_A \leq 0$, H_A: $\beta_A > 0$. Cannot reject H_0 since $|+1.244| < 1.711$.

C: H_0: $\beta_C \leq 0$, H_A: $\beta_C > 0$. Cannot reject H_0 since $|-1.10| < 1.711$ or since -1.10 does not have the sign of H_A.

b. Reject all null hypotheses.

c. Reject null hypotheses for T, J, and S. Cannot reject null hypotheses for F (since $|-1.47| < 1.645$) or B (since $|-1.33| < 1.645$ or since -1.33 does not have the sign of H_A).

5-16. **a.** All five tests are one-sided, so $t_c = 1.706$ throughout.

GDPN: H_0: $\beta \leq 0$, H_A: $\beta > 0$. Reject H_0 because $|6.69| > 1.706$ and 6.69 is positive as in H_A.

CVN: H_0: $\beta \geq 0$, H_A: $\beta < 0$. Reject H_0 because $|-2.66| > 1.706$ and -2.66 is negative as in H_A.

PP: H_0: $\beta \leq 0$, H_A: $\beta > 0$. Do not reject H_0 because $|1.19| < 1.706$.

DPC: H_0: $\beta \geq 0$, H_A: $\beta < 0$. Reject H_0 because $|-2.25| > 1.706$ and -2.25 is negative as in H_A.

IPC: H_0: $\beta \geq 0$, H_A: $\beta < 0$. Do not reject H_0 because $|-1.59| < 1.706$.

b. Reject H_0 of no effect because $F = 22.35$ is larger than the critical F_c value of 2.59 (interpolated).

c. Our confidence interval equation is $\hat{\beta} \pm t_c^* SE(\hat{\beta})$, and the 10 percent two-sided $t_c = 1.706$ (the same as a one-sided 5 percent t_c), so the confidence interval equals $\hat{\beta} \pm 1.706 \cdot SE(\hat{\beta})$, or:

GDPN: $1.07 < \hat{\beta} < 1.79$
CVN: $-0.98 < \hat{\beta} < -0.22$
PP: $-3.13 < \hat{\beta} < 17.75$
DPC: $-27.45 < \hat{\beta} < -3.81$
IPC: $-23.59 < \hat{\beta} < 0.83$

d. Yes. The important signs were as expected and statistically significant, and the overall fit was good.

e. Little would change: for the first two coefficients, such a specification change would alter the coefficient sizes but not their signs or significance; for the coefficients of the three dummy variables, even though the coefficient sizes would change dramatically, it's unlikely that their signs and significance would change.

Chapter Six

6-2. Expected bias in $\hat{\beta} = (\beta_{omitted}) \cdot f(r_{omitted, included})$
  a. Expected bias $= (-) \cdot (+) = (-) = $ negative bias.
  b. $(+) \cdot (+) = (+) = $ positive bias; this bias will be potentially large since age and experience are highly correlated.
  c. $(+) \cdot (+) = (+) = $ positive bias.
  d. $(-) \cdot (0) = 0 = $ no bias; it may seem as though it rains more on the weekends, but there is no theoretical relationship between the two.

6-4. **a.**
Coefficient	β_E	β_I	β_T	β_V	β_R
Hypothesized sign:	−	+	−	−	−
Calculated t-score:	−3.0	1.0	−1.0	−3.0	3.0
$t_c = 1.682$, so:	sig.	insig.	insig.	sig.	sig. but unexp. sign

  b. Both income and tax rate are potential irrelevant variables not only because of the sizes of the t-scores but also because of theory. The significant unexpected sign for β_R is a clear indication that there is a potential omitted variable.
  c. It's prudent to attempt to solve an omitted variable problem before worrying about irrelevant variables because of the bias that omitted variables cause.
  d. The equation appears to show that television advertising is effective and radio advertising isn't, but you shouldn't jump to this conclusion. Improving the specification could change this result. In particular, although it's possible that radio advertising has little impact on smoking, it's very hard to believe that a radio anti-smoking campaign could cause a significant *increase* in cigarette consumption!
  e. *Theory:* Given the fairly price-inelastic demand for cigarettes, it's possible that T is irrelevant.
  t-score: β_T is insignificant.
  $\bar{R}^2$: $\bar{R}^2$ remains constant, which is exactly what will happen whenever a variable with a t-score with an absolute value of 1 is removed from (or added to) an equation.
  Do other coefficients change?: None of the other estimated coefficients change significantly when T is dropped, indicating that dropping T caused no bias.

Conclusion: Based on these four criteria, it's reasonable to conclude that T is an irrelevant variable.

6-6. **a.**

Coefficient	β_1	β_2	β_3	β_4
Hypothesized sign:	+	+	+	−
Calculated t-score:	5.0	1.0	10.0	3.0
$t_c = 2.485$ (1% level), so:	sig.	insig.	sig.	unexpected sign

b. The significant unexpected sign of $\hat{\beta}_4$ is evidence of a possible omitted variable that is exerting positive bias. The omitted variable must either be correlated positively with X_4 *and* have a positive expected coefficient or else be correlated negatively with X_4 *and* have a negative expected coefficient. The fairly low calculated t-score for β_2 is not strong evidence of a specification error.

c. A second run might add an independent variable that is theoretically sound and that could have caused positive bias in $\hat{\beta}_4$. For example, X_5 = the number of "attractions" like movie theaters or shopping malls in the area would have a positive expected coefficient and be positively correlated with the number of nearby competing stores.

6-8. **a.** Nothing is certain, but the best guess is: X_1 = number of students, X_2 = chain price, X_3 = temperature, X_4 = Cooler price.

b. X_4 has the only negative coefficient, and Cooler price has the only negative expected sign. Number of students (in thousands) should be the most significant and have the largest coefficient. Weather should be the least significant and also have a small coefficient (since that variable can be the largest in size). X_2 = chain price by elimination.

c. Note that developing hypotheses includes determining the desired level of significance. A possible rerun would be to drop (or reformulate to absolute degrees difference from optimal hamburger-eating range, if there is such a thing) the weather variable. If there is omitted variable bias, it is positive on $\hat{\beta}_4$ (advertising?).

6-10. **a.** Consumers and producers can react differently to changes in the same variable. For example, price: a rise in price causes consumers to demand a lower quantity and producers to supply a greater quantity.

b. Include variables affecting demand ("demand-side variables") only in demand equations and variables affecting supply ("supply-side variables") only in supply equations.

c. Review the literature, decide whether the equation you wish to estimate is a supply or a demand equation, and, when specifying the model, think carefully about whether an independent variable is appropriate for a demand or supply equation.

6-12. a. No bias $(+ \cdot 0)$ unless weather patterns indicate a correlation between rainfall and temperature. If it tends to rain more when it's cold, then there would be a small negative bias $(+ \cdot -)$.

b. Positive bias $(+ \cdot +)$.

c. Positive bias $(+ \cdot +)$.

d. Negative bias $(+ \cdot -)$ given a likely negative correlation between hours studied for the test and hours slept.

6-14. a.

Coefficient	β_P	β_L	β_A	β_N
Hypothesized sign:	+	+	+	+
Calculated t-score:	3.3	1.5	−0.6	13.5
$t_c = 1.677$ (approx.), so:	sig.	insig.	insig.	sig.

b. The inclusion of N means that the other variables probably should be aimed at differences between the situations of farm women and rural nonfarm women, but they are not, probably because such data are unavailable. Thus, the equation certainly has omitted variables. If they can be found, then L, A, and possibly even P might be irrelevant.

c. Add a variable measuring the average income of farm women in the ith state, if possible as a ratio to the average income of rural nonfarm women in the state. Note that this is a sample of states, so suggesting adding a variable relating to specific women would create a mismatch in the data set.

d. *Theory:* if L is the best proxy available for the relative income of farm women, then it has a strong theoretical basis until the preferred variable can be found.

t-score: insignificant at the 5 percent level (but significant at the 10 percent level).

$\overline{R}^2$: $\overline{R}^2$ is not given, but it turns out that the deletion of any variable with a t-score greater than one in absolute value will lower $\overline{R}^2$, in this case not by much.

Bias: none of the coefficients change significantly.
Thus, the four criteria are inconclusive. As long as relative income data are unavailable, L probably should be retained.

Chapter Seven

7-2. **a.** Semilog [where $Y = f(\ln X)$]; as income increases, the sales of shoes will increase, but at a declining rate.
  b. Linear (intercept dummy); there is little theory for any other form.
  c. Semilog (as in part a above) or linear are both justifiable.
  d. Inverse function [where $Y = f(1/X)$]; as the interest rate gets higher, the quantity of money demanded will decrease, but even at very high interest rates there still will be some money held to allow for transactions.
  e. Quadratic function [where $Y = f(X,X^2)$]; as output levels are increased, we will encounter diminishing returns to scale.
  f. Although functional form should be chosen on the basis of theory, one outlier is capable of shifting an estimated quadratic unreasonably; in such cases, a double-log function might avoid the problem.

7-4. **a.**

Coefficient	β_1	β_2
Hypothesized sign:	+	+
Calculated t-score:	4.0	2.20
$t_c = 1.708$ at the 5% level, so:	$H_0: \beta \le 0$ can be rejected for both.	

  b. It is the sum of the constant effect of omitted independent variables and the nonzero mean of the sample error term observations; it does not mean that salaries (logged) could be negative.
  c. For this semilog function, the slopes are $\beta_1 SAL_i$ and $\beta_2 SAL_i$, which both increase as the Xs rise. This implies that a one-unit change in ED_i will cause a β_1 *percent* change in SAL_i, which makes sense for salaries.
  d. The $\overline{R}^2$s cannot be compared because the dependent variables are different. To do so, you would need to calculate a "quasi-R^2."

7-6. **a.** The Midwest (the fourth region of the country).
  b. Including the omitted condition as a variable will cause the dummies to sum to a constant (1.0). This constant will be perfectly

collinear with the constant term, and the computer will not be able to estimate the equation.

c. Positive.

d. Most correct = III, least correct = I.

7-8. Let PCI_i = per capita income in the ith period, GR_i = rate of growth in the ith period, and ϵ_i = a classical error term.

a. $GR_i = \alpha_0 + \alpha_1 PCI_i + \alpha_2 PCI_i^2 + \epsilon_i$ where we'd expect $\alpha_1 > 0$ and $\alpha_2 < 0$.

b. A semilog function alone cannot change from positive to negative slope, so it is not appropriate.

c. $GR_i = \beta_0 + \beta_1 PCI_i + \beta_2 D_i + \beta_3 D_i PCI_i + \epsilon_i$, where $D_i = 0$ if $PCI_i \leq \$2,000$ and $D_i = 1$ if $PCI_i > \$2,000$. ($\$2,000$ is an estimate of the turning point.)

7-10. a. The expected signs are β_1, + or ?; β_2, + β_3, + ; β_4, +.

b. AD_i/SA_i: the inverse form implies that the larger sales are the smaller will be the impact of advertising on profits. CAP_i, ES_i, DG_i: the semilog functional form implies that as each of these variables increases (holding all others in the equation constant), PR increases at a decreasing rate.

c. β_2, β_3, and β_4 all have positive expected signs, so $(+) \cdot (+) = (+)$ = positive expected bias on β_1 if one of the other Xs were omitted.

7-12. a. The estimated coefficients all are in the expected direction, and those for A and S are significant. $\overline{R}^2$ seems fairly low, even for a cross-sectional data set of this nature.

b. It implies that wages rise and then fall with respect to age but does not imply perfect collinearity.

c. With a semilog function form ($\ln Y$), a slope coefficient represents the percentage change in the dependent variable caused by a one-unit increase in the independent variable (holding constant all the other independent variables). Since pay raises are often discussed in percentage terms, such a functional form frequently is used to model wage rates and salaries.

d. It's a good habit to ignore $\hat{\beta}_0$ (except to make sure that one exists) even if it looks too large or too small.

e. The poor fit and the insignificant estimated coefficient of union membership are all reasons for being extremely cautious about using this regression to draw any conclusions about union membership.

	7-14.	**a.**	Coefficient	β_B	β_S	β_D

Coefficient	β_B	β_S	β_D
Hypothesized sign:	+	+	−
Calculated t-score:	−0.08	1.85	−1.29
$t_c = 1.682$, so:	insig.	sig.	insig.

The insignificance of $\hat{\beta}_B$ could be caused by an omitted variable, but it's likely that the interaction variable has "soaked up" the entire effect of beer consumption. Although we cannot reject the null hypothesis or $\hat{\beta}_D$, we see no reason to consider D to be an irrelevant variable because of its sound theory and reasonable statistics.

b. The interaction variable is a measure of whether the impact of beer drinking on traffic fatalities rises as the altitude of the city rises. For each unit increase in the multiple of B and A, F rises by 0.011, holding constant all the other independent variables in the equation. Thus, the size of the coefficient has no real intuitive meaning in and of itself.

c. H_0: $\beta_{BA} \leq 0$
H_A: $\beta_{BA} > 0$
Reject H_0 because $|4.05| > t_c = 1.682$ and 4.05 is positive and thus matches the sign implied by H_A.

d. Although there is no ironclad rule (as there is with slope dummies) most econometricians include both interaction-term components as independent variables. The major reason for this practice is to avoid the possibility that an interaction term's coefficient might be significant only because it is picking up the effect of the omitted interaction-term component (bias).

e. The exception to this general practice occurs when there is no reason to expect the interaction-term component to have any theoretical validity on its own. We prefer Equation 7.27 to 7.26 because we don't believe that altitude typically would be included as an independent variable in a highway fatality equation. Of our other three specification criteria, only the increase in $\bar{R}^2$ supports considering A to be a relevant variable. However, even moderate theoretical support for the inclusion of A on its own would result in our preferring Equation 7.26.

7-16. **a.**

Coefficient	β_T	β_E	β_P	β_H
Hypothesized sign:	−	+	+	−
Calculated t-score:	−1.33	2.16	+0.82	−7.09
$t_c = 2.447$, so:	insig.	insig.	insig.	sig.

b. At first glance, all three econometric problems seem possible.

c. Since S and H are inversely related by theory, an inverse functional form should be used.

d. Positive, because as H gets bigger, 1/H gets smaller and S gets smaller.

e. All of our four specification criteria favor Equation 7.29, but the theory behind the inverse functional form is so clear-cut that we would stick with the inverse even if the other criteria favored Equation 7.28.

f. $\overline{R}^2$ can indeed be used to compare the fits of the equations because the dependent variable has not been transformed.

Chapter Eight

8-2. **a., c.**

8-4. Likely dominant variables = a and d. In a. # of games won = # of games played (which is a constant) − # of games lost, whereas in d., # of autos = (# of tires bought)/(# of tires per car, which = 4 if no spare is sold with the cars or = 5 if a spare is included).

8-6. **a.**

Coefficient	β_F	β_S	β_A
Hypothesized sign:	+	+	+
Calculated t-value:	2.90	−1.07	5.97
$t_c = 1.699$ at the 5% level, so:	sig.	insig.	sig.
		unexpected sign	

b. All three are possibilities.

c. Multicollinearity is a stronger possibility.

d. Yes; the distribution of the $\hat{\beta}$s is wider with multicollinearity.

8-8. **a.** Don't change your regression just because a fellow student says you are going to have a problem; in particular, even if you do have multicollinearity, you may well end up doing nothing about it.

b. There is a reasonable $\overline{R}^2$ (.36) with all low t-scores (the highest is 0.84). Furthermore, the simple correlation coefficient HR and RBI is 0.93, which is significant at the 5 percent level. In addition, the VIFs for HR and RBI are >5.

c. Since multicollinearity is a sample problem and a sample of eight is extremely small, the first solution to try is to increase the sample size. In this particular case, a larger sample doesn't rid the equation of damaging multicollinearity, so we'd favor dropping one of the redundant variables. There is also at least one omitted variable—whether the player's team made the playoffs.

8-10.

a.

Coefficient	β_C	β_P	β_E
Hypothesized sign:	+	+	+
Calculated t-value:	31.15	−0.07	−0.85
t_c = 1.684 at the 5% level, so:	sig.	insig.	insig.
			unexpected signs

b. There is definite multicollinearity in the equation.

c. The payroll for defense workers and the number of civilians employed in defense industries are redundant, however; they measure the same thing. As a result, one or the other should be dropped.

8-12.

a. 2.35, 2.50, 1.18.

b. 9.17, 1.12, 9.52.

c. Since X_1 and X_2 are the only independent variables in the equation, $VIF(X_1)$ must equal $VIF(X_2)$ and hence $VIF(X_1)$ = 3.8.

d. In a two-variable equation, $r^2 = R^2$. Thus $R^2 = (0.80)^2$, and $VIF(X_1) = VIF(X_2) = 1/(1 - 0.64) = 2.78$.

8-14.

a.

Coefficient	β_Y	$\beta_Y{}^2$	β_H	β_A
Hypothesized sign:	+	−	+	+
Calculated t-score:	3.00	−0.80	6.50	−1.00
t_c = 1.282, so:	sig.	insig.	sig.	insig.
				unexpected sign

b. The functional form appears reasonable. The coefficient of Y can be greater than 1.0 since Y^2 is in the equation with a negative coefficient.

c. A and H seem potentially redundant.

d. The high VIFs strengthen the answer.

e. Either drop A or, if the purpose behind A was to measure the differential eating habits of children, change the two variables to A and $(H - A)$.

8-16. a.

Coefficient	β_T	β_S	β_O	β_R	β_W
Hypothesized sign:	−	−	−	−	+
Calculated t-score:	−4.20	−2.89	−0.03	0.26	0.69
$t_c = 1.725$, so:	sig.	sig.	insig.	insig.	insig.

b. Both the simple correlation coefficients and VIFs indicate potential multicollinearity (large mines tend to be more technologically advanced and more productive, causing T, S, and O to move together).

c. Yes. In fact, although this formula looks new, the underlying principle (adjusting each variable by its mean) is almost identical to that presented in the text.

d. We prefer Equation 8.28; the t-score of the estimated coefficient of O is insignificant, $\overline{R}^2$ rises when O is dropped, and the other coefficients do not change significantly when O is dropped. Most importantly, T and O are both measures of mine technology, making O potentially redundant.

e. There is no evidence that the Federal Mine Safety Act of 1952 had a significant impact on mine fatalities, even if slope dummies are used.

f. The equation for nonfatal injuries in year t (NF_t) is:

$$\widehat{NF}_t = 72.6 - 0.43T_t + 0.12S_t + 6.21O_t - 0.75R_t - 5.48W_t$$
$$\qquad\quad (0.10) \quad (0.11) \quad (2.98) \quad (1.97) \quad (2.03)$$
$$t = -4.31 \quad 1.11 \quad 2.08 \quad -0.38 \quad -2.70$$

The answers for the NF equation are identical to those for mine fatalities with three exceptions. First, $\hat{\beta}_S$ has an insignificant unexpected sign. Second, $\hat{\beta}_O$ is significantly positive, a result not expected by Andrews and Christenson but one that supports a union claim that higher output levels lead to more nonfatal accidents. This theoretical conflict suggests that a two-sided test of $\hat{\beta}_O$ is more appropriate in the nonfatal model. The final exception is that since $\hat{\beta}_O$ is significantly different from zero, it's difficult to justify even considering dropping O from the equation, so part d is no longer relevant.

Hints for Section 8.7.2: The SAT Interactive Regression Learning Exercise:

1. Severe multicollinearity between APMATH and APENG is the only possible problem in this regression. You should switch to the AP linear combination immediately.

2. An omitted variable is a distinct possibility, but be sure to choose the one to add on the basis of theory.

3. Either an omitted or irrelevant variable is a possibility. In this case, theory seems more important than any mild statistical insignificance.

4. On balance, this is a reasonable regression. We see no reason to worry about theoretically sound variables that have slightly insignificant coefficients with expected signs. We're concerned that the coefficient of GEND seems larger in absolute size than those reported in the literature, but none of the specification alternatives seems remotely likely to remedy this problem.

5. An omitted variable is a possibility, but there are no signs of bias and this is a fairly reasonable equation already.

6. We'd prefer not to add PREP (since many students take prep courses because they did poorly on their first shots at the SAT) or RACE (because of its redundancy with ESL and the lack of real diversity at Arcadia High). If you make a specification change, be sure to evaluate the change with our four specification criteria.

7. Either an omitted or irrelevant variable is a possibility, although GEND seems theoretically and statistically strong.

8. The unexpected sign makes us concerned with the possibility that an omitted variable is causing bias or that PREP is irrelevant. If PREP is relevant, what omission could have caused this result? How strong is the theory behind PREP?

9. This is a case of imperfect multicollinearity. Even though the VIFs are only between 3.8 and 4.0, the definitions of ESL and RACE (and the high simple correlation coefficient between them) make them seem like redundant variables. Remember to use theory (and not statistical fit) to decide which one to drop.

10. An omitted variable or irrelevant variable is a possibility, but there are no signs of bias and this is a fairly reasonable equation already.

11. Despite the switch to the AP linear combination, we still have an unexpected sign, so we're still concerned with the possibility that an omitted variable is causing bias or that PREP is irrelevant. If PREP is relevant, what omission could have caused this result? How strong is the theory behind PREP?

12. All of the choices would improve this equation except switching to the AP linear combination. If you make a specification change, be sure to evaluate the change with our four specification criteria.

13. To get to this result, you had to have made at least three suspect specification decisions, and you're running the risk of bias due to a sequential specification search. Our advice is to stop, take a break, review Chapters 6–8, and then try this interactive exercise again.

14. We'd prefer not to add PREP (since many students take prep courses because they did poorly on their first shots at the SAT) or ESL (because of its redundancy with RACE and the lack of real diversity at Arcadia High). If you make a specification change, be sure to evaluate the change with our four specification criteria.

15. Unless you drop one of the redundant variables, you're going to continue to have severe multicollinearity.

16. From theory and from the results, it seems as if the decision to switch to the AP linear combination was a waste of a regression run. Even if there were severe collinearity between APMATH and APENG (which there isn't), the original coefficients are significant enough in the expected direction to suggest taking no action to offset any multicollinearity.

17. On reflection, PREP probably should not have been chosen in the first place. Many students take prep courses only because they did poorly on their first shots at the SAT or because they anticipate doing poorly. Thus, even if the PREP courses improve SAT scores, which they probably do, the students who think they need to take them were otherwise going to score worse than their colleagues (holding the other variables in the equation constant). The two effects seem likely to offset each other, making PREP an irrelevant variable. If you make a specification change, be sure to evaluate the change with our four specification criteria.

18. Either adding GEND or dropping PREP would be a good choice, and it's hard to choose between the two. If you make a specification change, be sure to evaluate the change with our four specification criteria.

19. On balance, this is a reasonable regression. We'd prefer not to add PREP (since many students take prep courses because they did poorly on their first shots at the SAT), but the theoretical case for ESL (or RACE) seems strong. We're concerned that the coefficient of GEND seems larger in absolute size than those reported in the literature, but none of the specification alternatives seems remotely likely to remedy this problem. If you make a specification change, be sure to evaluate the change with our four specification criteria.

Chapter Nine

9-2. **a.** Reject H_0 of no positive serial correlation ($d < d_L = 1.03$).
   b. Cannot reject H_0 of no positive serial correlation ($d > d_U = 1.25$).
   c. Inconclusive ($d_L = 0.98 < d < 1.73 = d_U$).
   d. Inconclusive $(4 - d_U = 4 - 1.63 = 2.37 < d < 4 - d_L = 4 - 1.13 = 2.87)$.
   e. Cannot reject H_0 of no positive serial correlation ($d > d_U = 1.57$).
   f. Reject H_0 of no serial correlation ($d < d_L = 1.04$).
   g. Inconclusive ($d_L = 0.90 < d < 1.99 = d_U$).

9-4. **a.** $\beta_0^* = \beta_0(1 - \hat{\rho})$, so to get β_0, divide β_0^* by $(1 - \hat{\rho})$.
   b. To account for the fact that the equation was estimated with GLS.
   c. $\hat{\beta}_0 = 26.7/(1 - 0.90) = 267$.
   d. The equations are inherently different, and different equations can have drastically different constant terms, because $\hat{\beta}_0$ acts as a "garbage collector" for the equation it is in. As a result, we should not analyze the estimated values of the constant term.

9-6. The same test applies, but the inconclusive region has expanded because of the small sample size and the large number of explanatory variables. As a result, even if the DW = 2 you cannot conclude that there is no positive serial correlation.

9-8. **a.** Except for the first and last observations in the sample, the DW test's ability to detect first-order serial correlation is unchanged.
   b. GLS can be applied mechanically to correct for serial correlation, but this procedure generally does not make sense; this time's error term is now hypothesized to be a function of *next* time's error term.
   c. First-order serial correlation in data that have been entered in reverse chronological order means that this time's error term is a function of next time's error term. This might occur if, for example, the decision makers accurately predict and adjust to future random events before they occur, which would be the case in a world of rational expectations and perfect information.

9-10. **a.** $\hat{F}_t = 13.99 - 0.700RP_t + 0.854P_t \qquad \bar{R}^2 = .288$
   $\qquad\qquad\quad (1.840) \qquad (0.250) \qquad n = 25$
   $\qquad\quad t = -0.38 \qquad\quad 3.41 \qquad\quad DW = 1.248$

b. The relative price coefficient is now insignificant, and the dummy variable is now significant in the unanticipated direction (that is, the Pope's decision significantly *increased* the fish consumption). In addition the DW is inconclusive in testing for serial correlation, but the DW of 1.247 is quite close to the d_L of 1.21 (for a 10 percent two-sided level of significance). Thus, the omitted variable has not only caused bias, it also has moved the DW d just about into the positive serial correlation range.

c. This exercise is a good example of why it makes sense to search for specification errors before adjusting for serial correlation.

9-12. a.

Coefficient	β_{lnY}	β_{PB}	β_{PP}	β_D
Hypothesized sign:	+	−	+	−
Calculated t-score:	6.6	−2.6	2.7	−3.7

$t_c = 1.714$ at 5 percent, so: all four are significantly different from zero in the expected direction.

b. With a 5 percent, one-sided test and n = 28, k' = 4, the critical values are $d_L = 1.10$ and $d_U = 1.75$. Since d = 0.94 < 1.10, we can reject the null hypothesis of no positive serial correlation.

c. The probable serial correlation suggests GLS.

d. We prefer the GLS equation because we've rid the equation of much of the serial correlation while retaining estimated coefficients that make economic sense. Note that the dependent variables in the two equations are different, so an improved fit is not evidence of a better equation.

9-14. a. Equation 9.26:

Coefficient	β_1	β_2	β_3
Hypothesized sign:	+	+	+
Calculated t-score:	0.76	14.98	1.80
$t_c = 1.721$, so:	insig.	sig.	sig.

Equation 9.27:

Coefficient	β_1	β_2
Hypothesized sign:	+	+
Calculated t-score:	1.44	28.09
$t_c = 1.717$, so:	insig.	sig.

(Note: The authors explain a positive sign for $\hat{\beta}_{SP}$ by stating that the Soviet leadership became "more competitive" after 1977, leading the USSR to increase defense spending as SP increased.)

b. All three statistical specification criteria imply that SP is a relevant variable: $\overline{R}^2$ increases when SP is added, SP's coefficient is significantly different from zero, and the other coefficient estimates do not change more than one standard error when SP is added. On the other hand, our original expectation was that the sign of β_{SP} would be negative (an idea supported by the fact that the authors obtained a negative sign for $\hat{\beta}_{SP}$ for the subset of the sample from 1960 to 1976) and that Equation 9.26 therefore has a significant unexpected sign caused by an omitted variable. No matter which sign you expect, however, SP cannot be considered to be irrelevant.

c. For both equations, DW is far below the critical value for a 5 percent one-sided test, so we can reject the null hypothesis of no positive serial correlation. (For Equation 9.26, 0.49 < 1.12, and for Equation 9.27, 0.43 < 1.21.) This result makes us worry that $\hat{\beta}_{SP}$'s t-score might be inflated by serial correlation, making it more likely that SP is an irrelevant variable.

d. Such a small improvement in the DW statistic is no evidence whatsoever that the serial correlation is impure.

e. Just as we suspected, running GLS makes $\hat{\beta}_{SP}$ insignificant, making it even more likely that SP is an irrelevant variable.

9-16. a. With a 1 percent, one-sided test and n = 19, k' = 1, the critical values are $d_L = 0.93$ and $d_U = 1.13$. Since d = 0.48 < 0.93, we can reject the null hypothesis of no positive serial correlation. (Impure serial correlation caused by an incorrect functional form tends to be positive.)

b. See the answer to Exercise 1-6c.

c. 1.22 > 1.13, so we can't reject the null hypothesis.

d. 9.30, but, as we'll learn in Chapter 13, neither equation is perfect because the $\hat{P}$s are not limited by zero and one, even though in theory they should be.

Chapter Ten

10-2. a. LIKELY: the number of professors, the number of undergraduates.

b. LIKELY: aggregate gross investment, population.

c. LIKELY: U.S. disposable income, population, and, less likely but still possible, U.S. per capita disposable income.

10-4. **a.** At the 1 percent level, $t_c = 2.787$; reject the null hypothesis of homoskedasticity.

   b. At the 1 percent level, $t_c = 4.032$; $t = 1.30$, cannot reject null hypothesis of homoskedasticity.

   c. It depends on the underlying theory that led you to choose Z as a good proportionality factor. If you believe that the absolute value of Z is what makes the variance of ϵ large, then there is no difference between -200 and $+200$. On the other hand, if you believe that the *relative* value of Z is important, then you are forced to add a constant (greater than 200) to each Z (which changes the nature of Z) and run the Park test.

10-6. $\epsilon_i = u_i Z_i$, so $VAR(\epsilon_i) = VAR(u_i Z_i) = E[u_i Z_i - E(u_i Z_i)]^2$. Since u_i is a classical error term, $E(u_i) = 0$ and u_i is independent of Z_i, so $E(u_i Z_i) = 0$ and $VAR(\epsilon_i) = E(u_i Z_i)^2 = E[(u_i^2)(Z_i^2)] = Z_i^2 E(u_i^2) = \sigma^2 Z_i^2$ (since Z_i is constant with respect to ϵ_i).

10-8. $nR^2 = 33.226 > 15.09 =$ critical chi-square value, so reject H_0 of homoskedasticity. Thus, both tests agree.

10-10. **a.**

Coefficient	β_1	β_2	β_3	β_4
Hypothesized sign:	+	+	+	+
Calculated t-value:	7.62	2.19	3.21	7.62
$t_c = 1.645$ (5% level) so:	sig.	sig.	sig.	sig.

   b. Some authors suggest the use of a double-log equation to avoid heteroskedasticity because the double-log functional form compresses the scales on which the variables are measured, reducing a 10-fold difference between two values to a 2-fold difference.

   c. A reformulation of the equation in terms of output per acre (well, stremmata) would likely produce homoskedastic error terms.

   d. Assuming the heteroskedastic error term is $\epsilon_i = Z_i u_i$, where u_i is a homoskedastic error term, Z_i is the proportionality factor, and $Z_i = X_{1i}$, then the equation to estimate is:

$$Y_i/X_{1i} = \beta_0/X_{1i} + \beta_1 + \beta_2 X_{2i}/X_{1i} + \beta_3 X_{3i}/X_{1i} + \beta_4 X_{4i}/X_{1i} + u_i$$

10-12. **a.** $Y_i/\sqrt{X_{1i}} = \alpha_0 + \beta_0/\sqrt{X_{1i}} + \beta_1\sqrt{X_{1i}} + \beta_2 X_{2i}/\sqrt{X_{1i}} + u_i$.

   b. $Y_i/X_{3i} = \alpha_0 + \beta_0/X_{3i} + \beta_1 X_{1i}/X_{3i} + \beta_2 X_{2i}/X_{3i} + u_i$.

   c. $Y_i/\hat{Y}_i = \alpha + \beta_0/\hat{Y}_i + \beta_1 X_{1i}/\hat{Y}_i + \beta_2 X_{2i}/\hat{Y}_i + u_i$.

10-14. **a.** Heteroskedasticity is still a theoretical possibility. Young pigs are much more likely to grow at a high percentage rate than are old ones, so the variance of the error terms for young pigs might be greater than that of the error terms for old pigs.

b. Yes, $|-6.31|$ is greater than the two-tailed 1 percent t_c of 2.576.

c. An analysis of the sign of the coefficient can be useful in deciding how to correct any heteroskedasticity. In this case, the variance of the error term *decreases* as the proportionality factor increases, so dividing the equation again by weight wouldn't accomplish much.

d. One possibility would be to regroup the sample into three sub-samples by age and return the WLS specification on each. This is an unusual solution, but since the sample is so large, it's a feasible method of obtaining more homogeneous groups of pigs.

Chapter Eleven

Hints for Section 11.7.2: The Housing Price Interactive Exercise:

The biggest problem most students have with this interactive exercise is that they run far too many different specifications "just to see" what the results look like. In our opinion, all but one or two of the specification decisions involved in this exercise should be made before the first regression is estimated, so one measure of the quality of your work is the number of different equations you estimated. Typically, the fewer the better.

As to which specification to run, most of the decisions involved are matters of personal choice and experience. Our favorite model on theoretical grounds is:

$$P = f(\overset{+}{S}, \overset{-}{N}, \overset{-}{A}, \overset{+}{A^2}, \overset{+}{Y}, \overset{+}{CA})$$

We think that BE and BA are redundant with S. In addition, we can justify both positive and negative coefficients for SP, giving it an ambiguous expected sign, so we'd avoid including it. We would not quibble with someone who preferred a linear functional form for A to our quadratic. In addition, we recognize that CA is quite insignificant for this sample, but we'd retain it, at least in part because it gets quite hot in Monrovia in the summer.

As to interactive variables, the only one we can justify is between S and N. Note, however, that the proper variable is not $S \cdot N$ but instead is $S \cdot (5 - N)$, or something similar, to account for the different expected signs. This variable turns out to improve the fit while being quite collinear (redundant) with N and S.

In none of our specifications did we find evidence of serial correlation or heteroskedasticity, although the latter is certainly a possibility in such cross-sectional data.

Chapter Twelve

12-2. **a.** $\hat{Y}_t \approx 13.0 + 12.0X_t + 0.48X_{t-1} + 0.02X_{t-2}$
(smoothly decreasing impact)
b. $\hat{Y}_t \approx 13.0 + 12.0X_t + 0.96X_{t-1} + 0.08X_{t-2} + 0.01X_{t-3}$
(smoothly decreasing impact)
c. $\hat{Y}_t \approx 13.0 + 12.0X_t + 24.0X_{t-1} + 48.0X_{t-2} + \cdots$
(explosively positive impact)
d. $\hat{Y}_t \approx 13.0 + 12.0X_t - 4.8X_{t-1} + 1.92X_{t-2} - \cdots$
(damped oscillating impact)
e. $0 < \lambda < 1$

12-4. **a.**

Coefficient	β_{Pt}	β_{Pt-1}	β_U
Hypothesized sign:	+	+	−
Calculated t-value:	4.55	0.06	−3.89
$t_c = 1.341$, so:	sig.	insig.	sig.

b. The hypothesis being tested here is that the impact of a change in price on wages is distributed over time rather than instantaneous. Such a distributed lag (in this case ad hoc) could occur because of long-term contracts, slowly adapting expectations, and so forth. P_{t-1} is extremely insignificant in explaining W, but it's not obvious that it should be dropped from the equation. Collinearity might be the culprit, or the lag involved may be more or less than a year. In the latter case, it would not be a good idea to test many different lags on the same data set, but if another data set could be developed, such tests (scans) would probably be useful.
c. The equation would no longer be an ad hoc distributed lag.

12-6. **a.** $h = 0.0372 < 1.96 = t_c$ (5 percent two-tailed), so we cannot reject the null hypothesis of no serial correlation. (Specific h-values vary because the Durbin–Watson d is so close to 2.0, but H_0 can never be rejected.)

b. LM = 0.135 < 3.84 = 5 percent critical chi-square value with one degree of freedom, so we cannot reject the null hypothesis of no serial correlation.

12-8. An *F*-test with I Granger causing Y, F = $[(123157.6 - 71709.2)/4]/$ $[71709.2/18]$ = 3.23. Since this observed F-value is greater than the critical F-value of 2.93 (5 percent level with 4 degrees in the numerator and 18 degrees in the denominator), we can reject the null hypothesis that the coefficients of the lagged I's are jointly zero.

An F-test Y Granger causing I, F = $[(84571.07 - 31078.5)/4]/$ $[31078.5/18]$ = 7.75. Since the observed F-value is greater than the critical F-value of 2.93, we can reject the null hypothesis that the coefficients of the lagged Y's are equal to zero. Since both null hypotheses are rejected, we are still unsure whether Y Granger causes I or I Granger causes Y.

12-10. a. Y(GDP)

ACF with k = 2: 0.989 (t = 34.30; critical t = 1.703)
ACF with k = 6: 0.983 (t = 25.68; critical t = 1.714)

b. r (the interest rate)

ACF with k = 2: 0.408 (t = 2.36; critical t = 1.701)
ACF with k = 6: 0.015 (t = 0.07; critical t = 1.711)

c. CO (consumption)

ACF with k = 2: 0.995 (t = 52.02; critical t = 1.701)
ACF with k = 6: 0.989 (t = 32.15; critical t = 1.711)

d. I (investment)

ACF with k = 2: 0.773 (t = 6.33; critical t = 1.703)
ACF with k = 6: 0.826 (t = 7.04; critical t = 1.714)

All of the variables appear to be nonstationary with the exception of the interest rate variable, r. 5% *t*-tests on the ACFs for the variables support this observation.

Chapter Thirteen

13-2. a. $D_i > 1$ if $X_i > 7$ and $D_i < 0$ if $X_i < -3$
b. $D_i > 1$ if $X_i < 10$ and $D_i < 0$ if $X_i > 15$
c. $D_i > 1$ if $X_i > 6.67$ and $D_i < 0$ if $X_i < 3.33$

13-4. Start with $\ln[D/(1 - D)] = Z$ and take the anti-log, obtaining $D/(1 - D) = e^Z$. Then cross-multiply and multiply out, which gives $D = e^Z - De^Z$. Then solve for $D = e^Z/(1 + e^Z)$. Finally, multiply the right-hand side by e^{-Z}/e^{-Z}, obtaining $D = 1/(1 + e^{-Z})$.

13-6. **a.** WN: The log of the odds that a woman has used a recognized form of birth control is 2.03 higher if she wants no more children than it is if she wants more children, holding ME constant.
ME: A one-unit increase in the number of methods of birth control known to a woman increases the log of the odds that she has used a form of birth control by 1.45, holding WN constant.
LPM: If the model were a linear probability model, then each individual slope coefficient would represent the impact of a one-unit increase in the independent variable on the probability that the ith woman had ever used a recognized form of birth control, holding the other independent variable constant.

b. Yes, but we didn't expect $\hat{\beta}_{ME}$ to be more significant than $\hat{\beta}_{WN}$.

c. β_0 has no theoretical importance. It's fair to say, however, that in this particular case the two positive variable-coefficient pairs make it very unlikely indeed that we would observe a positive intercept.

d. We'd add one of a number of potentially relevant variables, for instance the educational level of the ith woman, whether or not the ith woman lives in a rural area, and so on.

13-8. **a.** There are only two women in the sample over 65. Because this causes a near singular matrix, many Logit programs, including EViews, will not be able to estimate this equation or will produce estimates quite different from ours.

b. We prefer Equation 13.15 because AD gives every appearance of being an irrelevant variable, at least as measured by the four criteria developed in Chapter 6.

13-10. **a.** All signs meet expectations except that of wait time.

b. The fact that the estimated coefficient of walk time is larger in absolute value than that of travel time supports this hypothesis, but the large positive coefficient for wait time does not.

c. Yes, if train commuters know train schedules and actually adjust their station arrival to minimize wait time, then setting the wait time for trains high allowed wait time to become a proxy for being the preferred mode of travel in Boston.

13-12. **a.**

Coefficient	β_F	β_M	β_Y	β_P	β_T
Hypothesized sign:	+	−	−	−	−
Calculated t-score:	1.86	−2.33	−2.16	−1.22	−0.23
$t_c = 1.669$, so:	sig.	sig.	sig.	insig.	insig.

For β_N, we'd use a two-sided test (H_0: $\beta_N = 0$ and H_A: $\beta_N \neq 0$). Since $|1.91| < 1.996$ (the 5 percent two-sided t_C), we cannot reject the null hypothesis of no effect.

  b. If we estimate a linear probability model, the only change in the signs and/or significance of the estimated coefficients is that $\hat{\beta}_N$ becomes significantly different from zero:

$$\hat{D}_i = -0.07 + 0.16F_i - 0.13M_i - 0.79Y_i - 0.09P_i - 0.03T_i + 0.03N_i$$
$$\phantom{\hat{D}_i = -0.07 +} (0.08) \quad (0.05) \quad (0.32) \quad (0.07) \quad (0.19) \quad (0.01)$$
$$\phantom{\hat{D}_i = -0.07 +} t = 1.96 \quad -2.64 \quad -2.45 \quad -1.25 \quad -0.18 \quad 2.45$$

  c. Two of the 78 predicted values for the dependent variable fall outside the 0–1 range. $R_P^2 = .744$.

  d. We prefer the logit in general for theoretical reasons and in this specific case because the linear probability model has two estimates outside the 0–1 range. Less importantly, the logit's R_P^2 is better.

  e. In the logit, the coefficient of S is 0.024 with a t-score of 0.28, while in the linear probability model, the coefficient of S is 0.0073 with a t-score of 0.47. Thus, neither model can provide evidence that would allow us to reject the efficient markets hypothesis.

Chapter Fourteen

14-2. **a.** All three equations are simultaneous.
  Endogenous variables $= Y_{1t}, Y_{2t}, Y_{3t}$
  Predetermined variables: $X_{1t}, X_{1t-1}, X_{2t-1}, X_{3t}, X_{4t}, X_{4t-1}$
  b. All three equations are simultaneous.
  Endogenous variables $= Z_t, X_t, H_t$
  Predetermined variables: $Y_t, P_{t-1}, B_t, CS_t, D_t$
  c. The equations are recursive; solve for Y_2 first and use it to get Y_1.

14-4. **a.** $P_t = \pi_0 + \pi_1 X_{1t} + \pi_2 X_{2t} + \pi_3 X_{3t} + v_{1t}$
  $Q_{St} = Q_{Dt} = \pi_4 + \pi_5 X_{1t} + \pi_6 X_{2t} + \pi_7 X_{3t} + v_{2t}$
  b. Step one: Set the two structural quantity equations equal to each other and solve for P_t:

$$\alpha_0 + \alpha_1 P_t + \alpha_2 X_{1t} + \alpha_3 X_{2t} + \epsilon_{Dt} = \beta_0 + \beta_1 P_t + \beta_2 X_{3t} + \epsilon_{St}$$
$$P_t = (\beta_0 - \alpha_0)/(\alpha_1 - \beta_1) - [\alpha_2/(\alpha_1 - \beta_1)]X_{1t}$$

$$- [\alpha_3/(\alpha_1 - \beta_1)]X_{2t} + [\beta_2/(\alpha_1 - \beta_1)]X_{3t}$$
$$+ [(\epsilon_{St} - \epsilon_{Dt})/(\alpha_1 - \beta_1)]$$

Step two: Compare this equation with the first reduced-form equation in part a:

$$\pi_0 = (\beta_0 - \alpha_0)/(\alpha_1 - \beta_1);$$
$$\pi_1 = -\alpha_2(\alpha_1 - \beta_1);$$
$$\pi_2 = -\alpha_3/(\alpha_1 - \beta_1);$$
$$\pi_3 = \beta_2/(\alpha_1 - \beta_1);$$
$$v_{1t} = (\epsilon_{St} - \epsilon_{Dt})/(\alpha_1 - \beta_1).$$

Step three: Substitute P_t into the structural Q_D equation, combine like terms, and compare this equation with the second reduced-form equation in part a:

$$\pi_4 = (\alpha_1\beta_0 - \alpha_0\beta_1)/(\alpha_1 - \beta_1);$$
$$\pi_5 = -\alpha_2\beta_1/(\alpha_1 - \beta_1);$$
$$\pi_6 = -\alpha_3\beta_1/(\alpha_1 - \beta_1);$$
$$\pi_7 = \alpha_1\beta_2/(\alpha_1 - \beta_1);$$
$$v_{2t} = (\alpha_1\epsilon_{St} - \beta_1\epsilon_{Dt})/(\alpha_1 - \beta_1).$$

Step four: Rearrange and solve simultaneously for the αs:

$$\alpha_0 = \pi_4 - \pi_0\alpha_1;$$
$$\alpha_1 = \pi_7/\pi_3;$$
$$\alpha_2 = \pi_5 - \pi_1\alpha_1;$$
$$\alpha_3 = \pi_6 - \pi_2\alpha_1;$$

c. First, the equation needs to be exactly identified; to see why this is so, try to solve for the βs of the overidentified Equation 14.5. Second, for equations with more than one or two slope coefficients, it is very awkward and time consuming to use Indirect Least Squares. Third, 2SLS gives the same estimates in this case, and 2SLS is much easier to apply.

14-6. a. There are three predetermined variables in the system, and both equations have three slope coefficients, so both equations are exactly identified. (If the model specified that the price of beef was determined jointly with the price and quantity of chicken, then it would not be predetermined, and the equations would be underidentified.)

b. There are two predetermined variables in the system, and both equations have two slope coefficients, so both equations are exactly identified.

   c. There are six predetermined variables in the system, and there are three slope coefficients in each equation, so all three equations are overidentified.

   d. There are five predetermined variables in the system, and there are three, two, and four slope coefficients in the first, second, and third equations, respectively, so all three equations are overidentified.

14-8. Stage one: Apply OLS to the second of the reduced-form equations:

$$Q_{St} = Q_{Dt} = \pi_0 + \pi_1 X_{1t} + \pi_2 X_{2t} + \pi_3 X_{3t} + v_{1t}$$
$$P_t \quad = \pi_4 + \pi_5 X_{1t} + \pi_6 X_{2t} + \pi_7 X_{3t} + v_{2t}.$$

Stage two: Substitute the reduced-form estimates of the endogenous variables for the endogenous variables that appear on the right side of the structural equations. This would give:

$$Q_{Dt} = \alpha_0 + \alpha_1 \hat{P}_t + \alpha_2 X_{1t} + \alpha_3 X_{2t} + u_{Dt}$$
$$Q_{St} = \beta_0 + \beta_1 \hat{P}_t + \beta_2 X_{3t} + u_{St}$$

To complete stage two, estimate these revised structural equations with OLS.

14-10. **a.** You don't know that OLS and 2SLS will be the same until the system is estimated with both.

   b. Not necessarily. It indicates only that the fit of the reduced-form equation from stage one is excellent and that $\hat{Y}$ and Y are virtually identical. Since bias is only a general tendency, it does not show up in every single estimate; indeed, it is possible to have estimated coefficients in the opposite direction. That is, even though positive bias exists with OLS, an estimated coefficient less than the true coefficient can be produced.

14-12. **a.** The serial correlation is so severe that it can be detected by the Durbin–Watson d test even though that statistic is biased toward 2. DW $= 0.98 < 1.30 = d_L$ for $n = 31, k' = 2$ at a 5 percent level of significance.

   b. Since the OLS and 2SLS estimates of this equation are similar, and since the serial correlation is quite severe, we'd choose to correct for serial correlation if we could correct for only one problem.

c. One possibility is a procedure first suggested by Fair.[1] This involves estimating a reduced form for YD_t that includes CS_{t-2} and YD_{t-1} on the right-hand side, and then substituting $\widehat{YD_t}$ into a GLS equation. This approach might be called "2SLS/GLS" since the 2SLS portion of the procedure is carried out before the GLS portion. A second possibility is to include an AR(1) term in a 2SLS model.

14-14. **a.** QU: −, −, −, +, +, +
UR: +, +, +, +, +
b. Yes, since UR and QU are jointly determined in this system.
c. This tells us that the UR equation is exactly identified but tells us nothing about the identification properties of the QU equation.
d. The lack of significance makes us wonder if UR and QU are indeed simultaneously determined. We should be hesitant to jump to this conclusion, however, because: one, the theory indicates simultaneity; two, multicollinearity or other specification problems may be causing the insignificance; and three, the pooled cross section/time-series data set makes it difficult to draw inferences.
e. Given the above reservations, we should be cautious. However, the results tend to confirm the theory that states interested in lowering their unemployment rates and lowering their budget deficits might consider lowering their unemployment benefits.

Chapter Fifteen

15-2. **a.** 73.58; 77.31; 74.92; 63.49
b. 117,276; 132,863; 107,287; Nowheresville
c. 14.07; 14.19; 14.52; 14.21

15-4. **a.** 160.82 ± 17.53
b. 800 ± 344.73

15-6. **a.** $Y_t^* = 1, 1, 1, 1, 1, 1, 1, 1, 1, 1, 1$
$Y_t^{**} = 0, 0, 0, 0, 0, 0, 0, 0, 0, 0$ (d = 1)

---

1. R. C. Fair, "The Estimation of Simultaneous Equation Models with Lagged Endogenous Variables and First-Order Serially Correlated Errors," *Econometrica*, 1970, pp. 507–516.

b. $Y_t^* = 0, 1, 1, 1, 1, 2, 2, 2, 3, 4, 5$
$Y_t^{**} = 1, 0, 0, 0, 1, 0, 0, 1, 1, 1$ (d = 2)
c. $Y_t^* = 1, 3, -3, 1, -2, 1, 2, -4, 3, 0, 2$
$Y_t^{**} = 2, -6, 4, -3, 3, 1, -6, 7, -3, 2$ (d = 0)

15-8.		Model A	Model T
a.	1997	30.50	29.50
	1998	30.25	30.25
	1999	30.13	29.87
b.	1998	31.50	28.50
	1999	30.75	30.75

c. Model A should exhibit smoother behavior because of the negative coefficient in model T.

15-10. **a.** For period one, this would be an unconditional distributed lag forecast.

$$\hat{S}_{t+1} = \hat{\beta}_0 + \hat{\beta}_1 \hat{Y}_{t+1} + \hat{\beta}_2 S_t$$

For period two, this would become a conditional distributed lag forecast:

$$\hat{S}_{t+2} = \hat{\beta}_0 + \hat{\beta}_1 \hat{Y}_{t+2} + \hat{\beta}_2 \hat{S}_{t+1}$$

b. For both periods, this would be a conditional distributed lag forecast:

$$\hat{S}_{t+1} = \hat{\beta}_0 + \hat{\beta}_1 \hat{Y}_{t+1} + \hat{\beta}_2 \hat{S}_t$$
$$\hat{S}_{t+2} = \hat{\beta}_0 + \hat{\beta}_1 \hat{Y}_{t+2} + \hat{\beta}_2 \hat{S}_{t+1}$$

c. Here, we'd build a (simultaneous) simulation model using the equations in part b with something like:

$$Y_t = \alpha_0 + \alpha_1 S_t + \alpha_2 T_t + \epsilon_t$$

Chapter Sixteen

16-2. Because these 100 professors have an average financial wealth of $40,000, their total financial wealth must be 100($40,000) = $4,000,000 (thus, the mean is $4,000,000/100 = $40,000). If the researcher mistakenly enters $4,000,000 instead of $400,000, total wealth increases to

$$\$4,000,000 - \$400,000 + \$4,000,000 = \$7,600,000$$

and average wealth rises to

$$\$7,600,000/100 = \$76,000$$

Such an error has no effect on the median, because it simply causes one high value to be replaced by another. This exercise illustrates the general principle that the median is less sensitive than the mean to measurement errors.

16-4. Because the numbers on each side are equally likely, we can reason directly that a six-sided die has an expected value of 3.5 and a four-sided die has an expected value of 2.5. Because the possibilities are more spread out on the six-sided die (1 through 6 versus 1 through 4), we know that the six-sided die has the larger standard deviation.

16-6. The z values and normal probabilities are:

$$P[x > 270] = P\left[\frac{x - \mu}{\sigma} > \frac{270 - 266}{16}\right] = P[z > 0.25] = 0.4013$$

$$P[x > 310] = P\left[\frac{x - \mu}{\sigma} > \frac{310 - 266}{16}\right] = P[z > 2.75] = 0.003$$

16-8. The high-school seniors who take the SAT are not a random sample because this test is taken by students who intend to go to college; these are generally students with above-average scholastic aptitude. The relationship between the fraction of a state's seniors that takes the SAT and the state's average SAT score is negative. If a small fraction of the state's seniors takes the SAT, it will mostly consist of the state's best students. As the fraction of a state's students taking the SAT increases, the group of students that takes the SAT is increasingly composed of weaker students, who bring down the state's average SAT.

16-10. The mean is 299,756.2174 and the standard deviation is 107.1146. Table B-4 in the appendix shows that with $23 - 1 = 22$ degrees of freedom, the appropriate t-value for a 99 percent confidence interval is 2.819. A 99 percent confidence interval does include the value 299,710.5 that is now accepted as the speed of light:

$$\bar{x} \pm t^*\left(\frac{s}{\sqrt{n}}\right) = 299{,}756.2174 \pm 2.819\left(\frac{107.1146}{\sqrt{23}}\right)$$

$$= 299{,}756.2 \pm 63.0$$

16-12. If x is N[215, 10] then for a random sample of size n = 20

$$P[\bar{x} \geq 257] = P\left[\frac{\bar{x} - \mu}{\sigma/\sqrt{n}} \geq \frac{257 - 215}{10/\sqrt{20}}\right] = P[z \geq 18.8] \approx 0$$

Dr. Frank's patients may choose to be medical patients because they have heart problems. Any trait they happen to share will then seemingly explain the heart disease; however, the standard statistical tests are not valid if these are not a random sample from the population of all people with earlobe creases.

16-14. The null hypothesis is that the population mean is 33.4 percent. The sample mean is 18.300, the standard deviation is 8.636, and the t value is −8.742:

$$t = \frac{\bar{X} - \mu}{s/\sqrt{n}}$$

$$= \frac{18.300 - 33.4}{8.636/\sqrt{25}}$$

$$= -8.742$$

Statistical Tables

The following tables present the critical values of various statistics used primarily for hypothesis testing. The primary applications of each statistic are explained and illustrated. The tables are:

Table B-1: The t-Distribution

The t-distribution is used in regression analysis to test whether an estimated slope coefficient (say $\hat{\beta}_k$) is significantly different from a hypothesized value (such as β_{H_0}). The t-statistic is computed as

$$t_k = (\hat{\beta}_k - \beta_{H_0})/SE(\hat{\beta}_k)$$

where $\hat{\beta}_k$ is the estimated slope coefficient and $SE(\hat{\beta}_k)$ is the estimated standard error of $\hat{\beta}_k$. To test the one-sided hypothesis:

$$H_0: \beta_k \leq \beta_{H_0}$$
$$H_A: \beta_k > \beta_{H_0}$$

the computed t-value is compared with a critical t-value t_c, found in the t-table on the opposite page in the column with the desired level of significance for a one-sided test (usually 5 or 10 percent) and the row with $n - K - 1$ degrees of freedom, where n is the number of observations and K is the number of explanatory variables. If $|t_k| > t_c$ and if t_k has the sign implied by the alternative hypothesis, then reject H_0; otherwise, do not reject H_0. In most econometric applications, β_{H_0} is zero and most computer regression programs will calculate t_k for $\beta_{H_0} = 0$. For example, for a 5 percent one-sided test with 15 degrees of freedom, $t_c = 1.753$, so any positive t_k larger than 1.753 would lead us to reject H_0 and declare that $\hat{\beta}_k$ is statistically significant in the hypothesized direction at the 95 percent level of confidence.

For a two-sided test, $H_0: \beta_k = \beta_{H_0}$ the $H_A: \beta_k \neq \beta_{H_0}$, the procedure is identical except that the column corresponding to the two-sided level of significance is used. For example, for a 5 percent two-sided test with 15 degrees of freedom, $t_c = 2.131$, so any t_k larger in absolute value than 2.131 would lead us to reject H_0 and declare that $\hat{\beta}_k$ is significantly different from β_{H_0} at the 95 percent level of confidence.

Another use of the *t*-test is to determine whether a simple correlation coefficient (r) between two variables is statistically significant. That is, the null hypothesis of no correlation between two variables can be tested with:

$$t_r = r\sqrt{(n - 2)}/\sqrt{(1 - r^2)}$$

where n is the number of observations. This t_r is then compared with the appropriate t_c ($n - 2$ degrees of freedom) using the methods outlined above. For more on the *t*-test, see Chapter 5.

TABLE B-1 CRITICAL VALUES OF THE t-DISTRIBUTION

Degrees of Freedom	One Sided: Two Sided:	10% 20%	5% 10%	2.5% 5%	1% 2%	0.5% 1%
			Level of Significance			
1		3.078	6.314	12.706	31.821	63.657
2		1.886	2.920	4.303	6.965	9.925
3		1.638	2.353	3.182	4.541	5.841
4		1.533	2.132	2.776	3.747	4.604
5		1.476	2.015	2.571	3.365	4.032
6		1.440	1.943	2.447	3.143	3.707
7		1.415	1.895	2.365	2.998	3.499
8		1.397	1.860	2.306	2.896	3.355
9		1.383	1.833	2.262	2.821	3.250
10		1.372	1.812	2.228	2.764	3.169
11		1.363	1.796	2.201	2.718	3.106
12		1.356	1.782	2.179	2.681	3.055
13		1.350	1.771	2.160	2.650	3.012
14		1.345	1.761	2.145	2.624	2.977
15		1.341	1.753	2.131	2.602	2.947
16		1.337	1.746	2.120	2.583	2.921
17		1.333	1.740	2.110	2.567	2.898
18		1.330	1.734	2.101	2.552	2.878
19		1.328	1.729	2.093	2.539	2.861
20		1.325	1.725	2.086	2.528	2.845
21		1.323	1.721	2.080	2.518	2.831
22		1.321	1.717	2.074	2.508	2.819
23		1.319	1.714	2.069	2.500	2.807
24		1.318	1.711	2.064	2.492	2.797
25		1.316	1.708	2.060	2.485	2.787
26		1.315	1.706	2.056	2.479	2.779
27		1.314	1.703	2.052	2.473	2.771
28		1.313	1.701	2.048	2.467	2.763
29		1.311	1.699	2.045	2.462	2.756
30		1.310	1.697	2.042	2.457	2.750
40		1.303	1.684	2.021	2.423	2.704
60		1.296	1.671	2.000	2.390	2.660
120		1.289	1.658	1.980	2.358	2.617
(Normal) ∞		1.282	1.645	1.960	2.326	2.576

Source: Reprinted from Table IV in Sir Ronald A. Fisher, *Statistical Methods for Research Workers,* 14th ed. (copyright © 1970, University of Adelaide) with permission of Hafner, a Division of the Macmillan Publishing Company, Inc.

Table B-2: The F-Distribution

The F-distribution is used in regression analysis to test two-sided hypotheses about more than one regression coefficient at a time. To test the most typical joint hypothesis (a test of the overall significance of the regression):

$$H_0: \beta_1 = \beta_2 = \cdots = \beta_K = 0$$
$$H_A: H_0 \text{ is not true}$$

the computed F-value is compared with a critical F-value, found in one of the two tables that follow. The F-statistic has two types of degrees of freedom, one for the numerator (columns) and one for the denominator (rows). For the null and alternative hypotheses above, there are K numerator (the number of restrictions implied by the null hypothesis) and $n - K - 1$ denominator degrees of freedom, where n is the number of observations and K is the number of explanatory variables in the equation. This particular F-statistic is printed out by most computer regression programs. For example, if $K = 5$ and $n = 30$, there are 5 numerator and 24 denominator degrees of freedom, and the critical F-value for a 5 percent level of significance (Table B-2) is 2.62. A computed F-value greater than 2.62 would lead us to reject the null hypothesis and declare that the equation is statistically significant at the 95 percent level of confidence. For more on the *F*-test, see Sections 5.5 and 7.7.

TABLE B-2 CRITICAL VALUES OF THE F-STATISTIC: 5 PERCENT LEVEL OF SIGNIFICANCE

	v_1 = Degrees of Freedom for Numerator											
	1	**2**	**3**	**4**	**5**	**6**	**7**	**8**	**10**	**12**	**20**	**∞**
1	161	200	216	225	230	234	237	239	242	244	248	254
2	18.5	19.0	19.2	19.2	19.3	19.3	19.4	19.4	19.4	19.4	19.4	19.5
3	10.1	9.55	9.28	9.12	9.01	8.94	8.89	8.85	8.79	8.74	8.66	8.53
4	7.71	6.94	6.59	6.39	6.26	6.16	6.09	6.04	5.96	5.91	5.80	5.63
5	6.61	5.79	5.41	5.19	5.05	4.95	4.88	4.82	4.74	4.68	4.56	4.36
6	5.99	5.14	4.76	4.53	4.39	4.28	4.21	4.15	4.06	4.00	3.87	3.67
7	5.59	4.74	4.35	4.12	3.97	3.87	3.79	3.73	3.64	3.57	3.44	3.23
8	5.32	4.46	4.07	3.84	3.69	3.58	3.50	3.44	3.35	3.28	3.15	2.93
9	5.12	4.26	3.86	3.63	3.48	3.37	3.29	3.23	3.14	3.07	2.94	2.71
10	4.96	4.10	3.71	3.48	3.33	3.22	3.14	3.07	2.98	2.91	2.77	2.54
11	4.84	3.98	3.59	3.36	3.20	3.09	3.01	2.95	2.85	2.79	2.65	2.40
12	4.75	3.89	3.49	3.26	3.11	3.00	2.91	2.85	2.75	2.69	2.54	2.30
13	4.67	3.81	3.41	3.18	3.03	2.92	2.83	2.77	2.67	2.60	2.46	2.21
14	4.60	3.74	3.34	3.11	2.96	2.85	2.76	2.70	2.60	2.53	2.39	2.13
15	4.54	3.68	3.29	3.06	2.90	2.79	2.71	2.64	2.54	2.48	2.33	2.07
16	4.49	3.63	3.24	3.01	2.85	2.74	2.66	2.59	2.49	2.42	2.28	2.01
17	4.45	3.59	3.20	2.96	2.81	2.70	2.61	2.55	2.45	2.38	2.23	1.96
18	4.41	3.55	3.16	2.93	2.77	2.66	2.58	2.51	2.41	2.34	2.19	1.92
19	4.38	3.52	3.13	2.90	2.74	2.63	2.54	2.48	2.38	2.31	2.16	1.88
20	4.35	3.49	3.10	2.87	2.71	2.60	2.51	2.45	2.35	2.28	2.12	1.84
21	4.32	3.47	3.07	2.84	2.68	2.57	2.49	2.42	2.32	2.25	2.10	1.81
22	4.30	3.44	3.05	2.82	2.66	2.55	2.46	2.40	2.30	2.23	2.07	1.78
23	4.28	3.42	3.03	2.80	2.64	2.53	2.44	2.37	2.27	2.20	2.05	1.76
24	4.26	3.40	3.01	2.78	2.62	2.51	2.42	2.36	2.25	2.18	2.03	1.73
25	4.24	3.39	2.99	2.76	2.60	2.49	2.40	2.34	2.24	2.16	2.01	1.71
30	4.17	3.32	2.92	2.69	2.53	2.42	2.33	2.27	2.16	2.09	1.93	1.62
40	4.08	3.23	2.84	2.61	2.45	2.34	2.25	2.18	2.08	2.00	1.84	1.51
60	4.00	3.15	2.76	2.53	2.37	2.25	2.17	2.10	1.99	1.92	1.75	1.39
120	3.92	3.07	2.68	2.45	2.29	2.18	2.09	2.02	1.91	1.83	1.66	1.25
∞	3.84	3.00	2.60	2.37	2.21	2.10	2.01	1.94	1.83	1.75	1.57	1.00

v_2 = Degrees of Freedom for Denominator

Source: Abridged from M. Merrington and C. M. Thompson, "Tables of percentage points of the inverted beta (F) distribution," *Biometrika,* Vol. 33, 1943, p. 73. By permission of the *Biometrika* trustees.

Table B-3: The F-Distribution

The F-distribution is used in regression analysis to test two-sided hypotheses about more than one regression coefficient at a time. To test the most typical joint hypothesis (a test of the overall significance of the regression):

$$H_0: \beta_1 = \beta_2 = \cdots = \beta_K = 0$$
$$H_A: H_0 \text{ is not true}$$

the computed F-value is compared with a critical F-value, found in Tables B-2 and B-3. The F-statistic has two types of degrees of freedom, one for the numerator (columns) and one for the denominator (rows). For the null and alternative hypotheses above, there are K numerator (the number of restrictions implied by the null hypothesis) and $n - K - 1$ denominator degrees of freedom, where n is the number of observations and K is the number of explanatory variables in the equation. This particular F-statistic is printed out by most computer regression programs. For example, if K = 5 and n = 30, there are 5 numerator and 24 denominator degrees of freedom, and the critical F-value for a 1 percent level of significance (Table B-3) is 3.90. A computed F-value greater than 3.90 would lead us to reject the null hypothesis and declare that the equation is statistically significant at the 99 percent level of confidence. For more on the *F*-test, see Sections 5.5 and 7.7.

TABLE B-3 CRITICAL VALUES OF THE F-STATISTIC: 1 PERCENT LEVEL OF SIGNIFICANCE

		v_1 = Degrees of Freedom for Numerator										
	1	2	3	4	5	6	7	8	10	12	20	∞
1	4052	5000	5403	5625	5764	5859	5928	5982	6056	6106	6209	6366
2	98.5	99.0	99.2	99.2	99.3	99.3	99.4	99.4	99.4	99.4	99.4	99.5
3	34.1	30.8	29.5	28.7	28.2	27.9	27.7	27.5	27.2	27.1	26.7	26.1
4	21.2	18.0	16.7	16.0	15.5	15.2	15.0	14.8	14.5	14.4	14.0	13.5
5	16.3	13.3	12.1	11.4	11.0	10.7	10.5	10.3	10.1	9.89	9.55	9.02
6	13.7	10.9	9.78	9.15	8.75	8.47	8.26	8.10	7.87	7.72	7.40	6.88
7	12.2	9.55	8.45	7.85	7.46	7.19	6.99	6.84	6.62	6.47	6.16	5.65
8	11.3	8.65	7.59	7.01	6.63	6.37	6.18	6.03	5.81	5.67	5.36	4.86
9	10.6	8.02	6.99	6.42	6.06	5.80	5.61	5.47	5.26	5.11	4.81	4.31
10	10.0	7.56	6.55	5.99	5.64	5.39	5.20	5.06	4.85	4.71	4.41	3.91
11	9.65	7.21	6.22	5.67	5.32	5.07	4.89	4.74	4.54	4.40	4.10	3.60
12	9.33	6.93	5.95	5.41	5.06	4.82	4.64	4.50	4.30	4.16	3.86	3.36
13	9.07	6.70	5.74	5.21	4.86	4.62	4.44	4.30	4.10	3.96	3.66	3.17
14	8.86	6.51	5.56	5.04	4.70	4.46	4.28	4.14	3.94	3.80	3.51	3.00
15	8.68	6.36	5.42	4.89	4.56	4.32	4.14	4.00	3.80	3.67	3.37	2.87
16	8.53	6.23	5.29	4.77	4.44	4.20	4.03	3.89	3.69	3.55	3.26	2.75
17	8.40	6.11	5.19	4.67	4.34	4.10	3.93	3.79	3.59	3.46	3.16	2.65
18	8.29	6.01	5.09	4.58	4.25	4.01	3.84	3.71	3.51	3.37	3.08	2.57
19	8.19	5.93	5.01	4.50	4.17	3.94	3.77	3.63	3.43	3.30	3.00	2.49
20	8.10	5.85	4.94	4.43	4.10	3.87	3.70	3.56	3.37	3.23	2.94	2.42
21	8.02	5.78	4.87	4.37	4.04	3.81	3.64	3.51	3.31	3.17	2.88	2.36
22	7.95	5.72	4.82	4.31	3.99	3.76	3.59	3.45	3.26	3.12	2.83	2.31
23	7.88	5.66	4.76	4.26	3.94	3.71	3.54	3.41	3.21	3.07	2.78	2.26
24	7.82	5.61	4.72	4.22	3.90	3.67	3.50	3.36	3.17	3.03	2.74	2.21
25	7.77	5.57	4.68	4.18	3.86	3.63	3.46	3.32	3.13	2.99	2.70	2.17
30	7.56	5.39	4.51	4.02	3.70	3.47	3.30	3.17	2.98	2.84	2.55	2.01
40	7.31	5.18	4.31	3.83	3.51	3.29	3.12	2.99	2.80	2.66	2.37	1.80
60	7.08	4.98	4.13	3.65	3.34	3.12	2.95	2.82	2.63	2.50	2.20	1.60
120	6.85	4.79	3.95	3.48	3.17	2.96	2.79	2.66	2.47	2.34	2.03	1.38
∞	6.63	4.61	3.78	3.32	3.02	2.80	2.64	2.51	2.32	2.18	1.88	1.00

(Left axis label: v_2 = Degrees of Freedom for Denominator)

Tables B4, B5, and B6: The Durbin–Watson d Statistic

The Durbin–Watson d statistic is used to test for first-order serial correlation in the residuals. First-order serial correlation is characterized by $\epsilon_t = \rho\epsilon_{t-1} + u_t$, where ϵ_t is the error term found in the regression equation and u_t is a classical (nonserially correlated) error term. Since $\rho = 0$ implies no serial correlation, and since most economic and business models imply positive serial correlation if any pure serial correlation exists, the typical hypotheses are:

$$H_0: \rho \le 0$$
$$H_A: \rho > 0$$

To test the null hypothesis of no positive serial correlation, the Durbin–Watson d statistic must be compared to two different critical d-values, d_L and d_U found in the tables that follow, depending on the level of significance, the number of explanatory variables (k′), and the number of observations (n). For example, with two explanatory variables and 30 observations, the 1 percent one-tailed critical values are $d_L = 1.07$ and $d_U = 1.34$, so any computed Durbin–Watson statistic less than 1.07 would lead to the rejection of the null hypothesis. For computed DW d-values between 1.07 and 1.34, the test is inconclusive, and for values greater than 1.34, we can say that there is no evidence of positive serial correlation at the 99 percent level of confidence. These ranges are illustrated in the diagram below:

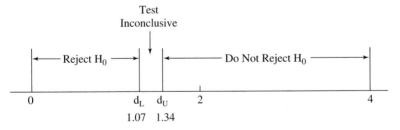

99 Percent One-Sided Test of $H_0 : \rho \le 0$ vs. $H_A : \rho > 0$

Two-sided tests are done similarly, with $4 - d_U$ and $4 - d_L$ being the critical DW d-values between 2 and 4. For more on this, see Chapter 9. Tables B-5 and B-6 (for 2.5 and 1 percent levels of significance in a one-sided test) go only up to five explanatory variables, so extrapolation for more variables (and interpolation for observations between listed points) is often in order.

TABLE B-4 CRITICAL VALUES OF THE DURBIN–WATSON TEST STATISTICS D_L AND D_U: 5 PERCENT ONE-SIDED LEVEL OF SIGNIFICANCE (10 PERCENT TWO-SIDED LEVEL OF SIGNIFICANCE)

n	k′ = 1		k′ = 2		k′ = 3		k′ = 4		k′ = 5		k′ = 6		k′ = 7	
	d_L	d_U	d_L	d_U	d_L	d_U	d_L	d_U	d_L	d_U	d_L	d_U	d_L	d_U
15	1.08	1.36	0.95	1.54	0.81	1.75	0.69	1.97	0.56	2.21	0.45	2.47	0.34	2.73
16	1.11	1.37	0.98	1.54	0.86	1.73	0.73	1.93	0.62	2.15	0.50	2.39	0.40	2.62
17	1.13	1.38	1.02	1.54	0.90	1.71	0.78	1.90	0.66	2.10	0.55	2.32	0.45	2.54
18	1.16	1.39	1.05	1.53	0.93	1.69	0.82	1.87	0.71	2.06	0.60	2.26	0.50	2.46
19	1.18	1.40	1.07	1.53	0.97	1.68	0.86	1.85	0.75	2.02	0.65	2.21	0.55	2.40
20	1.20	1.41	1.10	1.54	1.00	1.68	0.89	1.83	0.79	1.99	0.69	2.16	0.60	2.34
21	1.22	1.42	1.13	1.54	1.03	1.67	0.93	1.81	0.83	1.96	0.73	2.12	0.64	2.29
22	1.24	1.43	1.15	1.54	1.05	1.66	0.96	1.80	0.86	1.94	0.77	2.09	0.68	2.25
23	1.26	1.44	1.17	1.54	1.08	1.66	0.99	1.79	0.90	1.92	0.80	2.06	0.72	2.21
24	1.27	1.45	1.19	1.55	1.10	1.66	1.01	1.78	0.93	1.90	0.84	2.04	0.75	2.17
25	1.29	1.45	1.21	1.55	1.12	1.66	1.04	1.77	0.95	1.89	0.87	2.01	0.78	2.14
26	1.30	1.46	1.22	1.55	1.14	1.65	1.06	1.76	0.98	1.88	0.90	1.99	0.82	2.12
27	1.32	1.47	1.24	1.56	1.16	1.65	1.08	1.76	1.00	1.86	0.93	1.97	0.85	2.09
28	1.33	1.48	1.26	1.56	1.18	1.65	1.10	1.75	1.03	1.85	0.95	1.96	0.87	2.07
29	1.34	1.48	1.27	1.56	1.20	1.65	1.12	1.74	1.05	1.84	0.98	1.94	0.90	2.05
30	1.35	1.49	1.28	1.57	1.21	1.65	1.14	1.74	1.07	1.83	1.00	1.93	0.93	2.03
31	1.36	1.50	1.30	1.57	1.23	1.65	1.16	1.74	1.09	1.83	1.02	1.92	0.95	2.02
32	1.37	1.50	1.31	1.57	1.24	1.65	1.18	1.73	1.11	1.82	1.04	1.91	0.97	2.00
33	1.38	1.51	1.32	1.58	1.26	1.65	1.19	1.73	1.13	1.81	1.06	1.90	0.99	1.99
34	1.39	1.51	1.33	1.58	1.27	1.65	1.21	1.73	1.14	1.81	1.08	1.89	1.02	1.98
35	1.40	1.52	1.34	1.58	1.28	1.65	1.22	1.73	1.16	1.80	1.10	1.88	1.03	1.97
36	1.41	1.52	1.35	1.59	1.30	1.65	1.24	1.73	1.18	1.80	1.11	1.88	1.05	1.96
37	1.42	1.53	1.36	1.59	1.31	1.66	1.25	1.72	1.19	1.80	1.13	1.87	1.07	1.95
38	1.43	1.54	1.37	1.59	1.32	1.66	1.26	1.72	1.20	1.79	1.15	1.86	1.09	1.94
39	1.43	1.54	1.38	1.60	1.33	1.66	1.27	1.72	1.22	1.79	1.16	1.86	1.10	1.93
40	1.44	1.54	1.39	1.60	1.34	1.66	1.29	1.72	1.23	1.79	1.18	1.85	1.12	1.93
45	1.48	1.57	1.43	1.62	1.38	1.67	1.34	1.72	1.29	1.78	1.24	1.84	1.19	1.90
50	1.50	1.59	1.46	1.63	1.42	1.67	1.38	1.72	1.34	1.77	1.29	1.82	1.25	1.88
55	1.53	1.60	1.49	1.64	1.45	1.68	1.41	1.72	1.37	1.77	1.33	1.81	1.29	1.86
60	1.55	1.62	1.51	1.65	1.48	1.69	1.44	1.73	1.41	1.77	1.37	1.81	1.34	1.85
65	1.57	1.63	1.54	1.66	1.50	1.70	1.47	1.73	1.44	1.77	1.40	1.81	1.37	1.84
70	1.58	1.64	1.55	1.67	1.53	1.70	1.49	1.74	1.46	1.77	1.43	1.80	1.40	1.84
75	1.60	1.65	1.57	1.68	1.54	1.71	1.52	1.74	1.49	1.77	1.46	1.80	1.43	1.83
80	1.61	1.66	1.59	1.69	1.56	1.72	1.53	1.74	1.51	1.77	1.48	1.80	1.45	1.83
85	1.62	1.67	1.60	1.70	1.58	1.72	1.55	1.75	1.53	1.77	1.50	1.80	1.47	1.83
90	1.63	1.68	1.61	1.70	1.59	1.73	1.57	1.75	1.54	1.78	1.52	1.80	1.49	1.83
95	1.64	1.69	1.62	1.71	1.60	1.73	1.58	1.75	1.56	1.78	1.54	1.80	1.51	1.83
100	1.65	1.69	1.63	1.72	1.61	1.74	1.59	1.76	1.57	1.78	1.55	1.80	1.53	1.83

Source: N. E. Savin and Kenneth J. White. "The Durbin–Watson Test for Serial Correlation with Extreme Sample Sizes or Many Regressors," *Econometrica*, November 1977, p. 1994. Reprinted with permission.

Note: n = number of observations, k′ = number of explanatory variables excluding the constant term. We assume the equation contains a constant term and no lagged dependent variables (if so see Table B-7).

TABLE B-5   CRITICAL VALUES OF THE DURBIN–WATSON TEST STATISTICS OF D_L AND D_U: 2.5 PERCENT ONE-SIDED LEVEL OF SIGNIFICANCE (5 PERCENT TWO-SIDED LEVEL OF SIGNIFICANCE)

n	$k' = 1$ d_L	d_U	$k' = 2$ d_L	d_U	$k' = 3$ d_L	d_U	$k' = 4$ d_L	d_U	$k' = 5$ d_L	d_U
15	0.95	1.23	0.83	1.40	0.71	1.61	0.59	1.84	0.48	2.09
16	0.98	1.24	0.86	1.40	0.75	1.59	0.64	1.80	0.53	2.03
17	1.01	1.25	0.90	1.40	0.79	1.58	0.68	1.77	0.57	1.98
18	1.03	1.26	0.93	1.40	0.82	1.56	0.72	1.74	0.62	1.93
19	1.06	1.28	0.96	1.41	0.86	1.55	0.76	1.72	0.66	1.90
20	1.08	1.28	0.99	1.41	0.89	1.55	0.79	1.70	0.70	1.87
21	1.10	1.30	1.01	1.41	0.92	1.54	0.83	1.69	0.73	1.84
22	1.12	1.31	1.04	1.42	0.95	1.54	0.86	1.68	0.77	1.82
23	1.14	1.32	1.06	1.42	0.97	1.54	0.89	1.67	0.80	1.80
24	1.16	1.33	1.08	1.43	1.00	1.54	0.91	1.66	0.83	1.79
25	1.18	1.34	1.10	1.43	1.02	1.54	0.94	1.65	0.86	1.77
26	1.19	1.35	1.12	1.44	1.04	1.54	0.96	1.65	0.88	1.76
27	1.21	1.36	1.13	1.44	1.06	1.54	0.99	1.64	0.91	1.75
28	1.22	1.37	1.15	1.45	1.08	1.54	1.01	1.64	0.93	1.74
29	1.24	1.38	1.17	1.45	1.10	1.54	1.03	1.63	0.96	1.73
30	1.25	1.38	1.18	1.46	1.12	1.54	1.05	1.63	0.98	1.73
31	1.26	1.39	1.20	1.47	1.13	1.55	1.07	1.63	1.00	1.72
32	1.27	1.40	1.21	1.47	1.15	1.55	1.08	1.63	1.02	1.71
33	1.28	1.41	1.22	1.48	1.16	1.55	1.10	1.63	1.04	1.71
34	1.29	1.41	1.24	1.48	1.17	1.55	1.12	1.63	1.06	1.70
35	1.30	1.42	1.25	1.48	1.19	1.55	1.13	1.63	1.07	1.70
36	1.31	1.43	1.26	1.49	1.20	1.56	1.15	1.63	1.09	1.70
37	1.32	1.43	1.27	1.49	1.21	1.56	1.16	1.62	1.10	1.70
38	1.33	1.44	1.28	1.50	1.23	1.56	1.17	1.62	1.12	1.70
39	1.34	1.44	1.29	1.50	1.24	1.56	1.19	1.63	1.13	1.69
40	1.35	1.45	1.30	1.51	1.25	1.57	1.20	1.63	1.15	1.69
45	1.39	1.48	1.34	1.53	1.30	1.58	1.25	1.63	1.21	1.69
50	1.42	1.50	1.38	1.54	1.34	1.59	1.30	1.64	1.26	1.69
55	1.45	1.52	1.41	1.56	1.37	1.60	1.33	1.64	1.30	1.69
60	1.47	1.54	1.44	1.57	1.40	1.61	1.37	1.65	1.33	1.69
65	1.49	1.55	1.46	1.59	1.43	1.62	1.40	1.66	1.36	1.69
70	1.51	1.57	1.48	1.60	1.45	1.63	1.42	1.66	1.39	1.70
75	1.53	1.58	1.50	1.61	1.47	1.64	1.45	1.67	1.42	1.70
80	1.54	1.59	1.52	1.62	1.49	1.65	1.47	1.67	1.44	1.70
85	1.56	1.60	1.53	1.63	1.51	1.65	1.49	1.68	1.46	1.71
90	1.57	1.61	1.55	1.64	1.53	1.66	1.50	1.69	1.48	1.71
95	1.58	1.62	1.56	1.65	1.54	1.67	1.52	1.69	1.50	1.71
100	1.59	1.63	1.57	1.65	1.55	1.67	1.53	1.70	1.51	1.72

Source: J. Durbin and G. S. Watson, "Testing for Serial Correlation in Least Squares Regression," *Biometrika,* Vol. 38, 1951, pp. 159–171. Reprinted with permission of the *Biometrika* trustees.
Note: n = number of observations, k' = number of explanatory variables excluding the constant term. It is assumed that the equation contains a constant term and no lagged dependent variables (if so, see Table B-7).

TABLE B-6 CRITICAL VALUES OF THE DURBIN–WATSON TEST STATISTICS D_L AND D_U: 1 PERCENT ONE-SIDED LEVEL OF SIGNIFICANCE (2 PERCENT TWO-SIDED LEVEL OF SIGNIFICANCE)

n	k' = 1		k' = 2		k' = 3		k' = 4		k' = 5	
	d_L	d_U	d_L	d_U	d_L	d_U	d_L	d_U	d_L	d_U
15	0.81	1.07	0.70	1.25	0.59	1.46	0.49	1.70	0.39	1.96
16	0.84	1.09	0.74	1.25	0.63	1.44	0.53	1.66	0.44	1.90
17	0.87	1.10	0.77	1.25	0.67	1.43	0.57	1.63	0.48	1.85
18	0.90	1.12	0.80	1.26	0.71	1.42	0.61	1.60	0.52	1.80
19	0.93	1.13	0.83	1.26	0.74	1.41	0.65	1.58	0.56	1.77
20	0.95	1.15	0.86	1.27	0.77	1.41	0.68	1.57	0.60	1.74
21	0.97	1.16	0.89	1.27	0.80	1.41	0.72	1.55	0.63	1.71
22	1.00	1.17	0.91	1.28	0.83	1.40	0.75	1.54	0.66	1.69
23	1.02	1.19	0.94	1.29	0.86	1.40	0.77	1.53	0.70	1.67
24	1.04	1.20	0.96	1.30	0.88	1.41	0.80	1.53	0.72	1.66
25	1.05	1.21	0.98	1.30	0.90	1.41	0.83	1.52	0.75	1.65
26	1.07	1.22	1.00	1.31	0.93	1.41	0.85	1.52	0.78	1.64
27	1.09	1.23	1.02	1.32	0.95	1.41	0.88	1.51	0.81	1.63
28	1.10	1.24	1.04	1.32	0.97	1.41	0.90	1.51	0.83	1.62
29	1.12	1.25	1.05	1.33	0.99	1.42	0.92	1.51	0.85	1.61
30	1.13	1.26	1.07	1.34	1.01	1.42	0.94	1.51	0.88	1.61
31	1.15	1.27	1.08	1.34	1.02	1.42	0.96	1.51	0.90	1.60
32	1.16	1.28	1.10	1.35	1.04	1.43	0.98	1.51	0.92	1.60
33	1.17	1.29	1.11	1.36	1.05	1.43	1.00	1.51	0.94	1.59
34	1.18	1.30	1.13	1.36	1.07	1.43	1.01	1.51	0.95	1.59
35	1.19	1.31	1.14	1.37	1.08	1.44	1.03	1.51	0.97	1.59
36	1.21	1.32	1.15	1.38	1.10	1.44	1.04	1.51	0.99	1.59
37	1.22	1.32	1.16	1.38	1.11	1.45	1.06	1.51	1.00	1.59
38	1.23	1.33	1.18	1.39	1.12	1.45	1.07	1.52	1.02	1.58
39	1.24	1.34	1.19	1.39	1.14	1.45	1.09	1.52	1.03	1.58
40	1.25	1.34	1.20	1.40	1.15	1.46	1.10	1.52	1.05	1.58
45	1.29	1.38	1.24	1.42	1.20	1.48	1.16	1.53	1.11	1.58
50	1.32	1.40	1.28	1.45	1.24	1.49	1.20	1.54	1.16	1.59
55	1.36	1.43	1.32	1.47	1.28	1.51	1.25	1.55	1.21	1.59
60	1.38	1.45	1.35	1.48	1.32	1.52	1.28	1.56	1.25	1.60
65	1.41	1.47	1.38	1.50	1.35	1.53	1.31	1.57	1.28	1.61
70	1.43	1.49	1.40	1.52	1.37	1.55	1.34	1.58	1.31	1.61
75	1.45	1.50	1.42	1.53	1.39	1.56	1.37	1.59	1.34	1.62
80	1.47	1.52	1.44	1.54	1.42	1.57	1.39	1.60	1.36	1.62
85	1.48	1.53	1.46	1.55	1.43	1.58	1.41	1.60	1.39	1.63
90	1.50	1.54	1.47	1.56	1.45	1.59	1.43	1.61	1.41	1.64
95	1.51	1.55	1.49	1.57	1.47	1.60	1.45	1.62	1.42	1.64
100	1.52	1.56	1.50	1.58	1.48	1.60	1.46	1.63	1.44	1.65

Source and Note: See Table B-5.

Table B-7: The Normal Distribution

The normal distribution is usually assumed for the error term in a regression equation. Table B-7 indicates the probability that a randomly drawn number from the standardized normal distribution (mean = 0 and variance = 1) will be greater than or equal to the number identified in the side tabs, called Z. For a normally distributed variable ϵ with mean μ and variance σ^2, $Z = (\epsilon - \mu)/\sigma$. The row tab gives Z to the first decimal place, and the column tab adds the second decimal place of Z.

The normal distribution is referred to infrequently in the text, but it does come in handy in a number of advanced settings. For instance, testing for serial correlation when there is a lagged dependent variable in the equation (distributed lags) is done with a normally distributed statistic, Durbin's h statistic:

$$h = (1 - 0.5DW)\sqrt{n/(1 - n \cdot s_\lambda^2)}$$

where DW is the Durbin–Watson d statistic, n is the number of observations, and s_λ^2 is the estimated variance of the estimated coefficient of the lagged dependent variable (Y_{t-1}). The h statistic is asymptotically distributed as a standard normal variable. To test a one-sided null hypothesis of no positive serial correlation:

$$H_0: \rho \leq 0$$
$$H_A: \rho > 0$$

calculate h and compare it to a critical h value for the desired level of significance. For a one-sided 2.5 percent test, for example, the critical h value is 1.96 as shown in the accompanying graph. If we observed a computed h higher than 1.96, we would reject the null hypothesis of no positive serial correlation at the 97.5 percent level of confidence.

TABLE B-7   THE NORMAL DISTRIBUTION

z	.00	.01	.02	.03	.04	.05	.06	.07	.08	.09
0.0	.5000	.4960	.4920	.4880	.4840	.4801	.4761	.4721	.4681	.4641
0.1	.4602	.4562	.4522	.4483	.4443	.4404	.4364	.4325	.4286	.4247
0.2	.4207	.4168	.4129	.4090	.4052	.4013	.3974	.3936	.3897	.3859
0.3	.3821	.3873	.3745	.3707	.3669	.3632	.3594	.3557	.3520	.3483
0.4	.3446	.3409	.3372	.3336	.3300	.3264	.3228	.3192	.3156	.3121
0.5	.3085	.3050	.3015	.2981	.2946	.2912	.2877	.2843	.2810	.2776
0.6	.2743	.2709	.2676	.2643	.2611	.2578	.2546	.2514	.2483	.2451
0.7	.2420	.2389	.2358	.2327	.2296	.2266	.2236	.2206	.2217	.2148
0.8	.2119	.2090	.2061	.2033	.2005	.1977	.1949	.1922	.1894	.1867
0.9	.1841	.1814	.1788	.1762	.1736	.1711	.1685	.1660	.1635	.1611
1.0	.1587	.1562	.1539	.1515	.1492	.1469	.1446	.1423	.1401	.1379
1.1	.1357	.1335	.1314	.1292	.1271	.1251	.1230	.1210	.1190	.1170
1.2	.1151	.1131	.1112	.1093	.1075	.1056	.1038	.1020	.1003	.0985
1.3	.0968	.0951	.0934	.0918	.0901	.0885	.0869	.0853	.0838	.0823
1.4	.0808	.0793	.0778	.0764	.0749	.0735	.0721	.0708	.0694	.0681
1.5	.0668	.0655	.0643	.0630	.0618	.0606	.0594	.0582	.0571	.0559
1.6	.0548	.0537	.0526	.0516	.0505	.0495	.0485	.0475	.0465	.0455
1.7	.0446	.0436	.0427	.0418	.0409	.0401	.0392	.0384	.0375	.0367
1.8	.0359	.0351	.0344	.0366	.0329	.0322	.0314	.0307	.0301	.0294
1.9	.0287	.0281	.0274	.0268	.0262	.0256	.0250	.0244	.0239	.0233
2.0	.0228	.0222	.0217	.0212	.0207	.0202	.0197	.0192	.0188	.0183
2.1	.0179	.0174	.0170	.0166	.0162	.0158	.0154	.0150	.0146	.0143
2.2	.0139	.0136	.0132	.0129	.0125	.0122	.0119	.0116	.0113	.0110
2.3	.0107	.0104	.0102	.0099	.0096	.0094	.0091	.0089	.0087	.0084
2.4	.0082	.0080	.0078	.0075	.0073	.0071	.0069	.0068	.0066	.0064
2.5	.0062	.0060	.0059	.0057	.0055	.0054	.0052	.0051	.0049	.0048
2.6	.0047	.0045	.0044	.0043	.0041	.0040	.0039	.0038	.0037	.0036
2.7	.0035	.0034	.0033	.0032	.0031	.0030	.0029	.0028	.0027	.0026
2.8	.0026	.0025	.0024	.0023	.0023	.0022	.0021	.0020	.0020	.0019
2.9	.0019	.0018	.0018	.0017	.0016	.0016	.0015	.0015	.0014	.0014
3.0	.0013	.0013	.0013	.0012	.0012	.0011	.0011	.0011	.0011	.0010

Source: Based on *Biometrika Tables for Statisticians,* Vol. 1, 3rd ed., 1966, with the permission of the *Biometrika* trustees.
Note: The table plots the cumulative probability Z > z.

Table B-8: The Chi-Square Distribution

The chi-square distribution describes the distribution of the estimate of the variance of the error term. It is useful in a number of tests, including the White test of Section 10.3.3 and the Lagrange Multiplier test of Section 12.2.2. The rows represent degrees of freedom, and the columns denote the probability that a number drawn randomly from the chi-square distribution will be greater than or equal to the number shown in the body of the table. For example, the probability is 10 percent that a number drawn randomly from any chi-square distribution will be greater than or equal to 22.3 for 15 degrees of freedom.

To run a White test for heteroskedasticity, calculate nR^2, where n is the sample size and R^2 is the coefficient of determination (unadjusted R^2) from Equation 10.12. (This equation has as its dependent variable the squared residual of the equation to be tested and has as its independent variables the independent variables of the equation to be tested plus the squares and cross-products of these independent variables.)

The test statistic nR^2 has a chi-square distribution with degrees of freedom equal to the number of slope coefficients in Equation 10.12. If nR^2 is larger than the critical chi-square value found in Statistical Table B-8, then we reject the null hypothesis and conclude that it's likely that we have heteroskedasticity. If nR^2 is less than the critical chi-square value, then we cannot reject the null hypothesis of homoskedasticity.

TABLE B-8   THE CHI-SQUARE DISTRIBUTION

Degrees of Freedom	Level of Significance (Probability of a Value of at Least as Large as the Table Entry)			
	10%	5%	2.5%	1%
1	2.71	3.84	5.02	6.63
2	4.61	5.99	7.38	9.21
3	6.25	7.81	9.35	11.34
4	7.78	9.49	11.14	13.28
5	9.24	11.07	12.83	15.09
6	10.64	12.59	14.45	16.81
7	12.02	14.07	16.01	18.48
8	13.36	15.51	17.53	20.1
9	14.68	16.92	19.02	21.7
10	15.99	18.31	20.5	23.2
11	17.28	19.68	21.9	24.7
12	18.55	21.0	23.3	26.2
13	19.81	22.4	24.7	27.7
14	21.1	23.7	26.1	29.1
15	22.3	25.0	27.5	30.6
16	23.5	26.3	28.8	32.0
17	24.8	27.6	30.2	33.4
18	26.0	28.9	31.5	34.8
19	27.2	30.1	32.9	36.2
20	28.4	31.4	34.2	37.6

Source: See Table B-7.

INDEX